D1252278

COGNITION
THEORY AND PRACTICE

COGNITION
THEORY AND PRACTICE

Russell Revlin

University of California–Santa Barbara

WORTH PUBLISHERS

Senior Publisher: Catherine Woods
Executive Editor: Kevin Feyen
Executive Marketing Manager: Katherine Nurre
Marketing Assistant: Stephanie Ellis
Developmental Editors: Jeannine Ciliotta, Melissa Mashburn
Editorial Assistant: Nadina Persaud
Media Production Manager: Eve Conte
Media Editor: Christine Burak
Photo Editor: Christine Buese
Photo Researcher: Julie Tesser
Art Director and Cover Design: Babs Reingold
Interior Design: Lissi Sigillo
Cover and Chapter Opener Art: Laura Militzer Bryant
Illustration Coordinators: Janice Donnola, Bill Page
Art Illustrators: Hans Neuhart, Precision Graphics, Maps.com
Director of Development for Print and Digital Products: Tracey Kuehn
Associate Managing Editor: Lisa Kinne
Project Editors: Laura McGinn, Robert Errera
Supplements Production Manager: Stacey Alexander
Production Manager: Sarah Segal
Composition: MPS Ltd.
Printing and Binding: RR Donnelley

Library of Congress Control Number: 2011941453

ISBN-13: 978-0-7167-5667-5
ISBN-10: 0-7167-5667-6

Printed in the United States of America

First printing 2012

Worth Publishers
41 Madison Avenue
New York, NY 10010
www.worthpublishers.com

To Scott and Paul and especially Nancy Jean

About the Author

RUSSELL REVLIN is associate professor of psychology at the University of California–Santa Barbara. His academic journey began when, as a biopsychology student, he came across a tattered book on reasoning and problem solving at UCLA that expanded his view of psychology. The following year he was a graduate student in cognitive psychology at Carnegie Mellon University, where he earned a PhD. After a postdoctoral fellowship in psycholinguistics from Stanford University, Dr. Revlin established his laboratory in human inference, focusing on how memory, language, and imaginal processes contribute to our ability to reason about novel situations and domains.

Brief Contents

Contents

Preface

This text is written for my students, to address their questions and to challenge them to grasp the methodologies, findings, and applications of basic research. To do this, I've looked back to the past century of cognitive research and asked the question, *what does the field of cognitive psychology know?* and *what can it tell us?* The chapters highlight the enduring theories, the most fruitful perspectives, and identify cognitive processes in everyday activities.

Allen Newell, a towering figure in cognitive science, taught his students that the purpose of science was to find the universals that hold across time, space, and people: *to capture the generalities*. In this way he followed in the long tradition of researchers from the psychiatrist Carl Jung, to the neuropsychologist Donald Hebb, and to the anthropologist Joseph Campbell, all of whom were searching for the principles and themes that unite us all. This book is written in that spirit of inquiry. It ties together cognitive research and theory in a way that captures many of the universal regularities of human thinking and plumbs the depths of cognitive processes that produce those regularities. It does not shy away from describing aspects of human thought that reflect the incredible variability of human cognition, but it does so always within the context of diversity's relation to commonality. Revealing how the components of our common cognitive architecture fit together is a major focus of the text.

Cognitive students of all stripes and backgrounds ask the same fundamental questions: How can I use these theories to understand my own behavior or that of my peers or my clients? Why do I open the refrigerator and forget why I'm looking inside? How is it that I can ski down a slope but not be able to instruct someone to do the same without showing them? Why am I unable to remember the names of people a few minutes after we are introduced? Cognitive research has long held the answers to these and a myriad of other common questions. It has awaited only a text that reveals the cognitive mechanisms basic to the full range of cognitive processes and that provides a seamless linkage between theory, experimental findings, and ordinary human activity.

Applying cognitive theory to everyday situations is a goal that is completely consistent with the history of cognitive psychology, which originated from efforts to solve real-world problems but required fundamental research in order to accomplish that goal. The 13 chapters within these covers are designed to help students develop a broad understanding of human thinking by integrating cutting-edge cognitive research and theory with daily experiences and clinical and neurological practice.

For the most part, the order of topics follows what one would expect in a typical cognitive psychology course, with some notable exceptions. First, the usual philosophical traditions of psychology are not covered. The space required to address viable research findings makes it less useful to list the authors of millennia-old, unresolved philosophical issues. The chapter that describes attentional processes precedes a discussion of pattern recognition rather than following it, as in most texts. This is because attention is a central domain of cognitive research and is the gateway to our memory systems; therefore, attention comes first.

Most important, neuroscience has been integrated into every chapter. Cognitive neuroscience first entered the field as an addendum, and cognitive texts typically have a single section with intriguing photos of the brain that contribute little more than curiosities to the development of cognitive theory. This text reflects the modern perspective that neuroscience can illuminate our understanding of cognition: It tests theories of basic psychological phenomena and creates new ways to represent what we know. As such, brain imaging research is taking its place as intimately connected to the broader discipline of cognition. Neuroscience is used to test and illuminate theories originally developed from traditional laboratory studies, and neuroscience research with clinical populations helps us to understand the effects of specific brain injuries on cognitive functioning.

The text is divided into four parts. The first two chapters are introductory: The first presents an overview of human cognition and the second an overview of the brain and its functions. Part One focuses on attention and pattern recognition. Part Two covers the basic memory systems, working memory and long-term memory. Memory is the container in which our basic cognitive processes operate. These memory systems determine how we experience and remember the world and are responsible for what we know, believe, and understand. Readers will gain a sense of how intimately connected these central topics are through comparisons of the cognitive impairments that befall people with Parkinson's and Alzheimer's dementia, as well as those who suffer repeated concussions in accidents and athletic events.

Part Three emphasizes another universal aspect of human cognition: natural language. The chapters in this section present a functional analysis of language and its development, as well as the neurological basis of language that makes it a human universal. The treatment conveys an understanding of how messages are constructed, interpreted, and remembered. Theories of speech encoding are described and are then applied to the reading process to explain how best to teach it. These chapters emphasize the properties that reflect the universals of human language, just as Part Two describes universals of human memory.

Part Four views the vast range of human problem solving, reasoning, and decision making through the lens of the memory processes described in Part Two. The chapters that make up this section review findings from laboratory and cross-cultural studies of reasoning and show that basic reasoning skills are universal aspects of human cognition. Individual and cultural differences do not reflect deviations from universal cognitive principles, but rather result from differences in how people represent sentences and situations and from individual variations in the capacity of working memory. Examples of human reasoning permeate our everyday lives. These chapters discuss how people reason about social rules and obligations; how human inference and judgment play out in the court room and in the therapist's office; and the ways in which neurological factors affect our ability to formulate and imagine goals, to understand possibilities, and to consider alternative interpretations of events.

Cognition: Theory and Practice includes pedagogical elements and features intended to motivate students and help them understand and remember the material. Each chapter begins with a **Chapter Outline** that serves as an advance organizer, signaling the chapter's content and making it more memorable. It also includes an **opening quotation** that provides an interesting take on the key cognitive process the chapter discusses. **Key Terms** are boldfaced and defined when they first appear in the text. A **Key Terms list** with page numbers appears at the end of each chapter, and all key terms in the text are listed alphabetically with their definition in a **Glossary**. Every major chapter section ends with a **Section Summary** that provides a brief, succinct review of key points, which serves as a comprehension check for students and provides retrieval cues for later recall. A **Chapter Summary** is placed after the final section summary in each chapter. **Questions for Review** appear after each chapter summary in order to provide students with an opportunity to review, apply, and elaborate upon key theories and concepts.

   Demonstration boxes in every chapter allow students to actively experience the cognitive phenomena and classic experiments they are reading about. Demonstration box topics include, for example, modern techniques for assessing attentional impairments that result from concussions; the methods used to examine thought processes while people are trying to resolve moral dilemmas; and how lexical ambiguity affects understanding punch lines in jokes. When new research techniques are first introduced in the text, **Focus on Methods** boxes highlight their importance and make their essential components clear to the reader. These boxes describe the attentional blink paradigm, memory scanning, reading span tests, and much more.

Media/Supplements

The Cognitive Psychology Tool Kit

by John Krantz, Hanover College, with contributions from Joe Morrissey, SUNY Binghamton

The Cognitive Psychology Tool Kit is a comprehensive online source of classic and modern experiments regarded as foundational in the cognitive psychology course. The Tool Kit offers more than 45 experiments—such as the Stroop Test and the inversion effect—all with manipulative variables (a first for a product of this kind) that help students learn the major themes of each experiment. The

Tool Kit can be used with any cognitive psychology textbook, and its download-able data are compatible with a variety of software packages.

Book Companion Site at www.worthpublishers.com/revlin1e

This companion site exists:

- To provide students with an opportunity to study concepts, practice ter-minology, and reinforce their understanding of the material in this book at any hour of the day or night.

- As a password-protected repository for instructors to find relevant lec-ture and assessment materials, including PowerPoint slides for each chapter, art from the text, and assignable quizzes for their students.

Instructor's Resource Manual

by Alexandra Y. Chambers, University of California–Santa Barbara
The instructor's resource manual offers suggestions for in-class presentations, handouts, assignments, student activities, suggestions for videos, and other presentation tools. The manual also contains a set of 75 test items per chapter.

Printed and Computerized Test Bank (Available on Diploma CD for Windows and Macintosh)

by Alexandra Y. Chambers, University of California–Santa Barbara and Richard D. Platt, St. Mary's College of Maryland
The test bank continues Worth's tradition of providing high quality resources for testing and contains over 1400 questions. The CD-ROM includes all the test bank items for the text. It guides instructors through the creation of a test, allows them to add or randomize questions, and even insert their own visual elements and links to other material. Included is a grade book that makes it possible for the instructor to record students' grades, sort them, view detailed analyses of test items, generate reports, weight grades, and more. The Computerized Test Bank will allow you to export into a variety of formats that are compatible with many Internet-based testing products. Versions formatted for your campus LMS (such as Blackboard or Desire2Learn) are available within a Course Cartridge or ePack.

Acknowledgments

Aligning the theories and the laboratory research with the everyday phenomena was a painstaking task repeatedly energized by questions from students at the University of California–Santa Barbara, and the Pacifica Graduate Institute. They asked for clarity and consistency in the expression of basic cognitive principles and in the critical components of research methods. These students were my unsus-pecting collaborators and critics; this text is better because of their contributions.

The following reviewers were good enough to read the various drafts of the manuscript and to provide comments and suggestions that were of great help in completing the text. I am indebted to them for their considerable expertise and encouragement.

Lise Abrams,
University of Florida

Jennifer Ackil,
Gustavus Adolphus College

Aneeq Ahmad,
Henderson State University

Mark Allen,
Brigham Young University

Thomas Alley,
Clemson University

John Andrews,
Vassar College

Pamela Ansburg,
College of Denver

Sarah Arkin Haisley

Jason Barker,
University of Illinois–Springfield

Ralph Barnes,
Hood College

Jonathan Baron,
University of Pennsylvania

James Bartlett,
University of Texas at Dallas

John Bechtold,
Messiah College

Charles Behensky,
Hope College

Wendy Beller,
Quincy University

Bryan Benham,
University of Utah

Dale Berger,
Claremont Graduate Center

Garrett Berman,
Roger Williams University

Paula Biedenharn,
Aurora University

Katherine Binder,
Mount Holyoke College

Tamra Jean Bireta,
The College of New Jersey

Nathaniel Blair,
California State University–Sacramento

Stephen Blessing,
University of Tampa

Jill Booker,
University of Indianapolis

Heather Bortfeld,
University of Connecticut

Preston Bost,
Wabash College

Karen Boswell,
Siena College

Mary Boyle,
University of California–San Diego

Gary Bradshaw,
Mississippi State University

Wendy Braje,
SUNY Plattsburgh

Gary Brase,
University of Missouri–Columbia

Bruce Bridgeman,
University of California–Santa Cruz

Deborah Briihl,
Valdosta State University

Kathleen Brown,
Claremont McKenna College

Mary Camac,
Roanoke College

Richard Catrambone,
Georgia Institute of Technology

Kyle Cave,
University of Massachusetts–Amherst

Christopher Chabris,
Union College

Alexandra Chambers,
University of California–Santa Barbara

Isabelle Cherney,
Creighton University

Seth Chin-Parker,
Denison University

Edward Cokely,
Florida State University

John Coley,
Northeastern University

Raymond Collings,
SUNY Cortland

Sean Conlan,
Texas State University

David Conner,
Truman State University

Heather Coon,
North Central College

David Copeland,
University of Nevada

Russell Coulter-Kern,
Manchester College

Amy Criss,
Syracuse University

Victoria Cross,
University of California–Davis

Rita Culross,
Louisiana State University and A&M College

Dale Dagenbach,
Wake Forest University

W. M. De Neys,
Centre National de la Recherche Scientifique (CNRS, France)

Peter Delaney,
University of North Carolina at Greensboro

Martin Dennis,
Augustana College

Ann Devlin,
Connecticut College

Joe Dixon,
East Carolina University

Wendy Domjan,
University of Texas at Austin

Thomas Donnelly,
Rutgers University–Camden Campus

Robert Donohue,
Framingham State University

Cynthia Dulaney,
Xavier University

Ann Dunlea,
University of California–Davis

Roger Dunn,
San Diego State University

Jane Dwyer,
Rivier College

Jennifer Dyck,
SUNY Fredonia

Raymond Dye,
Loyola University–Lake Shore

Shimon Edelman,
Cornell University

Laird Edman,
Northwestern College

Julie Evey,
University of Southern Indiana

Kara Federmeier,
University of Illinois–Urbana-Champaign

Ira Fischler,
University of Florida

Robin Flanagan,
Western Connecticut State University

Jonathan Flombaum,
Yale University

Paul Foos,
University of North Carolina at Charlotte

Gregory Francis,
Purdue University Medical School

Thane Fremouw,
University of Maine

Carol Furchner,
University of New Mexico–Los Alamos

Danielle Gagne,
Alfred University

Michael Gardner,
University of Utah

William Gehring,
University of Michigan–Ann Arbor

John Geiger,
Cameron University

Dedre Gentner,
Northwestern University

David Gerkens,
*California State University–
Fullerton*

Morton Ann Gernsbacher,
University of Wisconsin–Madison

Kristen Gilbert,
University of Montevallo

Gerald Gillespie,
Kansas Wesleyan University

Arnold Glass,
*Rutgers University New
Brunswick*

Jonathan Golding,
University of Kentucky

Timothy Goldsmith,
University of New Mexico

Joana Gonsalves,
Salem State College

Kerry Goodwin

Lawrence Gottlob,
University of Kentucky

Bea Grosh,
*Millersville University of
Pennsylvania*

Robert Guttentag,
*University of North Carolina at
Greensboro*

Reza Habib,
Southern Illinois University

Lynda Hall,
Ohio Wesleyan University

Diane Halpern,
Claremont McKenna College

Neth Hansjoerg,
Rensselaer Polytechnic Institute

Mary Hare,
*Bowling Green State University–
Main*

William Hauselt,
*Southern Connecticut State
University*

Mary Hegarty,
Southern Connecticut State University

Gary Heiman,
SUNY Buffalo

Steve Hekkanen,
University of Tampa

Laurie Heller,
Brown University

Linda Henkel,
Fairfield University

Elizabeth Hennon,
University of Evansville

Beth Hentges,
University of Houston–Clear Lake

Andrew Herbert,
Rochester Institute of Technology

Lorna Hernandez Jarvis,
Hope College

Jean Hill,
*New Mexico Highlands
University*

Robert Hines,
*University of Arkansas–
Little Rock*

Andrew Hollingworth,
University of Iowa

Joseph Hopfinger,
*University of North Carolina at
Chapel Hill*

Keith Hutchison,
Montana State University

Maria Janicki,
Douglas College

Tiffany Jastrzembski,
Florida State University

Vikram Jaswal,
University of Virginia

Timothy Jay,
*Massachusetts College of Liberal
Arts*

Margaret Jelinek Lewis,
Lonestar College–Tomball

Andrew Johnson,
Park University

Kathy Johnson,
*Indian University–Purdue
University*

Sarah Johnson,
Moravian College

Philip Johnson-Laird,
Princeton University

Elaine Justice,
Old Dominion University

Todd Kahan,
Bates College

Michael Kalish,
University of Louisiana at Lafayette

Yasmine Kalkstein,
University of Minnesota–Twin Cities

Michael Kane,
University of North Carolina at Greensboro

Katrina Kardiasmenos,
Bowie State University

Jeffrey Karpicke,
Purdue University

Cynthia Kaschub,
University of Florida

James Kaufman,
California State University–San Bernardino

William Kelley,
Dartmouth College

Jeffery Kellogg,
Stockton College

Nancy Kim,
Northeastern University

Gary Klatsky,
SUNY Oswego

Futoshi Kobayashi,
Northern State University

Christopher Koch,
George Fox University

Steven Koch,
University of Indianapolis

Barbara Koslowski,
Cornell University

Aaron Kozbelt,
Brooklyn College, CUNY

David Krauss,
Boston College

Roger Kreuz,
University of Memphis

Stan Kuczaj,
University of Southern Mississippi

James Lampinen,
University of Arkansas

Susan Lima,
University of Wisconsin–Milwaukee

Diana Linden,
Occidental College

Tania Lombrozo,
University of California–Berkeley

Robert Lorch,
University of Kentucky

Mark Ludorf,
Stephen F. Austin State University

John Marazita,
Ohio Dominican College

Carrie Margolin,
Evergreen State College

Shelly Marmion,
University of Texas at Tyler

Heath Marrs,
Fort Hays State University

Lisa Martin,
Metro State

Marion Mason,
Bloomsburg University of Pennsylvania

Tamar Mather

John Mavromatis,
St. John Fisher College

Richard Mayer,
University of California–Santa Barbara

Christopher Mayhorn,
North Carolina State University

Jennnifer McCabe,
Marietta College

Michael McGuire,
Washburn University of Topeka

Kanoa Meriwether,
University of Hawaii at West Oahu

Wayne Messer,
Berea College

Glenn Meyer,
Trinity University

Katharine Milar,
Earlham College

Antoinette Miller,
Clayton State University

Kenneth Milles,
*Edinboro University of
Pennsylvania*

Keith Millis,
Northern Illinois University

LeeAnn Miner,
Mount Vernon Nazarene College

Jeffery Mio,
*California Polytechnic State
University–Pomona*

Mine Misirlisoy,
Florida State University

Christopher Monk,
George Mason University

Miguel Moreno,
Texas A&M University

Kevin Morrin,
*Lockhaven University of
Pennsylvania*

Dan Mossler,
Hampden-Sydney College

Jeffrey Mounts,
SUNY Geneseo

Kristi Multhaup,
Davidson College

Martha Munger,
Davidson College

Walter Murphy,
Lenoir-Rhyne College

John Murray,
Georgia Southern University

Dana Narter,
University of Arizona

Rolf Nelson,
Wheaton College

Jeffrey Neuschatz,
University of Alabama–Huntsville

Erik Nielsen,
Lewis and Clark College

Laura Novick,
Vanderbilt University

Caroline Noyes,
Oglethorpe University

Crystal Oberle,
Texas State University

Robyn Oliver,
Roosevelt University

Padraig O'Seaghdha,
Lehigh University

Daniel Osherson,
Princeton University

Amy Overman,
University of Pittsburgh

Brian Parry,
Mesa State College

Stephen Paul,
Robert Morris University

Nicole Peck,
Kansas State University

Jennifer Peluso,
Florida Atlantic University

Bruce Perrin,
Washington University

John Philbeck,
George Washington University

Shane Pitts,
Birmingham Southern College

Richard Platt,
St. Mary's College of Maryland

Devereaux Poling,
Ohio University Zanesville

Christine Porter,
College of William and Mary

Mathew Prull,
Whitman College

Jianjian Qin,
*California State University–
Sacramento*

Jennifer Queen,
Rollins College

Nancy Rader,
Ithaca College

James Rafferty,
Bemidji State University

Christopher Ramey,
Drexel University

Cathy Reed,
Claremont McKenna College

Daniel Reisberg,
Reed College

Glenn Rice,
Keene State College

John Rieser,
Vanderbilt University

Tony Ro,
Rice University

Bret Roark,
Oklahoma Baptist University

Craig Rogers,
Campbellsville University

Carrie Rosengart,
California University of Pennsylvania

Edna Ross,
University of Louisville

Justin Rueb,
University of Wisconsin–Stevens Point

Eric Ruthruff,
University of New Mexico–Main Campus

Lili Sahakyan,
University of North Carolina at Greensboro

Lelyn Saner,
University of Pittsburgh–Main

Kymberlie Schellin,
California State University–Long Beach

Mark Schmidt,
Columbus State University

William Schmidt,
SUNY Buffalo

Matthew Schulkind,
Amherst College

Eric Schumacher,
Georgia Institute of Technology

Miriam Schustack,
California State University–San Marcos

Wendy Schweigert,
Bradley University

Tanya Scott,
College of Staten Island/SUNY Stony Brook

Sheila Seelau,
Chatham University

Sandra Sego,
American International College

Rachael Seidler,
University of Michigan–Ann Arbor

Robert Seidenstadt,
Seattle University

Irina Sekerina,
College of State Island

Priti Shah,
University of Memphis

Tanya Sharon,
Mercer University

Raymond Shaw,
Merrimack College

Sonya Sheffert,
Central Michigan University

Ellyn Sheffield,
Salisbury University

Wendy Shields,
University of Montana

Arthur Shimamura,
University of California–Berkeley

Maria Shpurik,
Florida International University

Cynthia Sifonis,
Oakland University

Patricia Siple,
Wayne State University

David Sobel,
Brown University

Kenith Sobel,
University of Central Arkansas

Myeong-Ho Sohn,
George Washington University

Amelia Spears,
Mercer University

Melanie Spence,
University of Texas at Dallas

Kathryn Spoehr,
Brown University

Rebecca Stoffel
West Liberty University

Dawn Strongin,
California State University–Staislaus

Bianca Moravec Sumutka,
Lynchburg College

Brian Sundermeier,
Williams College

John Surber,
University of Wisconsin–Milwaukee

Evelina Tapia,
University of Houston–University Park

Michael Tarr,
Brown University

Vivien Tartter,
The City College of New York, CUNY

Annette Taylor,
University of San Diego

Holly Taylor,
Tufts University

Donald Tellinghuisen,
Calvin College

Lucien Thompson,
University of Texas at Dallas

Ruth Tincoff,
Wellesley College/Bucknell University

Meral Topcu,
Ferris State University

Richard Topolski,
Augusta State University

Leslie Valdes,
St. Cloud State University

Cynthia Vance,
Piedmont College

Michelle Verges,
Indiana University, South Bend

Paula Waddill,
Murray State University

Jeffrey Wagman,
Illinois State University

Rachel Walker,
Charleston Southern University

Thomas Ward,
University of Alabama

Charles Weaver,
Baylor University

John Webster,
Towson University

Lori Werdenschlag,
Lyndon State College

Wythe Whiting,
Washington and Lee University

Emily Wickelgren,
California State University–Sacramento

Mareike Wieth,
Albion College

Daniel Willingham,
University of Virginia

James Wise,
Washington State University–Tri-Cities

Michael Wolfe,
Grand Valley State University

Randall Wolfe,
Limestone College

Geoffrey Woodman,
Vanderbilt University

Karen Yanowitz,
Arkansas State University–Main Campus

Aaron Yarlas,
Grand Valley State University

Karen Yu,
University of the South

Nicholas Yeung,
Carnegie Mellon University

Otto Zinser,
East Tennessee State University

Worth Publishers have been true collaborators in producing this book, starting with Catherine Woods, senior publisher, who was a congenial host and made me feel that the endless drafts and revisions were appreciated. My thanks of course go to Kevin Feyen, executive editor, who encouraged, cajoled, bought lunches, guided the process from its early inception, and was endlessly patient. Kevin worked collaboratively with Jeannine Ciliotta, my gem of a development editor, who jumped into the breach, guided every aspect of the writing, and taught me so much about writing and communicating.

In the halls of Worth was Tracey Kuehn, director of development, who dazzled me with her understanding of the writing-to-publishing process. My writing days began with an e-mail from Robert Errera, the project editor, who shepherded the copyediting, was gentle with his criticism, kept me on track, and who, I assume, never sleeps. There are nearly 2,000 references in this book. Thank goodness for Linda Elliott, who verified each one and made sure that they met the highest standard of scholarly integrity. Just looking at the text, you have to marvel at the skills of Babs Reingold, the art director, who designed the book and is responsible for the wonderful cover. For all educators who adopt this text, I have Katherine Nurre, Steve Rigolosi, and the marketing staff to thank for bringing it to the attention of the broad community of scholars. Unseen by me, but much appreciated, are Christine Buese, photo editor, and Sarah Segal, production manager. They must have endless energy. There are supplements to this text for which I owe gratitude to the expertise of Nadina Persaud, Stacey Alexander, and Jenny Chiu. The online presence of this text is a result of the digital wizardry of Christine Burak, the media editor. My thanks go to them all and to their cohorts, who worked creatively to bring this work to press.

Most of all, I express my appreciation to my wife Nancy. Her encouragement and her endurance though the years of writing made this text possible. There is no book without Nancy.

COGNITION
THEORY AND PRACTICE

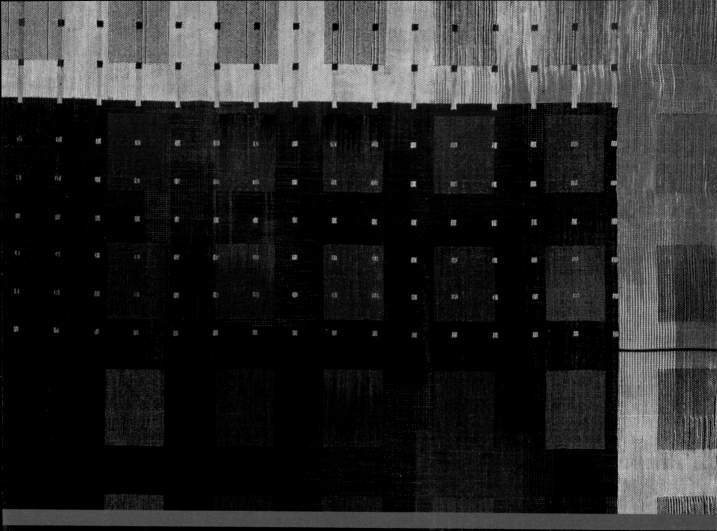

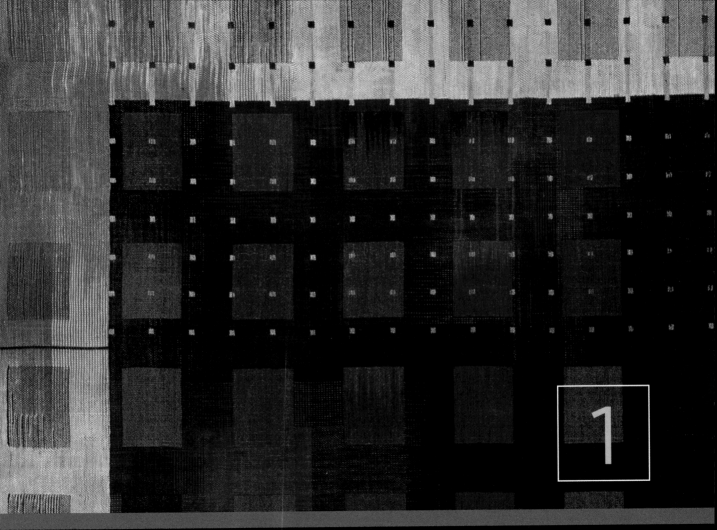

> "Life does not consist mainly—or even largely—of facts and happenings. It consists mainly of the storm of thoughts that is forever blowing through one's head."
>
> —Mark Twain

How do people think? As you read this book, you may be surprised to learn that you are already something of an expert on this topic. Our brains contain a vast store of factual knowledge, life memories, and beliefs that we use to interact with other people and the world around us. Our interactions with other people are not always successful, however, because the mental processes that allow us to make use of these extensive stores of different kinds of knowledge are limited.

A good example of our limited processing capabilities is seen in driving. Imagine that you are driving down a street and looking for a particular address—saying the address over and over to yourself—all the while talking to a friend on your cell phone. How easily will you be able to drive, find the address, and actively participate in the conversation with your friend? Research shows that you won't be able to perform all three of these activities equally well. The reason? In addition to the difficulty of driving, two of the tasks are verbal activities and they interfere with each other because they compete for the same memory resources (Baddeley, 1976). If, on the other hand, you are just driving down a street looking for a parking spot, a nonverbal task, it will be much less difficult for you to attend to a cell phone conversation. As we will see in Chapter 3, however, research also shows that talking on a cell phone while driving is never a good idea.

The branch of psychology that identifies our mental processes and how they affect our ability to interact with the world around us is called **cognitive psychology**. Cognitive psychology is more simply defined as the scientific study of cognition, a term defined in detail in the next section. The multidisciplinary contributions to cognitive psychology, as well as key cognitive psychology research methods and the major themes and organizing principles of this text, will be discussed in later sections of this chapter.

Defining Cognition

Although we know that we can think and that we have minds, it does not mean that it is easy for us to define what thinking is or what the stuff of the mind might be. Efforts to develop concrete and intuitively acceptable definitions of these terms date back at least to the teachings of two Greek philosophers. The first was Plato (429–347 BCE), who proposed that we could understand the world by identifying basic principles and use rational processes to create our knowledge. In modern terms, this view is called *rationalism*, advocated by the philosopher René Descartes and the modern linguist Noam Chomsky. The second Greek philosopher was Aristotle (384–322 BCE), who believed that we could understand the world by basing our knowledge on observations of the world outside ourselves. This view of human thinking has come down to modern times as *empiricism*, advocated by philosophers such as John Locke and psychologists such as B. F. Skinner. The ancient Greek philosophers started the science of the mind on its way by telling us that investigating the mind is discovering what makes humans human.

"Cognition" is a word that dates back to the 15th century when it meant "thinking and awareness." This definition may be intuitively appealing, but it lacks the precision required by modern scientists. Fortunately, we have a good working definition available that comes from the first textbook devoted to cognitive psychology, which defined **cognition** as

> those processes by which the sensory input is *transformed, reduced, elaborated, stored, recovered,* and *used* [emphasis added]. (Neisser, 1967, p. 4)

Each of the italicized terms emphasizes a key process that underlies cognition. Let's examine each of these important elements.

Cognitive Processes Transform Information

We live in a world filled with so much stimulation that it could potentially overload our senses. In order to understand what our eyes see, what our ears hear, and what we touch and taste, sensory signals must be transformed into a code that our brains can process. To take one example, although there are more than 140 million photoreceptors in the human eye, we do not experience millions of dots of light and dark when we look at a crowded street. Instead, we see shapes and color. This experience is the result of mental processes that transform the electrical and chemical stimulation of our receptors into perceptual experience. To gain a sense of such mental transformations, try Demonstration 1.1.

Behavioral psychologist B. F. Skinner in 1964, at work in a Harvard lab training brown rats in a Skinner box.

Nina Leen/Time & Life Pictures/Getty Images

■■■ DEMONSTRATION 1.1

Mental Transformations

Below are two pairs of circles, labeled A, B and A, C. Look at each pair and, as quickly as you can, decide which circle is the biggest.

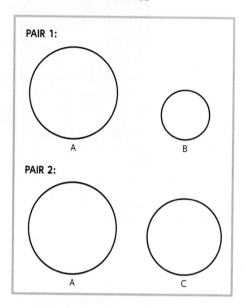

PAIR 1:

A   B

PAIR 2:

A   C

Did you notice a difference in how long it took you to identify the larger circle in Pair 1 versus Pair 2? People typically take slightly less time to judge the A, B pair than the A, C pair. If this was true of you, your impression matched previous findings; this demonstration is modeled after Moyer and Bayer (1976; see also Moyer, 1973).

The activity in Demonstration 1.1 is similar to an experiment that was conducted by Moyer and Bayer (1976). The surprising finding in the original study was that participants identified the largest circle in Pair 1 (A, B) more quickly than they identified the largest circle in Pair 2 (A, C). Since the absolute size difference between the paired circles is obvious to anyone who looks at them—people rarely make errors on this task—then the difference in time to make the judgments isn't the result of the impression of the circles on our eyes. It must be the result of a mental transformation of the visual stimulus by our brains. It is our internal processes—transformations of physical stimulation—rather than what our senses perceive that account for the judgments we make.

The demonstration illustrates a widely experienced phenomenon: The larger the difference in size between objects, the faster the judgment of which is larger. This phenomenon is called the **symbolic distance effect** (e.g., Banks, 1977; Péruch, Chabanne, Nesa, Thinus-Blanc, & Denis, 2006). This pattern holds true for blind as well as sighted people. In another version of this study, the experimenter tells the participants two clock times. They are then asked to imagine a clock face and decide which time would show the biggest angle between the clock hands. For both blind and sighted people, the bigger the difference between the two sets of hands, the faster the judgment—just as with the circles in the demonstration box (e.g., Noordzij, Zuidhoek, & Postma, 2007). The symbolic distance effect will be discussed in detail in Chapter 8, Imagery: Special Representation in Memory.

Cognitive Processes Reduce Information

If you were trying to describe your recollection of a television show to someone who hadn't seen it, you would not describe every detail of the lighting, the actors' vocal intonations, or their movements, unless those details were critical to the story. You would focus instead on the essential aspects of the show: the plot and the characters. Our recollections of events are not perfect recordings; instead, we reduce events to their crucial elements. In the same way, our cognitive processes tend to reduce our lived experiences. You can get a sense of this phenomenon of reduction yourself by trying Demonstration 1.2. The human tendency to store reduced, fragmentary representations of what we experience in our memory will be discussed more fully in Chapter 6, Long-Term Memory.

■■■ DEMONSTRATION 1.2

Information Reduction

Here are the lyrics to a Midwestern U.S. folk song. Read them rapidly and then answer the questions at the end without looking back at the words.

My mother and father were wonderful folks, but they both had a weakness for practical jokes, so when I was born, they both of one mind, said that I could have all of the names I could find. So . . . (refrain)

Jonathon, Joseph, Jeremiah,
Timothy, Titus, Obadiah,
William, Henry, Walter, Sim,
Ruben, Rufus, Solomon, Jim,
Nathanial, Daniel, Abraham,
Roderick, Frederick, Peter, Sam,
Simon, Timon, Nicholas, Pratt,
Christopher, Dick, and Jehoshaphat.

When I got married, the case was so bad, the parson stared at me as if I were mad. He said "my young man, it's a terrible shame your parents denied you a sensible name." He went on to say, without reason or rhyme, "you'll have to get married a piece at a time," So . . . (refrain)

Now, for the test. Without looking back, does the name Scott appear on the list of names (yes/no)? Does the name Benjamin appear on the list (yes/no)?

Students rarely say yes to Scott, but many will say yes to Benjamin. Alas, neither of these names appeared on the list! If you were to reduce the list to its essential features, you would say it had old-fashioned names, Biblical names, male names, and so forth. Adults accept Benjamin because it has properties that overlap with those of the list. They reject Scott because it does not share many features with the list. This false recognition based on the meaning of the words (or their association) is characteristic of adult recognition or recall. However, children around the age of 5 do not show the same effect. They recognize the words based on their sounds and they are more likely to falsely recognize one of the names if it rhymed with some of the names on the list, rather than if it were meaningfully related (Dewhurst & Robinson, 2004).

Perhaps you thought that the reduction of the items in memory in Demonstration 1.2 is a result of them being new to us. To see that cognitive processes also reduce visual details of objects that we've seen tens of thousands of times, try Demonstration 1.3.

■■■ DEMONSTRATION 1.3

Recognition Memory
Look carefully at the 15 coins and try to decide which one is the real penny. The answer is at the bottom of the box.

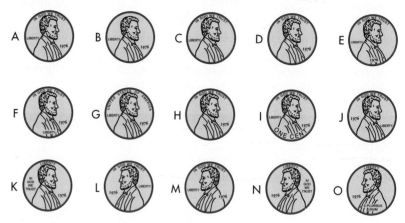

In the original task (Nickerson & Adams, 1979), 85% of college undergraduates selected the wrong penny. The correct answer is A. How did you do? No matter how often we have seen an object, we only process it down to the details that would be useful to us to recognize it and use it when we need to.

Cognitive Processes Elaborate Information

Just as we store information in a reduced form, we tend to elaborate on it when we remember it or try to tell it to someone else. People sometimes go too far in their elaboration and embellish their memories when recalling an event. For example, students participating in a cognitive psychology experiment heard a list of randomly ordered words and were later asked to recall them. The list fell into four categories: animals (e.g., lion), vegetables (e.g., carrot), occupations (e.g., teacher), and proper names (e.g., Harold) (Bousfield, 1953; Bower, Clark, Lesgold, & Winzenz, 1969; Kintsch, 1968; McDermott, 1996). Frequently, students "recalled" a word that had not been on the list, but was consistent with one of the categories on the list (e.g., bear). In addition, they tended to recall words from the same category together, even though they were not presented together.

This pattern is called *category clustering* and is typically shown by most people. It is not shown by people who are diagnosed with schizophrenia (e.g., Robert et al., 1997) or who suffer from Parkinson's dementia (Faglioni, Saetti, & Botti, 2000). The phenomenon of category clustering illustrates that human recollections tend not to be perfect duplications of what we originally learned, but are more like reconstructions that elaborate on a theme. It also illustrates the role of specific brain mechanisms in how we naturally use categories. This process will be discussed further in Chapter 7, Knowledge.

Cognitive Processes Store and Recover Information

Our cognitive processes help us to function in the world—to store information in memory so we can use it at the right time. A considerable portion of cognitive research is dedicated to understanding the mechanisms of **memory**: the mental operations that store information as well as recover or retrieve it at the appropriate times. Of course, we all occasionally fail to retrieve something we want to recall. This too requires a scientific explanation. Retrieval and nonretrieval are two sides of the same mechanism, as a French philosopher wittily observed:

> How is it that our memory is good enough to retain the least triviality that happens to us, and yet not good enough to recollect how often we have told it to the same person? (La Rochefoucauld, 1678/1871)

Memory processes will be the subject of Chapters 5–8. Questions related to retrieval of information from memory will be discussed in Chapter 6, Long-Term Memory.

Cognitive Processes Use Information

Our cognitive processes mediate every interaction that we have with the world around us, even when we react automatically "without thinking." Cognitive processes are present when we remember that an exam is coming up or forget to buy the birthday present we had planned to buy (*prospective memory*); when we comprehend what people say to us (*language understanding*); or when we don't know the answer to the question "Do they grow coffee in Paraguay?" and we say to ourselves, "They grow coffee in Brazil and Paraguay is next to Brazil, so they probably grow coffee in Paraguay" (*reasoning*). These are just some of the ways in which we use our cognitive processes to get along in the world, as you will see in the following chapters.

SECTION SUMMARY ▪

Defining Cognition

Cognition may be defined as "those processes by which the sensory input is *transformed, reduced, elaborated, stored, recovered*, and *used* [emphasis added]" (Neisser, 1967, p. 4). These mental processes allow us to function in the world. Although the operations of our cognitive processes are usually invisible to consciousness, their effects are present in everything we do.

▪ ▪

The Origins of Cognitive Psychology

Cognitive psychology focuses on how people think. For centuries, people have referred to their thoughts and have loosely described their experiences of self as their *mind* (e.g., Klein, Loftus, & Kihlstrom, 1996). An exception to this occurred in the early 20th century when some psychologists decided not to talk about the mind because it was unseen and therefore "unscientific" to refer to entities that could not be observed by others (Watson, 1925). This group of psychologists, called **behaviorists**, believed that to understand humans, scientists must look exclusively at their behavior rather than hypothesizing mental processes. Radical behaviorists believed that thinking and speaking were associated with muscle activity, not mental activity. Indeed, early psychology theorists (Curtis, 1899/1900; Watson, 1916) defined *thought* as "nothing but talking to ourselves" and "subvocal speech" (Watson, 1925, p. 6).

These views have not held sway. To appreciate this, just think back to the penny demonstration above. All of our experiences (rewarded behaviors) with pennies would predict that people should have perfect identification of the correct penny; clearly, they do not. More is going on in the recognition process than mere rewarded behaviors. Behaviorist principles were at odds with people's common experiences, and clever researchers developed experimental designs that allowed them to investigate mental processes. It became clear that any explanation of human activity ultimately required theories of mental processes (Chomsky, 1959): The discipline of cognitive psychology was needed. Today, a search of the University of California catalog of journals will show more than 160 scholarly journals worldwide with the words "cognitive" or "cognition" in the title.

Cognitive psychology as a field of study emerged out of researchers' attempts to understand the structure and processes of human mental life. This effort was informed in its early days and continues to be informed by four lines of work: research in human perception, human factors research, computer simulations of human behavior, and the emerging field of cognitive neuroscience. Cognitive psychology is not only a discipline of study, it is also a way of thinking about human behavior called **information processing**. This approach to human behavior analyzes the flow of events both in the external environment and in the internal environment of the person and shows how our past knowledge helps us understand present events. It reveals how we select, from among the repertoire of possible responses, just the ones that will yield positive results and makes our behavior intelligent. Information processing characterizes the four research areas that are the origins of cognitive psychology, to which we now turn.

Gestalt Psychology and Human Perception

Some of the earliest research in human perception was performed by scientists who wanted to understand how people take in what they see, hear, touch, or smell and transform them into organized patterns. For example, what do you see when you look at **FIGURE 1.1A**? Do you see a white line running through three disks? Look closer and you will see that the line is an illusory contour: It isn't really there. You can see how your mind creates the illusion by looking at **FIGURE 1.1B**, the same diagram, but without the breaks in the circles. Similarly, when we hear music, we perceive a melody rather than just a sequence of individual notes: We construct a whole that is something more than the sum of its parts. Experiencing the whole form or pattern, rather than the individual components, is expressed by the German word *gestalt,* and the related area of research is called **Gestalt psychology** because it seeks to discover the principles that determine how people's perception of the whole is derived from their perception of individual parts. It is a source of important ideas for cognitive psychology and is discussed in greater detail in Chapter 4, Pattern Recognition.

Human Factors

Human factors research is concerned with helping people to perform tasks efficiently and safely. The human factors approach has been an important early contributor to cognitive psychology because its research focuses on the limits of our mental capacities and how they constrain our actions. Human factors engineers design environments to compensate for our cognitive limitations so that we can achieve our goals.

Human factors grew out of military efforts during World War II to train people from different backgrounds to perform potentially complex tasks safely and effectively, such as flying airplanes, watching radar screens for hostile aircraft, and repairing equipment. This area of research was originally called *human engineering* and was concerned with why pilots crashed (e.g., Fitts, 1947), and why radar operators failed to see the blips on their screen or failed to hear auditory alarms that might signal the approach of enemy aircraft (Cherry, 1953; Karwowski, 2006). These early efforts to understand how people function under different conditions focused psychologists' attention on people's limitations and on differences among people in performing basic tasks. For example, Norman Mackworth, director

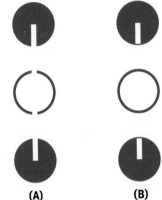

(A)   **(B)**

FIGURE 1.1 An Illusory Contour Illusory contours are a form of visual illusion where edges and lines are perceived when in fact none are there. This is due in part to a tendency for people to apply gestalt principles of continuation that complete lines and gaps. In (A), people see a white line running across circles because they "fill the gaps" in the circles. In (B), the gaps are not filled and the illusion is not present.

Navy Control Tower Operator at Work Human factors research grew out of efforts during World War II to train people from different backgrounds to safely and effectively perform potentially complex tasks such as flying airplanes, watching radar screens for hostile aircraft, and repairing equipment. Trying to understand how people function under different conditions focused psychologists' attention on limitations and differences among people in performing basic tasks.

U.S. Navy photo by Journalist 3rd Class David P. Coleman

of the renowned Applied Psychology Unit in Cambridge, England, discovered that radar operators started missing critical information after 20–30 minutes of staring at their instruments (Mackworth, 1948). Today, this finding affects the schedules of people in many different occupations, from military personnel to lifeguards (see Chapter 3).

Computer Simulation

At first, the computer simulation approach was used to create models of thinking by integrating the findings of gestalt and human factors research. More recently, the models have incorporated mechanisms based on studies of learning. These models carry with them a metaphor for talking about the mind. Today, it is natural to speak about human intellectual activity in terms of *memory capacity*, *storage*, *retrieval*, *encoding*, and *decoding*. All of these terms are derived from the computer metaphor, which is so ubiquitous that we hardly notice that it influences how we think about ourselves (Calvin, 1983). Psychological research has contributed a tradition of experimentation to cognitive psychology. Computer simulation, on the other hand, has helped researchers create theories of human cognition and has been a constant source of new ideas and new vocabulary.

The importance of computer simulation to cognitive psychology became clear at the very first cognitive psychology symposium, held at MIT in 1956 (Miller, 2003). Many of the papers described projects that used computer programs to capture the essence of human cognition. The goal of computer simulation is to have a computer respond to a problem by producing an output that matches the behavior of a real person confronted with the same problem. A computer program able to do this may be considered an embodiment of a theory of human cognitive processes (Simon, 1996).

Until the 1950s, computers were primarily used to make it easier to compute laborious calculations for mathematical tables. Then, as part of a research project at the RAND Corporation, Allen Newell and J. C. "Cliff" Shaw found that they could program a computer to simulate the blips on a radar screen produced by airplanes as they moved across the sky. Although this accomplishment might seem trivial by today's standards, in 1952 it was startling that computers could mimic "intelligent" systems like a radar screen.

This breakthrough changed thinking about computers and led to efforts to write computer programs that would match human problem-solving processes. For example, it was soon possible to program a computer to solve logic problems by mimicking the procedures that a human would use to tackle the same task (Newell & Simon, 1956). Today, computer programs are used to simulate how people understand language (McClelland & Elman, 1986), answer questions (Greenbaum & Revlin, 1989; Voorhees, 1999), and learn (Anderson, 2005b). These computer-based systems can also be used to become a more effective teacher (e.g., Fu et al., 2006; Sleeman & Brown, 1982).

Computer models have contributed to cognitive psychologists' understanding of how people such as physicians make decisions (e.g., Patel, Arocha, & Zhang,

2005) and also how they ought to make decisions (e.g., Chandrasekaran, Smith, & Sticklen, 1989). Broadly speaking, there are two major types of computer simulation models. First, *serial processors* describe the sequential processing of information, from the moment a question is asked, to the encoding of the question, to the search of one's knowledge for the relevant information, and finally, the production of a response. These models are at the heart of our understanding of human memory and problem-solving processes (e.g., Logan, 2002).

The second type of computer model sees human information processing as a series of decisions and actions that are produced at the same time; they occur in parallel and are sometimes called *parallel distributed processing* or *neural networks*. They provide excellent descriptions of human pattern recognition. For example, our ability to detect danger or sense when another person is sad or, in the case of a physician, what disease a person might have (e.g., Kara & Güven, 2007; Mofidi, Duff, Madhavan, Garden, & Parks, 2006), is made nearly instantly—not sequentially. You can appreciate this if you think about how you decide that a photograph of a family member is actually your mother. Do you analyze the shape of her ears, the size of the eyebrows, or the placement of her mouth with respect to her nose? You may do all of these things, but probably without conscious awareness, and you do it all at once—in parallel. Neural networks are not only useful models to understand basic pattern recognition, they have an applied benefit as well: They have been useful in helping law enforcement's efforts to identify terrorists (e.g., Latora & Marchiori, 2004; Zhao, Chellappa, Phillips, & Rosenfeld, 2003).

Cognitive Neuroscience

Cognitive neuroscience is the scientific study of the relationship between brain structures, neurological activity, and cognitive function. One of the most significant early scientific approaches to understanding the relationship between the brain and cognitive function is linked to the original work of Pierre Paul Broca, a French physician who described the autopsy of a patient named Leborgne. Because of a brain tumor, Leborgne had lost his ability to produce language. He was nicknamed "Tan" by the medical staff because that was the only sound he could voluntarily make (Broca, 1861). Broca's research identified a specific area of the brain that was important for speech. His work was an early step in the creation of the field of cognitive neuroscience. (Broca's work will be discussed in greater depth in Chapter 2.)

Cognitive neuroscientists hope to accomplish three important goals: to discover how the brain contributes to cognitive activity, to use neurological findings to test cognitive theories about how the mind works, and to find treatments for debilitating neurological diseases. In its early days, research in cognitive neuroscience was largely restricted to performing autopsies on people with cognitive deficits to find out what brain areas were

Pierre Paul Broca, ca 1875
Hulton-Deutsch Collection/Corbis

damaged. Modern researchers are able to assess an individual's brain activity when the person is conscious and performing a task. A description of these brain-imaging techniques and what they can tell us about the functioning human brain is presented in Chapter 2, The Brain and Cognition.

Today, research and theory in cognitive psychology and cognitive neuroscience are part of an even larger enterprise called **cognitive science**, an interdisciplinary field that embraces research and theory from many areas of specialization that are devoted to studying mental activity and intelligent behavior. Cognitive science includes researchers from fields such as anthropology, artificial intelligence, linguistics, and philosophy, as well as all of those working within cognitive psychology and cognitive neuroscience. Even though they come from many different academic disciplines, cognitive scientists are united by their common focus on how people are able to interact intelligently with their environment and how human behavior reflects the way that people mentally represent and use knowledge to produce new understandings and new behaviors.

SECTION SUMMARY ■

The Origins of Cognitive Psychology

Modern cognitive psychology, the scientific discipline that investigates how people think, emerged from four disciplines: research in human perception, human factors, computer simulation of human behavior, and neuroscience. The research in human perception, beginning with Gestalt psychology, focused on how people organize their experiences into structured patterns. Human factors research is concerned with human performance and focuses on how mental processes influence people's abilities to perform their tasks. In the 1950s, scientists began creating computer simulations in which the computer's output attempted to match the behavior of a real person. These computer simulations allow cognitive psychologists to test cognitive theories. Cognitive neuroscience studies the biological basis of mental activity and intelligent behavior. It originated in observations of the linkage between areas of the brain and cognitive and emotional difficulties experienced by individuals with neurological diseases.

■ ■

Cognitive Psychology Research Methods

Cognitive research is designed to identify and examine the fundamental processes that produce our thoughts and behaviors. Cognitive psychology relies on research methods that test theories and provide reliable data needed to develop new theories. Because cognitive processes are invisible to us when we view another person—or even when we view ourselves—methods have been developed to reveal their presence and how they work. This section describes several of the standard laboratory methods for obtaining cognitive data that psychologists have used for nearly 100 years.

Response Accuracy

One common method used in cognitive psychology is to place a person in a challenging situation and determine whether or not the participant makes a correct response in a specified period of time. For example, a participant is asked to answer questions that yield answers like yes or no, true or false, old or new. Consider our ability to recognize faces: We are surrounded by faces from the moment of birth and in general are quite good at it. However, in one study (Yin, 1969) university students were asked to study pictures of male faces for 3 seconds each and then were asked to decide whether a test picture had been previously studied (a yes/no judgment). When the test picture was right side up, the students were 85% accurate, but when the pictures were upside-down, the students were only 17% accurate in recognizing the faces. This simple measure of accuracy tells us that people recognize faces by noticing how facial features (eyes, nose, mouth, etc.) fit together rather than just using the individual features by themselves.

Sometimes groups show no difference in the performance of a task even when our intuition would lead us to expect a difference. In one study, participants had to look at a clock face and detect a subtle change in the movement of the clock's hand. This is called a *vigilance task* and is similar to the cognitive demands that are made on aircraft controllers looking at radar screens. Our preconceptions lead us to expect that alcohol use would affect performance. Yet, studies have shown that having a hangover from binge drinking the night before does not affect accuracy on the vigilance task: Volunteers who drank heavily the night before were just as accurate on the vigilance task as a group that had merely downed a glass of orange juice (Verster, van Duin, Volkerts, Schreuder, & Verbaten, 2003). Simple measures of accuracy can often reveal new patterns that run counter to our intuitions.

Produced Response

Recording the actual responses that participants make when they freely recall an event is a second important measure in cognitive research. This kind of measure is often used when a participant reconstructs the details of a story he or she has just heard. Such reconstructions give the researcher an idea of how the person interpreted the story, what aspects of the story he or she thought were important to attend to, and what strategies people use when they try to recall a story (Schacter, 2001). Take, for example, a study of how U.S. and Mexican students recalled events in a narrative. Students read stories about the first day at school that reflected either Mexican or U.S. culture. A week after reading them, the students were asked to recall the stories. U.S. students mistakenly recalled events from the Mexican stories in ways that were consistent with U.S. culture; Mexican students mistakenly recalled events from the U.S. stories in ways that were consistent with Mexican culture (Harris, Schoen, Lawrence, & Hensley, 1992). These findings show that we interpret events in other cultures in a way that is consistent with our own (e.g., Bartlett, 1932; Roediger & McDermott, 1995) and that our recollections reflect our interpretations as well as our memories. This is a powerful illustration of the importance of analyzing the subtleties of participants' responses.

Response Latency

Many cognitive studies measure the amount of time each participant takes in making a response. This third experimental measure is called **response latency**, also known as **response time** or **reaction time**. This measure is usually considered to be the time between the moment a stimulus is presented and the moment a response is made by the participant. Cognitive psychology assumes that reaction time is filled with specific cognitive processes (Donders, 1868/1969). An assumption that motivates the use of this method is that the more difficult a mental task is, the more time it should take to complete. If you look back at Demonstration 1.1, response time was the basic measure that revealed the presence of internal processes, contributing to the symbolic distance effect.

One of the inventive studies using this method investigated the mental processes of children when they learn how to add numbers (0–10) in their heads: a process called *mental arithmetic*. In a simple procedure, first graders were shown arithmetic problems (such as 3 + 5) and were timed as they produced the sum. Although the children seemed to perform the arithmetic without much effort, the time they took was puzzling: They took less time to add 1 + 5 than to add 3 + 5, and the same amount of time to add 1 + 6 (Groen & Parkman, 1972; Parkman & Groen, 1971). What sequence of mental processes could combine to give such results?

The researchers hit upon a simple theory. The children were not physically counting with their fingers, but they were mentally counting with them. First, they would look at the problem presented; second, they would find the bigger number; and third, they would count up (as if using their fingers) starting from the bigger number. This is called the *min* method of mental arithmetic because the child is counting the minimum number of fingers. **FIGURE 1.2**

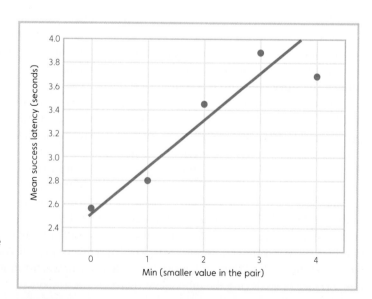

FIGURE 1.2 Response Latency and the Min Method
This graph shows the time it takes schoolchildren to add two numbers (each less than 10). Children start by identifying the larger number and then mentally count up by the smaller one (the minimum number) as if they were counting on their fingers. Because of this, the time to calculate the sum of two numbers increases with the size of the smaller one.

Source: After Groen & Parkman, 1972

graphs the time that the children needed to make their decisions (the vertical axis) and the size of the smaller number in the addition problem (the horizontal axis). It shows that children take about 2.5 seconds to study the numbers and identify the bigger number and the smaller or minimum number. Then it takes them 0.34 seconds to count each of the digits of the minimum number. For 3 + 5, the child starts with 5 and mentally counts up three digits: 6, 7, 8. For 1 + 5, the child only has to count one minimum digit starting with 5 (+ 1). This theory explains why children take less time to solve the equation 1 + 5 than they take to solve 3 + 5 (Groen & Parkman, 1972; see review by Ashcraft, 1995).

Of course, college-age students do not appear to use the min method. The time they require to do simple arithmetic reflects their ability to directly access the sums as if they were looking at a mental arithmetic table (e.g., Ashcraft & Stazyk, 1981). Such studies illustrate the techniques of information processing: identification of interesting patterns in the data and then accounting for them based on separate, time-dependent processes that account for each moment of time between a stimulus and a response.

Transfer of Training

When researchers want to discover whether one method of presenting information contributes better to students' understanding than another method, they will often measure whether the student can use the information in new circumstances. This is called **transfer of training** or **transfer of learning** (Thorndike & Woodworth, 1901). For example, Mayer, Heiser, and Lonn (2001) wanted to know whether students would have a deeper understanding of a science lesson on the causes of lightning if they saw slides about lightning with descriptions in captions or if they saw a multimedia display with pictures and heard a voice describing the facts. Students' memory for the facts was not affected by how the information was presented. However, students were better able to use the information to solve novel problems, such as "How can you prevent the damage of lightning?" when they viewed the multimedia presentation. This research suggests that different modes of presenting a lesson may have no effect on recalling the material, but may affect how well a student understands the material and its implications. In this example, the transfer of training method allows researchers to measure the effectiveness of one teaching method over another.

SECTION SUMMARY ▪

Cognitive Psychology Research Methods

Cognitive research uses a variety of methods to identify the internal mental processes that contribute to human behavior. One key laboratory method is to record the accuracy of participants' responses when making decisions. Another method is to have participants respond with their own conclusions and decisions in order to see how well they understand a situation presented to them. A frequently used experimental method is to record the overall response latency: the time participants consume in making their decisions. Research using this method estimates how many and which cognitive operations are required to perform a task and consume the overall time. Finally, transfer of training is used to determine whether different ways of presenting a set of facts promote the ability to use those facts in novel ways to solve problems.

About This Text

This book introduces you to theories and models derived from cognitive laboratories and from real-world experiences such as driving, reading, remembering, and speaking. Everyday applications of cognitive psychology are included throughout the text because cognitive psychology examines fundamental mental processes that have an impact on the way we live. Cognitive psychology as a field has matured sufficiently to give back the fruits of its research to society—if not to change the way humans behave, then at least to begin to explain why we behave the way we do.

Linking Research, Theory, and Practice

One of the primary goals in writing this text is to describe and explore the connections among research, theory, and practice. In addition to well-grounded findings from cognitive research, the next 12 chapters will convey how cognitive theory and research from the laboratory can help us to understand and help people outside the laboratory—from patients in hospitals to children in classrooms. For example, using cognitive methods, physicians are now able to administer a test that can identify, with 75% accuracy, whether a patient is suffering from Parkinson's or Alzheimer's dementia, and to plan an appropriate treatment for either of these maladies (Bronnick, Emre, Lane, Tekin, & Aarsland, 2007).

Police Lineup Cognitive research has been used to help police learn how to avoid biases when they create lineups.

John Lund/Sam Diephuis/Getty Images

This is important because different drugs affect the two diseases differently, and an incorrect diagnosis can harm the patient.

Cognitive psychology has also been at the forefront of research on what makes someone a skilled reader (e.g., Clifton, Staub, & Rayner, 2007; Just & Carpenter, 1987), and why there are individual differences in how people read and comprehend text (Demb, Boynton, & Heeger, 1997; Gibbs, 1989; Shaywitz, Morris, & Shaywitz, 2008). Such theories about reading skills are used to guide educators in presenting schoolwork so that it is easier for students to overcome individual obstacles to learning (e.g., Moreno & Mayer, 1999).

Cognitive research has provided a theoretical basis for treating depression using *cognitive behavioral therapy* (e.g., Beck, 1976; Budney, Moore, Rocha, & Higgins, 2006), a therapeutic method that focuses on helping people reinterpret the events in their lives. According to the American Psychiatric Association (2000), cognitive behavioral therapy has the best-documented effectiveness for the treatment of major depressive disorder. Cognitive research has also benefited the criminal justice system: Chapter 6 includes information on cognitive research that has revealed potential biases in eyewitness testimony, as well as difficulties in correctly identifying people in lineups (e.g., Valentine, Harris, Piera, & Darling, 2003). This research has been used to help police learn how they can avoid such biases when they interview witnesses (Geiselman & Fisher, 1997) and create lineups (Wright & Stroud, 2002).

Identifying Universals

The goal of cognitive psychology is to discover the psychological principles that apply to all of humanity regardless of cultural, social, and biological differences. Throughout this text, we will discuss the universality of cognitive processes with regard to human development. It is important to do this because the cognitive processes we share are sometimes obscured by the individual and group influences that differentiate us. For example, although there are nearly 6,000 different languages spoken in the world, we should not lose sight of the fact that most of the six billion human beings around the world will learn how to speak at least one of those languages. Individual facial characteristics vary significantly according to age and race (e.g., Bar-Haim, Ziv, Lamy, & Hodes, 2006; Sangrigoli & de Schonen, 2004). Yet, the visual pattern that all human infants recognize earliest and most rapidly is the human face (e.g., Fantz, 1963; Pascalis, de Haan, & Nelson, 2002; Valenza, Simion, Macchi, Cassia, & Umiltà, 1996). Since this preference for gazing at faces comes within the first 24 hours of life, it is not the result of learning or culture: It emerges from basic human brain structure and is a biologically based universal.

Interestingly, preference for attractive faces is greater than for unattractive faces (e.g., Slater, Bremner, et al., 2000; Slater, Quinn, Hayes, & Brown, 2000; Slater & von der Schulenburg, 1998). In a typical experimental design exploring this finding, newborn infants (1–3 days old; half boys and half girls) are shown two side-by-side photographs of a face. One face has been judged to be attractive by 14 adults, while the other photograph has been judged to be unattractive by the same panel. Two independent raters measure how much time each infant spends looking at each photo. The infants gaze longer at the photo of the attractive face (e.g., Slater, Bremner, et al., 2000) than at the photo of the unattractive face. **FIGURE 1.3** on the following page shows an example of this research procedure.

An Infant and His Father The visual pattern that all human infants recognize earliest and most rapidly is the human face. Their preference for gazing at faces comes within the first 24 hours of life; it is a biologically based universal.

Cultura Creative/Alamy

FIGURE 1.3 Preference for Attractive Faces In a series of studies, newborn infants were shown pairs of faces similar to the three pairs shown here. Infants gaze longer at a human face rated as more attractive than one rated by adults as less attractive. At 3 months of age, infants show a similar preference for faces of animals rated as attractive, even when they have had no prior experience looking at the animals. This preference must have some biological basis.

Source: Quinn, P. C., Kelly, D. J., Lee, K., Pascalis, O., & Slater, A. M. (2008). Preference for attractive faces in human infants extends beyond conspecifics. *Developmental Science*, *11*, 76–83; Slater, A., Bremner, G., Johnson, S. P., Sherwood, P., Hayes, R., & Brown, E. (2000). Newborn infants' preference for attractive faces: The role of internal and external facial features. *Infancy*, *1*, 265–274; Photo courtesy of Russell Revlin.

This preference for attractive faces is evident even when infants look at animal faces. In a recent study of the face preferences of 3-month-old infants (also illustrated in Figure 1.3), infants were shown pairs of animal faces (cats, tigers, etc.). One face in each pair was rated by 20 adults as being attractive; the other face was rated as unattractive. Here again, the infants preferred to look at the attractive faces even when they have had no prior experience looking at the animals (Quinn, Kelly, Lee, Pascalis, & Slater, 2008). Since the environment cannot have influenced such preferences, this finding suggests that the preference is biologically based. Because human brains are similarly structured, these findings argue for a universal, biological basis for judgments of relative attractiveness. Of course, the measure of attractiveness might only mean attention demanding, not "pretty." In any case, something in our brains causes us to attend to certain kinds of faces at such an early age when environmental factors are minimal. Perhaps it is the result of the structural characteristics of faces, which are biologically based (Grammer & Oberzaucher, 2008). Cognitive universals that appear to result from biologically based mechanisms will be discussed throughout the text.

Acknowledging Differences

One challenge for cognitive scientists is to separate the differences among people that result from basic biological factors from those that are affected by strategy, past experience, or culture. Take human memory, for example. A universal aspect of human cognition is that we all have a collection of memory systems: One system is useful for remembering things for a short period of time and another is effective for holding knowledge for a lifetime. Humans differ, however, on the parameters of these systems. People vary in the capacity of their memory span (e.g., how many numbers they can remember for a brief period of time). This difference is related, in part, to how rapidly individuals can repeat lists of words or numbers to themselves—either silently or out loud (e.g., Baddeley, Thomson, & Buchanan, 1975; Hulme, Thomson, Muir, & Lawrence, 1984)—in addition to other factors (Henry, 1994; Tehan & Lalor, 2000). Such seemingly small differences in basic memory abilities can have large effects on human behavior. For example, the memory spans of children and adults predict their difficulty in reading (e.g., Daneman & Carpenter, 1980; Daneman & Hannon, 2007; Das & Mishra, 1991).

Some differences among people are based on cultural environment and are not the result of differences in biology or in basic cognitive processes. Take color names in different languages, for example. Some languages have only two color terms, roughly the equivalent in English for black and white. Two such languages are Bassa (from Sierra Leone in Africa) and Dani (from Indonesian New Guinea; e.g., Berlin & Kay, 1969). A far greater number of cultures have 11 color terms that are commonly used within the culture, such as the terms found in European languages. Yet, there is no evidence that speakers of any of these languages differ in their basic ability to see color (Rosch, 1973b). Color perception is a universal property of human vision; how it is manifested in behavior results from cultural factors. Cognitive methods can be used to separate differences that are biologically based from those that are experientially based.

Our experiences greatly shape how we understand the world around us and shape our approach to solving even the simplest of problems. Take a look at the following two problems.

1. A ladder is attached to the side of a barn. Floodwaters are rising at 1 foot per hour. The rungs of the ladder are 1 foot apart. How many rungs will be covered by the floodwaters in 3 hours?

2. A ladder is attached to the side of a boat in the harbor. The tide is rising at 1 foot per hour. The rungs of the ladder are 1 foot apart. How many rungs will be covered by the tide in 3 hours?

With simple calculations for Problem 1, most people would conclude that three rungs will be covered. But what about Problem 2? It is superficially similar to Problem 1, which might lead someone without a knowledge of boats to draw the same conclusion—three rungs. However, if the reasoner's long-term memory of buoyancy is accessed, the reasoner will conclude that no rungs will be covered because the boat *rises* with the tide. Our experiences, stored in our long-term memory, contribute to how we represent problem situations and solve them. This will be explored in Chapters 11–13.

Organization of This Book

An enduring finding from cognitive research is that people benefit from knowing the organization of new materials before they are asked to learn the specific details. Sometimes these preview materials, called **advance organizers**, are formatted as a diagram that provides a visual schematic showing the interplay of topics (Ausubel, 1968; Mayer, 1979; Novak & Gowin, 1984). **FIGURE 1.4** reveals the interplay of topics in this text. It is loosely based on a structural theory of memory called the Atkinson–Shiffrin model (Atkinson & Shiffrin, 1969), which will be discussed in Chapter 3. The diagram is made up of four sections: red, green, blue, and yellow. The red section can be viewed as the interface between the world outside us and our internal experience, including sensory memory,

FIGURE 1.4 The Organization of the Text At the core are discussions of sensory and memory processes, which then are shown to inform the cognitive systems of language, problem solving, reasoning, and decision making.

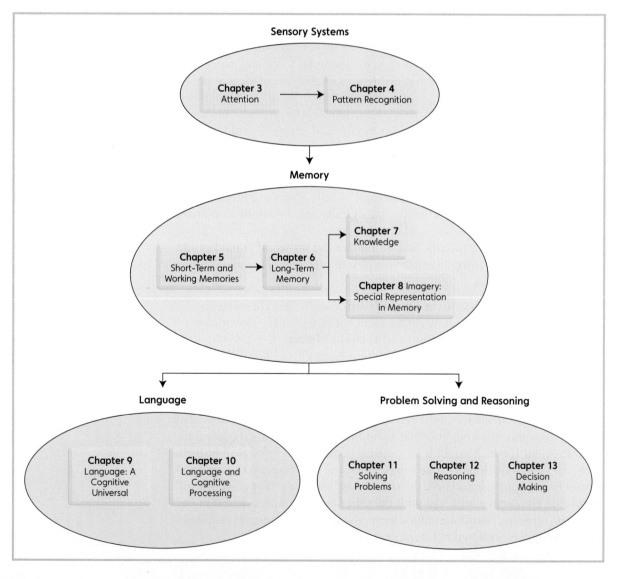

attention, and pattern recognition. The green section highlights the cognitive container within which all human mental processes are active. This includes two memory systems that will be described in Chapters 4–8: short-term/working memory and long-term memory. These memory systems interact and are the resources that language and human reasoning (represented by the blue and yellow boxes, respectively) depend upon.

The language system, the blue box, allows us to carry on conversations, understand an instruction manual for using an mp3 player, or mentally describe a route to find our way home. Human language operates according to its own rules and processes, but it relies on memory to provide the meaning of words, the importance of context, and the ongoing themes of a conversation. Language topics are discussed in Chapters 9 and 10.

The section outlined in yellow represents the human reasoning system. The arrows leading from the memory and language systems indicate the collaboration between our memory systems and language system to help us solve problems and make decisions. Although our reasoning and problem-solving abilities rely on other cognitive systems to some extent, these processes also operate according to their own rules. Chapters 11–13 are devoted to understanding how we reason, solve problems, and make decisions.

Before we launch into areas rich in content and theory, Chapter 2 offers a review of brain structure and function as well as cognitive neuroscience imaging methods that allow cognitive scientists to create and test their theories.

SECTION SUMMARY ▪

About This Text

This textbook introduces the research, theory, and practice of modern cognitive psychology. In describing critical elements of cognitive theory and how they are tested in scientific studies, the book also points to how these findings can be used to help people struggling with neurological and psychological difficulties and to explain phenomena from our everyday lives. The chapters of this book seek to draw out the universality of cognitive processes that underlie human behavior, while also acknowledging differences in cognitive processes that are biologically based or the result of environmental or cultural influences. The effort of cognitive psychology to understand the universal would not be complete without addressing the nature of individual differences.

This text is divided into four key parts in addition to this chapter and the next chapter, which provides a review of brain structure and neuroscience imaging methods. Chapters 3 and 4 cover sensory systems, which are the interface between the outside world and our internal experience. Human memory systems are the topics of Chapters 5–8. The language system is described in Chapters 9 and 10 in terms of its unique processes as well as its connections with and dependence on memory systems. Reasoning, problem solving, decision making, and the extent to which these processes depend upon our memory and language systems are covered in Chapters 11–13.

▪ ▪

CHAPTER SUMMARY

Cognitive psychology describes and explains those processes by which sensory input is transformed, reduced, elaborated, stored, recovered, and used (Neisser, 1967). Cognitive psychology emerged from the research fields of Gestalt psychology and human perception, human factors, computer simulation, and cognitive neuroscience. Cognitive psychology is not only a discipline of study, it also reflects a way of thinking about human behavior called information processing. It developed at a time in the early 20th century when psychologists often thought it was unscientific to investigate mental processes. In spite of this early opposition, cognitive research has thrived because it has been able to enrich our understanding of individual human behavior and illuminate the common threads that unite human beings.

Cognitive psychologists are concerned with basic processes of thought, including human memory, language, and reasoning. Researchers have developed special measures to acquire knowledge about cognitive processes: response accuracy, the actual response that is made, response latency, and transfer of training. Each provides a different kind of information about how we learn, remember, and solve problems.

The relationship between research, theory, and practice in cognitive psychology is a major emphasis of this book. It promotes an understanding of the universal aspects of human cognitive processes as well as research related to cognitive differences among groups of people and those expressed by individuals over time. This emphasis on universal processes and individual differences helps to explain the behavior of people as they live their daily lives.

KEY TERMS

cognitive psychology, p. 2

cognition, p. 3

symbolic distance effect, p. 4

memory, p. 7

behaviorists, p. 8

information processing, p. 8

Gestalt psychology, p. 9

human factors, p. 9

cognitive neuroscience, p. 11

cognitive science, p. 12

response latency (response time; reaction time), p. 14

transfer of training (transfer of learning), p. 15

advance organizers, p. 20

QUESTIONS FOR REVIEW

Check Your Knowledge

1. How do scientists define cognition?

2. What is the symbolic distance effect and why is it used as an illustration of internal processing?

3. Is a person's memory of an event more like a photocopy or more like a jigsaw puzzle?

4. What four disciplines contributed to the rise of modern cognitive psychology?

5. What point of view does cognitive psychology reflect?

6. What issues did Gestalt psychologists study?

7. What is human factors research, and what contributions did researchers in this area make to cognitive psychology?

8. What metaphors for cognition come from the field of computer simulation?

9. What is cognitive neuroscience?

10. What aspects of the field of cognitive neuroscience have been most useful to cognitive psychology?

11. What is cognitive science, and what is its relationship to cognitive psychology?

12. Describe response accuracy. What does it measure?

13. What is the produced response method? Provide examples.

14. Explain response latency. What sorts of cognitive phenomena does it measure?

15. What three-step procedure do children use when they are asked to add two numbers (e.g., $2 + 5$)?

16. What do cognitive psychologists assume fills the time between a stimulus and a response? In other words, what accounts for response time?

17. Why do cognitive psychologists measure transfer of training (also called transfer of learning)?

18. What contributions has cognitive psychology made to understanding human functioning?

19. Why is it important to understand and document human universals?

20. Why is it important to understand and document human differences?

21. What do newborn infants prefer to look at? Is this preference learned?

22. What are advance organizers, and how are they helpful?

23. What four basic aspects of cognition will be examined in this textbook?

Apply Your Knowledge

1. Assess Neisser's (1967, p. 4) definition of cognition. Make a list of the cognitive processes that you think you regularly use. Categorize each of these processes according to Neisser's definition: "*transformed, reduced, elaborated, stored, recovered,* and *used* [emphasis added]." Are any of the processes you have listed left over? Does Neisser's definition leave out any key parts of cognition?

2. Because infants spend more time staring at faces that adults think are attractive, does that mean that there are aspects of faces that humans around the world would see as contributing to attractiveness?

3. If thinking and speaking are human universals, and nearly everyone can think and speak, why do we have philosophy courses on how to think clearly and courses that teach grammar?

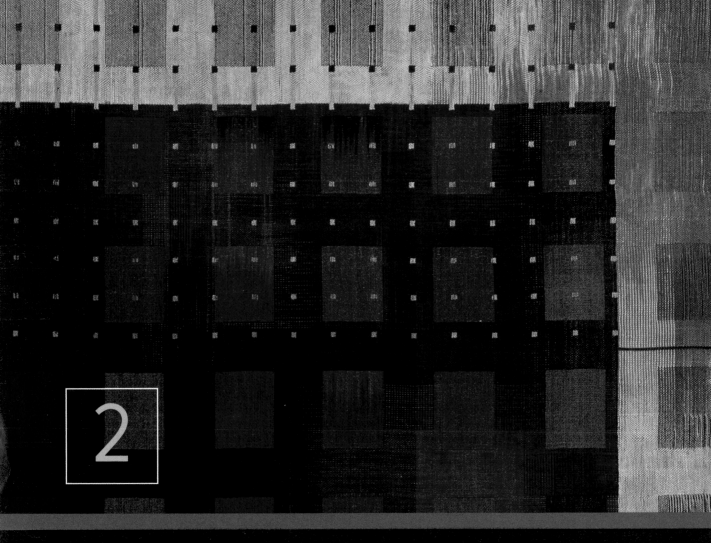

2

The Brain and Cognition

"[from the brain] come joys, delights, laughter and sports, and sorrows, griefs, despondency, and lamentations. And by this, in a special manner, we acquire wisdom and knowledge, and see and hear, and know what are foul and what are fair, what are bad and what are good, what are sweet and what unsavory."

—Hippocrates of Cos

The study of brain functioning over the past four decades by cognitive neuroscientists has had a tremendous impact on cognitive psychology. Interest in the brain is not new, however. Long before the first cognitive psychologists entered a laboratory, people wondered what the purpose of the brain might be. Ancient humans sensed a connection between brain and behavior and practiced a form of brain surgery on people with emotional difficulties. The surgery, called **trepanning** (or **trephining**), is performed by making a hole or holes in a person's skull (see **FIGURE 2.1**). Anthropologists believe that ancient humans performed these surgeries in order to allow evil spirits to escape or to invite the soul to return (Harris, 2004). Trepanning is probably the oldest surgical operation known: Evidence for it has been

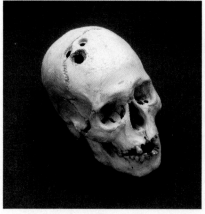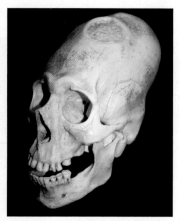

FIGURE 2.1 Trepanned Skulls Trepanning is a form of surgery dating back thousands of years. A hole (sometimes multiple holes) was cut into the skull with a round saw (*trepan*) in order to let evil spirits out or good ones in. The round piece of bone that was removed was worn for good luck. (A) shows a skull with multiple holes, and (B) is a skull that shows evidence of healing. Some people lived after the ordeal, most did not.

SSPL/Getty Images, Sabena Jane Blackbird/Alamy

(A)   (B)

found in 40,000-year-old Cro-Magnon sites and in archaeological digs around the world (Finger & Clower, 2003; Stone & Urcid, 2002). The brain's influence on behavior seems to be one of the earliest medical concepts. The Father of Medicine, Hippocrates (460–375 BCE), whose quote about the brain begins this chapter, wrote detailed instructions on how to perform skull trepanning as a treatment for most medical conditions (see Gross, 1999).

Our knowledge of what the brain does did not progress very rapidly from the early Greeks, partly because Roman law and later religious restrictions prevented European physicians from examining the brains of dead people. Scientific knowledge of the human brain and how our bodies work was so stifled, in fact, that until the 17th century most medical students did not know that their medical texts were based on the anatomy of monkeys (Barbary macaques) and not humans (Siraisi, 2001).

Brain Structure and Function: A Brief Review

Modern knowledge of the brain and its functions has come a long way since the ancient Greeks considered the brain a mass of tissue too inert to produce a thought. As late as the 17th century, Sir Thomas More, the English philosopher, is reported to have said of the brain: "This lax pith or marrow in man's head shows no more capacity for thought than a cake of suet or a bowl of curds" (quoted in Zimmer, 2004). On the face of it, More's perspective isn't too far-fetched. Look at the brain shown in **FIGURE 2.2**: It looks like a mass of clay with some hills and valleys in it. In fact, you are looking at a diagram of the brain of world-renowned physicist Albert Einstein, discoverer of the theory of relativity and one of the great minds in human history.

Of course, it's not how the brain looks but how it performs that counts. When we focus on the brain and its ability to produce cognitive processes, it is still a mystery how the physical operations of a concrete substance like the brain are able to evoke the mental experiences of thought. This is called the *mind–body problem*. We often look to the writings of the 17th-century French mathematician, scientist, and philosopher René Descartes (especially to *The Passions of the Soul*, 1649/1989) for early scientific thinking on how these two systems are connected. Alas, virtually none of his conjectures have withstood the test of time—the problem still awaits keen minds to solve.

Neurons: Building Blocks of the Brain

The human brain is made up of cells and the fibers connecting those cells, which are all immersed in a chemical environment. These circuits of specialized cells and their interconnections are called **neurons**. The typical adult's brain consists of more than 10 billion neurons (Shepherd & Koch, 1998; Williams &

FIGURE 2.2 Albert Einstein's Brain Human brains have valleys (*fissures* or *sulci*) and hills (*gyri*). The brain of Albert Einstein, one of the great geniuses of the 20th century, had less-developed fissures, which may have allowed the neurons of his brain to communicate better than the typical person.

BSIP/Photo Researchers

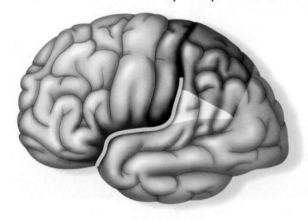

Herrup, 1988) that allow us to learn, think, and behave by transmitting signals throughout the nervous system. A diagram representing the structure of a neuron is shown in **FIGURE 2.3**. Notice that the neuron contains three major parts: (a) a cell body, which processes and transmits information; (b) fibers, called *dendrites*, which conduct input to the cell body; and (c) an axon, which conducts electrical activity from the cell body to a junction with other cells, called a synapse. The mass that we see when we look at the surface of the brain, called the **cortex**, is composed of the cell bodies and their axons. Hidden from view in the figure are the axons that connect neurons to one another and convey signals from the cell bodies at a rate upward of 220 miles per hour (100 msec). This is slightly faster than the highest average winning speed at the Indianapolis 500 race of 186 mph, achieved by Arie Luyendyk, in 1990.

If the brain were merely a large net of interconnected nerves, however, we humans would respond to events much like a jellyfish. We would be incapable of the novel, unpredictable actions independent of external events that mark much of human behavior. The key to our dynamic nervous system is the **synapse**, a junction that allows neurons to communicate. A synapse is basically a gap between neurons that fills with packets of chemicals called **neurotransmitters** when an electrical signal is transmitted down the axon. To appreciate the role synapses play, it is crucial to understand a puzzling thing about the human nervous system: Neurons are independent units; one neuron is not "wired" to another, but connects to other neurons across the synapse. When neurotransmitters are released into the synaptic gap, they act as switches that either allow an electrical impulse to occur on the other side of the gap or prevent an electrical signal.

When a signal is allowed, it is then transmitted to the cell body of the next neuron or, depending upon the strength of the electrical impulses, to the cell bodies of a number of neurons that have been activated. After they have done their job, neurotransmitters break down into their component parts or are washed out of the synapse. Research in cognitive neuroscience has shown that our ability to focus attention and solve problems relies on the contribution of these neurotransmitters to the smooth functioning of the neuron's synapses. In fact, many cognitive difficulties that people experience are the result of deficits in one or more of these neurotransmitters (e.g., Kolb & Whishaw, 2001; Vercelletto, Bourin, Lacomblez, Verpillat, & Derkinderen, 2005). The neurotransmitter dopamine, for example, stimulates nerve cells that control the muscles. People with Parkinson's disease typically have lost at least 80% of the cells that produce dopamine. Because of this, their motor system nerves have difficulty controlling

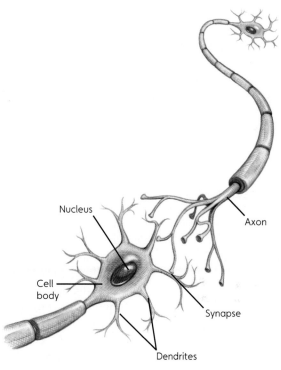

Nucleus

Axon

Cell body

Synapse

Dendrites

FIGURE 2.3 The Neuron The typical adult's brain contains billions of neurons that consist of a cell body that processes information, dendrites that bring inputs to the cell body, and an axon that conducts electrical activity from the cell to other neurons. When we look at the surface of the brain, it appears to be gray and is composed mainly of neuronal cells.

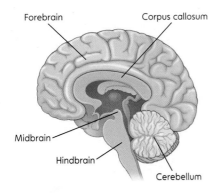

FIGURE 2.4 Sections of the Human Brain Key sections of human brain as seen from an interior view: hindbrain (including the cerebellum), midbrain, and forebrain.

movement and coordination. Symptoms characteristic of individuals with Parkinson's disease are muscle tremors, slow movement, poor balance, and difficulty walking.

Major Divisions of the Brain

The brain is roughly divided into three main sections from bottom to top: hindbrain, midbrain, and forebrain (see **FIGURE 2.4**). These three sections contribute to our cognitive functioning in specialized ways. Starting at the bottom or ventral portion is the **hindbrain,** which controls automatic processes that regulate basic life-support functions such as breathing, heart rate, swallowing, and sleep cycles. The hindbrain keeps us alive; damage to the central area of the hindbrain can result in coma or death. An important area of the hindbrain is the cerebellum. Its primary function is balance and the coordination of voluntary movements. Damage to the cerebellum makes it difficult to coordinate movements such as walking, kicking, typing, or throwing a ball. The reason drunken drivers can't pass the field sobriety test ("close your eyes, put out your arms, and touch your nose with your index finger" or "walk the white line") is that alcohol affects the cerebellum and makes these ordinary tasks difficult (e.g., Ivry, Spencer, Zelanik, & Diedrichsen, 2006; Sullivan, Deshmukh, Desmond, Lim, & Pfefferbaum, 2000).

The cerebellum also plays an important role in the ability to perform high-level cognitive tasks (e.g., Akshoomoff & Courchesne, 1992). Children who are born with a genetic disorder called Joubert syndrome have damage where the two halves of the cerebellum come together. These children not only have balance, coordination, and breathing difficulties, but they almost always show some form of mental retardation (Braddock, Farmer, Deidrick, Iverson, & Maria, 2006; Merritt, 2003).

The **midbrain** is the relay center for sensory information entering the brain, such as hearing and vision. A bundle of fibers associated with voluntary movement also passes through the midbrain. Damage to the midbrain can cause problems in hearing, seeing, and motor control. People who are diagnosed with Parkinson's dementia or epilepsy often have damage to a part of the midbrain called the *substantia nigra* ("black substance"), which produces a key neurotransmitter, dopamine (Frank, 2005; Sabatino, Gravante, Ferraro, Savatteri, & La Grutta, 1988; Theodore, 2006). Maintaining the proper level of dopamine is critical for attention, memory, motivation, and problem solving (e.g., Ashby, Isen, & Turken, 1999; Nieoullon, 2002) as well as muscle control.

It is also possible to have too much of a neurotransmitter. For example, excess dopamine is associated with a thought disorder called *schizophrenia* (van Rossum, Tenback, & van Os, 2009; Weinberger, 1987). Antipsychotic drugs used for treating schizophrenia are effective because they reduce excess dopamine levels (e.g., Seeman & Kapur, 2000; Strange, 2001).

The **forebrain** surrounds the midbrain and contains the cerebral cortex. This part of the brain regulates higher mental processes and enables people to engage in complex learning, memory, thought, and language. As already noted, the wrinkled outer portion of the forebrain, shown in Figure 2.2, is the cortex. The deep wrinkles or valleys in the cortex are called *sulci* and allow more surface area to be squeezed into the skull. To experience how sulci expand the surface area of the brain, take a piece of standard 8½ by 11 inch paper and try to fit it into a coffee cup. It only fits if it is crunched into a tight ball and forced in. When you pull the paper out, it is nearly as wrinkled as the surface of your brain. If laid flat, the average individual's cortex would cover approximately 2½ square feet (Peters & Jones, 1984).

Brain Lateralization

The brain is divided into two halves, split down the middle from front to back. Each half is called a **hemisphere**, and research has revealed that each hemisphere serves different cognitive functions (Geschwind & Levitsky, 1968; Kolb & Whishaw, 2001). Moreover, if ancient physicians had been allowed to examine the brains of cadavers, they might have noticed that the human brain is not symmetrical. Studies examining many human brains have revealed that the right frontal part of the brain is typically longer and larger than the left frontal part of the brain, and the left rear part of the brain is typically larger than the right rear part of the brain (Chui & Damasio, 1980; Galaburda, LeMay, Kemper, & Geschwind, 1978; Narr et al., 2007).

The right and left hemispheres are connected by giant collections of fibers called *commissures*. The largest is the **corpus callosum** (see Figure 2.4); others include the *anterior* and *hippocampal commissures*, and especially the *fornix*. When the corpus callosum's band of fibers is cut (typically in treatments for epilepsy; e.g., Ivry & Robertson, 1998; Wilson, Reeves, & Gazzaniga, 1982) or when it is not fully developed at birth (Moutard et al., 2003), people experience a **split brain** (or **divided brain**) in which one hemisphere has little knowledge of the signals that the other hemisphere is processing (Gazzaniga, 2005; Sperry, 1964). On a daily basis, people with split brains are mostly unaware of their condition because the areas of the brain that create conscious awareness reside in the left hemisphere and are cut off from their natural collaboration with the right hemisphere (Roser & Gazzaniga, 2004).

Each hemisphere has a particular relationship to the body. The right hemisphere generally controls the left side of the body, and the left hemisphere generally controls the right side of the body. For example, if particular parts of the motor areas of someone's brain are damaged on the right side, he or she will not be able to move certain parts of his or her left arm, left leg, or the fingers on the left hand. A similar pattern is shown for the left hemisphere. In addition, the right hemisphere registers the sensations originating from the left side of the body and the left hemisphere registers the sensations originating from the right side of the body.

The hemispheres also generally perform different functions. For example, the left hemisphere in most people controls the basic language functions of speech production, grammatical analysis, and comprehension, while the right hemisphere language centers participate in understanding figurative language and metaphor. People with impairments in the right hemisphere language areas often fail to understand jokes or sarcasm (Code, 1987; Foldi, Cicone, & Gardner, 1983; Winner & Gardner, 1977). People with this type of brain damage will interpret the metaphor for sadness, "John has a heavy heart," as "John's heart is big and weighs a lot" (Winner & Gardner, 1977).

Brain Localization

The hypothesis that different functions of thought are performed in different locations in the brain is called **localization of function**. Although it is a core assumption of much of the research in cognitive neuroscience, it has been around for only 200 years and was the result of a misguided view of the brain that gained popularity in the early 19th century.

Franz Josef Gall (1758–1828), German anatomist and physiologist, and the founder of phrenology, anticipated many modern neuroscientific discoveries when he argued that the brain was the organ of the mind and that different mental abilities were localized in different areas of the brain (Gall, 1835). Gall believed that the size of these areas was in proportion to the amount of the specific ability ("faculty") that a person possessed. Gall even provided a map locating the positions of 37 different mental and moral functions in the brain, which is shown in **FIGURE 2.5**.

Unfortunately, Gall and his colleagues diverged from science into quackery when they proposed that it was possible to identify these areas by looking at bumps on the skull: the larger the bump, the bigger the brain development under that area of the skull, according to their claims. The study of these bumps was called *phrenology* (Spurzheim, 1815). Although phrenologists unfortunately took money from people in order to "read" the bumps on their skulls, the concept that mental functions were localized in the brain was largely correct. It soon led to discoveries by Pierre Paul Broca (1861) and others about how language was produced by the brain and how higher mental processes could be related to the functioning of specific areas of the brain (Broca and his research will be described in Chapter 9).

We know now that in addition to having designated brain areas more devoted to some tasks than others, the brain generally acts in concert, with many areas contributing to a particular function or memory (e.g., Kroger et al., 2002; Uttal, 2001). For example, some parts of the brain increase activity while other parts decrease activity as tasks become more complex (Fox et al., 2005).

FIGURE 2.5 Gall's Phrenology Chart A phrenologist's atlas of the human brain, which identifies important mental functions with specific places in the brain that can be observed by identifying bumps on the skull.

ARPL/Topham/The Image Works

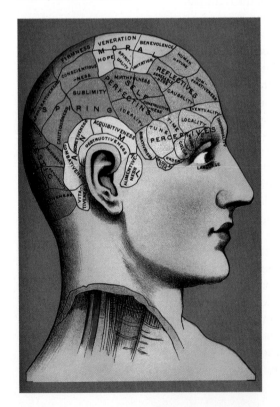

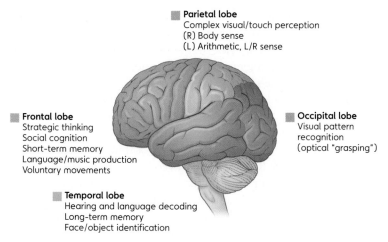

Parietal lobe
Complex visual/touch perception
(R) Body sense
(L) Arithmetic, L/R sense

Frontal lobe
Strategic thinking
Social cognition
Short-term memory
Language/music production
Voluntary movements

Occipital lobe
Visual pattern
recognition
(optical "grasping")

Temporal lobe
Hearing and language decoding
Long-term memory
Face/object identification

FIGURE 2.6 Lobes of the Brain and Their Major Functions There are four major divisions of the cortex: the occipital, parietal, temporal, and frontal lobes. Each lobe is associated with higher cognitive functions.

The bumps on the brain that fascinated the phrenologists are called *gyri* and between the bumps are deep grooves, called *fissures*. Fissures divide the cortex into four sections called *lobes*: the occipital, parietal, temporal, and frontal lobes (see **FIGURE 2.6**).

The primary visual area of the cortex is located in the **occipital lobe**, which does the complex job of processing the signals from our eyes (Hubel, 1989). In fact, the organization of the retina of the eye is mapped onto a key area of the occipital lobe called the *primary visual cortex*. Damage to the occipital lobe can lead to cortical blindness, which is a visual impairment even though the eyes are intact.

The **parietal lobes** (one in each hemisphere) are located above the occipital lobe and register our sensory experiences including touch, taste, and sight. The parietal lobes are also responsible for our ability to locate objects in space after they are identified by the occipital lobe (Mishkin, Ungerleider, & Macko, 1983), and play a role in spatially based, mathematical thinking. The parietal lobes' major functions were clearly evident in a study of the brain of Albert Einstein (see Figure 2.2). In most respects, Einstein's brain was typical of other adults his age. However, the lower portion of his parietal lobe was considerably more developed, making it 15% wider than would typically have been expected (Witelson, Kigar, & Harvey, 1999). The increased size of Einstein's parietal lobe may have contributed to the creation of Einstein's extraordinary mathematical theories.

The human brain has two **temporal lobes,** one in each hemisphere. The temporal lobes process sound, language, and long-term memories. Because we have two temporal lobes, damage to one does not necessarily produce complete loss of cognitive functioning. For example, complete deafness does not occur when there is damage to the left temporal lobe because there is a similar area in the right temporal lobe. The temporal lobes also contribute to our ability to retain auditory experiences in memory for a brief period of time (Buchsbaum & D'Esposito, 2008).

The **frontal lobe** performs many functions, especially those related to attention, memory, problem solving, and communication. Damage to specific parts of the frontal lobe results in different deficits. Brain injuries to the frontal lobe may result in difficulties in solving problems (e.g., Polk, Simen, Lewis, & Freedman, 2002), remembering events in one's life (e.g., Habib, Nyberg, & Tulving, 2003), or paying attention (E. E. Smith & Jonides, 1999; Volle et al., 2008). For example, if the left part of the frontal lobe is damaged due to a stroke or injury, people will typically lose the ability to speak fluently. This deficit may be so severe that they cannot form words and are restricted to a speaking vocabulary of only one or two words (see G. Martin, 2003; R. C. Martin & Freedman, 2001). Surprisingly, some people with this type of injury can sing songs that they knew prior to the brain damage (Yamadori, Osumi, Masuhara, & Okubo, 1977). An explanation for this odd outcome is that the person has neurological damage in the left frontal lobe, but the right frontal lobe, which contains the knowledge of song lyrics and melodies, is preserved. This finding is the basis of an effective treatment for stroke-related language difficulties called melodic intonation therapy (MIT). In it, patients are trained to speak with a melody by planning ahead what they want to say and creating a minisong to express it (Robey, 1994).

Brain Plasticity

One of the most fascinating properties of the brain is its organizational flexibility, which allows us to recover from injuries and other deficits (Ofan & Zohary, 2007; Ptito, Moesgaard, Gjedde, & Kupers, 2005). For example, when children are born with lesions or holes in one area of their brain, other regions will take over the functions that would have been performed in the damaged area (Reilly, Bates, & Marchman, 1998). Researchers describe the brain as "plastic" because it is capable of being modified by experience (Kolb, 1995; Rakic, 2002).

The occipital lobe was described previously as processing visual information. It is also capable of supporting other functions. Although it is reasonable to suppose that the occipital lobe would perform few functions for people who are blind from birth, it is actually active when visually impaired people read Braille—a touch-based writing system. In contrast, sighted people who read Braille do not show activation in the occipital lobe (Sadato et al., 1998). Clearly, the brain can change its functioning to accommodate special needs.

Another example of the brain's plasticity is shown in the effectiveness of the MIT procedure for helping people who have speech impairments as a result of a stroke in the prefrontal cortex. Not only does the person's speaking ability improve, but the previously damaged brain areas become partially reactivated as a result of the training (Belin et al., 1996).

The brain's plasticity should not come as a great surprise because we are all capable of learning new facts, new ways to behave, and new patterns to recognize. All of this requires some new growth and reorganization of the brain. Before birth and throughout life, brain cells grow new connections, a process called **neurogenesis** (Kandel, 2007). It allows for the overwhelming plasticity of the nervous system.

SECTION SUMMARY ▪

Brain Structure and Function: A Brief Review

In spite of the breadth of differences in appearance and experiences, all human beings have similar brains. The human brain consists of a vast, interconnected network of neurons, which are made up of cell bodies, dendrites, and axons. Neurons communicate with each other at a connection site called a synapse. The activity at the synapse depends on the presence of chemicals called neurotransmitters, which either promote transmission of signals from one neuron to another or turn off electrical transmission in the adjacent neurons.

The brain has three main structural levels: hindbrain, midbrain, and forebrain. The hindbrain regulates basic life-support functions such as breathing, heart rate, and swallowing. The cerebellum, a part of the hindbrain, controls motor coordination and some intellectual activities. The midbrain is the relay center for sensory information entering the brain, such as hearing and vision. It also contains a center important for attention and the production of the neurotransmitter dopamine.

The forebrain has a lateral organization: It is divided into two hemispheres. The right hemisphere controls signals to and from the left side of the body and the left hemisphere controls signals to and from the right side of the body. The hemispheres are connected by bundles of fibers, the largest of which is the corpus callosum. When these fibers are severed, one side of the brain does not know what the other side is experiencing. The top of the forebrain is the cortex, which is divided into sections called lobes, each having its own specialized functions. The occipital lobe at the rear of the brain is a major processor of visual information. The parietal lobes (one in each hemisphere) process sensory and spatial information. The temporal lobes (one in each hemisphere) are important to language, hearing, and memory. Activity in the frontal lobe is associated with attention, memory, problem solving, and communication.

Although different cognitive functions are localized to specific areas of the brain, the brain is said to be plastic: capable of rewiring itself to accommodate general psychological experiences as well as physical insults. The concept of neurogenesis tells us that all experience—even into adulthood—is coded in the brain as new neuronal connections. At the level of the neuron, our brains are always rewiring themselves to provide for new knowledge, understanding, or skills.

▪ ▪

Brain Imaging Methods and Cognitive Research

Cognitive scientists have a wonderful array of tools at their disposal to examine the relationship between neurological activity and cognitive processes. These research methods fall into the general category of **neuroimaging**, which refers to methods that reveal the structure and functioning of the brain. To give an example of the usefulness of these imaging methods, consider the mental arithmetic study discussed in Chapter 1. A common observation is that elementary schoolchildren take longer to successfully perform mental arithmetic than do college students. The question is why. Do the two age groups apply different methods to perform mental arithmetic, or are adults simply much faster at everything?

Neuroimaging provides an answer to this question. Students aged 8 to 19 years were asked to perform mental arithmetic problems while their brains were scanned (Rivera, Reiss, Eckert, & Menon, 2005). As a result, researchers found that the task activated different parts of the younger and older students' brains (see **FIGURE 2.7**). The areas in the frontal lobe (the prefrontal cortex) were most active in the younger participants; the areas in the parietal lobe were most active for the older participants. This reveals that the increased speed with

FIGURE 2.7 Speed of Mental Arithmetic and Age Neuroimaging methods can answer basic questions about cognitive processes. Here, scanning the brain (A) when a person is performing mental arithmetic (B) reveals that adults use different areas of the brain (activation shown in red) and therefore a different set of processes than do children (activation shown in blue) to perform mental arithmetic (C).

Photo courtesy Prof. Vinod Menon, Stanford University

(A)

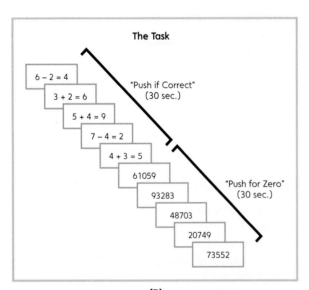

(B)

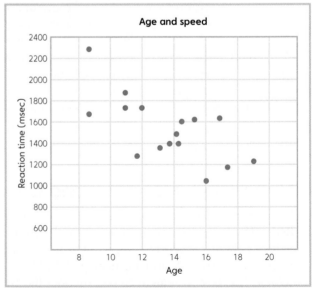

(C)

which older participants solve arithmetic problems is a result of using a different method for the calculation. That is, as we age a change occurs in how we use our brains (Ashcraft, 1982, 1995; LeFevre, Sadesky, & Bisanz, 1996). This is just a small example of how neuroimaging methods can help cognitive psychologists answer basic questions about human mental processes.

The three most commonly used brain imaging methods for cognitive neuroscience research are the electroencephalograph (EEG), positron emission tomography (PET), and functional magnetic resonance imaging (fMRI). These techniques have advanced our understanding of the relationship between human cognition and neurological structure and have been invaluable in testing theories developed from laboratory studies, such as the mental arithmetic models just discussed.

Electroencephalography (EEG)

Electroencephalography (EEG) is the oldest imaging method of all those currently employed. It uses electrodes on the scalp to record the electrical activity of the brain. A person wearing a typical electrode cap is shown in **FIGURE 2.8A**. The

FIGURE 2.8 EEG Diagrams (A) A volunteer wears a cap with EEG electrodes. (B) Diagrams showing brain waves taken from people who are experiencing different levels of consciousness (excited, relaxed, drowsy, asleep, coma). These brain waves vary in height (*amplitude*) and how rapidly they repeat (*frequency*).

Sean Gallup/Getty Images

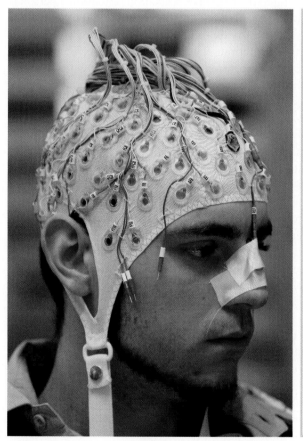

(A)

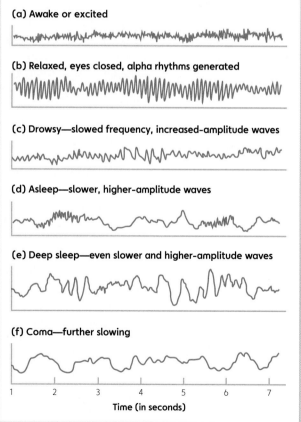

(a) Awake or excited

(b) Relaxed, eyes closed, alpha rhythms generated

(c) Drowsy—slowed frequency, increased-amplitude waves

(d) Asleep—slower, higher-amplitude waves

(e) Deep sleep—even slower and higher-amplitude waves

(f) Coma—further slowing

Time (in seconds)

(B)

EEG waves, sometimes called *brain waves,* reflect the total electrical output of neurons near the electrodes. There is always some electrical activity in the brain: Even when a person is resting and not performing any task, the brain is still active. However, the EEG signals vary with the person's state of arousal. To illustrate this, **FIGURE 2.8B** shows a sample of waves taken from people who are experiencing different levels of consciousness (excited, relaxed, drowsy, asleep, coma). Notice that the brain waves shown vary not only in height (*amplitude*), but also in how rapidly they repeat (*frequency*). These factors are used to diagnose the alertness of a person (S. J. Smith, 2005). Notice that the amplitude of someone in deep sleep is about the same as someone in a coma. However, the frequency of the two kinds of waves is quite different. Now compare the brain waves obtained when someone is sleeping with those measured when a person is deeply relaxed. The wave pattern of a relaxed person (*alpha rhythm*), exhibits high amplitude and high but rhythmic frequency.

EEGs are frequently used in clinical settings to diagnose conditions that affect the brain, such as epilepsy, tumors, and physical damage to the brain. They have also been used to help paralyzed people communicate. The frequency of brain waves changes according to the degree of relaxation or tension a person is feeling. If paralyzed individuals are hooked up to a computer that uses an EEG to record their brain waves, the individuals can select letters displayed by an assistant merely by thinking of something that makes them tense. This changes the brain waves, and the computer informs the assistant that the letter has been chosen. Simple messages may be communicated in this way, allowing an otherwise isolated person to make their wishes known (Kotchoubey, Lang, Winter, & Birbaumer, 2003; Pham et al., 2005).

Another important use of the electroencephalogram is to identify momentary changes in the EEG signal that occur as an immediate response to something that the participant has observed or thought about. These electrical responses are called **event-related potentials (ERPs)**. They occur at different time delays following a psychological event. In one study, ERPs were collected as young adults watched a screen that displayed colored slides of people, places, and paintings taken from a variety of print sources. The graph of the average of all participants is presented in **FIGURE 2.9A** and shows that about 300–400 msec (0.30–0.40 sec) after the slide was presented, the observer's brain responded to it. The amplitude of the response varied according to whether or not the observers recognized the objects in the slide (the more negative—downward—the ERP, the greater the recognition) and their degree of surprise in seeing particular objects (the more negative the response, the greater the surprise, as shown in **FIGURE 2.9B**) (Neville, Snyder, Woods, & Galambos, 1982). The brain of an observer registers a surprise response to events even before the observer is aware of what is happening. ERPs can reveal a full range of human sensitivities, from an emotional response (Vuilleumier, Armony, Driver, & Dolan, 2001) to the awareness that a sentence is ungrammatical or ambiguous (e.g., Kutas & van Petten, 1994).

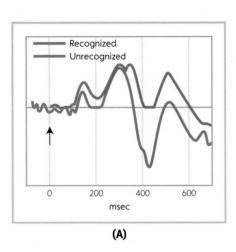

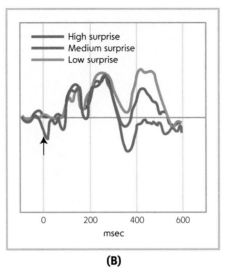

(A) **(B)**

FIGURE 2.9 Evoked Potential
Event-related potentials reflect the momentary changes in the EEG signal that occur as an immediate response to something the participant has observed or thought about. (A) The blue line is the response to the recognition of a picture; the red line is the response when the observer does not recognize a picture. (B) The blue line shows a high degree of surprise, the red line shows a medium degree, and the green line shows a low degree of surprise.

Source: From Neville, Snyder, Woods, & Galambos, 1982

One reason why EEG is so useful for cognitive research is that it answers the questions, when does it happen? and where does it happen? Notice in Figure 2.9 that the most downward point in the wave occurs around 300–400 msec after the stimulus is presented. This tells the researcher that it takes this much time for the brain to register the surprise. When the participant recognizes the pictures, the largest responses occur at electrodes over the frontal lobe, the parietal lobe, and the center of the skull. When the person does not recognize the pictures, the largest responses are in the parietal area. This suggests that even the simplest instance of surprised recognition requires the activity of several areas of the brain.

Positron Emission Tomography (PET)

The use of EEG techniques is helpful in identifying *when* broad areas of the brain are involved in specific cognitive events. Other methods have been effective in more precisely identifying *which* specific brain areas are active during cognitive events. One of these techniques is **positron emission tomography (PET)**. The basic idea behind the use of PET is that the more an area of the brain is involved in a cognitive task, the more blood will flow there. The PET system indirectly measures the amount of blood flow. To do this, a radioactive dose of glucose (the body's main source of energy) is injected into the bloodstream. The glucose emits particles called *positrons* as it is processed by the neurons. The brain is scanned to detect the energy that is released when the positrons interact with the electrons of the brain cells.

The PET camera, shown in **FIGURE 2.10**, identifies the location of this energy and creates an activity map of the brain. It does this by using a "subtraction" method. A participant engages in two types of tasks: one that requires minimal processing of information and a second that requires the cognitive functioning that the researcher is interested in studying. The brain areas activated during the first task

FIGURE 2.10 PET Scanner After a radioactive dose of glucose is injected, the PET (positron emission tomography) camera identifies where energy is released when blood flows to an area of the brain during a cognitive task. Using this method, researchers can create an activity map of the brain.

3D4Medical/Photo Researchers

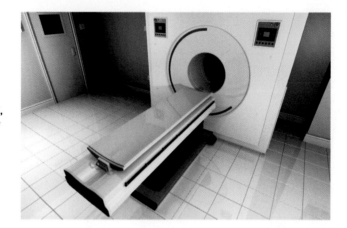

are subtracted from the brain areas associated with the second task. The difference in activation is due to the cognitive processing of interest (Posner & Raichle, 1997).

An illustration of this method can be seen in a study of mental imagery. Do the first three notes of the children's song, "Three Blind Mice," ascend or descend? Kosslyn, Ganis, and Thompson (2001) reported that when asked this question, most people say that they "hear" the song in the process of deciding. This is not the same as retrieving the answer from memory: People claim that they are actually "playing the tune" in their head.

One such study is illustrated in the Focus on Methods box. It shows that the right temporal lobe and other areas of the brain are involved in *both* hearing and imagining

FOCUS ON METHODS ■■■■■■■■■■■■■■■■■■■■■■■■■■■■

How Does the Brain Process Music?

Do we use the same brain circuits when we imagine musical lyrics as we do when we hear them? To investigate this question, American and Canadian researchers (Zatorre, Halpern, Perry, Meyer, & Evans, 1996) asked a dozen volunteers to judge the pitch of two words from familiar tunes (e.g., "Jingle Bells," "Joy to the World") while their brains were being scanned using the PET device (shown above).

Procedure

There were three conditions:

In the *perceptual* task they heard familiar songs while two words from the song were presented on a screen. The volunteers had to decide whether the second word had a higher or lower pitch than the first word. The components of this task include reading and listening.

In the *imagery* task they had to just read the words and imagine the song. The components of this task include reading and imagining.

In the *control* task they had to read the words and decide which word was longer. The component of this task was reading.

The control task was used to identify the brain areas that were activated when the participant was just reading. These areas were subtracted from the areas activated in the other two tasks. Then the brain area activated in the perceptual condition was subtracted from that in the imagery condition to see whether imagery required the same or different brain circuits.

Results

The PET scans resulting from the two conditions are shown on the next page. They illustrate that imagining a tune activates brain areas within a few millimeters of the brain areas that are activated when you actually hear the same tune. Mental imagery requires the same brain areas that actual perception requires. It's a wonder we can tell the difference between what we imagine and our perceptions of real events.

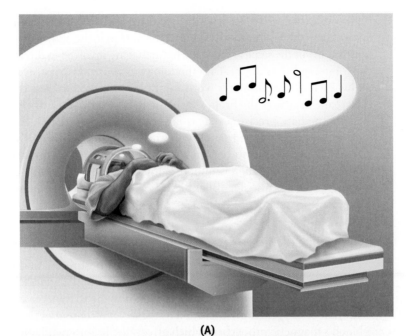

(A)

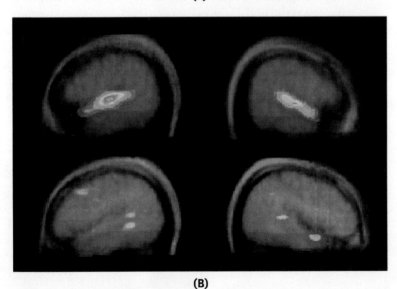

(B)

(A) A volunteer's brain is scanned while he hears or imagines a tune. (B) PET data are coded by a color scale ranging from dark for the lowest activation to white for the highest. The top brain scans show the activation in the left and right hemispheres when the person is hearing a tune. The lower brain scans show the activation that is the result of just imagining the tune. Note that imagining a tune activates brain areas within a few millimeters of the areas that are activated when you actually hear the same tune.

Zatorre, R. et al., "Hearing in the Mind's Ear: A PET Investigation of Musical Imagery and Perception," *Journal of Cognitive Neuroscience, 8:1* (Winter, 1996), pp. 29–46. © 1996 by the Massachusetts Institute of Technology.

the music (Halpern & Zatorre, 1999; Kosslyn et al., 2001). Besides helping us understand how the brain processes music, this research also shows that mental imagery uses many of the same areas of the brain that are involved in direct perception.

Timing limits the PET methodology in two ways. First, even though a stimulus such as a picture or a word might be presented for less than a second, the machine measures the brain's response over several seconds. Therefore, it lacks the immediate precision that is possible when using EEG. Second, the tracer chemicals are absorbed quickly by the brain, thus limiting the time in which researchers can study a person's activities. Another concern about PET methodology is that it depends upon the injection of a radioactive chemical—other methods are less invasive (Buckner & Logan, 2001). Some of these limitations are overcome by magnetic resonance imaging.

Functional Magnetic Resonance Imaging (fMRI)

FIGURE 2.11 BOLD Response
fMRI Magnet: (A) The participant performs a cognitive task that results in a change in the oxygen content of the blood flowing to different brain areas. (B) This alters the blood's magnetic signal (called the BOLD response), which is recorded by the electromagnetic system surrounding the participant, who rests in the cylinder.

Gregory G. Dmimjian/Photo Researchers

Functional magnetic resonance imaging is the most recent of the new technologies being used by researchers to study the brain and cognition. When a region of the brain is active, the amount of blood flowing to it increases and so does the amount of oxygen. This alteration of the oxygen content of the blood affects the blood's magnetic properties, which affects the brain's magnetic signal. This signal is called the BOLD (<u>b</u>lood <u>o</u>xygen <u>l</u>evel <u>d</u>ependent) response and is recorded by an electromagnetic system that creates an image of the electrical activity, called **functional magnetic resonance imaging (fMRI)**. This BOLD signal is an indirect measure of the amount of blood flow and therefore the amount of brain activity (Kwong et al., 1992; Ogawa et al., 1992; see also Heeger, Huk, Geisler, & Albrecht, 2000). The magnetic device shown in **FIGURE 2.11A** is a common

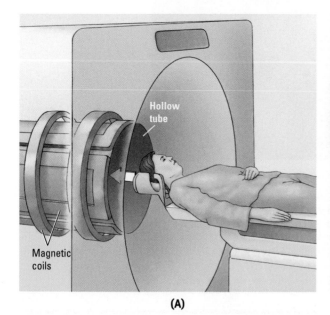

(A)

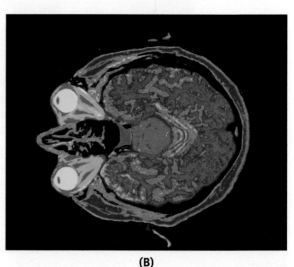

(B)

diagnostic instrument in medicine that is used to draw a static map of the brain and other parts of the body. A typical brain at rest is shown in **FIGURE 2.11B**. Research designs using this method typically involve subtraction in which two sets of conditions are compared, as in the PET studies described previously.

Functional MRI is the source of interesting new findings linking areas of the brain to specific cognitive function. It is important to be cautious in drawing conclusions from this research, however. For example, the fact that a specific area of the brain is more active when a person is solving arithmetic problems does not mean that the active area is the "arithmetic center." The finding could simply mean that the area of interest is just one of many areas that are part of a circuit involved in solving arithmetic problems, or it could be that math is stressful to the person whose brain is being imaged and the active area reflects a stress response. Many studies are needed to draw a definite conclusion from neuroimaging findings. Even though one area may be more active than another, no area is completely inactive in the normally functioning brain.

Repetitive Transcranial Magnetic Stimulation (rTMS)

TMS is a method that influences the electrical activity of an area of the brain by creating a weak electrical current using magnets that are held over the area of a participant's head. When the magnetic pulses are repetitive, it is called **repetitive transcranial magnetic stimulation (rTMS)**. It can cause an increase or decrease in a specific brain area's activity and help identify its function (e.g., Kosslyn et al., 1999; Pascual-Leone, Walsh, & Rothwell, 2000). Not only is rTMS useful in the laboratory, it may ultimately be a therapeutic tool to help individuals with neurological dysfunctions by either disrupting or enhancing brain activity (George, Lisanby, & Sackeim, 1999).

SECTION SUMMARY ▪

Brain Imaging Methods and Cognitive Research

Recent innovations in brain imaging allow cognitive researchers to observe the functioning human brain when people perform a task. These methods either record electrical waves produced by the brain, such as EEG and event-related potentials (ERPs), or they identify the amount of ongoing activity generated at a specific area of the brain as indicated by the amount of blood flow to that area. In the latter case, researchers either use positron emission tomography (PET) or functional magnetic resonance imaging (fMRI). The imaging devices are large magnets that register the change in the electrical activity of a brain area. These methods assume that the more a task demands of a specific area of the brain, the greater will be the blood flow to that area. They can also test the importance of specific brain areas by activating or inhibiting them using repetitive transcranial magnetic stimulation (rTMS). Brain imaging techniques help researchers to create a model of how the normal brain works and to test theories of cognitive processing. These methods also help identify the basis for cognitive difficulties shown by individuals who experience deficits in brain function. Although the different imaging techniques help to identify important areas that contribute to cognitive activity, we must always be mindful that the brain acts as a whole: Even though one area may be more active than another, no area is completely turned off.

CHAPTER SUMMARY

The universality of cognitive processes is largely due to the fact that human beings possess similar brains. Our brains contain a basic communication system whose fundamental unit is the neuron, composed of a cell body, dendrites, and an axon. Neurons communicate with each other at synapses, which are gaps filled with packets of chemicals called neurotransmitters that allow electrical signals to cross the gap to activate or deactivate the next neuron.

Scientists describe the brain as possessing three major divisions: hindbrain, midbrain, and forebrain. Each has its own separate function that regulates life support and cognitive processing. The cortex, the top portion of the forebrain, is divided into lobes, sections that are identified with broad cognitive functions such as attention, memory, language, sensation, motor control, and consciousness of our present condition.

Observing cognitive changes that result from neurological deficits, such as tumors, strokes, and lesions, broadens our understanding of how cognitive functions are localized within the brain. The results of this research help us to appreciate the brain's plasticity: its ability to compensate for brain damage.

Innovations in neuroimaging, using brain imaging methods such as electroencephalography (EEG), positron emission tomography (PET), functional magnetic resonance imaging (fMRI), and repetitive transcranial magnetic stimulation (rTMS), continue to help researchers identify localized brain functions. Cognitive neuroscience research has also helped cognitive scientists develop better cognitive theories and design more precise treatment methods.

KEY TERMS

trepanning (or trephining), p. 25

neurons, p. 26

cortex, p. 27

synapse, p. 27

neurotransmitters, p. 27

hindbrain, p. 28

midbrain, p. 28

forebrain, p. 29

hemisphere, p. 29

corpus callosum, p. 29

split brain (or divided brain), p. 29

localization of function, p. 30

occipital lobe, p. 31

parietal lobes, p. 31

temporal lobes, p. 31

frontal lobe, p. 32

neurogenesis, p. 32

neuroimaging, p. 33

electroencephalography (EEG), p. 35

event-related potentials (ERPs), p. 36

positron emission tomography (PET), p. 37

functional magnetic resonance imaging (fMRI), p. 40

repetitive transcranial magnetic stimulation (rTMS), p. 41

QUESTIONS FOR REVIEW

Check Your Knowledge

1. What is trepanning?

2. What are the three main sections of the brain? What are their primary functions?

3. What is phrenology and what are its basic assumptions?

4. What is the concept that mental functions could be located in specific brain areas called?

5. What are the basic biological units of the nervous system?

6. Humans have at least (a) 1 million, (b) 100 million, (c) 1 billion, or (d) 10 billion neurons?

7. What are the three basic components of the neuron?

8. What is a synapse?

9. What is a neurotransmitter? What does it do?

10. What is the largest band of fibers that connects the two brain hemispheres?

11. Which side of the body is controlled by the right hemisphere?

12. What are the lobes of the brain and what are their primary functions?

13. What does EEG measure?

14. What are the limitations of EEG as a research method?

15. What does PET measure?

16. What is a limitation of PET?

17. What does fMRI measure?

18. What is a limitation of fMRI?

Apply Your Knowledge

1. Certain areas of the brain seem to be important to specific cognitive functions. If two people's brains were organized differently, would they see the world in the same way?

2. One source of cognitive universals is the fact that humans have similar brains. Do you think our environments also contribute to cognitive universals? Do you think environment plays a role in universal aspects of brain structure and function?

3. If you were able to look inside someone's brain while the person was thinking, you wouldn't be able to see any thoughts; you would only be able to measure blood flow, oxygen consumption, electrical activity, and similar physiological phenomena. If you can't observe a thought, how do you know it has occurred?

4. If the portion of your brain associated with self-control is underdeveloped from birth and you suffer from poorly controlled emotional outbursts, is it your fault? To what extent should you be held responsible for your behavior?

3

Attention

> "We consider ourselves as defective in memory, either because we remember less than we desire, or less than we suppose others to remember. . . . The true art of memory is the art of attention."
>
> —Samuel Johnson

As soon as we wake up in the morning, we are immersed in a sea of stimulation and confusion: people asking questions, news on the TV, and pets (or children!) wanting food. At the same time, we are trying to juggle a variety of mental tasks. We may need to plan our day, remember where we put our keys, and decide what we want to eat for breakfast. This sensory input was described by one of the first American psychologists, William James (1842–1910) as a "blooming, buzzing confusion" (1890, p. 462) that starts at birth and never stops. Yet, most of us effortlessly focus on the important events of the moment and tune out irrelevant stimulation: the creak of the stairs, people we see getting on a bus, or the hum of fluorescent lights in a classroom. We notice some things and don't notice others. Meanwhile, other sorts of sights or sounds come in and out of focus, as when we register the tight fit of our shoes when we first put them on and then stop noticing their presence on our feet within a minute or two. At other times we seem to be able to focus on two things at once, such as driving a car while listening to the radio. Our attentional system allows us to achieve this broad array of mental feats.

What Is Attention?

Attention describes a set of cognitive processes that allow us to concentrate on one set of events in our environment while ignoring other events. Attention controls our mental environment by choosing the events that will enter our consciousness. When we are aware of the contents of our consciousness and react to them, we say we are paying attention. Not every event in our environment is allowed to pass through our attentional filter. For example, in the early part of the 20th century, the canneries in Monterey, California (made famous in the writings of John Steinbeck) used a unique series of whistles to alert their workers to the arrival of fishing boats in the early morning. Workers seemed to wake up to the distinctive tones of the whistle for their own cannery and sleep through the other whistles.

Our attentional system, by deciding what we should focus on, also affects how we perceive the incoming stream of stimuli. For example, when our attention is directed toward a painting, we actually experience its colors differently from the colors and textures of objects on the periphery of our attention. We see color and other properties better when we are paying attention (Carrasco, Ling, & Read, 2004; Prinzmetal, Presti, & Posner, 1986; Talgar, Pelli, & Carrasco, 2004).

Properties of Attention

For all the wonders that our attention can accomplish for us, it seems also to constrain what we can be aware of and for how long we can focus on a single event. Over a century of research has shown that our attentional system is limited in how much it can take in and selective in what it offers us. Perhaps the most important fact is that attention is basic to everyone's cognitive system.

Attention Is Limited How long are you able to pay attention and stay on task? The answer probably depends on how interesting the task is and what kind of distracters you experience. During World War II, the British Navy was interested in how long it should keep people staring at radar screens or listening for beeps on sonar. These are important but incredibly tedious military tasks. To answer this question, Mackworth (1950) developed a task that bears his name (the Mackworth Clock), which was briefly described in Chapter 1. Mackworth had young recruits stare at a clock-like face with an arm (emulated in **FIGURE 3.1A** with a dot) and press a button when the clock arm moved in a jerking motion (skipping 2 seconds). He found that errors in missing the jerking motions (called targets) increased with the time spent staring at the clock. **FIGURE 3.1B** shows that by the end of the first 30 minutes, the observer missed 15% of the targets, and this error rate nearly

FIGURE 3.1 Mackworth Clock To determine whether attention diminishes over time, volunteers stared at a dot moving around a clock-like face (A). The observers had to be vigilant and announce when the dot skipped a stop. The graph (B) shows that the longer the observers performed the task, the more misses they made.

Source: Based on Wellbrink & Buss (2004)

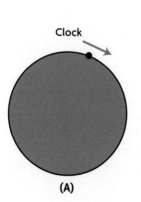

(A)

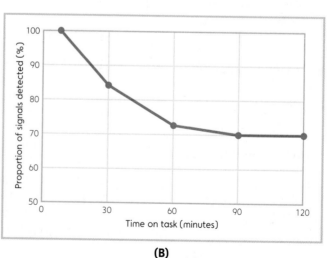

(B)

doubled in the next 30 minutes. Performance on the task is even worse when the temperature of the room is above 84°F (e.g., Matthews, Davies, Westerman, & Stammers, 2000; Wellbrink & Buss, 2004; Wickens, 1992). Mackworth also performed studies in which participants listened for tones or beeps over headsets and recorded similar results. Human attention is a limited capacity system: It is able to focus on a limited number of activities for a fixed period of time.

Attention Is Selective Focusing on something—attending to it—is only half the story. In order to sustain our attention to one event in everyday life, we must filter out other events: We must be *selective* in our attention by focusing on some events to the detriment of others. This is because attention is like a resource that needs to be distributed to those events that are important (e.g.,Wickens, 1992). William James (1890) put it this way:

> Everyone knows what attention is. It is the taking possession by the mind, in clear and vivid form, of one out of what seem several simultaneously possible trains of thought. . . . It implies withdrawal from some things in order to deal effectively with others." (pp. 403–404)

This ability to home in on a relevant event to the exclusion of all else can occur so rapidly that the perceiver may be momentarily unaware of all the stimuli that have been excluded. This is sometimes referred to as **preattentive processing** (or **preattentive analysis;** Treisman & Gelade, 1980; Treisman & Gormican, 1988; Zhaoping & Dayan, 2006) and reflects the role of the mind's automatic reaction to events. You can experience preattentive processing by looking at **FIGURE 3.2A** and searching for the round object. If you are like most observers, you did not look at each object in the figure one at a time to find the circle, it just popped out. Even though the circle is the same color as the other objects, it has a unique feature: its shape.

FIGURE 3.2 Preattentive Processing When searching for a red circle among red squares, as in (A), the circle "pops out" because it is unique and requires only effortless, preattentive processing that examines all features at once. In contrast, when a target shares features with other objects in a display, as when looking for a red circle among other things that are either red or circular (B), the task requires focused attention—features are assessed sequentially and with effort.

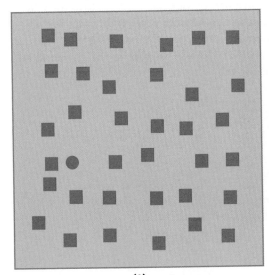

(A)

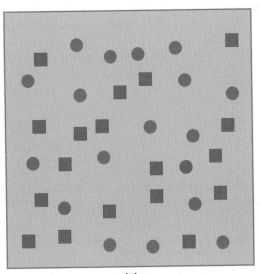

(B)

Preattentive processing is activated by the unique item and not activated by any of the other ones. In contrast, look for a red circular object in **FIGURE 3.2B**. Did it pop out to you? Probably not. That is because the target object shares features with other objects in the display. In this case, you had to use your attention more deliberately in order to look at each object because preattentive processes could not be effective. This is called **focused attentional processing**.

Attention Is Part of Everyone's Cognitive Architecture

Attention is a universal component of the human cognitive architecture. It is part of our basic biology to react to any distinctive change in the environment and turn our attention to it. These **orienting reflexes** ensure that we pay attention to important stimuli and changes in our environment. One example of this is the rooting reflex. If you touch the cheek of a newborn infant, she will turn in the direction of the touch and open her lips (presumably to nurse). Similarly, a newborn infant will turn her head in the direction of a loud sound in the first days of life (Morrongiello & Clifton, 1984). A loud noise or a sudden movement by a pregnant woman can elicit an immediate startle reaction from her fetus by age 9 weeks (DiPietro, Hodgson, Costigan, Hilton, & Johnson, 1996). There is also some evidence of orienting toward sound in near-term fetuses (Lecanuet, Granier-Deferre, & Jacquet, 1992). In everyday life, such orienting reflexes can have a positive benefit. When our attention is captured by a sound, it also helps our visual system attend to what is in the direction of the sound (McDonald, Teder-Sälejärvi, Di Russo, & Hillyard, 2003).

Directing our attention toward an unexpected stimulus helps us to identify it (Loftus & Mackworth, 1978). When novel stimuli are presented to people of all ages, there is an increase in activity in a part of the brain referred to as the **where/what circuits** (see **FIGURE 3.3**). These two circuits process information about the spatial location of objects and allow us to name them. The where circuit runs from the visual cortex to the parietal lobe in the case of visual stimuli and from the auditory cortex to the parietal lobe in the case of sound (Pavani,

A newborn turns toward a stimulus, displaying the orienting reflex.

Blend Images/Alamy

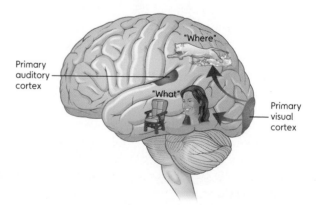

FIGURE 3.3 Where/What Circuits for Visual and Auditory Stimuli When people sense novel stimuli, there is an increase in activity in two circuits of the brain, called the where and what circuits, shown to the right for both visual and auditory stimuli. One circuit processes information about the spatial location of objects and the other activates areas of the brain that allow us to recognize and name them.

"Where"

Primary auditory cortex

"What"

Primary visual cortex

Ladavas, & Driver, 2002; Pinek & Brouchon, 1992; Rauscheker, 2011). The what circuit runs from the visual or auditory cortex to the temporal lobe. This circuit allows memories to be activated in order to recognize the object.

It makes sense that we would turn toward novelty. This reflex has survival value, whether we need to be alert to a jaguar in the jungle or the sound of tires screeching around the corner. Interestingly, when a stimulus is no longer novel, we don't orient toward it because it does not capture our attention. This is called **habituation** and accounts for how we get used to the tight shoes mentioned at the beginning of the chapter or the traffic noise outside our window. The strange sounds of a new house may initially make you nervous and disturb your sleep, but after a few days you will rarely notice them. When students attend a class for the first time, the sounds and slides in the lecture are novel. However, after a few class meetings, students habituate to the environment and may have to struggle to stay alert and attentive. College professors often try to maintain the attention of their students by creating interesting images and pacing the lecture with new topics (for a review of habituation across the animal kingdom, see Dethier, 1987).

The Spotlight: A Metaphor for Attention

Imagine you are walking in the woods on a moonless night with a powerful flashlight. You shine the flashlight in the direction of a startling sound and a pool of light—a spotlight—illuminates a creaky old tree. The center of the pool of light is strong and clear and you can see the bark of the tree and the outline of a branch in detail; as your eye moves away from the center to the edge of the spotlight, the light is dimmer (called the *spill light*) and what you see is less easy to identify. Suddenly, your eye catches a movement at the edge of the light, so you shift the spotlight in order to identify the source of the movement. It's only a cat—you have just enough time to identify it before it runs out of the pool of light into the darkness.

This spotlight example conveys some important ideas about how attention works. Most people have a sense that while they are attending to one event (such as a conversation), there are other events (such as an unfamiliar person walking by) at the periphery of their attention. They often can't quite focus on this person unless they shift attention from the current activity to the peripheral one. These intuitions are supported by research, which suggests that we have something like an **attentional spotlight**, a cognitive ability to focus in or sharpen our attention, just as we do when we move the beam of a flashlight or focus a zoom lens (Broadbent, 1982; Castiello & Umiltà, 1990; Cave & Bichot, 1999; C. W. Eriksen & Yeh, 1985; Jonides, 1983; LaBerge, 1983; Podgorny & Shepard, 1983; Posner, 1980). Of course the spotlight metaphor refers to internal mental processing; we are not talking about moving our eyes to focus on something else, only moving our attention.

The spotlight metaphor provides a useful way to talk about basic elements of attention (Fernandez-Duque & Johnson, 1999): (a) attention can be moved and refocused like a spotlight; (b) it takes time to shift attention from one thing

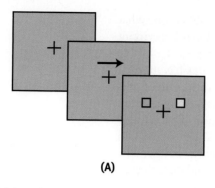

(A)

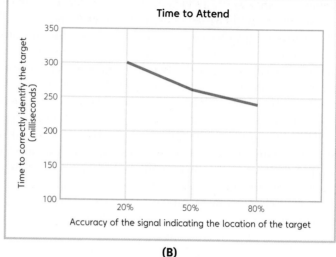

(B)

FIGURE 3.4 Attention Task
(A) Participants stared at a plus sign in the center of a screen and pressed a button when they detected the presence of a bright square on the periphery that they could see *without moving their eyes*. An arrow indicated with varying accuracy where the target would appear (left or right).
(B) Participants' speed varied with the accuracy of the arrow—fast for high accuracy, slow for low accuracy. These results are not surprising until you remember that the participants' eyes did not move: only their attentional spotlight moved.

Source: Based on Posner, Snyder & Davidson (1980)

to another, just as it takes time to shift the focus of a spotlight; and (c) attention has a limited range, just as the light in a spotlight is dimmer at its periphery. Although the term *spotlight* suggests that it refers only to visual attention, the spotlight could also refer to an auditory experience such as listening to someone speaking to you and not attending to other nearby conversations.

An illustration of how the spotlight works can be seen in a classic study by Posner, Snyder, and Davidson (1980). In it, participants were asked to stare at a plus sign in the center of a screen and press a button when they detected the presence of a bright square on the periphery that they could see without moving their eyes. The display is shown in **FIGURE 3.4A**.

During each trial, the participants could see an arrow that would be displayed to indicate with 80% accuracy where the target would appear (left or right). On some trials, a double arrow would appear that pointed in both directions and was clearly uninformative. The results are what you would expect: Participants' attention followed the directional arrow. They were faster and more accurate when the cue was correct (80% of the time) than when it was incorrect (20% of the time). Their accuracy and speed were intermediate on the uninformative condition (50% of the time). These results are not surprising until you remember that the participants' eyes did not move. They stayed fixed on the central plus sign. The movement that occurred was internal, within their attentional system. This shows that people can shine their attentional spotlight on their mental representation of a display just as they can flash a spotlight on an external display.

Because it is commonplace for people to have to shift their attentional spotlight, cognitive psychologists have wondered how long this might take. The answer can be seen in the experiment by Posner et al. (1980). Participants were obliged to move their attentional spotlight when they shifted their attention from an incorrect location to a correct one. The time to shift attention can be computed by comparing the time taken to make the judgment when the arrow is correct

(240 msec) with the time to make the judgment when the arrow points incorrectly (300 msec). The latter situation requires the observer to shift attention from the wrong spot to the correct one. The graph in **FIGURE 3.4B** shows that people take about an additional 60 msec (0.06 sec) to move their spotlight when the prompt is incorrect. We often don't notice events that occur this rapidly; for example, people often claim they can read the newspaper and listen to a conversation at the same time. In fact, their attentional spotlight is simply switching back and forth so rapidly that it seems as if they are processing two events at once.

The spotlight metaphor tells us that a person's attention has a limit or boundary. The *flanker task* has been developed to estimate the extent of this attentional boundary (A. Cohen & Shoup, 1997; B. A. Eriksen & C. W. Eriksen, 1974). Participants are asked to look at a string of five letters and to focus on the central letter (see below). The participant pushes a lever to the right if the center letter is either an *H* or a *K*, and pushes the lever to the left if the center letter is an *S*.

(a) K K H K K [lever right]
(b) S S H S S [lever right]
(c) H H S H H [lever left]

If the attentional spotlight is very narrow—say, the size of a single letter—then the observer should not be aware of the letters to the right and left of the center *H*. In this case, the ability to identify the *H* should not be influenced by what letters are on the periphery. The speed and accuracy in all three conditions ought to be the same: Press the lever to the right for (a) and (b), left for (c). However, if the attentional spotlight is wider than a single letter, the participants may be aware of the letters on the edges of attention and may confuse those letters with the center *H*. If the *K* on the periphery enters consciousness, the participants may think that *K* is the center letter, but they will still press the lever to the right in (a) because the rule is "press for either an *H* or a *K*." However, if the letter on the periphery is an *S* and it is unconsciously perceived, the participants may get confused and press the lever to the left in (b), responding as if the center letter were an *S*. Or, the participant may get confused in (c), thinking that the center letter is an H.

As it turns out, this is what happens. People are faster and more accurate at identifying the *H* in the first string than in the second string (b) and equally confused by the peripheral letter in (c). The findings show that the letters on the periphery, called the *flankers*, are analyzed by the attentional system even though the observers are directed to look only at the center letter. This effect of the flanking letters occurs only if they are within 1° from the center target. How wide is this attentional boundary? At arm's length, the nail of your index finger (the one next to the thumb) casts an image of 1° on your retina. Therefore, in terms of attention to the visual world, we are able to attend immediately to anything that casts an image of 1° or less from the center of our attention (Posner, 1980; see also Intriligator & Cavanaugh, 2001).

Is there a limit to how many items we can attend to within the 1° spotlight? Put another way, how much can we attend to at once without incredible effort? Philosophers refer to this as our **span of apprehension**. Before you read about how we measure this span, try the task in Demonstration 3.1.

Subitizing

Select seven or eight coins, all of the same size, and place them in a bag. Now, reach into the bag and grab a handful of coins (without looking at how many are in your hand) and place them on a table so that they fall near each other. Your job is to say how many you see as quickly as you can. Do this repeatedly for different numbers of coins. People typically require more time to make their judgment as the number of objects in a collection increases. In one of the earliest studies of this task, philosopher William Hamilton (1859, p. 177) noted that

> If you throw a handful of marbles on the floor, you will find it difficult to view at once more than six, or seven at most without confusion; but if you group them into twos or threes, or fives, you can comprehend as many groups as you can units.

The task you just performed is called **subitizing**: "the rapid labeling of small quantities of simultaneously presented items" (Kaufman, Lord, Reese, & Volkmann, 1949, p. 520). A typical display for subitizing is shown in **FIGURE 3.5A**. Research findings from this kind of task show that a maximum of four objects appears to fit into the basic attentional spotlight. We know this because when people are timed in estimating the number of dots on a screen, there is a break in the curve. **FIGURE 3.5B** shows that for one to four items, each additional item requires an extra 40 to 80 msec to estimate. However, from six to nine items, people require about 200 msec per additional item to estimate. This has led to the conclusion that we are able to automatically estimate four or fewer items but have to physically count objects in larger amounts (e.g., Gallistel & Gelman, 1992; Trick & Pylyshyn, 1994).

In a subitizing task such as the one in Demonstration 3.1, students often report that the pattern made by two coins is experienced by them as a line, three coins as a triangle, and four coins as a quadrilateral (Mandler & Shebo, 1982). However, in spite of people's personal impressions, PET studies of the brain (see Chapter 2)

FIGURE 3.5 Subitizing How many things can a person count in a single glance? (Consider the groupings of dots in [A].) Research on subitizing shows that we can nearly instantly identify up to 4 dots at a time (B). Groupings of more than 5 dots require effortful processing that needs about 200 msec for every additional item.

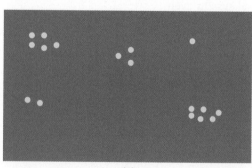

(A)

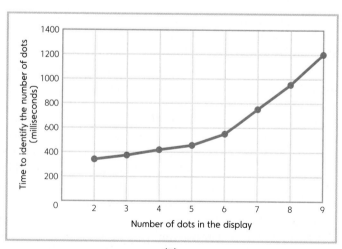

(B)

have found that the same brain areas are involved whether you are looking at four objects or nine. But what actually changes is the amount of brain activation: As the number of items increases, the activation in the visual cortex also increases (Piazza, Mechelli, Butterworth, & Price, 2002; see also Balakrishnan & Ashby, 1991, 1992). This research on subitizing helps identify the boundaries to the attentional spotlight and shows that the concept of the boundary has a biological basis.

SECTION SUMMARY ■

What Is Attention?

Attention is a critical element of the human cognitive architecture. The human attentional system consists of a set of cognitive processes that permits people to mentally focus on some items or events in their environment and to filter out others. Attention is limited in terms of how many events it can focus on and how long it can maintain its focus. It is also selective, but its action can occur so rapidly that it is completely inaccessible to conscious awareness, in which case we refer to it as preattentive processing. All humans, from the moment of birth (and possibly before), possess an orienting reflex that allows them to orient toward novelty and other potentially important events through the attentional system.

The attentional spotlight is a useful metaphor for how we are able to pay attention. Cognitive research has shown that just as with a spotlight, attention can be moved and refocused on relevant objects and topics, and it takes time to shift our attention from one to another. Human attention has a boundary of about 1° in the visual system: The strength of our attention diminishes outside our central area of focus, just as the light in a spotlight is dimmer at its periphery. Within the spotlight we are able to immediately grasp the number of objects we are observing, up to about four items. After this quantity we can make judgments of numbers only by actually counting the objects.

■ ■

Times Square in New York at night bombards the individual with sensory stimulation: lights, noise, people, vehicles, movement.

Alexandre Fagundes De Fagundes/ Dreamstime.com

The Platform for Attention: Sensory Storage

Although common sense suggests that we cannot pay attention to more than one thing at a time, we are in fact bombarded on a regular basis by information flowing to us along many dimensions at once. It takes time and cognitive effort to identify the events that we face, to decide what to react to first, and to focus on the relevant stimuli. Fortunately, nature has provided us with a memory system called **sensory storage**, which acts as a buffer memory system to host the incoming stream of information long enough for us to pay attention to it. Sensory storage is called a *buffer memory* because it separates the incoming stimuli from everything

else going on in our cognitive system. Sensory storage performs a similar kind of insulating function with incoming information.

The nearly unlimited stream of sensory events comes at us so rapidly that we need a way of holding back the tidal wave of information long enough to comprehend what we are experiencing. We need to buffer the environment around us. Cognitive psychologists refer to sensory storage by different names, including **sensory memory** and **sensory information storage (SIS)**. By whatever name it is called, sensory storage is a hidden memory system because we are rarely conscious of its actions in everyday life.

Sensory storage has separate buffer memories for each type of sensory input: sight, sound, touch, smell, and so on. The need for such buffers is easy to illustrate. Suppose someone asks you a question and you miss a key word because you were not processing the individual words quickly. You reflexively say "What?" and the speaker begins to repeat the question; however, all of the words in the question have actually made it into the auditory buffer of sensory storage (called *echoic storage*). By the time the person has repeated the question, you have accessed your memory of the words, picked up the missing one, and perhaps have begun answering the speaker's question while she is still in the process of repeating it—much to her annoyance. Sensory storage is important to normal visual processing as well. When people read, the movements of their eyes, called **saccades**, are ballistic: They rapidly dart from point of fixation to point of fixation, at which time most information is gathered. During these rapid eye movements, we do not experience a blur or "smear" of the visual signal. This is because the visual processing shuts down (called *saccadic suppression*) during the movements (Burr, Morgan, & Morrone, 1999), but perception appears smooth and continuous because sensory memory provides a persistence of the images, which bridges the gap between the fixations. (More will be said on this in Chapter 10.) This is another way that sensory storage buffers our experience so that we can focus on just the important events.

The distinctive properties of sensory storage can be revealed in the answers to four questions. These same four questions will also be used to gain an understanding of the memory systems described in Chapters 4–8.

1. **Capacity**: How much information can the memory system hold?
2. **Duration**: How long is the information held?
3. **Forgetting**: Why do we forget information?
4. **Coding**: How do we retain the information?

The Capacity of Sensory Storage

Because sensory storage is invisible to our conscious, everyday activities, it requires clever tasks to investigate how it works. Cognitive research on sensory storage was given a boost by Sperling (1960). He displayed cards on which numbers and letters were written. The cards contained 2–12 items and were shown to the participants for only 50 msec (0.05 sec) by means of a machine called a *tachistoscope.* The 2-, 4-, and 12-item displays look something like the following (see **FIGURE 3.6**).

The displays were set at a distance so that the information would be presented to the center of the observer's eyes and at a speed that prevented any eye movements. At best, the observer would only be able to scan the mental display, not the physical one. The results are shown in **FIGURE 3.7**. You can see that participants were good at reporting back what they saw as long as the display had fewer than five items. However, as the number of items in the display exceeded five, participants were still only able to repeat back between four and five items. This would normally indicate that the capacity of sensory storage is only 4.5 items. However, participants claimed they saw more than they could report.

Sperling (1960) thought that the reason people could not report more than 4.5 items was that the information was leaving their memory faster than they could report it. By the time they were able to report about five items, the rest had disappeared from memory. To test this, he used a technique called the **partial report procedure,** which is discussed in the Focus on Methods box.

After using the partial report procedure, the estimates of what observers can see in a brief visual presentation are shown in Figure 3.7. As the number of items presented increases, so does the number of items that an observer can report with only a brief delay. This suggests that perhaps there is no limit to the actual capacity of sensory memory. The limiting factor is how quickly we can report what we have experienced.

Duration and Forgetting of Information in Sensory Storage

How rapidly is information lost from sensory storage and why? To examine this, Sperling (1960) waited different amounts of time to signal the observer to report the top, middle, or bottom lines. He found that by 300 msec (0.30 sec) after the

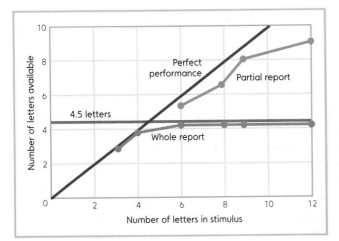

FIGURE 3.6 Three Different Stimuli for Tests of Span of Apprehension To see how many objects a person can grasp (apprehend) in sensory memory, practiced volunteers are shown displays of letters for about 50 msec. Here are different cards that have 2, 4, or 12 letters. The observers are supposed to verbally report the letters they saw. The results are shown in Figure 3.7.

Source: Sperling (1960)

FIGURE 3.7 Span of Apprehension This is a graph of the number of letters a volunteer can accurately name after they are seen for 50 msec. The graph labeled "whole report" shows that people are accurate up to about 4.5 letters. This is the typical span of apprehension. However, using the partial report procedure (described in the text) shows that sensory memory holds much more information than we can report.

Source: Sperling (1960)

FOCUS ON METHODS ■

Span of Apprehension

It has long been known that people sense they have seen more events than they can recall (e.g., Gill & Dallenbach, 1926). The basic findings of sensory storage show that information disappears so quickly that it is difficult to estimate just how much people can apprehend. To get a sense of what people really see in a brief presentation, Sperling (1960) used what is now called the partial report procedure, in which he asked the participants to report back only selected parts of a display, not the entire set. For example, after Sperling presented the card with three rows of letters, the participants heard a high-, medium-, or low-pitched tone. These tones indicated whether the observer was to report back the top, middle, or bottom lines of the display. Because the display disappears before the tone is presented, the participant can only use the tone to scan the mental image of the card in sensory storage.

The principle of the procedure is similar to taking an exam. It is often not physically possible to be tested on each and every item that you learned in the course. It would take too long to take such an exam. Consequently, the instructor creates a test that samples from each of the possible topics. The student's score (a percentage of the exam) is extrapolated to represent a

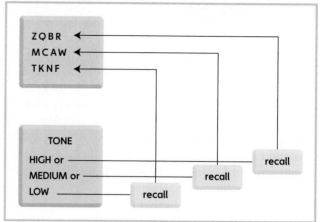

percentage of all the information he or she could have known. Sperling assumed that whatever percentage of a particular line students were able to recall reflected the percentage of all information that was available in memory.

So, for example, if a student reported 75% of a line (e.g., 3 out of 4 items on a line), this reflected the fact that the student possessed (however briefly) 75% of the total 12-item display (i.e., 9 of the 12 items).

letter cards were taken away, nearly half of the information in the buffer had disappeared from participants' memory. If the delay was 1 sec, the observers could not report any more information with the partial report procedure than they could with the whole report procedure (the standard "tell me everything you saw"). The results are summarized in **FIGURE 3.8**, which shows how rapidly information is lost from sensory storage.

Suppose there are two stimulus events: Event 1 and Event 2. Event 1 is presented to a person, is stored in the sensory buffer, and disappears in less than a second. If Event 2 occurs while Event 1 is still in the buffer, Event 2 can interfere with Event 1 and displace it from sensory storage. This phenomenon is called **masking** (Breitmeyer & Ganz, 1976; Breitmeyer, & Ogmen, 2000; Enns & Di Lollo, 2000; see also Holding, 1975) because one event masks or hides the other event from conscious awareness. The degree of masking reflects the time between the two events. If the two events are very close in time, about 80 msec or less, then to the observer they will appear to overlap and will be seen as a single event (Averbach & Coriell, 1961; Loftus, 1983). If the spacing of time is greater than 150 msec, the two events seem to clash and interfere with the identification of either one. With even longer spacing in time between the two events (say

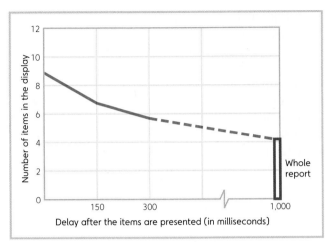

FIGURE 3.8 Duration of Sensory Storage To determine the duration of information in sensory storage, participants perform a partial report memory task (described in Focus on Methods, p. 56) and are asked to wait different amounts of time before they hear a signal to report what they can recall. The graph shows that with a delay of 300 msec, sensory memory retains roughly 6 out of 12 letters. By the time one second (1,000 msec) has passed, sensory memory possesses about 4.5 letters—roughly the same as the whole report procedure illustrated in Figure 3.7.

350 msec), the first event will have already been processed and the second, potentially masking event, will be seen as distinct.

The findings from studies of masking allow an answer to the question of why there is forgetting from sensory storage. As we experience the stream of stimulation to our senses, one event hides or removes a previous event. If the spacing between them is great enough, our attentional system will capture them and they will be processed and more permanently stored. Otherwise, we are left with only a dim impression that we saw something but can't quite grasp what it was. We are immersed in a sea of stimulation that continuously plants and then removes information in sensory storage.

The Coding of Information in Sensory Storage

Sensory storage holds information in an unanalyzed way: The material held in this storage is close to its basic, sensory form. As a result, there are limits to what can be done with the information until it has been analyzed by later processing in long-term memory and short-term memory. **TABLE 3.1** presents a summary of the findings of many studies using the partial report procedure. The table displays what a person can be signaled to do with the information while it resides

TABLE **3.1**	
Results of the Partial Report Procedure and the Sensory Store	
You can signal sensory storage to retrieve:	**You cannot signal sensory storage to retrieve:**
Letter size (small vs. large letters) Brightness (bright vs. dim) Location (top, middle, bottom row)	Categories (letters vs. numbers) (vowels vs. consonants)

in sensory storage (Chow, 1986, 1991; but see Coltheart, 1980; Loftus, 1983; Merikle, 1980; Mewhort & Butler, 1983).

In the original partial report procedure, students could be signaled to recall the top, middle, or bottom lines of a display. Table 3.1 shows that other basically sensory elements of a display can be signaled as well. But there are limits. This is because sensory storage is **precategorical storage**, which means that it stores information before it has been categorized. A person can access different sizes of letters, but cannot distinguish between letters and numbers. To do this requires access to long-term knowledge. Once information is categorized, it is no longer in the buffer but is processed by other memory systems, which are explored in later chapters in this text.

SECTION SUMMARY ■

The Platform for Attention: Sensory Storage

The incoming stream of events in our lives can occur so rapidly that they challenge the ability of our attentional system to focus its spotlight and evaluate the events. Fortunately, humans possess a buffer memory, called sensory storage, which hosts the elements of the incoming stream of events long enough for attention to identify and help categorize the events. The capacity of sensory storage is unlimited. The events are held for less than a second, either until the information fades away or is replaced by the next incoming event, called masking. The items kept in sensory storage are in a raw, unanalyzed, precategorical format. If the time in sensory storage is sufficient, attention will be able to focus on the event, which allows other memory systems to identify what we have just experienced.

■ ■

Attention As a Filter of Sensory Input

Sensory storage is like a tray that holds events long enough for our attentional system to grasp the right items. Within the first second after an event is captured by sensory storage, it is processed by the attentional system, an activity called **attentional processing**. Unfortunately, the stimuli come so rapidly that the attentional system has to decide which packet of information to process first, because trying to process everything could result in an information bottleneck and attentional confusion. The attentional spotlight is sometimes directed to events in the environment depending on their physical characteristics, such as sound or brightness. Our attention may be automatically directed toward a police siren or a rainbow in the sky. The attentional spotlight can also be directed by the content of the event—its meaning or relevance for the observer. This could be the topic of a conversation, a person's name, or the announcement "All aboard." Of course, attention can also be directed by both the physical and the content characteristics of the stimuli, as occurs in the case of someone screaming "Help!"

Attending to Physical Features

Perhaps when you were young, you played outside your house after school. Amid the noise and sounds of your games, you could always hear your mother's or father's voice calling you inside. This was called the **cocktail-party phenomenon** by British psychologist E. C. Cherry (1953) because it is typical of a party situation where you are deep in conversation with someone in a loud and crowded room when suddenly your attention is "grabbed" by someone across the room uttering your name (Moray, 1959; Shapiro, Caldwell, & Sorensen, 1997; Wood & Cowan, 1995). Not only do you hear your name called even when you are not expecting it, but you can also detect the sound of a familiar voice (such as your parents') emerging from the noise of others. Sometimes our attentional system focuses on stimuli based on their physical characteristics (e.g., Broadbent, 1956, 1958). For example, Cherry noticed that aircraft controllers could have many voices speaking to them over the same speaker, yet they were able to associate pilot voices over their headsets with particular flights and were able to keep the messages straight to prevent an accident (Kantowitz & Sorkin, 1983). To be able to study this phenomenon in a laboratory, Cherry developed a *shadowing* task, illustrated in the Focus on Methods box.

When people are shadowing one channel, attention seems to filter out all but the most basic physical characteristics of the unattended channel, although

FOCUS ON METHODS ■

Dichotic Listening

E. C. Cherry (1953) was fascinated by our ability to attend selectively to one message or word amid many voices and messages. To study this, he developed a shadowing task (sometimes called a *dichotic listening task*). In it, the participant wears a special headset that presents a different message to each ear.

The participant is asked to repeat aloud (called *shadowing*) the message as it is being heard in a specified ear (called a *channel*). Typically, in these studies there are two messages, one on the channel that the participant is expected to attend to and another one on the channel that is supposed to be unattended. Typically, the listener only notices physical changes to the unattended message, such as when there is a change in the gender of the speaker or a change in volume. Using this procedure, researchers have found that while listeners attend to one input, they are unaware of the content of the message on the unattended channel. For example, listeners cannot detect that the language has

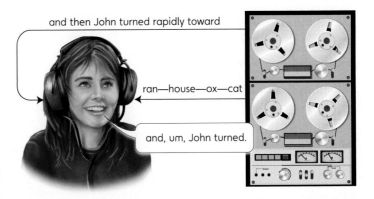

and then John turned rapidly toward

ran—house—ox—cat

and, um, John turned.

changed or that the sentences on the unattended channel are nonsensical (e.g., Egan, Carterette, & Thwing, 1954; Wood & Cowan, 1995). Findings such as these led another British psychologist, Donald Broadbent (1956), to theorize that there was an attentional filter on the early processing of signals that prevents information from getting through.

some important items still get through, for example, the listener's name can be detected. This was shown in a shadowing task by Moray (1959), where a word on the unattended channel was repeated 35 times, yet most participants did not notice. However, a majority of them did hear their own names spoken on the unattended channel, just as in the cocktail-party phenomenon. It is not only people's names that can command our attention. If the message presented to the unattended ear contains sexually explicit words, then people notice them immediately (Nielsen & Sarason, 1981).

Attending to Content

It is clear from Moray's (1959) study and others (see Norman, 1968, 1976) that people can also distinguish signals based on their content. In one study (Treisman, 1960, 1964), students were asked to attend to a message in the right ear and ignore the message in the left ear. The message in the right ear was a coherent narrative taken from the novel *Lord Jim* (by Joseph Conrad). Without warning the listener in advance, the content of the message shifted from the right ear to the left after about 25 words. Even though the students were highly practiced at staying attended to one ear, they typically switched ears for a word or two in order to follow the message. Treisman (1964) asked: How did they know that the message had switched to the unattended ear if that message was unattended? The answer was unavoidable. The nonshadowed message had been given some attention, if only to process its basic semantic content. Humans are capable of focusing both on low-level features of messages as well as high-level, conceptual features. Put simply, continuously throughout the day, our attentional system is activated by both the sensory characteristics of the input and by what our memory system considers pertinent or important to our ongoing lives. This view of human attention is illustrated in **FIGURE 3.9** (see Deutsch & Deutsch, 1963; Norman, 1968, 1976).

FIGURE 3.9 Model of an Attentional Filter After stimuli enter the sensory storage, they are captured by the overall attentional system, which includes long-term memory, short-term memory, and the pattern recognition process. Some physical features allow the stimuli to pass through an early attentional system for further processing. However, events that do not match the filter are not deleted (such as a cough); they are reduced or attenuated in intensity and are still available for processing somewhat later when our memory system identifies a physical event as having intrinsic importance (such as hearing our names). They are so pertinent to our lives that they too are followed when they are processed.

Source: Deutsch & Deutsch (1963)

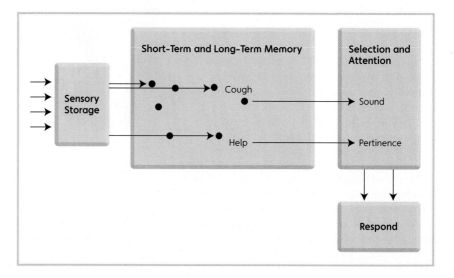

The figure shows the flow of stimulation as it passes through sensory storage and how it commands our attention at different levels of processing. Sometimes our attention is captured by sensitivity to the physical features of the stimulus. If we are listening to a concert and someone starts to cough, the coughing can be momentarily distracting and command our attention. Because attention to physical properties of a stimulus comes early, we say that attention shows an **early-selection filter** (Broadbent, 1956, 1958). Another way to look at it is that the coughing doesn't completely eliminate our ability to process the music, it simply reduces or *attenuates* the attention to the music (Treisman, 1964).

Elementary loud sounds like coughing are not the only dimension that can interrupt our mental activity. Whispering can also command our attention because human speech may be relevant to us even though its volume would not suggest that it should pass through an early filter. Figure 3.9 makes this general point and also shows that some messages—no matter what their physical characteristics—are so important that they are permanently set to be relevant or pertinent (e.g., the sound of your name, the scream "Help!", the odor of mold, or even an angry face). These are examples of attentional processing called **late-selection filter** (e.g., Deutsch & Deutsch, 1963). Such stimuli are not necessarily related to your ongoing activities, but may be important to your life.

Attending to Relevance

The fact that both the physical characteristics and the content of what people experience help them to direct and focus their attentional spotlight implies that an enormous amount of processing is brought to bear in order to identify and react to the physical stimulus. It is as if our attentional system waits for all of the information to combine before it makes its decision to focus the spotlight. This understanding of attention has been called the **late-selection theory**. It presumes that even the supposedly unattended message actually enters our sensory storage and is only filtered out late in the process if it is not relevant.

An illustration of how the late-selection filter can affect what we experience is shown in a study by Corteen and Wood (1972). They presented a series of words to participants who received a mild electric shock to some of the words (they were not hurt by this procedure). Later, the participants shadowed words in one ear and occasionally a word in the nonshadowed ear would be one that was associated with electric shock. If the words in the nonshadowed ear were truly being filtered out of attention, then the participants should show no reaction when one of the shock-associated words was presented. However, the presence of these words elicited a *galvanic skin response* (GSR): a change in electrical conductance of the skin (similar to the response measured by a lie detector device). This indicates that these words were detected (unconsciously) even though the participants were supposed to filter them out. The researchers not only found a GSR to the previously shocked words, but also to words that were synonyms of the shocked words. This definitely shows that our attention can be recruited on the basis of meaning and that the early filtering of attention can be overruled by the late selection of pertinent events (e.g., MacKay, 1973).

SECTION SUMMARY ■

Attention As a Filter of Sensory Input

The human attentional system filters the information coming in through our senses that is momentarily stored in sensory storage. The attentional filter is normally set to "relevance" and allows those sights and sounds that are relevant to pass through a series of filters for our ongoing activity. Sometimes these filters are set to an early filter to attend to the physical aspects of events (e.g., a cough can capture our attention in a theater); sometimes it is captured by a late filter that detects events pertinent to our lives (e.g., the sound of our name heard across a noisy room). It also focuses its spotlight and allows people such as aircraft controllers to track the speech of many pilots at the same time, and sets our filters so that we are not disturbed by low-level events like the whir of a fan or the cough of another audience member while we are watching a film.

■ ■

Automatic and Controlled Processes of Attention

Are we always in control of our attentional spotlight? Sometimes it seems that our attentional system is operating independently of any conscious control on our part. Imagine driving on a highway at 65 mph (95 feet per second), listening to music, and thinking about a scene from a movie you have just seen. How are you able to adjust to subtle changes in the speed of the cars in front of you or cars that are merging into your lane? Has it ever surprised you that you are able to take your eyes from the road to adjust the radio, yet you continue driving effortlessly? Some of these adjustments to the events around you are being handled automatically by your attentional system, which alerts you to danger. These are called **automatic processes** because they produce decisions that are not consciously controlled. You are not at the whim of these automatic processes; you can reign them in by conscious effort. For example, you can deliberately attend to the distance between your car and the one in front of you. This is called **controlled processing**.

Characteristics of Automatic Processing

Automatic processes are evoked without making decisions or necessarily intending them to occur. They can be wired in, as are simple reflexes, or they can be a learned combination of reactions that repeatedly go together. The operation of automatic processing can be easily illustrated by a phenomenon called the **Stroop effect**. Observers are shown words printed in different colors. Their task is to name the color of the ink in which the color word (red, brown, etc.) is printed. To experience the effect for yourself, go to Demonstration 3.2 and do the exercise there before reading on.

■■■DEMONSTRATION 3.2

The Stroop Effect

In the original Stroop (1935) Color–Word Interference Test, students were shown words that were printed in different colors. Their task was to name the color of the ink in which each word was printed. To get a sense of how the participants in the original study reacted to the task, look at the list of words to the right and name the color of the ink for each item on the list. Do this *as quickly as possible* and notice where you pause or stumble.

Which items did you have problems with? Were the first three words easy? These words and their ink color match. However, the next five words named a color that did not match their ink. Did you stumble over these words? Stroop's students took nearly 75% longer to identify the color of the ink when the ink was inconsistent with the color name, compared with the time required to name patches of the same color without the words.

RED
ORANGE
GREEN
GREEN
BLUE
YELLOW
RED
YELLOW

The interference effect illustrated by the Stroop task occurs because of a conflict between the color's name and the name of the word (e.g., J. D. Cohen, Dunbar, & McClelland, 1990). Skilled readers cannot stop themselves from reading the word, even though it is not relevant to the task. Indeed, reading is so automatic that efforts to have people avoid reading the words have been unsuccessful (T. L. Brown, Joneleit, Robinson, & C. R. Brown, 2002). The memory code for the word is automatically activated while the student is trying to name the color. When the color word is different from the name of the color, the two names interfere with each other and processing is slowed and prone to error. However, when we ask students to read just the color words (and not name the color), there is no interference (Dunbar & MacLeod, 1984; see also Melara & Mounts, 1993).

Another characteristic of automaticity is that it occurs rapidly and does not require a lot of attentional resources for its operation (Posner, 1975). In the Stroop task, reading the words is an automatic process and it is not slowed down by having people identify the color of the ink, which is a more laborious task (T. L. Brown et al., 2002). Yet another characteristic of automatic processing is that how it occurs is generally impenetrable to conscious awareness (Posner & Snyder, 1975; Shiffrin & Schneider, 1977). You can test this yourself. Read the next two sentences and decide whether each is grammatical in English.

1. We wented to the store.

2. We heard the bird.

If you are a fluent speaker of English and more than 6 years old, you indicated that the first was ungrammatical and the second was grammatical. While you may be able to state a grammar rule that the first one violated, you probably can't explain precisely how you made the initial assessment. This is because you are so skilled in language that these kinds of judgments truly occur with little awareness or effort and command few attentional resources.

Automatic processing can get us into trouble. As we go about our daily lives, we sometimes react automatically to other people as if they were categories, rather than people. If we are accidentally jostled in a crowd, we may automatically register superficial characteristics of the other person, such as the color of the person's skin or gender, and associate rudeness with the person's characteristics (Wegner & Bargh, 1998). Because of this, automatic processing is said to be "mindless" because we are using categories in a way that are irrelevant to a current situation (Langer, 1975).

Characteristics of Controlled Processing

Controlled processes, in contrast with automatic ones, are often available to conscious understanding: You know when they are operating (Norman & Shallice, 2000). When you see flashing lights in the rearview mirror as you drive down the highway, your attention system alerts you to this important turn of events (automatic processing). As a result, you decide to pull over and prepare your speech to the police officer (controlled processing). In general, conscious processes are willful: either intentionally performed or deliberately not performed.

Controlled and automatic processes are different, but they are not absolute opposites of one another. You can think of them as either on a continuum or as overlapping. The act of breathing provides a useful analogy. Breathing occurs reflexively and unconsciously. However, you can deliberately stop breathing for a minute or two, as you do when you hold your breath underwater. Automatic and controlled attentional processes can interact seamlessly. Sometimes when you recognize a face, you have an automatic feeling of knowing the person, but the person's name does not come to mind immediately. Indeed, if you are like most people, about 20% of the time you will have difficulty remembering the name of a person that you recognize (Young, Hay, & Ellis, 1985) and you have to consciously search your memory to try to retrieve the name.

When you begin to perform a new task such as driving a car, learning another language, or snowboarding, you expend considerable conscious effort trying to make the correct response to a situation by selecting among a large number of possible responses. But as a result of vast amounts of practice, the non-relevant responses drop away and the correct ones are reinforced. Novice typists, for example, focus on typing individual letters and often look at the keyboard to

A skilled typist at work on a laptop computer, hands flying, typing quickly.

RTimages/Alamy

check their accuracy. Skilled typists, on the other hand, look at whole words on the paper and rarely need to refer to the keyboard because typing has become an automatic skill.

Typing is usually considered a **closed skill**, where the learner's intention is to be able to precisely duplicate the behavior under a variety of *predictable* circumstances (e.g., keyboards may vary in angle or elevation and the keys vary in size and touch). Closed skills like typing are automated and encapsulated as if they are independent units. In contrast, **open skills** are applied in *unpredictable* circumstances and the person must commit attentional resources to the environment to compensate for the variability they encounter. This might occur when speaking to people with unfamiliar regional accents, playing a piano that produces a different quality of sound than the musician is used to (e.g., Allard & Starkes, 1991), or snowboarding on radically different terrain from season to season. Open and closed skills make different demands on attentional reserves, and the same skill may be closed or open depending upon the way a person has mastered it. For example, if someone learning a second language treats acquisition of the language as a closed skill and memorizes vocabulary printed on 3×5 inch cards or studies lists of verbs grouped by conjugation rules, he or she is likely to develop a kind of skill that is appropriate to classroom question-and-answer exercises, but not appropriate to speaking under normal circumstances (Segalowitz, 1997, 2000).

Just because many of our responses to the environment are under our conscious control does not mean that we always make thoughtful decisions. People who learned to drive a car many years ago were taught to pump the brakes to prevent them from locking up when trying to stop on a slippery surface. Now that antilock brakes (ABS) are standard on most cars, the appropriate way to stop is to depress the brake pedal firmly and keep your foot there until the car stops (the braking system does the pumping electronically much faster than a person could). Unfortunately, a common occurrence for people unused to driving cars with ABS is that they pump the brakes, which interferes with the braking mechanism. In this example, "accidents that could be *prevented* in the past by our learned behavior can now be *caused* by the same behavior" (Langer & Moldoveanu, 2000, p. 3). This is an instance of **mindlessness**: Even though we are engaged in a controlled process, we fail to evaluate what we are doing when we exercise control (Langer, 1975). It is as if we perform activities mechanically or by rote, that is, we are not "paying attention."

Why Are There Two Types of Attentional Processes?

What is the benefit to people to have both controlled and automatic processes? One benefit is that while controlled processes have the advantage of permitting reflection and thoughtful adjustment to what is happening to us, they are demanding of our cognitive resources and need to recruit attentional capacity to perform their functions. This is one reason why we are unable to actively attend to many tasks at the same time. In contrast, automatic processes make minimal demands on our attentional resources (e.g., Kahneman, 1973; Posner, 1975) and allow us to respond more quickly to events than we can when using controlled processes. If we reacted to the world only through controlled processes, we could not walk and think at the same time. Thanks to the joint use of controlled and automatic processing, we are able to focus our attention on critical, demanding tasks that are not easily automated while handling a seemingly unlimited number of concurrent tasks that make minimal demands on our attentional resources (e.g., Anderson & Lebiere, 1998).

The Dangers of Automaticity

Without automatic processes, our attentional system would be sluggish and ineffective; however, with a reliance on its greater efficiency comes the possibility of inappropriate responses. In the world outside the laboratory, attentional failures can be devastating. On February 9, 2001, the commander of the U.S. submarine *Greeneville*, after following standard procedures, ordered the submarine to surface. Too late, the commander realized that he had surfaced with another ship, the Japanese fishing vessel *Ehime Maru*, directly overhead, causing the death of 9 students on board. According to the U.S. National Transportation Safety Board (2005), the *Greeneville* crew was behind schedule and operating under time pressure; they were rushed and distracted by the presence of 16 civilian observers on board. The crew relied on their automatic attentional processing skills to identify dangers and spent only 80 seconds scanning the horizon with the periscope rather than the usual 3 minutes of controlled attention.

Under the demands of the social situation, neither the captain nor the officer of the deck saw the fishing ship, though it must have appeared in the periscope. The sonar picked up the *Ehime Maru*, but the sonar operator did not see it because his attention (though not his eyes) was focused on finishing a 10- to 15-minute job in 6 minutes. This is a case where normal attentional processes were misdirected to another task (dealing with visitors). Clearly, we cannot always rely on our automatic processes to perform flawlessly, especially when those processes are interrupted by having to attend to another task. This is especially the case when a task demands controlled attentional processing.

One framework for understanding tragedies like the *Greeneville*'s sinking of the *Ehime Maru* is the generic error modeling system (GEMS; Reason, 1990). According to this theory, many accidents are a result of two types of situations: (a) when automatic processes are *not* interrupted and taken over by conscious processes when they should be; and (b) when there is an unusual or unpredicted interaction between automatic and conscious processes.

The first situation happens to most people every year. In the first week of January, people frequently put the wrong date on their checks or papers even though they consciously know the year has changed. The second type of situation occurs when our automatic processing is interrupted and we have to apply

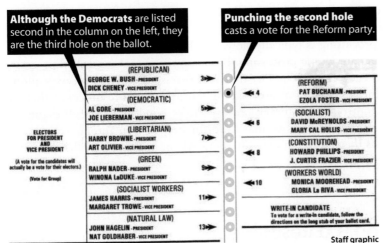

Although the Democrats are listed second in the column on the left, they are the third hole on the ballot.

Punching the second hole casts a vote for the Reform party.

Staff graphic

FIGURE 3.10 Florida Election Ballot The Florida ballot for the 2000 U.S. presidential election conflicted with normal attentional processes. The arrangement violated Gestalt principles, since the numbering of the holes did not correspond to the boxes for the candidates. The arrangement also violated typical left-right scanning: If the voter scanned left to right, from the name of the political party (in capital letters), the voter's gaze would land on the wrong hole. Ballots need to be congruent with voters' cognitive processes.

Sun-Sentinel Graphic

conscious attention in an unfamiliar way. A good example of this sort of violation of attentional processes occurred in the 2000 U.S. presidential election. The so-called butterfly ballot used in Palm Beach County, Florida, was an example of a design that promotes erroneous behavior because it is inconsistent with normal automatic processing. Inspection of **FIGURE 3.10** shows that the arrangement of the holes is incongruent with the arrangement of names. This in itself may have caused voters to misalign the names with the holes.

The role of automaticity in reading also comes into play here. English is read from left to right and reading quickly sets up an expectation that the holes corresponding to the names will be directly to the right of each name. They are not! You may think that the arrows will correct for the misalignment because they point to the correct hole. However, the arrows are not next to the names, so a reader would have to scan backward from the tip of the arrow in order to understand the name–arrow correspondence. For these reasons the construction of the butterfly ballot is not in keeping with normal cognitive processing and with the way our attentional system functions. According to newspaper reports at the time (e.g., "Presidential votes," 2000), nearly 10,000 votes were disqualified because voters punched more than one candidate for the same office and approximately 5,000 votes were punched for the wrong candidate. This ballot and its consequences would certainly justify the kind of human factors research described in Chapter 1.

SECTION SUMMARY ▪
Automatic and Controlled Processes of Attention
Human attention is a balanced system composed of two broad types of processing: automatic and controlled. Automatic processes are rapid and make minimal demands on our cognitive resources. They normally operate without conscious

awareness of their functioning details. Controlled processing occurs when we consciously direct our attention and are aware of its deliberate functioning. Controlled processing is typically slower and requires more of our attentional resources than automatic processing. Both automatic and controlled processes complement each other. The fact that we possess automatic processes allows us to attend to tasks without overloading our attentional resources so that we can engage controlled attentional processes to respond to important events. In critical situations, however, we may unfortunately rely on automatic processes to function as they do in familiar situations when, in fact, controlled processes need to take over.

Attention Is a Resource

When people think of attention, they often imagine they only have some limited quantity of it to distribute. This reflects most people's sense that they are not able to pay attention to more than a few items or events at a time. The idea that attention is a resource distributed among tasks is embodied in the **capacity theory of attention** (Kahneman, 1973). It says that our ability to focus attention varies with the number and complexity of the tasks and how mentally energized we are at the time. The difficulty we encounter in performing simultaneous multiple tasks involves the resource *cost*: the amount of resources needed to perform the task. If the cost is too high, we are less than optimal in our performance. If this sounds a bit like a theory in economics, it's probably because its developer, Daniel Kahneman, received the Nobel Prize for his work in economics in 2002. The idea of resource limitation can be seen in four phenomena that challenge commonsense ideas about attention: attentional blink, repetition blindness, change blindness, and inattentional blindness.

Attentional Blink

Suppose that you point your flashlight at some important object and then, after looking at it, you turn off the flashlight. Although for a brief moment after you turn off the flashlight the level of ambient light bouncing off the walls or still being emitted from the bulb may be sufficient to see something, it quickly becomes dark. If a new object is presented for your consideration, it will take a moment for you to turn your flashlight back on and have the illumination increase sufficiently to attend to the new event. This period between the moment the light is too dim to see and the moment that you turn the flashlight back on to attend to something new is like quickly closing and then opening your eyes—a blink. In terms of attention, the **attentional blink** (a term coined by Raymond, Shapiro, & Arnell, 1992) is the moment when you are shifting your attentional focus and are unable to attend fully to a new target event. In terms of Kahneman's (1973) capacity theory of attention, there is a cost when we selectively attend to a visual event

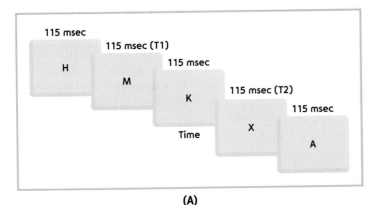

(A)

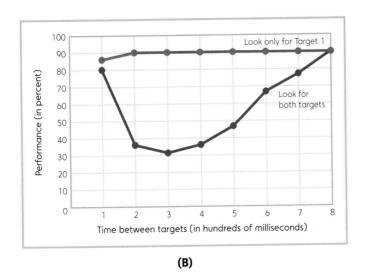

(B)

FIGURE 3.11 Attentional Blink Paradigm Volunteers look at letters presented in rapid order (A). If they see either an M (Target 1) or an X (Target 2), they must press a button. If they press the button for the M, they sometimes miss pressing the button for the X if it occurs a few hundred milliseconds after the M. It is as if the attentional system "blinked." The graph (B) shows how accuracy is affected by the blink.

and this cost is a kind of functional blindness to other unattended events (Jolicoeur, 1999; Kanwisher, 1987; Mack & Rock, 1998; Simons & Levin, 1997).

Attentional blink has been studied in the laboratory using a method called *rapid serial visual presentation* (RSVP) shown in **FIGURE 3.11A** (Raymond, Shapiro & Arnell, 1992; Shapiro, Arnell, & Raymond, 1997). In it, many letters are presented one at a time on the screen. The observer is looking for two possible targets and presses a button when a target is seen. When the observer finds one of the targets, it is difficult to find the second one if it occurs soon after the first (Shapiro, Raymond, & Arnell, 1994). This is shown in **FIGURE 3.11B** (After Wagemans, Verhulst, & De Winter, 2003). The graph indicates that for a typical college student, the attentional blink is about a half second. That is, after a target is identified, the attentional system's resources are depleted and the observer will not be able to identify the next target for about a half second. The blink occurs for both auditory and visual events (Mondor, 1998).

Why would humans be plagued by such a limitation to the attentional system? We can only guess that an attentional blink is a way for the brain to ignore distractions so that it can focus its processing on the first target (Maki & Padmanabhan, 1994). If two events follow nearly simultaneously (e.g., less than 0.10 sec apart), then the brain grabs them as if the two were a single item and is able to process them both. When there is a substantial delay between the two events, the brain has to finish processing one item before it grabs the next; however, it will miss the second item if that item occurs at a critical time.

How does the attentional blink affect everyday cognition? Suppose you are driving along a freeway, paying attention to the distance between your car and the one in front of you, as well as to other cars around you. All of a sudden, you notice that a friend is driving a car in the lane next to you. You focus attention to make sure it's your friend. This impairs your ability to attend to the car in front of you for slightly less than a half second. This effect is smaller for younger adults (aged 17–30 years) than for older adults (aged 62–77 years; Lahar, Isaak, & McArthur, 2001; Widner, Otani, Adams, & Mueller, 1998). Interestingly, the amount of disruption (how long the blink lasts) depends on how physically close you are to your friend's car. If you glance left and your friend is right there in the car next to you, your blink is longer than if you see your friend a bit ahead and two lanes over (Kristjansson & Nakayama, 2002).

Repetition Blindness

Repetition blindness is defined as a decrease in the ability to perceive repeated stimuli during a rapid serial presentation of items. For example, if letters are flashed at you in rapid order and two consecutive letters are both *B,* then you may only remember having seen one *B.* This is not due to an inability to visually separate the letters, because the effect occurs even when the letters are in different cases (i.e., **B** and **b**) or are in different sizes (i.e., **B** and B; MacKay & Miller, 1994; Miller & MacKay, 1994). To experience this for yourself, do the exercise in Demonstration 3.3 before reading on.

■■■DEMONSTRATION 3.3

Repetition Blindness

Try reading the following sentences aloud as fast as you possibly can. Do this by using a piece of paper and moving it across each sentence so that your eyes can't look back at a previous word. Try to take only a second or two to read each sentence.

1. Unless they are hot enough, hot dogs don't taste very good.

2. They wanted to play sports, but sports were not allowed.

3. They wanted to play sports today, but sports were not allowed.

If you are like most people, you slowed down at the second occurrence of a word or word fragment such as *hot* in *hot dog* in Sentence 1, or actually did not read the second instance of these words. This is repetition blindness. Because of repetition blindness, our visual system fails to record the second instance of *hot* as a unique event (Kanwisher, 1987; Kanwisher & Potter, 1990).

Like the attentional blink, the more items (or more syllables) between the two targets, the greater the accuracy in identifying the repeated word. For example, in Sentence 2 the lag between the repeated instances of the word *sport* is a single word (*but*); however, in Sentence 3 the lag is two words (*today* and *but*). The repetition blindness is less in Sentence 3 than in Sentence 2.

Cognitive psychologists study this phenomenon by rapidly presenting the individual words from a sentence to an observer. The observer's task is to press a button every time a target word is shown on the screen (Kanwisher, 1987). Many people are surprised when they read a sentence like the first one, because they fail to notice that *hot* is repeated (Kanwisher, 1987; Kanwisher & Potter, 1990). It is as if, when we perceive events, we need to create "objects" to be stored as "indicators" of what we have experienced (Kahneman & Treisman, 1984). We occasionally fail to do this when we don't treat the second repetition as a different object from the first. It is as if the two items compete for our attentional resource and our awareness of their existence and we can't tell whether there were two objects or one. We saw this phenomenon in the attentional blink studies. But here the "blink" is specific to a repeated word rather than just any word that is presented during a critical period (Morris, Still, & Caldwell-Harris, 2009). Similar to the findings regarding attentional blink, older adults show an increased rate of repetition blindness compared with younger adults (MacKay, Miller, & Schuster, 1994; see also Borovsky & Abrams, 2001).

Repetition blindness not only causes observers to miss words or letters, it can also cause observers to create illusory words. For example, if the words *lake*, *brake*, and *ush* are presented rapidly, one after another, for about 100 msec with a 15 to 30 msec break between the words, observers report seeing *lake* and *brush* and are astonished when told that *brush* was never presented (Morris & Harris, 1999).

Change Blindness

Change blindness is an everyday phenomenon that is somewhat similar to the attentional blink. Imagine you are looking at two photographs of Notre Dame Cathedral in Paris that are slightly different (see **FIGURE 3.12**). When you place the photographs side by side and compare them section by section, you can readily see the difference in just a few moments. However, if the pictures are flashed one after another repeatedly on a screen, each for about 250 msec with a gap of about 80 msec between pictures, you will find it difficult to discern any difference between the pictures (e.g., Grimes, 1996; Rensink, O'Regan, & Clark, 1997; Simons & Levin, 1997, 1998). This is especially true for changes that occur in parts of the scene that are not of central interest (notice how obscure the differences are in the pictures of Notre Dame in Figure 3.12).

FIGURE 3.12 An Illustration of Change Blindness Notre Dame in Paris, as seen from Quai de Conti along the river Seine. Can you spot the differences between the two images? In the experiment, two pictures are flashed with a gap of about 8o msec. The difference between the pictures is subtle. The typical person requires many such flashes to spot the change. However, when they are side-by-side, the changes take only a few seconds to identify. The changes are easier to identify when they are central to the attentional spotlight.

J. Kevin O'Regan
Laboratoire de Psychologie
Expérimentale, Centre National de
Recherche Scientifique, Paris, France

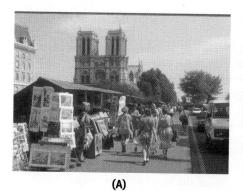
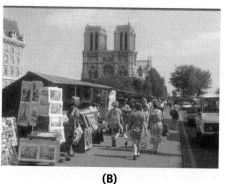

(A)   (B)

Since these details are not what the pictures are about, observers tend to take a long time to notice the changes. Changes in objects included in the center of the attentional spotlight are detected earlier than changes in objects at the periphery of the spotlight (Rensink et al., 1997), although occasionally even changes at the center of the spotlight are not detected (Angelone, Levin, & Simons, 2003).

Change blindness can occur in situations outside the laboratory. In one study (Simons, 2000; Simons & Levin, 1998) the experimenter stops a person on campus and asks for directions holding a map. While the person is speaking to the experimenter, workers carrying a door pass between the experimenter and the person giving directions, blocking that person's view of the experimenter. During this brief interval, which lasts 1 or 2 seconds, the experimenter joins the workers by walking behind the door and an accomplice, dressed similarly, takes the place of the experimenter and begins talking to the unsuspecting person, who usually continues giving directions—apparently oblivious to the change in the person. When asked about their experience later, more than half of the participants had not noticed that they wound up giving directions to a different person. Those who noticed the change were primarily from the same age group as the experimenters.

Why are the participants blind to the change that has occurred? One answer has to do with the number of changes occurring in their immediate environment and the need to conserve attentional resources. The participant's attentional spotlight is focused on the task of giving directions—everything else is on the periphery of attention. Often the participant senses that a change has occurred, but is unable to identify automatically where it has occurred. As a result, he or she attributes change to the major event (the door) and not to the person to whom they were giving directions (Gegenfurtner & Sperling, 1993), as long as the two people who exchanged positions were from the same social categories (occupation, race, gender, etc.). In general, change blindness is greatest when the changed object is inanimate (furniture, boxes, etc.) rather than animate (people, dogs, etc.; New, Cosmides, & Tooby, 2007). This may be a result of the kind of environments in which humans evolved that linked survival to an ability to detect predators or prey—an ability all humans inherit (Rees, 2008).

Inattentional Blindness

The human attentional spotlight can sometimes cause observers to miss entire events—not just a letter or a word. This was demonstrated with college students who were asked to look at a video of two teams (one in white shirts, the other in black) rapidly passing a basketball around. One group of observers was instructed to count the number of passes by either the white- or black-shirted team. A second group was given a more difficult task and told to keep separate counts of bounce and aerial passes. These are attention-demanding tasks (Neisser, 1979). During one version of the video a woman carrying an umbrella walked through the scene. In another version a person in a full gorilla suit walked through. Less than half of the observers reported seeing the woman or the gorilla (Most et al., 2001; Simons & Chabris, 1999). The students performing the more difficult task reported seeing the gorilla less often than those in the easier task.

Low-level, automatic attentional processing might indicate to the observers that there was some object moving across the screen, but the ongoing demands of the controlled attentional processes took up the resources necessary to identify the moving object. Since observers rely on the automatic processes to identify the moving object, they may simply assume that the object is a basketball player rather than someone wearing a gorilla suit!

The research on **inattentional blindness** can help us understand one cause of traffic accidents. Any activity that consumes attentional resources, (i.e., controlled processing) will have an effect on performance on another attention-demanding task (Kahneman, 1973). Driving performance can be affected by memory tasks (Alm & Nilsson, 1995; Briem & Hedman, 1995), mental arithmetic tasks (McKnight & McKnight, 1993), and verbal reasoning tasks (I. D. Brown, Tickner, & Simmonds, 1969). This is also true of attention-demanding motor tasks, such as dialing a phone number or even the act of pressing a button to answer a phone call (e.g., Briem & Hedman, 1995; Brookhuis, De Vries, & De Waard, 1991). These findings are consistent with what we know about the effect on performance of controlled attentional processing, and they point to the potential disruption to driving that comes from talking on a cell phone.

Of the 137 million cell phone owners in the United States, 85% (120 million) use their phones while driving (Strayer, Drews, & Johnston, 2003). Studies using a simulated driving environment found that when students engaged in phone conversations about topics in which they were interested, they reacted more slowly to traffic signals and actually missed some of them altogether, compared with students not engaged in phone conversations (Strayer & Johnston, 2001). Strayer et al. (2003) found that students were more likely

Using a cell phone while driving affects your driving performance in a negative way, no matter what your age.

jabejon/iStockphoto

to be involved in traffic accidents when speaking on a cell phone when many cars were present than when just a few were present. The accidents tended to be rear-end collisions.

Using a hands-free phone does not appear to benefit attention over a handheld phone. Although a handheld phone may impair steering, it does not by itself affect controlled attentional processing. Both handheld and hands-free phones affect driving performance. Talking on a cell phone while driving has an equal overall affect on people of all ages: roughly 17% slower in reaction to highway conditions. However, when younger participants (20-year-olds) are talking on their cell phones, they are as slow as older participants (70-year-olds) who are not talking on their cell phones (Strayer & Drews, 2006, 2007).

Research shows that listening to a conversation, the radio, or books on tape does not impair driving performance (Briem & Hedman, 1995). While these are potentially demanding activities, you can momentarily disengage from them to focus on driving with only marginal impact. Engaging in a conversation with a passenger is not like conversing on a phone because a passenger can adjust the conversation depending on road conditions. Also, the driver can pause a conversation without appearing rude. In demanding situations when the driver is really distracted, a passenger can also warn the driver of danger.

SECTION SUMMARY ■

Attention Is a Resource

Our attentional processing is limited by the resource demands placed on it by external stimuli and requirements of the tasks in which we are engaged. Four examples of this limitation have been explored by cognitive psychologists: attentional blink, repetition blindness, change blindness, and inattentional blindness. These phenomena stem from the fact that our attentional resources require time to replenish themselves. We experience an attentional blink when we commit resources to identify one important event and it impedes our ability to identify the next important event because we have not recovered from the first attention-demanding event. The blink typically varies with the age of the observer. It is longer for older people than for younger people. Repetition blindness occurs when two important events occur within 100 msec of each other: They are caught in the same spotlight and treated as one event. Change blindness and inattentional blindness occur when our attentional spotlight focuses on a few critical elements in our environment. It frequently misses elements on the periphery of attention because of the need to alternate automatic and controlled processing. We tend to show less blindness for scenes that contain animals, which may reflect skills that our genetic ancestors needed for survival. Inattentional blindness has modern implications. The ability to attend to one event, such as the distance between your car and the one ahead, can be affected by the demands made on your attentional system by a cell phone call or seeing something important in the adjacent lanes of traffic.

The Neuropsychology of Attention

Slips of attention can happen to everyone. They can be as benign as failing to correct a spelling error or as dangerous as causing an automobile accident because you were answering your cell phone. Accidents are called accidents because they are unexpected and seem unavoidable. There are people, however, whose difficulties in paying attention are unfortunately not accidental, but are the consequences of neurological deficits. Four key disorders that affect attention are discussed in this section: simultanagnosia, hemispheric neglect, attention-deficit/hyperactivity disorder, and Parkinson's dementia.

FIGURE 3.13 Stimulus Used to Test for Simultanagnosia People with Bálint's syndrome suffer from simultanagnosia. When they observe a scene with many objects, their attentional system can focus on only one of them; the rest of the scene is patchy. In this drawing, people with Bálint's syndrome can see only one of the objects.

Damasio, A. R. (1985a). Disorders of complex visual processing: Agnosia, achromatopsia, Balint's syndrome, and related difficulties of orientation and construction. In M. M. Mesulam (Ed.), Principles of Behavioral Neurology. Philadelphia, PA: Davis.

Simultanagnosia

Unfortunately, some people's attentional focus is so limited that they cannot see objects to the right or left of where they are attending. Their situation is called **simultanagnosia,** which refers to a difficulty in recognizing two or more objects at the same time (Farah, 1990; Michel & Henaff, 2004; Rizzo & Vecera, 2002). Clinical psychologists refer to simultanagnosia as Bálint's syndrome (Damasio, 1985a; Rizzo, 1993). When people who suffer from this condition observe a scene with many objects, they are not able to identify more than one of the objects unless their attention is deliberately guided to those objects. Notice the drawing in **FIGURE 3.13**. It is composed of the overlap of four objects. Do you see all four? People with Bálint's syndrome can see only one of them. They cannot move their gaze around the picture to identify the remaining objects. This is sometimes the result of stroke damage in the parietal lobe (Damasio, 1985a). Life with this syndrome can be difficult because sufferers frequently bump into objects that fail to activate their attentional system.

Losing Sides: Hemispheric Neglect

Neurologist Oliver Sacks (1985, p. 77) described the case of an older woman with attentional problems:

> Sometimes (when eating) she complains that her portions are too small, but this is because she eats only from the right half of the plate—it does not occur to her that it has a left half as well. Sometimes, she will put on lipstick and make up the right half of her face, leaving the left half completely neglected.

This malady is known as **hemispheric neglect** (or **hemineglect**); it occurs when people are unable to focus their attention on a portion of their visual field. It is as if they are blind to one half of what they should be able to see. However, their vision is completely intact (Mesulam, 1998). This disease is an attentional blindness, not a visual one. Hemineglect is a symptom of a broader neurological difficulty called *parietal lobe syndrome* (Bisiach & Luzzatti, 1978; Driver & Mattingley, 1998). **FIGURE 3.14** (from Bloom &

Model   **Patient's copy**

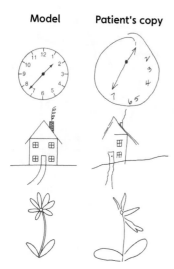

FIGURE 3.14 Pictures Drawn from Memory by a Patient with Hemineglect Patients with hemineglect typically have a stroke in their right hemisphere and cannot focus on the left side of a visual scene, as illustrated in these drawings. Their eyes do register the missing elements, but their attentional system neglects the visual input to their brains.

Source: Bloom & Lazerson (1988, p. 300)

Lazerson, 1988/2001) shows drawings made from memory by individuals with hemineglect. Notice that people with this disease draw an object from their right side and typically neglect their left side (Marshall & Halligan, 1994). When these individuals are asked to divide a picture or page in half with a vertical line, they will position the line too far to one side (Ferber & Karnath (2001).

Another test for hemineglect is to see if a person disregards one of his or her hands (left or right) when asked to take a ball and move it back and forth between the two hands. If there is consistent neglect of the left hand, this is evidence for a lesion (a structural change) in the nondominant (right) hemisphere (Driver & Mattingly, 1998). This malady is not unique to humans; hemineglect has also been shown in cats and monkeys (e.g., Payne, 1993). Curative treatments have been developed for these species (see review by Payne & Rushmore, 2003). However, the difficulties experienced by people with hemineglect can only be partially improved by medical treatment (Fleet, Valenstein, Watson, & Heilman, 1987; Hurford, Stringer, & Jann, 1998). The neurological damage is typically the result of a stroke, with the symptoms being most severe immediately after the stroke. Fortunately, the symptoms diminish with time, although the individual rarely returns to prestroke levels of functioning.

Hemineglect is clearly related to the attentional system and not the visual or auditory systems: The same objects that are neglected when they are in the left visual field are reacted to in the right field. When people begin to recover from this malady they show a peculiar pattern, similar to repetition blindness. They are asked to look straight ahead and indicate when two objects, brought from both sides of their head, appear in their periphery. When the two objects are different, say a coin and a key, they report them equally, and well within normal range for peripheral vision. However, when the two objects are identical, they fail to report one of them. Again, this is an attentional failure, not a result of a malady of the visual system.

Just because someone with hemineglect does not experience "seeing" something, that does not mean that the object does not have an unconscious effect on them. When a psychologist presents words to the left visual field of individuals with hemineglect (the left visual field corresponds to their impaired right hemisphere), the hemineglect individuals can only identify the word with great effort. However, their ability to identify the word improves with each presentation (e.g., Erickson & Allred, 2001; Ratcliff, Hockley, & McKoon, 1985). The low-level sensory information gets through the attentional filter, but the neurological problem prevents higher-level, controlled attentional processes from identifying the stimuli. These data suggest that hemineglect is the result of reduced attention, not blindness. This is one way that cognitive research has helped us to understand this troubling problem.

Attention-Deficit/Hyperactivity Disorder (ADHD)

Between 3% and 10% of school-age children are affected by **attention-deficit/ hyperactivity disorder (ADHD),** a common neurobehavioral problem. Boys suffer from ADHD 2 to 3 times more often than do girls (Barkley, 1990). According to the *Diagnostic and Statistical Manual of Mental Disorders* (*DSM–IV–TR;* American Psychiatric Association, 2000) symptoms of ADHD include distractibility and inattentiveness, as well as restlessness and difficulty in self-control. For 65% of affected children, the symptoms persist into adulthood. ADHD probably has many causes. However, studies suggest that there is some genetic link: 25% of the biological parents of children with ADHD have a history of the condition, but only 4% of adoptive parents have this condition (Kendall & Hammen, 1995).

The term *attention deficit* may be a misnomer because it suggests somehow that the diagnosed children are showing neglect of stimuli. The opposite is actually the case. These children absorb or are affected by too many stimuli in their environment and have difficulty filtering out unnecessary information, so they are easily distracted. Their attentional spotlight tries to focus on too many stimuli. This is illustrated in a study by R. S. Cherry and Kruger (1983), who had children perform the kind of dichotic listening task with headsets mentioned at the beginning of this chapter. The children, ages 7 to 9, were instructed to point to the picture of a word that was presented on one channel. In the other ear, the children heard either nothing, random static, backward speech, or forward speech. Both the ADHD children and a control group of the same age performed equivalently on this task when the unattended channel was quiet. However, ADHD children performed poorly under all other conditions, and especially poorly when the unattended channel had forward speech. In contrast, the control children were unaffected by the information on the unattended channel. This illustrates that ADHD is not a failure to notice something, but a difficulty in inhibiting responsiveness to competing stimuli: Children with ADHD notice too much. From this perspective, the diagnosis of *attention deficit* ought to be called *inhibition deficit.*

Attention deficit has a biological source. In general, children with ADHD show decreased blood flow to the frontal lobes compared with age- and IQ-matched peers (Gaddes & Edgell, 1994). For years, a common practice has been to treat the condition with versions of the drug methylphenidate, an amphetamine (Ritalin®, Concerta®, Methylin®, etc.) that tends to improve concentration and reduce restlessness in about 70% of cases. This medication, like amphetamines in general, has a stimulative effect in non-ADHD populations. It therefore surprises many people that it can have a positive effect on some children with hyperactivity. The basis for its effect with ADHD populations is threefold. First, it increases blood flow to the frontal cortex, which may have an influence on increased attention. Second, the frontal cortex influences activity

FIGURE 3.15 The Dopamine Circuit Attention deficit has a biological source. An abnormally low level of the neurotransmitter dopamine can cause three of the symptoms of ADHD: inattention, impulsivity, and hyperactivity. Dopamine is produced deep within the brain in the basal ganglia, as shown in the figure. Children with ADHD have smaller basal ganglia than same-age children matched for IQ.

Source: Kolb & Whishaw (2011, p. 371)

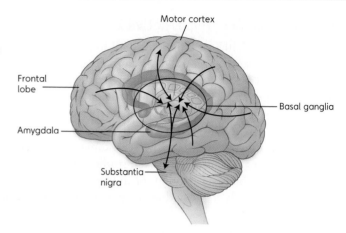

in lower brain centers; this decreases the volume of blood in the motor cortex, thereby reducing motor activity so they are less fidgety. Third, and perhaps more important, the methylphenidate tends to maintain the availability of dopamine, an important neurotransmitter that affects attention (Volkow, Fowler, Wang, Ding, & Gatley, 2002). This is also the basis for the effectiveness of other commonly administered medications for ADHD that are amphetamine derivatives (e.g., Dexedrine®, Dextrostat®, and Adderall®).

Researchers believe that the neurotransmitter dopamine is important to ADHD because an abnormally low level of dopamine can cause three of the symptoms of ADHD: inattention, impulsivity, and hyperactivity. Dopamine, which fuels the control of these functions in the frontal lobe, is produced deep within the brain in the basal ganglia (see **FIGURE 3.15**), and children with ADHD have smaller basal ganglia than same-age children matched for IQ (e.g., Aylward et al., 1996). The importance of the neurotransmitter dopamine for attentional processes has been revealed in recent neuroimaging studies that compared the brain activity of children with ADHD with the neural activity of children with no diagnosis.

In one study (Vaidya et al., 1998) 16 boys (half diagnosed with ADHD and half without ADHD) between the ages of 8 and 13 were asked to play a mental game while lying in a magnetic resonance chamber. One of their tasks was to respond whenever a consonant (e.g., B, D, W) appeared on the screen, but they were not to respond when an X appeared. Because most of the letters were not X, the children developed a bias to press the button and needed to control their impulse to press the button when they saw an X. As shown in **FIGURE 3.16**, both groups, but especially the ADHD boys, showed widespread activation in the frontal cortex as they developed impulse control. (The greater activation in those areas for the ADHD boys may indicate how much greater effort they need to achieve good performance.)

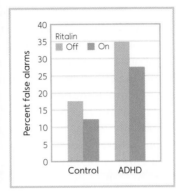

FIGURE 3.16 fMRI of Attention-Deficit/Hyperactivity Disorder During Inhibition Task The brain activity of children with ADHD is compared with the neural activity of children with no diagnosis, the control group. Both groups performed a task that measured their ability to control impulses (see text). When both groups were given Ritalin to increase their level of dopamine, they made fewer errors and increased the activity in the frontal lobes that helps self-control.

Adapted by permission from Macmillan Publishers Ltd: Molecular Psychiatry. Vaidya and Gabrieli, 1999.

The boys performed this task for two sessions, one without taking medication and one with an appropriate dose of Ritalin®. Both groups improved in their performance when taking Ritalin, but the effect of the drug was different in the brains of the two groups. The fMRI brain scans presented in the boxes outlined in yellow in Figure 3.16 show that the boys with ADHD have more activity in the structures highlighted (called the *striatum*) when taking the drug than when not, and their level of activity in this region is the same as the control group boys without a drug. When they have taken the drug, the control group boys actually show less activity in this area of the brain (Vaidya et al., 1998). This demonstrates that children with ADHD have specific brain areas that respond differently than those of children without ADHD.

Parkinson's Disease

Parkinson's disease (or **Parkinson's dementia**) is an irreversible, degenerative disease that typically affects people over 50 years of age. Mohammed Ali and Michael J. Fox are two well-known people who suffer from this disease. The readily identified symptoms of this malady are tremors when muscles are relaxed. It is this type of tremor that attracted the attention of James Parkinson (1817/2002), who described a "shaking palsy" experienced by some of his patients. However, one symptom that often goes unnoticed is the attentional difficulties that accompany advanced stages of Parkinson's. The attentional problems manifest: (a) when the patient needs to engage in activity that is not well learned or must formulate and evaluate a hypothesis; (b) when the patient needs to suppress an habitual response or resist a temptation; and (c) when the patient needs to keep focused and not be distracted in performing a task. You may notice that these symptoms are highly similar to those that are typical of children with ADHD.

These symptoms map onto circuits that involve the prefrontal cortex. Like ADHD, they involve the basal ganglia, specifically a part called the *substantia nigra* (dark substance) that contains dopamine-producing neurons (shown in Figure 3.15). Most individuals with Parkinson's disease have lost 80% of their dopamine-producing cells (R. G. Brown & Marsden, 1988, 1990; Dubois, Defontaines, Deweer, Malapani, & Pillon, 1995). This can have far-reaching effects because dopamine is probably involved in regulating many of our habitual, routine thoughts and behaviors, that require only our automatic attentional processing (Schultz et al., 1995). In addition, dopamine may be especially useful for learning and maintaining adaptive behavior in situations where several choices are available (Taylor & Saint-Cyr, 1995). Many patients respond to chemicals, such as levodopa (L-dopa), which stimulates the production of dopamine-producing cells. Another treatment is to stimulate those cells into productivity electrically using a technique called *deep brain stimulation*.

ADHD and Parkinson's dementia are two widespread conditions that affect the ability to maintain attention. The cognitive symptoms of people with ADHD and Parkinson's are similar, and so are the underlying brain mechanisms of these disorders. Further research by cognitive scientists may help medical researchers develop common treatments for these and other forms of attentional difficulties.

SECTION SUMMARY ■

The Neuropsychology of Attention

Attention works so seamlessly that we often are unaware of its importance until we have difficulty paying attention. A host of maladies falls under the general heading of attentional difficulties. People who suffer from simultanagnosia, for example, have difficulty switching their attention from one object to another. As a consequence they frequently bump into objects that their visual system registers, but to which their attentional system is blind. A similar malady is called hemispheric neglect. It occurs when a person's attentional system (but not the visual system) is blind to objects in half of that person's visual field, typically the left visual field. Their brains register the missing information, but their attentional system cannot react to it. For some people, paying attention is always difficult because of neurological problems. Although they do not have conscious awareness of events in the left visual field, these events can still have an unconscious influence on their behavior.

Attention-deficit/hyperactivity disorder (ADHD) is a common form of attentional difficulty in which both children and adults show distractibility. Although it is referred to as attentional deficit, its source is the inability of the attentional system to filter out irrelevant input. People with ADHD attend to too many stimuli, which suggests that it should be called inhibition deficit. It has a genetic component and is related to the presence of dopamine, a neurotransmitter that affects functioning of the frontal lobes. It is similar in many ways to Parkinson's dementia, a disease affecting roughly 1% of people over 80 years old in the United States. These individuals have difficulty switching their attention to new events or ideas.

CHAPTER SUMMARY

The term *attention* describes the cognitive processes that allow us to concentrate or focus on one set of events in our mental environment while ignoring others. When we are consciously aware of this happening, we are said to be paying attention. We are limited in how long we are able to focus our attention and it is selective: When we attend to one set of events, we stop attending to others. There are two broad types of attentional processes. The first of these, automatic processes, occurs when attention instantly reacts to signals with barely any conscious awareness or control. Automatic processes are developed with practice and experience and by themselves make minimal demands on our cognitive resources. In contrast, controlled processes are typically slow, time-consuming, and involve conscious awareness. They can place automatic processes under their control. When controlled processes interact with otherwise automatic ones, processing priorities can become confused, making us subject to potentially devastating errors and accidents.

Attention acts like a spotlight. Both automatic and controlled processes can direct where it points. At the attention spotlight's center are the events that are most important and demand the majority of our resources. The spotlight of attention is capable of moving and being attracted to different sources of stimulation based on simple visual and auditory cues, or familiar content like the sound of our own name or what is most pertinent to a situation and important to our lives. Attention works in conjunction with sensory storage, which momentarily retains what happens to us in a raw sensory form so that our attention spotlight can illuminate a portion of it. Sensory storage provides this brief form of memory for all sensory dimensions: vision, hearing, taste, and the like.

Sometimes our attentional system focuses on stimuli based on their physical characteristics (e.g., Broadbent, 1958), such as hearing a siren in the middle of the night, or based on the pertinence of an event to us, such as hearing your name spoken across a noisy room. It is as if human attention contains a filtering system that allows us to select stimulation that is worthy of further analysis from the limitless events that confront us at any moment.

Our attentional system acts like a cognitive resource that can be limited by the set of demands placed on it at any moment and what is required to replenish that resource. Life events can overwhelm our attention and make great demands on attentional resources, from which it takes considerable time to recover. During this period, our attention shuts down and we miss important stimuli. Similar blinks occur when people miss a repeated sound or word (repetition blindness) or when they focus their attention on one event and completely disregard another, potentially more important, event (as are the cases with change blindness and inattentional blindness).

The cognitive approach to attention can be applied to understanding biologically based conditions that interfere with normal attentional functioning: simultanagnosia, hemispheric neglect, Parkinson's disease, and ADHD. These and other interruptions to the smooth functioning of attention involve the frontal lobes of the brain and the neurotransmitter dopamine. Studies of neurological deficits combined with basic cognitive research have shown that paying attention to one object or event also means not paying attention to others. This is best illustrated with ADHD. The chief characteristic of ADHD is an attentional spotlight that contains too many stimuli competing for consideration, so the affected individuals have difficulty preventing themselves from attending to irrelevant events. Medications that are helpful to people with these disorders have helped psychologists understand the biology of attention.

KEY TERMS

attention, p. 45

preattentive processing
(or preattentive analysis),
p. 47

focused attentional
processing, p. 48

orienting reflexes, p. 48

where/what circuits, p. 48

habituation, p. 49

attentional spotlight, p. 49

span of apprehension, p. 51

subitizing, p. 52

sensory storage, p. 53

sensory memory, p. 54

sensory information
storage (SIS), p. 54

saccades, p. 54

capacity, p. 54

duration, p. 54

forgetting, p. 54

coding, p. 54

partial report procedure,
p. 55

masking, p. 56

precategorical storage, p, 58

attentional processing, p. 58

cocktail-party
phenomenon, p. 59

early-selection filter, p. 61

late-selection filter, p. 61

late-selection theory, p. 61

automatic processes, p. 62

controlled processing, p. 62

Stroop effect, p. 62

closed skill, p. 65

open skills, p. 65

mindlessness, p. 65

capacity theory of
attention, p. 68

attentional blink, p. 68

repetition blindness, p. 70

change blindness, p. 71

inattentional blindness,
p. 73

simultanagnosia, p. 75

hemispheric neglect (or
hemineglect), p. 75

attention-deficit/
hyperactivity disorder
(ADHD), p. 77

Parkinson's disease (or
Parkinson's dementia),
p. 79

QUESTIONS FOR REVIEW

Check Your Knowledge

1. Can you define attention?

2. How does the length of time spent performing a task affect your ability to attend to it?

3. If you were a lifeguard, how long should you stay in one place looking at a specific area of the pool before you started to miss important events?

4. What are the earliest signs of attention in the life of a child?

5. Sometimes we don't notice repeated events. What process accounts for this change in attention?

6. What are the properties of attention described by the spotlight metaphor?

7. How long does it take a typical person to move his or her attentional spotlight?

8. How wide is the spotlight in the visual domain?

9. What is subitizing?

10. How many things can we automatically identify?

11. Sensory storage is the memory system on which attention relies. Describe the four properties

of this system: capacity, duration, forgetting, and coding.

12. What is the dichotic listening task (shadowing)?

13. Attention can filter out new sensory events. What is an example of an early-selection filter?

14. What is an example of a late-selection filter?

15. Define automatic processing and give an example.

16. Define controlled processing and give an example.

17. What is the difference between an open and closed skill?

18. What is the key source of danger with automatic processing?

19. What is the attentional blink and how is it affected by the age of the person?

20. What is repetition blindness?

21. What is change blindness?

22. Which type of objects' changing are you more likely to be blind to?

23. What is inattentional blindness? Choose a real-world situation that embodies this phenomenon.

24. Which is more disruptive of driving: listening to the radio or talking on a hands-free cell phone?

25. What is Bálint's syndrome and why do people who suffer this malady develop bruises?

26. Is hemineglect the result of poor eyesight? Why?

27. What is attention-deficit/hyperactivity disorder?

28. What does the text think it should be called?

29. What other neurological maladies are similar to ADHD?

30. Why do amphetamines help people with ADHD?

Apply Your Knowledge

1. What are the benefits of an attentional system with both automatic and controlled attention?

2. What would life be like if we possessed only automatic attention processes? What would life be like if we possessed only controlled attention processes?

3. Suppose you are driving on a highway, closely following the car in front of you, and you notice a police car in your mirror. Aside from the issue of getting a ticket, why does research on attention advise you to slow down and increase the distance between your car and the car in front?

4. In light of research findings on inattention, what would your advice be to people who talk on their cell phones while driving? What do you think the data imply for using hands-free versus handheld cell phones?

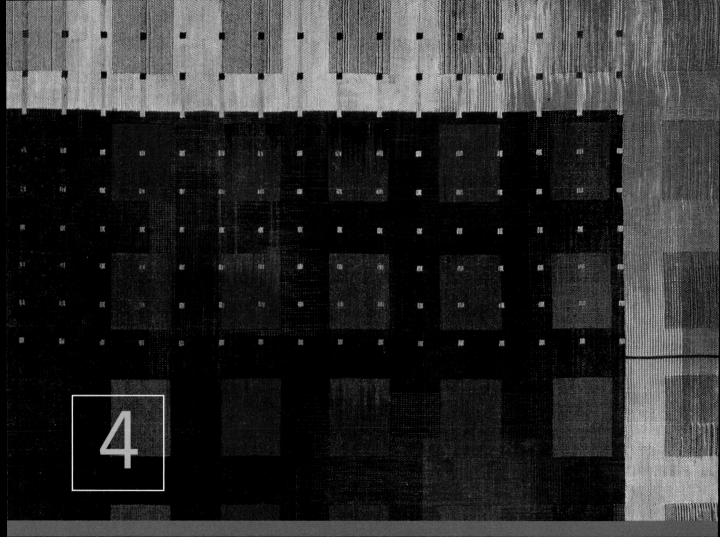

❝What we see depends mainly on what we look for.❞

—Sir John Lubbock

Imagine that you are driving a car on a crowded highway. In order to operate your car safely, you must make nearly instantaneous decisions with only bits and pieces of information to rely on. You must detect signs that the car in front is braking and slowing down (you see its brake lights flash), or that the cars on either side are about to merge into your lane (subtle movement in their lanes toward your car). Safely making your morning commute or even a drive to the grocery store relies on a process called **pattern recognition**, in which a person uses fragmentary pieces of sensory stimulation to create a higher-level identification of what he or she has just experienced. The activities of sensory memory and attention are the basic components that make pattern recognition possible, because in order to recognize a pattern, we must attend to it. In order to attend to something, it must register in sensory memory long enough for the attention system to focus on it and provide information to long-term memory so it can perform the recognition. Although pattern recognition seems to occur instantaneously, often years of experience are required to develop the ability to recognize patterns effortlessly. For example, in Chapter 3 we noted that skilled readers are able to recognize words and derive their meaning at the rate of about 0.10 to 0.20 seconds (100–200 msec) per word, yet it takes many years of practice to perfect this skill. Cognitive psychologists study how we come to acquire this ability.

Recognizing Patterns: The Problem of Perception

In order to survive, we need to perceive and react to objects in the world around us, but what we perceive is not a perfect copy of those objects. **Perception** is the act of becoming aware of something through our senses. This awareness is based on an inference from the stimulation of our sense organs. Suppose you are walking down the street and see a 10-foot tree. You are able to experience the tree because light bounces off it and stimulates cells on the retinas of your eyes. However, the imprint on the retina barely resembles the tree. Although the tree is 10 feet tall, the stimulation of cells on the retina is less than an inch high. The tree is a 3-D object, while the retina is a 2-D surface. The retinal cells transmit signals to specific regions of the visual cortex in your brain and cause you to "see" or "perceive" the tree. How do people accomplish these feats of perception and identify what they are experiencing?

One answer provided by researchers is that our attention is directed to a stimulus (e.g., the tree) and we extract primitive features from it, which are then compared with known patterns of stimulation that are stored in long-term memory. Cognitive scientists call this **bottom-up processing** (or **bottom-up analysis**) because it proceeds from basic elements and creates a higher level of understanding. But the pattern recognition process does not stop at general recognition based on the basic features of an object. Once a preliminary guess is made, the pattern recognition process tries to reduce the set of alternative possibilities by selecting just those low-level features from the input that appear worthy of further analysis in order to complete the identification. Researchers call this reassessment of the input features **top-down processing** (or **top-down analysis**). Thus, every perceptual experience results from a balance between bottom-up and top-down processing. To identify objects and events, we take into consideration both the basic aspects of objects like their edges and textures and our individual expectations of what objects (including people) are supposed to look like and how they are supposed to behave.

People are rarely aware of the elementary perceptual features in their recognition of patterns. The 19th-century French painter Seurat noticed this and created artistic works from tiny dots of color that observers are unaware of unless they deliberately focus their attentional spotlight on them. This technique is called *pointillism*. Look at the painting in **FIGURE 4.1A**. At first glance, did you notice the points of color or did you perceive a landscape? The concept of pointillism has been extended to a computer-based process, called *photomosaic*, which creates images from the combination of thousands of different photographs such as the picture of Abraham Lincoln

FIGURE 4.1 Invisible Bottom-Up Features (A) *Bathing at Asnièrs* by Georges Seurat, 1884. This painting is created from thousands of color dots using a technique called *pointilllism*. Just as with bottom-up processing in vision, we are unaware of the elementary features and perceive the whole idea or scene. (B) The photomosaic image of Abraham Lincoln is created from over a thousand tiny Civil War photographs, which we barely observe as a result of automatic, bottom-up processing.

National Gallery, London/Art Resource, NY; Photomosaic® by Robert Silvers, www.photomosaic.com

(A)   (B)

shown in **FIGURE 4.1B**, which is based on over a thousand photos from the Civil War era. Cognitive psychologists have sought to understand how we are able to create meaning from elementary features without seeming to be aware of them. These efforts began with the research of German psychologists at the beginning of the 20th century, which is the topic of the next section.

SECTION SUMMARY ▪
Recognizing Patterns: The Problem of Perception
Pattern recognition is a process by which we attend to aspects of sensory stimulation and identify what we have just experienced. The ability to recognize patterns requires three systems working in concert: a database of knowledge, a spotlight of attention to focus on the incoming stream of sensory experience, and an analysis of the relevant aspects of the sensory information. Long-term memory provides the database; attention focuses the spotlight; and perceptual processes provide the analysis. This perceptual analysis is described as either bottom-up or top-down. Bottom-up analysis reflects attention to low-level features of an object that are automatically extracted for later processing to create a preliminary identification. Top-down analysis reflects the person's expectation of what an object is likely to be. This usually involves the reassessment of which low-level features are important in light of expectations or because of the person's knowledge of the context in which the object appears.

▪ ▪

Gestalt Principles

When you hear music, you perceive a melody first, rather than just a sequence of individual notes. This is an example of how people experience the global features before the specific ones, just as we saw with the pointillist illustration. The idea that we perceive the form or configuration of things before we understand their parts is called **gestalt,** a German word that roughly translated means "configuration" or "whole." A German word is used because the original developers of the theory were professors at German universities, including many who emigrated to the United States in the 1930s when the Nazis came to power. The psychologists who studied this aspect of perception were called *Gestalt psychologists*. Some of their findings can be summarized as six universal (cross-cultural) laws of perceptual grouping that help create what can be considered the highest level of the bottom-up recognition process.

Before describing the individual laws, it's important to note a principle that permeates our perceptual judgments and is the source of the six laws: the **principle of Prägnanz.** The German word *Prägnanz* (pronounced /prek-nonce/) means "conveying the essence of something" (Koffka, 1935). Put simply, our perception of a stimulus will be organized into as cohesive a figure as possible: symmetrical, simple, closed, and regular. Gestalt psychologists called this a "good" figure (Koffka, 1922). Suppose individuals were shown a square superimposed on top of a triangle, as in **FIGURE 4.2A**. Their perceptual experience will not be the combination of

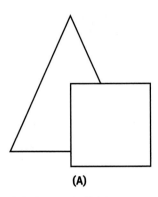
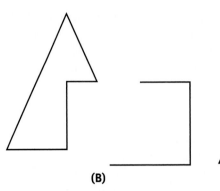
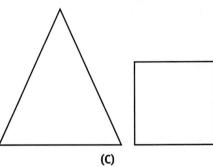

(A)   **(B)**   **(C)**

FIGURE 4.2 Applications of Prägnanz The principle of Prägnanz says that our perception of a stimulus as in (A) will be organized into as cohesive a figure as possible: symmetrical, simple, closed, and regular. We see the figure in (A) as two regular figures in (C) and not the actual lines in (B).

complicated shapes shown in **FIGURE 4.2B**, but rather the overlapping of two complete figures, individually shown in **FIGURE 4.2C**—making a good figure.

This tendency to simplify what our senses experience helps us recognize objects, but at the same time can make us susceptible to visual illusions (Buffart, Leeuwenberg, & Restle, 1983). Look closely at **FIGURE 4.3**. At first, you should see four columns surrounding the pool of water—this is the functioning of Prägnanz. If you scan the picture more carefully, however, you will notice something odd about the top of the columns. Once you make this observation, your entire mental construction of the scene dissolves into a kind of perceptual ambiguity because it becomes what Gestalt psychologists call an *impossible figure*.

Prägnanz underlies a general gestalt concept that the whole is greater than the sum of the parts. Humans tend to perceive the general connection among parts, rather than the parts themselves. To experience this, look at **FIGURE 4.4**. Most people see dots amid a field of white. At some point, these elements merge into an image of a Dalmatian dog (Gregory, 1970). Trying to perceive the individual elements of ear, nose, feet, and the dots that compose them does not create the perception of the dog. The dog emerges all at once: When perceivers experience the whole, they seem not to notice the fragmentary nature of the dots and lines that

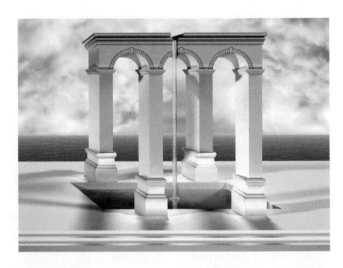

FIGURE 4.3 Impossible Figure and Prägnanz In this picture, Prägnanz causes you to focus either on the bottom of the columns or the top of them. It is only on closer inspection that we are forced to conclude that the picture is impossible.

Paul Fleet/Alamy

FIGURE 4.4 Immediate Perception of the Whole As you stare at the points of black and white, they begin to merge all at once into the image of a Dalmatian dog.

Courtesy of Ronald James

Illusory Conjunction?

create the picture. Gestalt psychologists focused on the nature of these "wholes" and discovered that they follow the principle of Prägnanz. They tend to be the simplest and purist possible forms. Gestalt psychologists have used the concept of Prägnanz to construct the following six basic principles or laws of automatic perceptual grouping (Wertheimer, 1923/1938): (a) proximity, (b) similarity, (c) closure, (d) common fate, (e) symmetry, and (f) good continuation.

Law of Proximity

Elements that are close together will be perceived as a coherent group and be differentiated from the items that are far from them. This is called the **law of proximity**. It is illustrated with the drawings in **FIGURE 4.5A**, where it is difficult for the perceiver to avoid seeing the four columns of triangles as two columns to the left of the center and two to the right. This law of proximity is often applied in the design of devices to help users identify buttons that share common functions, as in the remote control device in **FIGURE 4.5B**.

FIGURE 4.5 Gestalt Law of Proximity (A) Notice that the columns of triangles appear as two groups with a big space between them. (B) The law of proximity is applied in the design of devices like the channel selector. Separate functions are differentiated by the spacing and shape of the buttons. The channels are in a 3 × 4 array; the different modes are grouped at the top in a 1 × 5 array, and so on.

Py2000/Dreamstime.com

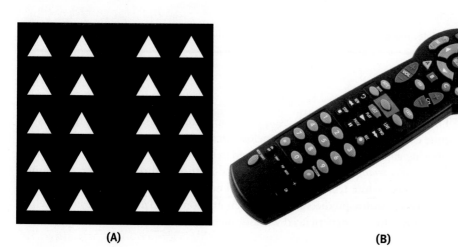

(A)   (B)

Law of Similarity

Elements that look similar will be perceived as part of the same form or group. The similarity can be based on size, brightness, color, shape, or even orientation. This principle along with the law of proximity helps differentiate the buttons in Figure 4.5B. The **law of similarity** is the basis for many tests of color blindness. To experience an application of this gestalt law, try the exercise in Demonstration 4.1.

■■■**DEMONSTRATION 4.1**

Color Blindness and Gestalt Similarity

Look at the two figures below, called *Ishihara plates* (invented by Dr. Shinobu Ishihara). A person who has red–green blindness will not be able to see the similarity of the green dots in (A) and will not group them together as the number 5. However, people with normal color vision and those with red–green blindness will automatically see the similarity of dots in (B), and group them together as the number 12.

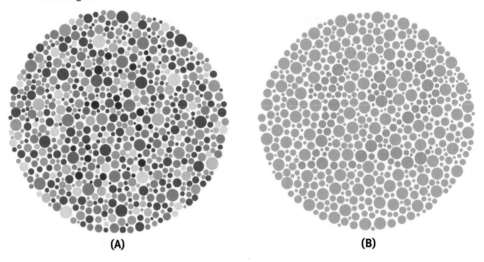

(A)   (B)

Alexander Kaludov/Dreamstime.com

Note: This demonstration is not a complete medical test for color blindness.

Law of Closure

The principle of Prägnanz is especially applicable in cases where a figure is not quite complete. Humans tend to enclose such spaces by completing a contour and ignoring gaps in the picture, as illustrated in **FIGURE 4.6A**, sometimes referred to as the *Kanizsa triangle*. You can either see the picture as three Pac-Men or, as most people do, a white triangle superimposed on three black circles (Kanizsa, 1976). The **law of closure** predicts a general phenomenon called *illusory contours* in which an enclosed form is experienced without such a form being on the retina of the eye.

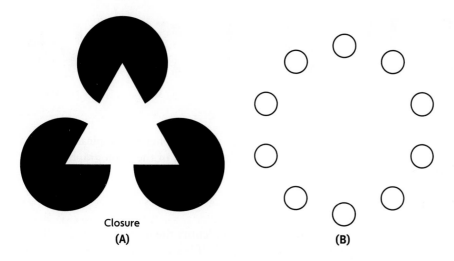

Closure

(A)

(B)

FIGURE 4.6 Gestalt Law of Closure (A) You can see the picture as three Pac-Men or as a white triangle superimposed on three black circles. Most people do the latter and complete the contours and ignore the gaps in the picture. (B) People find it difficult to see this figure as a set of 10. They automatically enclose the gaps and perceive them as one large circle.

Closure also describes the experience of seeing a figure as a closed unit, even when the observer knows there are open spaces (see also Figure 4.4). Who can resist seeing the dots in **FIGURE 4.6B** as a big circle?

Law of Common Fate

If two or more objects—cars, people, arrows—are moving in the same direction and at the same speed, they will tend to be perceived as a group and to share a common destiny. When we see flocks of birds like Canada geese or starlings flying in the same direction at the same speed, for example, we tend to perceive them as a group, in contrast with clouds in the sky or other birds flying nearby. Cars driving at the same speed on the highway may seem to be grouped together as well. These phenomena are grouped under the concept **law of common fate**. This pattern recognition process is used by artists and photographers to create an expectation of the lines of direction. If a photograph of horses shows them running to the right, as in **FIGURE 4.7**, the observer expects them to stay together

FIGURE 4.7 Gestalt Law of Common Fate When multiple objects move at the same speed and direction, they are seen as a group, sharing a common fate. It is natural to perceive these horses as running together from the left to a common end point on the right.

JTB Photo/Photolibrary

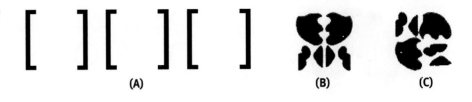

FIGURE 4.8 The Gestalt Law of Symmetry (A) People naturally experience the symmetry in this visual display. Even 4-month-old infants prefer to stare at the symmetrical figure in (B) than at the asymmetrical figure in (C).

Source for (B) and (C): Bornstein, Ferdinandsen, & Gross, 1981

and continue to run in that direction. A photographer will typically frame a photograph so the horses are placed in the left half of the photograph and will be perceived as having room to run!

Law of Symmetry

Most living things are symmetrical. If you identify the middle of a person from head to foot, you will notice that the right half is a reflection of the left: People are symmetric. The gestalt **law of symmetry** claims that humans are sensitive to symmetry in nature. The law of symmetry has two parts. First, images that are perceived as symmetrical are experienced as belonging together. Second, people tend to find symmetry in a figure even if it is otherwise disorganized. Notice in **FIGURE 4.8A** you can see the brackets as groupings of objects that are close together. Alternately, you can see them as three pairs of left–right brackets. The law of symmetry suggests you will do the latter. There is a biological basis for this preference. For example, 4-month-old infants prefer to look at vertically symmetrical objects like that in **FIGURE 4.8B** rather than asymmetrical objects like that in **FIGURE 4.8C** (Bornstein & Krinsky, 1985). Our ability to notice symmetry may have survival value; predators and possible mates are symmetric, whereas the background rocks, water, and trees are not (Chen & Tyler, 2010).

Law of Good Continuation

Another law identified by Gestalt psychologists is called the **law of good continuation**. It refers to the fact that people tend to connect elements in a way that makes the elements seem continuous or flowing in a particular direction. This is illustrated in **FIGURE 4.9A**, which is often perceived as two lines crossing

FIGURE 4.9 The Gestalt Law of Good Continuation The law of good continuation says that people will tend to connect elements in a way that makes them seem continuous. (A) This figure is often perceived as two lines crossing each other rather than two V-shaped configurations intersecting. (B) When you look at the dots, do you see it as a spiral?

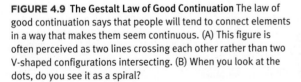

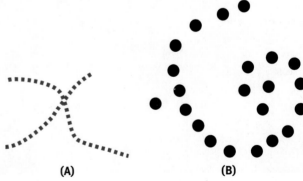

each other rather than two V-shaped configurations intersecting. Continuation can exercise a powerful affect on what we perceive. In **FIGURE 4.9B**, the dots don't necessarily form a spiral, but few people can resist seeing a spiral of dots.

SECTION SUMMARY ▪

Gestalt Principles

Before we recognize the components of a shape, we perceive its global form, its gestalt. There are six laws that describe how humans around the world accomplish this governed by a basic principle called Prägnanz, the tendency to capture the essence of what we perceive. The six gestalt laws are proximity, similarity, closure, common fate, symmetry, and good continuation. These laws summarize our tendency to see the entirety of an object and disregard minor deviations from a good figure.

Bottom-Up Processing

As noted in the introduction, every perceptual experience results from a balance between bottom-up and top-down processing. To identify objects and events we must deal both with the basic aspects of objects (such as their edges, colors, and textures) and use our expectations about how objects (and people) are supposed to look and behave. There are at least four different descriptions of how we employ basic bottom-up processes. These accounts are not mutually exclusive; they often operate at the same time. The bottom-up processing theories in the following sections are organized progressively as steps along the way from the stimulation of our sense organs and the analysis of elementary features to a global interpretation (a guess) of what we are experiencing.

Distinctive Features Theory

The core idea of bottom-up processing is that people recognize patterns based on their individual, basic perceptual characteristics. The modern version of this approach is called the **distinctive features theory** (Gibson, 1969), which assumes that all complex perceptual stimuli are composed of distinctive and separable attributes called *features*. Distinctive features are cues that allow observers to distinguish one object from another. To see how this works, look at the list of features that characterize the capital letter A shown in **FIGURE 4.10**. The list of A features includes a horizontal line, two diagonal lines, and the fact that the diagonal lines intersect each other. Compare the distinctive features of the letter A with those of other letters of the English alphabet shown in Figure 4.10. You will notice each letter can be differentiated from every other letter by a unique set of features. Distinctive features theory suggests that pattern recognition is accomplished by mentally assessing the presence or absence of a checklist of critical features. The observer then compares those features to a storehouse of features

Features	A	E	F	H	I	L	T	K	M	N	V	W	X	Y	Z	B	C	D	G	J	O	P	R	Q	S	U
Straight																										
Horizontal	+	+	+	+		+	+								+				+			+				
Vertical		+	+	+	+	+	+	+	+	+					+	+		+				+	+			
Diagonal /	+							+	+		+	+	+	+	+											
Diagonal \	+							+	+	+	+	+	+	+	+								+	+		
Curve																										
Closed																+		+			+	+	+	+		
Open *V*																				+						+
Open *H*																	+		+	+					+	
Intersection	+	+	+	+		+	+						+			+					+	+	+			
Redundancy																										
Cyclic change		+							+			+				+									+	
Symmetry	+	+		+	+		+	+			+	+	+	+		+	+	+			+					+
Discontinuity																										
Vertical	+		+	+	+	+	+	+	+					+								+	+			
Horizontal		+	+			+	+								+											

FIGURE 4.10 Gibson's Distinctive Features for Letters of the Alphabet All complex stimuli such as letters of the alphabet can be analyzed as composed of features that allow us to distinguish between them. Choose any letter and list its features; it will not match any other letter.

Source: Gibson, 1969

in long-term memory that correspond to objects a person has already encountered. According to this theory, pattern recognition depends upon identifying only those features that distinguish one object from some other objects.

It follows from the distinctive features theory that letters that share many critical features should be more difficult to discriminate than those that share few features. Figure 4.10 shows that the two letters P and R share many features. The theory correctly predicts that it takes longer for people to tell them apart than to tell G and M apart, two letters that share no common features (e.g., Briggs & Hocevar, 1975; Gibson, 1969). For an example of how feature-based pattern recognition works, see Demonstration 4.2.

■■■DEMONSTRATION 4.2

Recognition of Features

To experience how the feature-based approach works, place your hand over the second column so that you cannot see its letters and then search as quickly as you can for the letter Z in the first column.

Column 1	Column 2
CQOGRD	EMVXWI
QUGCDR	IVWMEX
QUGCDR	ANXEHM
QUGCDR	NFTVYLA
DUZGRO	WVZMXE
GRUQDO	IEVMWX

Now, uncover the second column and search for the letter Z there. Did it take you longer to find the Z in the second column than the first? Column 1 consists of round letters that are distinctively different from the features of Z. People typically find the Z in this group quickly; it just pops out. In contrast, Column 2 consists of angular letters that have similar features to Z; people are considerably slower at finding the Z in Column 2 than in Column 1 (Neisser, 1964).

People often confuse letters or objects that have similar features. Suppose you are asked to name letters flashed on a screen as fast as you can, such as the letter G. You are likely to make an occasional error in naming the letter. Distinctive features theory holds that if observers make an error (i.e., they identify a letter other than G), they are more likely to say that they saw a C or an O (letters with similar features) than any other letter. This is just what research has found. In one study, feature-consistent errors made up 93% of the errors of recorded identifications (Kinney, Marsetta, & Showman, 1966, reported in Anderson, 2005a).

All features are not equally detectable. Certain features are more easily detected than others because they may be "wired" in. Neurological evidence for this has been provided by Hubel and Wiesel (1962), who recorded the electrical activity of the visual cortex of a cat's brain and discovered that some neurons respond maximally to horizontal lines, while others respond maximally to diagonals. This is true for primates as well (Hubel & Wiesel, 1968; Maunsell & Newsome, 1987). If we can generalize from these findings, it suggests that many creatures, humans included, may use these features to recognize patterns without much training. Indeed, with a little training, even robots can successfully detect objects (e.g., Adams, Breazeal, Brooks, & Scassellati, 2000).

Global and Local Features The idea that people use features for bottom-up pattern recognition must deal with the fact that any visual scene is potentially composed of an unlimited number of features combined in an uncountable number of ways. How does the mind reduce the number of possibilities so that it can concentrate on one thing? A partial answer is that we start with global features and progress to more local ones. Navon (1977, 2003) asked observers to listen to the name of a letter and decide whether a visually presented large letter was the same or different from the one they heard. Some examples of the displays are shown in **FIGURE 4.11**, called

Global Features are First
(Navon Pictures)

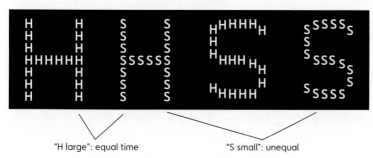

"H large": equal time   "S small": unequal

FIGURE 4.11 Navon Figures In Navon figures, large letters are composed of small letters. When participants heard the letter name *H*, they responded yes equally quickly to the large letters, no matter what the small letters were—these low-level features did not affect the global judgment. However, when deciding the name of the small letters, they were affected by the name of the capital letter—the global features are processed first.

Reprinted from *Cognitive Psychology, 9*, David Navon, Forest before trees: The precedence of global features in visual perception, 353–383, Copyright 1977, with permission from Elsevier. Courtesy David Navon.

Navon figures. You can see that the visual stimulus consisted of a large character (the global level) made out of small characters (the local level). When they heard the letter name *H*, participants responded yes equally quickly, regardless of whether they were shown the letter on the left (made up of *H*'s) or the letter on the right (made up of *S*'s) in the figure. This finding suggests that the low-level feature (*s*) did not affect the global judgment. However, when observers were asked to determine whether the letter name was consistent with the small letters, the observers took longer to respond yes to the capital *H* letter composed of small *s*'s than they did to the capital letter *S* composed of small *s*'s. This suggests that to access the local features, observers have to endure the early processing of the global features. The global features are processed first. This also affects the ability to read and to recognize letters within words (i.e., the word-superiority effect, described later in the chapter).

The importance of global and local features adds to our understanding of hemineglect (discussed in Chapter 3 as part of the clinical aspects of attention). You'll recall that people who suffer from hemineglect typically have difficulty processing objects presented to their left visual field even though their visual system is working properly. When such individuals participate in a recognition task with Navon's figures, they show the deficit only when they are processing the low-level local features, but not when they are processing the global features. People with hemineglect and people without hemineglect are equally able to identify the capital letter in displays like that shown in Figure 4.11. However, when participants are asked to cross out the small letters in any figure, those with hemineglect can only do so when the small letters are on the right side of the global letter (Marshall & Halligan, 1995). This is another piece of evidence that tells us that perception of the whole figure is not dependent upon noticing the features for the elementary parts, but is based on more global level analysis.

Recognition by Components Theory

Distinctive features theory focuses on how humans and other animals may recognize patterns by attending to low-level features of objects, such as lines, angles, and dots. Another feature theory, called **recognition by components theory** (or **RBC theory**; Biederman, 1987), describes the pattern recognition process in terms of how people recognize 3-D objects by identifying basic features that comprise the objects. These basic elements are composed of an alphabet of 36 primitive shapes, called **geons** (geometric ions), the basic building blocks for identifying 3-D objects. Some of these geons (along with the objects they are part of) are shown in **FIGURES 4.12** and **4.13**.

Like distinctive features theory, RBC theory suggests that people identify an object as an entity by noting its edges. Then, in order to recognize what the

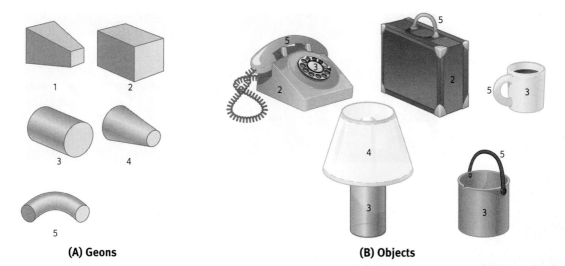

(A) Geons   **(B) Objects**

FIGURE 4.12 Geons (Geometric Ions) Geons are the basic building blocks for identifying three-dimensional objects. Some of them are numbered and shown in (A). You can see how these geons compose common objects by matching the numbers in (A) with numbers on the objects in (B).

Source: Adapted from I. Biederman, "Recognition by Components: A Theory of Human Image Understanding," *Psychological Review, 14*(2), 115–147, Figures 3, 6, 7, and 11. Copyright 1987 by the American Psychological Association. Reprinted by permission.

object is, such as the flashlight in Figure 4.13A, the observer proceeds through three stages:

1. The observer subdivides the object into sub-objects by noticing where lines intersect. For example, the flashlight in Figure 4.13A has lines that form the top and the bottom, which are intersected by a curved line (the light).

2. Each sub-object is then classified into 1 of 36 geons. The collection of geons is like an alphabet of shapes for constructing objects, just as letters comprise an alphabet for building up words.

3. Once observers have identified the geons, they are able to recognize the object as the pattern composed from these geons. To complete the alphabet metaphor, just as people build up their recognition of written words by identifying letters, we recognize each geon as part of the process of identifying the object.

Some simple predictions spring from RBC theory. First, if your view of the object is degraded in some way, the portion of a geon you can or cannot see is important. If something obscures the sides of the flashlight, for example, you can still tell what it is if you can see the intersection of the geons (see Figure 4.13B). However, as shown in Figure 4.13C, if the intersection of the handle and the surface or the surface and the round light are obscured, you will have difficulty recognizing the flashlight.

Biederman (1987) presented drawings to observers for 100 msec and asked them to identify what they saw. When they saw diagrams like the one shown in Figure 4.13C, they made nearly twice as many errors as when they observed objects as they appear in Figure 4.13B. This shows that RBC can not only account for recognizing more than a million patterns, but perhaps more important, it can explain how we are able to recognize objects even when we can't see all of them

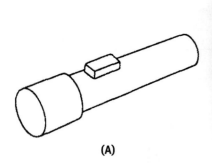

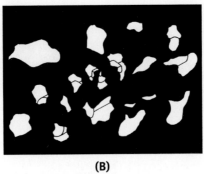

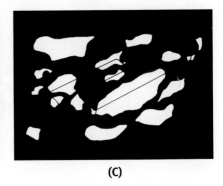

(A)   (B)   (C)

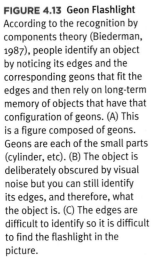

FIGURE 4.13 Geon Flashlight
According to the recognition by components theory (Biederman, 1987), people identify an object by noticing its edges and the corresponding geons that fit the edges and then rely on long-term memory of objects that have that configuration of geons. (A) This is a figure composed of geons. Geons are each of the small parts (cylinder, etc). (B) The object is deliberately obscured by visual noise but you can still identify its edges, and therefore, what the object is. (C) The edges are difficult to identify so it is difficult to find the flashlight in the picture.

Biederman, I. (1987). Recognition-by-Components: A Theory of Human Image Understanding. *Psychological Review, 94*, 115–147.

(as when they are in a shadow or blocked by some other object). Recognition using geons offers a way to account for the incredible ability of humans to recognize a limitless variety of objects seen from different points of view. Biederman (1995) calculated that various combinations and intersections of three geons at a time can create 306 billion possible objects: more than 20 times the number of seconds in a 100-year lifetime.

Template-Matching Theory

The use of features in pattern recognition is undeniable, but it is not enough to account for our ability to identify objects so rapidly, consistently, and accurately. To do this, a portion of the recognition process must be able to assemble the features to see the whole object. The **template-matching theory** accounts for this portion of the process. This theory assumes that we have stored away an unlimited number of patterns, literal copies corresponding to every object that we have experienced. These patterns are labeled with the name of the object. Whenever we see a new instance of one of these objects, it is matched to a stored template that is instantly activated and informs us of the name of the pattern we have just experienced. This theory goes back to the ancient Greek philosopher Democritus (460–370 BCE), who argued that miniature copies of objects in the world enter our minds through tubes (nerves) and that we know instantly what these objects are because they are identical, except for size, to real objects that we have previously observed.

Template matching works well in situations where the objects to be identified are easily discriminated from other objects and when all of the possible configurations of an object have been previously seen. If you have a bank check, look at the bottom numbers printed on it. Do you see that the numbers resemble normally printed numbers except that they are somewhat distorted? These subtle distortions allow specialized machines to read the account numbers even if the check is upside down. The machines know the orientation of the check because the string of numbers is surrounded by MICR (magnetic ink character recognition) characters. The machines that use these characters can identify bank accounts, zip codes on envelopes, or the bar codes on merchandise in stores by comparing the characters with a vast storehouse of similar patterns.

Is template-matching theory a good model for how humans recognize objects, words, and numbers? It is elegant in its simplicity and works well when we have considerable experience with the set of possible objects. It is highly impractical, however, when the set of possible patterns is very large. For example, imagine that your task is to identify the handwritten word, *hello*. To do this, you not only have to be able to read *hello* right side up or upside down, but also in all degrees of rotation. Because the word could be written in a large number of typefaces or in a wide variety of individual handwriting styles, the number of possible templates to recognize this one word would be enormous, and so would the time required to find a match by searching one template at a time. In addition to its inefficiency, a template-matching system fails to account for our ability to recognize new objects. How, for example, do we manage to read the handwriting of a person we just met?

Prototype Theory

The limitations of template theory can be dealt with by imagining that the template is not a literal match with an object, but is an average or typical instance of the many different views of that object. This average is called a **prototype** and the theory that uses them for pattern recognition is called **prototype theory**. To gain an intuitive understanding of this, ask yourself what example you would show to a child to convey the category *bird*. Would it be a robin or an ostrich? Most people would say robin (e.g., Smith, Shoben, & Rips, 1974) because it is a better reflection of the typically encountered bird. According to the prototype view, pattern recognition occurs when the features of the object to be recognized overlap in some way with the features of the prototype. To get a sense of how this works, try Demonstration 4.3.

■■■DEMONSTRATION 4.3

Prototypes

Make a list of 10 features that come to mind when you think of the word *bird*. These do not have to be dictionary definitions. Now do the same for *sparrow* and *ostrich*. When you look across the three lists, which two have the most features in common? For people the world over, the prototype of *bird* (flies, lives in trees, small) matches those of the most common bird, in this case *sparrow*. You should also find that some of the features of *ostrich* (tall, lives on ground, buries head in sand) do not match those of *bird*, because when you think of *bird* you imagine the most typical ones, and certainly an *ostrich* is not a typical bird.

Using prototypes to recognize patterns does not require an exact match between the object and the prototype, nor does it require the storage of patterns for every possible view of an object. The observer only needs to find a match between the central properties of the to-be-identified object and the stored categories. In this way a prototype-based pattern can identify the same object even if it appears in many different views and orientations.

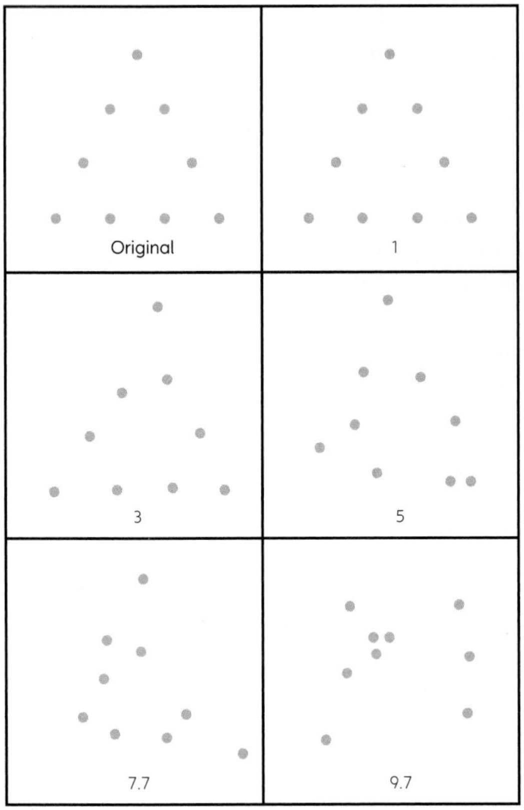

FIGURE 4.14 Posner and Keele Prototypes Students learned to label dot patterns that were distortions from the original prototype. They were later able to correctly label new distorted patterns, but they were especially effective in labeling the original prototype that they had not previously seen.

Source: Posner, Goldsmith, & Welton, 1967

One of the earliest studies to show the use of prototypes was performed by Posner & Keele (1968), who created dot patterns that represent a triangle. The dot pattern for a triangle is illustrated in **FIGURE 4.14**. Each dot pattern was then mathematically distorted so that the original patterns were progressively changed to being ultimately dissimilar to the distorted patterns. Notice that the bottom right triangle does not resemble the original in the top left box. In the learning phase of the study, participants only saw the distortions of the three original dot patterns and not the original prototypes. Their task was to sort each of the distorted dot patterns into one of three categories (call them A, B, and C categories). After participants were successful at doing this they were shown new distorted patterns. They correctly categorized these about 85% of the time even though they had never seen them before. This showed that they understood the underlying commonality among the stimuli in each category. The most interesting result occurred when the participants were shown the original prototypes of the triangle. These originals had not previously been shown to the participants, but they were able to classify these prototypes correctly. Observers, then, are able to induce the true but unseen prototypes when they are asked to observe patterns or objects. This suggests that when observers are identifying individual patterns, they use prototypes to decide what category the patterns fall into (Keele & Mayr, 2005).

These early studies of prototypes used rather unnatural stimuli: the dot patterns. For decades, however, cognitive psychologists have sought to conduct experiments based on how people operate in the real world. When experiments can do this, they are said to have **ecological validity** (Neisser, 1976). Many of the later prototype studies have used stimuli that are more similar to situations in which we might normally find ourselves. For example, Solso and McCarthy (1981) created three prototypical faces from the Identikit used by police to help eyewitnesses and victims of crimes identify perpetrators. The Identikit contains plastic templates for various facial features such as hair, eyes, nose, and so on. For each prototype, the researchers created a series of exemplars of the prototype that varied in the degree of similarity to the prototype (from 75% down to 0% similar). Some of these are shown in **FIGURE 4.15A**.

After the participants saw the exemplar faces, they were told to look at a new set of faces and to judge each one as old or new and to rate their confidence in their judgment on a 5-point scale (Old = 0 to +5, New = 0 to −5). This new set contained some of the original faces, some new ones that were similar to their respective prototypes, and some actual prototypes. **FIGURE 4.15B** shows a graph of the confidence judgments participants reported. Notice that they rated the

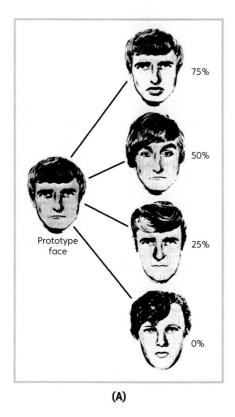

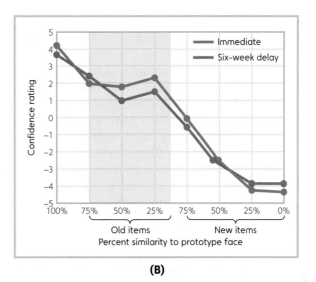

(B)

FIGURE 4.15 Solso and McCarthy Prototypes (A) Solso and McCarthy (1981) created prototypical faces from a police Identikit. For each prototype, they created exemplars that varied in their degree of similarity to the prototype (from 75% down to 0% similar). In this learning phase, the participants had not seen the prototypes. Later, they had to judge whether new and some old faces had been seen before. (B) The data were graphed, showing that participants rated the prototypes as old (even though they had never seen them before), and were more confident of that judgment than all others. The old and new exemplars were rated as old based on their similarity to the prototype.

Source: Prototype Formation of Faces, Solso & McCarthy (1981). *British Journal of Psychology. 72,* 499-503. Reproduced with permission of John Wiley & Sons, Ltd.

prototypes as old (even though they had never seen them before), and were more confident of that judgment than all others. This study shows that prototypes are part of the recognition process for realistic objects (e.g., human faces).

SECTION SUMMARY ▪

Bottom-Up Processing

The core idea of bottom-up processing is that people recognize patterns based on their basic perceptual characteristics, such as edges, colors, and textures. Some of these features are considered global and others are local. Four classes of theories describe how people make use of these features in bottom-up processing for recognizing patterns: (a) distinctive features; (b) recognition by components; (c) template-matching, and (d) prototype theories.

The distinctive features theory assumes that all objects are composed of features that will distinguish them from all others. The observer is able to recognize objects by finding a stored pattern whose features match the object. This theory correctly predicts that we will be confused when two objects have similar features.

The recognition by components theory notes that most objects can be decomposed into 36 primitive shapes called geons. These are the basic perceptual features that jointly comprise the human mental representation of an object. In order to recognize an object, a person must match the geons of an object to what has been stored in long-term memory. Objects can be recognized in any configuration.

Template-matching theory assumes that images of objects we have experienced are stored in long-term memory. The process of pattern recognition involves a match between the object in front of us and a stored image that includes the name of the object. This theory is best applied when the object is distinctive and easily discriminated from other objects.

Finally, prototype theory claims that we store away the "average" of our experience of a type of object so that the recognition process involves a comparison between the basic features of the object being identified and the features of the prototype: the average of all the similar objects we have experienced. The match doesn't have to be exact; it only has to be close enough for us to recognize the pattern.

FIGURE 4.16 Top-Down Processing and a Mountain Scene
Fishing at Eagle Rocks by J. Van Straalen. The first impression of this picture is a mountain scene. As you look at it, the global features give way to the local ones and you see that the mountain, rocks, and meadows are composed of animals.

© John Van Straalen, VSgrafx.com

Top-Down Processing

Human perception is not only based on activation by the sensory data as it comes in (bottom-up processing), it is also the result of expectations and contextual factors: top-down processing. Look at **FIGURE 4.16** for just a second or two and then return to this paragraph. Most people will describe the picture as a mountain scene, with several eagles. Is that what you saw? Now look at the figure again, but this time you should notice that the mountain and rocks are formed from the shapes of animals. How many bears and eagles can you count now? This illustrates, once again, that our first impression of a visual input generally reflects the global features of the scene (e.g., it's a kitchen or a mountain). But it also suggests that our expectations help to support that impression. If our expectations change—as when you learned that the rocks in the picture form animal shapes—so does our analysis of both the local and global features. Our expectations of what we will see influence what we perceive.

What would our lives be like if we were not able to use top-down processing and had to rely solely on bottom-up processing? The question comes to life in a poignant story told by neurologist Oliver Sacks (1995). The story concerns Virgil, a 50-year-old Oklahoma man who became blind at about the age of 6. Because Virgil could see light and faint shadows, a local ophthalmologist suggested that it might be possible to restore his sight through surgery. Surgery was ultimately done on the right eye; a thick cataract was removed and a new lens implanted. When the bandage was removed, Virgil said that he could see light, forms, movement, and color, but that they were all mixed up in a confusing blur. Only when the doctor started to speak did Virgil realize that he was staring at a face. The operation allowed him to become sensitive to the visual features of objects, but he was unable to perceive or recognize shapes and objects because he had very little top-down processing to rely upon since he had been blind nearly his entire life.

Speech Understanding

The acoustic signal that we identify as speech is so variable that it is a wonder we can recognize speech at all. The sounds of speech differ considerably depending on whether they are being uttered by a man, a woman, or a child, or even by the same person twice or with different emotions (Banse & Scherer, 1996; Scherer, 1986). To understand speech, humans need top-down processing. One way that top-down processing is revealed is in the importance of context for the perception of speech. Psychologists have known for a long time that people are able to recognize words more quickly when the words are consistent with their semantic, syntactic, and thematic contexts (Miller & Isard, 1963; Röder, Demuth, Streb, & Rösler, 2003). In fact, we may "hear" words that were never spoken if those words fit with the context (Warren, 1970).

In one study, students heard recorded sentences where a critical sound was replaced with a cough. Afterward they were asked what the sentence was and where the cough occurred. One sentence was "The *eel was on the shoe" (the asterisk indicates where the cough occurred). The students perceived the word "heel" and said that the cough was just background noise. In another sentence, "The *eel was on the axle," they heard the word "wheel" (Warren & Warren, 1970). More skilled speakers of a language are more likely to replace the missing speech sounds, called *phonemes*, than are less skilled speakers (Warren & Sherman, 1974). These studies show that we hear more than what reaches our ears and that people seem to be aware of the content of the message before they understand all of the individual words.

We can get a sense of the importance of top-down processing for speech understanding by considering what happens when it is not available. This occurs to people who experience neurological damage that results in **pure word deafness**: the ability to hear words, but only as sounds, not as language. Such individuals are able to hear speech well enough to repeat it, just as they might repeat the sound sequence of music or repeat the pattern of footsteps. However, they are unable to identify speech sounds as words. For example, these individuals are able to identify nonspeech sounds such as the telephone ringing, but cannot tell whether "hello" is a word or even what it might mean (Poeppel, 2001). People afflicted with pure word deafness can read, write, and even speak. You might imagine that if they can speak, then they can hear themselves; however, one person reported, "It's as if there were a bypass somewhere, and my ears were not connected to my voice" (Saffran, Marin, & Yeni-Komshian, 1976, p. 211). This malady suggests that understanding speech requires a full measure of top-down processing.

The Word-Superiority Effect

Reading in alphabetic languages such as English relies on bottom-up processing to identify the letters of a word, but it also relies on top-down processing of knowing the words and their context. In fact, having identified a word helps people recognize the word's letters—the reverse of what you would normally expect. This idea was first illustrated many decades ago by Cattell (see Miller, 1991), who showed that letters are easier to read when they form a word than when they do not. To see this, time yourself as you read the letters aloud in String 1 and then in String 2 below.

1. FONHGTAEW
2. FOG HAT NEW

If you are like the students in the original study, it took you longer to say each letter aloud in String 1 than in String 2. Both strings contain the same letters, but String 2 arranged the letters as words.

A carefully constructed study that further illustrates this point was performed by Reicher (1969), who used the two-part task shown in **FIGURE 4.17**. In the first part of the task, he presented a word such as WORD briefly on a screen. Immediately after the four letters making up WORD were shown, the letters were replaced with *X*'s and *O*'s to mask the entire word. Then the observer's task was to decide whether a *K* or a *D* was present in the initial word that had been flashed. In a second part of the task, the observer was shown a single letter instead of a word and had to decide afterward whether a *K* or a *D* had been presented. The surprising results were that observers are more accurate at detecting the existence of the *D* in a real word than when the letter was presented alone. This is called the **word-superiority effect**: People are better at recognizing letters when they are embedded in real words than when those letters are seen in random strings of letters or when the letters appear alone. If reading were a purely bottom-up process, people would be more accurate in identifying letters

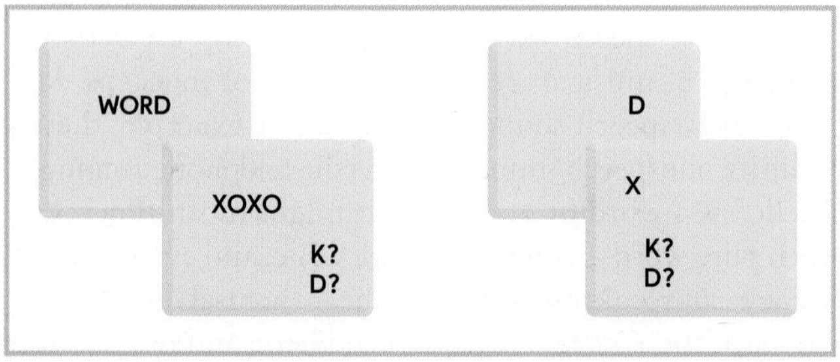

FIGURE 4.17 Reicher Word-Superiority Paradigm An observer sees either a word or a single letter on the screen, which is then masked with X's and O's. The observer must decide whether a K or a D was present in the initial stimulus. People are more accurate at detecting the presence of the D in a real word than when the letter was presented alone. This shows the impact of top-down processing on reading.

Source: Reicher, 1969

This sentence is very easy to read, but it is not just because you can see all of the letters in each row.

This sxntence is missixg a few letxers, but it can be read wxth little extra exfort.

In txis sxntexce, exery xourxh lexter xas bxen rxplaxed wxth ax x, bux you xan sxill xead xt.

Cax yox rexd txis xenxenxe, ix whxch xvexy txirx lextex is xisxinx?

Hxw xbxux txix oxe, ix wxixh xvxrx oxhxr xextxr xs xoxe?

FIGURE 4.18 Top-Down Processing and Reading: John Anderson's Paragraph Skilled readers do not read every letter of every word. They use the shape of the word, the grammar of the sentence, and its theme to derive a meaning from the stream of letters and spaces. This is the essence of top-down processing.

Source: Anderson, 2005a

in isolation (when there is only a single letter to identify) than when they are presented within a word surrounded by other letters. The word-superiority effect shows the impact of top-down processing on reading.

Pattern Recognition and Reading

When you read this page, you are engaged in pattern recognition. You are identifying words or groups of words and making sense of them. Even though your intuition may tell you that before you can read the words you must recognize the individual letters, the data on reading show that you are barely noticing the letters when you read. To illustrate this, look at the paragraphs in **FIGURE 4.18**. Your task is to read aloud each paragraph rapidly, starting from the top. As you read, move your finger from word to word.

Were you surprised at your ability to read sentences with missing letters? This demonstration shows that although students slow down as they get to sentences with fewer correct letters, they are still able to read them. Now look at the last sentence. Every other letter is missing, were you able to read it? Most people can if they start the exercise by reading the first sentence. However, if someone were asked to read the last line without having read the prior ones, they would find it quite difficult because the early sentences activate the critical words in memory as well as the general ideas of the sentences. While the words in the first sentence can be read without contextual help, the last sentence is completely dependent on meaning and context. That is, reading the last sentence depends on top-down processing.

SECTION SUMMARY

Top-Down Processing

Our perception of incoming information, captured by our attention, can be influenced by what we already know or expect. This is called top-down processing. We are confronted with a myriad of features from which we must recognize a pattern in a fraction of a second. We accomplish this feat by generating expectations of what we are experiencing and test these expectations against the incoming stream of information. Although we don't just perceive what we expect to see, the expectations allow us the luxury of not having to examine every bit of information or each and every stimulus feature as it comes in. When we look at a painting, we assess its individual features in order to recognize its patterns. This is bottom-up processing. However, when the title of the picture or a suggestion about what we should see alters our experience, top-down processing is at work.

Speech understanding is a common example of how much of our pattern recognition reflects top-down processing: People are able to recognize words more quickly when the words are consistent with their semantic, syntactic, and thematic contexts than when they are not. We hear more than what reaches our ears—people seem to be aware of the content of the message before they understand all of the individual words. Pure word deafness shows what happens when top-down processing is disconnected from speech. This is a malady in which people can identify sounds, but not understand that they are words.

The word-superiority effect is an example of top-down processing in reading. It shows that we are able to recognize letters when they are embedded in words faster than when they are alone, because all of the letters in the word contribute somewhat to the activation of our identification of the word, and this in turn helps us to see or recognize the letter pattern more readily.

■ ■

Face Recognition

The single most frequent and perhaps the most important pattern that people everywhere need to recognize is the human face. It is easy to imagine that recognizing the faces of friends or foes—and telling the difference between the two—has been important to human survival. Of course, before we can identify a particular face, we need to know that it is, in fact, a face. Research conducted on 2- to 3-week-old infants suggests that we may be born with the ability to appreciate the "faceness" of objects. This is revealed in infants' ability to imitate facial gestures (Meltzoff & Moore, 1977, 1997). The researchers presented adult's facial gestures (e.g., tongue thrust and mouth opening) to infants and observed how often they imitated those gestures. Pictures of infants' imitations are shown in **FIGURE 4.19**, along with a graph of how often the infants engaged in the imitative responses.

The graph not only shows that the infants are producing the imitative behavior, but that their actions are not just the result of being excited. The infants make tongue thrusts mostly when the experimenter does and open their mouths mostly when the experimenter does. They appear to be able to recognize the face and its elements and must appreciate the correspondence between what they see and their own faces, mouths, and tongues. These specific responses to the adult suggest that infants are recognizing facial patterns and imitating them even though they can't see themselves making the response. (A theory of how infants happen to be able to do this is presented in Meltzoff & Moore, 1997; see also Gopnik, Meltzoff, & Kuhl, 1999; Meltzoff & Prinz, 2002.)

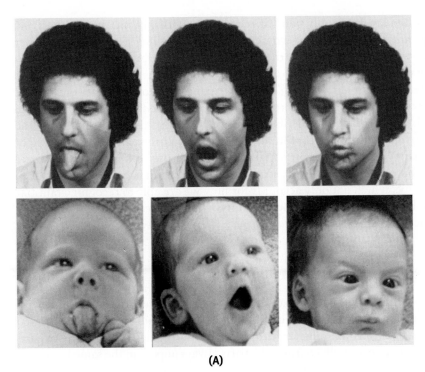

FIGURE 4.19 Infants Imitating and Recognizing Faces Humans come prepared to interact with the world with minimal training. (A) 2-to- 3-week-old infants imitate mouth opening and gestures of people around them without any explicit rewards. (B) The graphs show that infants' behavior is specific to what they see the adult doing. In (a) the adult is protruding his tongue. In (b) the adult is opening his mouth.

From: A. N. Meltzoff & M. K. Moore, "Imitation of facial and manual gestures by human neonates." *Science*, 1977, 198, 75–78. Reprinted with permission from AAAS.

(A)

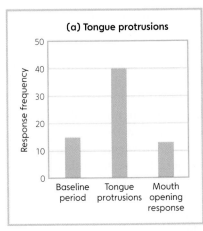

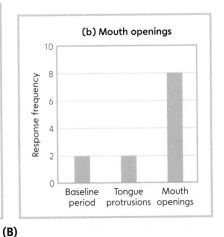

(B)

The fact that the ability to recognize faces occurs so early in life indicates that there are innate, biological mechanisms that we all share, which allow every normally developing infant to recognize the human face. The biological, and therefore universal, basis for this pattern recognition ability is further supported by a difference in the way boys and girls process faces. Boys tend to show greater reactivity to faces in the right hemisphere, whereas girls tend to show greater reactivity to faces in the left hemisphere (Everhart, Shucard, Quatrin, & Shucard, 2001).

Adults are incredibly good at recognizing faces. In one study, observers were shown 14 pictures of women's faces for about 3 seconds each. Either right away or two days later, they were shown the original pictures as well as many new ones. Their job was to indicate whether they had seen the pictures before by saying old or new. The participants correctly identified new and old faces 71% of the time, a result 5 times more accurate than mere chance (Goldstein & Chance, 1971). How are we able to accomplish this feat? One cognitive theory claims that humans inherently possess an understanding of the structural organization of faces, which we use to encode and retrieve faces that we encounter. This structural organization is embodied as a facial prototype, which not only accounts for how we are able to recognize familiar faces, but also accounts for the difficulty we have in recognizing the faces of people from other races.

Facial Prototypes

Faces are highly varied and except in rare circumstances, no two are alike. Yet they share significant similarities. Researchers Joseph and Tanaka (2003) pointed out that faces have a similar structure: They always contain the same set of parts (e.g., eyes, nose, mouth, etc.) and the parts always appear in the same basic configuration (e.g., nose centered below the eyes and above the mouth). We expect that every face we encounter will possess this familiar, frequently encountered spatial organization. Just like the prototypes for objects described previously, prototypes for faces are based on our experience with faces. For example, newborn infants were shown photographs of female faces. Some of the faces they had never seen before and some were composites of faces that they had seen before. The composites were the equivalent of a prototype of the faces they had experienced. Infants stared longer at the composite faces than the totally new faces (Walton & Bower, 1993). Just a few brief experiences with faces can create a prototype, which in turn will be reflected in infants' preference for faces, including the well-known preference for their mother's face (e.g., Bushnell, Sai, & Mullin, 1989; Walton, Armstrong, & Bower, 1998) (see Focus on Methods).

The effect of face prototypes can be seen in the human talent for recognizing faces when faces are right side up and looking forward; they are worst when faces are upside down (Yin, 1969). The fact that we are poor at recognizing upside-down faces suggests that we don't have practice seeing faces in that position (e.g., H. D. Ellis, 1975; A. W. Ellis & Young, 1989; Farah, Wilson, Drain, & Tanaka, 1998; Yin, 1969). We have only developed a prototype for right-side-up faces (Diamond & Carey, 1986; H. D. Ellis, 1975; Young & A. W. Ellis, 1989; Valentine, 1988). When we are presented with faces in a right-side-up position, we process them in a typically gestalt-like manner, using spatial relations among the face parts to construct a holistic view. However, when the face is rotated, holistic face processing is disrupted and we switch to noticing the individual facial features—the component information—that is

FOCUS ON METHODS ■■■■■■■■■■■■■■■■■■■■■■■■■■■■

Infants' Preferences for Faces

Within a few hours after they are born, infants show a preference for viewing their mother's face compared with the face of another woman (e.g., Walton et al., 1998). One behavioral method that shows this preference is called the *high-amplitude sucking procedure* (HASP; Siqueland & DeLucia, 1969). As early as a few hours of age, neonates can be trained to suck in order to see or hear a stimulus. The HASP mechanism consists of a nipple that contains no nutrition for the infant. The nipple is connected to a pressure-sensitive device that records whenever the infant sucks on the nipple. The device can control what the infant hears or sees, depending on how hard or how frequently the infant sucks.

Using this procedure, every time a neonate sucked on a nipple, a picture of a woman's face was presented. After seeing four faces, the infant's suck produced a face that was the average of the previous four faces or an average of four faces that the newborn had not seen. These averages were created by a computer morphing program. The infant spent nearly twice as long looking at the composite of familiar faces (not sucking to change the picture) than at the unfamiliar faces (sucking to change the picture). In less than a total of 1 minute of looking, the newborn had formed a general impression (a schema) for familiar faces (Walton & Bower, 1993).

These composites are the equivalent of a prototype of the faces they had experienced. The infants stared longer at the composite faces than at the totally new faces (Walton & Bower, 1993). Just a few brief experiences with faces can create a prototype, which in turn will be reflected in a newborn's preference

HASP Technique

- HASP: High-Amplitude Sucking Procedure
- Sucking on a non-nutritive nipple
- Sucking produces desired outcome

Krista Byers-Heinlein, Janet F. Werker's Infant Studies Centre, University of British Columbia

for faces, including the well-known preference for her or his mother's face (e.g., Bushnell et al., 1989; Walton et al., 1998).

Newborns store in memory a composite of faces that they have seen. The more a face is seen, the more it contributes to that composite. Since the mother's face is the most often seen, over time it forms the basis of the composite. In addition, there is an effect of the order that faces are seen. The first face the infant sees is always the preferred face. Because the mother's face is usually the first unmasked face in a delivery room that the newborn sees, the typical newborn will quickly develop a preference for her face (Walton et al., 1998).

---

more commonly used for identifying nonface objects (Carey & Diamond, 1977; McKone, Martini, & Nakayama, 2001).

To experience how dependent we are on right-side-up faces, try the exercise in Demonstration 4.4 before reading on. Adults as well as children (age 6 and older) are only able to focus on the individual presence or absence of the facial features and have difficulty maintaining the configuration when the faces are rotated. That is why adults and children fail to notice the grotesque results of switching facial features in the inverted pictures (Lewis, 2003).

■■■DEMONSTRATION 4.4

The Thatcher Illusion

Look at the pair of figures on the following page. Do they look normal even though they are upside down? Now, rotate the page so that the pictures are right side up. Are you surprised? The typical person will notice that the face previously on the right is "weird" after the figure has been rotated from the upside down position to the vertical position (Lewis, 2003). This demonstration was originally called the *Margaret Thatcher illusion*, named after the British prime minister whose face was the original model (Thompson, 1980, p. 483).

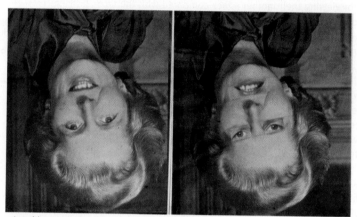

Perception 9(4), 483–484. Peter Thompson, 1980, "Margaret Thatcher: a new illusion." Pion Limited, London.

Recognizing Faces of Other Races

Although our ability to recognize faces is incredibly sophisticated, people have difficulty recognizing the faces of people from a different race. This is the **cross-race effect** (Chance, Goldstein, & McBride, 1975; Malpass & Kravitz, 1969) in which the recognition accuracy for faces of people of a different race is poorer than for your own race (MacLin & Malpass, 2001; O'Toole, Deffenbacher, Valentin, & Abdi, 1994; Valentine & Endo, 1992; Vokey & Read, 1992). This effect is not just the result of having more experience with faces of your own race (Meissner & Brigham, 2001). White students in Singapore, for example, show just as poor recognition of Asian faces as do White students in Ontario, Canada (Ng & Lindsay, 1994).

The cross-race effect may reflect that as we have experiences with our own-race faces, we develop an expectation of what the configuration of a face is supposed to look like—our experience affects top-down processes. This is another aspect of the development of facial prototypes. In a comparison of the face recognition ability of White children (6–7 years old) and adults (20 years old), the children recognized both White and Asian faces equally well, but older White people recognized White faces significantly better than Asian faces (Chance, Turner, & Goldstein, 1982). This suggests that the development of a facial prototype begins in childhood.

Categorizing faces by race also appears to affect face recognition. It seems that a number of superficial features, such as hairstyle and color, help people identify a face as falling into a category of own or other race, and this

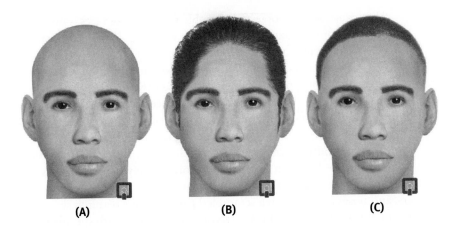

(A)   **(B)**   **(C)**

FIGURE 4.20 **Racially Ambiguous Faces and the Cross-Race Effect** (A) The ambiguous race face is missing the facial marker (hair). (B) When a Hispanic hairstyle is added to this ambiguous race face, the face is perceived as Hispanic. (C) When a Black hairstyle is added to the ambiguous race face, the face is perceived as Black. Hispanic students are more likely to recognize faces perceived as Hispanic than those perceived as Black. Because the faces are nearly identical, top-down categorization as same race or other race must contribute to the decision.

Perception, 2003, volume 32, pages 249-252. MacLin O. H., Malpass R. S., The ambiguous race face illusion. Pion Limited, London.

categorization contributes to recognition judgments. In a study testing this idea (MacLin & Malpass, 2001), students looked at faces created by a computer program. A feature that might act as a racial marker (in this case the length and style of the hair) was added to identical, racially ambiguous faces (see the examples in **FIGURE 4.20**). The study found that ambiguous race faces with a Black hairstyle were judged by students as having a darker complexion, narrower face, deeper eyes, and a wider mouth than the ambiguous race faces with a Hispanic hairstyle, even though the faces were *identical*.

Students also performed a recognition memory task, judging whether the faces were old or new. Consistent with the cross-race effect, Hispanic students were more likely to recognize faces with Hispanic racial features than those with Black racial features. Since the faces in each image were technically identical, the recognition judgment cannot be the result of experience with the faces alone. The top-down categorization as same race or other race must contribute to the decision.

The cross-race effect has practical implications. Police lineups in Britain, for example, are required by law to contain the suspect and eight people who look as similar to him or her as possible. This makes it difficult for the eyewitness to select the perpetrator from the lineup since the observer needs to have a good memory for the person's features. Because primarily White police construct these lineups, lineups of White suspects are more carefully constructed than lineups of other racial groups. Valentine, Harris, Piera, and Darling (2003) reported that a survey of the outcome of over 600 lineups organized by the Metropolitan Police in London found that White suspects were less likely to be identified from a lineup than suspects from ethnic minorities (Wright & McDaid, 1996).

Neuropsychology of Face Recognition

The cognitive research described above shows that the ability to recognize faces is a universal property of humans and is seen in infants soon after birth. This research has led to the identification of a broad circuit in the brain that is important for face recognition and helps us understand the neurological circumstances

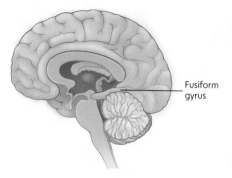

Fusiform
gyrus

FIGURE 4.21 Fusiform Gyrus
The fusiform gyrus is critical for
face recognition, which shows
that humans come adapted to
look at and recognize faces. In
this drawing, the orange area
represents the fusiform gyrus.

that cause some people to be unable to recognize faces—even their own (Bloom, & Lazerson, 1988; Bruce & Young, 1986, 1998; Damasio, 1985b; Sergent & Signoret, 1992; Szpir, 1992).

An area of the brain that seems to be central for face recognition is the *fusiform gyrus*, shown in **FIGURE 4.21** (Kanwisher, McDermott, & Chun, 1997). When volunteers are placed in an MRI scanner and are asked to look at photographs of objects and faces, the fusiform gyrus is more active when they look at faces than when they view an array of common objects (Sergent, Signoret, Bruce, & Rolls, 1992). In fact, the fusiform gyrus is also more active when volunteers view entire faces rather than pictures that contain facial features such as eyes, ears, and noses displayed in a scrambled pattern. This research shows that the fusiform gyrus is important for face recognition. People with specific neurological problems have severe difficulties recognizing faces. Three conditions are discussed in the following sections: prosopagnosia, schizophrenia, and autism.

Prosopagnosia People who are unable to recognize familiar faces are said to have **prosopagnosia**, which is sometimes referred to as *face blindness*. Prosopagnosia is not the result of visual, intellectual, or memory difficulties. Individuals who suffer from this malady may be able to recognize people by their voices, names, or by superficial features such as hair color. They are even able to detect aspects of a face that offer a hint to a person's gender or age or whether they are happy or sad. However, they are still not able to recognize the face itself (Farah, 1990).

One of the earliest reported cases was provided in 1947 by Dr. Bodamer, who noticed that one of his patients, as a result of a bullet wound to the right hemisphere, was unable to recognize previously familiar faces, including those of his family and friends, and even his own face in the mirror. Such individuals are not blind to the face. They know that they are looking at a face, but they cannot say to whom the face belongs unless the person speaks or moves in a distinctive way.

Individuals with prosopagnosia process faces differently from most people, who rely on facial prototypes and past experience. They are able to perform some face recognition, but tend not to use holistic processing. Because of this, their ability to recognize a face is not affected by inverting the face, as it would be for the typical person. For example, LH (a 40-year-old man who acquired prosopagnosia after an automobile accident when he was 20) is unable to recognize friends, neighbors, or even his wife and children. However, LH is better at recognizing inverted faces than right-side-up ones (see also de Gelder, Bachoud-Levi, & Degos, 1998). This is evidence that people with prosopagnosia are probably recognizing faces using detailed features rather than prototypes (Duchaine & Nakayama, 2005; Farah et al., 1998).

Broadly speaking, there are two forms of prosopagnosia: acquired and developmental. People with the *acquired* type possessed typical face recognition abilities prior to suffering a stroke, head trauma, or a degenerative disease, but are no longer able to recognize faces they previously recognized. *Developmental* prosopagnosia occurs in children who have not developed normal face recognition abilities. Children with developmental prosopagnosia are often unaware that they cannot recognize faces as well as other children.

The difficulty that individuals with prosopagnosia have in recognizing faces is a source of data for cognitive theories of face recognition. Scanning the brains of people with this malady has shown that they generally have damage to the fusiform gyrus in at least the right hemisphere (e.g., De Renzi, 2000). This is one more piece of evidence that highlights the importance of the fusiform gyrus in face recognition.

Schizophrenia People with **schizophrenia** typically suffer from a collection of mental difficulties (collectively called a *syndrome*): chiefly, abnormal perceptions, moods, and actions as well as difficulty expressing themselves in a logical manner. One additional symptom of this disorder is difficulty in identifying faces (e.g., Whittaker, Deakin, & Tomenson, 2001). In one study, participants with and without schizophrenia viewed 24 photographs of faces, one at a time, and tried to remember each one. Their recognition memory was tested immediately and again after 30 minutes. The participants with schizophrenia consistently showed poorer recognition memory (approximately 12%) for the faces than did the control participants. The degree to which the participants with schizophrenia showed poorer performance on the delayed memory condition correlates with the degree to which their fusiform gyrus was smaller than the participants without schizophrenia. Overall, people with schizophrenia have a smaller fusiform gyrus (on average a 10% smaller volume in both hemispheres) than people without schizophrenia (Onitsuka et al., 2003). Here we see a direct relationship between brain structures and cognitive activity.

Individuals with schizophrenia not only show poor recall of faces, they also tend to have difficulty in processing the faces that they identify. Although their recall is equivalent to people without schizophrenia in identifying whether a face belongs to a man or a woman, they have difficulty identifying the emotion expressed by the face, such as disgust, fear, and happiness (Bediou et al., 2005).

Autism *The Diagnostic and Statistical Manual of Mental Disorders* (American Psychiatric Association, 1994) defines **autism spectrum disorder** as a congenital condition involving deficits in social and communication skills. It is a *spectrum* disorder because it covers a range of symptoms and a degree of intensity of symptoms, not all of which are exhibited by everyone diagnosed with autism. With this in mind, by and large, children with autism do not appear to attend to faces in early childhood as much as children typically do (Joseph & Tager-Flusberg, 1997; Osterling, Dawson, & Munson, 2002). These children also show reduced social interaction and fewer communication skills when compared with more typical children. This may result from the different way they process faces, which makes it difficult for them to perceive and understand the communication signals of other people.

When autistic children do look at faces, they do not rely on holistic processing, as do their non-autistic peers. For example, children with autism are not as susceptible

FIGURE 4.22 Face Memory in Children Can you tell the difference between these two faces? Typically developing children and autistic children attend to different features of the human face, paying more attention to the eyes than to the mouth. Children with autism showed the reverse pattern—they attended to the mouth more than the eyes.

Joseph R. M., Tanaka J. Holistic and part-based face recognition in children with autism. *Journal of Child Psychology and Psychiatry*. 2003.

to the Margaret Thatcher illusion. They show only a small effect of face inversion, which suggests that they are relying primarily on features rather than prototypes.

People with autism are clearly impaired in their ability to recognize faces (Boucher & Lewis, 1992; Hauck, Fein, Maltby, Waterhouse, & Feinstein, 1998; Korkman, Kirk, & Kemp, 1998). For example, in one face memory task (Joseph & Tanaka, 2003), children were shown a photograph of the face of a child their own age. Four seconds later they were shown two photographs: the same photograph and one that looked nearly the same, but with one different facial feature (eyes, nose, or mouth). A sample pair of photos is shown in **FIGURE 4.22**. Can you tell the two apart? Typical 9- and 11-year-old children performing this task were able to recognize the original photograph 80% of the time when the only difference between the two photographs was the eyes. They were accurate 70% of the time when the difference was based on the mouth. This shows that typical children pay more attention to the eyes than the mouth to recognize a face.

The reverse pattern was shown for children with autism. They are more accurate at detecting changes in the mouth (70% correct) than the eyes (62% correct), which suggests that they tend to rely on the mouth as the critical facial feature aiding their efforts to recognize faces (Langdell, 1978; Tanaka & Farah, 1993). It makes sense that children would focus on the mouth when they are gazing at faces because the mouth moves more than the eyes and the mouth produces sounds that are consistent with the mouth movements. But the eyes can reveal the emotionality of the speaker in ways that the mouth does not. Autistic adults are more likely to focus on the mouth when they are asked to identify the emotion of the speaker (Spezio, Adolphs, Hurley, & Piven, 2007).

Research using fMRI methods consistently shows that when non-autistic people look at faces, activity in the fusiform gyrus increases (e.g., Kanwisher et al., 1997; Puce, Allison, Gore, & McCarthy, 1995). In contrast, people with autism show weaker activity in the fusiform area: somewhat at the same level of activation that is shown by non-autistic people when they are looking at objects other than faces (Pierce, Muller, Ambrose, Allen, & Courchesne, 2001; Schultz et al., 2000).

SECTION SUMMARY ▪

Face Recognition

The human ability to recognize faces comes early in a child's development and has a biological basis. Two-week-old infants can imitate the tongue and mouth movements of adults without being able to see their own faces. People become incredibly proficient at recognizing faces and retaining a memory of those faces over a considerable period of time. It is surprising then that people are so poor at recognizing and remembering the faces of people of other races than themselves. This cross-race effect illustrates that we use face schemas—prototypes—to recognize faces and that we know the prototypes best for people that we see most often (generally members of our own race).

When we are not able to use our prototypes to recognize faces, we tend to rely on recognizing individual facial features. This is especially the case when people suffer from neurological problems, as do children with autism or children and adults who develop prosopagnosia or schizophrenia.

▪ ▪

CHAPTER SUMMARY

Our perception of the world is a reconstruction created from the aspects of objects that the human attentional spotlight shines upon. Some patterns take many experiences with objects to identify rapidly and automatically. Other patterns, such as the human face, seem to require minimal experience to recognize and suggest the universality of our ability to recognize faces. The principles that help us fill in the blanks and identify broad patterns among objects are called gestalt principles, which are universal laws of proximity, similarity, closure, common fate, symmetry, and good continuation. The cognitive processes that allow us to recognize objects fall into two broad categories. The first is bottom-up processes, which include those mechanisms that extract features from the pattern of sensations and compares them to stored knowledge. The second is top-down processes, which are those mechanisms that rely on expectation and context to select and weigh the basic features. Bottom-up processes make use of simple, sensory-based features that are matched with geons, templates, and prototypes stored in memory. Top-down processes allow us to use our expectations to emphasize certain features

over others and thereby affect our perceptions and our ability to recognize patterns and objects.

An important aspect of human pattern recognition is our ability to see and recognize faces. Under normal conditions, people seem to be skilled at immediately identifying upright faces and the prototypes of faces that we normally encounter. People around the world are far more accurate and rapid in recognizing faces from their own race, a phenomenon that cognitive researchers call the cross-race effect. Our ability to recognize faces is supported by brain areas that seem to be specialized for recognizing faces; the most important of these areas seems to be the fusiform gyrus. People who have suffered damage to this area or whose fusiform gyrus has not been fully developed tend to have difficulty recognizing faces. To aid them in face recognition, many have learned to attend to individual facial features, such as eyes, hair color, and hair length, rather than making a holistic judgment. The fact that face recognition depends upon the functioning of specialized areas of the human brain underscores the universality of face recognition as emerging from the similarity of all human brains.

KEY TERMS

pattern recognition, p. 85

perception, p. 85

bottom-up processing (or bottom-up analysis), p. 86

top-down processing (or top-down analysis), p. 86

gestalt, p. 87

principle of Prägnanz, p. 87

law of proximity, p. 89

law of similarity, p. 90

law of closure, p. 90

law of common fate, p. 91

law of symmetry, p. 92

law of good continuation, p. 92

distinctive features theory, p. 93

recognition by components theory (RBC theory), p. 96

geons, p. 96

template-matching theory, p. 98

prototype, p. 99

prototype theory, p. 99

ecological validity, p. 100

pure word deafness, p. 103

word-superiority effect, p. 104

cross-race effect, p. 110

prosopagnosia, p. 112

schizophrenia, p. 113

autism spectrum disorder, p. 113

QUESTIONS FOR REVIEW

Check Your Knowledge

1. What are the three critical cognitive systems that allow us to perform pattern recognition?

2. What is the fundamental problem of perception?

3. Is our ability to see photomosaics as complete pictures without gaps due to top-down or bottom-up processing, or both?

4. What does the term *gestalt* convey about pattern recognition?

5. What is the underlying principle of Gestalt psychology?

6. What are the six laws of Gestalt psychology? Think of an example of each one.

7. What aspect of pattern recognition is captured by the term *bottom-up processing*?

8. What is the general principle of distinctive features theory?

9. According to distinctive features theory, which letter would you most likely confuse with a G: C or T?

10. Think of an example where you focus on global rather than local features of an object.

11. What are the components of recognition by components theory?

12. Template-matching and prototype theories seem similar. How are they the same and how are they different?

13. Which of the bottom-up theories would best account for your ability to read words written in handwriting that you had not seen before?

14. What pattern recognition process captures the importance of context and expectation?

15. Why does pure word deafness demonstrate the importance of top-down processing for perceiving words?

16. Someone hands you a photograph of a person whom you know. Are you faster at recognizing the face if the photograph is right side up or upside down? Why?

17. When the photograph is upside down, does the typical person rely on holistic processing to recognize the face or feature-based processing?

18. What does the Margaret Thatcher illusion demonstrate?

19. Are children with autism subject to the Margaret Thatcher illusion?

20. When looking at a photograph of another child, would a child with or without autism focus more on the mouth?

21. What neurological deficit do people with prosopagnosia and schizophrenia have in common?

Apply Your Knowledge

1. Suppose you are looking at a picture of a human face and a tree blocks half of the view. What do the theories of distinctive features and bottom-up processing (recognition by components, template-matching, and prototype theories) predict about how you will perceive the picture?

2. Imagine that this drawing on the right is flashed on a screen to three people. One is told before seeing the picture that it is about someone praying. A second is told that it means someone is fishing. A third person is told that it is a Japanese hiragana vowel (pronounced /za/). Later, the three people are asked to draw the character from memory. Given what you know about top-down processing, how might you expect the drawings to be different?

ざ

3. When we perceive the world we tend to employ both bottom-up and top-down pattern recognition processes. Suppose you are crossing a busy street, what would the benefit be in relying on top-down processing to identify objects moving toward you?

4. Many people with prosopagnosia are able to recognize familiar people by paying attention to nonfacial features such as hair, voice, and size. Do you ever rely on these features to recognize someone? Do you fail to recognize someone when they have changed one of these typical facial characteristics?

5. People with autism tend to have difficulty having social relations with others. How might their face recognition processes influence their social contacts and their memory for people?

" You have to begin to lose your memory, if only in bits and pieces, to realize that memory is what makes our lives. Life without memory is no life at all. . . . Our memory is our coherence, our reason, our feeling, even our action. Without it, we are nothing. **"**

—Luis Buñuel

To a large degree, our sense of who we are depends upon what we know, and what we know depends upon our ability to remember what we have learned. **Learning** is defined as the permanent change in behavior that results from experience. But this learned information must be stored within us in order to be retrieved later. This process of storage is **memory**: the mechanism that allows us to retain and retrieve information over time. Memory is an essential, underlying cognitive process that supports learning and makes it possible for us to acquire new knowledge and remember new information as we encounter new situations. This chapter and the three that follow comprise a unit that describes the different memory mechanisms we all possess, and how what we know helps us to learn more and function effectively.

A major goal of this unit is to explain some of the subtleties and complexities lurking just below the surface of the memory processes that we generally take for granted. We begin by describing what has been called **short-term memory (STM)**, the memory that contains our moment-to-moment conscious thoughts and perceptions. Short-term memory is fleeting: Its contents endure only as long as we are paying attention to them. Psychologists have historically found it easy to do research on the nature and limits of STM because people have immediate experience of its presence. In contrast, we have less awareness of **working memory (WM):** the set of mechanisms that underlies STM and also communicates with long-term memory (LTM), the semipermanent memory store that endures for a lifetime and aids us in learning new information. LTM will be the focus of Chapters 6–8. In this chapter we will discuss STM and its structural support, WM.

Short-Term Memory (STM)

Short-term memory reflects our conscious awareness. We rely on STM as we carry out everyday activities like remembering a phone number long enough to call it, remembering the play signaled by the third-base coach before taking a swing, or thinking about our next response in a conversation. In order to understand this memory system, we will consider its properties in terms of the same basic questions that were used in the previous chapter to understand sensory memory:

- What is the capacity of STM?
- How long does information last in STM?
- Why do we forget facts held in STM?

The Capacity of Short-Term Memory

As its name implies, our short-term memory allows us to retain information for a brief period of time. How much information can STM hold? Researchers have devised a number of precise procedures for determining STM capacity (see Focus on Methods). These procedures have yielded data showing that a typical adult's memory span is approximately 7 (between 5 and 9) unrelated items (Miller, 1956). STM capacity typically increases as people age until it reaches a maximum in young adulthood (Dempster, 1981; Huttenlocher & Burke, 1976) and starts to decline in old age (Kail & Salthouse, 1994).

FOCUS ON METHODS ■

Short-Term Memory Capacity

The typical way of measuring STM capacity, also called *memory span*, is to present a sequence of numbers, letters, or words aloud to a person at the rate of about 1 second per item. The research participant is instructed to repeat the sequence verbally, either in the order each item was presented or in a backward order (Bunting, Cowan, & Saults, 2006; Wilde & Strauss, 2002). The length of the sequence is continually increased until the person is correct only 50% of the time.

Another procedure is to average the number of items in the three longest sequences that the person gets 100% correct and call that the memory span. To make sure that the person being tested doesn't know how many items are in the list, and thereby develop a special memory strategy that artificially increases their memory span, a *running memory span* test is used in which the number of items on the list varies from list to list (Pollack, Johnson, & Knaff, 1959). The Table shows that STM capacity increases with age until, on average, people remember 7 items by age 18. Researchers have proposed three explanations for the expansion of STM capacity as we age. One explanation is related to neurological development, another

concerns strategies that people employ as they get older, and the third is related to how the coding of information changes with age. These explanations are discussed later in the section on working memory.

Memory Span Across Age Level	
Age (in years)	**Memory Span (for digits)**
2	2
4	3
6	4
8	5
10	6
12	6
18	7

Source: From Dempster, 1981

The basic findings concerning memory capacity go back to the research of Ebbinghaus (1885/1913), who sought to identify basic memory processes that are independent of people's past knowledge. To do this, Ebbinghaus used nonsense syllables (formed by inserting a vowel between two consonants) as the items to be remembered, and determined how many runs through a list of nonsense syllables it would take to recite a list perfectly. Try this yourself by doing the exercise in Demonstration 5.1.

■■■DEMONSTRATION 5.1

Ebbinghaus Test of Memory Capacity

Over 100 years ago Ebbinghaus used what he called the "anticipation method" to study primary memory—what we now call short-term memory. To experience the kind of task used in this classic study, do the following: Take 10 pieces of paper and on each write one of the following: MEB, GEC, TER, BOL, CUV, FIK, DAL, HOK, PUV, and JUH. After turning the stack of papers upside down, lift each one, turn it over, read it for 2 seconds, and place it aside (face up, but don't look at it). After you read all 10 pages, turn the stack over again and try to guess the syllable written on each page. Check to see if you are correct, and then do the same for the next page until you've gone through the whole list. Keep doing this until you are able to anticipate the syllable on each page in the correct order. How many runs through the list did you require to get 100% correct? Now read on in the text to see how your efforts compared with Ebbinghaus's findings.

In Ebbinghaus's primary research, he used himself as the only participant to be sure that the data were reliable. He used lists of nonsense syllables that varied in length. If a list had 1 item, it only took one look at the item to be able to recall it perfectly. With lists of 7 items he required a single run through the list to recall the items with 100% accuracy. With a list of 10 items (just like the one you were given in the demonstration), it took 16 viewings of the list to remember the list correctly. How well did you do? The relationship between the length of the list and the number of viewings that a person needs in order to have a perfect memory for the list is shown in **FIGURE 5.1**. The important point is that Ebbinghaus discovered that there is a discontinuity—a jump in the curve—between the length of the list and the number of viewings needed to recall it perfectly. Notice that in Figure 5.1 this discontinuity occurs at about 7 items. The number 7 holds fast for lists of nonsense syllables, unrelated pictures, words, whatever you can think of as long as the individual items are unrelated. Cognitive researchers have tested memory for all of these items in their efforts to determine STM capacity.

Chunking and Short-Term Memory It is tempting to think of STM as a kind of empty bag with a limited holding capacity. However, cognitive research reveals that STM is not just a formless reservoir, it has a structure. For example, during an assessment of a person's memory span, if the pacing of the items is broken up with pauses between every third and fourth item, the person's memory span will be greater than if no pauses are inserted (McLean & Gregg, 1967; Ryan, 1969; Wickelgren, 1964). It is no accident that when radio and television advertisers

FIGURE 5.1 The Ebbinghaus Learning Curve The graph shows how many times Ebbinghaus needed to look at lists of different lengths before he could recall them perfectly. The sharp elbow in the curve at 7 items reflects the maximum he could store in STM. This discontinuity holds for any list as long as the individual items are unrelated.

Source: Based on Ebbinghaus, 1885/1913, Figure 6

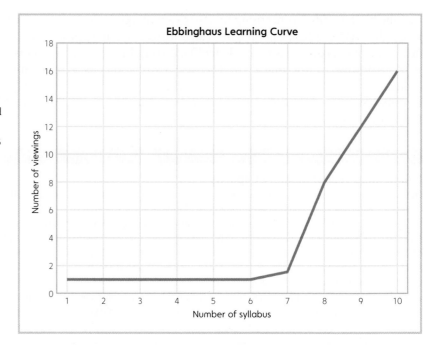

recite a phone number they pause between every three or four digits. Otherwise, the listener will have difficulty retaining the sequence. In a sense, the spoken digits between the pauses have become a single unit or **chunk** of information.

The idea that information in STM can be grouped, which increases the capacity of memory, was proposed by Miller (1956) in "The Magical Number Seven Plus or Minus Two: Some Limits on Our Capacity for Processing Information." Miller concluded that the capacity of STM was really between 5 and 9 meaningful items or chunks of information for the typical adult. In this case, the word "meaningful" refers to whether the person is able to find a way of relating the items to what he or she already knows. This process is called **chunking.** Take the following series of 12 numbers, for example. Assume that someone presents this list to you at a rate of 1 number per second and that you have been asked to memorize the list:

1 4 9 2 9 0 2 1 0 7 1 4.

If these numbers were presented to you verbally (you could hear but not see them), and you didn't pay much attention to the relationship among the numbers, you might be able to recall about 7 of them in the correct order. On the other hand, if the numbers activated information stored in your long-term memory, then you would notice 1492 (Columbus's discovery of America), 90210 (the title of a TV show), and 714 (the area code for Orange County, California—the O.C. and Surf City). The person who noticed these three chunks of information would most likely be able to recall the entire 12 digits and would be judged to have an enormous memory span. The effect is striking even with a single word. Take for example, "abracadabra." To someone unfamiliar with magical words in fairy tales ("hocus pocus" or "wingardium leviosa"), this would simply be a series of 11 letters or five syllables. Such a person would have difficulty recalling this string of letters perfectly. However, because of the chunking process, someone familiar with this word will see it as a single entity and will be able to recall it with little effort. The important message here is that what we have learned and stored in LTM can play a useful role in retaining information in STM.

The Importance of Prior Knowledge To be a chunk, something needs to fit together readily as a pattern distinct from the things around it (e.g., Gobet et al., 2001). For words or pictures to be a chunk, they need to be familiar to the person (Miller, 1956) and available in long-term memory. This illustrates that STM overlaps with—and relies upon—LTM to function efficiently. The depth and breadth of our knowledge in any given subject can influence our memory for new information related to that subject. This is one reason why someone may exhibit phenomenal memory ability in one class at school, but may perform at an ordinary level in another. The difference is due to what the person already knows.

Since prior knowledge affects everyone's ability to chunk and therefore retain information in STM, our estimates of a child's memory span may greatly depend on how familiar the child is with the testing materials being used (e.g., Huttenlocher & Burke, 1976; Santos & Bueno, 2003). For example, if a child is not familiar with numbers at the age of 4, but knows common one-syllable words, the child may show a memory span of 2 for numbers, but a span of 3 for words. Memory span tests, therefore, should be tailored to the person. There are no *pure* tests of memory that work for everyone: What is meaningful for one person may be meaningless for another.

This fact is illustrated by a study conducted by Chi (1978), who tested 10-year-old advanced chess players and found, not surprisingly, that their memory span using numbers was inferior to an adult group of inexperienced chess players. Chi then asked the children and the adults to look at a chessboard for 20 seconds and try to reconstruct the configuration of pieces that were on the board (14 pieces). On this task, the children performed better than novice chess-playing adults. This shows that for both children and adults, memory span is influenced by preexisting knowledge (Bjorklund, 1987): long-term memory.

Duration, Forgetting, and Short-Term Memory

We know that information is kept in short-term memory for a short period of time (hence its name). But, how short is *short*, and why are items lost from STM? The standard method of calculating the duration of information in STM is called the Brown–Peterson task after the researchers who separately developed the procedure (Brown, 1958; Peterson & Peterson, 1959). Try the task yourself by following the instructions in Demonstration 5.2.

■■■DEMONSTRATION 5.2

The Brown–Peterson Task

To perform this task, you will need paper and a timer (a buzzer, a watch with a sweep-second hand, or a stopwatch will work). You will need a friend to help you with this demonstration. For each of the three cases listed below, set your timer for the seconds listed to the right of the letter/number combination. Have your friend read aloud the triplet of letters and then the three-digit number next to it. Immediately after you hear the number, count backward by threes from the three-digit number (e.g., if the number is 780, you would recite 777, 774, 771, etc.). Stop counting when the timer goes off and try to write down the triplet of letters. Try this procedure three times using Items 1-3 below, each of which calls for a different time duration. Ready?

Letter/No. Combination	Duration	Recalled Letters
1. VZN 823	0 seconds	
2. LQB 282	10 seconds	
3. XHR 941	20 seconds	

How did you perform? If you are like the students in the original study, the number of letters in each triplet that you are able to recall declined the longer you were asked to hold the letters in memory by counting backward by threes.

Two important findings related to the duration of STM have come out of research using the Brown–Peterson task: First, the number of items that can be kept in STM rapidly decays with the passage of time. You can see this in **FIGURE 5.2**, which shows that nearly perfect recall occurs with a 0-second delay and only about 10–20% recall occurs with an 18-second delay. For a realistic

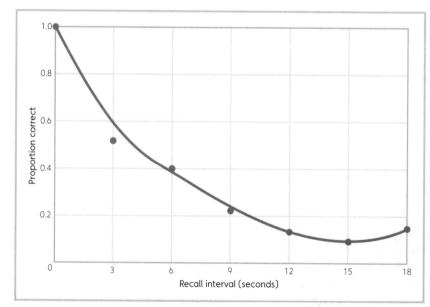

FIGURE 5.2 The Brown–Peterson Task
The number of items that can be kept in STM declines rapidly without rehearsal. The graph shows that items in STM are perfectly recalled when there is only a 0-second delay. But recall declines to 10–20% accuracy when there is a delay of 18 seconds.

Source: From Peterson & Peterson, 1959

example of this, imagine you are told a street address and then are immediately distracted by a question. In this situation, your ability to recall the street address would be significantly impaired within 18 seconds. To use a common metaphor in cognitive psychology, it's as if the items in STM decay with time. The duration of unrehearsed information in STM is approximately 18 seconds. In the demonstration, did the number of letters you were able to remember decline as the time to count backward increased?

The second finding from this research is that the duration of items in STM is related to the number of chunks that are present. For example, three unrelated letters, such as C-H-J (equivalent to three chunks), show the same loss of information over time as three words, such as CAT-HAT-JUG (Murdock, 1961). In contrast, a single word (or a single letter) in STM shows virtually no loss. The number of chunks influences our ability to keep information in STM. It appears that the more items or chunks in STM, the more opportunities there will be for them to become confused with one another. This confusion is called *interference* and is an important contributor to our inability to recall items in our STM.

Interference Interference may be broken into two broad categories: retroactive and proactive. **Retroactive interference** occurs when what you know now makes it difficult to recall something that occurred previously. (Trying to remember your current phone number may make it difficult to recall one you had many years ago.) In contrast, when something that you have already learned interferes with your ability to recall more recent events, it is called **proactive interference**, which is a source of interference that plagues performance in memory tasks and in everyday life. (If you take a class in Spanish and then take one in French, Spanish words will typically intrude upon your consciousness as you try to speak French.) Proactive interference can be embarrassing as well as frustrating, such as when you call a new romantic partner by a former partner's name. Proactive interference influences memory performance on the Brown–Peterson task discussed previously. The first time students participate in the task, they show very little loss of information (Keppel & Underwood, 1962), but after many trials, the curve shown in Figure 5.2 emerges because the task becomes more difficult with each new trial. Letters from earlier trials start to be mistaken for letters appearing in more recent trials. Fortunately for people who are trying to memorize facts for school or work, proactive interference does not last forever. It can be stopped if the information people are being asked to remember is changed to a different type of information. For example, there seems to be little proactive interference when participants switch from having to remember letters to remembering numbers (e.g., Wickens, Born, & Allen, 1963), or switch to remembering words from a different subject area (e.g., Loess and Waugh, 1967; Wickens, 1970). This explains why taking a break during study sessions can be so effective. Doing something else for a while reduces proactive interference, thereby increasing recall of what you are trying to learn (Loess & Waugh, 1967).

Something has caused the members of this jury in a federal court to pay close attention. Paying attention, or rehearsal, is one way we retain information in STM.

Alina Solovyova-Vincent/iStockphoto

Rehearsal Although pieces of information in STM last only about 18 seconds when we are not attending to them, those same pieces of information can endure in STM as long as we pay them attention. The act of paying attention is called **rehearsal**. Focusing our energies on the form and meaning of the thing we are trying to retain—rehearsing it—allows us to keep it fresh in STM. There are two kinds of rehearsal: maintenance rehearsal and elaborative rehearsal. **Maintenance rehearsal** is typically accomplished by saying something repeatedly in order to keep it in mind. This sort of rote rehearsal maintains the items in STM, but does not guarantee your permanent ability to recall the items freely after you stop rehearsing them (Glenberg, Smith, & Green, 1977). However, such rote memorizing can help you recognize the items later (Green, 1987). Maintenance rehearsal is a good strategy if you want to keep a phone number in memory long enough to call it, or if you want to be able to pick a number out of a list later on, but it is not a good way to be able to call the same number tomorrow (Craik & Lockhart, 1972). **Elaborative rehearsal** is accomplished by thinking about the meaningful relationships among the items to be learned and focusing on how they connect to other things that you know (Craik, 2002). This type of rehearsal strategy often results in enhanced long-term recall and recognition of things to be remembered (e.g., Benjamin & Bjork, 2000; Franklin et al., 2008; Mandler, 1980).

Why would either type of rehearsal be effective in helping us to retain information in STM? Whenever we rehearse an item, we are paying attention to it. One might say that each time we attend to something, whether it is an idea or a flower in our front yard, we enhance the energy of that item, sometimes called its *activation* (J. R. Anderson, Bothell, Lebiere, & Matessa, 1998). If we stop paying attention to something, its activation level decays and it becomes more difficult to recall. Keeping things activated in memory has the effect of keeping them available for recall. Elaborative rehearsal is a more effective means of retaining and recognizing items over a long period of time. That is because having many connections associated with something to be remembered increases its level of activation so that its retrieval is more likely to be triggered by a simple cue or reminder.

Retrieving from Short-Term Memory

Having examined the capacity and duration of STM, we turn to how information is retrieved from STM. Suppose you are told to go to a store and buy six items (e.g., apples, bread, soup, peanut butter, cereal, milk) and within a few seconds someone asks you whether milk is on the list. How do you search your memory to decide whether an item is stored in STM? To determine the processes that we use to retrieve facts from STM, Sternberg (1966, 2004) developed a task that bears his name: the Sternberg task. The structure of the task is illustrated in **FIGURE 5.3**. In it, a participant is given a set of up to seven items, which are presented rapidly, one at a time, over the course of a few seconds. Soon after, a memory test item, called a *probe* (e.g., milk), is presented and the participant must determine whether or not the probe is part of the memory set.

Many theories of how people scan their STM have been rigorously tested. The theory researchers now believe to be correct requires some uncommon sense to understand, and illustrates that our intuitions about how our minds work are not always correct. Researchers refer to this theory as **serial exhaustive search.** This theory proposes that we search every item in our STM in response to a question and do not stop searching even when we find the item in memory. Rather, we search our STM in its entirety—exhaustively. **FIGURE 5.4** shows what the data confirming the serial exhaustive search theory look like. The graph contains a positive line and a negative line. The positive line reflects the time it takes people to correctly say, "Yes, the probe is in my STM." The negative line reflects the time to correctly say, "No, the item is not in my STM" when it has not been found. The exhaustive search theory assumes it will take a person just as long to scan memory for a positive probe as for a negative probe because the entire list must be searched in both cases. In addition, the lines illustrate that as the size of the memory set increases (goes up on the right), so does the time needed to answer the question about what is in STM because the more items to be searched, the longer it takes.

The graph contains information that reveals two important aspects of STM search. First, the lines have a slope: the angle of the line compared with the horizontal. For every new item to be searched in STM, the line goes up 30–40 milliseconds on the vertical axis. Second, when, in theory, the set size is empty, the

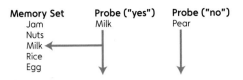

Memory Set — Jam, Nuts, Milk, Rice, Egg

Probe ("yes") — Milk

Probe ("no") — Pear

Note: In typical studies, the list of items to be scanned contains numbers or letters.

FIGURE 5.3 Sternberg Task Diagram To determine how people retrieve items from STM, participants in the Sternberg task are given a set of up to 7 items to store in STM. The items are presented rapidly, one at a time, over the course of a few seconds. Soon after, a memory test item (called a probe) is presented. Participants must decide whether or not the probe is contained within their STM.

Source: After Sternberg, 1966

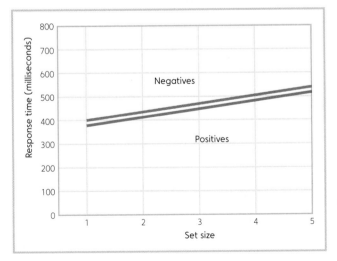

FIGURE 5.4 Memory Scanning The data in this graph confirm the serial exhaustive search theory. The positive (red) line reflects the time it takes a participant to correctly say, "Yes, the probe is in my STM." The negative (blue) line reflects the time to correctly say, "No, the probe is not in my STM" when it has not been found. The time to scan STM increases with the number of items in memory (40 msec/item), and a participant will take as long to scan for a positive probe as for a negative probe because the entire list must be searched in both cases.

Source: After Sternberg, 1966

lines intersect the vertical axis. The time at this point of interception is about 400 milliseconds. This point of interception represents the time needed to make the overall decision, including the time to press the button and the time to read the question, irrespective of what is in STM.

The serial exhaustive search theory shows that sometimes the correct hypothesis runs counter to our intuitions (e.g., Roberts, & Sternberg, 1993): Who would have thought that even after you find a probe item in STM, you would continue the search? Serial exhaustive search makes sense, however, if you imagine that you are in a ski race and want to see if your best friend is watching as you barrel down the hill in a slalom. You could proceed in two ways. One way would be to follow a self-terminating search procedure: You could ski slowly down the hill, examining each spectator until you find your friend and then, having terminated your search, you could speed up to the bottom—undoubtedly losing the race. In contrast, following a serial exhaustive search procedure, you could charge down the hill as quickly as possible while still searching the spectators for your friend. It might take you a few seconds after you spot him or her to be aware that your friend was actually watching you race. By that time, you would have reached the bottom of the course. The more spectators you scan, the more efficient is the serial exhaustive search. The serial exhaustive search explanation has been critically tested in many studies (e.g., J. A. Anderson, 1973; Theios, 1973; Townsend, 1971, 1990) and is still the dominant explanation of how we scan our STM.

These findings with healthy populations allow us to gauge the memory processes of clinical populations, such as people with Parkinson's or Alzheimer's dementia (e.g., Ferraro & Balota, 1999). **FIGURE 5.5** shows the different slopes

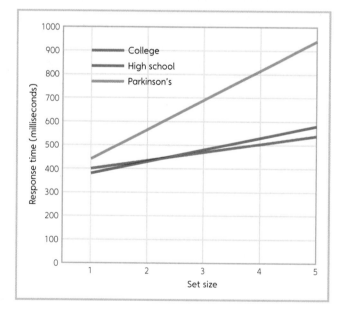

FIGURE 5.5 Memory Scanning Data for Different Groups In this graph, the slope of the lines reflects the time to compare items in memory. Individuals with Parkinson's disease require considerably more time per item to compare two things in memory than do healthy high school and college students. All three groups are equivalent in their overall time to read and respond, as reflected by where the lines would intercept the vertical axis. Memory-scanning procedures help researchers identify the sources of difficulty in memory retrieval as well as to assess the effectiveness of different treatments.

Source: After Hunt, 1978

and intercepts for three groups using this memory search task (Hunt, 1978). You can see from this graph that although individuals with Parkinson's respond as rapidly as typical high school students, they require considerably more time per item to compare two things in memory. The use of this kind of standard task enables researchers to identify sources of difficulties in memory retrieval as well as to assess the effectiveness of different treatments. For example, if a drug improves memory scanning, it should affect the slope of the line. However, if it merely makes someone faster in responding, but not better at memory search, it should affect only the intercept.

SECTION SUMMARY ▪

Short-Term Memory (STM)

Short-term memory is the memory system that contains our moment-to moment conscious thoughts and perceptions: from admiring the beauty of a sunset to remembering where we put our keys. STM is fleeting: Its contents endure only as long as we are paying attention to them. The capacity of STM increases with a person's age until it reaches a maximum of 5 to 9 meaningful items, called chunks. These chunks reflect the continuous connection between short-term and long-term memory. As long as we are able to rehearse, or pay attention to the information in STM, it can reside there indefinitely. However, without rehearsal, the information is lost from STM in about 18 seconds. Interference among the items is the primary contributor to the loss of items from STM. There are two types of interference: retroactive interference (new information preventing the retrieval of old information) and proactive interference (old information preventing the recall of new information). We can keep information in our STM by using two major kinds of rehearsal methods: maintenance and elaborative rehearsal. Both methods keep information active in STM, but only elaborative rehearsal promotes recall over a longer period of time.

To answer a question about the contents of their STM, people perform a serial exhaustive search. They check each item in STM against the item mentioned in the question. Unlike reading a list of items on a piece of paper and stopping when we have found the target, our memories are scanned completely. The more items in STM, the longer it takes to decide whether or not a questioned item is present in memory. Different populations of people can be compared based on how much time it takes them to decide whether an individual item is in memory and how much time it takes them to respond overall. This information can be used to gauge the effectiveness of therapies designed to improve STM.

The Serial Position Effect

When we try to remember a list of items in any order, the accuracy of our retrieval of the items shows an interesting relationship to the original list: Items at the beginning and end of the original list are much more likely to be remembered than items in the middle of the list. This phenomenon is called the **serial position effect** because the probability of recalling an item tends to be related to its position among other items on a list. This is illustrated in **FIGURE 5.6** for lists that are presented aloud and in writing. The serial position effect is found in studies testing memory for lists of numbers, facts, states, colors, pictures, and even ideas within paragraphs or the final scores of soccer games over an entire season (e.g., Beaman & Morton, 2000; Manning, 1980; Phillips & Christie, 1977; M. J. Watkins & O. C. Watkins, 1974). Each memory curve in **FIGURE 5.7** shows that the early part of the list is remembered better than the middle part of the list. This is called the **primacy effect.** Similarly, the last items on the list (those items most recently encountered) are also remembered better than the middle items. This is called the **recency effect** (Phillips & Christie, 1977). Notice that the serial position effect holds for all of the list sizes and conditions in the graph in Figure 5.7.

The serial position effect is another example of the interaction between short-term memory and long-term memory. To experience this first hand, try the task in Demonstration 5.3.

FIGURE 5.6 Serial Position Effect The serial position effect is found in studies testing memory for lists of numbers, facts, states, colors, pictures, and even ideas within paragraphs or the final scores of soccer games over an entire season. The ability to recall items from a list reflects where in the list the items come from and whether they are presented in a visual mode or an auditory mode.

Source: After Beaman & Morton, 2000

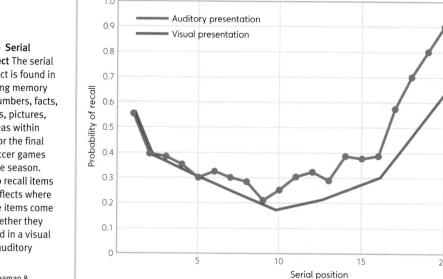

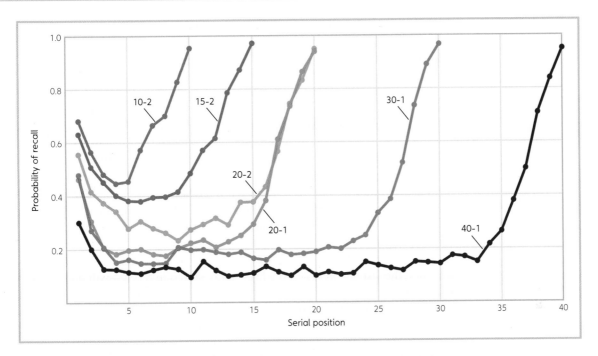

FIGURE 5.7 Serial Position Curves for Lists of Different Length The graph shows a serial position effect for all list lengths and presentation rates. The first number attached to each curve indicates the length of the list (e.g., 10, 20, 30, or 40 items). The second number tells how many seconds each word was presented (1 or 2 seconds).

Source: From Murdock, 1962

▪▪▪ DEMONSTRATION 5.3

The Serial Position Effect

Memorize the following list of nine words in the correct order. You will need a clock with a sweep-second hand and a piece of paper to cover the words on the list. You may use a maximum of 4 seconds to memorize each word. Read the first word on the list with the rest covered, try to memorize it for 4 seconds, and then go on to the next word. As you move on to a new item, continue to rehearse the preceding items. Remember you have only 4 seconds. Every time you rehearse an item, make a mark next to the word to keep track of the amount of rehearsal each word receives. Here is the list:

BLINK	APPLE
CLEAR	DREAM
PLANT	FIELD
ALLOW	GRAIN
TROOP	

When the time is up, try to recall the entire list on a separate piece of paper. Students typically have the most marks at the beginning of the list. Next in order are the last two words on the list (rehearsed as the person prepares to write down the list). The fewest marks are typically next to the middle of the list.

The demonstration illustrates that the primacy portion of the curve (the first items to be committed to memory) generally reflects more rehearsal and attention because there is nothing before them that competes for a person's attention. This helps make these early items accessible to STM and LTM. Fewer rehearsals of items are possible as the list increases in length (Atkinson & Shiffrin, 1969; Tan & Ward, 2000). As a result, more attention is given to the early items than to the later ones. In contrast, the information at the end of the list, the recency portion, consists of words or other items that are newly placed in STM, which makes them immediately available, but only temporarily. Students typically recall these items immediately (e.g., Beaman & Morton, 2000).

The separation between STM and LTM has been tested in many ways. These tests show that some learning conditions affect the first part of the serial position effect but not the last part, while other conditions can affect the last part of the serial position effect but not the first part. For example, if students are forced to wait 30 seconds before trying to recall a list that they have just committed to memory, the last few items on the list—those stored in STM—will not be easily recalled because the delay is over 18 seconds. This phenomenon is called **negative recency** (Craik, 1970). Such delays don't affect recall for the information from the first part of the list, however, because those items are better rehearsed and are more likely to be encoded into LTM. Negative recency is not limited to recalling arbitrary lists of words: It has been shown to hold true for recalling commercials during a TV show (Terry, 2005). After a delay, observers have difficulty recalling the last few brand names touted by the most recent commercials.

Alternately, if people find it difficult to rehearse the first few items on a list, the primacy effect—memory for the early part of the list—can be eliminated. For example, researchers presented lists of words at fast rates (two words every second) and at slow rates (one word every 2 seconds). They found that the faster the rate of presentation, the poorer the recall of the words at the beginning of the list, although speed of presentation had no effect on memory for the last few items on the list (e.g., Murdock, 1962). This "speed effect" can be seen if you glance back at Figure 5.7 and compare the curves for 20 items (1 second) and 20 items (2 seconds). The ability to rehearse the first few items is critical to the serial position curve.

Implications for Memory

The serial position effect not only reflects rehearsal conditions (Bjork & Witten, 1974; Van Overschelde, 2002), it also reflects whether the items to be remembered are presented visually or auditorily. In one study, participants either read digits silently to themselves, or listened to the digits as they were read aloud. The results can be seen in Figure 5.6, which shows two serial position curves: one for visual information presented to students and one for auditory information. You can see from the figure that students had more difficulty recalling the last few items of a list when they were visually presented (read silently to themselves) than when they were auditorily presented (Beaman & Morton, 2000). This is called the **modality effect** (Crowder & Morton, 1969; O. C. Watkins &

M. J. Watkins, 1980) because there is a different recall pattern depending on the stimulus modality (visual or auditory) being used. This effect shows how important auditory rehearsal is to STM.

Perhaps you have noticed that immediately after someone speaks to you, the words "disappear" and you must rely on your STM to understand fully what was just said. Because of this, humans may have developed sound-based rehearsal to keep information available for processing. In contrast, our cognitive system does not always have to compensate for the loss of visual information because visual events are not usually as fleeting as sound—even moving objects can be kept in view for some time period.

Getting Around the Serial Position Effect

One way to circumvent the power of the serial position effect is to make the information distinctive, and therefore more memorable. For example, if you are studying with a friend and want to help him remember a list of vocabulary words, you can say his name periodically during the session (e.g., "good, Eric"). This will redirect your friend's attention to the new information and create the equivalent of a new list. Or, if you are trying to remember portions of a text that you have highlighted, keep changing the color of the pen you are using; this breaks up the "list" of facts and makes the first few items in the new color more memorable than they would be otherwise.

Another way around the serial position effect is to find a way to connect the information you are trying to remember. The U-shaped curve associated with the serial position effect is typical for items that are unrelated to each other, but not for lists of things that are related. Suppose you are trying to remember a list of items to buy at the grocery store. The serial position effect predicts that you are likely to forget the items in the middle of the list within a minute. However, if you form a visual image of each item and create a combined picture of the first item with the second and the second with the third, and so forth, then when you get to the store, recalling any item will help you recall the others on the list. As a result, you will probably not show a serial position effect (Bower, 1970). You can gain firsthand experience of this memory technique by trying Demonstration 5.4.

■■■ DEMONSTRATION 5.4

Ways Around the Serial Position Effect

Have you ever played the game "my grandfather owns a grocery store and he sells . . ."? This is a game where the first person states an object in the store, and each succeeding person repeats the already stated objects and then adds a new one to the end of the list. By creating a mental image of each object and picturing how it connects to the preceding object on the list, the serial position effect can be eliminated—a winning strategy for the game and for improving your memory of a list of items. You can experience this effect by applying the strategy to the following list of 15 words. To do so, form a visual image of each object and then connect each new image to the previous one. For example, say "apple" and imagine an apple, say "knife" and imagine a knife and an apple together, then say "plate" and put the apple–knife combination on the plate, and so on. The knife stabbed into the apple (maybe with a little blood) should do the trick (e.g., Kroll & Tu, 1988)! The key factor in this demonstration is not the use of imagery, but that, as we will see in Chapter 8, memory is enhanced when we create relationships among the items to be remembered. One further hint: The more bizarre the image you create, the better the recall.

APPLE	DOOR	BOWL
KNIFE	BELT	RAISINS
PLATE	BROOM	CEREAL
GLASS	TOWEL	CUP
MILK	SOAP	CRACKER

Another way around the serial position effect is simply to accept that people will forget the ideas in the middle of a message and remember only the information at the beginning and end of messages. Commercials for prescription medicines typically place the description of the drug's possible side effects in the middle of the commercial. This helps to make the negative information less memorable. The product's name is spoken at the beginning and end of the advertisement in order to make it more memorable.

SECTION SUMMARY ■

The Serial Position Effect

The items in the middle of a list are not as likely to be recalled as those at the beginning or end of a list and it doesn't matter whether the list is made up of TV advertisements, introductions to people at a party, or the main points in a textbook paragraph. This phenomenon, called the serial position effect, is represented visually as a U-shaped curve and reflects the dual operation of short-term memory and long-term memory. For STM, it is more distinctive for auditory presentations of information than for visually based presentations; this is called the modality effect. Each portion of the curve can be separately affected by the conditions in which the information is presented. If information is presented rapidly, it is difficult for a person to attend to each item so the primacy portion (first part of the curve) will show poor performance. If a delay occurs between the time the list is presented and the time it is recalled, the recency portion of the curve (last part of the curve) will show poor performance. Methods exist to help individuals avoid the serial position effect. These methods involve making each item in a list meaningful and mentally connecting list items to one another to form a memorable image.

■ ■

Working Memory: The Structure Beneath Short-Term Memory

We have seen that STM behaves differently depending on whether the things to be remembered are presented visually or auditorily, rapidly or slowly, or whether the items activate information stored in long-term memory and where in a sequence of facts a critical item falls. Cognitive psychologists have developed a theory of the underlying mechanisms of STM not only to explain the properties of STM, but also to explain how STM helps us interact with the world and accomplish our goals. This emphasis on the active and structural aspects of STM began with the work of Miller, Galanter, and Pribram (1960). They called STM *working memory* to emphasize that it serves as our support system for doing cognitive work, such as reasoning, listening, or making decisions.

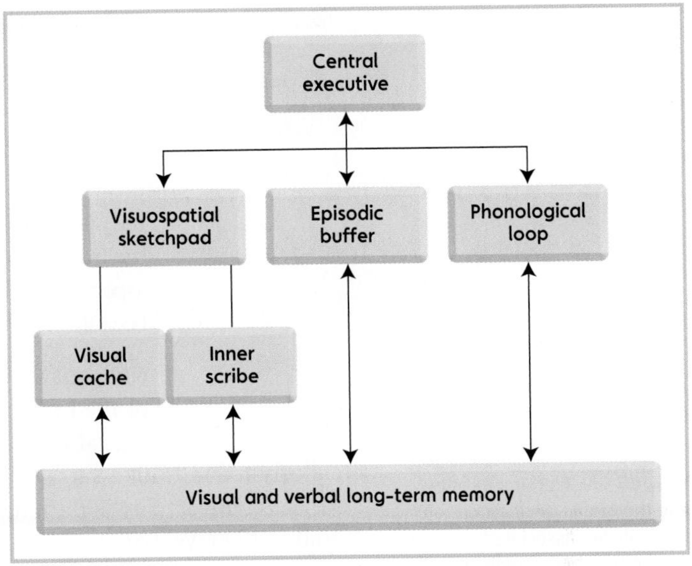

Great progress in this effort to replace the static model of STM with a more process-oriented model of working memory was made by Baddeley and Hitch (1974, 1976, 1977). They defined working memory as a limited capacity system that allows us to store and manipulate information temporarily so that we can perform everyday tasks. Their model of working memory is composed of the four divisions shown in **FIGURE 5.8**: a phonological loop, a visuospatial sketchpad, an episodic buffer, and a central executive. The goal of the remainder of this section is to describe the cognitive functions performed by each of these WM components and to show how the properties of short-term memory can be explained by the mechanisms of working memory.

FIGURE 5.8 Working Memory System Baddeley and Hitch formulated a process-oriented model of working memory that is composed of four divisions: a phonological loop, a visuospatial sketchpad, an episodic buffer, and a central executive.

Source: After Baddeley, 2000; Logie, 1995

The Phonological Loop

Sound is a primary means of conveying information. Even when we read silently, we often generate internal (subvocal) speech: a sound-based (phonological) representation of the visually presented words (e.g., Bookheimer, Zeffiro, Blaxton, Gaillard, & Theodore, 1995). Like the serial position effect, sound is one of the basic codes of STM. Not surprisingly, one of the subsystems in working memory is dedicated to the temporary storage of phonological information. This system is called the **phonological loop** and it contains two components: the **phonological store**, a reservoir in which an acoustic or phonological representation of the stimulus is stored; and the **articulatory control process** (like maintenance rehearsal), which automatically refreshes and maintains the elements in the phonological store. This control process refreshes the items in the phonological loop as if they were being rehearsed, though of course the process is subvocal, no sound is actually made.

Without the articulatory control process, the phonological store would be roughly equivalent to the original description of STM, because without the constant activation of the articulatory control process, items to be remembered would be lost over time. According to the WM model, the articulatory control process "refreshes" or automatically gives energy to each element in roughly a 2-second cycle. Any sounds (names, numbers, etc.) that can be repeated in 2 seconds can be maintained in WM

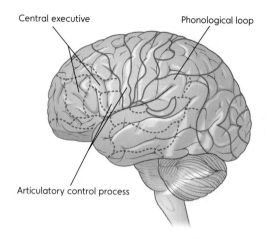

Central executive

Phonological loop

Articulatory control process

FIGURE 5.9 Working Memory and the Brain Specific areas of the brain are associated with the functions of the phonological loop and other divisions of working memory.

(Schweikert & Boruff, 1986). If a set of items requires more than 2 seconds to be repeated, some loss of information from memory will result because there is a trade-off in WM between the rate of loss and the rehearsal rate. When the items in the phonological loop are numerous or difficult to pronounce, the articulatory control process cannot keep up with refreshing all of the information in the phonological loop: The more information you have to process, the more information you will lose from working memory. This aspect of WM accounts for the fact that STM capacity has a limit because of the work required by the articulatory control process.

Neuropsychology of the Phonological Loop Specific areas of the brain are associated with the functions of the phonological loop and other divisions of working memory. These are illustrated in **FIGURE 5.9**. The basic storage function of the phonological loop is associated with activity in the left parietal region (Nyberg & Cabeza, 2000; Shallice & Vallar, 1990; Warrington, 1971). It may also connect just below the left parietal region to the superior temporal lobe (Buchsbaum & D'Esposito, 2008), a central area for language processing, which will be discussed in Chapters 10 and 11. The refreshing of items within the phonological loop is associated with activity in the prefrontal cortex (Awh, Jonides, Smith, Schaumacher, Koeppe, & Katz, 1996; Paulescu, Frith, & Frackowiak, 1993). This part of the brain helps people understand human speech (see Chapter 9) and is connected to an area of the cortex, called the motor area, which gives commands to the muscles that allow us to speak. The fact that the areas of the brain related to WM are also important to speech supports the hypothesis that the articulatory control process is speech based. Moreover, the fact that the brain areas associated with storage of words are separate from the area that refreshes those words is evidence that the phonological loop is separate from the functioning of the articulatory control process.

The Visuospatial Sketchpad

Sometimes we are called upon to remember a picture, a dance sequence, or imagine a route through a new neighborhood. The cognitive processes that are mobilized to perform these actions rely on another component of working memory: the **visuospatial sketchpad** (see Figure 5.8). This WM component is responsible for storing visually presented information such as drawings or remembering kinesthetic (motor) movements such as dance steps. For example, when you read the word "cat" you see the letters and store them; however, if time permits you might also retrieve a visual image of your favorite cat and store that in the sketchpad along with the written letters. It works the other way as well: If you see a picture of a cat, you may implicitly verbalize something like the word "cat" (Glanzer & Clark, 1964; Smith & Larson, 1970). However, this requires the participation of the central executive, described later. The importance of the visuospatial sketchpad is evident when reading a textbook like this one that has words, figures, and illustrations that are related to one another. In this case, both the sketchpad and the phonological loop are working together to combine the information that is presented on the page as both words and pictures. The sketchpad maintains the visual representation of stimuli as well as their spatial position on the page (Hegarty & Just, 1989; Schacter, Wagner, & Buckner, 2000).

The visuospatial sketchpad contains two structures: the **visual cache** and **the inner scribe** (Logie, 1995, 2003; illustrated in Figure 5.8). The visual cache temporarily stores visual information that comes from perceptual experience and contains information about the form and color of what we perceive (Smyth & Pendleton, 1989). And, as if it were storing a picture, it also contains some spatial information about what is perceived. In contrast, the inner scribe performs at least two functions. First, it refreshes all of the stored information contained in the visuospatial sketchpad. Second, it briefly stores spatial relationships associated with bodily movement. The two together are involved in our common experience of visual imagery. The visual cache holds the images and the inner scribe can manipulate them. Both require the involvement of part of the central executive called the *visual buffer* to create our images (Logie, 1995; see also Bruyer & Scailquin, 1998; Pearson, 2001). Visual imagery will be an important topic in Chapter 8.

The cognitive processes that allow us to follow and remember a route on a map, like this one of Montclair, New Jersey, rely on the visuospatial sketchpad, a component of working memory.

© Google

In an experiment to determine whether the visuospatial sketchpad and the phonological loop are independent divisions, university students were asked to memorize a miniature checkerboard with black and white squares: a perceptual task associated with the visuospatial sketchpad (Cocchini, Logie, Della Sala, MacPherson, & Baddeley, 2002). At the same time, the students either engaged in a motor task (also associated with the visuospatial sketchpad) or a verbal task (associated with the phonological loop). The motor task consisted of using a computer stylus to track a "ladybug" moving on a computer screen. The verbal task required the students to repeat back an ever-changing sequence of numbers (a typical digit-span procedure). Consistent with the concept of a visuospatial sketchpad, tracking the ladybug interfered with remembering the checkerboard (a spatial task). The digit-span task associated with the phonological loop, however, did not interfere with remembering the checkerboard. Thus, a spatial motor task interferes with perceptual information stored in the visuospatial sketchpad, but a phonological task does not. These findings support the theory that the visuospatial sketchpad and the phonological loop are separate, independent divisions.

Neuropsychology of the Visuospatial Sketchpad The visuospatial sketchpad is represented in the brain in a manner similar to the phonological loop (see Figure 5.9) except that it is represented primarily on the right side of the brain (Courtney, Ungerleider, Keil, & Haxby, 1997; Smith et al, 1995). Cognitive neuroscience provides evidence in support of the theoretical distinction between the visual cache and the inner scribe. The functioning of these divisions is associated with separate neurological areas (Levy & Goldman-Rakic, 2000; Sala, Rama, & Courtney, 2003).

Clinical cases also provide evidence for two subdivisions. In one case, an individual with a lesion in the right prefrontal cortex had difficulty remembering spatial relationships among objects (information associated with the inner scribe), yet had no difficulty perceiving those same objects (information associated with the visual cache; Carlesimo, Perri, Turriziani, Tomaiuolo, & Caltagirone, 2001). The same effect can be seen in laboratory experiments. In one study researchers were able to "knock out" the ongoing electrical activity of the part of the brain associated with the functioning of the inner scribe using a procedure called *repetitive transcranial magnetic stimulation* (rTMS). By doing so, they were able to interfere with a volunteer's ability to remember the arrangements of dots (illustrated in **FIGURE 5.10**), but not a volunteer's memory for pictures. When the researchers

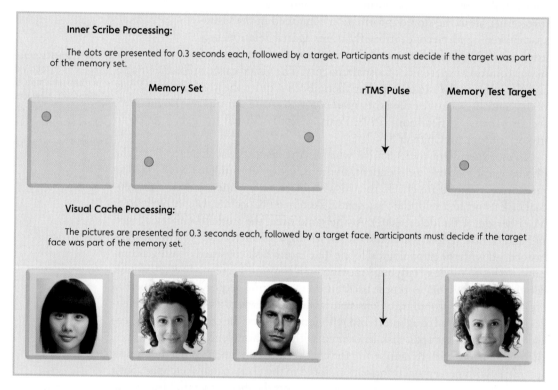

FIGURE 5.10 The Scribe and the Cache Are Separate Divisions In this study, researchers were able to show that the inner scribe and the visual cache are separate divisions. Volunteers performed two tasks: spatial memory for the pattern of dots (using the inner scribe) or memory for faces (using the visual cache). When performing these tasks, volunteers had targeted areas of their brain briefly knocked out by a pulse of repetitive transcranial magnetic stimulation (rTMS). When the rTMS pulse is sent to the area where the inner scribe functions (the dorsolateral medial prefrontal cortex) the dot pattern task is interrupted, but not the face recognition task. In contrast, when the rTMS pulse is sent to the visual cache area (ventrolateral prefrontal cortex), the face memory task is interrupted, but not the dot pattern memory task.

Source: Mottaghy, Gangitano, Sparing, Krause, & Pascual-Leone, 2002; Jason Homa/Getty Images; Image Source Black/Alamy; Photodisc/Getty Images

subsequently used rTMS to knock out the brain area associated with the visual cache, they were able to interfere with memory for pictures, but not memory for the spatial arrangements of dots (Mottaghy, Gangitano, Sparing, Krause, & Pascual-Leone, 2002). This testing procedure demonstrates the independence of the two components of the visuospatial sketchpad.

The Episodic Buffer

When people are engaged in a conversation, they have to keep track of what has been said, the responses to what has been said, and their assumptions about what individual speakers intended by their remarks. It is as if every conversation is a ministory or "episode" with a beginning, middle, and end. To keep track of such episodes, researchers argue that WM contains an **episodic buffer**, which acts as an integrative division that places events occurring in the visuospatial sketchpad and the phonological loop into a coherent sequence along with memory for the goals that initiated those events (Baddeley, 2000). Because the episodic buffer keeps track of the sequence of sentences that are spoken to us, it is natural to suppose that some part of the phonological loop would be connected to episodic memory. This is just what neuroscientists have found: The lower portion of the parietal lobe (near where the phonological loop seems to function) acts as an interface between episodic memory and the executive systems. Of course we should not think that the episodic buffer is localized only to this area of the brain. Rather we must always suppose that this part of the brain operates in coordination with other regions of the brain to perform the basic WM functioning (e.g., Vilberg & Rugg, 2008).

To appreciate the usefulness of the episodic buffer, remember that STM research has found that the typical person can remember a list of about 5 to 9 unrelated words. Yet, when those words are organized as a normal sentence, memory span increases to 15 or 16 words (Baddeley, Vallar, & Wilson, 1987). This phenomenon is most evident in people whose attention is working well (Baddeley & Wilson, 2002). The episodic buffer strings the sounds and words together to form a connected, time-based sequence to hold the words together as a sentence (as when we are able to chunk a sequence of words). It is the episodic buffer that also accounts for how people remember lists of unrelated items (not in a sentence), which was described earlier as the serial position effect.

The concept of the episodic buffer helps us to understand an oddity in the clinical literature. There are individuals who suffer from a kind of amnesia that affects their short-term memory. Their memory span might be one or two unrelated words presented either aurally or visually. They can't repeat back more words than that and they have a great deal of difficulty understanding what is going on around them. However, if they are presented with words that form a sentence, the number of words they are able to repeat is often doubled (Baddeley & Wilson, 2002). This suggests that there is a sequencing process that is able to hold items together with a kind of time-based glue. This sequence works through the episodic buffer. The episodic buffer does not seem to have a unique area of the brain that performs its functions. It is probably redundantly represented in a number of places (Baddeley, 2002). This is sensible because the buffer is called upon to organize so many systems.

The Central Executive

According to Baddeley's model, working memory contains a fourth component, the **central executive**, which coordinates the activities of the visuospatial sketchpad, phonological loop, and episodic buffer, and also communicates with long-term memory via the episodic buffer (Baddeley, 1998, 2002). The central executive is not a memory store: It is a control system that guides attention and allocates resources to maximize performance. The attention system was discussed in Chapter 3 along with the basic spotlight metaphor. Sometimes the spotlight is moved by automatic processes and other times by more controlled processes. The central executive is the main system for controlling attention.

Researchers have designed a task to test the central executive's effectiveness in different people (Daneman & Carpenter, 1980, 1983; Daneman & Merikle, 1996). In this task, participants are supposed to read a series of short sentences and remember the last word of each sentence. Then they are tested on how many of the last words they are able to recall. The number of such words that a participant is able to recall reflects the ability of the central executive to control two tasks at once: reading sentences and remembering unrelated words. WM span, which basically determines WM efficiency (Turner & Engle, 1989), varies among people and correlates with standard measures of fluid intelligence (the ability to reason and make decisions on the fly; Kyllonen & Christal, 1990). As we will see in the chapters on language, WM span also predicts reading comprehension (Conway, Kane, & Engle, 2003; Swanson & Jerman, 2007).

The central executive coordinates, manipulates, and updates the content of the WM divisions (Baddeley & Logie, 1999). In general, executive functions, such as planning and paying attention, are centered in this area of the prefrontal cortex where the central executive is identified (see Figure 5.9). People who have damage to the region suffer an inability to plan an action (Owen, Evans, & Petrides, 1996), difficulty attending to relevant aspects of their environment, or difficulty handling multiple tasks at once (D'Esposito, Detre, Alsop, & Shin, 1995).

A test that measures central executive functioning is the Paced Auditory Serial Addition Task (PASAT; see **FIGURE 5.11**). The PASAT requires participants to add aurally presented consecutive numbers at a rate of about 2.4 seconds per number and announce the sum. This is more difficult than you might assume because the participant must not confuse the addition that he or she has just stated aloud with the next number presented. For example, if the first number is 4 and the second number is 6, the answer is 10. If the third number is 3, the answer is 9 (6 + 3). The participant must resist the temptation to say 13 (10 + 3) (Gronwall, 1977).

A person's score on this test is the number of correct additions. This test makes only minor demands on arithmetic knowledge, but puts a premium on the individual's ability to do three things at once: add two numbers, keep track of the previously presented digit in working memory, and inhibit the sum of the previous two digits. The PASAT score relates to central executive functioning in the real world and is positively correlated with a person's level of vigilance: his or her ability to detect the presence of unlikely events (Weber, 1988). It also relates somewhat to a person's IQ (Spreen & Strauss, 1991; Wiens, Fuller, & Crossen, 1997). The PASAT has a diagnostic use: People who have recently suffered a concussion have greatly diminished PASAT performances (Erlanger, Kutner, Barth, & Barnes, 1999; Gronwall & Sampson, 1974).

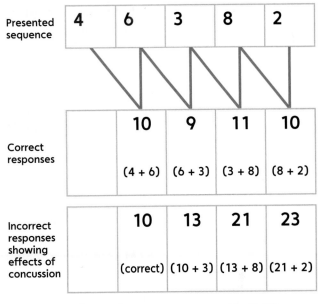

FIGURE 5.11 The PASAT Procedure The Paced Auditory Serial Addition Task (PASAT) measures central executive functioning. It requires participants to add aurally presented consecutive numbers at a rate of about 2.4 seconds per number and announce the sum. The difficulty is that the participant must not confuse the addition he or she has just stated aloud with the next number presented. The PASAT score relates to central executive functioning in the real world and is positively correlated with a person's level of vigilance. The test also has a diagnostic use: People who have recently suffered a concussion show greatly diminished PASAT performances.

Source: After Gronwall, 1977

It has already been mentioned that the PASAT is a measure of central executive functioning. Most studies indicate that both age and intelligence affect performance on the PASAT. In general, older people (50-year-olds) perform worse than younger people (20-year-olds), and those with higher IQ scores have stronger PASAT performance than those with lower IQ scores (Wiens et al., 1997). These effects suggest a biological basis for the efficiency of the central executive in working memory. Added to this is the effect of brain trauma on central executive functioning. Not only is the PASAT sensitive to the changes in cognitive functioning that result from concussions, it is also sensitive to more permanent cognitive damage following traumatic brain injury (Sohlberg & Mateer, 1989).

A word of caution is useful here. Although it is easy to point to the functioning of the frontal lobes as the location of the central executive, we must remember that the frontal lobes are connected to so many other areas of the brain that we can be confident neuropsychological research will show that additional areas outside the frontal lobes are likely to contribute to executive control.

SECTION SUMMARY ■

Working Memory: The Structure Beneath Short-Term Memory

Most cognitive researchers view short-term memory as reflecting a set of structures and processes called working memory. The working memory model consists of four divisions interacting with each other: the phonological loop, visuospatial sketchpad, episodic buffer, and central executive. The first three of these are limited-capacity memory structures that hold different representations of what we experience: sounds, visual and kinesthetic images, and sequential patterns that coordinate these representations. The central executive is responsible for attending to each of the memory divisions and ensuring that any event we experience is properly coded so that it may be retained and used. Many functions of working memory are performed in the parietal lobe and prefrontal cortex. Neurological studies have shown that the processing of each subdivision is performed in distinct areas of the brain, except for the episodic buffer, which seems to be redundantly represented in a number of places because it participates in so many memory functions. Neuropsychological findings have provided evidence for the functional independence of the working memory divisions.

Phenomena Explained by Working Memory

The following applications of the WM model illustrate how the four components of working memory function to explain three typical findings associated with STM: phonological confusions, word-length effect, and irrelevant speech effect.

Phonological Confusions

Phonological confusions occur when people try to remember lists of words or sentences (such as might occur in a poem) and find that their memory is worse for items that sound alike than for items that sound different. As a result, the person trying to remember a series of words or letters that sound alike will be judged to have a smaller STM span than a person trying to remember a sequence that does not sound alike. You can experience phonological confusion by trying Demonstration 5.5.

■■■ DEMONSTRATION 5.5

Phonological Confusions
Read aloud the string of seven letters in Set 1 as rapidly as you can, then close your eyes and try to recall the string of letters in the correct order.

Set 1: P-G-T-C-D-Z-B

Now do the same for Set 2.

Set 2: R-H-X-S-F-M-K

If you are like most adults, Set 1 felt like you were reading a tongue twister and typically takes longer to read than Set 2. How well were you able to remember each string? When people are asked to repeat back the letters, in exact order, Set 1 is more difficult to remember than Set 2.

Phonological confusion occurs not only when the letters are presented aloud, but also when they are presented visually (Conrad & Hull, 1964; Wickelgren, 1964). Working memory provides two explanations for these sound-based confusions. First, when the articulatory control process rehearses the phonological codes of the letters, it may confuse similar sounds and rehearse one sound or word more than the other because it can't tell which one it has already rehearsed. Second, these confusions occur even when the letters are visually presented because the central executive transfers a copy of the visual items to the phonological loop in the form of a phonological code. Once again, the articulatory control process becomes confused in its rehearsal of the sounds (Larsen, Baddeley, & Andrade, 2000).

Word-Length Effect

You have probably noticed that when you try to memorize vocabulary in a foreign language, the long words are more difficult to remember than the short ones. This pervasive phenomenon, investigated years ago by Hawkins and Shigley (1970), is termed the **word-length effect**: STM span decreases as the length of words to be memorized increases. For example, when students are asked to repeat one-syllable words like "mumps," "Maine," and "zinc," they are considerably more accurate than when they are asked to repeat words like "tuberculosis," "Yugoslavia," and "aluminum" (Baddeley, Thomson, & Buchanan, 1975). How does working memory explain this effect? Words with more syllables increase the number of sounds the articulatory control process must rehearse. Notice that long words not only have more syllables than short ones, they take longer to pronounce. To experience how time to pronounce affects your phonological loop, try Demonstration 5.6.

■■■**DEMONSTRATION 5.6**

Word-Length Effect

Read the words in Set 1 aloud as rapidly as you can. As soon as you finish, write down all the words you can remember. Then, do the same for Set 2.

Set 1: COERCE, HUMANE, MORPHINE, MOONBEAM, ZYGOTE, BASEBALL, PAINTING

Set 2: TABLE, EMBER, HACKLE, PILLOW, WIGGLE, CLEVER, TENNIS

Did you remember more or fewer words from Set 1? The two sets of words have the same number of syllables. However, when you pronounced them aloud you should have noticed that the syllables in Set 1 take longer to say than those in Set 2. Pronouncing the syllables in Set 1 exceeds the roughly 2 seconds for the articulatory control process. As a result, most people remember more words from Set 2 than from Set 1.

To study the relationship between word length and the time to rehearse, Baddeley et al. (1975) created word sets that had the same number of syllables and letters, but took different amounts of time to pronounce in English, as is the case with the words in Demonstration 5.6. Participants were better at pronouncing and remembering words with short sounds (e.g., PICKET) than words with long sounds (e.g., PARLOR). A rule of thumb for estimating a person's memory span is: *If the articulatory control process can rehearse an item within 2 seconds, it will be retained in the phonological loop.* It is this time-based limitation imposed by the articulatory control process that sets the limit for the capacity of short-term memory. The typical memory capacity of 7 items, mentioned earlier in the chapter, is really the consequence of how long it takes to say the names of the items (e.g., Avons, Wright, & Pammer, 1994). For example,

A background conversation may reduce what you are able to recall after studying. This irrelevant speech effect happens only when the background sounds are the same as the sounds you are trying to remember: Speech interferes with reading but music without lyrics does not.

Huntstock/Getty Images

Mandarin-speaking adults show a greater memory span for digits than do English-speaking adults (9.9 vs. 6.6 items). This perfectly coincides with how rapidly the two groups can articulate numbers. Mandarin speakers are faster at repeating numbers than English speakers (265 vs. 321 ms/digit; Ellis & Hennelly, 1980; Hoosain & Salili, 2005). Working memory shows that the speed of articulation is the key to the capacity of short-term memory.

Irrelevant Speech Effect

Suppose you are intensely studying a text and two people are having a conversation nearby. Although this background conversation is irrelevant to what you need to learn, it may reduce what you are able to recall in comparison to a situation when you are able to study in silence (Neath, 2000). The ability of inconsequential background speech to interfere with silent verbal rehearsal is called the **irrelevant speech effect** (Colle & Welsh, 1976). It can occur even when the language being spoken is different from the language of the text you are reading. This is because the speech sounds from the irrelevant speech enter the phonological loop and are added to the sounds associated with the words that you are trying to remember. Just like the word-length effect, sometimes the phonological loop holds so many speech sounds that the articulatory control process can't rehearse them in under 2 seconds.

Fortunately for people who like to listen to music when they study or balance their checkbook, the irrelevant speech effect occurs only when the irrelevant sounds are in the same category as those sounds that people are trying to remember: Speech will interfere with reading, but musical notes will not interfere with reading unless lyrics are embedded in the music (Salame & Baddeley, 1989). There are differences between men and women in the effect of lyrics and music: Women are more sensitive to the meaning of lyrics when they are embedded in music than men. The opposite is true when lyrics are presented in written form (Iverson, Reed, & Revlin, 1989).

SECTION SUMMARY ■

Phenomena Explained by Working Memory

Baddeley's model of working memory is able to explain many of the unusual phenomena associated with short-term memory: phonological confusion, word-length effect, and irrelevant speech effect. All of these effects are related to how WM codes what we see and hear and how the visuospatial sketchpad, the phonological loop, and the central executive retain information. All of these STM effects are connected to the way the articulatory control process of the phonological loop is able to maintain the viability of the information.

Working Memory and Emotion

Everyone experiences stressful events, but some life stressors are so extreme that they intrude unexpectedly into everyday thoughts and compete for working memory resources (Klein & Boals, 2001b). Efforts to suppress negative or stressful thoughts compete with WM resources to deal with ordinary tasks such as reasoning, remembering, and problem solving (e.g., Baradell & Klein, 1993). One reason for this is that emotional stimuli capture our attention and tell us they are important in ways that nonemotional stimuli often do not. This is called the *attentional capture hypothesis* (Yantis, 1993). These emotional stimuli could be anything from seeing a threatening face, reading a taboo word, or something that signals danger (e.g., Holmes, Vuilleumier, & Eimer, 2003; Mackay, Shafto, & Taylor, 2004; Taylor & Fragopanagos, 2005). Emotional events in our lives can be relentless in dominating our thoughts and consuming our WM resources (e.g., Mikels, Reuter-Lorenz, Beyer, & Frederickson, 2008). The relationship between emotional events, life stress, and WM capacity was examined in an experiment designed by Sarason, Johnson, and Siegel (1979). College students were asked to complete the Life Experiences Scale (Sarason et. al., 1979), which lists 47 significant life events (death of a family member, obtaining a new job, etc.). The students were also asked to take a WM test. On the test, students read a simple equation and marked the answer true or false. Each equation was followed by a different word that the student was expected to remember (e.g., "$4 \times 2 = 6$, back"). After reviewing sets of two to seven problems, students were asked to write down all the words paired with the equations that they could remember. The people with the greatest life event stress performed the poorest on this task. The higher the number of stressful events in one's life, the greater the demands on WM and the poorer the performance on WM-relevant tasks.

In a related study, Klein and Boals (2001a) asked college undergraduates to write either an essay about a negative event they had unwanted thoughts about, or an essay about a positive event in their lives. A control group of students was asked to write an essay about the day they were having. Students wrote for 20 minutes a total of three times over a 2-week period. At the end of the study, the students' WM capacity was measured and compared to their WM score when the study began. Students who had been asked to write about a negative event showed an 11% increase in WM capacity. Those who had written about a positive experience and those in the control group showed less than a 4% improvement in their WM score. This finding suggests that images of negative or traumatic experiences often intrude on our thoughts and tax WM's ability to inhibit the negative event so that we can focus on the tasks before us.

Writing the essay allowed the students to understand the negative emotional events and organize their thoughts about them. The negative thoughts were then less likely, in Klein's (2011) words: "to come unbidden to our conscious minds." This allowed the central executive to operate more efficiently on the

WM tasks, resulting in an improved score. Klein and Boals (2001b) further showed that this has a lasting effect. Those students who showed the greatest improvement in WM score also had the highest college grades a semester after the study was completed. These findings support the belief that emotions can tax the resources of the central executive and also underscore the possible value of keeping a diary.

The influence of emotion on the central executive can help explain cognitive impairments that are often attributed to neurological deficits. Cognitive impairments related to multiple sclerosis (MS) are a case in point. MS is a disorder of the central nervous system that results in the destruction of the white matter (in particular, the myelin) in the brain. More than a million people worldwide suffer from MS. In advanced stages of the disease, individuals with MS experience difficulty in processing information (Archibald & Fisk, 2000; Lengenfelder, Chiaravalloti, Ricker, & DeLuca, 2003). D'Esposito et al. (1996) asked participants with MS and a control group of healthy participants to perform concurrent tasks like judging the angle of lines while humming, tapping, or reciting the alphabet. The more difficult the concurrent task, the more impaired the participants with MS were in comparison with the control group.

Some of these findings may be the result of the negative emotions that individuals with MS experience as a result of their unpredictable and often debilitating condition, rather than neurological deficits resulting from the disease. In an independent test of depression and WM capacity, researchers found that depressed individuals with MS had a lower WM capacity than nondepressed individuals with MS or nondepressed individuals without MS (Arnett et al., 1999). This suggests that some of the effect of neurological diseases on WM may be a result of the emotional reaction and psychological state of the individual with MS, rather than a direct effect of the neurological damage.

Positive emotions should have a beneficial effect on WM because we know that happy moods are related to the flow of the neurotransmitter dopamine to the frontal lobes (Ashby, Isen, & Turken, 1999; Berk et al., 1989), which results in improved problem-solving abilities. However, positive moods do not seem to have as consistent an effect as negative moods. In one study, participants watched a comedy film or ate candy. As a result, they showed improvement in creative problem solving (Isen, Daubman, & Nowicki, 1987). However, the opposite results were shown in another study in which students, who watched a comedy film and experienced a positive mood as a result, showed poorer performance on tasks that required central executive functioning (Oaksford, Morris, Grainger, & Williams, 1996). Although positive moods have different effects on working memory, we know that negative moods diminish working memory. This may be because negative mood has a direct influence on blood flow to various regions of the brain having to do with memory and learning (e.g., Bush, Luu, & Posner, 2000; Liotti, Mayberg, McGinnis, Brannan, & Jerabek, 2002).

SECTION SUMMARY ▪

Working Memory and Emotion

Our emotions interrupt the continuous flow of cognitive processes and affect the efficiency of working memory. In particular, negative thoughts compete for WM resources. The more stress in one's life, the lower the efficiency of WM in performing simple cognitive tasks. Students who performed exercises that reduced the intrusion of negative thoughts showed an increase in their WM capacity. The decline in WM capacity shown by some people with multiple sclerosis may be a result of their depression in reaction to having the disease, rather than to the direct effect of the neurological damage associated with the disease. Mood states (positive or negative) can have an influence on the neurotransmitter dopamine, which in turn can affect problem solving.

▪ ▪

CHAPTER SUMMARY

Memory, broadly speaking, refers to our ability to retain information. Short-term memory (STM) is a memory system that allows us to retain items for a short period of time and may form the basis of our long-term memory and knowledge. STM is a limited-capacity system that increases from childhood to adulthood. The typical adult's STM span is between 5 and 9 unrelated items, called chunks. The amount of information that can be grouped as a chunk depends on whether a person is able to find a way of relating the items to one another and to what is already stored in long-term memory. People are able to retain information in STM for about 18 seconds without paying attention to it. Rehearsal (paying attention) helps to keep items in STM. There are two major types of rehearsal: maintenance and elaborative. Only elaborative rehearsal makes it easier to store new information in long-term memory. A major source of forgetting in STM is the interference among the items to be retained. The basis of interference is determined by the coding of the items. The major code in STM is sound based. People are able to verify the contents of their STM by using an exhaustive search procedure. The Sternberg task, which measures STM search, allows researchers to assess the effects of drugs and other treatments on memory.

Long-term memory and short-term memory interact when we try to remember a list of things in the precise order in which the list was presented. In this case, the proportion of the information we are able to recall tends to be related to the position of the items on the list. This phenomenon is called the serial position effect. According to the serial position effect, items at the beginning and end of a list are recalled more easily and accurately than items in the middle of the list. One way to overcome the power of the serial position effect is to make the information in the middle of a list more distinctive or to find a way to relate the items.

Short-term memory is a global term that describes a host of memory mechanisms that are called upon to help us interact with the world. An entire system of cognitive processes exists below the surface, which works to make STM visible and allows us to solve problems, make decisions, and remember and retrieve facts. This system is called working memory (WM). It is a multicomponent system composed of three limited-capacity subsystems: a phonological loop, a visuospatial sketchpad, and an episodic buffer. In addition, there is an attentional system called the central executive that coordinates the activities of the other subdivisions. The coordination of these subdivisions contributes to our smooth performance in reciting a poem or playing a sport, and explains selective impairments to memory that result from damage to various parts of the human brain, especially the frontal and parietal lobes.

WM components are able to explain three basic phenomena associated with STM. Phonological confusions result from similar sounding words being rehearsed by the articulatory control process in the phonological loop, as well as visually presented words in the visuospatial sketchpad. The word-length effect results from some words requiring more time to rehearse, which exceeds the refresh rate of the articulatory control process. The irrelevant speech effect occurs when unfiltered speech sounds enter into the phonological loop and interfere with rehearsal.

Nonspeech sounds like a melody do not contribute to the irrelevant speech effect.

Human emotion can influence the flow of blood and neurotransmitters to brain areas that are critical for the optimal functioning of WM. Negative affect and depression can reduce WM capacity and interfere with cognitive performance. Positive mood has, in some cases, been shown to increase problem-solving effectiveness.

KEY TERMS ■

learning, p. 119

memory, p. 119

short-term memory (STM), p. 119

working memory (WM), p. 119

chunk, p. 122

chunking, p. 122

retroactive interference, p. 125

proactive interference, p. 125

rehearsal, p. 126

maintenance rehearsal, p. 126

elaborative rehearsal, p. 126

serial exhaustive search, p. 127

serial position effect, p. 130

primacy effect, p. 130

recency effect, p. 130

negative recency, p. 132

modality effect, p. 132

phonological loop, p. 135

phonological store, p. 135

articulatory control process, p. 135

visuospatial sketchpad, p. 136

visual cache, p. 137

inner scribe, p. 137

episodic buffer, p. 139

central executive, p. 140

phonological confusions, p. 142

word-length effect, p. 143

irrelevant speech effect, p. 144

QUESTIONS FOR REVIEW ■

Check Your Knowledge

1. What is the definition of learning?

2. What is the relationship between learning and memory?

3. State the three questions that scientists ask regarding short-term/working memory.

4. What are the answers to these questions with regard to STM?

5. Do children have the same STM capacity as young adults or older adults?

6. What is the memory span test?

7. What is a chunk and how is it related to STM capacity?

8. How is chunking helped by long-term memory?

9. What are the two categories of interference? Give an example of each one.

10. What are the two categories of rehearsal? Which one improves storage in LTM?

11. What search procedure do we use when we search our STM for a particular item?

12. If you graph the time to scan STM, what does the slope of the curve tell you?

13. If you are given a drug that doesn't affect the slope of the curve but only affects where the curve intercepts the vertical axis, what has the drug done?

14. When you read a paragraph and are tested on your recall of it right away, which part of the paragraph will you recall best: the beginning, middle, or end? What is this pattern called?

15. How can you improve your recall for the different parts of a paragraph?

16. What are the four main divisions of working memory?

17. In which portion of WM do we rehearse the sounds of words? What is the typical rehearsal rate for this part of WM?

18. How does the rehearsal rate affect STM capacity?

19. What are the two parts of the visuospatial sketchpad and what are their main functions?

20. Why does a concussion affect a person's ability to pay attention? What part of WM is affected by concussions?

21. What system is responsible for keeping track of steps in problem solving and where you are in a conversation?

22. What are phonological confusions?

23. What is the word-length effect?

24. What is the irrelevant speech effect?

25. How do our emotions affect our STM capacity?

Apply Your Knowledge

1. Using Baddeley and Hitch's theory of working memory, how can you account for the claim that adult STM capacity is 7 plus or minus 2?

2. The serial position effect is seen even when people are trying to remember the main points discussed in a paragraph. Design an instructional method to help students avoid falling prey to the effect when they are reading a textbook.

3. Some people are able to read with the radio or TV on in the background. This fact seems to conflict with the irrelevant speech effect predictions discussed in this chapter. Using what you have learned about the subsystems of working memory, explain how some people are able to avoid the effect.

4. As discussed in the text, some people with MS have difficulty with central executive functioning. This may be the result of an emotional reaction to a neurological problem rather than a direct physical effect of that problem. How might it be possible for a clinician to determine when memory difficulties result from emotional rather than physical causes?

6

Long-Term Memory

"When to the sessions of sweet silent thought I summon up remembrance of things past, I sigh the lack of many a thing I sought**"**

—Shakespeare, Sonnet 30

Most Americans can sing the lyrics to the *Star Spangled Banner* without difficulty, but are unable to recite the words without mentally "playing" the music that accompanies them. People typically can recall their first trip to an amusement park and often the name of their first-grade teacher, but they cannot remember their first step or the first full sentence they uttered. And some of us can recall a vast number of historical facts, yet can't remember to take a daily vitamin supplement. We rely on memory to get us through the day and complete tasks at work and in the classroom, but our memory processes perform perfectly in some areas and are deeply flawed in others. This chapter and the next describe the inner workings of long-term memory and the properties associated with this component of memory.

Long-term memory (LTM) is the aspect of our memory system that consists of all the experiences and knowledge we gather throughout our lifetime. Long-term memory is the repository of information as varied as our knowledge of language and social rules, our ability to read and write, what we believe about life and the universe, and how to find our way home from an unfamiliar neighborhood. As noted in Chapter 4, our ability to cross the street safely or decode the meaning of words spoken to us relies on the pattern recognition process. The vast library of patterns that we depend upon daily to go about our lives is stored in long-term memory. As we learned in Chapter 5, the central executive in working memory coordinates the use of this library of patterns in our daily lives.

A brief demonstration shows how even our ability to understand what we are reading relies on information stored in long-term memory. The following paragraph is based on the doctoral dissertation of G. E. Rawlinson (1976) at the University of Nottingham in England. Its words should be unreadable, but if you force yourself to ignore the spelling errors, you can read and understand this passage easily:

Aoccdrnig to a rscheearch at Cmabrigde Uinervtisy, it deosn't mttaer in waht oredr the ltteers in a wrod are, the olny iprmoetnt tihng is taht the frist and lsat ltteer be at the rghit pclae. The rset can be a total mses and you can sitll raed it wouthit porbelm. Tihs is bcuseae the huamn mnid deos not raed ervey lteter by istlef, but the wrod as a wlohe.

We owe our skill in reading this paragraph to the ability of long-term memory to recognize entire patterns and words based solely on fragmentary input. LTM also creates a coherent meaning from the individual words, which in turn facilitates further pattern recognition and understanding. This illustrates how seamlessly our long-term memory is able to contribute not only to our ability to read, but more generally to our ability to function. LTM creates a scaffold that supports who we are and everything we do (e.g., Kihlstrom, Beer, & Klein, 2003).

Divisions of Long-Term Memory (LTM)

As these examples demonstrate, long-term memory encompasses a broad array of information. Researchers divide LTM into two main systems: explicit/declarative memory and implicit memory (e.g., Tulving & Craik, 2000). These two main systems have been further divided into the subdivisions shown in **TABLE 6.1** (after Schacter & Tulving, 1994; Rosenbaum et al., 2005).

Explicit/Declarative Memory

Explicit memory includes all memories that we consciously seek to store and retrieve. These memories are also called **declarative memories** because they include events that we have deliberately learned, such as "I enjoyed playing poohsticks in Sussex" or facts, such as "they grow coffee in Brazil,"

TABLE 6.1

Divisions of Long-Term Memory

	Long-Term Memory				
	Explicit/Declarative			Implicit	
		Episodic			
	Semantic	Retrospective	Prospective	Procedural	Perceptual
Question (Prime)	Who invented the snowboard?	What did you do the last time you went down the slope?	Will you remember to pack snow chains?	Describe, in words only, how to turn right on a snowboard.	Look at the slope (deep powder); how will you take it?
Memory	[Burton]	[I Fell]	[Oops]	[You lean this way, then you lean that way.]	[Automatically: Put weight on back foot and keep nose up above snow.]

and can be described or "declared" to others (Milner, 1965). Explicit/declarative memory is further subdivided into semantic and episodic memory.

Semantic Memory   **Semantic memory** is the aspect of LTM that retains conceptual knowledge stored as an independent knowledge base. It is the library where discrete facts like "dogs bark" and "robins are birds" are stored. Your memories of where you were when you first learned such facts, however, are considered part of episodic memory.

Episodic Memory   **Episodic memory** is the portion of LTM that stores and connects the specific times, places, and events in an individual's life—it is autobiographical in nature. Our use of episodic memory gives rise to the conscious experience of recollection (Tulving, 1982, 1985; Wheeler, Stuss, & Tulving, 1995, 1997). Episodic memory allows us to travel back mentally in time to earlier moments in our lives not only to retrieve a fact, but in many cases, to relive the experience (Boyer, 2008). This aspect of episodic memory is called **retrospective memory**. However, episodic memory also allows us to travel forward mentally in time in order to remember to do things in the future. This aspect of episodic memory is called **prospective memory** and is at work when we need to remember to take a pill before breakfast, to go to class at 11:00 a.m., or to set the alarm to wake up in time for an exam. Although these types of memory have their distinct properties, they also interact with each other. Planning for a future action often requires consideration of past events—to know what needs to be done or needs to be avoided. Retrospective and prospective memories are two sides of the same coin.

Implicit Memory

Our cognitive system is designed for efficiency. In order to free up resources so that we can focus our energies on demanding tasks, it allows us to put important mental functions that can be performed automatically in the background. This semiautonomous memory system is called **implicit memory**. As a result of implicit memory's functioning, we are able to learn without being aware that we are doing so (e.g., Graf & Schacter, 1985), and we can retrieve or use that information without being aware that we have stored it in memory.

When a commercial appears during an episode of your favorite TV show, do you watch it carefully or not pay much attention to it? Although people are notoriously poor at recalling the names of products in TV commercials when tested several minutes later (using their explicit memory), they purchase the products at a significantly high level when prompted by the situation depicted in the commercial, such as having a headache (Lee, 2002). In the 1960s, for example, there was a headache commercial with annoying images of hammers pounding heads. People hated these commercials and often could not recall the name of the product, Anacin. But when they went to a pharmacy, they bought vast quantities of the product (Roman, 2009).

This illustrates the functioning of implicit memory, where the knowledge that we possess influences our behavior, yet we are unable to deliberately recall the pieces of information on which our behavior relies. When learning conditions affect one type of memory but not another, the types of memory are said to be *process-dissociated* (Jacoby, 1991) and the results argue for the relative independence of the processes required of the types of memory. Some of the effects of implicit memory have been shown in laboratory situations. In one study, geometric shapes were presented to student participants so rapidly that they complained that they could barely see them. Afterward, the students were shown pairs of shapes, one member of which they had seen before and one they had not. When they were asked which object they had seen before (a standard question that assesses explicit memory), they could not tell the difference between the two shapes. Yet, when they were asked which they preferred (a standard implicit memory task), they reliably chose the one they had previously seen but could not remember (Kunst-Wilson & Zajonc, 1980). Implicit memory allows us to be influenced by experiences that we cannot deliberately recall.

As Table 6.1 shows, researchers divide implicit memory into two subsystems: procedural memory and perceptual memory.

Procedural Memory **Procedural memory** refers to stored knowledge that allows us to behave skillfully in spite of the fact that we cannot remember learning the individual skills needed to perform a particular task. Nor are we able to give a complete account of how the task should be performed. Tasks or actions included in procedural memory range from typing on a keyboard to sipping through a straw. Riding a bicycle is a useful example of the functioning of implicit memory. It is a skill acquired over many attempts, some of which are likely to be completely forgotten. You would also have difficulty clearly explaining how you ride a bicycle to someone else.

Perceptual Memory Throughout people's lives—whether they live in Bujumbura, Burundi, or in Brussels, Belgium—they acquire long-term perceptual knowledge of their surroundings: the smell of native flowers, the sight and sounds of friends and family members, and the taste of familiar foods. These examples of **perceptual memory** consist of perceptually based patterns that are often difficult to describe, but nevertheless are recalled effortlessly (e.g., Graf & Schacter, 1985; Schacter, 1996). A test of perceptual memory is useful to see perceptual processing in action. The Gollin Test (Gollin, 1960) is used to assess processing in people who have suffered strokes and other debilitating brain damage; it is described in the Focus on Methods box.

Riding a bicycle is a useful example of the functioning of implicit memory. It is a skill acquired over many attempts, some of which are likely to be completely forgotten.

Greenland/Dreamstime.com

FOCUS ON METHODS ▪▪▪▪ ▪

Perceptual Memory: The Gollin Test

The Gollin Test is often used to assess memory skills. The procedure consists of showing a person a series of line drawings so that each succeeding drawing projects a more detailed view of a familiar object. The top row below is a fish and the bottom row is a car. If you put a piece of paper covering all but the first image on each line, you will experience how difficult the identification can be even though you know the final identity of the object.

The person being tested is shown each drawing in order of increasing complexity until he or she is able to guess the object. Then, an hour later, the sequence is repeated. Adults typically are able to identify the objects with fewer presentations on the second trial than on the first. Even completely amnesic individuals, who cannot recall having ever been presented with the pictures when they are shown to them a second time, can improve on this task. This test supports the fact that perceptual memory improves with practice and suggests that learning can occur without any verbal rehearsal.

SECTION SUMMARY ▪

Divisions of Long-Term Memory (LTM)

Cognitive psychologists divide long-term memory into two broad systems: explicit/declarative and implicit memory. Explicit/declarative memory includes memories that help us store and retrieve semantic information, such as facts that we have learned about world geography or the names of streets in our neighborhood. It also contains episodic information, such as what it was like living in our first house or shopping at a local grocery store. Episodic memory is divided into retrospective memory (which stores past events in a person's life) and prospective memory (which stores memories related to future actions, such as going to a dental appointment or taking a pill). Implicit memories may be either procedural or perceptual. Procedural memories include complex actions that are difficult to describe clearly, such as how to drive a car. Perceptual memories are the source of our pattern recognition skill (see Chapter 4). Like procedural memories, they are automated and difficult to decompose into constituent parts.

▪ ▪

Characteristics of Long-Term Memory

Cognitive research on LTM has explored four primary characteristics of memory: capacity, duration, forgetting, and coding. These findings are described later and will reveal the ways in which long-term memory is a distinct memory system.

Capacity of Long-Term Memory

People often joke that learning new things means that they forget facts they already know. While this is a common belief, research has shown that the capacity of LTM has no obvious limit: Learning new facts does not expel or obliterate memories of old facts. Rather than actually losing information from LTM, the capacity limits that we experience seem to be based on our difficulty in finding a piece of information amid the vast knowledge that we possess. Thus, our ability to retrieve facts is as crucial as our ability to learn them. To gain a better appreciation of the retrieval process, try the exercise in Demonstration 6.1 before starting the next section.

•••DEMONSTRATION 6.1

Retrieval from LTM

Can you recall the names of 25 birds in less than 5 minutes? Most students think they cannot (at least when they are asked to do so in front of their classmates). Try writing down as many bird names as you can. If you get stuck, look below at the first prompt to see if it allows you to list some additional birds. Use the other prompts as needed until you have listed 25 different types of birds. Relax and don't rush yourself. When you are finished writing down 25 bird names, look at the prompts again and see if you can recall even more!

Prompts

> Live in cages
>
> Served at dinner
>
> Live at the seashore
>
> Has a color word in its name (e.g., blue)
>
> Large predators
>
> Large nonpredators

Adults of all ages are able to freely recall the names of 22 to 25 birds (Roediger, 2003) with only a few prompts, and people are capable of recognizing nearly 3 times that many names. Why? Because they have been accumulating these names from early childhood and storing them in long-term memory. The prompts help in retrieval because they provide cues or features that can be used to search memory. Our efforts to freely recall bird names or a myriad of other facts rely on a search of memory using the properties of our goal topics. The prompts add properties and thus help us search more specifically. When we do locate a searched-for element, we then recognize the items we encounter: Some are what we are searching for (*canary*) and some are not (*stool pigeon*).

Duration and Forgetting in Long-Term Memory

The knowledge stored in long-term memory endures nearly forever. This surprising finding is supported by a series of studies (Bahrick, 1984; Bahrick, Bahrick, Bahrick, & Bahrick, 1993; Bahrick & Phelps, 1987) that evaluated students' recollections of their academic knowledge from their high school and college Spanish courses. The researchers tested 587 people (including high school and college students) at periods ranging from 1 year after completion of a Spanish course to more than 49 years later. **FIGURE 6.1** shows two sets of scores. The top lines reflect participants' ability to recognize the correct answer to the Spanish questions, and the lower lines show participants' efforts to freely recall the Spanish information. Comparing these lines shows that our ability to *recognize* the correct answer is substantially better than our ability to freely *recall* the correct answer. Notice the right- and left-hand sides of the graph. The left side shows that not all of the learning is retained—there is a pronounced loss of information during the first few years. But then notice the right side. Both recognition and recall show a flat memory curve that reflects a kind of **permastore** starting 3 years after Spanish language training and continuing for nearly 50 years. Once information is firmly stored in LTM, it is not lost: It may be difficult to retrieve, but it is still there.

This does not mean that all of our recollections from LTM are always precisely correct or that they are even verbatim retrievals, as if LTM consisted of a stack of 3 × 5 inch cards with facts written on them. Much of our retrievals reflect reconstructions from the facts we possess. Take, for example, the question of whether you lived on a two-way street or a one-way street when you were 10 years old. You may have factual information stored in memory, but the way you retrieve this is most probably by accessing images from your memory of the neighborhood and testing whether these can form plausible support for a one-way or two-way street

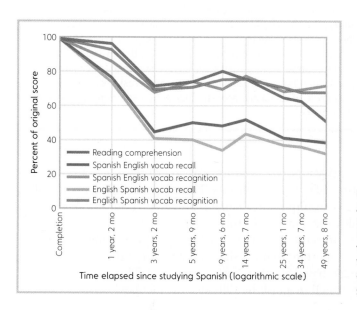

FIGURE 6.1 Recall and Recognition of Spanish Vocabulary Across Decades Participants of different ages were able to recognize correct Spanish vocabulary decades after they had taken their first Spanish class. Their ability to recall the vocabulary from an English prompt declined more severely with time, but still showed relatively stable memory across a lifetime.

Source: Bahrick, 1984

(e.g., Schmidt, Peeck, Paas, & van Breukelen, 2000). It may surprise you to learn that stage actors, who seem to have perfect, verbatim recall of their lines, are actually uttering paraphrases of their lines about 30% of the time (Schmidt, Boshuizen, & van Breukelen, 2002). They reconstruct their memory for the scripts in response to cues from the actions and words of the other actors.

Codes in Long-Term Memory

As we discussed in Chapters 4 and 5, memory systems code information in unique ways. Chapter 5 emphasized that sound- and spatially based information seem to be favored by working memory. Long-term memory is able to work with these perceptual codes and many others. In fact, the coding of information in LTM can be along any perceptual dimension you can experience. Visual coding can help you visualize the room you slept in when you were 12. You get a sense of auditory coding when you read a letter from a friend and imagine his or her voice saying the words. Kinesthetic codes come into play when you ski or snowboard for the first time each year and make unconscious adjustments in your posture until you know your body feels "right." We are often unaware of the LTM codes that we employ. To get a sense of this, try the activity in Demonstration 6.2.

■■■DEMONSTRATION 6.2

Coding and Long-Term Memory

Take only a minute to do the following activity. In the margin of your paper, write down the names of all the U.S. states you can remember that end with the letter a. Did you notice that you're able to do this with only a little effort, even though you have never memorized state names by their last letter?

Typically after five or six names, people begin to have difficulty writing down any more states and they start to use different retrieval schemes. Many start to imagine an alphabetical list of states and visualize whether the last letter is an a (in fact, 20 of the 50 states end in a). Did you try to recall a rhyme of state names learned in childhood ("Fifty nifty United States . . .")? Many people use an imagery strategy by imagining they are flying over a map of the country reading the state names. Did you do this? The visual scheme helps people access the names. This demonstration provides an example of visual and acoustic coding. Sometimes people have equal access to both types of encoding.

Semantic Codes and Memory for Sentences Word meanings are stored as packages or collections of meaning elements. These meaning elements are called **semantic features**. For example, our mental representation for *man* is probably made up of the following semantic features: human, male, and adult.

When we listen to sentences or read a passage, it is the meaning of the words that is most important to us. It should not be surprising, then, that our memory for language-based events relies on semantics. This reliance on word meanings was illustrated in a task by Fillenbaum (1966), who asked students to listen to 96 sentences until the meaning of each sentence was clear. The researcher then showed students a set of sentences and asked them to pick the one from the set that they had heard before. For example, a student might hear a sentence such as "The door was open." Later on the student would be shown the quartet:

(a) The door was open.

(b) The door was closed.

(c) The door was not open.

(d) The door was not closed.

The student's job is to pick the sentence that matches the original. Of course, most of the time students are able to make the correct selection and choose option (a) in the above example. The important result, however, is the decision that students make when they pick the wrong sentence. Of the three incorrect sentences, (d) is the most physically dissimilar to (a): two of its five words do not match (a). Yet (d) is the only one that semantically matches the original and this is the sentence that students most often choose if they fail to correctly identify (a). This demonstrates that students are remembering the *gist* (the meaning of the original sentence) and using that as the basis for retrieval.

Semantic Codes and Memory for Sentences in a Paragraph Students use semantic cues even when sentences are embedded in a paragraph. In one study (Sachs, 1967) students first heard a paragraph like the one shown below and then were asked to judge whether a test sentence had appeared in the paragraph. Some of the students were tested immediately after the key sentence (a delay of 0 syllables), some students were tested 80 syllables later, and still others were tested 160 syllables after the key sentence. Here is one of the paragraphs used in the study:

> There is an interesting story about the telescope. In Holland, a man named Lippershey was an eyeglass maker. One day his children were playing with some lenses. They discovered that things seemed very close if two lenses were held about a foot apart. Lippershey began experimenting, and his "spyglass" attracted much attention. *He sent a letter about it to Galileo, the great Italian scientist.* [0 syllables] Galileo at once realized the importance of the discovery and set about to build an instrument of his own. He used an old organ pipe with one lens curved out and the other in. On the first clear night he pointed the glass toward the sky. He was amazed to find the empty dark spaces filled with brightly gleaming stars! [80 syllables] Night after night Galileo climbed to a high tower, sweeping the sky with his telescope. One night he saw Jupiter, and to his great surprise discovered near it three bright stars, two to the east and one to the west. On the next night, however, all were to the west. A few nights later there were four little stars. [160 syllables] (Sachs, 1967, p. 438)

Some test sentences that students had to respond to were verbatim matches with the original (e.g., *He sent a letter about it to Galileo, the great Italian scientist*); some

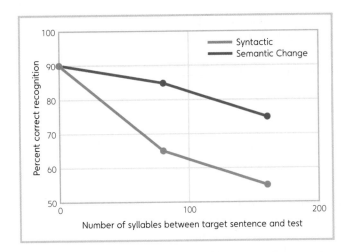

FIGURE 6.2 Memory for Sentences in a Paragraph Students were tested on their ability to detect changes in sentences they had read less than a minute before in a factual paragraph. Their ability to detect slight wording changes was at chance level with a delay of 80 syllables (approximately 27 seconds).

Source: Sachs, 1967

sentences were semantically dissimilar (e.g., *Galileo, the great Italian scientist, sent him a letter about it*); some were semantically similar but with slight wording changes (*A letter about it was sent to Galileo, the great Italian scientist*). The results are graphed in **FIGURE 6.2**. You should notice three patterns in the graph. First, students are good at detecting changes in meaning (semantic change). Second, they are not as good at detecting changes in sentence form (syntax only). Third, the ability of people to detect any change in the original sentences declines as the time between reading the passage and being tested increases. But this decline in accuracy is greater for syntactic change than it is for semantic change. Semantic features (*meaning*) last longest. Perhaps this is because meaning is the core of LTM storage.

SECTION SUMMARY ■

Characteristics of Long-Term Memory

This section describes four basic characteristics of LTM: capacity, duration, forgetting, and coding. It shows that there are no practical limits to how much information we can store in long-term memory. LTM duration is sometimes said to be like a permastore: a nearly lifelong retention of information, including facts and autobiographical episodes. Information that is fully integrated into LTM is retained for at least 50 years. We do not forget things once they are stored in LTM even though we may have difficulty retrieving them. These hard-to-retrieve facts only require effective retrieval cues to make them available. LTM contains a vast array of knowledge that is organized by basic codes. LTM stores information coded according to any dimension that we may experience, including sensory codes (visual, auditory, kinesthetic, etc.) and episodic and semantic codes. Semantic codes relate to the intrinsic meaning of an event or piece of information. The semantic features of words, sentences, and paragraphs are a major way humans code information in LTM. Effective retrieval cues make use of one or more of the multitude of codes.

■ ■

Metamemory

People often have a sense that they know something but are unable to recall it. This experience is called a **feeling of knowing** (e.g., Hart, 1965; Koriat, 2000) and relies on our **metamemory**: Our awareness of our memory system and what resides there. If you have ever watched game shows like *Jeopardy!* on television, you have probably seen contestants make a quick button press indicating that they can answer a question, after which they have difficulty producing an answer. Sometimes, the contestant who pressed the answer button first provides an incorrect answer. These are examples of metamemory at work. Contestants have a sense that they know the answer to a question, they press the button based on their feeling of knowing, then they must go about the difficult task of retrieving the correct information from LTM. To experience the feeling of knowing, try the activity in Demonstration 6.3.

•••DEMONSTRATION 6.3

Feeling of Knowing

In a typical feeling-of-knowing procedure (e.g., T. O. Nelson, Gerler, & Narens, 1984), participants look at a series of common knowledge questions to answer. Some questions they cannot answer, but are asked to indicate how strong their feeling of knowing is about the question. Before you attempt the second part of the demonstration (from the FACTRETRIEVAL computer program; Shimamura, Landwehr, & Nelson, 1981), look at the 10 questions below and rate them on a scale from 1 (*I couldn't possibly know this*) to 10 (*I know that I know it and can recognize the answer*).

1. Who painted the *Mona Lisa*?

2. What is the largest desert on earth?

3. What is the capital of New York?

4. In what country is Mount Everest?

5. Where is the Eiffel Tower?

6. What is the northernmost state in the continental United States?

7. Which continent has the most countries?

8. Where is the lowest spot in the continental United States?

9. Who is the primary author of the Declaration of Independence?

10. Who was the first person to walk on the moon?

For your next task, look at the recognition questions below and for each pair of possible answers in the parentheses, circle the one that you think is the answer to the question. Check the actual answers given at the end of the chapter.

1. Who painted the *Mona Lisa*? (Da Vinci, Galileo)

2. What is the largest desert on earth? (Gobi, Sahara)

3. What is the capital of New York? (New York City, Albany)

4. In what country is Mount Everest? (Tibet, Nepal)

5. Where is the Eiffel Tower? (Paris, London)

6. What is the northernmost state in the continental United States? (New Hampshire, Minnesota)

7. Which continent has the most countries? (Africa, Europe)

8. Where is the lowest spot in the continental United States? (Death Valley, Salton Sea)

9. Who is the primary author of the Declaration of Independence? (Jefferson, Hancock)

10. Who was the first person to walk on the moon? (Neil Armstrong, Buzz Aldrin)

You can analyze your own data by grouping the questions based on the rating of feeling of knowing that you gave them and indicating how many of each category that you answered correctly: high (7–10), medium (4–6), low (1–3).

If your data are similar to those typically found in psychology experiments, you got more of the high feeling-of-knowing group correct than those in the low group (e.g., Koriat, 2000). One of the amazing characteristics of LTM is that people seem to have good *metamemory*, an intuitive knowledge of what their memory contains.

People effectively use their metamemory to help decide whether a fact that doesn't immediately come to mind is worth a retrieval attempt or whether they should just give up and say, "I forgot" or "I don't know." Of course, sometimes the time to perform the search exceeds a deadline, such as with the overeager *Jeopardy!* contestant, and we fail to retrieve the fact. However, a key advantage of metamemory is that it allows us to judge whether we know something based on whether the topic seems familiar. This phenomenon is called *cue familiarity* (Aggleton & Brown, 1999; Eichenbaum, Otto, & Cohen, 1994; Mayes, 1992; Wickelgren, 1979).

We can get a sense of this when we are asked questions about which we are certain that we are ignorant. If you ask a typical American, "what is the name of the largest department store in Russia?" most will answer that they do not know and respond so rapidly that they must not be doing much of a search of their memory (Kolers & Palef, 1976). A flowchart of how this approach to retrieval from LTM works is shown in **FIGURE 6.3**. It shows that when asked a question, people rely on their metamemory to provide a quick yes/no feeling-of-knowing judgment. If the judgment is yes, then people proceed to search their memory.

Research shows that people tend to be correct in their feeling of knowing even when they can't give a correct answer right away (e.g., Hart, 1965; Schraw, 1995; Shimamura & Squire, 1986). When a possible target for the

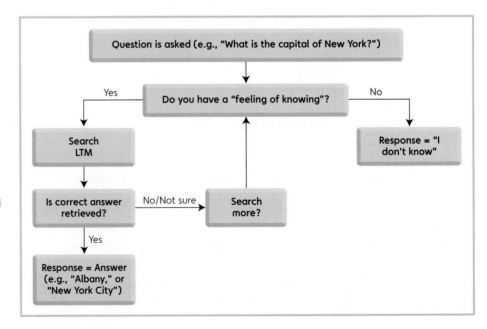

FIGURE 6.3 Feeling of Knowing When we are asked a factual question, a feeling of knowing motivates the search of our memories for an answer—even an incorrect one. The steps we take are described in this flowchart.

Source: Kolers & Palef, 1976

answer is encountered in LTM, people must judge whether it is correct or not. If they are confident that their response is correct, they respond with the information; if they are not, they evaluate whether to continue the search. Even people with **amnesia**, who have difficulty storing and retrieving new facts, make use of their metamemory and their feeling of knowing. One study of people with different forms of amnesia showed that their ability to recognize the answer to questions was predicted by their feeling of knowing (Shimamura & Squire, 1986).

Metamemory and feeling of knowing decline as we age (Perrotin, Isingrini, Souchay, Clarys, & Taconnat, 2006). One reason for this is that our metamemory and our ability to estimate what we know rely on the optimal functioning of our frontal lobes (e.g., Klein, German, Cosmides, & Rami, 2004), whose functioning also tends to decline with age (Raz, 2000; Salthouse, 1996; Souchay, Isingrini, & Espagnet, 2000).

Even with a well-functioning brain we can have a high feeling of knowing, but still find ourselves unable to retrieve the word we are searching for. When this happens, we often say that the word is on the tip of our tongue (e.g., A. S. Brown, 1991; R. Brown & McNeill, 1966; Smith, 1994). This experience is called the **tip-of-the-tongue (TOT) phenomenon**, the temporary inaccessibility of a word in memory. To get a sense of TOT, try the activity in Demonstration 6.4.

■■■DEMONSTRATION 6.4

The Tip-of-the-Tongue Phenomenon

Written below is a definition of a word. After you read the definition, write down the word that corresponds to it. If you write down the word right away, fine. If not, write down the words that come to mind along the way. Some will be relevant and some won't. Here is the definition (the correct word is written at the bottom of the page):

A navigational instrument used in measuring the angular distance of sun, moon, and stars at sea.[1]

Guess the word:

Words that come to mind:

Guess the first letter of the word:

Guess the number of syllables in the word:

When students know the word but can't quite recall it, they have a feeling-of-knowing experience and typically are able to write down a word similar in meaning to the target word. In fact, they can often guess the first letter and the number of syllables in the word (e.g., R. Brown & McNeill, 1966; Schacter, 2001). This shows that the word resides in LTM, but that the person simply can't retrieve it (Burke, MacKay, Worthley, & Wade, 1991). Try to find a name:

The first name of Scrooge in "A Christmas Carol" by Charles Dickens.[1]

---

[1] After completing the exercise, turn page for answers.

The TOT phenomenon may be universal. A study of 51 languages found that nearly 90% of them refer to TOT states. Terms for TOT vary across languages. In Korean, the term roughly translates as "sparkling at the end of the tongue," while in the Cheyenne language it can be translated as "I have lost it on my tongue" (Schwartz, 1999). Although it appears to be a universal state, TOT occurs more often in older adults than in younger ones (James & Burke, 2000).

The TOT phenomenon shows that sound-based codes play a role in word retrieval, just as semantic coding plays a role. For example, to help yourself when you experience TOT, try to generate words that you think may sound like the word you're searching for (James & Burke, 2000). This technique works with people who are sensitive to the sounds of words. However, children with language disabilities who have difficulty encoding the sound component of words are not helped by such a sound-based technique (Faust, Dimitrovsky, & Davidi, 1997).

SECTION SUMMARY ▪

Metamemory

Retrieval depends greatly on our willingness to continue the search for the missing information. This search is controlled by our metamemory, which conveys a sense of how our personal LTM works and what it contains. Metamemory processes are able to communicate a feeling of knowing. When the feeling is weak, we decide that our memory does not contain a sought-for fact; as a result, we do not pursue the missing fact. When the feeling of knowing is high, we pursue the search. People often experience what is called the tip-of-the-tongue phenomenon, in which they have difficulty retrieving a word about which they have a high feeling of knowing: It's on the tip of their tongue.

▪ ▪

Encoding Specificity

Our ability to retrieve information from long-term memory is affected by whether the questions we are asked match the way we have coded the information in LTM. As an illustration of how this works, Barclay, Bransford, Franks, McCarrel, and Nitsch (1974) showed two groups of students a series of sentences. One group saw sentences like the first one, and the second group saw sentences like the second one (there were many more sentences than just these).

(a) *The man tuned the piano.*

(b) *The man lifted the piano.*

Notice that (a) implies the idea of music, whereas (b) implies heaviness or weight. Later on, the students were asked to recall the piano sentences, but they were given different cues to help them. Students given the cue "something heavy" were 3 times more likely to retrieve (b) than students who were given the cue "something melodious." This illustrates that the way you think about information when you store it has an effect on what sort of retrieval cue will be useful in

---

[1] Answers from Demonstration 6.4: sextant; Ebenezer

helping you recall the information. This phenomenon is **encoding specificity**: A retrieval cue is an effective reminder when it helps re-create the specific way an experience was initially encoded (Tulving & Thomson, 1973). Of course, there is no guarantee that a cue will be equally helpful to everyone. People may experience and therefore code the same event very differently from the way others experience the same event.

Psychologists say that each of us has our own unique encoding of events: We have our own **subjective organization** (Chaffin & Imreh, 2002; Johnson, Hashtroudi, & Lindsay, 1993; Tulving, 1962). Suppose your friend is trying to remember the name of a stranger he met at a party. You try to help by asking questions about what the person looks like. These cues won't be helpful if your friend's encoding of the person is in terms of occupation, college, or regional accent rather than appearance.

The concepts of encoding specificity and subjective organization are best illustrated in a laboratory study by Tulving and Osler (1968), who had four groups of students learn a list of words for later testing. Two of the groups were given poor cues while they were learning the words. For example, one of the nouns was *ground* and the cue was *cold*. It is a poor cue because hearing it does not make you think of the target word (*ground*). The other two groups were given no cues. A 2 × 2 table (**TABLE 6.2**) describes the design of the study.

Half of the students learned the list without a cue and half with a cue. Half of the students were reminded of the cue at the time of test and half were not. The results were surprising. The groups with the best recall were Groups I and IV. Why is this? Group I had lots of help in recalling the list of words. They were given the cues to help them encode the material, and then at test time they were given the cues to help them retrieve the material. In terms of the ideas that introduced this section, the cues ensured a specific encoding of the materials and the cues at recall ensured that the retrieval cues were mentally available and were specific to the encoding—even though the cues would normally be considered mediocre. So it is easy to see why the participants readily recalled the material.

In contrast, the students in Group IV were left to their own devices. They did as we normally do: They studied the material carefully and tried to think of their own cues to help them learn the list. These students used subjective organization at learning and retrieval. They were not given confusing information at retrieval and therefore did well.

What about the students in the other groups? Those in Group III used a personalized, subjective organization when they learned the list. Unfortunately, the cues provided at recall were inconsistent with the subjective ones used at storage; the students in Group III had difficulty finding the list in memory because the retrieval cues were inconsistent with the encoding cues. Group II's participants were given special cues at encoding, but those cues were not provided at recall to help them remember the list. Groups II and III showed the poorest recall.

TABLE 6.2

Importance of Subjective Organization

Condition	Cue at Test	No Cue at Test
Cue at Learning	Group I (LT)	Group II (LO)
No Cue at Learning	Group III (OT)	Group IV (OO)

Note. LT = cue at learning, cue at test; LO = cue at learning, no cue at test; OT = no cue at learning, cue at test; OO = no cue at learning, no cue at test.

The educational implications of this research are straightforward whether you are a student or a teacher:

1. When you learn a set of materials, create or provide an organizational structure into which the material fits. If the material does not lend itself naturally to a particular structure, create one of your own and stick with it.

2. When you prepare to take an exam, study the materials in a way that reminds you of the material's organizational scheme.

Context-Dependent Retrieval

Psychologists have known for a long time that when we learn something for the first time, we associate the entire environment with our learning experience (Guthrie, 1935). We also know that the context can be an effective cue for retrieving information. To demonstrate this, three groups of students were asked to learn 80 words in a distinctive room and then were given a recognition test on some of the words (so that they would think that this phase of the experiment was over and wouldn't rehearse the words during the next 24 hours). The next day all three groups were given a surprise recall test. Group I was tested in the same room and recalled 22% of the list; Group II was tested in a different room and recalled 15% of the list; and Group III was tested in a different room but was told to first think about the distinctive room. Group III's results were nearly identical to Group I's results. Group III recalled 21.5% of the list (Smith, 1979).

This photo of the September 11, 2001 attacks on the World Trade Center is almost iconic: All who were there that day or who saw the TV coverage will instantly recall the moment. Researchers have found that many people were so traumatized that they unwillingly relived earlier traumatic events in their lives.

AP Photo/Carmen Taylor, File

The importance of context as a cue for retrieval has been shown in many studies where the researchers compare learning and testing either under the same or different conditions: underwater or on land (e.g., Godden & Baddeley, 1975); in a room smelling of chocolate or in a room with a different odor (Schab, 1990). The results of these studies are consistent with the concept of encoding specificity: The elements that are present when we encode items can be effectively used when we want to retrieve those items.

State-Dependent Retrieval: Your Mental State As Context

Researchers have found that after the September 11, 2001 terrorist attacks, many people were so traumatized that they unwillingly relived earlier traumatic events in their lives (e.g., Huber et al., 2001). In this case, the emotional response to an event served as the retrieval cue for earlier events.

Using a variety of techniques to elicit particular emotional states in volunteers, cognitive researchers have found that recall of a list of words is best when the mood at the time of retrieval is the same as the mood at encoding (e.g., J. C. Bartlett & Santrock, 1979; Bower, 1981). This holds true not only in tasks related to memory for lists of words, but also in those related to memory for life events. For example, Gilligan and Bower (1983, 1984) asked participants to record in a diary for a week, rating their experiences as either positive or negative. The participants were later hypnotized to feel happy or sad. Under post-hypnotic suggestion, they were asked to recall the events in their diary. Events rated happy in their diary were more likely to be recalled when the participant was in an induced happy state than in an induced sad state. The opposite was found for the sad events. Thus, even our moods can affect encoding specificity and affect our ability to retrieve memories (e.g., Bower & Forgas, 2000).

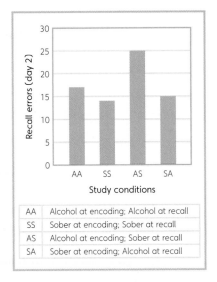

AA	Alcohol at encoding; Alcohol at recall
SS	Sober at encoding; Sober at recall
AS	Alcohol at encoding; Sober at recall
SA	Sober at encoding; Alcohol at recall

FIGURE 6.4 State-Dependent Memory Four groups of medical students learned and were tested on their memory for sentences. They were either sober or intoxicated. The sober learners (SS and SA in the figure) made fewer errors than the intoxicated ones (AA and AS). Students made fewer errors when they tried to freely recall information under the same body–state conditions as the original learning (AA and SS).

Source: Goodwin, Powell, Bremer, Hoine, & Stern, 1969

State-Dependent Retrieval: Your Physical State As Context

Your mood is one aspect of your body's physical state. The process of encoding specificity also applies to how your body is functioning, such as when you are drunk or sober. To examine this aspect of state dependency, 48 male medical students performed memory tasks either while sober (they had a soft drink) or intoxicated with alcohol (8–10 ounces of 80-proof vodka). In one task, the students memorized four 5-word sentences. You can see the results in **FIGURE 6.4** (Goodwin, Powell, Bremer, Hoine, & Stern, 1969). There are two major findings. First, as you might have anticipated, sober learners (SS and SA in the figure) recalled more than intoxicated learners (AA and AS in the figure). Second, performance was better when they tried to freely recall information under the same body-state conditions as the original learning (AA and SS). This is called **state-dependent learning**. This principle predicts the surprising finding that if one learns a set of facts while intoxicated, there is no advantage in trying to recall the information when sober. Notice, however, that learning when sober has an advantage over learning when intoxicated. State-dependent learning has been supported in research using a host of other drugs, such as nicotine, that have effects on the mind and body (e.g., Peters & McGee, 1982; Warburton, Skinner, & Martin, 2001).

SECTION SUMMARY ▪
Encoding Specificity
How we code the facts and experiences of our lives has an effect on our ability to retrieve those facts and experiences when we are asked a question about them. Encoding specificity is the process that mediates between the question we are asked and the way we have coded the relevant information. People vary widely

in how they encode material; this is called subjective organization. If the nature of the question fits with the coding of the information in our memory, then our answer will be more accurate and our ability to retrieve the information will be more rapid. The full context of our experiences, including our emotional and physical states, is part of the encoding in memory and can serve as retrieval cues for successful recall.

Autobiographical Memory

Imagine that you are getting ready to leave your house one morning and you have forgotten where you put your keys the day before. One way to retrieve your keys would be to walk around your home looking for them. Another option would be to travel back mentally in time to the moment you last recall having your keys and then imagine where you went after that point in time (e.g., Tulving, 2002). This deliberate, episodically based retrieval process taps into your **autobiographical memory**, which is memory of your personal past experiences: your retrospective memory (Tulving, 1972, 1984) of events that have occurred to you in your life. As we learned earlier, episodic memory also includes prospective memory, to allow you to project into the future and expect certain events to happen. The key to autobiographical memory is that you are the central actor, the coordinating element that ties the episodes together. In a sense, your personal identity, your sense of self, is the common thread that connects the events (e.g., Klein, Loftus, & Kihlstrom, 2002).

According to a recent theory (Klein et al., 2004), we must possess three essential elements in order to have a fully functioning autobiographical memory:

1. A capacity for self-reflection (the ability to reflect on your own mental states);

2. A sense of personal ownership (the feeling that your thoughts and acts belong to you);

3. The ability to think about time as an unfolding of personal happenings centered around yourself.

In addition to our sense of self, our autobiographical recollections reflect a combination of episodic and semantic elements (e.g., Rajaram, 1993; Squire, 1992; for a different point of view, see Glenberg, 1997). For example, when you use semantic memory you recall that 1/4 is a smaller quantity than 1/2. When you use episodic memory you recall that your second-grade teacher illustrated the difference in fractions by asking you whether you wanted 1/4 or 1/2 of a candy bar. The joint activation that occurs when recalling facts and simultaneously recalling the experience of learning those facts illustrates that we encode multiple aspects of events in our lives when we store them in LTM.

To get a sense of the interplay between episodic and semantic memories in autobiographical memory, consider the case of people with amnesia (loss of memory). There are two broad categories of amnesia. One is *retrograde amnesia*, where people cannot recall events or facts in their lives that occurred prior to some critical event that affected their brain (e.g., an accident or a stroke). The other is *anterograde amnesia*, a failure to add to memory after a critical event. Episodic and semantic memories have been documented in R. S., a man whose amnesia resulted from stroke damage to a part of his brain called the hippocampus. R. S. has considerable retrograde amnesia (he can't recall most of his past) and he has nearly total anterograde amnesia (he can't remember new events). A clinician who studied R. S. described his memory deficits this way:

> R. S.'s knowledge of the state of affairs in his own life seems not to have been updated since his stroke. He believes that he, and his wife and children are 13 years younger than they really are, and that his mother is still alive. He does not know what year or season it is and, when asked, states that he believes his memory to be "about the same" as his neurologist's (Kitchener, Hodges, & McCarthy, 1998, p. 1314).

Researchers assessed R. S.'s episodic memory with an *autobiographical memory interview* (Kopelman, Wilson, & Baddeley, 1989). This assessment collects examples of information from three life periods: childhood, early adulthood, and the past few years. There are two categories of facts required in the test: semantic facts (e.g., names of friends, teachers, addresses) and personal episodes (e.g., describe an incident that occurred in the period before you went to school). The results of the interview showed that R. S. has lost episodic memory covering his entire lifetime, including events that happened prior to his stroke. R. S. can accurately identify events that have occurred in his life, but can give no information about them other than their occurrence.

However, R. S.'s semantic memory system has not been totally obliterated: He has been able to acquire some factual knowledge since his stroke. He can recognize a few famous faces and knows some current events. R. S.'s ability to recognize some people and events suggests that episodic and semantic memories are somewhat independent.

Although true autobiographical memory requires memory for episodes, it is possible for people to lead productive lives without episodic memory. For example, three young people (12–19 years old) suffered damage to their hippocampi and other brain areas when they were very young children (Vargha-Khadem et al., 1997). As a result, they cannot form episodic memories for any life events, yet they have normal IQs, perform well in school, and show good vocabulary development and language comprehension. Their semantic memories are functioning well.

Infantile (or Childhood) Amnesia

Although our life experiences generally appear to be part of LTM's permastore, children have difficulty recalling experiences during their first 2–3 years of life. This difficulty in retrieving autobiographical memory of early childhood

FIGURE 6.5 Percent Recall Scores As a Function of Age
College students showed infantile amnesia; they had difficulty recalling events that occurred when they were 2 years old or younger. In contrast, they had accurate recall of events that occurred when they were 4 or 5 years old. For some events, like going to the hospital or someone dying, they had no knowledge at all.

Source: Usher & Neisser, 1993

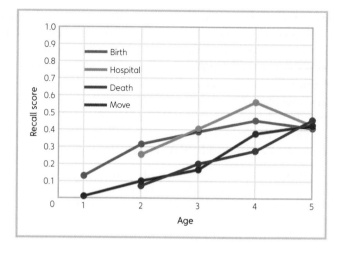

experience is referred to as **infantile (or childhood) amnesia** and was first described as a symptom of clinical processes by Sigmund Freud (1901/1974), the 19th- and early 20th-century clinical psychologist. A steep drop in recall accuracy typically exists for events that occurred prior to 3 years of age (Crovitz & Shiffman, 1974; Kihlstrom & Harackiewicz, 1982; Rubin, Wetzler, & Nebes, 1986). For example, college students were asked specific questions about four targeted events: birth of a sibling, a hospitalization, death of a family member, or a family move to a new home. For the birth of a sibling, they were asked: "Who told you that your mother was going to the hospital?". The findings are shown in **FIGURE 6.5**. The graph shows that students could not recall much of anything if the event occurred prior to the age of 2. In contrast, they had accurate recall if the events occurred when they were 4 or 5 (Usher & Neisser, 1993).

Infantile amnesia may be the result of three cognitively related factors. First, the brain mechanisms that are needed to maintain information over many years of a lifetime may not be sufficiently mature in the first 2 years of life (Morcom, Good, Frackowiak, & Rugg, 2003; Nadel & Zola-Morgan, 1984; C. Nelson, 1995), even though memory over a shorter period of days or weeks has already developed.

A second factor contributing to infantile amnesia is that children do not immediately pay attention to the context of their life events: the *when* and *where* of an event. This is common in cases of negative memories, which tend not to be recalled as early as positive memories (e.g., Joseph, 2003; Usher & Neisser, 1993). A child may actually retain the knowledge of an event but be unable to contextualize it in time and space, and therefore be unable to freely recall it.

A third factor, also related to the loss of contextual information, is the gap between a person's current worldview and his or her encoding of the original event in infancy. This is an application of the concept of encoding specificity.

As we grow older we learn to communicate our episodic and semantic events through narrative. The narrative format is not present in the encoding of infants and therefore retrieval of nonnarrative encoded events is difficult. Pillemer and White (1989) proposed that the early retention of actions and imitative sequences acquired by infants relies on nonverbal, image-based memories. In contrast, the development of narrative memories takes time and is related to language ability. Because people remember themselves as the central character of their own narrative memories, infantile amnesia may indirectly reflect the late development of the concept of the self (Howe & Courage, 1993).

Although the period of infantile amnesia marks a time in our lives that we cannot describe to ourselves and others, it does not mean that nothing is retained in our memories. This is the period in our lives when we learn to walk and talk, and discover that cookies taste good. This was illustrated in a simple study (e.g., Rovee, & Rovee, 1969; Rovee-Collier, 1999): Infants (2–3 months old) had a silk cord attached to their foot that was connected to an overhead mobile above their crib. Whenever the infants kicked, the mobile would move and make a novel sound. Even 24 hours later, the infants kicked more in the presence of the mobile than when it was not there. They were capable of learning and retaining information in memory for a day—a long period of time for a newborn. Infancy represents a period of fast learning even though we have difficulty recalling the episodes of that learning (Rovee-Collier & Giles, 2010).

Reminiscence Bump

When older adults look back on their lives and recollect autobiographically relevant events, their recollections are organized by periods in their lives (e.g., Fitzgerald, 1988, 1996; Hyland & Ackerman, 1988; Jansari & Parkin, 1996; Rubin & Schulkind, 1997a, 1997b). For example, when people in their 50s are given cue words and asked to recall significant events in their lives related to those words, the number of recollections of life events has a strange distribution. They can recall a great number of memories for the last few years (age 40–50) as one might expect. However, beyond that, the distribution of memories over decades has an inverted U-shaped function. People recall the largest number of memories for events that occurred between the ages of 10 and 25. The top of this inverted U is called a **reminiscence bump** (Rubin et al., 1986). This heightened recall includes autobiographical events as well as memories of favorite films, places visited, and other aspects of life (Rubin, Rahhal, & Poon, 1998).

In a study using volunteers from the Internet (Janssen, Chessa, & Murre, 2005; Janssen & Murre, 2008), researchers showed that the true top of the bump probably averages around 15 years of age: American women showed a bump at age 13 and men at age 17. The reminiscence bump was apparent for all research participants regardless of age or educational background. Moreover, the bump is evident whether researchers are asking about episodes in a person's life or factual information related to specific periods in a person's life (Rybash, Monaghan, & Brynn, 1999).

FIGURE 6.6 Reminiscence Bump Across Cultures
Participants were given 1 hour to recall as many episodes in their lives as they could and when they occurred. A reminiscence bump at around the age of 15 to 20 is shown in the memories of people from many cultures.

Source: Conway, Wang, Hanyu, & Hague, 2005

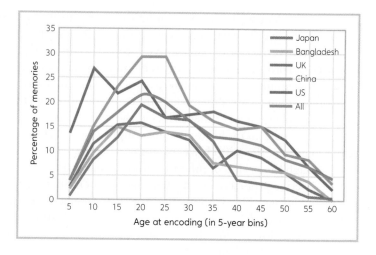

The reminiscence bump in LTM is related to what we learned about the serial position effect in Chapter 5. You may recall that memory for items at the beginning of a list or paragraph is greater than for items in the middle of the list. The characteristic reminiscence bump occurs during the second decade of one's life, a period that is typically filled with firsts, such as getting a driver's license, leaving home, and starting a full-time job. Indeed, there are so many firsts that this period can be construed as the beginning of adulthood. It is the beginning of one's "life list" and the serial position effect tells us that recall would be the greatest for this period. Because the serial position effect is a universal phenomenon in human cognition, we should anticipate that the reminiscence bump would also be universal. The results of a study of autobiographical memories in Japan, China, Bangladesh, England, and the United States are shown in **FIGURE 6.6**. Participants were given one hour to recall episodes in their lives and indicate when they occurred. The reminiscence bump is manifested in the memories of people from all of these cultures (Conway, Wang, Hanyu, & Hague, 2005).

Episodic Codes and Flashbulb Memories

Most people believe that under special circumstances they are able to form detailed, perfect memories of a distinctive, surprising, or significant event. Such memories are called **flashbulb memories** (R. Brown & Kulik, 1977) because they are experienced as if someone had taken a photograph of an event and stored it away in LTM. People describe flashbulb memories as highly detailed and etched in their memory, seemingly forever. Recent research, however, suggests that these reports are not always as accurate as they seem.

On September 11, 2001, terrorists crashed jetliners into the World Trade Center in New York City, the Pentagon in Washington, DC, and a field in Pennsylvania, killing nearly 3,000 people. That deadly event provided the most recent opportunity for a series of studies on flashbulb memories. In one study

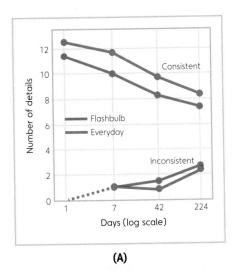

(A)

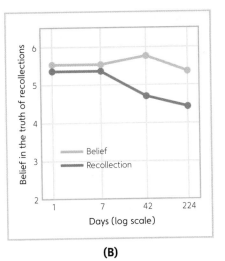

(B)

FIGURE 6.7 Accuracy of Memory: Flashbulb and Ordinary Events (A) University students answered questions about the 9/11 attacks or an everyday event on September 12 and many weeks after. There was no special memory for the flashbulb event: The effect of time had the same impact on the amount retained from flashbulb and everyday memories. However, (B) shows that the students were most confident in the accuracy of their flashbulb memories.

Source: Talarico & Rubin, 2003

(Talarico & Rubin, 2003) 54 university students answered questions about the 9/11 attacks on September 12, as well as an everyday event (of the participants' own choosing) that occurred before the attacks. Students were tested a second time either 1 week, 6 weeks, or 32 weeks later for recollections of both the 9/11 and ordinary events. The results in **FIGURE 6.7A** reveal that recollections were similar for both flashbulb and ordinary memories. Notice that the effect of time was the same for both the flashbulb and ordinary memories. The effect of time also had the same impact on the number of elements retained (consistent recollections) and the number of incorrect events recalled (inconsistent recollections) on both types of memories. Despite these findings, **FIGURE 6.7B** shows that students are confident that their recollections of 9/11 are more accurate than for everyday events. Taken together, these findings suggest that there is no special accuracy related to memories of these important historic events; there is only a *sense* of accuracy because the flashbulb event was so emotional and important. Indeed, it may be that the higher belief in the accuracy of a flashbulb memory is because it is a significant event and unlike any other event in a person's life (Talarico & Rubin, 2009).

One characteristic of flashbulb memories is their intense, emotional component. You might expect that the greater the emotional experience, the better your autobiographical memory would be for these events. To see if this is true, nearly 2 months after 9/11, three groups of students completed a questionnaire about their memory for the events of 9/11 and for their autobiographical recollections (e.g., where they were, how they received the news, etc.; Pezdek, 2003). The students were located at three distances from the East Coast: New York, California, and Hawaii. As you would expect, the New Yorkers, so close to the events, expressed the most emotional reaction and were the most factually correct about the events. However, you would also expect that if flashbulb memories were substantially different from ordinary memories, then the students' flashbulb recollections should be best for the New Yorkers and poorest for the Hawaiians and Californians. This was not the case. The New York participants had the least accurate of the flashbulb elements (where they were and how they felt). Once again, this tells us that flashbulb memories are not like mental photographs of an episode in your life, but are similar to other intense emotional experiences—some accurately recalled and some not.

Prospective Memory

Just as our autobiographical memory allows us to reminisce and mentally travel into the past, it is also relied on to aid us in doing things in the future: remembering to take our medicine at a certain time each day, paying our bills before a deadline, or taking cupcakes out of the oven before they burn. All of these actions rely on prospective memory: remembering to carry out a future action at the right time (Harris, 1984; Meacham, 1982; Meacham & Singer, 1977; Winograd, 1988). Prospective memory is a form of autobiographical memory projected into the future.

Prospective memory is not an isolated system; it interacts with retrospective elements of autobiographical memory. People are constantly retrieving from the past in order to carry out activities in the future: knowing that you need to go to class this morning isn't sufficient to get you there. You have to retrieve stored information such as the time your class begins, the building it is in, and the classroom's location. Prospective memory not only includes retrospective memory, but also planning and remembering when an event should occur. When you look at a bottle of medicine, you may remember what it is, but not what you are supposed to do with it (e.g., Kvavilashvili, 1987; McDaniel & Einstein, 1993). It has been estimated that nearly half of our everyday memory failures are failures of prospective memory rather than the mere forgetting of a fact (Crovitz & Daniel, 1984).

Having a good retrospective memory for facts does not mean that you will have a good prospective memory. This was shown in a simple study with undergraduates who were given a list of unrelated words that they had to recall immediately after reading the list. The best quarter and the poorest quarter of the students on the list memory task were then given a prospective memory task that simulated the burden of having to take medications at certain times. They were asked to carry a small box with them for a week and to press a button on the box each day at 8:30 a.m., 1:00 p.m., 5:30 p.m., and 10:00 p.m. Students who were best on the list memory task were poorest at the prospective memory task and those who were worst on the list task were best on the prospective memory task (Wilkins & Baddeley, 1978). The authors of the study referred to this as the "absent-minded professor effect." The critical factor for college-age people is the kind of tasks that they are engaged in while trying to remember to perform the prospective task. The good list learners are making personal demands on their working memory continuously throughout the day and may have few resources left over for the prospective task, while the poor list learners are not making as many demands on working memory and have plenty of resources available to remember to press a button in the prospective task (Marsh & Hicks, 1998).

Sometimes we believe that people have poor prospective memory, when in fact they have not adequately encoded the initial, explicit information. Take the case of searches for missing children that rely on photos placed at supermarket exits. People tend not to be able to identify the faces of the children later on. However, Lampinen, Arnal, and Hicks (2009) found that people are only glancing at the photos and are not deeply encoding the faces or the listed characteristics of the children. They show poor prospective memory because their initial encoding is poor.

Prospective memory develops quite early in life. To explore how early, Guajardo and Best (2000) asked 3- to 5-year-olds to watch a computer screen that showed interesting pictures. The children were told to press the space bar when a picture of a house appeared. The prospective aspect of the task was that they were supposed to ask for a sticker and then close the door when the task was done. There was a definite difference in prospective memory for the two different ages: 83% of the 5-year-olds asked for the sticker, but only 52% of the 3-year-olds remembered to ask for a sticker. Seventy-five percent of the 5-year-olds remembered to close the door without prompting, but only 25% of the 3-year-olds did so. Boys and girls in each age group performed similarly on the prospective memory task. These findings indicate that even very young children are sensitive to event-related tasks that need to be performed in the future and that prospective memory improves with age. The next section describes deficits that come as people age.

The Neuropsychology of Autobiographical Memory

A puzzling condition exists in case histories of people with brain damage and amnesia. Some people have retrograde amnesia for autobiographical information, yet they are still able to retrieve semantic information. And, as mentioned before, there are people who have anterograde amnesia and thus are not able to store new episodes in their life, but are able to store some factual and language-based information. These findings suggest that semantic and episodic information are maintained in separate systems and that they involve different areas of the brain. Damage to one system does not necessarily damage the other.

Episodic Memory The neuroscientific findings concerning episodic memory are summarized in the hemispheric encoding–retrieval asymmetry (HERA) model (e.g., Tulving, Kapur, Craik, Moscovitsch, & Houle, 1994). The areas of the brain related to the HERA model's principles are shown in red (indicating activation; Habib, Nyberg, & Tulving, 2003) in **FIGURE 6.8**.

Let us start by comparing the left, prefrontal cortex in the figure on the left with the right prefrontal cortex in the right picture. It suggests that the left hemisphere is more involved than the right hemisphere in *encoding*

FIGURE 6.8 HERA Model The frontal lobes play an important part in storage and retrieval of episodic events. Encoding information into episodic memory activates the left hemisphere more than the right, while retrieval of episodic memories activates the right hemisphere more than the left. Other areas of the brain are involved, but this asymmetry shows that encoding and retrieval are separable processes.

Reprinted from *Trends in Cognitive Sciences, 7*, Habib, R., Nyberg, L., and Tulving, E. Hemispheric asymmetries of memory: the HERA model revisited. 241–245, 2003, with permission from Elsevier.

Left (encoding)   Right (retrieval)

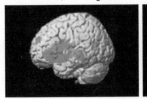 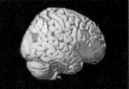

information into episodic memory. Damage to the left hemisphere tends to result in more difficulty than damage to the right hemisphere in remembering new episodes that occur after the damage takes place (anterograde amnesia)—the events do not get encoded. What about retrieval from episodic memory? The right prefrontal cortex (shown in the right photo) is more involved in *retrieval* from episodic memory than the left hemisphere. Damage to the right hemisphere leads to more retrieval difficulty for events that occurred before the damage (retrograde amnesia). We must not assume, of course, that these distinct areas are sitting idly by until episodic information is presented. Every brain area has a multitude of functions. Nor should we assume that these are the only areas involved in autobiographical memory. What the data do suggest, however, is that autobiographical memory is a biologically based system of long-term memory.

Prospective Memory Older adults generally perform more poorly on prospective memory tasks than do younger adults. To explain this, it is important to understand that there are two kinds of prospective situations: those where you are reminded by external factors to do the task (*event-based situations*), such as turn off the oven when the buzzer sounds, and those where actions are self-initiated (*time-based situations*), such as take the pill at 5:00 p.m. (Balota, Dolan, & Ducheck, 2000; Einstein & McDaniel, 1990). The primary effect of age on prospective memory is found in relation to time-based situations (Einstein, McDaniel, Richardson, Guynn, & Cunfer, 1995; Harris & Wilkins, 1982).

Time-based and event-based prospective memories are associated with activity in the frontal lobes (e.g., Maujean, Sum, & McQueen, 2003; McDaniel, Glisky, Rubin, Guynn, & Routhieaux, 1999). However, because the attentional demands are much greater for time-based prospective memory, there is a greater reliance on effective frontal lobe functioning (Marsh & Hicks, 1998). Therefore, we should expect that the development of the frontal lobes after birth would be associated with improvement in prospective memory. Guajardo and Best's (2000) study indicated that 5-year-olds performed better on a prospective memory task than 3-year-olds. To examine whether children show a different pattern of prospective memory from adults, 7- to 12-year-olds were tested for prospective memory using a video game with racing cars. The prospective memory task was a requirement that the children monitor their gas levels. If they ran out of fuel they would lose all their points. In order to monitor the fuel level, children could press a button to display the fuel level for 3 seconds. The older children did a better job of monitoring their fuel than the younger children, showing once again that prospective memory develops with age. This improvement of prospective memory is also associated with the physiological development of the frontal lobes (Kerns, 2000). In contrast, deterioration of the frontal lobes is associated with a decline in time-based prospective memory, which is typical as adults age.

The Neuropsychology of Semantic Memory

As we noted before, the major division within explicit/declarative memory is between episodic and semantic memory. The importance of the frontal lobes for episodic and autobiographical memory as well as, to a lesser extent, for semantic memory was described in the previous section. This section describes the temporal lobes of the brain and the devastating effects that damage here has on semantic as well as episodic memory.

Amnesia and the Hippocampal Region The temporal lobe of each hemisphere of the brain contains a structure called the *hippocampus* (see **FIGURE 6.9A**). When both hippocampi are not working properly, people experience amnesia. The importance of the hippocampus for memory storage has been known for at least 50 years as a result of the case of H. M., who died in 2008 after providing cognitive researchers with an invaluable understanding of how the brain is able to learn and store new information. H. M., whose real name was Henry Molaison (pictured in **FIGURE 6.9B**), had anterograde amnesia. Although his working memory functioned normally, he was unable to acquire new explicit memory from the age of 27 until the end of his life.

During his early life H. M. suffered from epileptic seizures that began when he was 10, perhaps as the result of a bicycle accident at age 9. In 1953, by the time he was 27, H. M. suffered frequent grand mal seizures. To alleviate these, Dr. William Scoville employed a new procedure (pioneered by W. Penfield) to remove a portion of the temporal lobe that contained the areas where the seizures began. As a result of that surgery, the right- and left-hemisphere hippocampal structures (as well as other structures; Corkin, Amaral, Gonzalez, Johnson, & Hyman, 1997) were removed. The surgery was successful in significantly reducing the epileptic seizures. H. M.'s personality seemed to be the same after

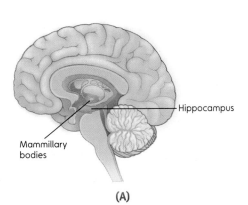

(A)   (B)

FIGURE 6.9 Temporal Lobes and Structures (A) The temporal lobe of each hemisphere of the brain contains a structure called the hippocampus. When both hippocampi are not working properly, people experience amnesia. (B) When he was 27, H. M. (Henry Molaison) underwent surgery to remove a portion of the temporal lobe that contained the areas where his epileptic seizures began. The right- and left-hemisphere hippocampal structures as well as other structures were removed. The surgery was successful in significantly reducing H. M.'s epileptic seizures, but he became profoundly amnesic: Until the end of his life, H. M. could not remember events that occurred after his surgery or people that he had met.

© Suzanne Corkin, used with permission of The Wylie Agency, LLC

surgery and he maintained his enthusiasm for detective stories and solving crossword puzzles. His IQ even increased 8 points (Milner, Corkin, & Teuber, 1968).

What made his situation famous is that he became profoundly amnesic: He could not remember events that occurred after his surgery or people that he had met. He could not remember the new home he was moved to after the surgery or even its floor plan. H. M.'s style of speech and words were basically frozen in the 1950s. He acquired a few new words after his surgery, such as *ayatollah* and *rock 'n roll* (Gabrieli, Cohen, & Corkin, 1988), but his semantic system was otherwise frozen in time. He would repeat stories endlessly unless redirected. He maintained the belief that Harry Truman was president of the United States and that he was about 30 years old until he died. H. M. volunteered a sense of his experience to neuropsychologist Brenda Milner:

> Every day is alone in itself, whatever enjoyment I've had, and whatever sorrow I've had. Right now, I'm wondering. Have I done or said anything amiss? You see, at this moment everything looks clear to me, but what happened just before? That's what worries me. It's like waking from a dream; I just don't remember. (Milner, 1970, p. 37)

H. M. lived in a care facility in the Hartford, Connecticut area, not far from where he grew up. Although he was told frequently about his great contribution to our understanding of human memory, he was unable to retain that knowledge. Until his death, he remained an amiable and considerate person and the people who worked with him enjoyed his company.

H. M. and other people with similar lesions (e.g., Squire, 1992) are able to demonstrate implicit learning. For example, they are able to show improvement on the Gollin Test (mentioned previously) and they are able to learn to recognize patterns and to follow simple procedures. They are also able to do the mirror tracing task (Milner, 1962, 1965) in which participants trace the outline of a star, but instead of looking straight at it, they can only look at the star and their hand reflected in a mirror (see **FIGURE 6.10**). This is a difficult task to master. The figure shows the learning curve of H. M. Notice that all participants rapidly

FIGURE 6.10 Mirror Tracing Task (A) People with amnesia (like H. M.) are able to demonstrate implicit learning in the mirror tracing task (Milner, 1962, 1965), where they must trace the outline of a star by looking at their hand reflected in a mirror. (B) The learning curve of H. M. is the same as a control participant without amnesia. Notice that both participants rapidly reduced the number of errors on this task and eventually made few errors.

Source: Milner, Squire, & Kandel, 1998

(A)

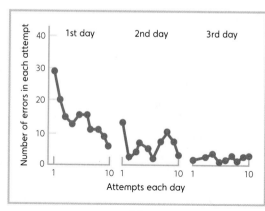

(B)

reduced the number of errors on this task until, on the 30th trial, H. M. and the control group were highly accurate and showed nearly identical performance. The only difference between the participants without amnesia and H. M. is that H. M. could not recall ever performing the task!

Case histories such as H. M.'s provide evidence that the hippocampus plays an important role in the storage of new information and may be the command center that links elements of memory together (e.g., Milner, Squire, & Kandel, 1998). To gain a clearer understanding of this, consider the complexity of your experiences. When you take a trip on an airplane, your memory is perceptual (the smell and noise of the plane, the appearance of the person sitting next to you), semantic (the reason for the trip), and episodic (the trip's emotional importance) to name just a few elements. These separate components are stored in different areas of the brain relevant to the dimension in question. The hippocampus ties these disparate elements together to make a coherent memory (Damasio, 1989; Schacter, 1996). Once that job is performed, other areas of the brain are used for retrieval. If the hippocampus is damaged so that new memories are not consolidated, there is no way for other brain areas to retrieve those events.

People with amnesia, however, are able to recognize patterns, such as those on the Gollin Test, because their implicit/pattern learning systems are intact, even though their hippocampus-based episodic systems are not. In addition, although people with amnesia have damaged hippocampi, the surrounding tissue, the *parahippocampal region*, is still functioning. Activity in the parahippocampal region is associated with a feeling of knowing as discussed with regard to metamemory and cue familiarity (Meudell, Mayes, Ostergaard, & Pickering, 1985).

Korsakoff's Syndrome and the Mammillary Bodies   One of the more frequently occurring amnesias is not a result of surgery, but is largely (though not exclusively) the consequence of malnutrition caused by excessive alcohol consumption. **Korsakoff's syndrome** (Korsakoff, 1889/1955) is associated with damage to the temporal lobes, specifically to a cluster of cells called the *mammillary bodies* as well as, in most cases, to the *mammillothalamic tract* (e.g., Barbizet, 1970). Individuals with this malady show symptoms like those of H. M. However, there are important differences between Korsakoff's syndrome and the type of amnesia exhibited by H. M. Korsakoff's syndrome tends to get progressively more severe over time. Although the progress of the disease can be arrested by stopping alcohol consumption and using nutritional therapy—especially increasing the amount of thiamine in the individual's diet—it can only be reversed in about 20% of cases. The most significant characteristic of Korsakoff's syndrome is that its sufferers tend to fill in missing information by **prevaricating**: They tend to make up answers to questions rather than indicate that they do not remember. Because of this, their feeling of knowing is typically incorrect (Shimamura & Squire, 1987). Korsakoff's syndrome offers additional clinical support to the idea that the temporal lobes are key to the storage of episodic information.

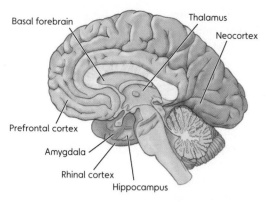

Basal forebrain

Thalamus

Neocortex

Prefrontal cortex

Amygdala

Rhinal cortex

Hippocampus

FIGURE 6.11 The Temporal Lobes and the Amygdala The area of the temporal lobes associated with emotionality is the amygdala. When the amygdala is damaged, the emotional component of the memory is lost.

Source: Kolb & Whishaw, 2011

Emotional Memory

Many episodes in our lives are memorable because they are linked with either positive or negative emotions. The area of the temporal lobes associated with emotionality is the *amygdala*. It is an almond-sized structure shown in **FIGURE 6.11** (Kolb & Whishaw, 2011) just in front of the hippocampus. The amygdala connects through a long set of fibers to the mammillary bodies. It receives stimulation from many areas of the brain, including the prefrontal cortex, and in turn it sends output to the *hypothalamus*, an area of the brain that regulates temperature, eating, blood pressure, and other physical activities. For example, when an emotional memory is activated, people sometimes experience increased breathing, sweating, and other stress reactions. When the amygdala is damaged, explicit memory functioning is still preserved, but the emotional component of the memory is lost (LeDoux, 1994).

Emotion is not just a feature that is added to an episode, but can affect what is actually stored and how it is retrieved. Loftus and Burns (1982) showed participants videos of staged criminal acts. They found that when observers experienced high levels of emotional arousal, they narrowed their attentional focus on the scenes in front of them and had heightened recall for the weapons involved. This is called *weapon focus* and shows that under threat, our emotional reaction directs our attention to threat-related stimuli.

Emotion also affects what is retrieved. For the typical person, recalling life experiences shows a distinct pattern that goes by the name **Pollyanna principle** (e.g., Boucher & Osgood, 1969; Matlin & Stang, 1978). There is a tendency to retrieve a greater number of pleasant memories than unpleasant memories. This is illustrated in the schematic graph in **FIGURE 6.12**. In one study, a researcher (Linton, 1979) wrote down at least two events from her personal life every day for 6 years. Each month she would randomly select from her pool of events and attempt to recall specific details surrounding them. She consistently found that she recalled more pleasant than unpleasant memories and that the negative events were not as strongly negative as when they had actually occurred. It seems that emotion associated with negative events fades faster in intensity than does the emotion associated with positive events (Walker, Skowronski, & Thompson, 2003).

This positivity in the recall of life experiences increases as a person ages. Participants (ages 47–102) were asked about a health and lifestyle questionnaire they had completed 17 years before. The older participants showed the Pollyanna effect more than younger participants, and this is especially the case when the older adults were asked to be accurate but mindful of their current emotional states (Kennedy, Mather, & Carstensen, 2004; Mather & Carstensen, 2005). The older adults in this study had a more positive view of their current life, and this can color their retrieval of their past.

How does this affect people who have negative feelings about their current life? The Pollyanna principle does not hold for depressed people. People who experience depression perceive their lives to be more negative than nondepressed people typically do. As the principle of encoding specificity would predict, depressed people retrieve disproportionately more negative episodes and attribute the negativity to themselves (Abramson, Metalsky, & Alloy, 1989). In one study (Walker, Skowronski, Gibbon, Vogl, & Thompson, 2003) people were divided into depressed and nondepressed groups. They were each asked to recall six emotionally intense incidents from the preceding 6 months of their lives and to rate their emotional intensity at the time the events occurred and then rate how they felt about the incidents now. For the nondepressed participants, the negative events faded in intensity more than the positive events did. However, for the depressed participants, the negative events did not fade in intensity any more than did the positive events. One suggestion from these findings is that there is a protective mechanism that induces people to have mostly positive recollections about their lives and feel good about themselves. Unfortunately, the emotional protective effect does not extend to people who are at least mildly depressed.

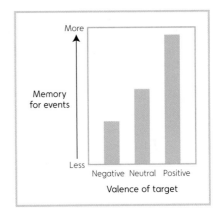

FIGURE 6.12 The Pollyanna Principle Information associated with positive emotion is remembered more easily than information associated with negative emotion.

Source: Kihlstrom, Eich, Sandbrand, & Tobias, 2000

SECTION SUMMARY ▪

Autobiographical Memory

Our autobiographical memory allows us to reminisce about the past and plan for future actions. To have autobiographical memory, we must have a sense of self that connects the episodes of our lives. To accomplish this requires three critical elements: a capacity for self-reflection, a sense of personal ownership, and the ability to think about time as an unfolding of personal happenings centered around ourselves.

In spite of our broad ability to retrieve life events, some periods in life are recalled more easily than others. We tend to have infantile amnesia for the first 2 years of life and a reminiscence bump in our ability to recall events that occurs at about 15 years of age. Although we believe that we have a specially enhanced memory for highly emotional events in our lives, flashbulb memories tend not to be any better recalled than less dramatic events that occurred about the same time.

Case histories show that retrograde and anterograde amnesia for episodes in our lives are the result of separate areas of damage in the brain. The HERA model of episodic memory points to separate areas in the frontal lobes that are critical for storage and retrieval. This is a biological demonstration of the independence of storage and retrieval of episodic information. The frontal lobes are also important for another aspect of autobiographical memory: prospective memory.

As we experience life events or seek to retain facts, structures in the medial temporal lobe of the brain consolidate the current contents of our consciousness into lifelong storage. These brain structures function as control centers to transfer information from short-term/working memory to long-term memory. When these centers are surgically removed or damaged, as is the case with extreme alcoholism, people suffer from anterograde amnesia and are unable to learn new facts or retain new episodes in their lives. When the surrounding brain areas remain intact, however, they help preserve a feeling of knowing for perceptual and motor patterns.

Human memories often have an emotional content that is used to retrieve those memories. The experience of emotional aspects of our lives is contributed by a structure deep within the temporal lobes called the amygdala. Extreme emotional experiences result from increased blood flow to the amygdala, which in turn helps to create emotional memories. Under normal conditions, the emotional aspects of our memories diminish over a lifetime, with the negative component being lost faster than the positive component. As a result, we tend to have a modest positive feeling for our life's events.

How Prior Knowledge Affects Memory

In 1932, Sir Frederick C. Bartlett asked people in Great Britain to read an unfamiliar story called "War of the Ghosts," a folktale of the Kwak'wala speaking people of Vancouver Island. At different times after this initial reading (from less than an hour to years later), Bartlett asked the participants to recall the story. To experience the situation yourself, read the story in Demonstration 6.5 and summarize what you think happened in it.

■■■DEMONSTRATION 6.5

"War of the Ghosts"

One night two young men from Egulac went down to the river to hunt seals and while they were there it became foggy and calm. Then they heard war-cries, and they thought: "Maybe this is a war-party." They escaped to the shore, and hid behind a log. Now canoes came up, and they heard the noise of paddles, and saw one canoe coming up to them. There were five men in the canoe, and they said:

"What do you think? We wish to take you along. We are going up the river to make war on the people."

One of the young men said, "I have no arrows."

"Arrows are in the canoe," they said.

"I will not go along. I might be killed. My relatives do not know where I have gone. But you," he said, turning to the other, "may go with them."

So one of the young men went, but the other returned home.

And the warriors went on up the river to a town on the other side of Kalama. The people came down to the water and they began to fight, and many were killed. But presently the young man heard one of the warriors say, "Quick, let us go home: that Indian has been hit." Now he thought: "Oh, they are ghosts." He did not feel sick, but they said he had been shot.

So the canoes went back to Egulac and the young man went ashore to his house and made a fire. And he told everybody and said: "Behold I accompanied the ghosts, and we went to fight.

Many of our fellows were killed, and many of those who attacked us were killed. They said I was hit, and I did not feel sick."

He told it all, and then he became quiet. When the sun rose he fell down. Something black came out of his mouth. His face became contorted. The people jumped up and cried.

He was dead. (F. C. Bartlett, 1932)

Without looking back to the story,

1. What happened in the story?

2. Who were the people that were fighting?

3. What happened to the young man after he returned home?

When Bartlett (1932) tested his participants, he discovered two things. First, very soon after they read the story, people did not agree on its details. Their recollections were not verbatim recollections of the story, but reflected the participants' cultural biases and interpretations. The second finding was that the participants' memories for the story changed over time. The retellings of the story became shorter, leaving out the folktale's supernatural components and ambiguities. The order in which the participants recalled the events was in keeping with British experiences of cause and effect. The reduction in information was quite extreme for one participant who said 2 years later, "It's about seals." Bartlett's findings led to the conclusion that human memory is reconstructive and not a verbatim recollection of our experience.

Our personal knowledge not only influences our memory for narratives, but, as Bartlett (1932) demonstrated, it can even affect our memory for the words that we see and hear. This was shown in a clever study by Deese (1959), who presented a list of words to students and asked for their immediate recall. One of the lists had words such as the following: *drowsy, bed, rest, awake, tired, pillow, pajamas, dream, wake.* A common error made by students was to report a word that had not appeared on the list, such as *sleep.* Indeed, students falsely recognized *sleep* 84% of the time: about the same rate at which they correctly identified words that were actually on the list (Roediger & McDermott, 1995). These basic memory studies show that sometimes people have difficulty distinguishing between the source of the information that is presented and ideas that spring to mind when the real information is presented. This is a cause for concern when we rely on eyewitness testimony.

Eyewitness Memories

An important type of episodic memory comes under the general heading of eyewitness reports, which are critical to the legal system. From the point of view of the witness, eyewitness memories

Margaret Kelly Michaels was a day care worker whose conviction on 1,170 charges of sexually abusing 20 young children was later overturned because eyewitness testimony was proved false. Here she arrives at court for the opening day of her trial in June 1987.

AP Photo/Mike Derer

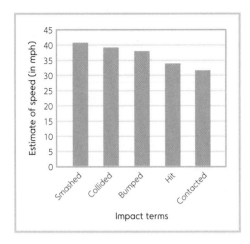

FIGURE 6.13 Effect of Leading Questions Students saw a film about an auto accident and were asked, "How fast were the cars going when they (*insert verb*) into each other?" The verbs used to fill in the blank were *smashed, collided, bumped, hit,* or *contacted.* The estimated speed varied with the type of verb, illustrating that someone trying to recollect an event can be misled by the type of question he or she is asked.

Source: Loftus & Palmer, 1974

are similar to flashbulb memory experiences because they are often associated with emotional events such as crimes. Like flashbulb memories, an observer's confidence in his or her report does not make it any more accurate. Two aspects of eyewitness reports affect accuracy: How questions are asked to elicit the report, and the observer's guessing strategy in generating facts.

Leading Questions Eyewitness descriptions are as fallible as other efforts to recollect events. In fact, they may be even more fallible because people trying to recollect an event can be misled by the type of questions they are asked. For example, Loftus and Palmer (1974) showed students a film purporting to be an auto accident. In fact, the cars did not really crash into each other and there was no broken glass. The participants were asked: "About how fast were the cars going when they (*insert verb*) into each other?" The verbs used to fill in the blank were either *smashed, collided, bumped, hit,* or *contacted. Smashed* produced higher estimates of speed than the other verbs, as illustrated in **FIGURE 6.13**. In a second experiment, a week after estimating the speed, students were asked a new question: "Was there broken glass?" Students who were asked the question with *smashed* as the verb said yes (on average, 32% of the time) more often than those who were asked the question with *hit* (16% of the time) or students who were not asked any leading questions (12% of the time). Note that there had been no broken glass at all in the film. **FIGURE 6.14** shows the probability that a student would say, "yes, I saw broken glass", depending on how fast they thought the cars were going and on the verb used.

The willingness of students to report broken glass depended on how they encoded the original event. The leading question affected students' estimates of speed; it also affected (at any speed estimate) their willingness to say there was broken glass. Leading questions can affect our recollections of everything from eyewitness descriptions of automobile accidents to estimates of the number of headaches a person experiences weekly (e.g., Loftus, 1975; Loftus & Zanni, 1975).

Memory and Guessing While leading questions can influence eyewitness recollections, they can also affect how people will guess when they aren't really sure of the answer. The classic study of this phenomenon was conducted by Loftus, Miller, and Burns (1978), who asked more than 1,000 undergraduates to watch a series of slides depicting an auto–pedestrian accident. Participants were shown a series of slides of a red car stopping at an intersection and then turning right and hitting a pedestrian. The students saw the car stopped either at a *yield* sign or a *stop* sign. Soon after, they were asked a series of questions about the slides. One of the questions asked was either consistent with the slides or misleading and followed this format: "Did another car pass the red Datsun while it was stopped at the _____ sign?" The consistent question mentioned the sign the observer had actually seen. The misleading question mentioned the other sign. Twenty minutes later, the students were asked to decide which of two pictures they had seen in the experiment. The students who were asked the consistent question were about 75% accurate in recognizing the sign that they had seen, but those who were asked the misleading question were only about 40% accurate in picking the correct sign. Members of a third group, who had not been asked about the signs earlier, accurately identified the sign they had seen about 60% of the time.

A week later, the undergraduate participants were all asked to pick the sign that they had seen. Those given misleading information picked the correct sign only 20% of the time, but the consistent and neutral groups showed only small declines in accuracy. It is clear from such studies that eyewitness testimony can be quite fallible and is easily affected by outside influences (Loftus, 1997).

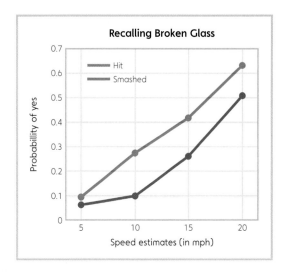

Source Monitoring

One reason the information in leading questions can confuse eyewitness memories is that we may have difficulty recalling whether the new information is something we actually observed or just heard about. Our ability to tell the difference is called **source monitoring** (Johnson et al., 1993; Zaragoza & Lane, 1994), which refers to the process of identifying where our knowledge comes from. By now it should be clear that our ability to identify the sources of our memories is far from perfect. We often ask ourselves questions like, "did I lock the door before I left or did I only think about locking the door?" or "did I really get bitten by a dog when I was a child or did I just dream it?" (Henkel & Franklin, 1998; Lindsay & Johnson, 2000).

Difficulties in source monitoring can lead to false recollections not only in the case of leading questions, but also when someone is forced by an interviewer to give false information. This situation is not as odd as it may seem. Interviewers sometimes try to get a witness to give an account of what the interviewer believes occurred, even when the witness does not remember the event in the same way, or perhaps never witnessed the event at all (Bruck, Ceci, & Hembrooke, 1998). In one study, university students watched an 8-minute movie about a summer camp that was filled with action and drama, and then were interviewed about their recollections. One group (the free group) was told to answer only those questions they were sure they knew. The other group (the forced group) was told to answer every question, even though some of the questions asked were clearly biased in a particular direction. For example, the forced group might be asked: "When Delaney fell on the floor, where was he bleeding?" Participants in the forced group knew that Delaney had not been injured in any way, but were pushed to make up an answer. In this latter situation, the experimenter either reinforced the answers by saying "yes, that is the correct answer" or just gave a neutral response by saying OK.

Four weeks later the participants were told to describe the events they had seen as accurately and in as much detail as possible. Students in the free group did not report any erroneous events. Students in the forced group recalled 27% of

FIGURE 6.14 Speed and Broken Glass Students were asked whether they saw broken glass in the film. This figure shows the probability that a student would say, "yes, I saw broken glass", depending on how fast they thought the cars were going and the verb used. Note: there was no broken glass. The leading question affected students' estimates of speed and also their willingness to say there was broken glass.

Source: Loftus & Palmer, 1974

the false events that had been given a neutral feedback (OK), but recalled 55% of the false events that had been given the positive feedback (yes). Interestingly, when asked about their recollections of the interview, they tended to correctly remember what they told the interviewer the first time, but not that they had been forced to lie (Zaragoza, Payment, Ackil, Drivdahl, & Beck, 2001, Experiment 2). When we are made to respond to leading questions or forced to lie about a situation, we create false memories and fail to remember their source. As a result, when we are asked to retrieve what we remember about an event, the false memories are recalled and it is difficult to distinguish fact from fantasy.

Recovered Memories

The research just described is based primarily on laboratory studies of emotionally neutral events. However, source-monitoring difficulties can also be found in real-life situations associated with strong emotions. For example, in one study, college students were asked to recall as much as they could about four events from their childhood. All but one of these events, the target event, had actually occurred (as verified by the participants' families). Examples of made-up target events included: "at age 5, knocking over a punchbowl at a wedding and spilling the punch on the bride's parents" and "going to a hospital for a high fever."

If students could not recall the target event presented to them, they were encouraged to think about the events for a couple of days. They were tested on their recollections 2 days later. The first time they were interviewed, students reported experiencing the false target event only 3% of the time. However, by the second interview, they reported the false event 27% of the time (Hyman & Billings, 1998; Hyman, Husband, & Billings, 1995; see also Loftus, 1993). It is therefore possible for people to be convinced that events have occurred in their lives simply by asking them about those events and asking them over a period of time to imagine the possibility that the event occurred.

This evidence suggests that we should be cautious in interpreting the truth of people's reports of having recalled some event from their early childhood decades after the event is said to have occurred. It is possible that these recollections are the result of interviews and suggestions made by others. At the same time, we should also be cautious in dismissing those recollections. The fact that memories can be planted does not mean that all memories have been planted.

The Cognitive Interview

The fallibility of human memory is a major concern to the legal profession, because legal findings depend on the accuracy and recollections of witnesses (e.g., Kassin, Ellsworth, & Smith, 1989; Wells, 1993). These concerns have prompted the development of interview techniques that try to enhance the accuracy of eyewitness testimony. One technique that is based on research findings is the **cognitive interview** (Fisher & Geiselman, 1992; Fisher, Geiselman, & Amador, 1989; Geiselman & Fisher, 1997). Cognitive interviews have three major components that are used to enhance recall of an event. The first of these is to interview the observers at the crime scene or have them imagine that they are back at the crime scene witnessing the event. This part of the interview uses the encoding specificity principle, which assumes that memory retrieval will be best when recall and storage are in the same context. This component alone adds considerably to the added recall associated with the use of this interview technique (Memon & Higham, 1999).

The second component is to have witnesses report everything that they can recall, even aspects that are incomplete or don't make sense. Encouraging these free-form recalls works against the tendency of people to edit out pieces of information that they think are unimportant, but may be ultimately relevant to investigators. It also allows the interviewer to record details that can be connected to those reported by other witnesses. The research cited previously on the effect of leading questions suggests that interrogators ought to use open-ended questions, such as "tell me what you have observed." Asking such a neutral question right after an event can associate the information with its original source and therefore protect it from distortion if misleading questions are asked later in the investigation (Geiselman & Fisher, 1997; Koriat & Goldsmith, 1996; Loftus, 1980; Reyna & Titcomb, 1997).

The third component of the cognitive interview is to have the observer recount the events in different sequences: "what happened next?", but also, "what happened just before that?" In the usual time-ordered sequence, observers tend to add pieces of information that may never have occurred, but which make sense given the sequence of recounted events. Asking for a recount of events in reverse order reduces the number of these intruded recollections, and also increases the number of correct recollections. For example, in one study participants were asked to report events in the standard (forward) order, followed by recalling them in the reverse order. These participants remembered more information than witnesses who reported the events twice in the forward order (Geiselman & Callot, 1990). An overall analysis of the many studies of the cognitive interview shows that it results in a 25% increase in correct recollections compared with other police methods (Geiselman & Fisher, 1997; Kohnken, Milne, Memon, & Bull, 1999).

SECTION SUMMARY ▪

How Prior Knowledge Affects Memory

What we know influences what we can learn because our prior knowledge affects how we encode new events. F. C. Bartlett's (1932) research on memory for stories shows that a person's cultural preconceptions and beliefs affect what that person will understand and view as important to remember. The subjective interpretation of text contributes to later confusion about what the person actually read or what the person merely inferred. The beliefs and attitudes that we possess can be mentally activated by having been asked leading questions, which in turn cause us to reinterpret what we have experienced. The effect of these activations is a source of confusion when we try to recall an event, because we forget the source of these new ideas: Did we create these new interpretations or are we just remembering what someone told us? We occasionally read about people who have recovered a memory for an event not previously recalled. Findings from scientific studies suggest that it is difficult to know whether these recovered memories are autobiographical memories from a prior experience or the result of leading questions posed by other people. The use of the cognitive interview can improve the accuracy of people's recollection of events and reduce difficulties with recalling the source of the information.

CHAPTER SUMMARY

Long-term memory (LTM) is the personal library of all the volumes of knowledge that we possess. Researchers divide LTM into two broad memory systems: explicit/declarative and implicit memory. Explicit/declarative memory includes facts that we have learned, memories of our life experiences, and our plans for future behaviors like taking our medicine. Our implicit memory includes procedures that we employ (typing or riding a bike) and patterns of stimuli that we have learned to recognize (an Apple iMac or a Burton snowboard). Many of our memories last a lifetime after a brief period in working memory.

LTM is an unlimited capacity system—at least as far as we can tell. Even though we may have difficulty recalling a fact, our metamemory tells us whether it is truly stored away and available or not. We see this in our feeling of knowing and when the word we are searching for is on the tip of our tongue. The information stored in LTM comes in a multitude of codes related to how we experience them. Forgetting information in LTM is essentially a failure to retrieve what is already there by using search cues that are a poor match with the way in which the stored information is coded. People possess a set of processes called metamemory, which informs them about what their memories contain. If they have a strong feeling of knowing the answer to a question, they will actively pursue a search of their memories. They are less likely to perform such a search when they have a low feeling of knowing.

Encoding specificity is the process that mediates between the question we are asked and the way we have personally coded the relevant information. When the question and our storage of the facts are congruent, our answers are accurate and rapid. When the question and the facts don't match, our answers may be flawed.

The episodes and semantic data associated with some periods in life are recalled more easily than those of other periods. In the first 2 years of life we tend to experience infantile amnesia and later on in life we cannot retrieve episodes that have occurred (declarative knowledge), even though we unconsciously acquire skills during this same period of time, such as motor control and the beginnings of language. Over the course of a lifetime, we have heightened recall for the period from about 10 to 25 years old, called the reminiscence bump. Although we believe that we have specially enhanced memory for highly emotional events across our life span, those special memories called flashbulb memories tend not to be any better recalled than less dramatic events that have occurred at about the same time.

Our ability to store and retrieve life events relies on different areas of our brain. The HERA model of episodic memory shows that the left hemisphere is more involved than the right hemisphere in *encoding* information into episodic memory. Damage here leads to anterograde amnesia. In contrast, the right prefrontal cortex is more involved in *retrieval* from episodic memory than the left prefrontal cortex. Damage to the right hemisphere leads to retrograde amnesia. The frontal lobes are also critical for people's ability to engage in prospective memory.

The temporal lobes are important for the storage of both episodic and semantic memory. Damage to both hippocampi or both mammillothalamic tracts leads to anterograde amnesia for declarative knowledge, but not for implicit memories. The temporal lobes also contain the amygdala, without which we could not retain the emotional content of our memories. In general, the positive aspects of our lived episodes endure longer than the negative aspects. This allows people to gain a sense of retrieving more positive than negative memories.

The human ability to acquire new knowledge is affected by what we already know because the way we encode future events depends on how we have already encoded past events. This results in cultural biases in recollections of stories or in mentally recording events in a way that makes personal sense rather than in the way it actually occurred. Although people are often able to make credible reports of events, they frequently forget the source of that information and attribute it to what they saw rather than what they were told. Cognitive psychologists have developed special methods, such as the cognitive interview, to elicit eyewitness testimony in a way that overcomes people's memory biases.

KEY TERMS

long-term memory (LTM), p. 151

explicit memory, p. 152

declarative memories, p. 152

semantic memory, p. 153

episodic memory, p. 153

retrospective memory, p. 153

prospective memory, p. 153

implicit memory, p. 153

procedural memory, p. 154

perceptual memory, p. 154

permastore, p. 157

semantic features, p. 158

feeling of knowing, p. 160

metamemory, p. 160

amnesia, p. 163

tip-of-the-tongue (TOT) phenomenon, p. 163

encoding specificity, p. 165

subjective organization, p. 165

state-dependent learning, p. 167

autobiographical memory, p. 168

infantile (or childhood) amnesia, p. 170

reminiscence bump, p. 171

flashbulb memories, p. 172

Korsakoff's syndrome, p. 179

prevaricating, p. 179

Pollyanna principle, p. 180

source monitoring, p. 185

cognitive interview, p. 186

QUESTIONS FOR REVIEW

Check Your Knowledge

1. Define long-term memory (LTM).

2. What are the two broad categories that make up LTM?

3. What is explicit/declarative memory? Give two examples.

4. Define episodic memory and semantic memory and give an example of each.

5. What is prospective memory? Give two examples of prospective memory.

6. What are the two broad categories of implicit memory? Provide examples of each category.

7. What is the capacity of LTM?

8. What is the duration of LTM? Why is the term *permastore* used to describe the duration of LTM?

9. What is the difference between failure to retrieve and forgetting?

10. How do we code information in LTM?

11. Which retrieval procedure is the best method for assessing what we know: recall or recognition? Which illustrates permastore?

12. What is cue familiarity and how does it explain people's willingness to search their memories?

13. How does memory for semantic features allow us to incorrectly recognize words from a list?

14. What is the tip-of-the-tongue phenomenon? Is it universal?

15. What role do semantic features play in recalling sentences and passages?

16. What is encoding specificity? How does it explain memory retrieval?

17. How can you use encoding specificity principles to help study for exams?

18. Can your performance on an exam be enhanced if you study in the same room where you will be tested? Why? What is the special name for this?

19. Can your mental state while studying for an exam affect your performance on the exam? In what way? What is the special name for this?

20. How do autobiographical amnesias support the idea that semantic and episodic memory systems are independent?

21. What are the three preconditions for autobiographical memory?

22. What is infantile amnesia?

23. Define the reminiscence bump.

24. Does research support the superiority of flashbulb memories?

25. How does age affect prospective memory?

26. What does the HERA model tell us about semantic and episodic memory?

27. What general principle does the answer to Question 26 support?

28. What is the overall cognitive role of the hippocampus? How does the removal of both hippocampi or damage to both hippocampi affect cognition?

29. What is the overall cognitive role of the mammillary bodies? How does damage to both mammillary bodies, or the removal of both mammillary bodies, affect cognition?

30. What does Korsakoff's syndrome teach us about long-term memory?

31. What role does the amygdala play in memory for emotional events?

32. In what ways does culture affect our interpretation of stories?

33. Given what you know about source monitoring, how good are the identifications of eyewitnesses?

34. Given what you know about LTM, how confident should we be in recovered memories?

35. What is the cognitive interview and what does it help us do?

Apply Your Knowledge

1. The reading example with the scrambled letters placed near the beginning of the chapter illustrates that we are able to read entire words without reading the individual letters. What does this say for how we may recognize people and objects? Why aren't we confused more often?

2. Given what you know about permastore and the encoding specificity principle, design a simple procedure to help people recall information over a lifetime.

3. Based on what you know about reconstructive processes in memory, how would you evaluate the verbatim knowledge required of game shows on TV (e.g., *Jeopardy!*, *Who Wants to Be a Millionaire?*, etc.): Is it reasoning, pattern matching, or search of memory?

4. Encoding specificity correctly predicts state-dependent learning. What are the pros and cons of using drugs or medications when you study?

5. Many people report a memory or two from their childhood before the age of 3. How is this possible given what you know of infantile amnesia?

6. The Pollyanna principle seems to claim that over time, we see our lives through rose-colored glasses. Does the evidence support this claim? What do you think might be the benefit of this retrieval process over a lifetime? What might be the costs?

7. How does what you know about prospective memory explain the fact that the stereotyped professors, with their detailed factual knowledge, could show absent-mindedness in meeting their appointments?

SOLUTIONS ━━━━━━━━━━━━━━━━━━■

Demonstration 6.3: Solutions to Questions

1. Da Vinci
2. Sahara
3. Albany
4. Nepal
5. Paris
6. Minnesota
7. Africa
8. Death Valley
9. Jefferson
10. Neil Armstrong

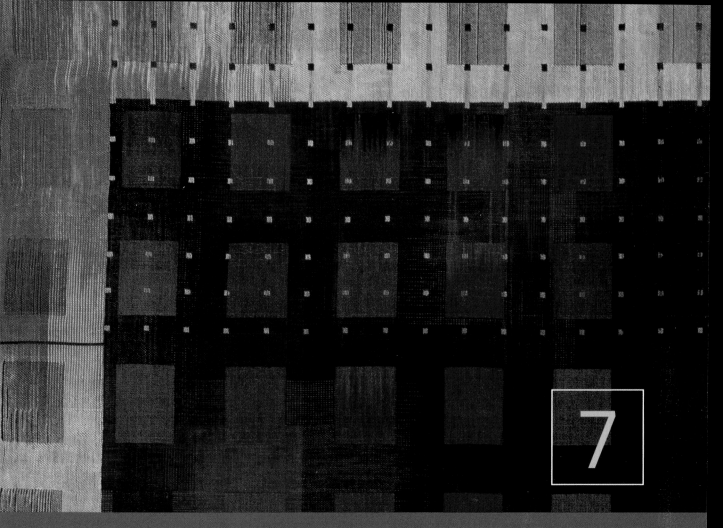

> **"It is a great nuisance that knowledge can be acquired only by hard work."**
>
> —Somerset Maugham

Your long-term memory is the repository of all that you know, but it is more than a mere dictionary of facts. It allows you to use those facts to deduce and create even more knowledge without having to deliberately memorize a new fact. For example, if you know particular facts about birds—they have feathers, lay eggs, and most can fly—and someone tells you that the Mindoro bleeding-heart is a bird that lives in the Philippines, you can effortlessly answer many questions about the bleeding-heart without learning one new fact about it; all you need to know is that it is a bird.

As we discussed in Chapter 6, the portion of LTM that encompasses these kinds of facts, as well as the inferences to be made from those facts, is *semantic memory*. Semantic memory is often compared to a vast library of abstract and concrete knowledge. Research has shown, however, that it also contains separate, specialized combinations of knowledge called *schemas* that are organized in different ways depending on how they are to be used. These specialized groupings of information will be discussed in this chapter after we examine four types of theories that seek to explain how knowledge is structured in semantic memory.

Theories of Knowledge

Researchers have proposed a variety of broad theories of knowledge to explain our ability to use the knowledge stored in semantic memory in order to draw inferences, answer questions, and effectively perform daily tasks. Four major types of theories have dominated cognitive psychology's research on human knowledge: Network, feature-based, perceptual, and connectionist theories have all shed light on how knowledge is structured for maximum usefulness and efficiency.

Network Theories

Network theories of knowledge assume that every category stored in semantic memory is potentially connected to every other category, like a giant net. To experience this general idea, try Demonstration 7.1.

▪▪▪DEMONSTRATION 7.1

Knowledge Network

For the strong of heart, do the following. Randomly select two words from a thesaurus. Call them Word 1 and Word 2. Try to find a connection between the two words by writing down the synonyms and antonyms for each of them (which may be a considerable list); then look up the synonyms and antonyms of the synonyms and antonyms you've just written down. Stop when you discover Word 2 when looking at the synonyms or antonyms of Word 1 (or vice versa). You should be able to find a connection between the two words, on average, in three or four links (Motter, de Moura, Lai, & Dasgupta, 2002). All word meanings are eventually connected to each other—a fact that network theories implicitly assume.

FIGURE 7.1 The Node–Link System As a Fishnet: The Knowledge Network Based on Quillian's Teachable Language Comprehender (TLC) The basic knowledge network is like a fishnet in which every node or fact is connected to every other one. One example of this is how objects share color names, shown at the bottom. The links have labels to indicate class-inclusion relations like *is a* or property relations like *has a*.

Source: Quillian, 1968

Network theories assume that the things you know, such as words, images, and facts, can be connected to other things that you also know, such as procedures, beliefs, and contexts. The things are represented in memory as *nodes*—specific locations in memory—and the connections between the nodes are *links*. This **node–link system** can be conceptualized as a fishnet with everything ultimately connected to everything else, as illustrated in Demonstration 7.1 and pictured in **FIGURE 7.1**. If you prefer, a node–link system can be conceptualized as resembling a tree with limited connections, as illustrated in **FIGURE 7.2**.

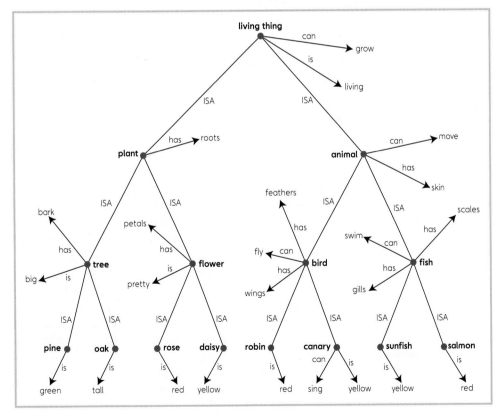

Network Model

FIGURE 7.2 The Node–Link System As a Tree Structure: A Cross-section of a TLC Network (a Hierarchy) The node–link system of Figure 7.1 can be redrawn to have multiple levels like a hierarchy. To determine whether there is a connection between one node and another requires a search up and down the links in the hierarchy.

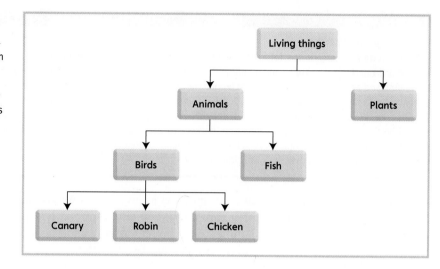

Quillian's Network Theory M. Ross Quillian developed one of the best-known and most thoroughly researched network theories in the late 1960s: the **teachable language comprehender (TLC)** (Quillian, 1968). It states that our semantic network has two main components: the node–link structure shown in Figure 7.1 and a question interface. The meaning of a concept is composed of all the links associated with it. Look at the node for *bird* in Figure 7.1. You will see that it is *an animal, with feathers, that has wings*, and in some cases *can fly*. A simplified version of the node–link structure in Figure 7.1 is redrawn as a hierarchy of knowledge in Figure 7.2. Specific facts are shown at the bottom of the hierarchy and progressively more abstract concepts at the top. For example, an individual's knowledge of canaries is represented by the node *canary*. Connected to this node are relevant facts and related ideas about canaries and other birds.

These nodes and links exist at one level of the network. At a more general level might be the concept *types of living things*. It is this hierarchical version of the TLC theory that has been tested most frequently (Collins & Quillian, 1969, 1970, 1972).

The second component of TLC, the **question interface**, refers to a sort of sensibility test that we use to determine whether we should pursue answering a question. For example, if someone were to ask a question such as, is a canary an arm? you would know immediately that a *canary* is an *animal*, and an *arm* is a *body part*. You might wonder whether the person was kidding or whether there is a special name for a *robot arm* called a *canary*. What you would not do is search your knowledge base to discover a possible connection between *arm* and *canary*. This is similar to what you do when you have a feeling of knowing as described in Chapter 6. The question interface prevents you from having to tax your attention in order to search for information that you would clearly not be able to find. The question interface serves a gatekeeping function for the knowledge network (Quillian, 1968) and is associated with people giving rapid answers to questions that deserve an immediate no (Glucksberg & McCloskey, 1981).

TLC makes three key assumptions about the mechanisms governing people's decisions when they are asked sensible questions: (a) equal link lengths in the hierarchy, (b) an efficient filing system, and (c) spreading activation.

Equal Links. The model assumes that all the links in the hierarchy are consistently of equal length. For example, the link between the *canary* and *bird* nodes is the same length as the connection between the *ostrich* and *bird* nodes. Links are important because it takes time for the cognitive system to travel from node to node across a link. Therefore, all questions that require accessing the same number of links will take the same amount of effort and time to answer.

Efficient Filing System. TLC assumes that the properties of an object are stored at the highest node in the hierarchy that is appropriate. For example, rather than noting that *canaries* have wings, feathers, and lay eggs and that *robins* have wings, feathers, and lay eggs, the model places these repeated properties with the category *bird*. Consequently, if you are asked whether a canary has feathers, you may say to yourself, canaries are birds and birds have feathers so canaries have feathers. This efficiency minimizes the demands on long-term and working memories (Greenbaum & Revlin, 1989).

Spreading Activation. Finally, TLC claims that when you are asked a question such as, does a canary breathe? you search to see if there is a connection in your network between the subject (*canary*) and the predicate (*breathe*). The TLC model assumes that the search is performed by a process called **spreading activation,** in which energy spreads from the nodes activated by the question in all directions at the same time, but one level or node at a time. This process also activates many unnecessary nodes along the way, which accounts for why irrelevant things come to mind when we are answering a question. A crucial implication of spreading activation is that the greater the distance between the subject and predicate terms in the network, the longer it should take to answer a question.

Keeping these three components in mind, let's see how TLC describes someone's process in answering questions about canaries. It should take longer to answer the question, is a canary an animal? than it would take to answer the question, is a canary a bird? because the concept of *animal* is more links away in the network from *canary* than is *bird*. **FIGURE 7.3** shows the relationship between the time to answer questions (*latency*) and the distances in the network that your search mechanism must travel. Two lines are graphed in Figure 7.3. The red line shows the time it takes to answer questions about classes, such as, is a canary a bird? The blue line shows the time it takes to answer questions regarding the properties of objects, such as, does a canary sing? or does a canary have skin? Notice that although property questions take longer to

FIGURE 7.3 Relationship between Time to Answer Questions (Latency) and Distances in the Network The farther apart two nodes are in the hierarchy, the longer it takes to discover they are related. The red line shows the time to answer questions for class-inclusion relations (*is a canary an animal?*), the blue line shows the time to answer questions for property relations (*does a canary have skin?*). Notice the fast latencies to false sentences.

Source: Collins & Quillian, 1969

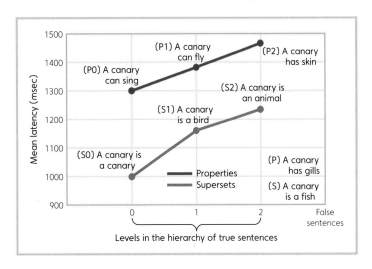

answer than class questions, they both show the effect of distance in the knowledge network. The fact that time to answer the question increases with the distance between categories is called the **semantic distance effect** and was a major discovery of the Collins and Quillian research.

One consequence of spreading activation as described by TLC is the **repeated path hypothesis**. Suppose you are asked two questions in quick succession. If the second question requires some of the same pathways as the first, you should respond a little faster on the second question than you might otherwise because the connections are already activated by the first question. In other words, repeating a path speeds processing (Collins & Quillian, 1970). For example, let us say that someone asked you the name of the current president of the United States and within a second or so asked you the name of the vice president. You would be able to retrieve the vice president's name more quickly in this instance than if the first question had been, what's the capital of South Dakota?

Collins and Quillian (1970) tested the repeated path hypothesis by asking ordinary people a series of questions involving dictionary definitions. For example, they asked participants: "Is a canary an animal?" To answer this question requires the activation of *canary*, *bird*, and *animal* nodes. Then they asked a follow-up question, such as "do birds breathe?" which requires the activation of *bird*, *animal*, and *living things*. They found that when a path was repeated in the follow-up question to the original question (in this example, *bird* and *animal*), people responded more rapidly than when a path wasn't repeated (e.g., as in the question "do fish have gills?"). This repeated path hypothesis is unique to network theories and is a source of support for TLC.

Rethinking Quillian's Network Theory In spite of the general support for network models like TLC, there are some phenomena that it does not explain. First, within a category such as *bird*, not all instances (the different types of birds) are equivalent in how much time it takes someone to answer a question about them. For example, you are faster at responding true to is a sparrow a bird? than to is an ostrich a bird? (Collins & Loftus, 1975; Smith, Shoben, & Rips, 1974). This difference in time to answer a question is called the **typicality effect**, where the typical or central members of a category (like *sparrow*) are more closely associated with the category (*bird*) than are untypical members (like *ostrich*).

Another phenomenon that challenges network theories is the **semantic relatedness effect**, which reflects the existence of inequalities across categories: people take longer to decide whether a canary is an animal than to decide whether a chicken is an animal. What this shows is that the relatedness of items is important for the judgments. Chickens seem to be more closely associated with animals than they are to birds and the opposite is true for canaries, even though canaries and chickens are both birds and animals. TLC cannot explain the typicality effect or the semantic relatedness effect without some crucial revisions to the original theory (e.g., Siakaluk, Buchanan, & Westbury, 2003).

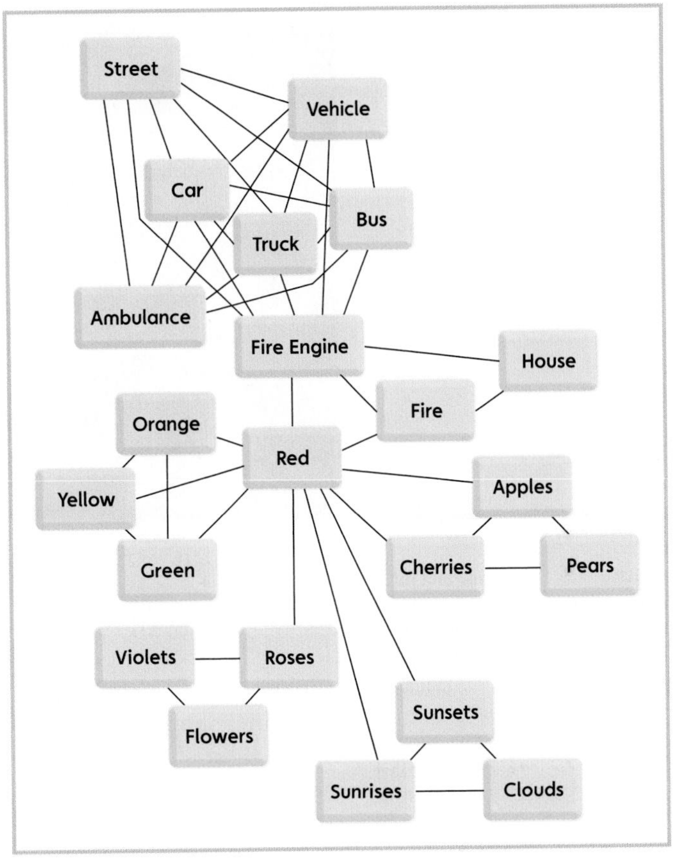

FIGURE 7.4 Semantic Relatedness Effect One way to represent knowledge is to group strongly related concepts close together and weakly related concepts farther apart. The stronger the association between concepts, the more rapidly a person can answer questions about their relationship.

Source: Collins & Loftus, 1975

TLC gives a better account of how people answer questions if the hierarchical nature of the knowledge system is envisioned as less rigid. One proposal modifies TLC to put more emphasis on the spreading-activation process and to allow the connections between the nodes to vary in strength (e.g., Collins & Loftus, 1975). For example, *car* is more often included in discussions of *vehicles* than is *ambulance*. As a consequence, there are more ways that *cars* and *vehicles* are connected than *ambulances* and *vehicles*. This is illustrated in **FIGURE 7.4**, where some concepts have stronger associations (shorter links) and are more readily connected (more links) than others. This implies that information may be stored in more than one place in the broader network and the associations between categories and their instances may vary considerably. The problem with such alternative versions of TLC is that they are difficult to test scientifically: There would be endless versions of the theory to fit each person's individual responses.

The need to explain the exceptions to the theory has resulted in many modifications to the basic TLC theory (e.g., J. R. Anderson, 1974; J. R. Anderson & Reder, 1999; Collins & Loftus, 1975; Greenbaum & Revlin, 1989). These alternate theories are like TLC in that they view human knowledge as a network of relationships stored in semantic memory. However, an alternate theory represents knowledge as a vast plain containing concepts and instances. That theory is the subject of the next section.

The Feature Comparison Model

An alternative to network theories of knowledge, the **feature comparison model (FCM)** (Rips, 1989; Smith et al., 1974) portrays human knowledge as a giant *semantic space*, a plain that contains clusters of hills and valleys representing our knowledge. The photo in **FIGURE 7.5** is a metaphor for the map in **FIGURE 7.6**. Notice that the clusters that represent categories of knowledge have a consistent pattern: The hills in the center of the clusters contain items that are more similar than those at the periphery of the cluster. This is because some instances are more central to the meaning of a category than others (see also Rosch & Mervis, 1975).

FIGURE 7.5 The Plain of Knowledge The feature comparison model portrays human knowledge as a giant semantic space: a plain that contains clusters of hills that represent our knowledge. The tighter the cluster of knowledge, the more similar the items are to each other and the easier it is to decide whether a proposed relationship (e.g., *robin is a bird*) is true.

Robin Smith/Photolibrary

FIGURE 7.6 Semantic Plain for Animal Names Students rated the similarity of different birds and different mammals. The result was a set of two clusters that are organized along the same two dimensions: size and predacity. The space of hills in Figure 7.5 is a metaphor for this kind of semantic relatedness.

Source: Rips, Shoben, & Smith, 1973

The prototype models discussed in Chapter 4 on pattern recognition are closely related to this approach. Those models propose that when we think of the categories we know—from *cat* to *throwing a baseball*—the examples that immediately come to mind are the best examples of the categories: the *prototypical cat* and *baseball throws*.

To see how this applies to understanding concepts stored in semantic memory, consider a study in which university students were asked to rate how similar pairs of concepts were to each other (e.g., *duck* and *chicken*, or *chicken* and *animal*). The researchers (Rips, Shoben, & Smith, 1973) transformed these judgments into a kind of map of the semantic space showing the closeness of the pairs of items. Figure 7.6 shows this map. Notice that some obvious birds such as a *robin*, are closer to the concept of a *bird* than are other birds such as a *chicken*. In fact, students rated *chicken* as closer to the concept of *animal* than to that of *bird*. The panel on the left shows how birds are related to each other and the panel on the right shows the relatedness of mammals. It is as if the two clusters exist as hills in the semantic space (e.g., Figure 7.5). These hills seem to be structured in the same way. Did you notice that the horizontal axis for each

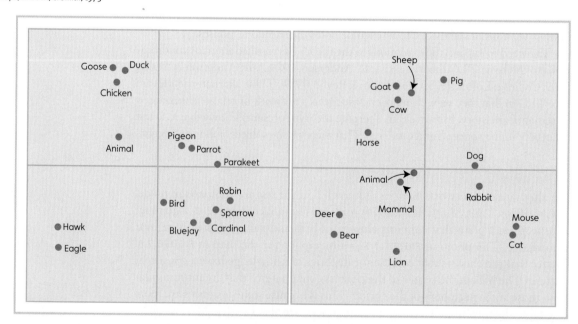

panel ranges in size from small creatures to large? What can you say about the vertical axis of each panel? Rips, et al. (1973) believed that the vertical axis reflected how predatory the animals were. Here we have a case of two different clusters of creatures and the clusters seem to be organized along the same principles.

The figures and your own intuitions will tell you that some instances of a category are more central to the category than are others. The basis for deciding how central an item is depends on the features (what TLC theory would call *properties*) the item possesses. The feature comparison model claims that some features are defining features, whereas others are characterizing features. **Defining features** are those that are necessary and jointly sufficient to specify the requirements for a category. For example, the potential to lay eggs is a necessary feature of birds, but other features are necessary as well, such as having wings and being covered in feathers. When these defining features (*lays eggs*, *has wings*, *covered in feathers*) occur in an animal, they are sufficient for us to be able to say that the animal is a bird. **Characterizing features** describe the commonly occurring characteristics of many (though not necessarily all) members of a category that we are most familiar with. So, *building a nest in a tree* is characteristic of birds, but it is not necessary to do this to be considered a bird. Penguins, for example, do not build nests in trees.

Three key aspects of the feature comparison model make it different from network theories like TLC in describing how people answer questions about their knowledge. The first is that this model assumes that when people think about categories such as birds or furniture or vehicles, they have an overall sense of the defining and characterizing features that comprise these categories. Another key aspect of the theory is that it assumes that in deciding whether one category is part of another category (e.g., whether a dog is a mammal), a person compares the total set of features associated with each category (*dog* and *mammal*) to see whether they overlap. Finally, in deciding whether two categories overlap sufficiently to consider one category a part of another category, people use their own personal standards. In this regard, the feature comparison model emphasizes the unique aspects of every individual's semantic memory.

FIGURE 7.7 is a flowchart that shows how these three aspects of the FCM participate in your knowledge judgments. In the first step (at the top of the flowchart), someone is presented with a question. In the process of understanding the question, the listener identifies the main terms (e.g., the subject and predicate terms of the question). In the second step, the listener retrieves all of the defining and characterizing features of these terms from semantic memory and compares them before making a final decision in the third step. As noted before, the FCM assumes that a final decision regarding the relationship of the subject and predicate is based on the individual's personal standard. If the overlap is close, the person will respond yes; if the overlap is slight, the person will respond no. Finally, if the overlap is intermediate (based on the individual's personal standards), the person will compare the features again, but this time restrict the comparison to the defining features: the essential ones that define membership in the category. Based on

FIGURE 7.7 Feature Comparison Model When people answer questions about their semantic knowledge, they access the defining and characterizing features of the categories from their long-term memory. This flowchart describes where these features play a role in the question–answer sequence, and it predicts which questions will be answered quickly and which will require more time.

Source: Smith, Shoben, & Rips, 1974

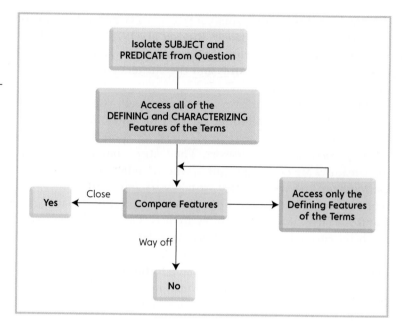

TABLE **7.1**			
Feature Comparison Model Predictions			
Question	**Similarity**	**Answer**	**Response time**
Is a robin a bird?	High	True	Fast
Is a robin an animal?	Medium	True	Slow
Is a robin a fish?	Medium	False	Slow
Is a robin a rock?	Low	False	Fast

Note: From Smith, Shoben, & Rips, 1974

this last comparison, if there is a match, the person will respond yes; if there is no overlap, the person will respond no.

The FCM flowchart specifies the steps a person will take to answer a question. This allows the theory to be scientifically tested. If its predictions correspond to what a person actually does, it will be supported. In contrast, if the theory doesn't match a person's behavior, the theory is wrong. The FCM can account for the typical pattern of responses to knowledge questions with the same pattern as in TLC. The different types of questions and their answers are shown in **TABLE 7.1**. Notice that the predicted times to answer questions are very close to what was shown in Figure 7.3 for yes answers. You can see from the table that FCM goes further and makes verified predictions about the pattern shown by students when asked questions that are clearly no (i.e., false). This ability of the feature comparison model to tell us something that research has not already shown makes it an important theory in cognitive psychology.

The Perceptual Theory of Knowledge

Network theories and the feature comparison model assume that human knowledge is organized around broad, abstract concepts and properties. Another approach to understanding human knowledge views seemingly abstract knowledge as perceptually based (Barsalou, 1999). For example, the first time we see a car, our perceptual system stores this information neurologically. Later, when we are thinking about cars or someone mentions one, our brains reactivate the image of the original car (or more recent cars we have seen, depending on our experience) as if we were simulating the initial visual input. We experience this retrieval process as a visual image (Barsalou, Simmons, Barbey, & Wilson, 2003).

The theory of knowledge that embraces this view is called a **perceptual symbol system** because it assumes that our understanding of things is based on the perceptual mode (visual, auditory, etc.) in which we experience them. For example, one study asked students to verify properties of objects such as, does a pony have a mane? The students were able to answer this question more quickly if they had just been asked whether a horse had a mane rather than if a lion had a mane. If only the abstract concept of a *mane* was relevant, then both questions should have produced the same effect on answering the second question. Notice, however, that the perceptual properties of a lion's mane are quite different from a horse's mane (Solomon & Barsalou, 2001), and only the question, does a horse have a mane? facilitated answering the question about a pony's mane.

This finding supports the idea that properties are represented with their perceptual characteristics in LTM and that our semantic knowledge includes concrete elements as well as abstract concepts. In fact, when we answer questions that seem to be conceptual (e.g., does a bird have wings?) we seem to first imagine a prototypical bird and "inspect" it to see if it has wings. Only after that do we seem to get the semantic knowledge, as proposed in TLC or the feature comparison model. The perceptual theory of knowledge is compatible with the structure of network theories and feature comparison theories. It demands only that the content of our knowledge be based on our raw experiences, and not just abstract ideas.

Network theories, the feature comparison model, and the perceptual theory of knowledge are all supported by scientific studies, and each provides us with insight into a portion of semantic memory. A theory that seeks to combine the insights of all these views is the connectionist model.

The Connectionist Model of Memory

There is a broad type of model of knowledge that borrows the best aspects of the specific theories we just covered. This type is called a **connectionist model** because it asserts that people's ability to respond to a question or identify a picture of a flower depends on the entire pattern of connections in the brain. Such theories are sometimes called *neural networks* because they seem similar to the way the nervous system works in coordinating human thinking (McClelland & Rogers, 2003). The connectionist model asserts that every node of knowledge is connected directly or indirectly to every other node and that perceptual experiences are a key component of the network. Some of these connections are strong and others are weak. The strength of a connection is determined by past experiences and whether they have been used successfully to answer a question. For example, in identifying the letter H, the feature *horizontal line* needs to be strong and *round line* (as in a Q) needs to be weak. The entire set of connections reflects the sum of your knowledge. Most critically, this approach assumes that when a person is asked a question or shown a picture, activation spreads over time across the person's entire knowledge network. This basic underlying assumption makes connectionist models unique because they suggest that we have access to our entire store of knowledge at once. They assume humans are parallel processors of information (e.g., McClelland & Rumelhart, 1981).

Like the perceptual theory of knowledge, connectionist models emphasize how we acquire information through experience. When you first encountered animals such as a robin or a sparrow, someone might have said, "see the birdie flapping its wings so it can fly." Because of such experiences, concepts like *bird*, *has wings*, and *flying* became associated. New creatures you encountered that were called *bird* would be connected to all the other birds you had encountered, even fanciful creatures like *Sesame Street*'s Big Bird.

Due to their common connections to additional nodes (called *units*) in memory, other properties of birds would be activated in your mind, even some that are not correct. For example, you might expect penguins to fly because they are birds and have wings, or you might think that an airplane was a bird because someone said it was flying. Of course, throughout your life you are corrected or supported in your conclusions so that the link between *sparrow* and *flying* is strengthened and the link between *penguin* and *flying* is not. **FIGURE 7.8** illustrates the connectionist model. Unlike the network model (shown in Figure 7.1), which is organized by categories like *plants*, *animals*, and *birds*, in the connectionist model the instances and the properties are all connected by common units that link the name of an object (e.g., *canary*) with a general property (e.g., *can*) and an output property (e.g., *fly*).

The connectionist models are quite useful. First, they can be modified based on a person's development of knowledge: They can account for the concept of learning. Second, they illustrate how people often confuse related information. Finally, they offer a systematic explanation for the loss of information resulting from brain damage, which occurs when people suffer from semantic dementia (Hodges, Graham, & Patterson, 1995; Snowden, Goulding, & Neary, 1989; Warrington, 1975). For example, a person with semantic dementia may be shown a series of pictures containing different animals and asked to name each one. The progress of the disease can be explained by connectionist models. Early in the malady, the person might respond correctly to many of the names and properties and only occasionally make an error. He or she might call a penguin a duck, or perhaps call a horse a dog, which is explained by the fact that both horses and dogs have four legs. At this point, the person would still remember that birds fly and lay eggs. After about 3 years with the malady,

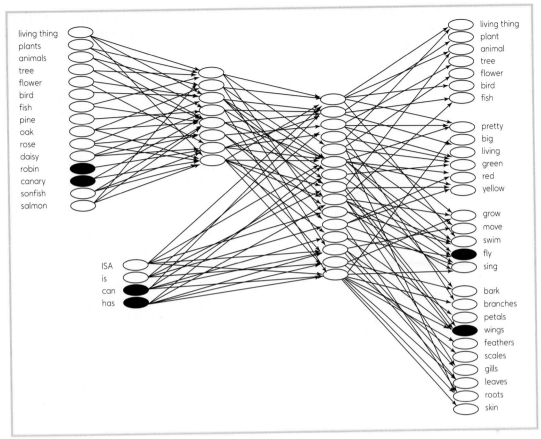

Connectionist Model

FIGURE 7.8 The Connectionist Theory The connectionist theory hypothesizes that instances and properties are all connected by common units that link the name of an object (e.g., *canary*) with a general property (e.g., *can*) and an output property (e.g., *fly*).

Source: McClelland & Rogers, 2003

the person becomes unable to name individual animals such as canary, and can identify them only by their generic name (bird). However, often he or she loses the link between the name and the category; the person might call a peacock a vehicle or a dog (see McClelland & Rogers, 2003). The person has lost the strong connections that define relationships, such as losing *is a* between robin and bird. Connectionist theories will someday allow physicians to look in specific areas of the brain to identify the type of damage that characterizes semantic dementia.

SECTION SUMMARY ▪

Theories of Knowledge

Four different types of theories have been used to explain how knowledge is structured in semantic memory and how humans add new knowledge and make inferences from their knowledge. Network theories envision knowledge as a vast net in which every fact is linked through a series of nodes to other facts. Some of these facts are abstract and conceptually based, such as Quillian's teachable language comprehender (TLC) theory, but others are experientially and perceptually based, such as the perceptual theory of knowledge. The fundamental retrieval mechanism posed by network theories is spreading activation, where the time to respond to a question about concepts in knowledge depends on the distance in the network between the terms being considered. Quillian's original network theory, the TLC, views human knowledge as hierarchically organized. The time to answer a question, according to this theory, is related to the distance between levels in the knowledge hierarchy.

A more spatial way of representing human knowledge is the feature comparison model (FCM), which focuses on the defining and characterizing features of categories. People answering questions about categories do so by deciding whether the terms of a question are similar. If they are very similar or very dissimilar, answers are rapid. If they are of medium similarity, the person requires more time to respond to the question because he or she needs to focus on the defining features of categories.

Finally, connectionist theories combine the perceptual and experiential view of knowledge with the network concept and create a parallel processing theory, where all knowledge is potentially accessed. It can account for the basic findings by assuming that facts in our knowledge vary in their strength of connection based on how often they are successfully used to identify a pattern or answer a question. In addition, it can correctly predict the gradual decline in ability to answer semantic questions that results from a malady called semantic dementia.

Schemas: The Structure of Knowledge in Everyday Life

If you wanted to create a map of your neighborhood so that visitors could find your house, would you draw a picture of every house, tree, and crack in the sidewalk, or would you draw a superficial sketch marking relevant street intersections and your house number? The picture is time-consuming to draw and is full of irrelevant details. In contrast, the sketch is easy to draw, has only the pertinent information, and may be easier to use. Many of our memories for what things look like or how to perform tasks are more like the sketch than the picture.

When our knowledge is like a sketch, it is called a **schema**, a piece of knowledge that can apply to many situations for many purposes (Bartlett, 1932; Head, 1926; Head & Holmes, 1911). Like the sketch of your neighborhood, schemas may be thought of as correct in overall form but perhaps wrong about (or missing) major details. Schemas represent knowledge in the kind of flexible way that reflects the human tolerance for "vagueness, imprecision, and quasi-inconsistencies" (Rumelhart & Ortony, 1977, p. 111; Fiske & Linville, 1980).

Consider the human face. Our faces are semi-elliptical objects that contain two eyes, two ears, a nose, and a mouth. This is our general idea of what a face should contain—a face schema. Yet our understanding of faces goes beyond this basic sketch. If we encounter a face with one of its features obscured, such as when a hat hides someone's eyes, we would still call it a face. Or consider the case of the Cyclops in Homer's *Odyssey*: Even though it had only one eye, we would not deny that it had a face. Outlaws in old Western movies wear bandanas that reveal only their eyes, but we know there are faces under the masks. A schema such as the face schema is useful because it allows us to apply our vast knowledge of faces to patterns where we only have fragmentary information. Schema knowledge is generally based on experience and differs from the knowledge we gain from looking up definitions in a dictionary. Schemas contain our knowledge of the world and provide an understanding of how real things are related. As a result, schemas change over time and evolve as our experiences increase and change (Rumelhart & Norman, 1981; Rumelhart & Ortony, 1977).

Outlaws in old Western movies wear bandanas that reveal only their eyes, but we know there are faces under the masks because of our face schema, which allows us to use our knowledge of what a face is when we have incomplete information.

Courtesy Everett Collection

One type of schema, called a **script,** tells us what behavior we should expect of ourselves and of others in certain kinds of situations (e.g., M. B. Brewer, 1999; Goffman, 1959; Neisser, 1976; Rumelhart, 1975, 1980; Rumelhart, Smolensky, McClelland, & Hinton, 1986). Schema knowledge in general, and scripts in particular, are organized hierarchically. Take our knowledge of restaurants, for example. At the most general, or highest level of a hierarchy, might be a schema that describes *types of restaurants*; at an intermediate level might be scripts describing *how to behave in a restaurant, how to order the food,* and *how to pay for the food*. At the lowest level of a schema hierarchy might be schemas describing details such as *the placement of knife and fork while dining* and *where to put your utensils between bites*.

Although schemas can be stand-alone knowledge structures, they generally interact with other schemas. A schema for performing a task will interact with a schema for how to interact with other people. Suppose you are a surgeon in an operating room. Your schema for performing surgery might include a separate schema for how to prepare for surgery (*how to put on surgical scrubs* and *wash your hands*); another might be a schema for how to perform the overall surgery; another for the professional way to talk with your assistants—even how to tell a joke and with whom you can joke. For example, the surgeon can tell a joke, but the scrub nurse cannot (Edmondson, 2003; Goffman, 1967; Solet, Norvell, Rutan, & Frankel, 2005). Finally, you might have a special schema for describing the outcome of the surgery to the patient's friends and family (Hetts, Werne, & Hieshima, 1995).

An important characteristic of schemas that contributes to their adaptability is that a schema can be modified depending on conditions, which are sometimes called *variables*. For example, if you're going to a restaurant with your friends, you might order food differently depending on whether it is a fast-food, takeout (*takeaway* in Britain), buffet, or sit-down establishment. In a sit-down restaurant you wait to be seated and are handed a menu and then the server asks you to order from the menu. At a takeout restaurant, the menu might be written on a list hanging on the wall. Customers at all of these eateries will order food, but how they do it depends on the type of restaurant. The *type of restaurant* is a variable in the overall restaurant schema.

Schemas Fill In Missing Information

Our ability to understand conversations or text is especially dependent on our ability to make inferences from what we hear or see (Graesser, Singer, & Trabasso, 1994). Since no conversation or text could include every possible fact about a scenario, speakers and authors rely on the listener or reader to "fill in" unstated information. For example, if someone were to tell you that she dined at the Jeanne D'Arc restaurant in San Francisco, you would be able to infer that she sat at a table, was shown a menu, and paid for the meal. All these items are part of the *dining* component of the restaurant schema and need not be described by the speaker unless they are important to the narrative. What kind of tablecloths covered the tables would never need to be mentioned unless someone was describing eating at Durgin-Park, a restaurant in Boston, where new tablecloths are placed on top of previously used tablecloths throughout the day, making the tables lumpy. A character in a horror film might look through a keyhole to see what is lurking on the other side of a door, only to see another eye peering back. We infer from that eye that an entire person (or perhaps a monster) is on the other side.

If you possess a schema that is relevant to a situation, it will speed up your ability to comprehend discussions or narratives about that situation. A computer metaphor helps to explain this. When you first set up your word processor, you will be asked whether or not you want "fast saves." This is a procedure in which the computer stores only the updates to what you are writing rather than rewriting the entire text to its hard drive. To improve efficiency, it stores only what is new. Similarly, when we understand a narrative, we too may be concentrating on what is new or what is inconsistent with the schema for the topic of conversation. What we already know does not concern us. However, information that does not fit into the schema may not be understood, or may be poorly understood. This explains why readers have a difficult time understanding a text on a subject they are not familiar with, even if they understand the meaning of the individual words in a passage.

To illustrate how schemas provide background knowledge, Schank and Abelson (1977) developed Script Applier Mechanism (SAM), a computer program that is able to analyze printed stories such as those from a newspaper, create paraphrases of them, and then answer simple questions about them. SAM does this by interpreting sentences not literally, but in reference to a script for how people and their environments interact. One of the schemas built into SAM is a restaurant schema, whose properties are shown in **TABLE 7.2**. This schema is similar to what you would expect a script of a play to contain: the name of the script, a cast of characters, and a list of scenes that describes what the characters do.

The computer program identifies elements from the narrative and searches its memory for an appropriate script, in this case a restaurant. It then matches parts of the narrative with the elements of the script in the same way a person might. **TABLE 7.3** shows a simple narrative and a paraphrase of it produced by SAM. The underlined parts of the paraphrase are ideas that match the narrative. Notice that most of the paraphrase is supplied by the schema for going to a restaurant and was never directly expressed in the narrative.

Schemas Can Mislead

One of the negative consequences of having a schema for an event or a concept is that we are prone to misinterpret what we have experienced. In the movie *Being There*, the main character is a man named Chance, a slow-witted gardener who emerges from virtual isolation in a mansion upon the death of his employer. People around him do not know he is a gardener because he fits their schema of a businessman: He speaks deliberately and is wearing the clothes of his deceased wealthy employer. Therefore, they treat everything he says as intelligent and deeply profound.

Because schemas are so rich with information, it can be difficult for people to distinguish between their own knowledge—as provided by the schema—and their actual memory for the experience. This is illustrated in the activity in Demonstration 7.2. Try it and then continue reading the text.

TABLE **7.2**
Restaurant Schema

Schema: Restaurant

Characters: Customer, hostess, waiter, chef, cashier

Scene 1: Entering

  Customer goes into restaurant

  Customer finds a place to sit

    He may find it himself

    He may be seated by a hostess

      He asks the hostess for a table

      She gives him permission to go to the table

  Customer goes and sits at the table

Scene 2: Ordering

  Customer receives a menu

    Customer reads it

    Customer decides what to order

    Waiter takes the order

      Waiter sees the customer

      Waiter goes to the customer

      Customer orders what he wants

  Chef cooks the meal

Scene 3: Eating

  After some time the waiter brings the meal from the chef

    Customer eats the meal

Scene 4: Exiting

    Customer asks the waiter for the check

    Waiter gives the check to the customer

    Customer leaves a tip (in U.S. restaurants)

      The size of the tip depends on the goodness of the service

    Customer pays the cashier

    Customer leaves the restaurant

Note: From Schank & Abelson, 1977

TABLE **7.3**
Narrative and Paraphrase Produced by SAM

Narrative

John went to a restaurant. The hostess seated John. The hostess gave John a menu. John ordered lobster. He was served quickly. He left a large tip. He left the restaurant.

SAM paraphrase

John decided he was going to go to a restaurant. <u>He went to one</u>. He asked the hostess for a table. She told him he could go to it. <u>He went to it. She went to it.</u> He sat down in a chair. <u>He got a menu from her.</u> He read it. A waiter saw John at the table. The waiter went to it. <u>John ordered lobster</u>. A chef cooked it. The waiter got it from the chef. The waiter <u>served it quickly to John.</u> He ate it. He asked the waiter for a check. John got it from the waiter. John remembered the waiter had served him quickly. <u>John left</u> the waiter <u>a large tip.</u> John paid the check. <u>He left the restaurant.</u>

Note: From Schank & Abelson, 1977

•••DEMONSTRATION 7.2

The Impact of Schemas on Memory
Read the following narrative at a normal pace and then answer the question below it.

> Chief Resident Jones adjusted his face mask while anxiously surveying a pale figure secured to the long gleaming table before him. One swift stroke of his small sharp instrument and a thin red line appeared. Then an eager young assistant carefully extended the opening as another aide pushed aside glistening surface fat so that vital parts were laid bare. Everyone present stared in horror at the ugly growth too large for removal. He now knew it was pointless to continue.

Look away from the story for about a minute and then return to the activity below.
Circle the words below that occurred in the story and then return to the text.

car

doctor

nurse

scalpel

table

building

If you are like the students in the original study (based on Pompi & Lachman, 1967, p. 144), you circled doctor, nurse, and scalpel. If you look back at the narrative, you'll notice that none of these words appear in the actual story, but readers often identify them as having been in the passage. One explanation is that the passage activates a surgery schema and the elements of the schema fill the participants' working memories with information that is not included in the actual passage (there are many similar findings; e.g., R. C. Anderson, Spiro, & M. C. Anderson, 1978; Bower, Black, & Turner, 1979; Spiro, 1977; Zangwill, 1972).

Schemas not only are able to mislead us in what we have read, they can occasionally distort our recollection of things we have personally experienced.

The photograph in **FIGURE 7.9** depicts a graduate student office used in a study by W. F. Brewer & Treyens (1981). Students were asked to wait in this office for about 35 seconds "before beginning the experiment." In fact, the experiment began when the students were in the room, because when they left it, they were informed that their real task was to remember what the office contained. The students were asked to recall the items verbally, or to recognize items from the room. They were reasonably accurate in recalling objects that were present and consistent with their expectations (e.g., chair and desk). They were poor at recalling objects that were present but unexpected (e.g., bulletin board and skull). However, their personal schemas of what such an office contained caused them to falsely recall the presence of expected (but absent) items such as books. In fact, of the 88 items they recalled on average, 19 (or 21%) were never presented. This distortion, based on their schemas, increased with the passage of time (Lampinen, Copeland, & Neuschatz, 2001).

FIGURE 7.9 Student Office in Brewer and Treyens Study Students waited in this room for about 35 seconds. When they left, they were asked to recall the items in the room verbally, or to recognize items from the room. Their memory was good for items that were consistent with their schema of a graduate student office, but not for those that were inconsistent.

Brewer, W. F., and Treyens, J. C. (1981). "Role of Schemata in memory for place." *Cognitive Psychology; 23,* Figure 1, pp. 207–230.

These findings show that schemas have a psychological reality: They help us fill in the blanks, but they also contribute to false recollections because we incorrectly assume the presence of script-consistent elements.

On the positive side, people are good at detecting when schema-inconsistent events occur in a story. These oddities appear to stand out with special clarity in our memory. We recall the schema-consistent information and then add these inconsistent events (Graesser, Gordon, & Sawyer, 1979; Graesser, Kassler, Kreuz, & McLain-Allen, 1998). Sometimes these special, unpredicted events are the most clearly recalled information from a particular event (Nakamura, Graesser, Zimmerman, & Riha, 1985). In one study on script memory (Bower et al., 1979), students recalled 53% of the inconsistent information, but only 38% of the schema-consistent information. People are very good at discriminating between unexpected events that occurred in a story and unexpected events that did not occur.

Cueing Schemas

The memory for a schema can be activated by the mention of key terms in a narrative, such as *chief resident* and *sharp instrument* in the example in Demonstration 7.2. The title of a narrative may also activate a schema (Ausubel, 1960; Mayer, 2003). In a study conducted by Sulin and Dooling (1974) a group of students read a passage about a fictitious character named Carol Harris, while another group read an identical story titled "Helen Keller" (a deaf and blind woman whose incredible accomplishments made her an admired person in the 20th century). Either immediately after reading one of the two passages or 1 week later, the

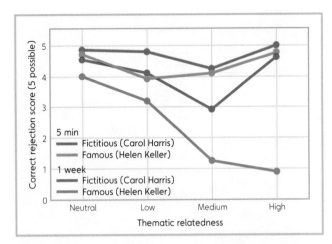

FIGURE 7.10 Correct Rejection Score For False Sentences (out of 5 possible) Participants read a passage about a fictitious character (Carol Harris) or a real person (Helen Keller) and were tested immediately or a week later on their memory for sentences that never appeared in the passage but were true of the real Helen Keller. After a week's delay, only those who thought the passage was about Helen Keller falsely recognized sentences consistent with their schema of her.

Source: Sulin & Dooling, 1974

students were tested on their recognition memory for critical sentences that were related (from poorly to highly related) to Helen Keller. For example, one critical sentence that was highly related to Helen Keller, but never appeared in the narrative was "She was deaf, mute, and blind." As shown in **FIGURE 7.10**, both groups of students were highly accurate in rejecting this sentence 5 minutes after they read the passage. However, 1 week later, the students who thought the passage was about Helen Keller falsely recognized this sentence as having been part of the narrative, whereas the students who read about the fictitious character Carol Harris did not make that mistake.

The presence of a particular schema at time of retrieval can also influence what we recall. In one study, students who had read the Carol Harris story were told just before the recognition test that the story was really about Helen Keller. They showed the same pattern of false recognitions as the people who had read the story with the title "Helen Keller" (Dooling & Christiaansen, 1977).

SECTION SUMMARY ■

Schemas: The Structure of Knowledge in Everyday Life

A schema is a piece of knowledge, generally gained from experience, that can apply to many situations for many purposes. Schemas contain our knowledge of the world and how real objects or events are related. When schemas are about behaviors, they are called scripts. The knowledge embodied in a schema is generally experience-based and may change considerably over a life span. The structure of a schema tends to be hierarchical, with broad specifications at the highest level (*what happens in a restaurant*), to specific details at the lowest level (*paying the bill*). Schemas possess variables that dictate which subtype of a schema should be employed. For example, the application of the restaurant schema varies with whether a person is in a fast-food or sit-down restaurant.

Schemas help us predict what will happen and fill in missing information: when we see a head hidden by a shadow, the body schema allows us to infer that an entire person is present; if we read a description of a surgery, we infer that the actors are surgeons and nurses. The reason we can make such inferences about other people is that schemas are often organized as if we were participants in a play and reading from a script. Schemas can be activated by special terms in a narrative or even the title of a story. When a schema is activated in long-term memory, it can help us interpret what we are seeing or reading. However, schemas can mislead us. Although scripts help us to interpret stories and remember the details, we often recall unstated details from narratives because they are an intrinsic part of the script.

Schema Development

We are born into the world with predispositions to react, and the world cooperates by providing the stimuli for those reactions. Swiss psychologist Jean Piaget (1926) conducted research showing that much of children's knowledge is derived from their interactions with the world, but they are biologically prepared to interact with the world through specific action sequences or schemas.

Behavior Sequences at Birth

Infants are born with a set of reflexes or innate mechanisms for interacting with the world (see **TABLE 7.4**). **Reflexes** may be considered to be wired-in action schemas: a package of coordinated sequences triggered by certain environmental conditions. It is easy to see the adaptability of some of these reflexes. The *blink reflex* (involuntary closure of the eye when a bright light is flashed or an object rapidly comes toward the infant) protects the eye. The *Moro reflex* occurs when infants hear a loud noise or feel a loss of support; their arms and legs extend and then come together as if to grab onto an object to prevent falling. Other reflexes seem intended to help infants acquire key motor skills. The *walking reflex* is seen when newborns are held upright and their feet come in contact with a surface and they exhibit a stepping motion. Although this reflex disappears within a few days, it reappears about a year later when infants start learning to walk.

Infants exhibit other schema-based predispositions as well, especially in response to faces. We saw in Chapter 4 that within a day of birth, newborns can imitate facial gestures such as smiles and frowns (Meltzoff & Brooks, 2001). Infants appear to have an innate preference for gazing at face-like images, such as a pair of round blobs, over a horizontal line (Johnson, 2001; Quinn, Eimas, & Tarr, 2001; Slater & Quinn, 2001). They prefer to look at an upright T shape (an abstract set of eyes and a nose) more often than an upside-down T shape (Simion, Cassia, Turati, & Valenza, 2001). They gaze longer at a picture of their mother's face than at a picture of any other female (e.g., Pascalis, de Schonen, Morton, Deruelle, & Fabre-Grenet, 1995; Walton, Bower, & Bower, 1992). It may be that our adult preference for faces comes from many experiences at an early age. In one study, 7-month-old infants raised by single mothers preferred to look at pictures of female faces, whereas those raised by single fathers preferred male faces (Quinn, Yahr, Kuhn, Slater, & Olivier, 2002).

TABLE **7.4**	
Newborn Reflexes	
Reflexive schemas	**Content**
Blink	Involuntary closure of the eye to a flash of light
Moro	Arms and legs extend and then come together as if to grab onto something
Landau	Reflexive crawling (raised head/arched back)
Protective	If cloth is placed over an infant's eyes and nose, infant will turn head from side to side
Palmar	Grasping reflex when object is placed on palm
Walking	When the soles of the feet touch a flat surface, infants place one foot in front of the other

The Development of Narrative Schemas

Schemas change over a person's lifetime because they are a consequence of experience and understanding. For example, the stories that a 2-year-old tells are about surprising or even startling events (Ames, 1966; Davidson, 1996; Hudson & Nelson, 1983; Lucariello & Mindolovich, 2002; Skarakis-Doyle, 2002) and consist of one or two words where the message is conveyed more by the *prosody* (word emphasis) than the information value of the words (Sutton-Smith, 1986). Such two-word stories tend to be separated by taking a breath. By 4 or 5 years of age, stories are a sequence of events that have a beginning, middle, and end and are typically tied together with "and then" (Kemper & Edwards, 1986). Just before children go to elementary school, the narratives they communicate to adults have a broader structure, and consist of a setting that gives information about the main character as well as the time and place for the event. These narratives also contain at least one episode that includes a starting event, and possible responses to it. In general, such narratives also include an ending where the problems that started the episodes are resolved (Stein & Glenn, 1979). These characteristics fit a basic structure called a **narrative** (or **story**) **schema**, which is a schema for telling a story that develops over time until it matches the full schema that characterizes adult stories with a plot structure: Plots are typically incorporated into story schemas by the time a child is 8 years old (e.g., Sutton-Smith, 1986).

As narrative schemas develop over time they become more complex and more interesting to adults. Research has identified four basic types of story schemas that develop: recounts, eventcasts, accounts, and fictionalized stories (Stein, 2002). **Recounts** organize the stories of speakers around their personal experiences. They are typically the first narratives children tell and are prompted by the questions of others. In school, you provide a recount when you are asked to describe your summer vacation. **Eventcasts** are running commentaries of events at hand or ones that will occur in the future (When we go to granny Doris's house, she'll make lots of cookies). **Accounts** are speaker-initiated narratives (Guess what . . .) similar to recounts. **Fictionalized stories** are imaginative narratives that fit one of the schemas, but are about fictional characters or events. Story schemas are discussed later in this chapter, but the critical point now is that the schemas that characterize narratives are diverse and unfold over time.

A Child Tells a Story in School. Narrative schemas develop over time; plots become part of story schemas by about the age of 8.

James Shaffer/Photo Edit

Our reliance on schemas to understand narratives endures for life, even though their basic structure changes. In fact, by the time we are adults, the use of schemas is automatic (Hess, 1985; Light & Anderson, 1983). One study (Zelinski & Miura, 1988, Experiment 2) compared memory for narratives in young adults (19–32 years old) and older adults (59–80 years old). Participants listened to a recording of a story in which the main character engaged in three scripted activities: (a) going to the doctor, (b) attending a lecture, and (c) going to a party. Although the young participants freely recalled more details than the older ones 24 hours later, both groups showed equal ability to recognize sentences from the passages that were consistent with the story schemas. These findings support the view that our reliance on narrative schemas does not decline with age.

SECTION SUMMARY

Schema Development

Some schemas seem to be activated at birth and then disappear with time. Others develop steadily across the life span. These more enduring schemas tend to begin as simple, generic behavior sequences, such as how we tell a story. When we are young these tend to be recounts that involve "I did this [*child takes a breath*] I did that." These stories progress through eventcasts, accounts, and fictionalized stories. By the time people are teenagers, their concept of a story includes plot structure, locations, episodes, and resolutions.

Schemas As Organizers

Schemas function as knowledge structures that organize how we learn and behave. They help us encode the stories that we read or hear and influence what we will remember about them. In everyday lives schemas also control what we expect of the people and objects around us.

Story Schemas

Last year, 160 million copies of Harlequin romance novels were sold worldwide in more than 23 languages. The Canadian publisher of this vast series of books claimed: "If you set out to read all of the Harlequin books sold over the past 10 years, and averaged about two hours per book, you would be reading for the next quarter of a million years" (www.millsandboon.com.au/aboutus.asp#history). These novels contain a basic story script: Boy meets attractive though rarely beautiful girl, boy loses girl because of a problem, and after 180 pages boy and girl reunite romantically with at least a happy ending and often with the possibility of marriage. The story structure is known and satisfying to readers.

A *Star Wars* Poster. The *Star Wars* stories follow a standard structure: Each episode revolves around the battle between good and evil. It is a type of story told by people all over the world.

Other popular genres also have a common story structure. The *Star Wars* stories follow a standard structure: Each episode is grounded by a contrast of good and evil. They all begin with the problem posed by evil: Darth Vader's spaceship attacking Princess Leia's spaceship, probes being sent out to find the rebels, Jedi fighters being fired on by a battle cruiser, and so forth. Then they quickly contrast these settings with "good" people. Once the problem is introduced, a series of sub-episodes follow in an effort by the good to defeat the evil, with a partial resolution occurring at the end. The progression of these stories is consistent with what Joseph Campbell (1949/2008) referred to as the "hero's journey." This standard schema appears universally in stories told by diverse groups of people all over the world.

Story Schema Constituents

What are the essential elements of a story schema, the basic structure of narrative? Every narrative has four primary categories or constituents: (a) setting, (b) theme, (c) plot with main characters and a causal chain of events, and (d) a resolution to the story (e.g., Mandler & Johnson, 1977; Thorndyke, 1977). **FIGURE 7.11** presents a story called "Circle Island" that has been used in many studies of story comprehension. The numbers in the narrative correspond to **FIGURE 7.12**, a tree structure that divides the story into the four main story schema categories. Notice that the branches of each category can be divided into subparts; for example, the setting category might have subcategories of location and time. The episode category has an initiating event, an attempt to deal with the initiating event, and an outcome of this attempt.

These elements are important for how people understand and remember stories. To illustrate this, Thorndyke (1977) showed "Circle Island" to undergraduates and asked them to freely recall the sentences of the story. He was interested in whether the recollections were best predicted by the order in which the sentences were presented or by the categories in the story schema. Thorndyke reasoned that if students are simply recalling the information sentence by sentence as presented in the narrative version of the story (Figure 7.11), then their ability to recall Sentence 5, for example, should be better if they recall Sentence 4 because they are remembering the story in order. However, if the categories used to create the story in Figure 7.12 are what the students understand and remember, then recall of Sentence 5 should be greater if it and Sentence 4 are

(1) Circle Island is located in the middle of the Atlantic Ocean, (2) north of Ronald Island. (3) The main occupations on the island are farming and ranching. (4) Circle Island has good soil, (5) but few rivers and (6) hence a shortage of water. (7) The island is run democratically. (8) All issues are decided by a majority vote of the islanders. (9) The governing body is a senate, (10) whose job is to carry out the will of the majority. (11) Recently, an island scientist discovered a cheap method (12) of converting salt water into fresh water. (13) As a result, the island farmers wanted (14) to build a canal across the island, (15) so that they could use water from the canal (16) to cultivate the island's central region. (17) Therefore, the farmers formed a procanal association (18) and persuaded a few senators (19) to join. (20) The procanal association brought the construction idea to a vote. (21) All the islanders voted. (22) The majority voted in favor of construction. (23) The senate, however, decided that (24) the farmers' proposed canal was ecologically unsound. (25) The senators agreed (26) to build a smaller canal (27) that was 2 feet wide and 1 foot deep. (28) After starting construction on the smaller canal, (29) the islanders discovered that (30) no water would flow into it. (31) Thus the project was abandoned. (32) The farmers were angry (33) because of the failure of the canal project. (34) Civil war appeared inevitable.

FIGURE 7.11 The Story of "Circle Island" The story of "Circle Island" has played a part in many studies of story memory. The numbers in the narrative correspond to elements of the story's structure shown in Figure 7.12.

Source: Thorndyke, 1977

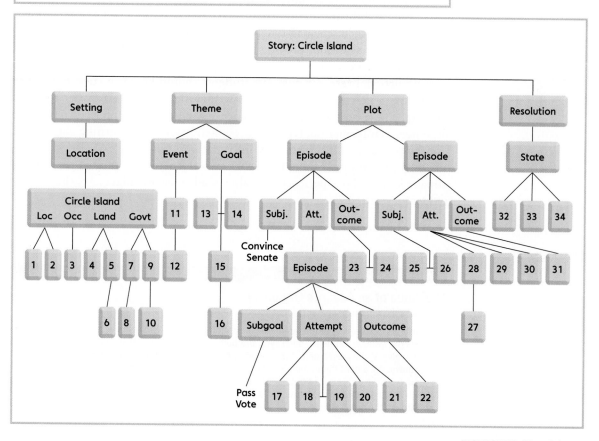

FIGURE 7.12 Story Schema of "Circle Island" This diagram portrays a story schema of "Circle Island" (Figure 7.11). It divides the story into the four main universal story categories that are important for how people understand and remember stories: setting, theme, plot, and resolution.

Source: Thorndyke, 1977

from the same category. Thorndyke tallied the recollections of students and found that the likelihood of recalling Sentence 5 if Sentence 4 is already recalled is quite high if both sentences are in the same category, but quite low if they are in different categories. This illustrates the importance of story elements for people's ability to remember the story. In fact, stories that conform to the structure of story schemas are better recalled than stories that conform less well (W. F. Brewer, 1996; Mandler & Johnson, 1977).

Schemas and Reading Comprehension

Reading comprehension is a significant component of academic performance in the early school years (Lorch et al., 1999). Cognitive research related to story schemas has been used to develop procedures to help schoolchildren make better use of their own memories. A major benefit of schemas is that they offer people a framework for understanding, storing, and retrieving new information. When students have difficulty learning new topics, it may be that their existing knowledge structure (their schemas) is not activated in the learning situation, and therefore, the schemas cannot provide the structural support the students need to encode new information.

Instructional research suggests students should be given cues in advance of reading a new text or story for how they should organize what they are reading. These cues were called **advance organizers** in Chapter 1. An advance organizer is information, typically presented prior to the learning experience, that helps learners interpret new information (Ausubel, 1963, 1968; Mayer, 1979) by providing a bridge between new information and what the learner already knows. To experience the value of advance organizers, try the activity in Demonstration 7.3.

■■■**DEMONSTRATION 7.3**

The Value of an Advance Organizer

Read the following passage and see if you can understand it.

> Bicycle tire pumps vary in the number and location of the valves they have and in the way air enters the cylinder. Some simple bicycle tire pumps have the inlet valve on the piston and the outlet valve at the closed end of the cylinder. A bicycle tire pump has a piston that moves up and down. Air enters the pump near the point where the connecting rod passes through the cylinder. As the rod is pulled out, air passes through the piston and fills the area between the piston and the outlet valve. As the rod is pushed in, the inlet valve closes the piston and forces air through the outlet valve.

(Mayer & Gallini, 1990, p. 721)

Memory Question: How many valves does the pump have?

Problem-Solving Question: How can a pump push more air?

One difficulty people have with remembering and using the information in this passage is the effort it takes to integrate the separate pieces of information into a coherent image of the entire device: a schema. A visual advance organizer can provide the necessary schema. Look at the diagram on the next page and then re-read the passage.

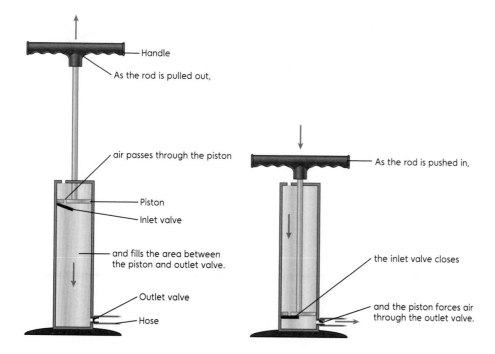

Handle

As the rod is pulled out,

air passes through the piston

Piston

Inlet valve

and fills the area between
the piston and outlet valve.

Outlet valve

Hose

As the rod is pushed in,

the inlet valve closes

and the piston forces air
through the outlet valve.

Did the diagram help you? Although the diagram does not add any words that are not in the text, Mayer and Gallini (1990) found that students who were shown the diagram recalled 4 times as much as students who read the text alone. Both groups were tested on their ability to solve a problem using the information given in the passage. The diagram group was 69% better at solving the problem than the text without diagram group.

Advance organizers do not always lead to an increase in overall recall of facts when they give irrelevant or distracting information, sometimes called *seductive details* (e.g., Mayer & Anderson, 1991; Rowland-Bryant et al., 2009). However, their primary advantage is in helping the learner transfer or apply the learned information to new situations (Mayer, 2003).

Teaching a simplified story schema to children as an advance organizer can increase their ability to remember stories (Beck & McKeown, 1991). An example of how this is done is shown in **FIGURE 7.13**, which illustrates a story-mapping exercise. Story maps lead to increased comprehension among young students compared with alternative instructional strategies (e.g., Davis, 1994; Gordon & Braun, 1983; Reutzel, 1985, 1986). This is especially the case for students with learning disabilities (e.g., Taylor, Alber, & Walker, 2002).

Schemas About People

Another universally used type of schema is the **person schema**. These schemas connect common personality traits (outgoing, shy, aggressive, etc.) with the behavior such traits commonly produce. For example, if a child tends to be clumsy and knock things over, the *clumsy* schema suggests that you might want to move

FIGURE 7.13 A Story-Mapping Exercise Teaching children to understand the structural elements of a story improves their story comprehension. One way to do this is with a story-mapping exercise, in which children are asked questions corresponding to levels in this chart.

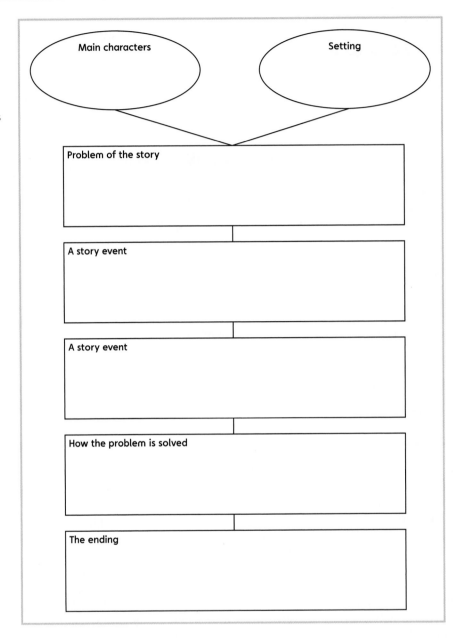

glasses of water away from the edge of the table when the child is around (Horowitz, 1991; but see Ross & Nisbett, 1991). Like all schemas, person schemas affect your interpretation of the events that you witness, your memory for those events, and what to expect in the future.

Person schemas are often extended to encompass the members of particular groups. A person schema applied to an entire group is a **stereotype**: an oversimplified understanding of the qualities of groups of people. The term has its origin in a method dating to 1798 of creating images in newspapers and books (a rigid print type that lacked depth or detail, but was easy to reproduce; Lippmann, 1922). Stereotypes may be founded on assumptions that a group has positive or negative traits, but these assumptions are nearly always inaccurate. Every member of a group rarely shares the same attribute or attributes with every other member of a group. Even using a positive stereotype of a group carries with it the implication that members of other groups don't have that positive trait.

FIGURE 7.14 Stereotyping: Drawing from Allport and Postman's Study Students were asked to study a picture in which a White man is holding a weapon and there is a second man (White or Black) in the picture. When they saw a picture with a Black man as the second man, students were 3 times more likely to recall the weapon being in the second man's hand than those who saw a picture in which the second man was White. Stereotypes are schemas that affect our perception and our memory.

Copyright 1987, Canadian Psychological Association. Permission granted for use of material.

Stereotypes lead to biased or prejudicial behavior (Allport, 1935; Nelson, 2006), and like other schemas can cause people to misrecall events so that they are consistent with the set of assumptions governing the stereotype (e.g., Lenton, Blair, & Hastie, 2001). Research shows that these distortions can occur even when people are warned not to allow their biases to operate (e.g., Peters, Jelicic, Verbeek, & Merckelbach, 2007). In one study, two groups of Scottish university students viewed a cartoon-like story depicting an interaction between two men on a subway (see **FIGURE 7.14**). In the last frame of the story, one man holds a knife. Group A saw a story in which both men were White and one of the White men held a knife. Group B saw a story where one of the men was Black and the other was White and the White man held the knife.

Forty-five minutes later, all the participants were given a recognition test (this is just one of the many conditions in the study) in which they were shown a picture from the story. Group A saw a test picture in which a *different* White man held the knife. (Group A was the control group to see just how accurate the participants were in remembering who had the knife.) Only 20% of the students made an error on this picture. Group B saw a test picture in which the Black man held the knife. This group showed the effect of a racial stereotype on remembering: 60% of the students incorrectly identified the Black man as holding the knife. Recall that, in the original picture, the White man held the knife (Boon & Davies, 1987). Findings such as these show we possess person schemas that, when activated, can lead to the same kind of inference and filling in of slots that we find in more prosaic situations like going to a restaurant. Obviously, the use of person schemas can lead to more serious consequences.

SECTION SUMMARY ▪

Schemas As Organizers

The stories we tell conform to a structure found in narratives that have universal themes. Story schemas make it easier for people to recall stories as well as to understand them. Most narratives contain four main categories: (a) setting, (b) theme, (c) plot with main characters and a causal chain of events, and (d) a resolution to the story. Like other schemas, when the stories do not correspond to the standard structure, the listener adds or reorganizes the story elements to correspond to the story schema. Cognitively based instruction advocates that students should be given schematic information in advance of reading a new factual text or story. This additional material, called an advance organizer, helps students understand the key concepts of what they are about to learn by providing an integrated framework on which to store the new information. Advance organizers can take the form of diagrams, metaphors, or background material. One effective form of advance organizer is to inform the young reader that the story can be divided into categories based on a story map. This procedure improves the reading comprehension of both skilled and poor readers.

Person schemas are applied to understanding and predicting the behavior of others. Sometimes these schemas are overgeneralized and used to describe the behavior of members of an entire group. These broad generalizations are called stereotypes. Research shows that stereotypes can lead not only to biased or prejudiced behavior, but to distorted memories of events as well.

Expertise, Knowledge, and Skilled Memory

There are many anecdotes of superb feats of memory in specialized areas such as music. Mozart is said to have heard a performance of Allegri's choral work, *Miserere Mei Deus,* in Rome at the age of 12. He wanted a copy of the score, but because no one was allowed to get a copy under threat of excommunication, Mozart is reputed to have committed the work to memory after hearing it only once. He returned home and wrote down all of the notes nearly perfectly. Toscanini, an early 20th-century conductor, is reputed to have memorized every note to be played by every instrument for hundreds of symphonic works (Neisser, 1982). He made use of his astonishing memory for music by conducting without a musical score in front of him. Toscanini had to rely on his incredible memory because he was extremely nearsighted and would not have been able to read the score while conducting. Finally, for more than a thousand years, the laws of Scandinavian countries were committed to memory by Lawspeakers, who were called upon to recite the laws from memory at legislative assemblies or in courts.

It may surprise you to learn that all of us exhibit heightened memory for some things. Take our ability to reconstruct stories as an example. We are all experts in how to read stories and, as discussed in the previous section, this translates into our enhanced ability to remember stories. If you were memorizing a list of 100 random words it might require at least 1 hour of hard work. However, if you were to memorize a story of 100 words (roughly seven lines on this page), it would be comparatively easy for you. In fact, a person reading a novel for 1 hour can reproduce and reconstruct the general theme and events quite well (Kintsch, Patel, & Ericsson, 1999). The key to our ability to remember events and facts is our background knowledge—our level of expertise. The next two sections describe how this works and concludes with a theory of memory that explains the phenomenon.

Expertise and Memory

People's past knowledge helps them learn new things. To show this, participants in a series of studies (Chiesi, Spilich, & Voss, 1979; Spilich, Vesonder, Chiesi, & Voss, 1979) were divided into two groups of college students: baseball experts and baseball novices. Both groups were asked to listen to a fictional account of half an inning of a baseball game and were then asked to summarize its contents. The participants were then given a written test. The baseball experts remembered more of the specific details, provided a more organized response, and included more details relevant to the outcome of the game than baseball novices. Although neither group had heard the information before, the experts could relate to the goals of the game and could understand the motivation of the players. The same findings were revealed a week later when the students were asked to recall the text. Clearly, the more you know about something, the easier it is to acquire new related information: The more you know, the more you can know.

The effect of expertise has been replicated in a variety of domains, such as card games (Charness, 1979), chess (Charness, 1989; Cooke, Atlas, Lane, & Berger, 1993; Horgan & Morgan, 1990; Simon & Gilmartin, 1973), and even memory for circuit diagrams by technicians (Egan & Schwartz, 1979). One characteristic of experts in any domain of knowledge is that their superior memory is restricted to facts within their domain of expertise: It does not carry over to any other domain. For example, Rajan Mahadevan, who can recall 31,811 digits of pi, is quite ordinary in his ability to perform a spatial memory task (Biederman, Cooper, Fox, & Mahadevan, 1992). At the printing of this text, Akira Haraguchi is the world record holder in memory for pi at 100,000 digits. Mr. Haraguchi is a retired engineer.

In order for cognitive psychologists to understand how people become experts and how they function in their area of expertise, we must first understand the way they have represented their knowledge and how that representation differs from nonexperts' representations. A brief summary of a group of such methods is described in the Focus on Methods box.

Three Principles of Skilled Memory

Memory experts have normal memory, and yet they are able to build on their areas of special knowledge to acquire staggering amounts of new information. The theory that explains how these experts can exhibit such astonishing memory in particular areas is called **skilled memory theory**, which consists of three basic principles that account for great feats of memory by experts in any domain (Chase & Ericsson, 1981): the meaningful encoding principle, the retrieval structure principle, and the speed-up principle.

Meaningful Encoding Principle Memory experts use their prior knowledge to encode new information in their area of expertise. This knowledge is often in the form of **memory chunks**, perceptual units that allow experts to see configurations of events that are invisible to the typical person. These chunks have been acquired through years of practice. For example, one waiter could memorize

FOCUS ON METHODS ■

Knowledge and Expertise

How is the expert's knowledge organized and how is it different from the nonexpert? One of the major researchers studying skilled performance is M. T. H. Chi (e.g., Chi, Glaser, & Farr, 1988), who has developed a broad listing of methods of studying expert cognitive processing, including three major methods described here: recalling, perceiving, and categorizing. Differences between experts and novices on these tasks have allowed researchers to understand how participants represent and use their knowledge.

Recall Tasks

One of the hallmark characteristics of experts is their superior recollection of information from their domain of expertise. They are faster and more accurate at freely recalling information whether the domain is recall of food orders by restaurant waiters, street routes by cab drivers, or chess moves by grand master chess players. These differences are not the result of superior memory ability. Although grand master chess players recall considerably more chess configurations on a board than do novice chess players, they are barely better than novices when the pieces are randomly placed on the board (Chase & Simon, 1973a, 1973b). This greater recall in domain-specific contexts has been found in other games such as Go (Eisenstadt & Kareev, 1975) and bridge (Charness, 1989), as well as special tasks such as recalling an electric circuit (Egan & Schwartz, 1979) or the blueprint for a building (Gobert, 1999). These studies show that experts possess many more memorized configurations of situations, which contain many more important components, than do nonexperts, and that these chunks are hierarchically organized in the knowledge of the experts.

Perceiving Tasks

Experts perceive their domains of knowledge differently than do nonexperts. Expert radiologists more readily spot tumors in X-rays than do skilled, but nonexpert physicians (e.g., Lesgold et al., 1988). The experts were not only better able to identify more important features, but also were better at inferring meaning from those features. This helps their diagnoses because experts tend to reason from their basic identification of patterns forward to a conclusion or diagnosis. Nonexperts try to formulate hypotheses and use them to calculate what to look for in the X-rays.

Categorization Tasks

In the standard categorization tasks, participants are asked to read or view situations that are either within or outside their

A Waiter Taking Orders Over time, experienced waiters develop strategies to memorize orders from a number of diners at once. The skill is part of their expertise.

Exactostock/SuperStock

areas of expertise. They are then asked to sort these situations in terms of how they best go together. In one study by Quilici and Mayer (1996), students were asked to sort statistics problems into groups (e.g., correlations, t tests, etc.). One statistics problem was as follows:

> A personnel expert wishes to determine whether experienced typists are able to type faster than inexperienced typists. Twenty experienced typists (i.e., with 5 or more years of experience) and 20 inexperienced typists (i.e., with less than 5 years of experience) are given a typing test. Each typist's average number of words typed per minute is recorded.

Experts were students who were given word problems to read and understand before they sorted the problems. The novices had received no instruction in statistics. Experts sorted the problems in terms of core concepts having to do with the kinds of samples involved or the kinds of questions the tests needed to answer, whereas the novices sorted based on superficial features of a problem (e.g., the problem was about typing). Because of this different representation of the problems (as reflected in their categorization), novices' sorting did not reflect the true nature of the problem. Such categorization methods reveal that experts have an entirely different structure of knowledge than do novices. The use of this different knowledge goes a long way in explaining differences in performance between experts and novices.

nearly 20 dinner orders at a time with simple strategies that he had developed over time (Ericsson & Polson, 1988). He would encode an item from a category (e.g., salad dressing) connected with all previous items from the same category in a clockwise order around a table. If a diner ordered blue cheese dressing, he would remember it as *B* and add it to the other orders making, for example, the word *BOOT*, standing for blue cheese, oil-vinegar, oil-vinegar, Thousand Island.

Retrieval Structure Principle When storing the information into a well-learned schema, skilled memorizers are sensitive to what is important. They attach specific retrieval cues to the material so that it can be readily accessed at a later time from LTM by means of those cues. The waiter's retrieval structure consisted of the clockwise order and the single word describing the dressings, connected to his long-term knowledge of the menu. The ability to establish these retrieval cues at time of encoding and use these cues in order to retrieve the information later depends on practice.

Speed-up Principle You have no doubt heard a version of Thomas Wilson's (1553) phrase, "practice makes perfect" (p. 4); it holds true for skilled memory performance. Practice speeds storage and retrieval. How does it do this? There are two reasons why practice and expertise result in a speed-up of storage and retrieval. First, as specific patterns and experiences are repeatedly presented to us, such as when we frequently practice retrieving the information, we begin to create links called *retrieval structures* between working memory and the relevant areas in long-term memory. These retrieval structures become so heavily used that it is not necessary for the expert to rehearse information in working memory before it is stored or retrieved in long-term memory; the connections are made immediately. In this way experts become more efficient in storing new information as their experience with doing so develops. Years of practice and, most important of all, a conscious, deliberate intent to improve their memories, are required to develop these retrieval cues (e.g., Gobet, 2000). Because of this seamless connection between working memory and long-term memory, the storage and retrieval process of expertise is called *long-term working memory* (Ericsson & Kintsch, 1995).

The second aspect of expertise that contributes to the speed-up principle is that the expert acquires a vast amount of information about a single topic and in so doing creates a hill of knowledge like those portrayed in Figure 7.5. These hills of knowledge are schemas where one fact can activate closely related facts, which in turn can activate still others so long as they are on the same hill. One of these hills becomes a semantic neighborhood, where bits of important information are located close to each other. Quick access of information, however, is limited to the neighborhood. Outside the neighborhood, where the retrieval structure does not apply, the person displays no special memory skills. Just because you may be an expert in golf doesn't mean you will show memory skills for any other sport or a special ability to remember a shopping list (Kintsch et al., 1999). Fortunately, we all have some such schemas carved out of LTM: In a sense, we are all experts at something.

SECTION SUMMARY ■

Expertise, Knowledge, and Skilled Memory

The knowledge that we possess helps us to acquire new knowledge in the same topic. Under special circumstances, feats of memory and understanding performed by experts are the result of possessing large amounts of knowledge about special domains. Possessing this specialized knowledge enhances their memory ability, but this is restricted to their area of expertise and does not generalize to unrelated topics. Experts demonstrate an ability to rapidly access and store away pertinent information about their area of expertise. The skilled memory theory accounts for the role of expertise in memory. It has three basic principles: meaningful encoding, retrieval structure, and speed-up. These three principles account for feats of memory in the domain of special knowledge, but not outside the domain.

CHAPTER SUMMARY

Humans possess both abstract knowledge (e.g., about robins and living things) as well as encapsulated knowledge called schemas, which allow us to apply abstract knowledge to concrete situations. There are four major theories about how people represent their knowledge of objects and categories in everyday life: (a) a network theory either with a hierarchical organization or one that is like a fishnet of relations, (b) a feature-based theory that relates instances and categories based on similarity, (c) a perceptually based theory with visual features serving as the fundamental building blocks of the representation of knowledge, and (d) a connectionist model based on how we have acquired our knowledge through our experiences of being asked questions about what we know.

Schemas are organized collections of knowledge that help us understand events and guide our own behavior and predict the behavior of others. Schemas possess default elements that allow us to infer the presence of components of the schema without having actually experienced them. Some schemas, in the form of reflexes, seem to be present at birth; reflex schemas seem to have some survival value in the early life of the infant. Others have been acquired over a lifetime and help us encode the world around us and provide retrieval cues for remembering what has occurred. When human recollections are not accurate, it may often be

the result of using schemas that indicate what the person should have seen and experienced rather than what he or she actually has experienced.

Schemas are present in the creation and understanding of narratives and stories. Once we learn about the schema elements (like advance organizers) we are better able to understand and recall stories. Knowledge of story schemas helps students with a range of reading skills to understand the stories.

All typical adults are experts in something, including their native language. Along with this expertise come special abilities to understand and remember. We are all capable of these skills in some domain because we possess unique hills of knowledge, called semantic neighborhoods. Access to this portion of knowledge makes use of long-term working memory. It is based on retrieval schemas that develop after considerable practice with special topics. This use of retrieval schemas is best illustrated by people who are memory experts and who appear to store and retrieve vast amounts of information in specified domains effortlessly, such as numbers, or names and addresses, or food orders in a restaurant. Although people demonstrate wonderful feats of memory in their areas of expertise, the skill does not carry over to domains outside their area of expertise.

KEY TERMS

node–link system, p. 193

teachable language comprehender (TLC), p. 194

question interface, p. 194

spreading activation, p. 195

semantic distance effect, p. 196

repeated path hypothesis, p. 196

typicality effect, p. 196

semantic relatedness effect, p. 196

feature comparison model (FCM), p. 197

defining features, p. 199

characterizing features, p. 199

perceptual symbol system, p. 201

connectionist model, p. 201

schema, p. 204

script, p. 205

reflexes, p. 211

narrative (or story) schema, p. 212

recounts, p. 212

eventcasts, p. 212

accounts, p. 212

fictionalized stories, p. 212

advance organizers, p. 216

person schema, p. 217

stereotype, p. 218

skilled memory theory, p. 221

memory chunks, p. 221

QUESTIONS FOR REVIEW

Check Your Knowledge

1. What kinds of facts are in semantic memory?

2. Is every word in the thesaurus ultimately connected to every other word?

3. What are the three main elements of Quillian's network theory?

4. Which will take less time to answer: (a) does a canary have feathers? or (b) can a canary breathe? Justify your answer.

5. What is the repeated path hypothesis and is there evidence in support of it?

6. The question, is a chicken an animal? is answered faster than is a chicken a bird? Why is this evidence against Quillian's network theory?

7. What is the name for the phenomenon in Question 6?

8. According to network theories without hierarchies, how are people able to answer semantic questions?

9. According to the feature comparison model, what is a defining feature?

10. According to the feature comparison model, what is a characterizing feature?

11. How are defining and characterizing features used in answering semantic questions?

12. In what way is the perceptual symbol system different from the standard network model? How are they the same?

13. According to the connectionist theories, how are concepts and properties related?

14. What is the basis for answering questions according to the connectionist theory?

15. What form of neurological malady does the connectionist theory explain?

16. What is a schema? What is a script?

17. How do schemas help us fill in missing information?

18. What source of error in our memory do schemas contribute to?

19. How do schemas help us understand situations and people?

20. How do people process schema-inconsistent information?

21. Name some of the behavioral schemas that humans seem to possess at birth.

22. What are these behaviors called?

23. What is a story schema?

24. What are the constituents of a story schema?

25. How are stereotypes really schemas?

26. How do stereotypes distort reality?

27. What are advance organizers, and how do they help readers?

28. Do advance organizers always help people recall information?

29. What is story mapping, and how is it an advance organizer?

30. What is the relationship between a story map and a story schema?

Apply Your Knowledge

1. If much of what we know and understand comes to us through the filter of our schemas, to what extent can we assume our memories are actually correct copies of what we experienced?

2. In what ways can schemas lead to miscommunications between two speakers? Imagine that there are two speakers from radically different cultures, how might their different cultural backgrounds (and schemas) contribute to miscommunication?

3. If our knowledge of how to behave in different situations is governed by schemas and scripts, does our ability to learn new behaviors mean we have a schema for how to learn new things?

4. There are many aspects of life in which everyone is an expert (e.g., how to speak our native language, how to recognize faces, how to dress ourselves). How can we use the topics of expertise, schema, and connectionist models to account for this level of skill?

8

Imagery: Special
Representation in
Memory

> " *Hamlet*: My father!—Methinks I see my father.
>
> *Horatio*: Where, my lord?
>
> *Hamlet*: In my mind's eye, Horatio. "
>
> —Shakespeare, *Hamlet* (act 1, scene 2)

Close your eyes and think about the following: your room, the face of a friend, the Taj Mahal, and what you did this morning after you woke up. In each of these cases it's typical to say that you are imagining, visualizing, or picturing something. **Images** are seemingly perceptual experiences that we have without the presence of an external source for the perception—the image comes from inside us, from our mind's eye. These mental images are not limited to the visual dimension. For example, music may be stored in a complete form and played back in our brains under certain circumstances, such as when we hear a tune in our head. In fact, during surgery for epilepsy, a woman was stimulated in her temporal lobe and reported hearing a song that would stop when the stimulation stopped and start again at the beginning when the electrical stimulation was restarted (Penfield & Perot, 1963; see also research by Crowder, 1989). Some imagery can be **motoric**, as when we mentally rehearse a dance or imagine making a great play on an athletic field. Images can also be **haptic**, as when we imagine touching sandpaper.

Mental images are a natural part of our everyday lives. Who has not mentally experienced the voice of a friend when reading a letter from that person, or in childhood imagined a monster lurking behind a door. However, images should not be confused with hallucinations, because images are under our control and we don't experience them as coming from outside of us as happens with hallucinations. Cognitive psychologists recognize that imagery is an important part of our mental life. They have developed special research methods to investigate the nature of our images and when they can help us to achieve our goals and when they are obstacles.

The Benefits and Limitations of Imagery

We all know that most people have some form of mental imagery—it comes with our cognitive system. In fact, written mention of images dates back to at least 2700 BCE in the *Gilgamesh* epic of ancient Sumeria (modern day Iraq; George, 2003). But of what use are images? Do they really help us solve problems and find our way in a new neighborhood, or do they contribute to error and lead us into blind alleys? Cognitive research has been directed to answering a basic question: What can we do with an image?

People often use images to help answer questions such as, was the window open when I left the house? did I leave my keys in the door? If you were asked whether your mother's car has a side-view mirror on its right side, you would most likely call up an image of her car and "inspect" the right side. We can mentally manipulate images depending on the question we are asked. This was shown in a study by Kosslyn (1975), who asked students to imagine a rabbit next to their mental image of an elephant or next to their mental image of a fly. When the students had created the mental image, they were asked a question that could be answered by inspecting the image, such as does the rabbit have whiskers? Kosslyn hypothesized that if images were similar to photographs, then the student would have to "zoom in" when the rabbit is standing next to the fly and "zoom out" when it is standing next to an elephant to get them both in the same image. Therefore, the size and details of the rabbit would be larger in the image where it is standing next to a fly than the one where it is standing next to an elephant. This prediction was supported by the data: Students were faster at answering questions about the details of the rabbit when it was next to the fly than when it was next to the elephant. This research shows that our images can be manipulated to achieve our goals. Some of these goals involve survival, including finding our way in the world.

Finding Your Way

When you wander around a strange city or walk in the woods, you may navigate and find your way back to your starting point or base camp by recalling images of your current location and some of the landmarks you have passed along the way. This is called **way finding** (or **route learning**), which refers to the cognitive processes people employ in a spatial environment in order to arrive at a goal (Arthur & Passini, 1992; Lynch, 1960). One of the most extraordinary examples of the use of imagery for way finding is how the people of Micronesia, who inhabit a territory of more than 600 islands in the Western Pacific, are able to navigate from one island to another.

For thousands of years these people have successfully traveled great distances by canoe, hundreds of miles outside the sight of land, without the benefit of charts or mechanical devices to guide them. Unlike western navigators, Micronesians do not imagine themselves moving through a static arrangement of islands. Rather, they view themselves as occupying a static space—the canoe is imagined as stationary. What moves are islands, birds, waves, and stars. There are other reference points, imaginary islands called *etaks* that are imagined to move

A person walking a trail in the woods finds his or her way by means of landmarks.

Chris Howes/Wild Places Photography/Alamy

with the stars. This "movement" helps navigators decide how far they have gone and where the target island is with reference to the etaks (Hutchins, 1996).

Remembering

Our images can help us remember. Schnorr and Atkinson (1969, 1970) taught students three lists of 32 pairs of words, for example, *dog–book*. The students' job was to recall the second item of the pair, given the first item. For half of the cases in each list, students were to memorize the pairs by rote learning—repeating the words to themselves as many times as they could. On the remaining half of the cases, students were asked to use imagery learning: They formed an interacting visual image of the items (e.g., a *dog* playing with a *book*). Using imagery resulted in better recall than did using the rote method. Why was the imagery condition best? To examine this more closely, Bower (1970) had three groups of high school students learn paired words (just like the participants in Schnorr and Atkinson's experiment). One group was told to rehearse the pairs aloud by repeating the words—the kind of thing we normally do in rote learning. The second group was told to construct two images, one for each member of the pair. The images were supposed to be independent pictures that did not interact with each other. The third group was to construct an image for each item of the pair, but the items in the image were supposed to interact (e.g., a *dog* reading a *book*).

The three groups of students were then given two types of tests: a recognition test for the pairs of words and a recall test where they freely recalled the word pairs they could remember. In the recognition test there was no special effect of imagery since all of the groups were equally accurate (about 85% correct). However, in the free-recall condition there were differences. The group that formed interacting images recalled about twice as many word pairs as the rote-learning and noninteracting-imagery groups. The fact that the rote-learning and noninteracting-imagery groups did not differ in their accuracy suggests that imagery by itself does not help people remember. The advantage of imagery comes when it provides an association—a link—between the items that people are trying to remember.

Some people have an extraordinary talent for using imagery to memorize things. Mental imagery has played an important role in the memory skills of a man named Solomon V. Shereshevskii, who is referred to in the scientific literature as S. (Luria, 1968). He was famous because he could recall lists of numbers that he had memorized decades earlier. His memory was so good that he was actually unable to forget what he had memorized. Noteworthy also was his remarkable visual imagery. It was so strong that sometimes imagination and reality had no firm boundaries: If he was given a long series of words or numbers, he would represent them in his mind as objects and then mentally "distribute" them along some roadway or street he visualized in his mind.

His remarkable ability to memorize lists of names or numbers could be overshadowed by his inability to notice the meaning of what he was representing. For example, S. could memorize a 50-digit table in 3 minutes, and take only

40 seconds to reproduce it. It has been suggested that S. could memorize a book in little more than the time it took him to read it, but he would have been totally unable to summarize its contents. Just being able to form a mental photograph of something does not mean that the representation is properly coded to be able to understand the inherent patterns without the photograph present. For example, S. could instantly memorize the following three rows of digits, but could not predict what the fourth row might be. Can you?

1 2 3 4

2 3 4 5

3 4 5 6

Problem Solving

Forming a visual image can sometimes enhance our ability to solve problems. To see this, try the problem in Demonstration 8.1.

▪▪▪DEMONSTRATION 8.1

Images in Reasoning

Try the following reasoning problem in two ways. First, imagine that a man is looking at a photograph and saying:

Brothers and sisters have I none; that man's father is my father's son?

Who is in the photograph? Take 1 minute to see if you can figure out the riddle logically. After trying it for 1 minute, try the problem again, but this time imagine the physical image of each of the people referred to in the problem.

Most people find it difficult to solve this problem without trying to imagine the characters. Only 17% of university students are successful at solving the riddle (Casey, 1993). Their typical answer to the riddle is that the man is looking at a picture of himself. However, when you imagine the people—maybe standing on each other's shoulders—you will see to your astonishment that the picture is of the man's son.

Of course, people are not always helped by their reliance on their imagery ability, as the story about S. shows. The limitations of imagery can be subtle. This was found in a study by Hayes (1973), who showed arithmetic problems such as those in (a) and (b) below to college students. The students were highly skilled in solving them in their heads; however, the speed of their decisions reflected their imaginal coding of the problems. The students took longer to solve problem (a) than (b) mentally (without paper or pencil). One reason given by the students is that there is a carry or remainder in the division, which needs to be mentally noted; the students reported that in (a) there is not enough "room" for them to place the remainder compared with (b), which has more space. Notice that all of the arithmetic operations are performed in their imagination.

(a) $4\overline{)392}$ (b) $4\overline{)3\ 9\ 2}$

How Are Images Represented?

Broadly speaking there are two ways of describing mental images. The first is to view them as having an **analog code**. Analog codes are like maps or moving pictures; they preserve the relationship among the elements of the image as if a person were experiencing them directly. For example, a map captures the distances and directions among locations; a mercury thermometer expresses temperature continuously as the height of the liquid; a watch with hands indicates the passage of time with the angle between the 12 and the small hand (in hours). Although these are physical systems, the information they convey is abstract: the map isn't the real terrain, the height of the mercury isn't itself the temperature, and the angle of the hands only indirectly suggests the passage of time. However, this type of code captures the essence of mental images because it corresponds to our experience of physical events while still being abstract. When we have these experiences of images, it is natural to think that they are stored in our brains as pictures, or at least stored in the same way as our perceptions.

An alternative way of describing images is to say that they embody a **propositional code**. Such a code is like a series of words or a sentence (although more abstract). Propositions are the smallest unit of knowledge that can be either true or false. In contrast, pictures or photographs or other analog metaphors for pictures can't be true or false. Propositions do not themselves resemble the physical stimulus as a mental picture might; however, propositions can express the underlying meaning of the stimulus. Take a map, for example: Some people prefer routes to be expressed as a list of directions (turn right onto Route 101, drive south until it turns into the 405, merge right, etc.). This would be similar to a propositional presentation. In contrast, other people prefer to have the directions from their house to their destination drawn out as a diagram with the correct route highlighted; this would be equivalent to an analog presentation. At core, the same information generates the route, only the presentation formats differ. However, whether the coding of images is analog or propositional may affect what you are able to do with the image, as illustrated in the following.

If mental images contain analog information, then people should be able to scan their images in much the same way as they scan a photograph. Common experience, for example, tells us that it takes longer to visually scan across larger distances than smaller ones. In one study (Finke & Pinker, 1982) college students briefly saw a display of four dots (as in **FIGURE 8.1**), then the dots disappeared and an arrow was shown in an unexpected location. The students' task was to indicate whether the arrow pointed to any of the previously seen (but now invisible) dots and

FIGURE 8.1 Coding and Imaginal Distance Observers looked at the left panel for 5 sec, then the middle panel was presented and the observer had to say whether the arrow was pointing to where a dot had been in the first panel. Time to respond correctly was related to the distance between where the arrow pointed and the original dot—showing that the observer was scanning a mental image depicted in the rightmost panel.

Source: From Finke & Pinker, 1982

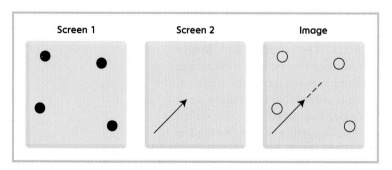

to press a button to indicate yes or no. One way to perform the task is to create a mental image of the dots and superimpose that image over the display with the arrow. Then, start at the tip of the arrow and scan out in the direction of the arrow. The distance between the tip of the arrow and an imagined dot was varied; the participants showed an increase in response time (and error rates) as the distance increased. This indicates that they were "scanning" their mental images to evaluate the spatial relationships. It is difficult to conceive of how the same task could be performed if our basic storage format was a set of propositions.

The Finke and Pinker (1982) study shows that images kept in short-term memory/working memory have analog properties. But what about images that are derived from our long-term knowledge, such as mentally scanning the room you lived in as a child, or estimating the distance of routes you traveled years before? This question was examined in a clever study by Kosslyn, Ball, and Reiser (1978). They had students look at a map of an island until they could draw it accurately (shown in **FIGURE 8.2A**). The map became part of their long-term memory. The map had seven landmarks, and the distance between the landmarks varied. The participants were asked to form a visual image of the map and answer questions about it. They were given the names of two of the landmarks (e.g., a hut and a tree) and then told to imagine that a black dot moved in a straight line from the first object to the second object (e.g., from

FIGURE 8.2 Spontaneous Imagery Scanning (A) The fictional map used to study the effect of distance on mental scanning time. Students memorized a map; when it was removed, they answered questions about how long a dot would take to move from one object on the map to another. (B) The time required for students to scan from one object to another in their mental image of the map was directly related to the distance between objects in their mental image.

Kosslyn, S. M., Ball, T. M., and Reiser, B. J. (1978). Visual images preserve metric spatial information: Evidence from studies of image scanning. *Journal of Experimental Psychology: Human Perception and Performance, 4,* 47–60. Figure 7.2. APA.

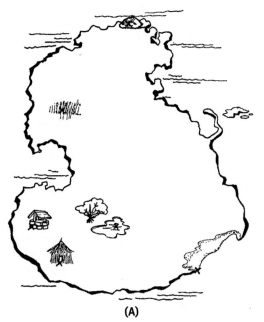

(A)

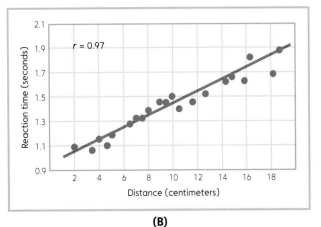

(B)

the hut to the tree). When the students experienced the imagined dot arriving at the second landmark in their image, they pushed a yes button. The no button was pushed if the student thought the second object did not exist. Try this yourself: Look at the map and imagine walking from the hut to the tree. Now imagine walking from the tree to the pond. Does one trajectory seem shorter than another? This would certainly be the case if you were simply scanning the picture of the island.

The times required by the participants to scan their images mentally are given in **FIGURE 8.2B**. It shows that they took longer to scan the distance between two far-off points on the map than to scan between two close-in landmarks (Kosslyn, 1983; Kosslyn et al., 1978). Of course, it is possible that people slow down or speed up their scanning because they "expect" some distances to require more time than others (Lea, 1975). In one test of this possibility, students were asked to imagine walking a familiar route carrying a cannonball. They took longer to imagine traversing the route with than without the cannonball (Intons-Peterson & Roskos-Ewoldsen, 1989). However, in another test of the importance of expectation, students were told that the farther the distance, the *faster* people would be moving (Jolicoeur & Kosslyn, 1985). This expectation did not affect their scanning rates. People still showed the linear effect of distance. Overall, these findings support the idea that although our expectations may be important for scanning rates, our images of spatial layouts preserve the spatial relations. When we scan our images, it is similar in many respects to actually scanning a physical picture. We are using an analog code.

There are limits to our ability to use images. Sometimes using our images is not like scanning a picture. Searching for hidden figures in a drawing is often a delightful task for young children and for adults as well. If our visual images were like pictures in the mind, then we ought to be able to search for hidden figures within our mental images of drawings as well as we do when we look at the drawings in front of us. To test this, Reed and Johnsen (1975) showed participants geometric shapes (illustrated in **FIGURE 8.3**) and asked them to form a visual image of the drawings. Afterward the participants were shown possible hidden components of the bigger figure. Their job was to say whether the test figure was hidden within the memorized, imagined figure. Most students correctly identified A and B as hidden figures. However, most students failed to identify the C figure as hidden. Yet, they readily identified picture C as a hidden figure when the pictures were in front of them. Clearly, images are not the same as having a physical object in front of us.

To experience the difficulty of reinterpreting or retrieving new information from images, try the activity in Demonstration 8.2. This activity illustrates that our mental images can have an abstract, categorical quality that can make it difficult to "see" something new in the image (Chambers & Reisberg, 1985, 1991, 1992). In spite of these examples, most research on imagery is consistent with the view that images are best described as possessing an analog code. The next section describes this research.

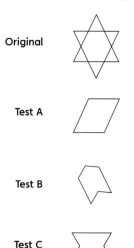

FIGURE 8.3 Searching for Hidden Figures in a Mental Image Mental images have limitations. Students memorized the original figure and then decided whether the other figures were hidden within their mental image. They were more accurate on some hidden figures such as C when the object was physically present than just a mental image.

Source: From Reed & Johnsen, 1975

Original

Test A

Test B

Test C

▪▪▪DEMONSTRATION 8.2

Rotating a Mental Image

Below are silhouettes of animals. Look at each one for 10 seconds and then put your hand over the picture and answer the question below it.

Source: From Slezak, 1991

Parrot With your eyes closed, rotate the animal 90° to the right. Name what you see.

Snail With your eyes closed, mentally rotate the animal to the right. Name what you see.

Duck With your eyes closed, mentally rotate the animal to the right. Name what you see.

Now look at the silhouettes and rotate the page to the right. Name what you see for the parrot, snail, and the duck. In the original study (Slezak, 1991) students were able to rotate the animals, but were unable to see that they became other animals after the rotation. However, they could tell that the parrot became a cat, the snail became a seahorse, and the duck became a rabbit when they physically rotated the page. This shows that images may not always function as mental pictures.

SECTION SUMMARY ▪

The Benefits and Limitations of Imagery

Throughout human history, people have been able to create images in their mind's eye that capture the essence of past experiences from their memory or create depictions of future experiences. We can hear the voice of a friend who is not present, imagine a monster lurking behind a door in a film, or mentally rehearse a dance step. Humans use images to find their way to their destination, remember the events in stories, and solve problems. Creating and using images are basic components of the human cognitive system.

Although most people experience mental images, it is still a challenge for cognitive psychologists to determine how such images are created in the brain and how they should be described within the human cognitive system. In general, images are viewed as possessing either an analog or propositional code. The term analog refers to a representation of a quantity that varies continuously such as temperature, distance on a map, or time of day. Many imagery experiences have the quality of being continuous, as if we were watching a film, or scanning a crowd looking for a friend. Laboratory studies show that we tend to scan our mental images in much the same way that we scan objects outside of us.

There is a limit to what we can do with our images, which suggests that perhaps they should be described as possessing a propositional code. Propositional refers to a representation that is like a set of words or logical structure. These mental sentences describe an experience, but do not themselves resemble the experience. Consistent with the propositional code, research with hidden figures shows that we are not able to manipulate mental images as we would a photograph or a line drawing, even though we experience the images as if they were pictures.

Research on Imagery

Cognitive psychologists have often used a particular type of task when trying to identify how images are coded. It is called the *dual-task method*. The idea behind the dual-task method is this: If you are asked to drive a car and sing a song at the same time, you can generally do both of these together as well as you do either of them alone. This is because the two tasks do not compete much for cognitive resources of memory and attention: They are both somewhat automatic tasks. However, if you are asked to listen to a lecture and at the same time try to remember all the things you are supposed to do after class, both tasks will be impaired because they are both attention demanding and require verbal processing. If people are asked to perform two tasks at once and it affects their ability to perform the tasks, then there is a basis for suggesting that they require the same or overlapping cognitive resources. To see whether imagery and perception overlap in the cognitive processes that they require, students were asked to do two tasks simultaneously (Brooks, 1968). One was a verbal task: The participants heard a sentence and had to mentally repeat it to themselves and identify each word as being a noun or not by responding yes or no. Some of the participants responded using a verbal medium by saying the answer aloud. Other participants responded using a visual medium, pointing to a *Y* (yes) or *N* (no). These letters were printed in a scattered array on a sheet of paper, as shown in **FIGURE 8.4A**. This response medium is considered visual because in order to find the correct response, the participant had to visually scan the array.

The second task involved visual imagery. Participants had to imagine the outline of a letter, such as a capital *F* (see Figure 8.4A) and then scan the mental image clockwise from the lower left. Their task was to indicate if the point of intersecting lines was at the top or bottom edge of the letter. If the point was there, a yes response was required. If the point of the lines was somewhere in the middle, a no response was required. For the *F* shown in the figure, the correct response would be yes, yes, yes, no, no, and so on. As in the verbal task, the response was made by either saying it aloud (verbal response) or by pointing to the *Y–N* display (spatial response).

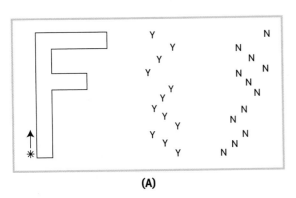

(A)

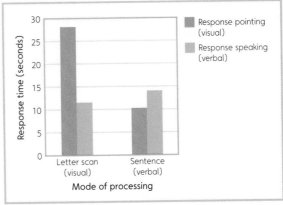

(B)

FIGURE 8.4 Dual Code Task Stimuli and Response Time
(A) Participants imagined the outline of a letter and then scanned their mental image clockwise. They indicated yes or no if the point of intersecting lines was at the topmost or bottommost level of the letter. They either spoke aloud (verbal response) or pointed to the *Y–N* display (visual response). In another task, they scanned a memorized sentence and indicated whether each word was a noun. (B) Graph shows the time for participants to respond in each condition. When the scanning task and the response required the same encoding format (verbal task/ verbal response or visual task/ visual response), participants required more time to respond than when the task and the response used different representational systems (verbal task/ visual response or visual task/ verbal response). This shows that scanning an image uses some of the same cognitive resources as scanning a picture.

Source: From Brooks, 1968

The time for the students to respond in each condition is shown in **FIGURE 8.4B**. When the task and the response required the same encoding format (verbal task/ verbal response or visual task/visual response), the students required more time than when the task and the response used different representational systems (verbal task/visual response or visual task/verbal response). This finding tells us that the process of scanning an image uses some of the same cognitive resources as scanning a picture; and furthermore, that the coding of images is more similar to the coding of pictures than it is to the coding of a string of words. This offers evidence that under some conditions, images have an analog code. The importance of analog codes for imagery is described in more detail in the following sections.

Mental Rotation

Are you able to manipulate the mental images of objects that you are visualizing in the same way you manipulate the real objects that they represent? Suppose you select a shape in a drawing program on your computer and you give the program a command to rotate the shape 90°. The program calculates the array of points at 90° and redraws the shape. In contrast, if you had a physical object on your desk that you wanted to rotate 90°, you would move it continuously, a fraction of a degree at a time (as rapidly as you could). When we rotate an object in the real world we are not merely redrawing it, we are literally turning it. Now, to return to the original question: When we manipulate an object mentally, do we do it in a way that is similar to the way we manipulate real objects, or do we act more like a computer program? To examine this question, Roger Shepard and his graduate students (Cooper, 1995; Shepard & Metzler, 1971) asked volunteers to view an *R* on a screen. Sometimes the letter was facing the correct direction, sometimes it was not. In addition, the angle of the letter could be anywhere around a 360° rotation (as on a clock face).

The participant's task was to determine if the letter would be pointing in the correct direction if it were in its upright position. The experimenters recorded

FIGURE 8.5 Time to Mentally Rotate Letters Students looked at a letter flashed in front of them that was rotated around 360° and had to decide if it would be pointing in the correct direction when it was in an upright position. The time taken to make the judgment increased continuously as the letter was rotated from 0° to 180° and showed that a mental image could be rotated just like a real object.

Source: From Cooper & Shepard, 1973

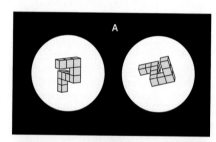

FIGURE 8.6 Mental Rotation Stimuli Students looked at pairs of 3-D objects and decided whether, if the one on the right had been rotated in some way, it would match the one on the left. In A, objects match if they are rotated in the picture plane; in B, objects match if they are rotated in the depth plane; in C, objects will not match. The time required to make this judgment is shown in Figure 8.7.

Source: From Shepard & Metzler, 1971

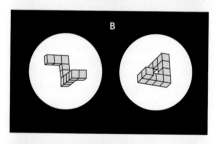

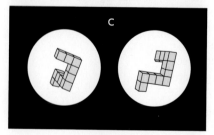

whether the judgment was accurate and how long it took to make the judgment. The times to make correct judgments are graphed in **FIGURE 8.5**. Notice that the time taken to make the judgment increased continuously as the letter was rotated from 0° to 180° (the point where the letter was upside down). The participant takes progressively less time to make the decision as the letter gets past 180°. Together, this shows that (a) people were rotating the image; (b) they were doing it over the "shortest" direction to the upright position (clockwise or counterclockwise); and (c) they were rotating the image continuously as if it were a concrete object and not part of a computer program.

Humans are able to mentally rotate 2-D figures continuously in a manner that is similar—called **isomorphic**—to the way we physically rotate 2-D objects, such as pictures. This pattern is also found for mentally rotating concrete, 3-D looking objects like those shown in **FIGURE 8.6**. Shepard and Metzler (1971) asked students to look at the standard 3-D object on the left and the target object on the right. The student's task was to decide if the target had been rotated in some way, would it match the standard. **FIGURE 8.7A** shows the time that the participants took to say yes for each degree of rotation to align the two objects in the picture plane. **FIGURE 8.7B** shows the amount of time the participants needed to rotate the target in the depth plane only. People seem to be mentally rotating the objects similarly in the picture plane and the depth plane. It requires approximately 17.5 msec to move the objects through each degree of rotation in each plane. It shows that people are not merely computing how the object should look as a computer would. It tells us that this kind of mental rotation is isomorphic to what we would do if we were rotating 3-D objects in front of us—as if our images had an analog code.

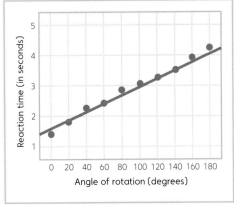

(A) Picture-Plane Pairs   **(B) Depth-Plane Pairs**

FIGURE 8.7 Reaction Time for Deciding that Pairs of Figures Are the Same (A) The graph shows how much time would be required to align the two objects in the picture plane. (B) The graph shows the amount of time participants needed to rotate the target in the depth plane. People need approximately 1 second to mentally rotate an image of a 3-D object 60°. This is similar to what we would do if we were rotating 3-D objects in front of us.

Source: From Shepard & Metzler, 1971

Symbolic Distance Effect

Chapter 1 described the **symbolic distance effect,** where the more discriminable two real objects are, the more quickly you are able to judge which is bigger or smaller. For example, people decide which I beam is bigger in the A–B pair more quickly than the same judgment in the A–B′ pair:

$$I \;\; {}_{I}$$
$$A \; B$$

$$I \;\; I$$
$$A \; B′$$

Studies have shown that the symbolic distance effect holds true for judgments about many different types of physical objects (e.g., Banks, Fujii, & Kayra-Stuart, 1976; D. M. Johnson, 1939; Parkman, 1971). It is not necessary for the objects to be in front of you; the same pattern is shown when you make size judgments of imagined objects. Suppose you are asked: Which is bigger, an elephant or an ant? You would answer this question more rapidly than if you had been asked: Which is bigger, an elephant or a cow? The pattern of responding is shown in **FIGURE 8.8**: As the difference in size increases, the time to make the judgment decreases. This pattern in judging mental images of animals is the same found when people judge the actual pictures of these animals (Moyer, 1973). The symbolic distance effect supports the idea that images can have an analog code.

The Neuropsychology of Imagery: Analog Codes and the Brain

Some people create such vivid images that they feel that they are actually looking at a scene (Galton, 1880/1907, 1883). This has prompted researchers to

FIGURE 8.8 Illustration of the Symbolic Distance Effect Which is bigger, an elephant or a dog? Which is bigger, a sheep or a squirrel? This graph shows that the larger the difference between objects, the faster the judgment. This pattern is called the symbolic distance effect and occurs when we are looking at objects or just reading their names.

Source: From Moyer, 1973

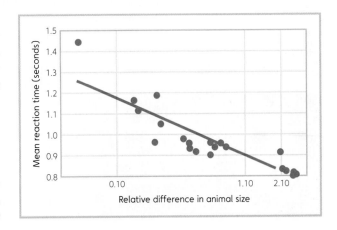

wonder whether imagining an object requires using the same areas of the brain that are used when someone actually perceives the object. If the same brain areas are used, it would be evidence that similar mental processes may be employed in both perception and imagining. In the typical person, the right hemisphere performs many functions important to the perception of spatial relations (e.g., Bradshaw & Nettleton, 1981; Kosslyn, Koenig, Barrett, & Cave, 1989). It is natural then to expect that the right hemisphere would also be important to the rotation of mental images if images are processed as if they are actually being perceived. This turns out to be the case.

Mental rotation appears to be easier when the right hemisphere is used rather than the left hemisphere. This was shown in a study of how a person with a **split brain** (or **divided brain**; Corballis & Sergent, 1988) performs on a mental rotation task. People with a split brain function with the right and left hemispheres independent of each other. For them, the **corpus callosum**, a bundle of fibers that connects the two hemispheres, has been severed. Consequently, information that comes to one hemisphere is not communicated to the other as would normally occur. Using a standard letter rotation task, such individuals are faster and more accurate doing the rotation when the letter is presented to the right hemisphere than when it is presented to the left hemisphere (see also Corballis & Sergent, 1992; LeDoux, Wilson, & Gazzaniga, 1977; Yamamoto & Hatta, 1980). This offers evidence that visual imagery is related to right hemisphere functioning.

More precise evidence that imagery and perception share processing is offered by PET measures of cerebral blood flow. When participants imagined small letters, a different area of the visual cortex was activated than when they imagined large letters. These areas are shown in **FIGURE 8.9**. They are the same areas that are activated when the participant is actually looking at either large or small letters rather than just imagining them (Kosslyn et al., 1993; see also Goldenberg, 1998). These findings have been confirmed by many studies where participants are required to imagine detailed images (see a review of the research by Kosslyn & Thompson, 2003). The conclusion from this research is that perceptual and imaginal processes share common brain areas.

Difficulty in perceiving and naming objects can be related to the ability to imagine those same objects. For example, a woman identified as J. R. was injured in an accident when she was 19 and as a result, suffered difficulty in naming objects and identifying line drawings of objects (a perceptual task). Ten years later, she was assessed for her ability to draw pictures from memory (imagery task). Although her perceptual ability did not deteriorate further, her ability to imagine objects (evaluated by her drawings of them) did deteriorate: In drawing an elephant from memory, for example, J. R. left out the trunk—a highly salient aspect of an elephant (Wilson & Davidoff, 1993).

FIGURE 8.9 Mental Imagery and the Brain Brain activity when a person is imagining a letter shows activity in different places depending on whether the mental image is small or large. The left side of the figure shows that when the imagined letters are small, the participant has activation in the posterior (backmost) portion of the occipital lobe, called area 17. The right side of the figure shows that when the imagined letters are large, activation is in the anterior portion (front part) of the occipital lobe.

Kosslyn, S. et al. (1993). Visual mental imagery activates topographically organized visual cortex: PET investigations. *Journal of Cognitive Neuroscience, 5*, 263–287.

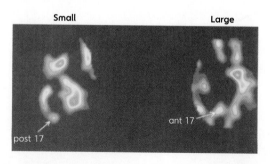

Small   Large

post 17   ant 17

A similar pattern was shown in the case of H. J. A., who suffered a stroke that resulted in damage to his occipital lobe where visual processing occurs. Nearly a decade after his stroke, his ability to name line drawings was still profoundly impaired. Most important, like J. R., he had difficulty drawing familiar objects from memory (Riddoch, Humphreys, Gannon, Blott, & Jones, 1999). These are cases in which difficulty in imagining objects goes along with a similar impairment in perceiving objects.

In Chapter 3 we discussed **hemispheric neglect** (or **hemineglect**). People with hemineglect are unable to attend to scenes or words that are shown to their left visual field. You'll recall that if such individuals look straight ahead at a plate, they see the food only on the right side and not the left. If they look directly at a word, they perceive only the letters in the right half of it. Individuals with hemineglect are said to *neglect* to process (i.e., to attend) to the information in the left visual field. Interestingly, they also have difficulty processing the left side of their own mental images. One person, for example, was asked to imagine a familiar square in Milan where he lived (the Piazza del Duomo) and to list the buildings that he could see in his mental image. When he imagined himself standing on the north side of the square (looking south), he could not name the structures on his left (the east side). When he imagined himself standing on the south side (looking north), he could not list the buildings on his left (the west side), but could identify structures on the east side of the square. This imagery neglect on the left side of his mental images is equivalent to what the person experiences when he is actually looking at the scene and not just imagining it (Bisiach & Luzzatti, 1978; Bisiach, Luzzatti, & Perani, 1979).

A view of the Piazza del Duomo in Milan.

Robert Harding Picture Library Ltd/Alamy

Imagery in the Blind

Do blind people experience mental images even if they are not visually based? This would be equivalent to having an analog coding of a perceptual—though not visual—experience. To see if blind participants would show the same imagery effects as sighted participants, Kerr (1983) replicated two of Kosslyn's (1975) studies mentioned previously. In one experiment, participants with **congenital blindness** (blind from birth) and sighted control participants were asked to imagine two objects next to each other. The size of the *target* object, such as a radio, was subjectively experienced differently depending on whether it was alongside a *context* object that was either very large or small. In all cases, participants were asked to verify whether a physical attribute (e.g., a knob) was a part of the imagined target object. Like other studies with sighted participants (Kosslyn, 1975), the time taken to verify a physical feature of a target object was greater when the context item was large and the target object was subjectively small, rather than when the context item was small. Both the congenitally blind and sighted participants showed a similar effect.

Kerr (1983) also replicated the map study described previously (e.g., Jolicoeur & Kosslyn, 1985; Kosslyn et al., 1978) with blind as well as sighted participants. They were asked to examine by touch a 3-D version of the map (see Figure 8.2A) and memorize the locations of several figures. Both groups were then asked to imagine the board and to mentally scan from one object to another. Like the earlier studies, there was a positive relationship between the distance between objects and the time to scan the distance mentally. This effect was shown for the congenitally blind as well as the sighted participants.

The letter rotation studies of Cooper and Shepard (1973) have also been replicated with congenitally blind students (e.g., Carpenter & Eisenberg, 1978; Marmor & Zaback, 1976). After studying letters by touching a wooden cutout, blind participants and blindfolded sighted students were presented a letter in some orientation between 0° and 300° from upright, just as in the original experiment (see Figure 8.5). They were timed while they judged whether the letter was a normal or mirror image of the target letter. Both the blind and the blindfolded sighted participants took more time to make their decisions the greater the angle of rotation. The data from these studies support the idea that blind people can mentally imagine objects and manipulate them and show that mental rotation can operate on a spatial representation that does not have any specifically visual components (e.g., Fleming, Ball, Collins, & Ormerod, 2004; Zimler & Keenan, 1983).

Telling the Real from the Imagined

Because our mental images and perceptions of the real world share some common processes and even common pathways in the brain, how are we able to tell the difference between the images derived from external stimulation and those that come seemingly full-blown from our heads? There is a long tradition in cognitive psychology of showing that people do have difficulty distinguishing between their images and reality. This is exemplified by the Perky experiments, so named because they originated with C. W. Perky (1910), who had participants look at a screen and imagine common objects like a banana. The participants were unaware that the experimenter was projecting a faint picture of the objects on the screen, using rear projection. Many participants seemed to be unaware that they were not experiencing their own mental image! In a similar study Segal (1971) had people imagine the skyline of New York while looking at a blank screen. Without the participants' knowledge, a faint image of a tomato was projected onto the screen. Many people reported experiencing the skyline at sunset! Under normal circumstances people can distinguish between events inside themselves and those outside themselves. They are occasionally confused, however, when they put effort into forming a visual image, because the internal events use some of the same cognitive processes as the external perceptual events (Segal, 1971; Segal & Fusella, 1971).

If people can be confused about inner and outer events when they are happening, how do they tell the difference between a recollection of a real event and one that they have only just imagined? This question falls under the general heading of **reality monitoring** (e.g., Henkel & Franklin, 1998; M. K. Johnson, Hashtroudi, & Lindsay, 1993): the ability to discriminate between genuine memories acquired from perceiving the external world from memories generated by the imagination. As discussed in Chapter 6, people are occasionally plagued with the need to monitor reality by inspecting their images: Did you lock the door when you left the house? Is your dog or cat in or out? Did you accidentally throw away an invitation with the trash? Are the visual images that you use to answer these questions generated internally or are they recollections of real events?

In general, recollections of actual experiences have more contextual details than recollections of imagined experiences. In contrast, those recollections based purely on imagination often have more information about the cognitive effort used to create them than do memories derived from perception (e.g., M. K. Johnson, Foley, & Leach, 1988; M. K. Johnson, Foley, Suengas, & Raye, 1988). Of course, people can be deceived when a particular imaginary memory is unusually vivid and readily comes to mind.

An explanation for how we assess the reality of our recollections is called *source monitoring* (M. K. Johnson et al., 1993), described in Chapter 6. It states that people determine the source of a specific memory by comparing its features to the typical features of their entire history of memories derived from perception and those derived from their imagination. In a sense we decide on the reality of our memories based on which set of typical features they are most like. Sometimes the features from an *imagined* memory are more similar to the average features for *perceptually* derived memories; this results in source errors (Intraub & Hoffman, 1992; M. K. Johnson, Foley, & Leach, 1988; M. K. Johnson, Raye, Wang, & Taylor, 1979). Source areas of the brain are at work when people say to themselves: Did I ride a pony when I was six, or did I just imagine that I did?

Even though imagery and perceptual processes have many similarities, they are definitely not the same thing. For example, some people are unable to form a mental image of objects that they have long known, and they cannot answer questions about them (e.g., Does it have a tail?). Yet, they are still able to recognize them when they are presented visually (Farah, 1988; Farah, Levine, & Calvanio, 1988; Riddoch, 1990). The opposite is also true; there are people who can imagine objects (pliers, saws, paper clips), but not recognize them when they are presented visually (e.g., Behrmann, Moscovitch, & Winocur, 1994). Finally, some people suffer from Charles Bonnet syndrome. They are blind and their imagery ability is so seriously impaired that they cannot imagine colors, yet they hallucinate seeing people and objects in color, although often in miniature (Ramachandran & Blakeslee, 1988).

This phenomenon has been simulated in the laboratory with university students who wore blindfolds for 5 days. During that time, a majority reported seeing people, objects, and landscapes. They knew that they were hallucinations, but could not stop them from appearing (Merabet et al., 2004). In these cases there is neither imagery nor visual sensation, but there is definitely perceptual experience.

SECTION SUMMARY ■

Research on Imagery

Use of the dual-task methodology shows that the process of mentally scanning our images uses some of the same cognitive resources as scanning a picture, but not the same resources as scanning a sentence. This is supported by studies of brain imaging, which show that manipulating images employs similar brain areas as manipulating real objects. Both sighted and blind people are able to mentally rotate 2-D and 3-D images continuously, as if they were pictures. Phenomena such as the symbolic distance effect show that the same cognitive processes are involved in estimating the sizes of imagined objects as performing the same operation on real objects.

Because imagery experience and perception of real events use many of the same brain areas and overlapping cognitive processes, it is sometimes difficult for people to discriminate between perceptually based memories and those generated by the imagination. The way people are able to accomplish this feat of reality monitoring is explained by source monitoring.

■ ■

Imagery, Memory, and Dual Codes

We don't experience everything as either an image or as word-based proposition. Sometimes words evoke images; sometimes seeing an object causes us to store an image as well as a verbal description of it. Take the word *chalk*. You can think of it verbally and define it as the substance of gypsum used to write on blackboards, coat a pool cue, and so on. You can also form a mental image of it from your school days. Or, if you're so disposed, you can imagine one of the great limestone pieces of chalk in the world: the White Cliffs of Dover, England. Surprisingly, if you repeat the word once a second for about five or six times, it loses all meaning. Try this yourself. This strange phenomenon is called *semantic satiation*. Young people are more susceptible to it than are older adults (Balota & Black, 1997; L. C. Smith & Klein, 1990). Did you notice that you were able to retain a mental image of chalk even though the meaning was disappearing?

Some words evoke few images, for example, the abstract word *idea*. You can think of it verbally, but it's difficult to imagine a mental picture associated with it (a culturally defined way of doing this is to imagine a lightbulb over a cartoon character's head). In general, it appears that concrete words like *chalk* have dual codes associated with them: both an image and a verbal semantic code. In contrast, abstract words tend to have only a single code: a verbal representation.

The fact that words can have multiple codes was discovered by Paivio (1969), who described it as the **dual code hypothesis** (or **dual coding theory**). The concept of dual code can be used to predict how easy or difficult it will be to remember different types of words.

The Dual Code Hypothesis

The dual code hypothesis states that some concepts, especially abstract ones (e.g., *idea* or *liberty*) are primarily represented verbally and not with a visual image. In contrast, other concepts, especially concrete ones, can be represented both by imaginal and verbal strategies. This does *not* mean that abstract concepts cannot be associated with visual images (e.g., *liberty* might be remembered with an image of the Statue of Liberty in New York or the one in Paris); however, only a small number of abstract concepts are so represented. Similarly, not all highly concrete words have dual codes: Some concrete concepts are difficult to express verbally. Can you verbally describe what a spiral staircase is without using your hands to make a spiral?

One consequence of storing a word or fact that has multiple codes is that if you forget one of the codes, you may still have another to help you retrieve the information. Suppose you are trying to recall the name of a handheld device that stores music. The name (the verbal code) is on the tip of your tongue. However, if you can recall what it looks like—its picture code—you may be able to use that to retrieve its name (iPod).

An iPod You can retrieve its name with a verbal code or a picture code.

Courtesy of Apple

Support for the reality of the dual code hypothesis has come from many directions. First, people feel that some words are more imaginable than others. Paivio and his colleagues (e.g., Paivio, Yuille, & Madigan, 1968) asked students to rate each word for its **imagery value** (*I*) from a list of 925 words: the higher the imagery value, the more vivid the image. In general, concrete nouns have higher *I* values than abstract nouns. Second, students' memory for a sample of these words in subsequent studies (e.g., Paivio, 1969, 1971) is related to the imagery value of the words. The *I* rating is the best predictor of how memorable a word will be: The greater the imagery value, the easier it is to remember the word in a memory experiment.

The Picture Superiority Effect

According to the dual code hypothesis, pictures should be better remembered than words because pictures are represented both imaginally in an analog code and verbally in a propositional code. In fact, for most people, pictures are easier to recognize than a list of words. This is called the **picture superiority effect** (e.g., Kinjo & Snodgrass, 2000; Kobayashi, 1986; Mintzer & Snodgrass, 1999; D. L. Nelson, Reed, & Walling, 1976; Paivio & Csapo, 1973; Paivio, Rogers, & Smythe, 1968; Stenbert, Radeborg, & Hedman, 1982). To illustrate this, in one study people viewed more than 600 pictures, one at a time, and were able to recognize 98%

of them accurately when tested immediately (Shepard, 1967). In a similar study, people were able to recognize photographs with 63% accuracy 1 year later (Nickerson, 1968). This superior recognition of pictures occurs as long as they are visually distinctive (horse vs. screwdriver), but not when they are similar (a cat vs. a dog; D. L. Nelson et al., 1976).

Neuroscience of the Dual Code Recent neurological findings support the dual coding hypothesis in explaining the picture superiority effect. In Kelley et al. (1998), volunteers' brains were scanned using fMRI techniques while they studied words, line drawings of common objects, and unfamiliar faces (pictures with no verbal labels). The results showed that the left prefrontal cortex was most active when encoding words; the right prefrontal cortex was most active when encoding faces (without names); and both hemispheres were active when encoding nameable objects. This pattern is the neurological embodiment of the dual code hypothesis. In addition, the medial temporal lobes showed the same pattern of activity during encoding, which we learned in Chapter 6 is associated with LTM and meaning. These results tell us that studying nameable pictures strongly activates both hemispheres and meaning circuits, whereas studying words alone strongly activates only one hemisphere. This neurological evidence of the dual code explains the picture superiority effect (Poldrack & Gabrieli, 1998).

Limits of Visual Memory In spite of the picture superiority effect, most studies show that our visual memory is not perfect. T. O. Nelson, Metzler, and Reed (1974) displayed one of four versions of photographs like the example in **FIGURE 8.10**. Participants either saw (a) the original photographs, (b) detailed drawings of the photographs, (c) nondetailed versions of the photographs, or (d) verbal descriptions of the photographs. Later on, after seeing many pictures, students were asked to pick out which version they had seen. The participants

FIGURE 8.10 Picture Memory: A Smiling Man Holds a Little Girl Students saw versions of a picture (simple or complex line drawings, a photograph, or a verbal description). They were no better at recognizing the photographs than the line drawings either immediately or 7 weeks later, even though the photographs had potentially greater detail (color photo in original study not available).

Source: Nelson, T. O., Metzler, J., & Reed, D. A. (1974). Role of details in the long-term recognition of pictures and verbal descriptions. *Journal of Experimental Psychology, 102,* 184–186.

(A) (B) (C)

were no better at recognizing the photographs than the line drawings, even though the photographs had potentially greater detail (including color in the original study) than the drawings. The authors concluded that as long as you can retrieve any critical area of the line drawing from memory, you can reconstruct the entire picture (e.g., Loftus & Bell, 1975; Loftus & Kallman, 1979; Pezdek et al., 1988; Suzuki & Takahashi, 1997). Even if our picture memory is not perfect, the superiority of picture memory makes it a useful medium for communication. For example, the picture superiority effect promotes the use of pictures in advertising because they not only make the product or brand more memorable, they are also associated with more favorable attitudes toward the products (e.g., Mitchell, 1986).

FIGURE 8.11 Meaningless Pictures Students memorized sketches like these; half had meaningful labels and half did not. Students were more accurate in recalling pictures that had meaningful labels than ones that did not.

Source: From Klatzky & Rafnel, 1976

The Dual Code and Meaning

Some pictures are not encoded with multiple codes. For example, if you are shown a drawing that has no compelling interpretation, such as a work of abstract art or a random line drawing, sometimes called a *droodle* (doodle + riddle), then when you see it, you have only a single pictorial code and therefore a lesser ability to recall the drawing later on. If the picture superiority effect occurs because pictures and images have multiple codes, then droodles, which are pictures with only a single code, should not be easily remembered. To test for the importance of a meaning code for recalling drawings, Klatzky and Rafnel (1976) showed droodles (Price, 1953) like those in **FIGURE 8.11** to students. Half of the pictures were associated with labels that made the droodles meaningful and half were not. The students' ability to freely recall what they had seen was much greater when the drawings were associated with meaningful labels (see also Bower, Karlin, & Dueck, 1975). In a second study (Rafnel & Klatzky, 1978), meaningful labels helped students distinguish between pictures that were consistent with the ones they had studied and pictures that were radically different. These studies show that meaning—and not merely a "picture in the head"—is the key to some of the benefits of using imagery.

SECTION SUMMARY ▪

Imagery, Memory, and Dual Codes

Some words, especially those that name concrete objects, evoke coherent images. Others, especially those that name abstract ideas, do not. Although our memory for the meaning of words is critical, for some words a pictorial/imaginal code is stored as well. By having multiple codes associated with words or concepts, these words are less susceptible to forgetting, because if we are unable to retrieve a word or concept using one code, we may be able to retrieve it using an alternative code. The dual code hypothesis not only accounts for the ability to remember certain words, but also for the superior memory for pictures.

Individual Differences in Imagery Ability

More than a century ago, Sir Francis Galton (1880/1907) asked people to mentally imagine something specific, such as their breakfast table that morning. He found that many people were surprised that they were able to describe their images in great detail, similar to what people might say if they were physically looking directly at the scene. The actual responses ranged from statements such as,

> Quite comparable to the real object. I feel as though I was dazzled, e.g., when recalling the sun to my mental vision (p. 61);

to those statements that denied imagery all together,

> To my consciousness there is almost no association of memory with objective visual impressions. I recollect the breakfast table, but do not see it (p. 64).

Since Galton's time, cognitive research has substantiated what he found: People differ in their ability to form and use images and this may have an impact in subtle ways on their lives. To understand this, we just have to remember S. and the uniqueness of his skill. His life was not idyllic, however. He had difficulty understanding abstract concepts, and reading words on a page disturbed him because what they looked like interfered with his ability to understand what they meant. At a less extreme level, ordinary people show differences in their ability to form visual images. In a typical study, students were asked to look at pictures and words; when they saw a printed word, they had to imagine the object it referred to. Later on, they were tested on their accuracy in deciding whether they had seen the pictures or the words. Overall, students are not highly accurate at this task and often cannot remember whether they originally saw a word or a picture (e.g., M. K. Johnson et al., 1979).

What is important is that the people who were characterized as vivid imagers made more errors than those who were less vivid imagers: Those who could create vivid images had the most difficulty distinguishing between what they had seen and what they had imagined (see also Anderson, 1984; M. K. Johnson & Raye, 1981). Recent research also shows that confusing memory for a picture with memory for words is related to activity in distinct brain areas (precuneus, inferior parietal cortex, and anterior cingulate cortex; see **FIGURE 8.12**). Correct identifications are associated with activity in other parts of the brain (prefrontal cortex and left anterior hippocampus; Gonsalves et al., 2004). People can differ substantially in the ability to

FIGURE 8.12 Brain Areas Associated with Recognition Confusions Some people have such vivid images of words that they confuse whether they have seen a word like *house* or a picture of a house. These kinds of confusions are associated with three brain areas labeled (A), (B), and (C). When people correctly recognize words and pictures, two different brain areas are involved, labeled (D) and (E).

Gonsalves, B., Reber, P. J., Gitelman, D. R., Parrish, T. B., Mesulam, M. M., & Paller, K. A. (2004). Neural evidence that vivid imaging can lead to false remembering. *Psychological Science, 13,* 655–660. Figure 2.

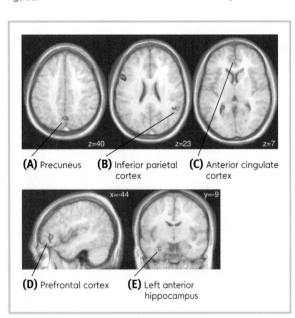

(A) Precuneus (B) Inferior parietal cortex (C) Anterior cingulate cortex

(D) Prefrontal cortex (E) Left anterior hippocampus

use images, and the findings suggest that this skill may be related to different activity patterns in their brains.

It is difficult to say why there is a difference among people in imagery experience. Some evidence supports the adaptive nature of visual memory and spatial ability. For example, Inuit children in Alaska score much higher on measures of visual memory than do nonnative children in Alaskan cities. It is easy to see how this could be related to a hunting culture that lives within the vast wilderness of the Arctic (Kleinfeld, 1971), especially because visuospatial ability is correlated with the ability to find one's way and to remember routes (e.g., Vanetti & Allen, 1988).

Visual Versus Spatial Imagery

The difference among people in the ability to form and use images is related to the type of imagery that is being used. There are two major types of imagery: primarily visual and primarily spatial. **Visual imagery** refers to the visual appearance of an object, such as its shape, color, or brightness. A typical visual imagery task might ask someone to state the color of an object that has a characteristic color, like a football. **Spatial imagery** refers to a representation of the spatial relationships between parts of an object or its location in space. An example of a spatial imagery task is called the Form Board Test (Likert & Quasha, 1970) and is shown in **FIGURE 8.13** (Hegarty & Waller, 2006). The participant is supposed to select a set of objects at the bottom of the figure that can be put together to form the object at the top (in this case a box). This requires a mental rotation of the object to find a match.

Visual and spatial imagery require separate mental processes. This has been shown by Farah, Hammond, Levine, and Calvanio (1988), who noticed that some individuals with brain lesions are impaired in visual imagery but show normal functioning in spatial ability tasks, whereas others show the reverse pattern. Recent studies of the usefulness of imagery have found that spatial imagery is the type of ability that makes the most important contribution to sentence understanding and problem solving (e.g., Hegarty & Waller, 2006).

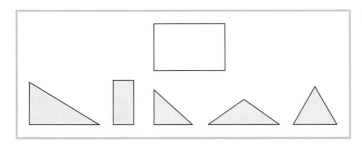

FIGURE 8.13 Form Board Test The Form Board Test is a way of assessing people's spatial imagery ability. Which objects at the bottom can be arranged (and rotated) to form the square at the top?

Source: After Hegarty & Waller, 2006

Imagery Ability and Mathematics

It has long been known that mathematical reasoning benefits from visual imagery and an ability to maintain images in memory (e.g., Battista, 1990; McGee, 1979; Sherman, 1979; I. M. Smith, 1964). The noted physicist Albert Einstein wrote about his thought processes to Jacques Hadamard, the great French mathematician:

> The words of the language, as they are written and spoken, do not seem to play any role in my mechanism of thought. The psychical entities, which seem to serve as elements in thought are certain signs and more or less clear images, which can be "voluntarily" reproduced and combined. . . . The above-mentioned elements are, in my case, of visual and some of muscular type.
>
> *(Hadamard, 1945, pp. 142–143)*

Many people describe themselves as either a visualizer or a verbalizer and often link their success in mathematics to this preference for certain types of information. **Visualizer–verbalizer** is the name of a cognitive style that expresses the degree to which people use visuospatial representations (images or diagrams) or words, especially while solving mathematics problems (e.g., Hegarty & Kozhevnikov, 1999; Krutetskii, 1976; Lean & Clements, 1981; Presmeg, 1992). In spite of popular belief about the importance of visual imagery for mathematics, some studies have shown that visualizers are not more successful at mathematics problem solving than are verbalizers (Lean & Clements, 1981; Presmeg, 1992). This is probably because there are really two types of visualizers: Those with high spatial ability and those with low spatial ability (Kozhevnikov, Hegarty, & Mayer, 2002). In one study, elementary schoolchildren were told about a man planting trees 5 meters apart on a path. The children were given the total length of the path and had to find the number of trees planted. High spatial visualizers drew a diagram of the path, marking the position of trees on the path and the distance between them, whereas the low spatial visualizers reported experiencing a mental image of the man planting trees. Although both groups of children were considered visualizers, the high spatial visualizers were more successful in solving the problem. The images of the high spatial visualizers embodied the spatial relations between objects described in the problem. The images of the low spatial visualizers did not reflect how the elements of the problem were related (Hegarty & Kozhevnikov, 1999).

These findings show that imagery ability by itself does not guarantee mathematical skill. This ought to have been clear from the example of Luria's (1968) study of S, who possessed enviable imagery skills but did not possess great problem-solving ability. If he had possessed greater spatial ability, he might have been better at problem solving (Ben-Chaim, Lappan, & Houang, 1986; McGee, 1979). Spatial visualization can lead to academic success in geometry (Battista, 1990), other forms of mathematics (Rhoades, 1981; I. M. Smith, 1964), chemistry (Pribyl & Bodner, 1987), and physics (Pallrand & Seeber, 1984) because it allows students to generate effective representations for information they will need in solving a problem. To appreciate how spatial ability contributes to our understanding of the world around us, read the Focus on Methods box, "Spatial Abilities and Mechanical Reasoning", which illustrates the experimental methods that are used to investigate spatial processing.

FOCUS ON METHODS ■

Spatial Abilities and Mechanical Reasoning

The difference between visual and spatial imagery can be seen in mechanical reasoning tasks. In a simple but inventive task, students were timed as they answered questions about the pulley system shown here.

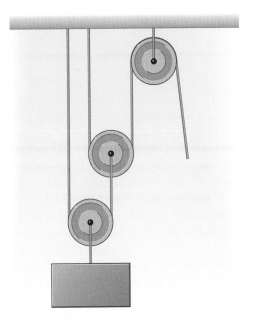

A Pulley System

Students were asked to look at the pulley system and to notice that the box at the bottom is a weight; the line at the top represents a ceiling; and the end of the rope is on the right. As they looked at the diagram, students were asked to answer questions such as the following:

1. True or False: The upper pulley is attached to the ceiling.
2. True or False: The upper pulley turns counterclockwise when the rope is pulled.

The answer to Question 1 is true; the answer to Question 2 is false. The first question asks about a *static property* of the picture and requires visual imagery to supply an answer. The second question asks about a *kinematic property* (the movement of one or more components) and requires spatial imagery to supply an answer. It is no surprise then that the ability to answer questions like the second one is correlated with a person's spatial ability (Hegarty & Sims, 1994).

Hegarty and her colleagues have shown that the ability to perform mental animation is highly correlated with spatial visualization ability (Hegarty & Kozhevnikov, 1999; Hegarty & Sims, 1994; Hegarty & Steinhoff, 1997). According to their findings, the more mechanical components people are asked to mentally animate, the more errors people make. However, people with low spatial ability make more errors than those with high spatial ability as the task becomes more complex.

One method employed by cognitive psychologists to understand what the experience is like in order to do this task is called *protocol analysis*. Students are either prompted to speak aloud when they are performing a task or immediately after the task. This method reveals the cognitive processes that are available to their consciousness (Ericsson & Simon, 1993). In this case, many participants reported that they were "watching" a dynamic system in operation when they were asked questions like the second one, but not the first one (Hegarty, 1992).

Their experience is as if they were "running a mental model" of a mechanical system (Hegarty, 2004). Here, a mental model refers to a representation of a situation that is similar in many respects to the physical situation that it reflects.

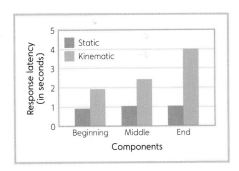

Latency Graph

Source: From Hegarty, 1992

To verify the accuracy of the protocol and the nature of the mental model independently, cognitive psychologists may make use of another method, *response latency* (or *reaction time*). Participants in the pulley study were timed as they answered questions. The results are shown in the graph, which displays the time to answer two types of questions:

(continued)

static questions (like Question 1) and movement (kinematic) questions (like Question 2). The graph shows that students required more time to verify a kinematic question that taps what is going on at the end of the chain of events than in the middle. This is what you would expect if people were mentally scanning a sequence of events from the beginning of the system, but not if they were running the pulley system all at once (as if it were a moving picture). In that case all the parts would be immediately accessible and there would be no difference in the time to answer questions that

asked about information at the beginning, middle, or end. The data show that observers mentally animate the pulley system only to the degree necessary to answer the question. The mental model is not a holistic system where everything is moving at once: The intuitions of the participants, as reflected in their protocols, are not a precise recording of the cognitive processes required to perform the task. Running a mental model is not like running a movie in your head. To discover this required the convergence of many experimental methods.

Environmental Spatial Ability

You may have noticed that even the most intelligent of your friends can become disoriented when they wander around a new office building or new campus—where the hallways and buildings all seem to be alike. People differ in their ability to integrate spatial information over time as they explore or navigate an environment. The ability to navigate in new places successfully is called **environmental spatial ability** (Hegarty & Waller, 2006), which includes the ability to form accurate mental representations of large-scale environments such as buildings, campuses, or cities. Hegarty and Waller described a study in which 12 people, who performed well on tests of knowledge of locations in Los Angeles, were compared to a similar group who performed poorly on tests of their city. The high-knowledge students (good mappers) also scored higher on tests of their ability to visualize space and remember visual information than the low-knowledge students (poor mappers). This suggests that spatial ability may have a real impact on the effectiveness of everyday activities such as finding our way (see review by Lawton & Kallai, 2002).

Eidetic Imagery

Some people's imagery ability is extreme: These people are called *eidetikers*. **Eidetic imagery** is the ability to maintain a mental image that has the quality of reviving an earlier perceptual event with great clarity (Allport, 1924). It is popularly referred to as *photographic memory* (Binet & Henneguy, 1894), as cited in Siegler (1992). Eidetic images should not be confused with afterimages. You may have experienced *afterimages* when you stared at a diagram or photograph for a long period of time and still "saw" it when you looked away. Afterimages move when the eyes move. In contrast, eidetic images are reported to be in the same physical place even if the eyes move. If the object is taken away, eidetikers feel that the details of the object are still located in the empty space (A. Richardson, 1969; Stromeyer & Psotka, 1970).

Eidetic Imagery in Children The incidence of eidetic imagery is higher in children than in adults. Woodworth (1938) described the phenomenon of eidetic imagery in preadolescent children: "If they examine any complex object or picture . . . and then shut their eyes, they can see the object as if it were still before them and can answer questions about it which they did not have in mind during the actual presence of the object. This image is not strictly photographic, but rather plastic, and likely to be modified by the subject's interest" (pp. 288–289). The phenomenon is rare. Haber and Haber (1964) gathered 150 children and showed each a picture for roughly 4 minutes and removed it. Only 12 children (8%) were able to demonstrate some degree of eidetic imagery. The percentage of children who could be characterized as showing full eidetic imagery is considerably smaller.

Eidetic Imagery in Adults The number of eidetikers in the adult population (those who possess the very highest in imagery skills) is negligible. They represent about 1 in a million adults—if that many (Crowder, 1992). This is not because the eidetic imagery ability of children is eliminated over time. Ten-year studies of such children show that the skills they possess do not diminish with time (Haber, 1979), but the number of people with the highest level of this skill is exceedingly rare. One explanation for this pattern is that as one gets older it is more efficient to employ verbal codes in order to deal with abstract concepts. Tests of eidetic imagery may not be sensitive to this shift in emphasis with verbal codes as we age (Kosslyn, 1980).

There have been a few cases of people with extraordinary imagery ability who have been studied in the laboratory. One woman (Elizabeth) is reported to be able to reproduce a poem, written in a language foreign to her, from bottom to top without hesitation (Stromeyer & Psotka, 1970). Her imagery ability is so extraordinary that when random dot patterns were presented successively to each eye, she was able to mentally fuse together the two images to form a single picture. Another woman (Sue D'Onim) had such incredible imagery that she could speak a 10-word sentence backward after having only a brief look at it (Coltheart & Glick, 1974). In spite of these special abilities to form an image, research has not shown any reliable relationship between having eidetic imagery and possessing any other cognitive or intellectual skills.

SECTION SUMMARY ▪

Individual Differences in Imagery Ability

Not everyone experiences visual images, and among those who do, tests reveal that there are two kinds of imagery that need to be distinguished: visual imagery and spatial imagery. People who score high on tests of visual imagery do not necessarily show heightened ability to manipulate objects mentally. People who score high on spatial ability perform best on tests of mechanical reasoning or way finding.

People who score the highest on visual imagery are said to have eidetic imagery and show the ability to maintain images that revive earlier perceptual events. These are the people who are often said to have photographic memories. Although children show a greater level of eidetic imagery than adults, the very highest levels are extremely rare in children or adults.

Using Imagery to Enhance Physical and Cognitive Functioning

Ninety percent of Olympic athletes and their coaches employ imagery techniques to improve their performance (Gould, Hodge, Peterson, & Giannini, 1989; Jowdy & Harris, 1990). Imagery can affect athletic performance in a number of ways, including development of skill, but it can also aid in reducing stress and increasing motivation (e.g., Feltz & Landers, 1983; Martin, Moritz, & Hall, 1999). Imagery has also been deliberately trained in order to develop better memory and study skills.

Imagery and Performance

Visual imagery activates selective areas of the visual cortex. We now know that **motoric imagery** seems to be related to similar activity in the motor cortex (e.g., Ingvar & Philipon, 1977; Jeannerod, 1994; Roland & Friberg, 1985) as well as in other motor-related areas of the brain such as the cerebellum (e.g., Naito et al., 2002). Does this activation of the motor cortex result in any change in actual performance? It is distinctly possible. For example, a group of volunteers allowed a cast to be put on their fifth finger in order to immobilize it. Half the participants imagined contracting the finger and the other half did not. After 5 weeks, the imagery group increased strength in the finger by nearly 50%, but the nonimagery group lost strength by about 12% (Yue, Wilson, Cole, & Darling, 1996). Of course, the imagery group might have been unconsciously flexing their fingers during the study. However, other studies do not have this problem.

Roure et al. (1999) recruited the aid of intermediate-level volleyball players (average age = 23) and divided them into two groups of roughly equal ability in passing a served ball to a target team member. One group practiced imagining the pass situation in 30-minute sessions three times a week for 2 months. The players in the other group met with the experimenters in social settings and did not mentally practice the skill. At the last rehearsal session, the researchers recorded physiological measures of arousal, such as heart rate and skin temperature. There were two main results. First, the imagers significantly improved in their volleyball performance from pre- to posttest, whereas the nonimagers did not reliably improve. Second, among the imagery group, those players who showed the greatest physiological arousal during the last imagery session and therefore, were most invested in the imagery practice, also showed the greatest gains in performance.

The improvement due to imaginal practice may not be due entirely to the practice itself, but may also be a result of increased motivation that comes from the practice. To test this possibility, beginner golfers were taught how to putt a golf ball and then were assigned to imagery or nonimagery groups. As expected, imagery practice resulted in an increase in final performance. Interestingly, the imagers spent more time mentally practicing the golf-putting task than did nonimagers, even though this was not required by the experiment. Interviews showed that the imagers also set higher goals for themselves and stuck to their training programs outside the study (Martin & Hall, 1995; Orliaguet & Coello, 1998).

Increased motivation may be the most important consequence of the imagery practice (Paivio, 1985). Motivation is not merely an overall desire to perform well. Performance motivation can be divided into two types. The first is a kind of motivation that leads to toughness, determination, and confidence to achieve mastery of a specific skill (Moritz, Hall, Vadocz, & Martin, 1996). The second type is a more generalized arousal that gets the performer energized for the task (e.g., C. Hall, Mack, Paivio, & Hausenblas, 1998). An increase in these two types of motivation can have a powerful effect on performance. In spite of all these benefits of imagery practice, it tends not to produce the same level of performance that is achieved by someone with the same motivation and real practice (Driskell, Copper, & Moran, 1994). You will not become a star performer by imagination alone.

Imagery and Mental Maps

Which city is farther north, Boston or Seattle? Which city is farther west, Reno or San Diego? You probably will want to look at a map to verify the answers to these questions: Seattle is farther north than Boston; perhaps the greatest surprise is that Reno, Nevada, is farther west than San Diego, California (see **FIGURE 8.14**). If you are like the university students who were originally asked these questions by Tversky (1981), you answered at least one of them wrong. These errors are not the result of ignorance; residents of San Diego were asked to indicate the direction of Reno (and

FIGURE 8.14 Map of U.S. and Landmark Cities People consistently misalign U.S. cities, both north-south and east-west, because they do not rely on their spatial knowledge, but instead use incorrect shapes of states to position the cities.

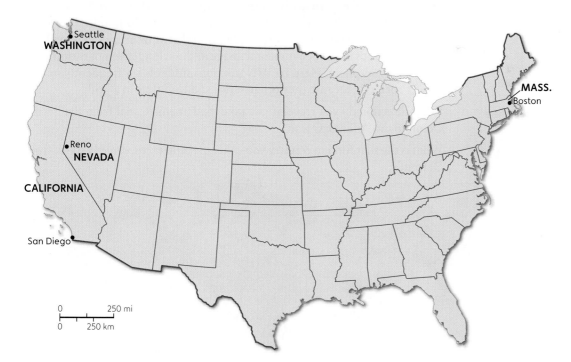

other cities) from San Diego. They ought to know the answer to these questions, yet most imagined that Reno was northeast of San Diego, not northwest.

When they mentally represent the locations of cities within states, most people organize the spatial locations hierarchically. They might think of Reno as a city in the state of Nevada and San Diego as a city in the state of California and then, because they also know that California is mostly west of Nevada, conclude that San Diego must be west of Reno (e.g., Stevens & Coupe, 1978). Perhaps you think that your mental image of the states is somehow based on your experience with the maps you have seen. However, you have never seen one where all of California is west of Nevada.

People's mental maps are not organized as a true picture, but as a configuration where states and countries line up as if they were rectangles rather than the way they really are: jagged, irregular shapes, occasionally tilted from the vertical (Tversky, 1981). People seem to employ a heuristic of making the irregular geographic boundaries fit a kind of grid as a way of keeping much of the information as straight as possible—at the cost of a loss of detailed information. To see this for yourself, inspect **FIGURE 8.15** and decide which map is more correct. People tend to pick the world map in Figure 8.15B as the correct map. It is horizontally aligned: The European continent is parallel to the frame, North America is aligned with Europe, and South America and Africa are aligned. Alas, the correct map is shown in Figure 8.15A.

Our image of the arrangement of states and countries seems to be along regular lines—neat and not messy. People tend to place locales at right angles even when their personal experience is consistent with angles other than 90° (Tversky, 1981). Although you have probably seen maps of the world hundreds or even thousands of times, you may be surprised to find that your images look nothing like the maps. Let's inspect your mental image of the arrangement of countries in the western hemisphere. Here are two questions students are frequently unable to answer correctly because they orient cities and countries in a grid:

What direction do you travel if you take the Panama Canal from the Pacific Ocean to the Atlantic Ocean?

What is the first foreign country you come to if you travel directly south from Detroit?

FIGURE 8.15 World Maps
(A) True map of the world where continents are not aligned.
(B) Imagined map of the world where continents and countries are aligned horizontally.

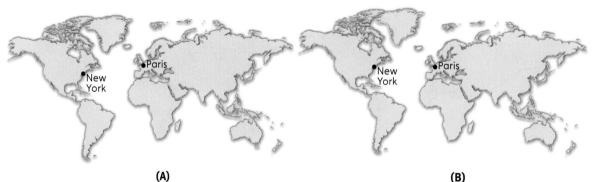

(A)   (B)

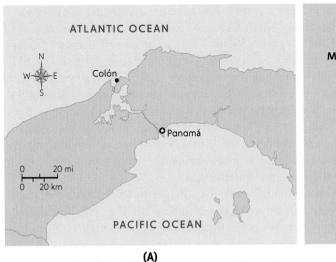

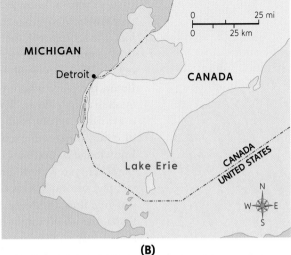

(A)   **(B)**

The correct answers to these questions are *west* and *Canada* (see **FIGURES 8.16A** and **8.16B**). This exercise illustrates that our mental images are more than merely photographs of a scene or a map.

FIGURE 8.16 Accurately Locating Areas (A) Panama Canal showing that the Atlantic entrance near the city of Colon is actually west of the Pacific entrance near Panama City. (B) A map showing that the country directly south of Detroit is Canada.

Mnemonics

People have tried to improve their memories for millennia by learning special memory-enhancing techniques. Such methods are called **mnemonics**, which are plans for retrieval that are well learned and stored in long-term memory. They are used in order to store and later retrieve information that would otherwise be stored in short-term memory. The techniques are named after Mnemosyne (ni-ˈmä-sə-nē), the Greek goddess of memory and mother of the nine muses. They often involve the use of visual imagery, though not always (Ericsson, 1988; Hunt & Love, 1972). One famous mnemonist was Simonides (556–468 BCE), a lyric poet from the Greek island of Ceos. He would attend banquets and create impromptu poems celebrating the people who attended the banquets. For this he needed to remember the names of the guests. One technique he commonly employed was to associate the names with the guests' seat locations. Legend says that he had a disagreement with his host, Scopus, and went outside. Soon afterward the building collapsed, crushing the guests. Simonides was able to identify the bodies based on their location in the room. The memory technique for associating information (in the form of images) with locations is called the **method of loci and imagines** (locations and images).

Method of Loci The method of loci is a mnemonic technique that was well known to Greek orators who could speak for hours and yet were able to maintain the correct order of their ideas (Yates, 1966). The method of loci, as well as other mnemonic schemes, involves four major steps. The first is to commit the basic structural knowledge to memory. The *structure* is a schema (see Chapter 7) that will hold together the information you want to remember. In the method of loci, the structure is memory for a location that is sufficiently detailed to allow the memorizer to mentally move about the location and have a firm image of its details. This is typically someplace that you know well. It could be your room at home, the place where you normally have dinner (as in the case of Simonides), or shelves in a closet. The important aspect of identifying this location is that it is available to you from your long-term memory. Most of the cognitive demand of using mnemonic schemes results from the setup costs of establishing the knowledge structure. Once that is done, acquiring new information by using the schema may, with practice, seem effortless.

The second step is to identify each item that is to be remembered and to imagine it as an object. For example, if the topic is the U.S. relationship with Cuba, the island might be represented by a cube of sugar (a major industry for the island); the Cuban revolution by a cigar (also a major industry, and also a symbol of Fidel Castro); the cigar could be sitting on a balance scale, indicating the early career of Castro (he was originally a lawyer), and so forth.

The third step is to combine the imagined items with the schema already in long-term memory. For method of loci, the individual items would be mentally "placed" in the designated location. The order in which the items appear in the schema corresponds to the order in which the information needs to be recalled.

The fourth step is retrieval. When you wish to recall the set of items, you mentally scan your location/schema and see each item placed there. Retrieval in the correct order is assured because the memorizer, called a *mnemonist* (ni-ʹmä-nist) scans the overall location in a predetermined, well-learned order. The more images stored at a specific mental location, the more nuanced the recollection can be. There is a limit: Research supports four items per location as an optimal number (Crovitz, 1971). Like other imagery effects, the uniqueness of the images reduces the likelihood that they will be confused with other ideas.

The method of loci has many advantages over ordinary efforts to rote memorization of lists of items (where the order of those items is important). One advantage is that it endures without rehearsal for at least a week (De Beni & Cornoldi, 1985). The method of loci has been shown to facilitate students' recollections of text. However, since the method relies on visual imagery, you will be more successful in using the method of loci if you are listening to a text while forming a visual image of it rather than reading a text while you are trying to memorize it because using the visual system to both read and memorize will introduce error into the memorization process (Cornoldi & De Beni, 1991; De Beni & Cornoldi, 1997).

Method of Loci and Age Older adults show dramatic benefits from the method of loci. In one study 10 people ranging in age from 63 to 82 years old were taught to use the method of loci to remember grocery purchases. When tested immediately they showed near maximum performance. Over time, however, many of the participants began to modify the method on their own and did not show as much benefit when they were tested 4 weeks later (Anschutz, Camp, Markley, & Kramer, 1985; see also Baltes & Kliegl, 1992; Verhaeghen & Marcoen, 1996).

Some older adults gain more from using the method of loci than do others. For example, older graphic designers, who have demonstrably greater spatial ability than other people of the same age, show a considerably greater benefit from using the method of loci than do ordinary people. It should be noted, however, that even with reliable gains from using the method, none of the older graphic designers showed as high a level of memory as did typical 19-year-old college students (Lindenberger, Kliegl, & Baltes, 1992).

Method of Story An essential element of the method of loci is that it spatially connects items in a specified order. The same thing can be accomplished by creating links that are not physical places, but thematic. This is what the method of story (or narrative) does. It links images that are in a thematic relationship with each other by fitting them into a story. Bower and Clark (1969) examined whether this adaptation of the method of loci would be effective in helping students remember many lists of words. In that study there were two groups of students: the mnemonic group and the control group (who received no special instructions). The first group used a narrative mnemonic and was given the following instructions:

> A good way to learn a list of items is to make up a story relating the items to one another. Specifically, start with the first item and put it in a setting, which will allow other items to be added to it. Then, add the other items to the story in the same order as the items appear. Make each story meaningful to yourself. Then, when you are asked to recall the items, you can simply go through your story and pull out the proper items in their correct order. (p. 181)

The control group was not given any special instructions. Both groups were shown a list of 10 words, which they studied at their own pace, and then were immediately tested on their recall of the items. They were then given a new list to study and the procedure was repeated for all 12 lists. Finally, they were then asked to recall each list in order.

The narrative and control groups did not differ on their immediate recall of each list after it had been presented; both groups scored over 99% correct. They did differ, however, in their ultimate recollection of all of the lists at the end of the study. Here the narrative group recalled 7 times as many words as the control group (93% and 13%, respectively). The narrative group used thematic ideas to hold the sentences together and was able to reconstruct the critical words from these ideas. **TABLE 8.1** is taken from the original study and shows that these

TABLE **8.1**
Sample Stories
A LUMBERJACK DARTed out of a forest, SKATEd around a HEDGE past a COLONY of DUCKs. He tripped on some FURNITURE, tearing his STOCKING while hastening toward the PILLOW where his MISTRESS lay.
A VEGETABLE can be a useful INSTRUMENT for a COLLEGE student. A carrot can be a NAIL for your FENCE or BASIN. But a MERCHANT of the QUEENs would SCALE that fence and feed the carrot to a GOAT.
One night at DINNER I had the NERVE to bring my TEACHER. There had been a FLOOD that day, and the rain BARREL was sure to RATTLE. There was, however, a VESSEL in the HARBOR carrying this ARTIST to my CASTLE.

Note: Memorized words are capitalized.

Source: From Bower & Clark, 1969, p. 181

narratives were not particularly brilliant, but were sufficient to include images of the critical words in a sensible order.

Method of Story and Age The method of story (or narrative) has been shown to be quite effective for improving retention of information with older adults. Residents of a retirement home were trained to use the method of story and then were given a list of 26 words to remember. Their ability to recall the list was superior to a control group (not taught the method) either immediately following the training session or 3 days later (Hill, Allen, & McWhorter, 1991). Of course, not everyone will benefit equally from such training. Older participants (72 years old and older) with larger working memory capacities tend to show the largest benefits for using the method of story (Drevenstedt & Bellezza, 1993).

Peg-Word Method Another well-known mnemonic technique also involves visual imagery and a fixed ordering, called the **peg-word method**. To use this method, the person first commits to memory a fixed set of visual images that are able to be called up at a moment's notice. These are called *pegs* because new items to be memorized are connected (or hung) on them. To experience how this works, try the activity in Demonstration 8.3.

■■■DEMONSTRATION 8.3

Peg-Word System

The first part of the method requires the memorizer to learn the pegs. Let's assume that you will need 10 pegs to learn 10 new words. To do this, you first memorize the following rhyme to create the mental pegs. This specific procedure was probably first described to modern audiences by Miller, Galanter, and Pribram (1960).

> *One is a bun,*
>
> *Two is a shoe,*
>
> *Three is a tree,*
>
> *Four is a door,*
>
> *Five is a hive,*
>
> *Six are sticks,*
>
> *Seven is heaven,*
>
> *Eight is a gate,*
>
> *Nine is a line,*
>
> *Ten is a hen.*

When you memorize this rhyme, you should form a visual image of each of the nouns: *bun, shoe, tree,* and so on. When you are done, you will be able to activate an image of one of these objects whenever you hear a number from 1 to 10. These objects are your pegs in long-term memory.

The next step is to take each new item to be memorized and form a visual image of it. This image will be hung on the peg associated with the same number. The list of to-be-remembered items might look something like the following (taken from Miller et al., 1960)

1. ashtray
2. firewood
3. picture

4. cigarette

5. table

6. matchbook

7. glass

8. lamp

9. shoe

10. phonograph

Your memory should have an image of an ashtray combined with an image of a bun; a bundle of firewood should be combined with a shoe, and so forth.

To retrieve the list, you could start with a number (e.g., 1), find the peg that rhymes with it (e.g., *bun*) and inspect the image to identify the object that is combined with the bun. In this case, it would be an *ashtray*.

Now, without looking back at the words, try to recall the first 5 words in order by starting with the number. What is the number of *lamp*? If you inspect your mental images, you may notice that a *lamp* is hanging from a *gate*, which rhymes with *eight*. Therefore, *lamp* is number 8.

The peg-word method is similar to the method of loci because the ordering in both cases is determined by a contextual image (either a location or a rhyme). For both methods there is an image for each item to be remembered. Retrieval consists of remembering a sequence that is available in LTM and then reading off an associated item that is linked to the peg or to the location.

Key-Word Method The **key-word method** has been used for decades as an aid to learning a new language or for remembering names and faces (e.g., Atkinson & Raugh, 1975; Kasper, 1993; Levin, 1981, 1993; Paivio & Desrochers, 1981; Shing & Heyworth, 1992; Wang, Thomas, & Ouellette, 1992). The technique is to form a bridge between a foreign word, for example, and one in your own language. By way of illustration, suppose you are trying to learn the Spanish word *carta*, which means *letter* in English. This is illustrated in **FIGURE 8.17**. In Stage 1, you listen to the Spanish word and find an English word that sounds like it, such as *cart*. *Cart* is the key word. In Stage 2 you link the key word (*cart*) with the English meaning of the Spanish word. The English meaning is represented mentally as an image (e.g., you might have an image of a mail carrier's cart filled with letters). In your image of the cart, you may have it pushed by a woman because *carta* in Spanish is feminine (*la carta*). When this is done, you can retrieve the English meaning of the Spanish word by just hearing the word in Spanish.

Two difficulties with this procedure are that the key word, over time, may be associated with more than one image depending on the vocabulary words

FIGURE 8.17 Key-Word Example When you hear the Spanish word *carta*, which means "letter" in English, you form a visual image of a cart pushed by a female letter carrier (*carta* is a feminine noun). Whenever you hear *carta*, you think of this image and you retrieve "letter."

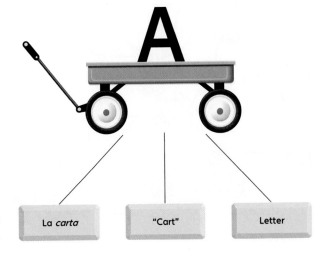

that are being studied. For example, *cart* may be associated with the mail cart, or a farm cart (from *la carreta*), or the driver of a cart (e.g., *el carretero*), and so on. Another difficulty is being able to remember the Spanish word given the English one. The word *letter* may be associated with an unlimited number of images so that hearing or seeing the word will not necessarily yield the key word or the original Spanish word.

In spite of such shortcomings, the key-word method has been effectively used for learning foreign languages. One reason for this may be that it leads to immediate improvement in the recall of vocabulary words (e.g., Atkinson, 1975). For children learning Spanish, the key-word system is as effective as the story method (Pressley, Levin, & Miller, 1981). However, for university students, who tend to be of high ability, the key-word system does not provide any advantage over what they normally do to aid their memory (J. W. Hall, Wilson, Patterson, 1981; McDaniel & Pressley, 1984). Fortunately, the key-word method has been effective in helping people with learning disabilities to remember events and facts from their lives, both inside and outside the classroom (e.g., King-Sears, Mercer, & Sindelar, 1992; Mastropieri, 1988; Mastropieri, Scruggs, & Fulk, 1990; Mastropieri, Scruggs, & Levin, 1985).

Key-Word Method and Age The key-word system has also been shown to be effective for older adults. Participants in one study (Dretzke, 1993; see also Levin, Shriberg, & Berry, 1983) were asked to learn information presented in short passages about fictitious cities. Here is an example:

> Belleview is attractively situated at the base of an inactive volcano, which last erupted in the eighteenth century. Hot air balloon rides provide a thrilling way for visitors to take in the lovely surroundings. A large automobile museum in the city boasts the best collection of turn-of-the century classics that can be found in this part of the country. This is also the home of skilled craftsmen known for handmade musical instruments. Every summer, thousands of folks from all over the world come here to compete against the best in an Olympic-style marathon.
>
> *(Dretzke, 1993, pp. 493–494)*

FIGURE 8.18 Key-Word Illustration Diagram Transformational illustration designed to represent details about the fictitious city of Belleview. Having a diagram that embodied all the details of a story improved the memory of participants of all ages.

Dretzke, B. J. (1993). Effects of pictorial mnemonic strategy usage on prose recall of young, middle-aged, and older adults. *Educational Gerontology. 19:* 489–502. Figure 1.

The three groups of participants were young (17–29 years old), middle-aged (40–50 years old), and older (60–84 years old) adults. They used their own personal strategies to learn the material, a key-word illustration strategy where pictures were provided for them, or their own key-word images. An example of the pictures provided is shown in **FIGURE 8.18**. Does this capture the salient aspects of the passage for you?

The key-word illustration and the imagery strategies resulted in significant increases in recall for all three age groups compared with those who used their own strategies. It should be noted that some in the older group did not improve as much as the others because they had difficulty in comprehending the passage and therefore difficulty in using the mnemonics. Although these data show the value of using mnemonic strategies, they also show that such strategies cannot overcome basic comprehension difficulties.

Songs and Rhymes Some mnemonics rely on wordplay, which may be a kind of auditory imagery. For example, rhyming or creating jingles is a useful technique to remember a set of facts. People of all ages seem to benefit equally from using songs or rhymes. In one study, college-age students and older adults (average age = 71 years) were asked to listen to a radio show that had two advertisements in it. For half the participants the advertisements used simple rhyming to present the name of the products. The other half heard similar ads but without any rhyming. Seven days later all participants were tested for their recall of the ads and the brands. The people who heard the rhyming advertisements recalled the brands better than those who heard the nonrhyming ads. There was no difference in the ability of the younger and older adults to recall the advertisements (M. C. Smith & Phillips, 2001). To experience how songs have played a role in your memory, try the activity in Demonstration 8.4.

▪▪▪DEMONSTRATION 8.4

Songs, Rhymes, and Memory

Write down the alphabet backward starting from the last letter. You should do this by writing at a slow, continuous pace across the page—not stopping other than to write down the letters. Some letters will be written down close to each other; sometimes there will be broad spaces between letters. Did you notice that the letters appear in groups with large spaces between the groups? If you spent your early years learning the alphabet by watching shows like *Sesame Street*, then the groupings (when looked at from the beginning of the alphabet) generally correspond to the phrasing of the alphabet song: abcdefg hijk lmnop qrs tuv w x y&z. This demonstrates the power of the rhyme to create structure in memory.

The "Alphabet" song is a melody that is typically well known to children: It is the melody to "Twinkle, Twinkle, Little Star." The melody and the associated rhyming sequences tie the words together. The phrasing also provides a kind of grouping of the letters of the song.

The use of songs for remembering is not restricted to children of the TV culture. Throughout history, the indigenous people of the Australian Outback have practiced the song method of holding together a sequence of facts (Chatwin, 1987). *Aborigines* (a term used universally to describe the original inhabitants of any land) believe singing is a creative act and that their semidivine ancestors sang the world and all its elements into existence. As a religious duty, they *walkabout*, retracing the routes their ancestors walked across the continent, re-singing everything back into life—giving them shape. Much of the ancient paths they tread are unmarked. They navigate via the sequence of landmarks described in the songs. In a sense, a musical phrase is a map reference. Although these paths can extend thousands of miles, the aborigines can correctly navigate their way across vast terrain by knowing the "land's song" (note that this description hardly does justice to the elaborate religious beliefs of these people).

Mnemonics in the Clinic People with mild forms of amnesia caused by head injuries frequently complain about having poor memories: They are forgetful about appointments, people's names, or plans for future actions. You might think that all the person would have to do is practice memorizing. Unfortunately, with regard to rote memory, practice alone does not make perfect. We have known this since William James, one of the earliest American psychologists, memorized 158 lines of poetry each day for 8 days. Then he went on for 38 days memorizing the first book of Milton's *Paradise Lost*—roughly 6,000 words. Then he returned to the book of poetry and discovered that his ability to memorize poetry had not improved at all. Many studies have had people practice for hundreds of hours memorizing pairs of words, only to find just a slight improvement in their ability (see review by Schacter, Chiu, & Ochsner, 1993).

Fortunately, people with memory impairments can benefit from practice on visual imagery to improve their memory retention (e.g., Canellopoulou & Richardson, 1998; Lewinsohn, Danaher, & Kikel, 1977; J. T. E. Richardson, 1992). When imagery is coupled with the method of story used by Bower and Clark (1969), the gains can be substantial. A version of this method has been developed by Kovner, Mattis, and Goldmeier (1983) to rehabilitate the memory processing of persons with memory impairments. They first teach the individual to read a humorous (ridiculous) story that already has the to-be-remembered words embedded in it. The person then tries to remember the target words. After many trials with this procedure, participants are asked to create stories themselves: They are given a list of words for which they are to create a story that will embed the words. This technique, sometimes called the *ridiculous image story* (RIS) procedure, results in benefits to individuals with amnesia and head injuries (e.g., Goldstein et al., 1988). It leads to even greater improvements in memory for individuals with multiple sclerosis (Allen, Goldstein, Heyman, & Rondinelli, 1998) and illustrates the effectiveness of imagery for improving memory (e.g., J. T. E. Richardson, 1992).

Mnemonics in the Classroom Mnemonic methods have been shown to enhance students' performance in the classroom (e.g., Carney & Levin, 2000; Uberti, Scruggs, & Mastropieri, 2003), especially for students with learning difficulties (e.g., Bulgren, Schumaker, & Deshler, 1994; Keeler & Swanson, 2001; Scruggs & Mastropieri, 2000; Swanson, 1999). Mnemonic methods are not limited to memory for strictly verbal material. For example, teaching mnemonic strategies can even help with learning math facts (Greene, 1999).

Children learning a foreign language and other facts have been shown to benefit from the key-word method (e.g., Raugh & Atkinson, 1975) just like older adults. In the classroom, words learned by the key-word method are retained at a higher level than those using a student's normal method. This was shown in a study of elementary schoolchildren who were trying to memorize the state capitals—a common activity for fourth- and fifth-grade U.S. students (Levin, Shriberg, Miller, McCormick, & Levin 1980). On the first day of the experiment, the children learned to associate 12 state names with 12 key words and were shown corresponding pictures by the experimenters. For example, for Maryland they saw the key word *marry* and for the capital they saw two apples representing *Annapolis*. Finally, the cartoon was a picture of two apples getting married. After learning these pairings, the students were 78% correct in recalling the capital when given the name of a state.

On the second day, the students learned an additional 13 state capitals, but were allowed to use any procedure they liked. For these, they were 65.9% correct. After 2 days' delay, the students were 71.2% correct in recalling the state capitals learned by key word, but only 36.4% correct in recalling state capitals learned by their own methods. These studies are just illustrations of a substantial body of data supporting the idea that imagery—even imagery prompted by other people's pictures—can have a positive effect in helping young and old people store and retrieve information.

SECTION SUMMARY
Using Imagery to Enhance Physical and Cognitive Functioning

People often use motor imagery to train in order to enhance their performance. There is clear evidence that imagery training can be effective. However, some of the benefits are derived from increased motivation that comes from the practice.

People's geographic knowledge demonstrates that visual and spatial imagery can be deceiving. This is because people do not necessarily access images that reflect maps that they have observed, but rather create images that fit their preconceptions. They tend to imagine that U.S. states are somewhat rectangular and assume that cities and states are organized hierarchically: If city A is in state X and state X is at least partially west of state Y, then city A is west of any city in state Y. People also align their map of the world so that continents are horizontal or vertical with respect to each other. These processing assumptions distort our mental maps.

Imagery has been used for thousands of years to aid memory. People who develop special memory skills are called mnemonists. They use schemas for storage and retrieval that are kept in long-term memory. Most of these methods rely on imagery ability. They include the methods of loci, story, peg word, key word, and songs/rhymes. Most mnemonics rely to some degree on visual imagery; however, they can also employ auditory imagery such as the use of songs and rhymes. Both older and younger adults benefit from learning any of these mnemonic techniques, although the younger ones tend to do better on memory tests. Among the older adults, those with heightened spatial ability tend to benefit most from the method of loci, which relies on imagining spatial layouts.

Teaching mnemonics to aid memory has a direct application to clinical cases; such techniques can mitigate difficulties that people with memory impairments experience. They show reliably greater improvement in memory performance than with more traditional rote methods. In addition, the key-word method, with its reliance on a combination of auditory and visual representations, is effectively employed in the classroom to help children remember vocabulary and stories.

CHAPTER SUMMARY

Creating and using mental images are experiences that seem similar to a perceptual experience, yet without the external stimulation that is normally associated with perception. Imagery has been documented as part of human thinking since earliest recorded history. We experience images in our dreams, in solving problems, in navigating or finding our way through space, and in retrieving past events and projecting future experiences. Images sometimes act as if they have continuous properties, as when you mentally imagine your room at home and count the number of windows. In this case we say that images are described as having an analog (continuous) code. Sometimes our images are best described as if they were discrete facts, as when we remember a sentence, in which case we say they have a propositional code.

Images can be so much like a picture that people can find it difficult to tell the difference between whether they have imagined a picture of a word's meaning or an actual drawing of the meaning. People often appear to scan their mental images of a map as they do with a real map in front of them, and they can mentally rotate images as if they were objects on a desk top. As useful and fascinating as images can be, they are not like photographs in the mind. Mentally generating an image of a map tends to be constrained as much by nonimagery concepts that we possess as by actual memory for the map. People have more difficulty searching for hidden forms in their images than they do in physical drawings.

There is considerable variation among people in ability to form a visual image or manipulate it once it has been formed. This seems to be independent of other cognitive abilities. Some people report never having visual images; in contrast, a rare few show exceptional ability called eidetic imagery. Most of the special imagery skills that are effective in problem solving and finding your way rely on spatial rather than verbal working memory.

A new use for imagery has been to provide mental practice of a skill. Use of imagery may not only improve the level of skill, but can be effective in reducing stress, increasing arousal, and increasing overall motivation to perform.

Special memory techniques, called mnemonics, often rely on forming visual images to help store lists of facts. Some of the commonly used techniques are the methods of loci, story, peg word, key word, and songs/rhymes. They have been successfully taught to children in the classroom and to adults with memory impairments.

KEY TERMS

images, p. 228

motoric, p. 228

haptic, p. 228

way finding (or route learning), p. 229

analog code, p. 232

propositional code, p. 232

isomorphic, p. 238

symbolic distance effect, p. 239

split brain (or divided brain), p. 240

corpus callosum, p. 240

hemispheric neglect (or hemineglect), p. 241

congenital blindness, p. 241

reality monitoring, p. 243

dual code hypothesis (or dual coding theory), p. 245

imagery value, p. 245

picture superiority effect, p. 245

visual imagery, p. 249

spatial imagery, p. 249

visualizer–verbalizer, p. 250

environmental spatial ability, p. 252

eidetic imagery, p. 252

motoric imagery, p. 254

mnemonics, p. 257

method of loci and imagines, p. 257

peg-word method, p. 260

key-word method, p. 261

QUESTIONS FOR REVIEW

Check Your Knowledge

1. What are examples of motoric and haptic imagery?

2. How do we distinguish between mental images and hallucinations?

3. What are some of the ways that we can manipulate our mental images?

4. What are some of the unusual images that navigators in Micronesia use?

5. Why do mental images help us remember?

6. The famous mnemonist S used images to enhance his memory, but what did he have difficulty doing with his images?

7. Give an example of how images can interfere with problem solving.

8. What are analog and propositional codes? Give an example of each.

9. Can we scan our visual images the way we scan a photograph?

10. Can we search for hidden pictures within our images the way we search a physical drawing?

11. Are people's representations for pictures the same as for words?

12. Can we rotate a mental image of a 3-D picture the same as a 2-D picture? Are the images of the two objects isomorphic to ones in the real world?

13. What is the role of images in the symbolic distance effect?

14. Do our brains respond to mental images the way they do to scenes or pictures? What evidence can you cite?

15. Is there such a thing as hemineglect for visual images the way there is for visual scenes?

16. What is the experience of "imagery" for a person who is congenitally blind?

17. How can we tell that we are remembering a mental image as opposed to an actual scene?

18. What is the dual code hypothesis, and how does dual coding predict memory ability?

19. What is the picture superiority effect? Is a picture remembered better than a line drawing?

20. Do most people experience visual images? How do you know?

21. What is the difference between visual imagery and spatial imagery? What can you do with one that you can't do with the other?

22. What is a good mapper and a poor mapper? How do they have different experiences?

23. What is eidetic imagery? How common is it?

24. Name some ways that imagery can affect athletic performance.

25. What are some ways in which people distort their mental maps? In general, how good are we at retrieving maps of the country and the world?

26. Name three mnemonic methods and describe how they work.

27. Which method is very effective for remembering foreign vocabulary words?

28. Do some mnemonics work better for older people than for younger people, or vice versa?

29. How does creating a ridiculous image story help people to remember?

30. What are the important ingredients for the key-word mnemonic?

Apply Your Knowledge

1. If our physical experiences and our imagination use the same brain circuits, how can we tell that we are behaving and not hallucinating? How can we tell what is real?

2. Perform the study that Galton's (1880/1907) participants took part in a century ago: Think of your breakfast table this morning. What can you see in your mind's eye? Rate your mental images on a scale from 1 (*very low*) to 7 (*highest*) for the dimensions such as brightness, color, sharpness, smell, and touch. Based on your scores, would you say that you have strong, weak, or no visual images?

3. One of the characteristics of Luria's (1968) patient S was that he was not able to forget things he memorized, even if he wanted to. Would you like to have a visual image of everything you have encountered, or do you see a value for being able to close your eyes and *not* form a visual image? Is there a benefit for not forming mental images?

4. When you imagine your room at home, you might be able to scan it and count the number of windows. When you do this, are you mentally looking at a photograph stored in your brain, or are you creating an image from bits and pieces of color and dark as is done by a computer screen? How real are images?

9

Language:
A Cognitive Universal

> **"Ef oona ent kno weh oona da gwine, oona should kno weh oona come from! [If you don't know where you are going, you should know where you come from!]"**
>
> —Gullah proverb (Penn Center)

Everyone has a language. The first section of this text describes the memory systems that every human possesses. Our memories are the containers for our cognition and affect the way we perceive and understand the world around us. Chapters 9 and 10 describe the cognitive processes of language and how language allows people to solve problems, communicate, and understand the world around them. Cognitive psychologists are interested in language because, like memory, language has universal components that are the same for everyone no matter where they live or their overall intelligence. In fact, language itself is universal.

All normally healthy people over the age of 4 years have a native language. More than 6,500 languages are spoken in the world (Grimes & Grimes, 2000), and at least half of the world's adult population speaks more than one language (Tucker, 1998). The ability to use language is as universal as walking. Yes, there are people with neurological difficulties who cannot walk or speak, but the vast majority of people learn to walk and speak without real training; all that is needed is an environment in which they are allowed to move and interact with people who are speaking.

This chapter describes the basis for the universality of language in terms of the human environment, both biological and external, and how our language influences other aspects of human cognition. But first, we must define language and its basic components.

The Four Necessary Components of Language

A first step to understanding the relationship between cognition and language is to specify the components of language. **Language** is a system of communication that presumes there is a speaker and a listener (interpreter). The speaker tries to get the listener to understand or to do whatever is intended by the message. The listener presumably wishes to understand the communication. The problem for the speaker, then, is to figure out the best way to communicate the message. The problem for the listener is to figure out the meaning of the message.

TABLE **9.1**		
Necessary Components of Language		
Four components of language		
Component	Rule-based system	Description
Message	Semantics	The sense conveyed by an utterance. It is affected by the context, syntax, and accompanying gestures.
Physical constraints	Syntax	Rules that arrange words into phrases and sentences. These, along with special markers, facilitate the extraction of meaning.
Medium	Articulation/Gestural	The two basic dimensions on which language is founded.
Social constraints	Pragmatics	Social rules that native speakers must acquire to know what can be said and how it must be done to cooperate with the listener for effective communication. These rules govern the speaker's performance and the listener's expectations.

In order for a communication system to be called a **natural language** (one that is the first or native language of a person), it must contain four basic components: a message, rules or physical constraints, a medium of communication, and social constraints. Each of these is described above and summarized in **TABLE 9.1**.

Before turning to a discussion of these language components, note that from here on we will refer to linguistic expressions as **utterances**, which may be either a speech sound or a gesture. Have you ever passed a friend at school who looked at you and said "*Tsup,*" accompanied by a quick jerk of the head upward? This greeting is more like a gesture than a sentence, but it is nevertheless a meaningful utterance. The term utterance captures the fact that people do not always speak in full sentences, but nevertheless manage to convey clear messages.

Message: Semantics

If an utterance is to be considered linguistic, it must seek to convey meaning. Humans possess an ability for taking the ideas that they want to express and translating them into words and gestures, then conveying those ideas to a listener. In a sense, the words and gestures reflect packets of meaning, which are collectively called **semantics**. Any system for communication, no matter how primitive, must have a semantic component. Even nonhuman "languages" communicate meaning. For example, animals use different warning cries depending on the degree of danger they are experiencing, and dogs display different sorts of growls depending on the situation confronting them (Seyfarth & Cheney, 2003). However, as far as we know, only human language can convey meaning about the message itself:

Imagine a dog barking, "Gee, what a great growl I just uttered." This type of animal utterance happens only in the movies.

How Do We Derive Meaning? One of the great mysteries of language is that we are able to figure out the intended meaning from what are basically arbitrary sounds. Imagine a situation that must occur thousands of times a day all over the world: A parent notices a bird flying by and points it out to a child and says something like "see the birdie." How does the child know that *birdie* refers to the entire creature and not merely its color, or the tree the bird came from, or the size of its wings, or the bug in its beak? Part of the answer lies in the context of the utterance, what the child is attending to, and what happens following it (Premack, 1985). Most important, the child's understanding of *birdie* seems to depend on what may be a biologically based, universal mental program that maps speech sounds with the properties of objects.

The program seems to follow three principles. The first is the **reference principle**. The child interprets words to be about objects and not merely the feelings of the speaker: *Birdie* does not refer to how happy the speaker is about seeing a bird; it is about the bird itself. This is reflected in the child's own first words. A universal characteristic of a child's 50 first words is that they are typically about things that move and movers of things. Young children put the words uttered around them into these two categories (Brown, 1973). This biases children's first words to be nouns (Bates et al., 1994; Gentner, 1982; Golinkoff, Mervis, & Hirsh-Pasek, 1994). When children begin to acquire two-word utterances, they emphasize objects. For example, "more cookie," "mommy come," and "no bath" are typical two-word phrases used by 18- to 24-month-old children. Although the content varies with the culture, children all over the world—in every imaginable linguistic environment—show the same speech pattern.

The second principle is the **whole object principle**, in which the child shows a preference for identifying words with whole objects rather than a part of an object (Macnamara, 1982; Markman & Wachtel, 1988). If someone says to a child "see the birdie," the child assumes the word *birdie* is the name of the whole creature and not its beak or wings (E. V. Clark, 1987; Golinkoff et al., 1994; Markman & Wachtel, 1988).

The third principle is the **nonredundancy of words principle**. Young children act as if there is only one name for an object and every name has only a single thing it points to—its referent. For example, a 4-year-old might protest when you call your mother *mom* because that's the name of her mother! When the child hears a word that is unfamiliar, she connects it with something in her field of vision whose name she does not know (Golinkoff et al., 1994). If an object already has a name, it can't have another (Markman & Wachtel, 1988).

Meaning Is More than Words As adults we understand that the meaning of an utterance can be greater than the sum of the meanings of the individual words in it, as in "John happily made love to his neighbor's friendly wife" (Osgood, 1971). This adult tendency to find meaning beyond what is superficially expressed begins in childhood between 18 and 36 months (McNeill, 1970) and is called **holophrastic speech**. A single word can convey an entire sentence of meaning, as when a 2-year-old says "Cookie!" This one-word sentence is often accompanied by finger-pointing or reaching. The child may even alter her pattern of saying words when she uses the same word in a different context (Barrett, 1982). These nonword elements are also part of the effort to convey meaning and are present from the child's first words to the adult's fully developed sentences. We will see that as a person develops, there are "rules" for the use of these nonword meaning elements when we take up the topic of pragmatics.

Arrangement of Words: Syntax

Words are not randomly placed into sentences. Each language has rules for how sentences should be put together, called **syntax**. By knowing the syntactic rules of a language, the speaker can convey distinctions such as tense (past, present, and future), mood (wishes, intentions, necessity), or aspect (conditions that are continuing or ending). These distinctions are necessary because of what humans talk about. You may be describing an event that occurred long ago (I studied for the exam) or one you wish had occurred but did not (If I had only studied for the exam). Because of syntax, English sentences can have different meanings even though they use the same words. Take, for example, sentences (a) and (b). They contain identical words but they are arranged in different sequences. Notice that the two sentences convey radically different meanings.

(a) The dog bit the man.

(b) The man bit the dog.

Even the meaning of individual words can change depending on where they occur within a sentence. For example, in sentence (c) *some* means at least one and doesn't specify any specific books. In contrast, the word *some* in sentence (d) suggests a specific set of books.

(c) All students have read some books.

(d) Some books have been read by all students.

Syntax and Animal Communication   Syntactic rules are largely missing from animal communication systems. This is because each behavior conveys meaning in a fixed way. For example, the "dance" of honeybees is used to communicate the location of honey. When a honeybee returns to the hive, it spreads out samples of the flower's nectar to the other bees. This gets their attention and creates a context for a dance. The honeybee then performs a dance that identifies the distance, direction, quality, and quantity of the food supply. Each "step" of the dance conveys a fixed piece of information. Although the order in which the steps occur is not relevant, the system is relatively inflexible. Some circumstances cannot be communicated by the honeybee's dance. In one study, the honey was deliberately located either above or below the hive (von Frisch, 1974). The honeybees were not able to provide direction via the dance because their "language" deals only in direct line-of-sight information. No combination of steps could be used to convey the true location of the honey.

Cues to Syntax   The listener's job is to use the available cues to understand the message. We have learned many of these cues without explicit instruction. Can you tell that sentences (e) and (f) convey subtly different meanings about the *ball* even though the wording is nearly identical?

(e) Katie kicked the green ball over the fence.

(f) Katie kicked a green ball over the fence.

The two sentences differ because they contain the articles *the* and *a*. In sentence (e) use of the definite article *the* tells the listener that the speaker assumes the listener already knows something about the ball. In sentence (f) the indefinite article *a* is noncommittal; the speaker conveys no assumption about whether the listener knows which ball it is (Osgood, 1971). Did anyone teach you the distinction between definite and indefinite articles? Probably not; their use reflects knowledge you picked up by using English.

Syntactic cues are also conveyed by the endings of words. For example, endings such as *ing, ed,* and *en* are cues that the words they are attached to are likely to be verbs; *s* and *es* are cues that the words may be nouns; and *y* at the end of a word can be a cue that it is an adjective. An illustration of how important these syntactic cues can be to our comprehension is shown in the poem *Jabberwocky*, reproduced in Demonstration 9.1. The poem appeared in *Through the Looking Glass and What Alice Found There* by Lewis Carroll (1871, pp. 56–57). Read the poem and see if the syntactic cues help you to create a mental image of the story. You may realize that the poem is about nothing. However, because the nonwords in the poem follow general syntactic principles, it is difficult not to derive sense from a heap of nonsense.

■■■**DEMONSTRATION 9.1**

Syntax and Meaning in a Poem
Jabberwocky

Wikipedia

'Twas brillig, and the slithy toves
Did gyre and gimble in the wabe;
All mimsy were the borogoves,
And the mome raths outgrabe.

"Beware the Jabberwock, my son!
The jaws that bite, the claws that catch.
Beware the Jubjub bird, and shun
The frumious Bandersnatch!"
He took his vorpal sword in hand.
Long time the manxome foe he sought-
So rested he by the Tumtum tree,
And stood awhile in thought.
And as in uffish thought he stood,
The Jabberwock, with eyes of flame,
Came whiffling through the tulgey wood,

And burbled as it came!

One, two! One, two! And through and through

The vorpal blade went snicker-snack!

He left it dead, and with its head

He went galumphing back.

"And hast thou slain the Jabberwock?

Come to my arms my beamish boy?

O frabjous day! Callooh! Callay!"

He shortled in his joy.

'Twas brillig, and the slithy toves

Did gyre and gimble in the wabe;

All mimsy were the borogoves,

And the mome raths outgrabe.

As you read the poem, you can see that in the first sentence, *slithy toves* looks like an adjective (*slithy*, a word ending in *y*) modifying a noun (*toves*, a word ending in *es*). Or, as Humpty Dumpty tells Alice, "*slithy* means lithe and slimy . . . it's like a portmanteau (saddle bag)—there are two meanings packed into one word. *Toves* are something like badgers . . . and lizards . . . and corkscrews that make their nests under sun-dials . . . and live on cheese" (p. 58).

Medium of Communication: Speech and Gesture

Messages can take many forms: They can be spoken, written, or gestured. Although poets say that language can be evocative as in "a language in her eye, her cheek, her lip, nay her foot speaks" (Shakespeare, *Troilus and Cressida*, act IV, scene 5), there are really only two recognized, universal media for language: voice and gesture. Voiced or spoken language is universal. All hearing children, exposed to a linguistic environment, will master a native language that has speech sounds as the essential medium. It is no accident that the word *language* has its origin in the Latin word *lingua*, the word for tongue.

A universal characteristic of all infants is that they begin babbling around 4 months of age. These sounds are typically consonant–vowel pairs. Infants the world over produce the same set of early babbling sounds independent of their caregivers' language (Nakazima, 1962; Oller, 1980). Deaf children, who could not be imitating the sounds in their environment, also produce these same early speech sounds (Oller & Eilers, 1988). Children acquire gesturing skills (e.g., sign language) when they are in an environment where adults are gesturing—as deaf parents do—much in the same way and at the same time as children acquire speaking skills in a speaking environment (Bonvillian, Orlansky, & Novack, 1983). Just as deaf and hearing children babble with their voices in their cribs, they also "babble" with their hands. Both deaf and hearing children progress in mastery of their native language (e.g., spoken American English and American Sign Language) through the same stages at roughly the same time (Poizner, Klima, & Bellugi, 1987). Development and environment have different effects on them, however, because hearing and deaf infants depart in the percentage of babbling in sound versus gesture by 10 months of age (e.g., Petitto & Marentette, 1991).

The similarity in language development between hearing and deaf children suggests that the universality of language is based on a common biology. Both hearing and deaf children process language in the left hemisphere. Although hand gestures would appear to be processed by the right hemisphere because of their spatial nature (see Chapter 8), the opposite is the case. Both deaf signers and hearing speakers have their language disrupted by damage to the left hemisphere. This suggests that language is processed by the same neurological structures for both hearing and gestural communication (Poizner et. al., 1987). The role of the separate hemispheres in language is described in the Neuropsychology of Language section later.

You might think that writing would be included as a third medium for language, since writing surrounds us in everyday life. All modern writing falls into three basic classes depending on the size of the language unit: sound, syllable, or whole word. One type of writing is sound based and is called a **phonological (or alphabetic) system**. In this case, a letter or group of letters corresponds to the sounds of the spoken language. English is an example of an alphabetic language: The word *cat* consists of the individual sounds of /k/+/ae/+/t/. A second type of writing is called a **syllabary system**. Here, a letter or symbol corresponds to a syllable of a spoken word. Two examples in modern Japanese are *hiragana*, which includes syllables and other elements related to spoken Japanese, and *katakana*, a syllabary used to write out the sounds of words from non-Japanese languages. For example, the English word *hotel* is written with three kana, ホテル (*ho-te-ru*). The third type of writing system uses a symbol to convey the meaning of an entire word. These are called **logographic** (literally meaning *word-picture*) **systems**. Chinese is a modern example of a whole-word system in which the "letters" are actually pictograms that correspond to individual words or concepts in the language. In Chinese, the word *hotel* is written as 館. (Japanese also uses pictograms, in combination with hiragana and katakana.)

Written languages are found all over the world, but writing is not universal. Although nearly every language user communicates within phonological or gestural media or both, not every language user develops written language. Many adults in the world are not literate. A United Nations (2009) survey estimates that as of the year 2000, 14.3% of the world's people over the age of 15 were illiterate (roughly 900 million people), and the percentage of illiteracy for some sub-Saharan countries was approximately 80%. Because children have to be deliberately taught written language but not spoken language, the latter is seen as universal; the former is not.

Social Constraints: Pragmatics

Semantics, syntax, and medium are the essential components of language, but knowing them does not tell us how language is actually used. To do that, we must imagine that utterances are acts of cooperation between speaker and listener. The system of rules for social cooperation is called **pragmatics** and includes limits on what can be spoken about, how to speak, and the listener's expectations about how the information will be presented. Pragmatics tells you when and to whom you can talk about your latest bout of stomach flu; when a question is asking for information (Are you going to school by car or by bus?); or when a question is rhetorical and its message is quite different from what appears on the surface (Are you going to wear *that* shirt to school?).

You have probably noticed that when people speak, they often use hand gestures or head movements. Pragmatics also describes the nonspeech elements that are used to coordinate with the spoken sentence to convey the message (Petitto, 1987). Take saying no, for example. Look at a child who is offered a distasteful medicine. In American culture, the child might shake his or her head from left to right in the nonverbal indicator of denial and say "I don't want any medicine." Although a speaker is free to add the head movement or other gestures, the timing of when it occurs is actually dictated by pragmatic rules. The gesture must occur in a critical period around the presence of the negative term *not*. Similar rules also occur when people communicate with American Sign Language (ASL; Emmorey, 1999; Liddell & Metzger, 1998).

Some gestures are universal, although their meaning may not be. For example, deaf and hearing children, as well as rhesus monkeys and gorillas, turn their faces away as a form of denial (Altmann, 1967). In American culture, head turning from side to side indicates denial or negation (*no*). However, in India a similar gesture (with head tilted) is used to indicate agreement. Pragmatic rules are critical to interpreting sentences. Further research on the relationship between pragmatics and sentence understanding is discussed in Chapter 10.

Language and Animals

If you have ever tried to talk to a parrot or cockatiel, you have noticed that they can repeat strings of sounds, but there is no evidence that they understand what they are saying. Your dog may understand the significance of the words *walk*, *biscuit*, or *leash* and may jump up and down or drool when he hears these words, but just add the clause "would you dislike a . . ." and see if he doesn't act the same way. There is no evidence that animal communication has syntactic or pragmatic rules. Animals do not naturally possess language as we have defined it here. This does not mean, however, that some animals do not possess the intelligence to acquire rudimentary forms of language. Many researchers who use behavioral methods (e.g., instrumental conditioning) have been effective in teaching simple grammars and providing opportunities for communication with other primates.

Four of these animals have achieved near-stardom. Two chimpanzees, Washoe (R. A. Gardner & B. T. Gardner, 1969) and Nim Chimpsky (Terrace, Petitto, Sanders, & Bever, 1979) as well as a gorilla, Koko, have been taught to sign words and short sentences in response to speech and gestures by their trainers.

Nim Chimpsky During a Training Session When psychologist Herbert Terrace shows him the puppet, Nim signs "hug."

Susan Kuklin/Photo Researchers

The most impressive of these primates is Kanzi, a bonobo chimpanzee that mastered language skills through auditory input. Kanzi is able to respond to requests by pointing to symbols on a board or acting out commands (Savage-Rumbaugh, McDonald, Sevcik, Hopkins, & Rubert, 1986). The behavioral techniques used with these primates have also proved effective in instructing autistic children in basic social and communication skills (e.g., Lovaas, Cross, & Revlin, 2006; McEachin, Smith, & Lovaas, 1993). The training technique has been used because, unlike their peers, many children with autism do not develop language skills naturally.

SECTION SUMMARY ▪

The Four Necessary Components of Language

The four conditions for language—meaning, structure, medium, and pragmatics—help us understand why possessing a natural language is exclusively a human activity. No animal language possesses all four components. Children are able to master the meaning (semantics) of words in their environment by following three basic principles: (a) the reference principle, in which words are thought to refer to objects—things that move and objects that make them move; (b) the whole object principle, in which words refer to the entire object, not just a part; and (c) the nonredundancy of words principle, in which there is only one name for an object. The arrangement of words to convey ideas is called syntax. Although people acquire the syntactic rules of their language, they often identify critical syntactic elements based on simple cues. There are two universal media of communication: sound and gesture. Written language is not universal. Language is a social means of communication and therefore all languages embody social limits on what can be said and to whom a message can be addressed. These limitations are called pragmatics.

Some Language Universals

You may have wondered how there came to be more than 6,500 human languages. The truth is that there is no scientifically based, definitive answer to this question. We can't tell if all languages developed from a single original language or if many languages emerged all at once. We do know, however, that wherever there are people, there will be language because we all possess similar language-related wiring in our brains. This universal in biology leads us to anticipate that there will be commonalities in the way languages are developed and created and that there will be similarities in the way all languages are structured.

Language Creation

The process of language creation has been repeated over thousands of years. It begins with two groups of people who speak different languages but come together for some purpose: to exchange goods and/or members of their group for marriage. If their languages are substantially different, over years of contact the groups develop common terminology to facilitate the exchange. These fragments of language, if they persist over time, are called **pidgins**—named after the Pidians, indigenous people who lived along the Orinoco River (in modern Venezuela) in the 17th century. The Pidians developed a fragmented English to engage in trade with Europeans (Kleinecke, 1959). Pidgins are found all over the world. Europeans sometimes gave them names, such as *Lingua Franca* (basic Italian and part Spanish, French, Greek, and Arabic) or *Pidgin English* (part English and part Chinese). Folklore has it that *pidgin* was based on the Cantonese effort to say "business," which they heard as *bigeon*.

Eventually pidgins become fuller and more expressive and took on character- istics of the grammar of the dominant group. When a pidgin becomes a **native language** (a language that is learned as the first language of children), it is called a **Creole** and enters the compendium of the world's 6,500 languages. Within the United States there are at least two major Creole languages: Hawaiian Creole, developed by Asian immigrants to the Hawaiian Islands, and Gullah/ Geechee, a language developed by isolated slaves on the islands off the coast of South Carolina and Georgia (Joyner, 2009). Gullah sounds like English, with a few words from its West African origins (Pollitzer, 1999). Were you able to understand the Gullah passage that begins this chapter? How about this:

'E tek'e foot een 'e han dry 'long so.
(He left quickly without a reason.)

Given the existence of thousands of languages, it is surprising to find many commonalities among them. These linguistic similarities may reflect com- monalities in our human genetic history. Anthropologists have shown that the ge- netic similarity between two chimpanzees randomly sampled from nearby troops is far less than the genetic similarity of any two humans randomly selected from the 6 bil- lion in the world (Ambrose, 1998). Perhaps, then, these language universals simply reflect our common biological heritage. A few other language universals are described below and summarized in **TABLE 9.2**.

Phonological Universals

Not only does every society have a spoken language, but human speech has many simi- lar features. For example, although the human

TABLE **9.2**	
Linguistic Universals	
	Linguistic universals
Types	**Examples**
Language itself	Every healthy child learns a native language at the same rate, everywhere.
Phonological charac- teristics	In each language, a small set of approximately 44 sounds characterizes the basic language.
Syntactic order	For three-word utterances, only three of six possible arrangements of subject, verb, and object appear in a sample of 2,000 languages.
Language-learning benchmarks	Children everywhere learn language in the same sequence, and roughly at the same rate.
Biology of language	The language centers of the brain are roughly equivalent for all humans.

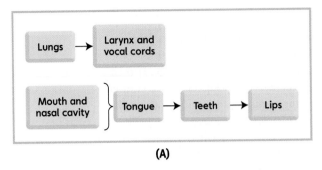

(A)

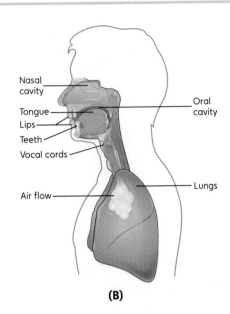

(B)

FIGURE 9.1 The Vocal Tract Speech sounds are the result of moving air from the lungs, over the vocal cords and the larynx in the throat, and into and then out of the mouth. To create a speech sound, the mouth must create an obstacle. An exception comes from people who speak languages with click sounds, including dozens of languages of Africa and the Damin language of Australia. For these sounds the obstacle is produced in the larynx (see Figure 9.1B).

voice mechanism is capable of producing an extraordinary array of sounds, there are only about 600 different consonants (e.g., /b/, /g/, /t/) and about 200 vowels (e.g., /i/, /a/, /o/) in the entire range of human speech. The sounds of a typical language vary from 2 to 25 vowels and from 6 to 100 consonants (with a few exceptions). English, for example, can be characterized by fewer than four dozen speech sounds (approximately 13 vowel sounds and over 30 consonants). Why is the speech of the world's people so limited? One explanation is that humans are limited in the number of meaningful distinctions their cognitive system can make from among auditory signals (G. A. Miller, 1956). A second explanation is that the biologically based human linguistic apparatus we all possess is tuned to these sounds. Whatever the explanation, it is clear that the phonological system for human languages is not composed of a random collection of elements. There is a common thread running through all speech systems.

How Speech Sounds Are Created The physical system that creates speech sounds is generally described by the flowchart in **FIGURE 9.1**. It shows that air is pushed out under pressure from the lungs and passes through the vocal cords. The tension on the cords is determined by signals from the frontal lobe of the brain that alter the muscle tension, causing the vocal cords to vibrate. You can get an experience of how this works by trying the activity in Demonstration 9.2.

▪▪▪DEMONSTRATION 9.2

Vocal Cords

To experience the effect of air moving past the vocal cords, try the following. Take a wide rubber band, stretch it out loosely, and place it lengthwise in front of your mouth (about ¹/₄ inch away). Now, blow on the rubber band. You should only hear the sound of the air coming from your mouth. Now, stretch the rubber band tightly and blow on it. You should be able to hear a sound from the vibration. Now stretch the rubber band tighter. The pitch of the sound should be even higher. Singers modify the tension on their vocal cords in order to alter the pitch and create the desired note. Your vocal cords are like the rubber band: The source of the air is your lungs, and the stretching of the vocal cords is initiated by signals to the muscles surrounding the cords.

In English, changes in pitch (fluctuations in tone from high to low) are not so much associated with individual words (we can speak in a monotone if we wish), but pitch is important to signal a question. Compare the sentence, "Jessie's at Pam's house" with "Jessie's at Pam's house?" In English, the pitch of the voice rises when there is a question (Shelly, 1996; Tannen, 1994b).

How Speech Is Produced Much research has gone into how people produce speech sounds by opening or closing their lips, making sounds in the throat, and placing the tongue in different parts of the mouth (e.g., Levelt, 1989). The great puzzle is that although scientists can specify individual sounds that make up words (called **phonemes**), this analysis tells us very little about how we actually hear those sounds. Take the word *cat.* Technicians can create machines that will produce the individual phonemes: /k/+/ae/+/t/. And, when people hear such a sequence, they can always discern the individual elements—the initial /k/ sound, followed by the middle /ae/, and so forth. In contrast, when real people say the word *cat,* the listener is barely able to hear the separation of the phonemes. We hear the word as a single sound. One reason is that the speaker produces the individual phonemes almost at the same time (Lieberman, 1984).

Syntactic Universals

If you have tried to learn a second language, you may have been struck by the complexity of another language's rules. Yet there are many similarities among the syntactic forms of all languages. For example, a basic three-word sentence contains a subject, a verb, and an object [e.g., Bambi (*subject*) ran (*verb*) home (*object*)]. If languages were just random arrangements of subject (S), verb (V), and object (O), there should be some languages in the world that correspond to each of the six possible arrangements of S, V, and O; some should have SVO, SOV, VSO, VOS, OSV, or OVS in roughly equal numbers. In a sample of 2,000 languages, however, we observe only three of the six arrangements (Greenberg, 1966): Examples are SVO (English), SOV (Japanese), and VSO (Arabic, Irish/Gaelic). There is little evidence for the remaining three (VOS, OVS, and OSV).

This is not to say that we cannot understand these invisible, syntactic arrangements. The *Star Wars* character Yoda occasionally used VOS syntactic structure ("Know things I do"; "Help you I can"). No doubt we understood these expressions because we are so familiar with the words that any arrangement would be understandable. The fact that human languages reflect only half of the possible syntactic arrangements suggests that there is a universal cognitive limitation to our ability to process information.

Language-Learning Universals

Children all over the world acquire their native language in the same age-related sequence; it doesn't matter where they live or how complex their language (Slobin, 1970). The ability of children to learn their language so quickly gave rise to the widespread belief that children are born knowing a language and that they actually acquire the language of their community as a second language. This belief prompted many efforts over the centuries to determine what this true, native language could be. It has led to many tales of how kings have sought the true language. In one,

> Herodotus, an ancient Greek historian, relates the story of an Egyptian king, Psamtik I, who believed that Egyptians were the original human race and that if children were not spoken to for the first two years of life, the first words they spoke would be the true language of all humans, Egyptian. Psamtik ordered a shepherd to raise two children normally in all respects, except that they could not be spoken to. When the children were two years old, it is reported that they ran to the shepherd, with their hands outstretched, and said "Becos," a word from the language of the Phrygians (who lived in what is now Turkey). Psamtik wisely concluded that the Phrygians were the oldest race of humans, but that Egyptians were the second oldest race.
>
> *(Bonvillian, Garber, & Dell, 1997, p. 219)*

One reason children can begin to acquire rudiments of language shortly after birth is that the child's sensitivity to language begins before birth in the third trimester (the last 3 months in the womb). This was revealed in a study by DeCasper and his colleagues (e.g., DeCasper & Spence, 1986; see also DeCasper & Fifer, 1980). Pregnant women read one of three children's stories out loud (such as Dr. Seuss's *The Cat in the Hat*; Geisel, 1957) twice a day during the last 6 weeks of pregnancy for a total of about 5 hours over the course of the experiment. A few days after the infants were born, they heard tape recordings of the mothers reading either the familiar story or another one. Which story the newborns heard was determined by how rapidly they sucked on a pacifier. This method is called the high-amplitude sucking procedure (HASP; described in Chapter 4). In one condition, a rapid rate of sucking produced the mother's voice, and a slow rate of sucking produced another voice or another story. Most of the newborns showed a distinct preference to suck for the story that they had been read in the womb, and also preferred to hear their mother's voice reading the story. The control group for this study consisted of infants who had not been read any of the stories during the last trimester. Those infants showed no distinct preference for any story, although they did prefer to hear their mother's voice.

Infants can tell the difference between their mother's voice and other voices. They can even distinguish between their mother's language (spoken in the third trimester) and other languages (Mehler et al., 1988). All this is possible because newborns are sensitive to the **prosody** of their mother's speech. Prosody refers to the rhythm, the stress, and the intonation pattern (singsong quality) of the voice (Ramus, Hauser, Miller, Morris, & Mehler, 2000).

The sound of the mother's voice in the womb influences the sounds that the infant makes after birth. One study of crying by French and German newborns showed a distinct difference between the two. **FIGURE 9.2** illustrates that the cries of infants of French-speaking mothers are characterized by a slow rise in pitch and then a rapid decline, whereas the cries of infants of German-speaking mothers show a quick rise and then a slow decline in pitch (Cross, 2009; Mampe, Friederici, Christophe, & Wermke, 2009).

Prosody is important to children even after they are born. Everyone who has seen parents interacting with their children has noticed that parents speak differently to preverbal infants than they do to adults. There is a melodic quality to the parents' speech, often called *motherese* or *caregiverese*. For example, when we say yes to an infant or give it a compliment, we tend to use a rising, singing quality in our voices. In contrast, when we warn or scold an infant, our voices tend to have a sharp, descending quality (Fernald, 1989). It is as if the melody in the caregivers' utterances carries the message rather than the words (e.g., Fernald, 1989; Fernald et al., 1989). This pattern has been shown to occur in languages as different as English, Japanese, and Hausa (an African language).

The sensitivity to prosody and its use is different between autistic children and adults and typical speakers. In one study (Shriberg et al., 2001) conversations between adults and children (ranging in age from 10 to 50 years old) were tape-recorded. Analysis showed that a majority of people with high-functioning autism showed a significant inability to use prosody correctly compared with typical language speakers of all ages, who rarely made a mistake in their speech.

Turnabout Although language-based interactions between infants and caregivers vary with culture, a universal form of the interactions is called **turnabout**, a technique used to get the infant to respond. When the mother, for example, touches her infant's nose (e.g., 3–6 months of age) and says "nose," "feel the nose," "touch the nose," the infant will occasionally either touch the mother's nose or her own. These responsive interplays are examples of the infant engaging in "conversation" with another. The parent is typically in charge of these interactions (Kaye & Charney, 1980). By

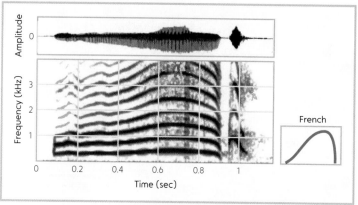

(A) Typical French Cry

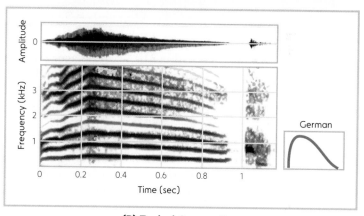

(B) Typical German Cry

FIGURE 9.2 Speech Contours: The Cries of French and German Newborns Infants become tuned to the prosody of the mother's language in the third trimester of pregnancy. When they are born, their cries capture distinguishing features of the speech sounds they heard in the womb. French infants tend to produce cries with a rising melody contour, whereas German infants tend to cry with a falling contour.

Source: From Cross, 2009

Mother and Child Playing Turnabout

Picture Partners/Alamy

10 months of age, the infant will respond or initiate a conversation by holding up an object (e.g., Lewis & Freedle, 1973) or pointing to an object or tugging at the caregiver's clothes (Bates, 1976).

In these turnabouts, mothers seem to treat their infants as full communicating partners, which both engages the infants' attention and also models communicative behavior for them (Kajikawa, Amano, & Kondo, 2004; Kaye & Charney, 1980). Mothers of normal-hearing 2-year-olds tend to control these interactions. In contrast, mothers of hearing-impaired infants tend to "share" the initiation of the turnabout interaction more equally with the child (van den Dikkenberg-Pot & van der Stelt, 2001). Perhaps this compensates for the greater difficulty the infant experiences in understanding parental speech.

The typical child achieves a basic understanding of his or her language within 3 or 4 years of age. This begins with a semantic understanding and progresses to a grammatical understanding (syntax plus semantics). This sequence was shown in a study in which children between the ages of 2 and 4 were told: "This cookie monster can't talk properly. He says things all the wrong way around." One of the other puppets was going to teach him how to talk properly. The child took the role of the teacher puppet and would correct sentences when they were wrong. All of the children were able to identify when the sentences were semantically incorrect and could correct them, as illustrated in **TABLE 9.3**. However, only the most linguistically advanced children were consistently able to identify and correct the syntactic errors (de Villiers & de Villiers, 1972).

By age 4, the child can tell the difference between grammatically acceptable and unacceptable utterances, even though the grammatical rules are never directly explained to the child and children are rarely corrected in their early use of language (Brown, 1973; Seidenberg, 1997). It is quite remarkable that children learn the grammar of their native language even though people all around them are not always speaking in complete (or even grammatical) sentences (Ramsey & Stich, 1991).

Children are able to understand the meaning of words that are not explicitly defined and can use those words appropriately in creating sentences they have never heard before. This phenomenon is referred to as the *poverty of the stimulus* (Chomsky, 1980). It means that the child could not have figured out the grammar from the sentences he or she has overheard. Therefore, the child must bring some innate linguistic ability to the situation. The universals of language emerge from this biological predisposition toward language.

TABLE **9.3**		
Semantic and Syntactic Judgment in 2- to 4-Year-Olds		
Judgment type	**Correct**	**Incorrect**
Semantic	Draw a picture	Ride a picture
	Drink the juice	Drink the chair
Syntactic	Eat the cake	Cake the eat
	Brush your teeth	Teeth your brush

Speech Discrimination in the First Year During the first year of life, infants the world over are biologically prepared to sense the speech sounds of any language—even languages they have never heard (Trehub, 1976; Werker & Tees, 1984). However, by the end of the first year, infants become more sensitive to speech sounds within their linguistic environment and less sensitive to the sounds of other languages. For example, Werker and her colleagues (Werker, Gilbert, Humphrey, & Tees, 1981) found that 6- to 8-month-old infants from an English-speaking community could discriminate sounds that are found in Hindi (originating in India) or in Nthlakapmx (pronounced /enklapem/), spoken by the Salish people living along the Thompson River in British Columbia. Yet by 1 year of age, this ability had significantly diminished (Werker & Tees, 1984). According to MacWhinney (1998, p. 202), "children spend much of the first year of life losing the ability to make contrasts that are not used in the speech they hear about them."

By the end of their first year, infants' pattern of speech sound discrimination resembles that of adults from their language community (Kuhl, Williams, Lacerda, Stevens, & Lindblom, 1992). After the first year of life, although infants have reorganized their sensitivity to speech sounds, they are still open to new possibilities. For example, 1-year-olds from English-speaking communities are still able to distinguish different Zulu click sounds (a South African language) from English sounds (Best, McRoberts, & Sithole, 1988). The unfolding of this language-learning system during the first 4 years of life allows typical healthy children to acquire the basic elements of their native language. **TABLE 9.4** shows some of the mileposts the language learner passes along the way.

TABLE **9.4**	
Stages in Language Development	
Level 1	
Age	**Benchmark steps**
0–6 weeks	crying
6–12 weeks	cooing (vowel-like)
20 weeks	cooing (consonant-like)
6 months	consonants (front to back) vowels (front to back) = (*babbling*)
12 months	frequent repetitions (*mama/dada*) clearly understands a few words less than 50 words produced
18 months	produces less than 100 words (*gimme cookie*)
24 months	two-word phrases; original phrases
Level 2	
3 years	3,000-word vocabulary; 80% understood by strangers (Carey, 1978)
4 years	basic language limited in complexity and vocabulary (8,000 words)

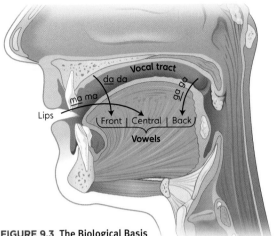

FIGURE 9.3 The Biological Basis for Speech Speech sounds are produced by the same anatomical structures in all humans. This diagram, showing how the first recognized speech sounds are produced by 6-month-olds, illustrates the role of the lips and tongue in producing specific consonants and vowels.

Producing Speech The child's production of speech-like sounds develops over the course of the first 6 months of life and culminates in the production of the consonants and vowels of the child's native language. Consonants are generally produced when the mouth is closed, vowels when the mouth opens. By 6 months, front consonants (/m/, /v/) are distinctly heard, as illustrated in **FIGURE 9.3**. The first vowels to appear are those produced when the tongue is in the front of the mouth (/e/ as in *beet*). The later appearing ones are produced when the tongue is farther back in the mouth (e.g., /u/ as in *put*). This sequence is universal and independent of the language and speech sounds in the child's environment. English-speaking parents typically identify the child's first speech sounds as consonant–vowel pairs such as *mama* or *dada* when they occur in strings of sounds such as *mamama* or *dadada*. These are not real words, but are duplications of babbling sounds.

What Children Say After children finally acquire the skills for producing the speech sounds of their native language, you may wonder what they say. What functions do children's speech serve, and is there universal content in their early speech? To answer such questions, Slobin (1970) culled descriptions of the two-word conversations of children who spoke one of the following languages: English, German, Russian, Finnish, Luo (from Kenya), and Samoan. He discovered that the speech of these children can be categorized into seven basic linguistic functions: locate and name, demand, negate, describe, indicate possession, modify, and question. Some of these functions are more difficult to express in some languages (e.g., Finnish) than in others (e.g., English); however, all children perform the same functions. Some examples are shown in **TABLE 9.5** from English and Luo for children ages 18–30 months. Note that Luo-speaking children have no questions recorded because Luo etiquette prohibits children from asking questions of visitors (Brown, 1973).

Regularization The language-learning trajectory is not always upward. Just when 4-year-old children are demonstrating competence with their native language and increasing their vocabularies at a rapid rate, they show a decline in ability to handle syntactic irregularities in their language. The process that explains this turnaround in language skill is called **regularization** and shows that

TABLE **9.5**		
Early Linguistic Functions in Two Languages		
Functions of two-word sentences in children's speech		
Functions	**English**	**Luo (Kenya)**
Locate, name	*There book*	*Ma wendo* (this visitor)
Demand, desire	*Give candy*	*Miya tamtam* (give candy)
Negate	*No wet; allgone milk*	*Beda onge* (my slasher absent)
Describe event	*Bambi go*	*Chungu biro* (European comes)
Indicate possession	*My shoe*	*Kom baba* (father's chair)
Modify, qualify	*Big boat*	*Piypiy kech* (pepper hot)
Question	*Where ball?*	

Note: In the negate function, a Luo 3-year-old is worried about where he put his machete! No questions are recorded for Luo-speaking children because etiquette prohibits children from asking visitors questions.

Source: From Slobin, 1970

children have been automatically applying language rules (Bybee & Slobin, 1982). For example, a 4-year-old who correctly creates a plural noun with an /ez/ sound, as in *boxes* or *glasses*, may begin to say *bookses* or *catses* or *mouses*. The same child at age 4 may have correctly used the past tense of irregular verbs such as *to go* (*went*) or *to come* (*came*). However, by the age of 4½, the child may tend to overly apply the *-ed* rule for creating past tense verbs. The child goes from saying *went* to saying *goed* or even *wented* and *camed* (Slobin, 1973). This pattern is illustrated with English here, but occurs in other languages as well, as long as they have syntactically irregular forms (e.g., Spanish; Clahsen, Aveledo, & Roca, 2002).

These errors are not random: They result from the application of standard grammatical rules (Marcus, 1996). It appears that children around the age of 4 are applying rules to what they had previously committed to memory. They overgeneralize the more frequent rules and make errors. But within a year, at the age of 5 or so, they begin to appreciate that there are irregular grammatical forms and are able to apply syntactic and phonological rules appropriately (Marchman & Bates, 1994). This journey is not always complete. You may know some adults who will occasionally slip and use one of the erroneous forms that are so typical of children. One explanation for this is that long-term memory does not erase itself. Chapter 6 showed that what was available in childhood is still available in adulthood, but much less accessible than more frequently used forms. We get a glimpse of the existence of these archaic forms when the speaker is under pressure or stress, or when the context promotes old habits of speaking.

SECTION SUMMARY ▪

Some Language Universals

Human language is everywhere and within everyone. Perhaps because of the universal need for communication and contact, the development of whole languages follows a consistent pattern worldwide. Even within an individual, we find universal patterns in language development. In spite of more than 6,500 human languages, the number of consonants and vowels used in any language is relatively small, and they develop in the same sequence for every child. The child's ability to hear and discriminate among speech sounds follows a systematic pattern: In the first year of life, the child can detect the speech sounds of every language. By the end of the first year, the child begins to focus on speech sounds in his or her own language and to lose the ability to detect those of other languages. Some of a child's preference for speech sounds begins to develop before birth because in the third trimester the fetus becomes sensitive to the prosody of the mother's voice.

Only three of the six possible syntactic arrangements of subject, verb, and object generally occur in the set of all human languages. This tells us that there may be a biological limit on how information packets can be communicated from one person to another. Other limitations seem to occur in what we talk about when we first begin to learn our native language. For example, when children first begin to produce consistent speech sounds that we would all call language, we find that the utterances of children the world over focus on seven basic functions: locate and name, demand, negate, describe, indicate possession, modify, and question. Children not only follow the same language-learning trajectory, they also show a similar downturn in language skill around the age of 4½. This downturn comes in the form of regularization, in which children replace the irregular forms in the language and make them consistent with the regular nouns and verbs. However, by the time children reach 5 or 6 years, this tendency is reversed and they return to using the regular and irregular forms in their language.

The Neuropsychology of Language

Language is a universal skill that binds all humans together. One source for this universality is that all humans possess a common biology: Our brains are similar, and our language emerges out of similar neural wiring. The first part of this section describes how language is manifest in the healthy brain; the second part illustrates the difficulties that occur when one or more of the language centers are impaired; and the final part describes language impairments that occur when language centers are only indirectly affected, as in dementia.

Language in the Hemispheres

For most people, the left hemisphere of the brain hosts the major language centers. The distribution of language functions and brain areas is shown in **FIGURE 9.4**. The consensus is that slightly more than 90% of right-handed people (called *dextrals*) have the dominant centers for language in the left hemisphere. Sixty to seventy percent of left-handed people (*sinistrals*) also have their dominant language centers in the left hemisphere. The remainder of dextrals and sinistrals have their dominant center in the right hemisphere or balanced between left and right hemispheres (Rasmussen & Milner, 1977).

One way that the dominant hemisphere for language has been traditionally assessed is by the means of the Wada test (Wada, 1949), in which an anesthetic (e.g., sodium amobarbital or sodium methohexital) is injected into the right or left carotid artery (or an artery in the thigh) while the person's arms and legs are raised. Since the carotid artery goes from the heart to the brain, the anesthetic "paralyzes" the hemisphere on the same side of the body as the injection, which causes the limbs on the opposite side of the body to drop. Paralysis of a hemisphere permits assessment of language, memory, or general cognitive functioning of both hemispheres. For example, just prior to the administration of the anesthetic, the person might be shown pictures and asked to name them or asked to recite a poem or count backward from 100. After the injection, if the person cannot continue to perform these tasks during the next 1–3 minutes, it indicates that the anesthetized hemisphere has language functions. If the person can perform these functions, then language functions are active in the hemisphere that was not anesthetized.

FIGURE 9.4 Language and the Brain The left and right hemispheres of the brain are involved in language comprehension and production. For most people, many of the dominant functions of language are performed using areas of the left hemisphere: Wernicke's area (semantic and some auditory processing), the angular gyrus (word categorization), and Broca's area (syntactic and semantic processing; communication with Wernicke's area; and activation of motor areas of cortex for speech production).

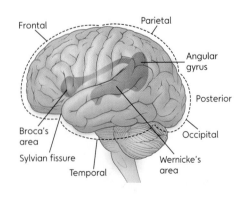

Frontal

Parietal

Angular gyrus

Posterior

Broca's area

Occipital

Sylvian fissure

Wernicke's area

Temporal

The Wada test has been effective in broadly identifying the dominant hemisphere for language. Currently, advances in the use of neuroimaging techniques (PET and fMRI) have allowed researchers to identify more specific localization of language functions in the brain (e.g., Michael, Keller, Carpenter, & Just, 2001).

Specific Language Centers

Three major centers in the cortex of the human brain are directly related to language functioning: Wernicke's area, the angular gyrus, and Broca's area, shown in Figure 9.4. These critical areas are not as far apart as the diagram makes them appear. A fascinating use of magnetic resonance imaging (MRI) allows us to take picture "slices" of a living brain and to reconstruct what a person's cerebral cortex would look like if somehow it could be unfolded into a flat sheet. This method shows that all the language areas are actually adjacent to one another, in one continuous territory (Gazzaniga, 1989). This region of the cortex (the area around the Sylvian fissure shown in the figure) might be considered to be the language organ that everyone possesses.

Wernicke's Area and the Angular Gyrus The first component of language we discussed at the beginning of this chapter was semantics—the meaning of the message. Two major brain areas are associated with this function: **Wernicke's area** and the **angular gyrus**. You can locate them in Figure 9.4 in parts of the brain called the *auditory cortex* and the *parietal lobe*. It is fitting that some of the language functions are performed in this auditory processing area because for many of us, language is essentially a spoken system. Semantic processing of the auditory signal largely depends on Wernicke's area, which performs a computation of the overall message and relies on an understanding of categories of words provided by the angular gyrus.

Broca's Area Often we derive the meaning of an utterance by also understanding its syntax. The syntactic rules of a language such as English dictate the arrangement of grammatical elements (called *constituents*), such as *articles* (e.g., the), *nouns* (e.g., boy), and *verbs* (e.g., laughed). When the arrangement of constituents is syntactically correct, the message is most effectively packaged for the listener. The area of the brain that performs syntactic and some semantic analysis is **Broca's area**. It is typically located in the left prefrontal cortex (see Figure 9.4). Broca's area has at least two primary functions. The first is to perform syntactic analyses on the incoming stream of words and communicate this back to Wernicke's area. The second function is to activate the motor areas of the cortex that are involved in speech production.

Language Impairments: Aphasias

Case histories of individuals have been invaluable in helping cognitive psychologists understand the contribution of different brain areas for language functioning. The language impairments of these individuals are generally called **aphasias,** and the most common forms are listed in **TABLE 9.6**. A few of these are described in the following.

TABLE **9.6**		
General Types of Aphasia		
Form of aphasia	**General locus**	**General symptoms**
Broca's (also called *cortical motor, expressive,* or *nonfluent aphasia*)	Broca's area	Grammatical functions impaired, often associated with dysarthria
Dysarthria	Connection between Broca's area and motor cortex; associated with many other neurological problems	Difficulty and/or reluctance to speak
Wernicke's (also called *cortical sensory, receptive,* or *fluent aphasia*)	Wernicke's area	Syntactically correct, but meaningless phrases; individual often unaware of the problem (*anosognosia*)
Word deafness	The connection between auditory cortex and Wernicke's area is severed	Unable to understand external speech including one's own; can speak articulately
Paroxysmal aphasia	Dysfunction of all language areas, often the result of epileptic seizure	Total aphasia, but can still comprehend the situation (no *anosognosia*)
Global aphasia (also called *total aphasia*)	Areas around the Sylvian fissure dysfunction	Total aphasia with no impairment of other cognitive functions
Automatic speech	Similar to global aphasia	Nearly total aphasia except for the ability to recite highly learned phrases or written passages
Mixed transcortical	Broca's and Wernicke's areas damaged	Cannot understand or generate novel sentences, but can repeat (with correction) sentences heard

Note: Causes of these neurological deficits vary, ranging from cerebrovascular disease to closed head injuries to strokes and tumors.

Damage to the Dominant Hemisphere Damage to the left hemisphere is more likely to disturb language functioning than damage to the corresponding regions in the right hemisphere. However, language functioning in the dominant hemisphere can return following trauma to the brain. A third of those suffering symptoms of aphasia are able to recover nearly full functioning within 3 months. In contrast, about the same percentage show little to no recovery years after the injury to the brain. The remaining percentage may require years of therapy to have just a portion of their linguistic skills return (Lenneberg, 1967).

The most frequently occurring aphasias are the result of strokes. **Strokes** cause damage to specific areas of the brain brought about by the loss of blood to those areas either by a blockage or because a blood vessel bursts. The effects of aphasias are slightly different in men than in women. Overall, women suffer slightly less from aphasia after left-hemisphere damage than do men, but it depends on where the damage occurs. When a stroke is in Wernicke's area, men are 3 times more likely to suffer aphasia than women. When a stroke is in Broca's area, the pattern is reversed: Women are about 2 times more likely to suffer aphasia than men (Kimura, 1993).

Both hearing and deaf people suffer the same consequences of hemispheric damage. This is especially the case for the approximately 10% of deaf people born to deaf parents, whose native language is a sign language. These individuals are less disrupted in their interpretation and production of language signs by damage to their right hemisphere than they are by damage to their left hemisphere (Poizner et al., 1987). The right hemisphere has primary responsibility for the kind of spatial processing that is important for identifying gestures (Hickock, Klima, & Bellugi, 1996), but when gestures become linguistic signs, they are processed in the same areas of the dominant hemisphere as spoken language for hearing people.

Damage to the Nondominant Hemisphere The nondominant hemisphere—typically the right hemisphere—makes an important contribution to language processing. Some individuals have damage (called **lesions**) in the right hemisphere in areas that are the mirror image of Wernicke's area in the left hemisphere. These individuals suffer a reduction in their ability to understand the intent or subtleties of a message (Shields, 1991). For example, a typical person with a right-hemisphere lesion will report: "I know what you're saying—I understand the words and the grammar—but I can't understand what the purpose is." Such individuals have difficulty understanding the moral of a story, or the metaphor, or even figurative language. For example, when individuals with a lesion in the right-hemisphere version of Wernicke's area are told that *Nancy had a heavy heart*, they can accurately convey the literal meaning of the expression (their left-hemisphere language centers are intact), but when shown pictures of (a) a person crying, (b) a heart, (c) a heavy weight, or (d) a person pulling a cart with a giant heart, half select (d), the bizarre but literal picture (H. Gardner, 1975). This form of aphasia in the nondominant hemisphere appears to be the same for hearing speakers and deaf signers (Hickok et al., 1999). These studies show cognitive psychologists how important the nondominant hemisphere is for language processing. Before reading on, try the exercise in Demonstration 9.3.

▪▪▪DEMONSTRATION 9.3

Making Connections with the Right Hemisphere
Read the following passage and then answer the questions at the end.

> This is very rewarding but tends to be quite expensive even if you own all that you need. The outfit does not really matter. One can get seriously injured without proper instruction even if it comes more naturally to some people than others. Some don't like the smell or the lack of control. So some people are scared to try it even if they've dreamed of it since they were a kid reading about it in books and watching it on television. A running start is uncommon, although there are some who do it. Typically, success requires that you start with your left leg, and make sure that it is securely in place. Then swing your body high into the air. The direction matters. Once you are settled, your thumbs should be pointing up. Sometimes there is no security but the animal's hair. Other times you can hang off to the side. In any case you will be sore if this is your first time.
>
> *(St. George, Kutas, Martinez, & Sereno, 1999, p. 1318)*

What does this passage describe?

As you were reading it were you trying to connect ideas . . . unsuccessfully?

The passage is about horseback riding. When it was originally presented without a title, students had difficulty understanding it or remembering any of it. The absence of a title taxed people's ability to make a sensible connection among the individual ideas in the passage. These are just the language functions performed by the right hemisphere.

In one study of brain functioning, volunteers read 16 passages like the one in Demonstration 9.3. Half of them had no title and were difficult to understand. While students were reading these narratives, their brains were being scanned using an fMRI procedure (St. George et al., 1999). The overall results are shown as a graph in **FIGURE 9.5A** and as a corresponding brain image in **FIGURE 9.5B**. Notice that when reading the passage with the title, there was some activation in the right hemisphere, but mostly in the left. However, when there was no title, the right hemisphere contributed a large portion of the brain activation. This illustrates the importance of the right hemisphere for generating alternative understandings and deriving the "big picture" of a narrative.

Hemispherectomy Sometimes it is necessary to remove the dominant hemisphere (a surgery called **hemispherectomy**) in order to relieve the effects of pathologies such as epilepsy when other treatments are not effective. How would this affect language? The consequences tend to be related to the age of the individual. The age-related outcomes (*prognoses*) are summarized in **TABLE 9.7**, which shows that if the individual is younger than 5 years, the prognosis is good for relearning linguistic functions; if the individual has reached adulthood, the prognosis is poorer for a return of language comprehension and fluency.

Table 9.7 illustrates the **plasticity** of the brain, its ability to make new connections and preserve its functions. If the damage occurs early enough, the nondominant hemisphere will take over. This plasticity is seen most strikingly in cases where a child is born with severe damage to part of one or both hemispheres. To determine how such damage affects the development of language, a group of children between 5 and 8 years old were asked to

FIGURE 9.5 The Role of the Right Hemisphere in Language Comprehension The results of fMRI brain scans of people reading short narrative passages: (A) shows that the right hemisphere is more active than the left when people read untitled passages and more active on the left when there is a title. This is because our brains need to work harder to understand the theme of the text when there is no title. (B) presents the actual scans. Note that the left hemisphere is shown on the right and the right hemisphere is on the left.

St. George, M., Kutas, M., Martinez, A., & Sereno, M. I. Semantic integration in reading: Engagement of the right hemisphere during discourse processing. *Brain*, 1999, 122, 7, 1317–1325 by permission of Oxford University Press.

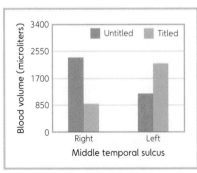

(A) Results of Study

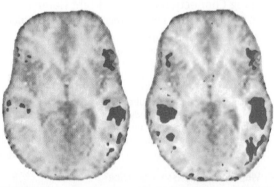

(B) fMRI Scans (left image: titled; right image: untitled)

TABLE 9.7

Effects of Complete Damage to Language-Dominant Hemisphere at Different Ages

Age	Normal language	Immediate effects	Prognosis
0–20 months	Cooing to words	Delay of onset	Normal development (opposite hemisphere can acquire functions)
21–36 months	Basic language	All language accomplishments disappear	Language reacquired through same sequence
3–10 years	Full grammar	Aphasia	Language reacquired; deficits in reading and writing
11–14 years	In U.S. second language acquired	Selective aphasia depending on locus	Problems with lateralization; learning disorders
over 15	Variable	Selective aphasia	Irreversible

Note: Based on descriptions by Slobin (1970) and Lennenberg (1967).

describe events and people in their lives. Some of the children had no lesions at birth; others had lesions in the left or the right hemisphere. The results are summarized in **FIGURE 9.6**. More than a dozen measures of language ability showed that there were no appreciable language deficits for any of the children, and there was no difference between children who had left- or right-hemisphere lesions from birth compared with children in the control group who had no lesions at all (Bates & Goodman, 2001; Denis & Whitaker, 1976; Reilly, Bates, & Marchman, 1998).

Localization of Language: Broca's Area Damage to Broca's area is often the result of a stroke, which impairs the ability to speak, called **Broca's aphasia**. It is named after Pierre Paul Broca, who in 1861 performed an autopsy on the brain of an aphasic man named Leborgne. (Leborgne was mentioned in Chapter 1 as Tan because that was the only syllable he used in response to prompts, along with an occasional swear word.) The autopsy showed that Leborgne had a large lesion in his left prefrontal cortex. After examining individuals with similar injuries, Broca concluded that linguistic ability was the province of the left hemisphere. Leborgne's brain is stored in a jar for all to see at Le Musée Dupuytren in Paris (see **FIGURE 9.7**).

Individuals with Broca's aphasia show difficulties in speaking in complete sentences. Often words that would normally appear at the beginning of a sentence are eliminated from speech (Goodglass & Kaplan, 1983). For example, the individual wants to say "The boy went to the store," but actually says "boy . . . there . . . store." In general, the individual produces halting, effortful speech, although it is typically understood, as in this example, where the

FIGURE 9.6 The Effect of Focal Lesions (Left Hemisphere) in Children and Adults The brain can rewire itself to perform cognitive functions. Eight-year-old children who were born with focal lesions (gaps) in their left hemisphere showed the same linguistic abilities as children born without lesions. They are as skilled as adults who have suffered strokes in the left hemisphere.

Source: From Bates & Goodman, 2001

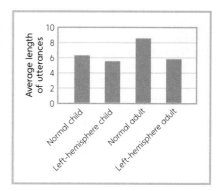

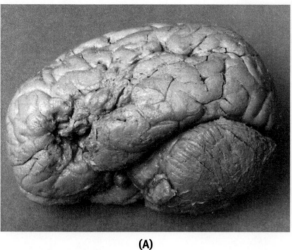 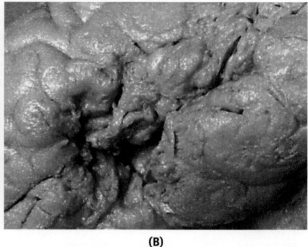

(A) **(B)**

FIGURE 9.7 Damage in Broca's Area (Leborgne's Brain) (A) This photograph shows the damage to Leborgne's brain that contributed to what is now called Broca's aphasia. His speech was limited to a few expressions and the word *tan*. (B) shows a closer look.

N. F. Dronkers, O. Plaisant, M. T. Iba-Zizen and E. A. Cabanis, Paul Broca's historic cases: high resolution MR imaging of the brains of Leborgne and Lelong, *Brain*, 2007, 130, 5, fig 3, by permission of Oxford University Press.

person is describing what he sees in a picture (see **FIGURE 9.8**): "Dog tree . . . girl arms . . . cat sleep . . . boots."

People with Broca's aphasia are aware of this difficulty and of how they sound. Their own comprehension of speech is best when they hear sentences that are unambiguous and when the context allows a direct interpretation, as in "he put the book on the table." The meaning is clear in any arrangement because while

FIGURE 9.8 Man In a Tree Picture The Boston Diagnostic Aphasia Examination is used to help diagnose people with various forms of aphasia. The person looks at the picture and describes what he or she sees. Someone with Broca's aphasia might say: "Dog tree . . . girl arms . . . cat sleep . . . boots". Someone with Wernicke's aphasia might say, "oh, my, many people there."

Nicholas, L. E. & Brookshire, R. H. (1993). A system for quantifying the informativeness and efficiency of the connected speech of adults with aphasia. *Journal of Speech and Hearing Research, 36*, 338–350.

you typically *put a book on a table*, you do not normally *put a table on top of a book*. Broca's aphasia is not limited to speech; individuals with Broca's aphasia have similar difficulties with written language. Because they have difficulty producing speech, the condition is called *nonfluent aphasia*.

Localization of Language: Wernicke's Area Wernicke's area was identified as important to language by Karl Wernicke (1848–1904). Damage here results in fluent but meaningless phrases and is called **Wernicke's aphasia**. Most often, such individuals produce effortless speech, but with ill-chosen words and phrases. Although the sentences sound like normal speech, they often make no sense to the listener. These individuals do not realize that they are not making sense and, as a result, they keep speaking. Those with Wernicke's aphasia have difficulty understanding writing, speech, and even their own recorded messages. All of this supports the notion that Wernicke's area is important to semantic processing.

Wernicke's aphasia is diagnosed by a variety of language tests. One of the most popular is the Boston Diagnostic Aphasia Examination (Goodglass & Kaplan, 1983). On one of the forms, the individual sees a picture depicting a scene such as the one in Figure 9.8. The individual describes the scene and the examiner evaluates his or her verbal fluency and ability to be understood.

It is sometimes difficult to tell the difference between Wernicke's and Broca's aphasias based on the ability to comprehend sentences. The diagnostic method often used is to have the individual with aphasia see a picture such as described in (g) and then present two sentences, as in (h) and (i). The individual is then asked which sentence matches the picture (e.g., Grodzinsky, Pinango, Zurif, & Drai, 1999).

(g) Individual sees picture: /a boy is pushing a girl/

(h) Individual hears: The boy pushed the girl.

(i) Individual hears: The girl pushed the boy.

Notice that the two sentences differ on who is performing the *pushing* action. Individuals with Wernicke's aphasia have more difficulty than those with Broca's aphasia in keeping the themes of the sentences straight when the sentences have a simple syntax (Grodzinsky, 2004), but individuals with both types of aphasia find the test difficult (Caramazza & Zurif, 1976).

Localization of Language: Angular Gyrus Figure 9.4 shows that the part of the brain next to Wernicke's area is the angular gyrus. Damage here results in a condition called **anomia**, in which the individual has difficulty retrieving instances of categories, such as the names of vegetables. These individuals sound inarticulate, as if they can't complete sentences and use the right nouns; however, their intellectual ability is not affected by damage to the angular gyrus. They are as conversationally skilled as before the injury, except that they avoid specific names of objects and people. Such a person might look at a drawing of a mother and child in a kitchen with the water running in the sink and say: "Filling there, but looking around to see things over here that are so nice."

This injury reflects retrieval difficulty rather than a loss of words. We know this because although individuals with anomia find it difficult to retrieve nouns from their mental dictionary, they can understand the nouns when they are used by others. A standard test that reveals anomia is called the Boston Naming Test (Kaplan, Goodglass, & Weintraub, 1983). Individuals are shown 60 line drawings of common objects (e.g., bread, tree, church, etc.) and are asked to say the common name for them. If they indicate that they need a hint, the examiner provides the general idea of the picture. If they still need help, the examiner provides the first sound of the word. The test is sensitive to left-hemisphere damage (anomia) as well as nonlanguage impairments in the right hemisphere. It has been used to assess Alzheimer's dementia, multiple sclerosis, and studies of the neurology of **bilingualism**, where people are fluent speakers of two or more languages (e.g., Hernandez, Martinez, & Kohnert, 2000).

Language and the Environment

Children learn their native language merely by being in an environment where their use of language has some utility. Listening to the radio or watching TV has little effect: A linguistic environment is the critical element. We know this because of what happens when there is no linguistic environment.

Over the last couple of centuries there have been many reported cases of *feral* (wild) children living alone outside human society. Once rescued, these children have never fully mastered speech. Perhaps you know the story of *Victor, the Wild Boy of Aveyron* (Itard, 1962), who was found in the woods in France at the end of the 18th century. A sculpture of him is shown in **FIGURE 9.9**. Victor was given care and shelter for 28 years but never really learned to communicate verbally, in spite of the best efforts of the people around him. More recently, there is the story of Genie, a socially isolated, abused child discovered in 1970. Genie, who was about 13, had been physically and socially restrained for more than a decade in a house in a suburb of Los Angeles. Although she heard people speaking, she was abused when she tried to do so herself. After her liberation, and with intense instruction in language and social interaction for 9 years, Genie developed fair comprehension and a workable vocabulary, but she used it sparingly. She preferred nonverbal forms of communication (Curtiss, 1977; Rymer, 1992a, 1992b).

FIGURE 9.9 The Wild Boy of Aveyron Victor was discovered in the forest of Aveyron, France, January 8, 1800. He was about 12 years old and had lived as a feral (wild) child for about 7 years. He could hear and make vocal sounds, but never truly learned language. He always showed kindness to Madame Guerin, who took care of him for the rest of his life.

Courtesy of EdithB

SECTION SUMMARY

The Neuropsychology of Language

The universality of human language is largely the result of the universal equivalence of the human brain. In the brain, the dominant hemisphere for language is the left hemisphere (90% of right-handed people and 60–70% of left-handed people). The right hemisphere is considered the nondominant hemisphere in most people. Its contribution to language processing is related to the interpretation of metaphor and the global message behind a communication.

Three major centers in the dominant hemisphere are directly related to language functioning: Wernicke's area, the angular gyrus, and Broca's area. Although each makes a contribution to semantics, Wernicke's area and the angular gyrus are the two major centers for language understanding. Broca's area is involved in syntactic analysis of language and the production of speech, because of its connection to the motor cortex. Cognitive neuroscientists have developed an understanding of these areas and how they communicate by observing the different types of aphasia that result from damage to each of these areas from strokes, tumors, and lesions. They have also understood the necessity for a linguistic environment from studies of children raised without one.

Intelligence and Language

The ability to use language is a truly universal skill that nearly every adult possesses, regardless of background or intelligence. Learning a first language does not depend greatly on a speaker's intelligence. Except for the most severely developmentally delayed people, everyone learns at least one language. To illustrate this independence of language and intelligence, we discuss the language skills of people with disabilities in five different groups: Down syndrome, Williams syndrome, Turner's syndrome, specific language impairment, and spina bifida.

Down Syndrome

The first of these groups consists of people with **Down syndrome**, a condition identified by Dr. J. L. H. Down in the 1880s (Down, 1886). Most cases of Down syndrome are caused by the presence of three (rather than two) copies of the 21st chromosome in each cell of the body. People with Down syndrome may be mildly to severely developmentally delayed. About 5% show mild symptoms (called *Down syndrome, mosaic type*) because they have an extra 21st chromosome in only some cells of their body.

Although linguistic progress is slower for children with Down syndrome than average children, by puberty most Down syndrome children have a basic working vocabulary and are capable of articulating and interpreting simple sentences. Unlike their average peers, Down syndrome children show little further linguistic development past the age of 14 or so (Lenneberg, 1967).

It is difficult to characterize people with this syndrome because the range of verbal and nonverbal abilities is quite large. For our purposes, however, it's important to focus on the fact that their tested intelligence tends to be low compared with the average person, and so too are their linguistic skills, which is evidence in favor of a direct relationship between intelligence and linguistic ability. But before you draw any conclusion, consider the next group of people.

Williams Syndrome

The second group consists of people with **Williams syndrome**, associated with a defective gene on chromosome 7 (involved in the production of *elastin*, a protein that provides strength to blood vessel walls). Williams syndrome was first identified in 1961 by Dr. J. C. P. Williams of New Zealand (Williams, Barratt-Boyes, & Lowe, 1961), who noticed that these individuals have an unusual appearance: short stature with narrow, elfin faces. Like individuals with Down syndrome, they have an IQ between 50 and 75 and find it difficult to perform even simple arithmetic functions or create simple drawings. They typically cannot draw circles, find their way, or tell left from right (even as adults). But they speak so clearly and effortlessly that they would be considered to have normal intelligence based on their language skills alone (e.g., Jones et al., 2001).

Even though they are often slow to start acquiring a language when they are children, people with Williams syndrome exhibit normal grammatical ability to understand sentences and to identify errors in sentences (Bellugi, Korenberg, & Klima, 2001). They are best known for being talkative and are extraordinary conversationalists (e.g., Jones et al., 2001), possessing exceptional social skills and a sophisticated vocabulary. Even their narratives, constructed by 5- to 10-year-olds, often exceed their normal peers in being socially engaging (Losh, Bellugi, Reilly, & Anderson, 2000). Comparing people with Down and Williams syndromes, we find nearly equivalent low IQs, but vastly different linguistic abilities (Bates & Goodman, 2001; Harris, Bellugi, Bates, Jones, & Rossen, 1997). People with Williams syndrome can be viewed as evidence against a direct relation between intelligence and linguistic skill.

Turner's Syndrome

A third group of people has **Turner's syndrome**, a chromosomally based malady described by Dr. Henry Turner (1938) that affects only females. Unlike most girls who possess two X chromosomes, girls with Turner's syndrome are born with only one X chromosome (occasionally the second X chromosome is present, but damaged). This results in a number of overt physical, cardiac, and hormonal difficulties. Such girls tend to score slightly below normal on verbal tests, and significantly below normal on spatial and social intelligence measures. They show difficulties in driving a car, social relations, and nonverbal problem-solving tasks. In contrast, their basic spoken language skills are definitely within the normal range (Hall, 2005; Romans, Stefanatos, Roeltgen, Kushner, & Ross, 1998). Women with Turner's syndrome offer another case where intelligence and language skills seem unrelated.

Specific Language Impairment

The fourth group is said to possess a **specific language impairment (SLI)**. They come to our attention because they possess more or less normal intelligence, but have not fully developed language (Merzenich et al., 1996). Unlike the first three groups, no clear genetic basis for the condition has been identified. People with SLI can understand normal speech, but their own speech tends to violate grammatical rules. By way of illustration, children with SLI make errors shown in sentences (j) to (l):

(j) The boy *eat* four cookie versus The boy *eats* four cookies.

(k) She *hurts* herself yesterday versus She *hurt* herself yesterday.

(l) Carol *is cry* in the church versus Carol *was crying* in the church.

Spina Bifida

The fifth group to show a separation between language and intellectual functioning is composed of people born with **spina bifida** (divided spine). This congenital defect leaves the vertebrae of the spinal cord exposed. Specific symptoms depend on the level at which the cord is divided. In many cases the child has excessive cerebrospinal fluid, which frequently results in learning difficulties, depending on where a shunt is placed to drain the fluid (Hunt & Holmes, 1975).

In spite of intellectual deficits, these children's language facility is typically preserved and in many cases substantially above average. They resemble people with Williams syndrome in their productive use of language, although they are often characterized as having difficulty in monitoring their speech for appropriateness or logic (Cromer, 1994). The outlook for many of these children is good if those around them help them maintain focus in their conversations and encourage them to verify their understanding of what has been said.

SECTION SUMMARY ■

Intelligence and Language

Taken jointly, five groups illustrate that the ability of humans to have language appears to be roughly independent of intelligence, or at least not dependent on intelligence in any obvious way after the brain has been formed. Four groups with a range of below-average IQ (Down syndrome, Williams syndrome, Turner's syndrome, and some children with spina bifida) have radically different language skills, and one group (SLI) with about average intelligence shows linguistic deficits. In sum, language and intelligence as broadly conceived systems appear to be largely independent. Language as a uniquely human system appears to be sufficiently independent of other cognitive systems to maximize the possibility that nearly any person can acquire a native language.

■ ■

Language As a Cognitive Filter

Language is a skill common to all humans, but at the same time 6,500 different languages also divide us. For the past 150 years experts on language have pondered the extent of this divide and conjectured that because we speak different languages, we also think differently (Lucy, 1992). They propose that if language shapes our thoughts, then people who speak different languages could never understand each other's view of the world (Au, 1983). A New England fire inspector, Benjamin Lee Whorf (1956), along with his mentor, Edward Sapir, spent his spare time studying anthropologists' reports of the languages of tribes in the American Southwest. He proposed what came to be called the **Sapir–Whorf hypothesis**: The language you speak unconsciously shapes your thinking about the world. This theory is called **linguistic relativity**.

The evidence that one's native language determines one's perceptions of the world has been linked to the assumption that Inuits (Eskimos) have more words for snow than English speakers and therefore those words allow Inuits to make subtle distinctions that English speakers fail to make. In spite of fanciful estimates (one report had the Inuit possessing 100 words for different kinds of snow), Inuits have no more words for snow (about 17) than English speakers who are avid snowboarders or skiers (*blizzard, California concrete, com/crud, gnar gnar, groomed, ice/glass, packed, powder/pow, shower, slush, spring*; see **FIGURE 9.10**; Martin, 1986). One reason the estimates were so high has to do with subtleties of Inuit syntax and the fact that their concept of snow also includes icebergs.

When necessity requires people to make distinctions, they will develop terms to deal with those distinctions no matter what their language. Having many terms in a language helps to communicate to other speakers what is culturally important. A modern-day example comes from the Inupiaq of Alaska who, to avoid marrying a relative, make fine distinctions among family members about who is related to whom; they have created many more words for *cousin* than English speakers, who don't typically require such distinctions.

FIGURE 9.10 Words for Snow
People learn special words to help them communicate. The Inuits (Eskimos) have been said to have 17 words for snow, which is supposed to affect how they understand snow. In contrast, skilled skiers in the United States are familiar with about 40 words for different kinds of snow conditions.

DigitalVision

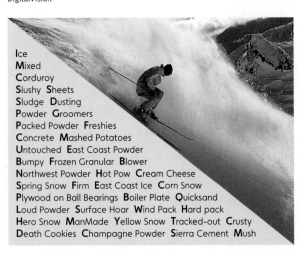

Ice
Mixed
Corduroy
Slushy Sheets
Sludge Dusting
Powder Groomers
Packed Powder Freshies
Concrete Mashed Potatoes
Untouched East Coast Powder
Bumpy Frozen Granular Blower
Northwest Powder Hot Pow Cream Cheese
Spring Snow Firm East Coast Ice Corn Snow
Plywood on Ball Bearings Boiler Plate Quicksand
Loud Powder Surface Hoar Wind Pack Hard pack
Hero Snow ManMade Yellow Snow Tracked-out Crusty
Death Cookies Champagne Powder Sierra Cement Mush

Does Language Control Cognition?

The basic premise of linguistic relativity is that language and thought are closely connected and that this relationship is embodied in two rules:

RULE 1. *If the number of words for a phenomenon in two languages differs, then speakers may understand the phenomenon differently.*

RULE 2. *If the number of words for a phenomenon in two languages is the same, then speakers will tend to understand them equivalently.*

Anthropologists and psychologists have tested these claims by examining language and cognitive distinctions from around the world. Two prime examples are words for color and words for logical relationships.

Color Categories Many cultures differ in the number of color terms in their language. For example, the Dani of Indonesian New Guinea (Irian Jaya), who are speakers of Dugum Dani, have 2 color words, the equivalent of black (*mili*) and white (*moda*), even though their environment is full of colors. The Pomo (California) have 3 terms: white (*totokin*), black (*likolkokin*), and *red*

The colorful tropical environment of the Dani is not reflected in their words for color. Their language has only two words for color, the equivalent of black and white.

Adrian Arbib/Corbis

(*tantankin*); a typical English speaker uses at least 11 color terms (*black, white, red, green, yellow, blue, brown, purple, pink, orange, and gray*). The principle of linguistic relativity would argue that the people who speak English and Dugum Dani would experience the world differently because they divide up the color spectrum differently.

Do people whose language has 2 color terms see colors differently from those whose language has 11 terms? To find this out, the participants in a study by anthropologists Berlin and Kay (1969) and their associates were shown a range of colors from a set of 329 color chips and were asked to group the colors. If red was one of the color groupings, a surprising finding was that the participants from many different language backgrounds selected the same color chip as the best example for the color red. In fact, they selected the same color chips for 8 colors: red, yellow, green, blue, brown, pink, orange, and purple. These are now generally referred to as **focal colors** (e.g., Rosch, 1973b). In a related study with 3-year-old U.S. children, who knew few if any color terms, the children were asked to look at a color chip pasted to a card, and then (without looking back), go across a room and pick out the same chip from among a large set of other chips. This task (called a *matching-to-sample task*) was difficult for these children and they made many errors. However, if the color chip that they were trying to match was one of the focal colors identified by Berlin and Kay (1969), the children were highly accurate in matching the sample. Their errors were made primarily when trying to match nonfocal colors (Mervis, Catlin, & Rosch, 1975).

These focal colors have other special properties; for example, facts associated with these colors in a learning task are easier to memorize and to recall. Rosch (1973a, 1973b) asked Dani children to learn to associate clan names with certain color disks taped to a card (the same colors used by Berlin and Kay, 1969). The children learned an association between clan names and colors more rapidly when the color was one of the focal colors (Rosch, 1973a; Rosch Heider, 1972). It is as if these colors act like cognitive pegs: Anything hung on the pegs is easier to learn. The important thing to know is that the adult Dani do not have names for these colors (just *light* and *dark*), so the ability to use these colors in learning and memory tasks does not rely on having names for them. Our words do not determine our concepts, as linguistic relativity would claim.

The anthropologists also discovered that the color terms used by different language groups fit a universal pattern. Berlin and Kay (1969) found that every language takes its basic color terms from only 11 color names: *black, white, red, yellow, green, blue, brown, purple, pink, orange,* and *gray*. When a language has only 2 terms, it uses not just any 2 at random, but rather *black* and *white*. When a language has just 3 colors, it always uses *black, white,* and *red*. The pattern can be expressed as a chart in which the brackets show the set from which the terms are selected.

$$
\left[\begin{array}{c} \text{black} \\ \text{white} \end{array}\right] - \left[\begin{array}{c} \text{red} \end{array}\right] - \left[\begin{array}{c} \text{yellow} \\ \text{green} \\ \text{blue} \end{array}\right] - \left[\begin{array}{c} \text{brown} \end{array}\right] - \left[\begin{array}{c} \text{purple} \\ \text{pink} \\ \text{orange} \\ \text{gray} \end{array}\right]
$$

If a language has 7 color terms, it will take the first 7 starting from the left (*black, white, red, yellow, green, blue,* and *brown*). If a language has 8 color terms, it will add 1 from the immediate right (*purple, pink, orange,* or *gray*) to the 7 from the left. You may wonder how many different ways there are to arrange 11 color terms. If the combinations of the 11 basic color terms were random, there would be 2,048 possible arrangements. The ordering shown here restricts that number to 33 (only 22 were actually observed in a sample of 98 languages). According to Berlin and Kay (1969): "Color categorization is not random and the foci of basic color terms are similar in all languages" (p. 10).

Words and Reasoning Another area where languages differ radically is in the use of "logical" terms, such as *if*, as in "If you finish your homework, you can watch TV." Linguistic relativity claims that members of different language groups may differ in their logical abilities when they use *if* differently. A clear test of this prediction has come in a study comparing native Mandarin and English speakers on their ability to do **counterfactual reasoning**. This is a fancy term to denote something we do all the time: pretend about situations that we know to be false, as in "If I had studied for the test, I would have gotten a good grade." Any native speaker of English will tell you this sentence means that

(m) You didn't study for the test.

(n) You didn't get a good grade.

(o) You believe that there is a causal relation between studying and grades.

Even though these three "facts" can be gleaned from the utterance, they are not explicitly stated in it (Fillenbaum, 1974). English speakers are helped in understanding counterfactual expressions by the grammatical form called *subjunctive conditional*: "If I had . . . I would have . . ." By using this syntactic form, the English speaker readily communicates to the listener that he or she is pretending. In contrast, Mandarin Chinese—a language spoken by more than a billion people—has no such construction. To illustrate, take the English sentence in (p) and compare it with the Mandarin translation in (q) and (r).

(p) If Mrs. Wong knew English, she could read the *New York Times*.

(q) Mrs. Wong does not know English.

(r) If Mrs. Wong knows English, she then can read the *New York Times*.

Clearly, the Mandarin form is less obvious in revealing its counterfactual nature. If an English speaker were just beginning to learn Mandarin, it would be difficult to understand that a counterfactual was being described. Therefore, consistent with the principle of linguistic relativity, Chinese speakers should have a great deal of difficulty doing counterfactual reasoning because it is not supported in a simple way in their language (Bloom, 1981).

To find out whether Sapir–Whorf's hypothesis held, Au (1983, 1984) tested the ability of Chinese/English bilingual high school students in China and Taiwan to reason counterfactually by having them read a gruesome story about a Dutch explorer who witnessed a tribe drinking a broth made from a dead human (see Focus on Methods box). She then asked the students to answer questions that tested their reasoning skills. The students who read the story in Mandarin answered questions about it just as accurately (97%) as Chinese students who read the story in English or students who were native speakers of English and read the story in English. According to linguistic relativity, the Mandarin and English speakers should not reason equally accurately. The fact that they did is a piece of evidence that disconfirms the theory (see also Bloom, 1984).

We have dealt with the first part of the Sapir–Whorf version of linguistic relativity and now turn to the second part, which says that if two languages are equivalent in their description of something, then the speakers of those languages should have equivalent understanding of it. Put another way, the theory is disconfirmed when two people possess the same linguistic form, but differ in their understanding and use of those forms. One simple test is right in front of us every day. Children typically use the same terms as adults, but do not possess the adult interpretation (E. V. Clark, 1970, 1971; Sinclair-de Zwart, 1967). This was shown in children's use of the comparative terms *less* and *more*, as in "May I have some more cookies?" Scottish children were asked

FOCUS ON METHODS ■■■■■■■■■■■■■■■■■■■■■■■■■■■■■

Understanding of Text by Two Bilingual Groups

A common method for studying the understanding of language among monolingual and bilingual participants is to ask both groups to read a story and answer questions that reflect their understanding. Sometimes the story is given to bilingual participants in either of two languages to see if they reason differently in the two languages. Such a method was used by Au (1983) to determine whether Mandarin and English speakers understood the logical implications expressed in a story. She asked 372 bilingual Mandarin and English students to read the following story and answer questions about it afterward. The purpose of such studies (there were five experiments in the original study) was to see if the students would draw the same counterfactual inferences if the stories were in Mandarin or in English. Normally, finding no difference between groups is called *accepting the null hypothesis* and is considered too easy to do unless there are many participants and many studies whose combined findings show no difference. Au avoided that criticism by employing large numbers of students in many studies. In Experiment 1, the students saw the following passage. There was no time limit for this task. Most students took less than a half hour to read the story and answer the questions.

> Once a Dutch explorer ventured into Central Africa and saw a tribe of natives gathered around a fire. Hoping to make some interesting discoveries, this Dutch explorer held his breath and observed the natives attentively from behind the bushes. He heard one of the natives shout in a language which he unfortunately did not know. He then saw the natives throw a dead human body into a big pot of boiling water. And when the "human broth" was done, the natives all hurried to drink some of it. Upon seeing this event, the explorer was absolutely astonished, and fled as soon as he could. If this explorer had been able to understand the language spoken by the natives and had not fled so quickly, he would have learnt that the dead native was actually a hero of the tribe, and was killed in an accident. The explorer would also have learnt that the natives drank the "broth" of their

hero because they believed that only by doing so could they acquire the virtues of their hero. If this explorer had been able to understand the language spoken by the natives and had not fled so quickly, he would have learnt that the natives were very friendly, and were not cruel and savage as he thought.

Please indicate, by choosing one or more of the following answers, which thing or things about the natives the Dutch explorer knew according to the above paragraph.

1. The dead native was a hero of the tribe.
2. The dead native was killed in an accident.
3. The natives believed that they could acquire a dead hero's virtues only by boiling the dead man's body in water and then drinking the "broth."
4. The natives were friendly and not cruel and savage as the Dutch explorer thought.
5. None of the above. (Please explain your opinion briefly.)

If the answer was none of the above they were given the following choices:

a. The Dutch explorer did not know the natives' language.
b. The Dutch explorer did not understand what the native was shouting about.
c. The Dutch explorer fled too quickly.
d. If the Dutch explorer had known these facts about the natives, he would not have fled so quickly. (The same idea expressed with the *if–then* construction in Chinese was also accepted because the justifications, in both cases, were instances of spontaneous use of the counterfactuals; Au, 1983, p. 163.)

Bilingual participants had little difficulty in understanding the counterfactual story, whether written in Chinese or English. The results showed that even though there is a distinct counterfactual marker in English and not in Chinese, bilingual Chinese are nevertheless just as inclined to reason counterfactually in Chinese as in English.

to look at two trees (shown in **FIGURE 9.11**) and indicate which of the trees had *more* apples and which of the trees had *fewer* apples (Donaldson & Balfour, 1968). Three- and 4-year-old children pointed to the same tree in response to both questions. They treated these two terms as meaning the same thing; *some* or *amount* (see H. H. Clark & E. V. Clark, 1977). Even though both terms were in the children's productive vocabulary, they treated them differently from the way adults would treat them.

All of this challenges the theory that language controls our thoughts. Research shows that people who speak languages that have different distinctions nevertheless show identical behaviors and perceptions. Children and adults who speak the same language show quite different behaviors.

Does Language Assist Cognition?

Even though there is no strong evidence that language controls thought, language can have an effect on how we understand simple concepts and use and retrieve them. There are examples all around us, and they have implications for how we educate children.

Arithmetic One example that has gained prominence recently is how the number terms in different languages can affect how readily children learn arithmetic. **TABLE 9.8** shows the number terms from 0 to 20 in four languages. Notice that in the columns labeled *Japanese*, *Mandarin*, and *Welsh*, there is a definite logic to the terms: The numbers after 10 are simple arrangements of the number terms from 1 to 10 (I use numerals here so as not to confuse words with numbers). For example, in these three languages the words corresponding to the number 11 are *ten and one*; for 12 they are *ten and two*, and so forth until 20, where they all refer to the number as *two ten*: the

(A)

(B)

FIGURE 9.11 Testing the Sapir–Whorf Theory Although people have the same words in their vocabulary, it doesn't mean that they understand them the same way. Three- and 4-year-old Scottish children were asked to look at two trees and indicate which of the trees had *more* apples and which had *fewer (wee-er)*; the children pointed to the same tree in response to both questions. They treated these two terms as meaning the same thing—*some* or *amount*—not what an adult thinks these terms mean.

Naturalis/Alamy

actual meaning of the number 20. A child learning any of the number terms in these languages gains a clear understanding of the relationship that holds over the number scale (K. Miller, Smith, Zhu, & Zhang, 1995).

Now take a look at the English terms for numbers greater than 10. If you had never seen the word *eleven* before, what would you think it referred to? Well if you spoke Old Norse you would know that it meant "one left over (after 10)" and that *twelve* meant "two left over." Alas, there aren't many of us who speak Old Norse. A child trying to learn the number terms after *ten* in English would be learning nothing more than a series of nonsense syllables. Perhaps this is the reason that in cross-national studies of arithmetic competency, children who are native English speakers score lower than speakers of Asian languages (e.g., Miura, 1987; Stevenson et al., 1990).

Experiments have evaluated the importance of vocabulary for arithmetic skills. K. Miller et al. (1995) tested the counting skills of Mandarin- and English-speaking children from ages 3 to 5 and found that the two groups of

TABLE **9.8**				
The Logic of Numbers Expressed in Four Languages				
Number	**English**	**Japanese**	**Mandarin**	**Welsh**
1	one	ichi	yi	un
2	two	ni	er	dau
3	three	san	san	tri
4	four	yon	si	pedwar
5	five	go	wu	pump
6	six	roku	liu	chwech
7	seven	nana	qi	saith
8	eight	hachi	ba	wyth
9	nine	kyu	jiu	naw
10	ten	ju	shi	deg
11	eleven	ju-ichi	shi-yi	un deg un
12	twelve	ju-ni	shi-er	un deg dau
13	thirteen	ju-san	shi-san	un deg tri
14	fourteen	ju-yon	shi-si	un deg pedwar
15	fifteen	ju-go	shi-wu	un deg pump
16	sixteen	ju-roku	shi-liu	un deg chwech
17	seventeen	ju-nana	shi-qi	un deg saith
18	eighteen	ju-hachi	shi-ba	un deg wyth
19	nineteen	ju-kyu	shi-jiu	un deg naw
20	twenty	ni-ju	er-shi	dauddeg

FIGURE 9.12 Counting in Two Languages English- and Mandarin-speaking children were asked to count to the highest number that they could. The children were equal in counting until the number 10 was reached. Counting in the *teens* was considerably easier for Mandarin speaking children because in Mandarin, number names follow a consistent rule, but in English, they do not. This effect of language contributes to an ultimate difference in mathematical achievement.

Source: From K. Miller et al., 1995

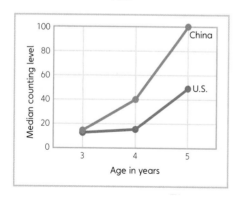

children diverge in their ability (Mandarin speakers learning faster than English speakers) when they begin to count numbers greater than ten. This is graphed in **FIGURE 9.12**, which shows that both groups of children had difficulty counting to twenty, but the difficulty was greater for the English speakers. In fact, the kinds of errors they made were quite telling. Some of the English-speaking children who were able to count to 29 would often count *twenty-eight, twenty-nine, twenty-ten* (instead of *thirty*). They were actually trying to count using the same decimal logic as the Mandarin speakers, who have the logic embedded in the number terms themselves.

Imagery Language can help us encode information in unintended ways. For example, in American Sign Language (ASL), when a signer describes a scene to another person, the observer (equivalent to the listener in speech) may have to mentally rotate the description to understand it from the signer's perspective. For example, when the signer describes something that is on the right side of a car, the observer actually sees it on the left side.

To determine whether practicing this skill of perspective taking for a lifetime affects the imagery ability of adult signers, Emmorey, Klima, and Hickok (1998) asked two groups of people to view a video of a board with objects appearing on it one at a time. One group consisted of ASL signers and the other group consisted of hearing nonsigners. The task of the two groups was to duplicate the arrangement on a board that either matched the one they observed or one that was rotated 180° from the original one. ASL signers did reliably better at the rotation task, which suggests that the skill developed in creating and using symbols in space promoted a broader cognitive skill.

Deaf office workers communicate in sign language.

Michael Newman/Photo Edit

SECTION SUMMARY ▪

Language As a Cognitive Filter

Research on the importance of language for cognitive processes suggests that a speaker's language can affect general cognitive processes. Just because two people speak widely different languages, however, does not mean that they see the world differently. Language is intimately connected to our thoughts. When we plan our day or read a letter from a friend, it is difficult to avoid hearing an "inner voice" talking to us. Although language does not necessarily control our thinking, special aspects of language (e.g., number terms or practice with sign language) can affect specific cognitive skills. The studies on the effect of language on arithmetic and mental rotation indicate that our language can affect how we pay attention to things, how we encode important elements (and therefore how easy it is for us to retrieve them), and how the names can make the concepts behind them more transparent to the observer.

CHAPTER SUMMARY

Cognitive psychologists study the development and use of language because, like the memory systems discussed in earlier chapters, language captures a human universal. All humans have language. Although we may differ in our overall linguistic accomplishments, the presence of a native language seems to be independent of geography, genetics, or general intelligence. Our first language unfolds in a more or less systematic way and with a consistent time course and sequence for everyone everywhere, beginning with the last few weeks in the mother's womb. The source of this universality is a result of commonalities in our brains. Linguistic functions appear to be localized in different areas of the brain. When there is damage to these areas (due to strokes, tumors, or lesions), the effects are predicted by the functional layout of the brain. Although language does not dictate how we think about the world, it can influence how we perform everyday tasks and skills. The next chapter considers language in more detail and illustrates how current research methods allow us to assess the cognitive processes that affect our language understanding.

QUESTIONS FOR REVIEW

Check Your Knowledge

1. Approximately how many languages are spoken in the world?
2. Why is language a cognitive universal?
3. Does every adult possess a language?
4. Name the four necessary components of a natural language.
5. What is the reference principle?
6. When a child hears "see the birdie," what principle does he or she use to know that *birdie* doesn't refer to the wing?
7. How would the nonredundancy of words help a child learn the name of an object?
8. What is holophrastic speech?
9. Define *semantics*.
10. Define *syntax*.
11. Does the bee language have syntax?
12. Name a universal medium of communication.
13. Is writing a universal medium of communication?
14. How does an alphabetic language differ from a logographic language?
15. Are there specific gestures that are used universally?
16. What is *pragmatics*?

17. What is the difference between a Pidgin language and a Creole language?
18. Name a Creole language used in the United States.
19. What part of the vocal system creates the pitch of speech sounds?
20. When do infants start to identify their mother's language?
21. What aspect of the mother's language do infants attend to?
22. By what age can a typical child tell the difference between a syntactically correct and incorrect sentence?
23. Name the seven functions of language in the child's early speech.
24. A child speaking English may say, "We *goed* to the store yesterday." What is this an example of? When does it occur and when does it end?
25. For right-handed people, what is the dominant hemisphere for language?
26. What does the nondominant hemisphere contribute to language?
27. What are three language centers? What separate functions do they perform?

28. What is the relationship between intelligence and language?

29. Does our language control our understanding of events?

30. Does the number of color words in our language affect our cognition?

31. Does our language assist our cognition? Give an example.

Apply Your Knowledge

1. Turnabouts in parent–child interactions suggest that language development is affected by our social environment. If turnabouts are universal, does it mean there is a biological basis for social-language behavior?

2. If humans are able to master their native language without special instructions, why do we go to school and study our language?

3. The theory of linguistic relativity doesn't hold true, but language can influence our perceptions about what is important. To see this, find someone who speaks another language and was raised in a different culture. You should each write down the 7 or 8 most emotional insults or swear words in each language/culture and then translate each to see what the cultures and languages regard as important.

4. What has language helped humans to achieve that nonlinguistic communication has not helped animals achieve?

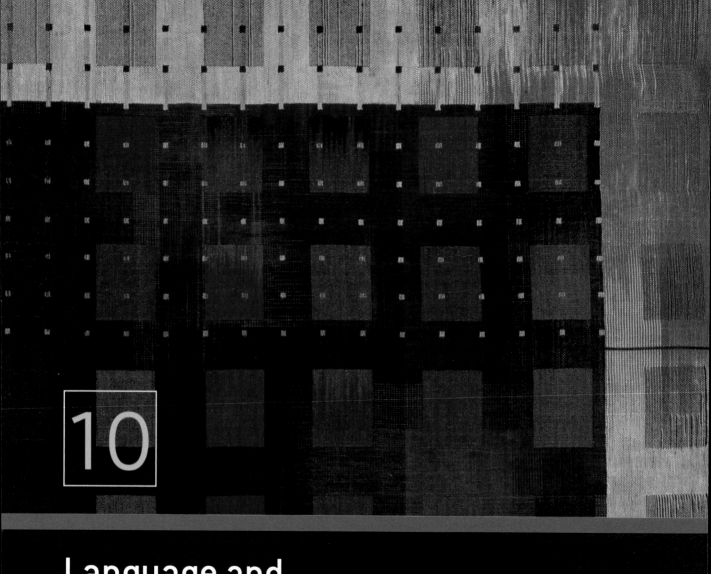

10

Language and
Cognitive Processing

❝Language is a city to the building of which every human being brought a stone.**❞**

—Ralph Waldo Emerson

I
n Chapter 9, we looked at some of the important universal patterns of human language and described how each of the components of language (semantics, syntax, medium, and pragmatics) interacts with every other component—all of the time. This chapter describes the sequence of cognitive processes that allows every human being to understand and produce language and what happens when normal language processes break down. It does this by tracing how we first experience a combination of sounds and silences, identify the speech segments as repeating sequences of sounds, and then use the melodic pattern to bind the communication together as a *message packet*. It also describes how we isolate semantic elements of words and use them to figure out what the message is about and how to respond to the speaker. Although reading is not a universal linguistic process, it is pervasive in many cultures. Because of this, in the latter part of the chapter we talk about the cognitive processes of reading.

Understanding Speech

Understanding sentences spoken in your native language seems effortless and automatic, but an unfamiliar foreign language can sound like the vocal equivalent of a machine gun. You can't tell when one word ends and another begins because you are unable to identify which sounds make up a word. So imagine how difficult learning a language must be for children, who have so little past experience identifying individual words (e.g., Jusczyk, 1997). It is as if, in order for children to know what they hear, they have to be able to hear what they know. Children everywhere solve this paradox of language processing in a similar way (Cooper & Aslin, 1990).

The typical child is surrounded by sound and is sensitive to it even in the womb. In the last 2 months of gestation, fetuses are so sensitive to sound that if a loud noise and a mild vibration are paired together, after about 20 pairings, the fetus will move in response to the mild vibration as it would to the loud noise (Spelt, 1948; see also Hepper, Dornan, & Little, 2005). In one study, pregnant women were conditioned to relax when they heard a piece of music. Shortly after birth, newborns showed that they had also been conditioned to the music along with their mothers: When the music played, the infants stopped crying and opened their eyes (Hepper, 1996). The ability of fetuses to hear in the womb prepares them to respond to sounds after they are born, especially to their mother's voice.

We saw in Chapter 9 that the newborn's sensitivity to the musical quality of the mother's voice puts the infant on the road to understanding his or her language. This early experience with sound may go further, however, and focus the newborn's attention on sound as an important medium of communication, thus making speech (and its gesture equivalent) special (Liberman & Mattingly, 1989).

Speech and Gesture Processing

Sounds and gestures make up sentences and convey meaning. The typical human brain can distinctly hear nearly 30 speech sounds per second (phonemes like [*buh*] and [*duh*]), especially when they are encapsulated within words (Liberman, 1982). We are capable of identifying words surrounded by noise or music. We can understand sentences spoken with different pitches: Think about the high-pitched speech sounds of a 3-year-old child and the lower pitch sounds of the average adult man. And we can understand sentences that are spoken at widely different rates. To get an appreciation of how well we are able to identify sentences, you might listen to a Rap artist such as Busta Rhymes (e.g., "Break Ya Neck"), where you can understand words at rates between 20 and 30 speech sounds per second. If you pay close attention to disclaimers on the radio—usually spoken at 10 to 15 syllables per second—it is actually possible to understand what is being said.

It is commonly thought that we are able to do this by identifying speech sounds because they are surrounded by silences. In fact, tape recordings of natural speech (e.g., Yeni-Komshian, 1998) show that the transition from one word to another is not filled with silence. The average conversational speech rate is approximately 2.5 words per second (Lieberman, 1970), with few or no "silences" between the words.

We are not always perfect in our ability to segment the speech sounds into words or larger collections of words, called *clauses* (a collection of words with a subject and a verb that does not stand alone as a sentence). Take, for example, a child's segmentation of a phrase from the *Star Spangled Banner*:

José can you see by the donzerly light?
    [Oh say can you see by the dawn's early light];

or from the Pledge of Allegiance:

and to the republic for witches stand
    [and to the republic for which it stands].

These "errors" in segmentation indicate that early stages of processing are imperfect because the listener lacks the information to figure out when one word ends and another begins and exactly what words are being spoken.

What we hear depends in no small part on what we expect to hear and how the stream of sounds or gestures fits with the syntax and semantics we know.

Theories of Speech Recognition

The acoustic signal that we identify as speech is so variable, it is a wonder we can recognize speech at all. The sounds of speech differ considerably depending on whether they are being uttered by a man, a woman, or a child, or even by the same person twice with different emotions (Banse & Scherer, 1996; Scherer, 1986). If people's understanding of speech were based simply on some acoustic analysis like that performed by an electronic device, they would experience **word deafness**: the ability to hear sounds, but not to identify what they are. This section reviews three theories of speech recognition that explain these phenomena.

Motor Theory of Speech Perception Have you noticed that you can understand speech more readily when you can see the face of the speaker? Or, as some people say, "I'll hear you better as soon as I put on my glasses." This is because people use a speaker's lip movements and facial muscles as cues to what is being said (Liberman & Mattingly, 1985). Special cameras that can detect eye movements show that fluent adult speakers—people who could easily understand speech in the dark or over the phone—spend nearly half the time in a speaker's presence looking at the speaker's mouth, especially when there is noise in the environment (Vatikiotis-Bateson, Eigsti, Yano, & Munhall, 1998). The **motor theory** says that listeners try to mentally simulate the creation of the speech sounds they hear. If the sound they simulate matches the sound that their brains have registered, then they are able to identify the speech sound they heard. Seeing the lips of the speaker helps this process, sometimes called *analysis by synthesis* (Corballis, 2002; Stevens & Halle, 1967).

Typically a speaker's articulation and the sounds we hear are coordinated. When they are not, the difference can be surprising. Have you ever watched a movie where the sound is out of sync with the speaker's lips or when the voices are dubbed in a different language? It throws off your speech processing—a reminder that we really are paying attention to lip movements. Laboratory studies have examined how listeners coordinate speech sounds with the facial features of the speaker (e.g., Massaro, 1998; McGurk & MacDonald, 1976). In these studies, the listener watches a speaking face (often computer generated) and hears sounds over headphones. When the speaker's lips and the sounds are coordinated, the listener identifies sounds accurately, but when lips and sounds do not match, the listener hears something that is neither in the mouth movements of the speaker nor in the auditory signal. This phenomenon is called the **McGurk effect**. For example, when the speaker's lips are configured to make a [*ga*] sound, but the sound presented to the listener's ears is equivalent to [*ba*], the listener reports hearing [*da*]. The McGurk effect isn't just for isolated sounds. If the sound coming to your ears is *bab pop me poo brive* and the speaker's mouth is saying *gag kok me koo grive*, you will perceive "dad taught me to drive"!

Watching the mouth of the speaker cannot be the only basis for speech perception, because we can hear in the dark or on the phone when we cannot see the speaker. Moreover, people who cannot speak and suffer from a condition called *dysarthria* are still capable of perceiving speech, and blind children are still able to learn to speak. Although visually impaired people are reported to have difficulties with subtle acoustic properties of speech (e.g., R. Campbell, Zihl, Massaro, Munhall, & Cohen, 1997), it would be best to think of articulation cues as one factor among many that we use to understand speech (Lewkowicz, 2002).

Interaction Models People interpret the speech sounds they hear and the gestures they see by evaluating the entire context, including the semantics of words, the syntax of the utterance, and the themes of the social interaction (Miller & Isard, 1963; Röder, Demuth, Streb, & Rösler, 2003). Theories of speech perception that rely on this interaction among linguistic and social elements are called **interaction models**. For example, we perceive words that were never spoken if those words fit with the context (Warren, 1970). In one study, students heard recorded sentences in which a critical sound was replaced with a cough. Afterward they were asked what the sentence was and where the cough occurred. For example, when they were presented the sentence, "The *eel was on the shoe" (the asterisk indicates where the cough occurred), students perceived the word *heel* and said that the cough was just background noise. In another sentence, "The *eel was on the axle," they heard the word *wheel* (Warren & Warren, 1970). More skilled speakers of a language are more likely to replace the missing phonemes than are less skilled speakers (Warren & Sherman, 1974). These studies show that we "hear" more than what reaches our ears and that people seem to be aware of the content of the message before they understand all the individual words. This interaction among linguistic elements is at the heart of two prominent interaction models: the cohort model and its sister theory, the TRACE model.

The **cohort model** (Marslen-Wilson, 1987) divides speech recognition into two stages at the word level. In the first stage we detect the component sounds at the beginning of a word, which activates all of the possible words in long-term memory that have a similar set of sounds, called a *cohort*. In the second stage of processing, all other possible sources of information are brought in to help eliminate words that are not the target word. These other sources include the broad context of the word, including syntax and semantics, as well as other acoustic information coming from other parts of the sound stream that makes up the word. The more we have of these additional elements, the more accurate we are at identifying the speech.

The way this works is illustrated in **FIGURE 10.1**. Let's assume that someone says to you, "Nancy looked at the map," and you were trying to identify the last word, *map*. The initial group of possible words would include all words with the initial sound /ma/, such as *mad*, *man*, *map*, *mat*. However, the set of possibilities is narrowed because the last sound heard is /p/. This is also where your knowledge of the world comes in: You know that "looked at the mad" makes no sense.

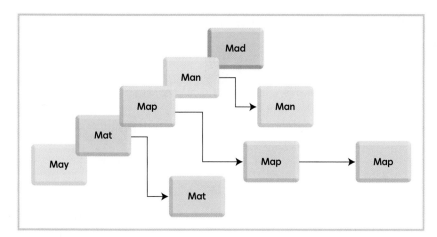

FIGURE 10.1 The Cohort Model of Speech Perception According to this model, our perception of a given word occurs in two stages: First, we determine a cohort of possible words based on an initial sound (shown as words *may* through *mad*); then we use all other sources of information to identify the most appropriate of these (*mat*, *map*, *man*) and then decide on *map*.

Source: After Marslen-Wilson, 1987

You also use information from the preceding sentences. If you were speaking about traveling, the listener would pare down the options to either *map* or *man*.

One test of this theory is whether it can account for the time-related sequence in comprehension. To examine this, students were asked to look at a computer display that contained pictured objects (e.g., a beaker, beetle, speaker, and a carriage). They were to move one of the objects on command. For example, the students heard the word *beaker* and a camera recorded where they looked on the screen. In the first 100 msec or so, the student's eyes switched rapidly between the beaker and the beetle (two objects whose names start with the same sound, /b/). However, after 400 msec, their eyes moved between the beaker and the speaker, objects whose names have similar overall speech sounds throughout (Allopenna, Magnuson, & Tanenhaus, 1998). Notice that this sequence of speech analysis corresponds to the description of the cohort model.

A related theory is the **TRACE model** (McClelland & Elman, 1986), which assumes the listener will use all the information at his disposal, all at once (in parallel) to identify what is being said. One special attribute of TRACE is that it works in a forward and backward process: People not only identify initial speech sounds, but when words are guessed at they then are used to correct the initial identification of speech sounds.

Fuzzy Logic Model Another popular theory of speech comprehension is the **fuzzy logic model**, illustrated in **FIGURE 10.2**. This model treats speech perception like all other forms of perception: It assumes that everyone has stored idealized or "prototypical" forms of speech sounds in their long-term memory and uses those prototypes to determine which sound they have just heard. Notice that this is similar to the pattern recognition models in Chapter 4. Why would prototypes of speech sounds be useful? The speech signal is highly variable, and a word can be pronounced in different ways at different times. This incredible variability in the speech signal is a challenge for any perceiver. Storing a prototypical speech form for every word that you have heard would be highly useful.

FIGURE 10.2 The Fuzzy Logic Model of Speech Perception According to this model, an incoming stream of sounds is first identified and matched against prototypes stored in memory (the evaluation stage); then, the reverse percentage is estimated (the integration stage); finally, the listener decides how good the overall match is (assessment and decision stages).

Source: After Massaro, 1987

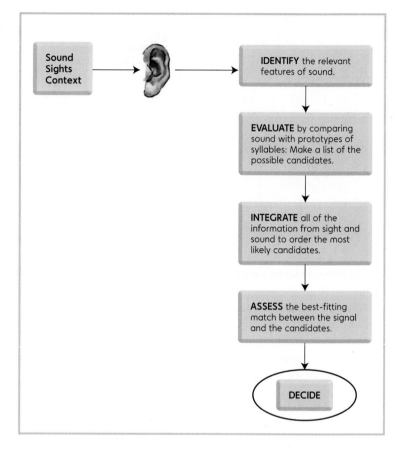

According to the fuzzy logic model, the listener matches the incoming stream of sounds against speech prototypes stored in memory. At this point, the listener estimates the percentage of the input features matching the prototype, called the *evaluation stage*. Then the listener estimates the reverse percentage (what part of the prototype matches the input), called the *integration stage*. Finally, the listener decides how good an overall match there is between the input and the prototype, called the *assessment and decision stage*. This model of speech recognition suggests that we take all possible factors into consideration and do the best we can (Massaro, 1998).

Bringing the Theories Together The fuzzy logic model differs from the interaction theories like the cohort and TRACE models, not so much by having multiple stages, but because the outcome of each of its stages is uncertain, whereas the cohort model produces a final, definitive guess. In the extreme we might say that we're never really sure we've heard the sentence correctly, but we use the speaker's nods, smiles, and gestures to increase our confidence and accuracy. It is difficult to predict at this point which of the theories will ultimately prove to be closest to the truth. What is important is that all of them assume the listener is attending to multiple aspects of the speech signal and processing them all at once (parallel processing of a sort).

The listener brings to bear a high level of contextual information as well as an analysis of low-level elements of the sound pattern in order to home in on recognizing the spoken word. One element that is common to these theories is that the recognition process is fallible: We don't always identify speech correctly. Fortunately, people possess sensory and working memories that are able to hold the sound input long enough to repair any misperceptions.

Speaker and Listeners A speaker makes a point to listeners, using both words and gestures. We use a speaker's nods, smiles, and gestures to increase our confidence that we have heard and understood the message.

Michael Newman/Photo Edit

Speech Recognition Pathologies

While the theories of speech recognition have each been confirmed in laboratory studies, they have also been tested in the laboratory of real life among people who suffer from neurological deficits that affect their ability to recognize speech. Two types of aphasia are directly related to the speech recognition theories: primary progressive aphasia and conduction aphasia. A third type of speech perception aphasia, pure word deafness, was described in Chapter 4.

Primary Progressive Aphasia One form of aphasia becomes progressively worse over a period of time. **Primary progressive aphasia** is characterized as a slow deterioration in the ability to understand language (Mesulam, 2001). Loss of comprehension is not the result of a general intellectual decline (such as might be seen in Alzheimer's dementia, for example). It begins with the person having difficulty understanding specific words. It is followed by a progressive deterioration in the ability to identify the names of objects, and then a reduction in general comprehension, although the ability to speak is initially retained. The sequence of language difficulties parallels the sequence in actually learning to recognize speech: understanding isolated words, names, sentences.

Initially, people who suffer from primary progressive aphasia can speak basic sentences, but cannot understand other people's speech or sign language; ultimately, they cannot understand written words and they become mute (Duffy & Petersen, 1992). Unlike other aphasias that are the result of strokes and can benefit from different forms of therapy, as of this writing, there is no procedure or medication that can arrest or reverse primary progressive aphasia (Cress & King, 1999; Weintraub, Rubin, & Mesulam, 1990).

This type of aphasia is usually diagnosed with a series of tasks. The first task typically tests the individual's ability to perform simple sound discriminations with nonsense syllables (Halstead–Reitan Battery; Boll, 1981). For example, "Are these the same or different: *BAK* and *TAK*?" The next level of task presents a spoken word and a collection of diagrams. The individual has to point at an appropriate picture (Sklar Aphasia Scale; Sklar, 1983) or follow progressively more complex commands, from a simple one like "touch the red square" to a more complex one, such as "before touching the yellow circle, pick up the red square" (Token Test; De Renzi & Vignolo, 1962, p. 672). The sequencing of these tests corresponds nicely with the speech perception theories by beginning with sound discrimination and progressing to interactions among syntactic, semantic, and contextual factors.

Conduction Aphasia **Conduction aphasia** is a rare form of language difficulty that occurs when a person can understand what is being said but cannot repeat it correctly. For example, a person asked to repeat back "no ifs, ands, or buts about it" might respond "no nifs nand nor but" (W. W. Campbell, DeJong, & Haerer, 2005). Although the person realizes he or she has made a mistake, even the corrections will be wrong (Bhatnager & Andy, 1995). Two major brain areas are involved: the *arcuate fasciculus* (a bundle of nerve fibers that connects Broca's and Wernicke's areas) and the auditory cortex of the left hemisphere. Individuals who suffer this aphasia can recognize speech if either the left or right hemisphere is intact. If the left hemisphere is damaged, however, they cannot produce a correct repetition of what they have just heard (Goodglass & Kaplan, 1983) and have difficulty reading aloud. When these individuals speak, they may distort words by adding syllables or by adding sounds to a word. But if the speech is spontaneous (not a repetition), it is largely unimpaired.

Speech comprehension of people with conduction aphasia is not perfect when sentences include complex elements such as prepositions (e.g., *above, below, before, after*). These individuals can understand, "Do you write with a pen?" but not, "<u>Before</u> you say hello, please stand." Their writing typically contains spelling errors and transpositions of words and syllables (Brookshire, 1997). This rare form of aphasia is important for cognitive theory because it shows that the brain area important for speech production is also associated with a brain area important for speech recognition (Damasio & Damasio, 1980; MacKay, Wulf, Yin, & Abrams, 1993).

Hearing speech is not enough, of course: Words must be linked to individual meanings. This is the topic we turn to next.

SECTION SUMMARY ■

Understanding Speech

Sensitivity to language comes early in a child's life, perhaps as early as 8 weeks before birth. Humans possess a special ability to hear and identify speech sounds that are presented at a high rate of speed so that there are virtually no pauses between the speech sounds. Our early experiences with language contain many errors because we lack the information needed to figure out when one word ends and another begins. What we hear is affected by what we expect to hear. Three theories jointly account for human speech perception: (a) the motor theory says listeners try to mentally create a match for the speech sounds they hear, and seeing the lips of the speaker helps this process; (b) interaction models such as the cohort and TRACE models tell us that listeners rely on an interaction among their library of similar sounding words, and linguistic and social cues to detect speech sounds; (c) the fuzzy logic model, in which speech perception, like other kinds of pattern recognition, involves matching sensory signals to stored prototypes of similar sounding words and then making a guess.

Two types of speech pathologies are related to the theories of speech recognition: primary progressive aphasia and conduction aphasia. The sequence of difficulties of primary progressive aphasia seems like the reverse of how people learn to recognize the speech of others and begin to speak themselves. Initially, sufferers can speak basic sentences but cannot understand other people's speech or sign language; ultimately, they cannot understand written words and become mute. Conduction aphasia is characterized by the inability to repeat speech a person has just heard. It reveals that human speech recognition is accomplished by areas in both hemispheres of the brain, although speech production generally relies on the left hemisphere. Both types of aphasia begin with insensitivity to speech sounds as unique sounds. The fact that the individual's hearing is not impaired suggests that speech is distinct from other nonlinguistic sounds.

Identifying the Meanings of Words

After you recognize a speech pattern or gesture and identify the word that has been uttered, your next task is to identify the meaning of the word in order to continue the process of speech comprehension. When you "look up" the meaning of the identified sound in your memory, you should have access to the *denotation* of the word, its dictionary-like definition as far as you know it. So for the word *bird*, you might know that it is "a small, two-legged animal with feathers and wings that procreates by laying eggs." You might also access your own personal *connotations* for the word *bird*: ideas that come to mind, but are not necessarily true. For example, *bird* might evoke "flying creature, lives in trees, and chirps" or "insulting gesture," or "a disparaging term for a young girl." All this information, and much more, is easily retrieved from a mental dictionary called a **lexicon**.

The Lexicon: The Mental Dictionary

If you were designing a language, you would want to make sure there was a one-to-one correspondence between a word and a meaning. One word would have only one meaning, and that meaning would have only one word to express it. Alas, human languages come close to this ideal, but not close enough. Words are often ambiguous, that is, they have multiple meanings. Here are three words with multiple meanings:

bank 1. sloping ridge typically beside a body of water; **2.** place to keep your money; **3.** to bounce an object off another object on an angle; **4.** an arrangement of objects (e.g., *bank* of tools).

straw 1. plant stalks (e.g., wheat or hay); **2.** plastic sucking device; **3.** not real (e.g., *straw* vote or *straw* man).

rate 1. total amount of a charge; **2.** proportion; **3.** price; **4.** speed.

Sometimes people pronounce words differently even though they are spelled the same because they have different meanings: *read* (e.g., Go to your room and *read* a book) and *read* (e.g., She *read* the expression of horror on my face). People also pronounce different words in the same way, such as my throat was *hoarse* when I rode the *horse*.

These examples show that our lexicon contains much more than standard, dictionary definitions. To illustrate this, take the two words *sugar* and *cup*; their simplicity is deceiving. Sugar (as granules) is called a *mass noun*, because when you describe its quantity (e.g., How *much* sugar do you want to put in the recipe?) you use the word *much* because sugar is uncountable. In contrast, when you're talking about cups or cups of sugar, you use the word *many* (e.g., How *many* cups of sugar do you want to put in the recipe?) because we can count the distinct cups; you wouldn't say "how *much* cups of sugar do you want?" Our lexicon must be quite dynamic to contain not only the specific definitions of words, but also **selection restrictions**, which are the conditions under which the definitions hold and how the word should be treated within sentences.

It is difficult to pin down the true nature of the lexicon because it is so rich in possibilities. In part, this is because what we retrieve from our lexicon is influenced by the context in which we perceive words. This is illustrated in the Focus on Methods box.

FOCUS ON METHODS ■■■■■■■■■■■■■■■■■■■■■■■■■■■■■■■■■

Recognition Memory

The ability of people to recognize a name or a face or a situation is often a better indicator of what they know than their ability to recall the same information verbally (e.g., Anderson & Bower, 1972; Glanzer & Adams, 1990; Watkins & Tulving, 1975). The method of testing recognition memory has also worked to reveal how people encode the meaning of words. This method has been successfully employed to examine the effect of context. Light and Carter-Sobell (1970) asked students to read 134 sentences that contained an adjective modifying an underlined noun; the students knew that they were going to be tested on their ability to recognize the nouns later on. For example, they might see pairs of words such as the following foods:

> sugar <u>cubes</u>
>
> soda <u>cracker</u>
>
> Virginia <u>ham</u>
>
> strawberry <u>jam</u>

Later on, the students were tested on their ability to recognize the words they had seen before as well as others that were new. Some of the words were in a context that would foster the same meaning for the noun as they had seen before:

> ice <u>cubes</u>
>
> saltine <u>cracker</u>

> baked <u>ham</u>
>
> raspberry <u>jam</u>

Other nouns were in a context that promoted a different meaning:

> geometric <u>cubes</u>
>
> safe <u>cracker</u>
>
> radio <u>ham</u>
>
> traffic <u>jam</u>

As long as the context words promoted a similar meaning for the target nouns as the one they had at the time of learning, such as jam (*a food you spread on bread*), students were about 65% accurate in recognizing words they had seen before. In contrast, accuracy averaged less than 25% when the context promoted a meaning for the noun that was different from the one the students had originally seen, such as jam (*traffic congestion*).

This method reveals that the lexicon may contain multiple meanings of a target word and that the meaning retrieved depends on the contextual demands of the situation. It also shows that just because we are able to retrieve one meaning of an ambiguous word, it does not mean that we are aware of its alternative meanings.

Ambiguity and Comprehension

Ambiguous sentences require more cognitive effort to understand than do unambiguous sentences. Read the following sentence:

> I was afraid of Tyson's powerful punch, especially since it had already laid out much tougher men who had bragged they could handle that much alcohol.

Notice that you are led down a garden path until the last word, where you encounter the word *alcohol* and realize your interpretation of a blow from a fist was not the intended meaning. This causes you to recover or reanalyze the meaning of the entire sentence (Ferreira, Christianson, & Hollingworth, 2001). Much humor is based on this kind of surprise. Indeed, we laugh because the joke is on us, as in Henny Youngman's comments:

> I told the doctor I broke my leg in two places:
> He told me to stop going to those places.

> My wife dresses to kill:
> She cooks the same way.

What are the psychological consequences of ambiguity? We have known for a long time that ambiguity within a sentence slows down the listener or reader. MacKay (1966, pp. 434–436; Olson & MacKay, 1974) asked students to complete sentence fragments, such as those shown below, as quickly as possible. He recorded how long it took the students to say the completions aloud. Some fragments were ambiguous and some were not. You might try the task yourself; begin with ambiguous sentences first and have someone time you.

Ambiguous	**Unambiguous**
(a) After taking the *right* turn at the intersection, I . . .	After taking the left turn at the intersection, I . . .
(b) Although Hannibal sent troops *over* a week ago . . .	Although Hannibal sent troops almost a week ago . . .
(c) Knowing that *visiting* relatives could be a nuisance, I . . .	Knowing that some relatives could be a nuisance, I . . .

Students took longer to complete ambiguous fragments than the unambiguous ones (nearly 2 seconds longer in some cases). The fragments with three or more meanings, such as sentence (c), took longer than those with just two meanings, such as sentence (a). MacKay noted that the multiple meanings loaded down the language processing of some students so severely that students were even likely to stutter on the ambiguous fragments.

How Long Does Ambiguity Last?

When you ask people about ambiguous sentences, they are often unaware of the multiple meanings. You might assume that people are unaware of the ambiguity because they access only one of the meanings—perhaps the most frequently occurring one. But if this were true, then ambiguous sentences should not take any longer to complete or read than unambiguous ones. One possibility is that our lack of awareness of ambiguity comes from the fact that we calculate the additional meanings of a word, but then drop them from working memory as soon as we choose the preferred meaning. How long do we carry the multiple meanings in our working memory before we drop them? In general, the more familiar you are with the ambiguous word, the longer you would retain its multiple meanings (Simpson & Burgess, 1985). Typically, the listener tends to retain multiple meanings until the end of the clause boundary.

A clause was defined earlier as a group of words that is like a sentence, but cannot stand alone, as in the sentence, "Hey Kelly, after you go sailing, call from the dock." A clause is formed by the words *after you go sailing*. We can see the role clauses play with ambiguous sentences by repeating MacKay's (1966; Olson & MacKay, 1974) experiment with ambiguous sentence fragments that do or do not contain a completed clause. Recall that the students were timed as they tried to complete the fragments.

Complete clause: Although flying planes can be dangerous, he . . .

Incomplete clause: Although flying planes can . . .

In both sentence fragments there are two potential meanings for *flying planes*. One is the act of putting an airplane into flight (a verb) and the other is a description of the type of plane (an adjective). Students require more time to complete sentences like the incomplete fragment. The authors of the study concluded that listeners are carrying around two meanings in that sentence fragment when they try to complete it, and they are slowed down by the burden of having to consider alternate meanings (Bever, Garrett, & Hurtig, 1973; Frazier & Rayner, 1982). In contrast, listeners have already unburdened themselves of the alternative meanings at the clause boundary in the first sentence fragment prior to completing it. We can conclude from this that when we hear a sentence, all of the word meanings are available until the clause boundary is encountered. Listeners make a commitment to a particular interpretation at the clause boundary and unburden themselves at that point.

Sometimes people keep the wrong interpretation. They are led down a garden path based on their favored interpretation. In comedic timing, the punch line must come long enough after the clause boundary to allow the listener time to pursue the wrong interpretation, but quickly enough to ensure that the original word or phrase that activated the multiple meanings is still available in working memory after the punch line (roughly 2 to 3 seconds; see Chapter 5). To see how this works, try the exercise in Demonstration 10.1.

▪▪▪**DEMONSTRATION 10.1**

Comedy and the Phonological Loop

Read the following one-liners to a friend (another Henny Youngman example) at different rates of speed to see that timing is everything. The one-liners are printed on two lines; for (a) use a 3-second pause between the first and second lines. In (b) read it with only a 1- or 2-second pause. Rapid pacing creates the humor.

(a) I bet on a horse at 10 to 1:
 It didn't come in 'til half past five.

(b) My grandmother is over 80 and still doesn't need glasses:
 She drinks right from the bottle.

SECTION SUMMARY ▪

Identifying the Meanings of Words

Our knowledge of words is stored in a mental dictionary called the lexicon. It contains denotations, connotations, pronunciation rules, and selection restrictions (the conditions under which the definitions hold and how words should be treated within sentences). The fact that words can be ambiguous and possess different meanings slows our comprehension process when we try to understand those words. When we read or hear ambiguous sentences, we carry in our working memories all the potential meanings until we reach the end of the clause and then we make a commitment to the most likely meaning.

Case Grammar: From Words to a Sentence

After the listener identifies the individual words of an utterance, the next task is to construct a message. Linguists have developed many different grammatical systems for analyzing sentences, and cognitive psychologists have worked long and hard to determine whether there is a particular grammar in the head of the average person to compute the meaning of an utterance (Pinker, 1994; Watt, 1970). One grammar identified by psychologists and linguists, called case grammar, has been shown to be successful in describing listeners' and readers' intuitions about the meaning of a sentence (Fillmore, 1968; Kintsch & Keenan, 1973).

Case grammar is a universal set of concepts that is expressed in the sentences of all languages (Brown, 1973; Chafe, 1970; Fillmore, 1968). The psychological claim is that when we hear sentences, we separate them into syntactic–semantic elements called *cases* in order to construct the speaker's message. **TABLE 10.1** defines five of the universal set of cases: agent, instrument, patient, object, and locative. Research on the ability of university students to identify cases from reading text shows that they are most sensitive to the agent, patient, and instrument (Shafto, 1973). A detailed analysis of the earliest two- and three-word utterances of children (Brown, 1973) revealed that children's speech reflects the use

TABLE 10.1

Cases and Their Definitions

Case	Definition	Example[a]
Agent	Animate instigator of an action	*Scott* hammered the nail. The nail was hammered by *Scott*.
Instrument	Inanimate force or object that brings about the action named by the verb	The *saw* cut the wood. Jesse broke the window with a *ball*.
Patient	Animate being that is affected by the action, which is named by the verb	Pam fed the *entire family*. Nancy gave the gift to *Kelly*.
Object	Inanimate recipient of an action	Paul built a *table*. Huck painted the *fence*.
Locative	Location of the action	The *front door* was open. *Paris* is beautiful.

[a]The case is italicized.

of cases in their communication. A sample of children's utterances during the earliest stages of language development are listed in **TABLE 10.2**.

These case components are so critical to understanding sentences that when the speaker leaves an important case out of a sentence, the listener mentally supplies it. Take instruments, for example. If you were told, "Jessie cut the ribbon," you would intuitively understand that:

Agent = Jessie

Object = ribbon

Instrument = scissors or a knife (but not a chainsaw or a sharp look of criticism)

TABLE 10.2

Role of Objects in Children's Sentences

Semantic function	English utterance
Demonstrative + Object	*There book*
Action + Object	*Give candy*
Agent + Object	*Eve lunch* (Eve is having lunch.)
Agent (Object) + Action	*Bambi go*
Possessor + Object	*My shoe*
Attribute + Object	*Big boat*
Location + Object	*Where ball?* *Allgone milk*
Action + Location[a]	*Go street*

Note: After Brown, 1973 (p. 173)
[a]Not present in Slobin's (1970) seven functions.

You know there needs to be an instrument because the verb *cut* assumes someone or something that is doing the cutting and something or someone that is cut. Since the speaker does not tell us what the instrument is, the listener takes a guess. Singer (1979) asked students to read brief passages that either explicitly stated an instrument, as in (a), or had one implied, as in (b):

(a) The sailor swept the floor with the broom.

(b) The sailor swept the floor.

Twenty minutes later, the students were shown sentences such as (a), and they had to indicate whether they had read the sentence before in the laboratory (recognition condition).

The data are summarized in **FIGURE 10.3**, which shows that people who had only read sentence (b) were slightly less confident that they had read sentence (a) than the students who actually did read the sentence. Other students were asked to verify whether the test sentence was true or false in comparison to what they had read (verification condition). The researchers did this because the students might have realized they had not seen the actual sentence, but that the test sentence might be consistent with how they understood the original sentence. Figure 10.3 shows that the proportion of students saying true is the same for students who had originally seen the test sentence as for those who had not. It is as if the reader *inserted* the missing instrument in order to make sense of the sentences either at the time the sentence was heard or later on in retelling it (Johnson, Bransford, & Solomon, 1973; Singer, 1979).

Children show a similar sensitivity to missing instruments. In one study (Paris & Lindauer, 1976), young children heard sentences such as (b) and later were given a cue, such as the word *broom,* to help them recall the sentence. Now *broom* should not be a useful cue because the instrument was never mentioned in the sentence. Yet the missing instrument was an effective recall cue for children as young as 7 years old. These studies illustrate that case has a psychological relevance to people's comprehension and memory for sentences. Even though they may not have been tutored in case grammar, people appear to have a natural intuition about the importance of case for communication. But what do we do with this case information? To answer that question, we must consult a model of pragmatic factors in sentence comprehension and use.

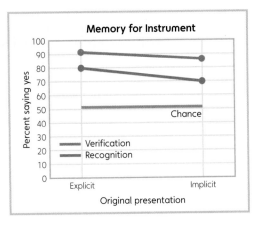

FIGURE 10.3 Memory for Cases Studies have shown that cases are so important for our analysis of sentences that we mentally insert them into sentences that don't contain them. The data here show that students who had read sentences with implicit instruments responded to sentence recognition and verification tasks as if they contained explicit instruments far greater than would be expected by chance.

Source: From Singer, 1979

SECTION SUMMARY ▪

Case Grammar: From Words to a Sentence

When people hear or read a sentence, critical elements called cases are identified in order to mentally construct the speaker's message. Five of the universal set of cases are agent, instrument, patient, object, and locative (defined in Table 10.1). People most readily identify the agent, patient, and instrument cases; even small children use these cases in their basic language. Cases are so much a part of the comprehension process that when a case is missing from the speaker's sentence, the listener often automatically adds the missing element to working memory as if it had been stated.

Sentence Comprehension: The Utilization Process

So far, we have discussed identifying individual words, accessing their meaning, and identifying the critical elements of a sentence. This section focuses on how the listener constructs the meaning of a sentence and figures out what the speaker wants the listener to do. This final stage of language understanding is called the **utilization process** (Clark & Clark, 1977), a reference to the fact that the listener is supposed to *use* the message in some way. A diagram of the utilization process

FIGURE 10.4 Flowchart Showing the Utilization Process The last stage of speech comprehension—constructing the message—can be broken down into a series of steps in which the listener interprets the intent of the speaker and responds (uses the message) accordingly.

Source: After Clark & Clark, 1977

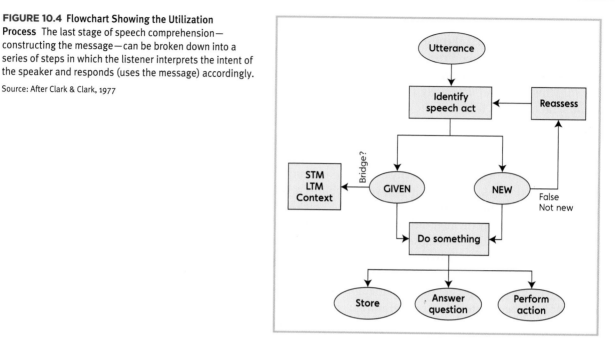

is shown in **FIGURE 10.4**. Notice that the bottom of the flowchart contains ovals that indicate what the listener is supposed to do with the incoming message: store it, answer a question, or take some other action.

The utilization process conveys the idea that language is a communication system intended to facilitate an exchange between speaker and listener. The speaker's goal is to get the listener to do something—if only to listen and remember what the speaker has to say. This places quite a burden on the listener because sometimes it may sound as if the speaker is asking a question, when in fact the speaker is making a request. For example, the speaker says, "can you pass the salt?" If you were not familiar with this indirect request, you might think that the speaker was inquiring about your physical ability to pass the salt. Even more indirect would be, "are you finished with the salt?" If you have ever used this expression at a family dinner with young children, you may have gotten yes or no as the answer because children have difficulty understanding the underlying intent of a question (Ervin-Tripp, Guo, & Lambert, 1990).

A Parent Yelling at a Child If language is a communication system intended to facilitate an exchange between speaker and listener, this speaker's goal is clear: to get the listener to do or to stop doing something.

David Young-Wolff/Photo Edit

Speech Acts

As we will see in the following, such requests are usually made when the listener is *not* in the process of salting the food. In this case, the speaker

TABLE **10.3**		
Speech Acts		
Speech act	**Content**	**Example**
Representative (assertion)	Represents the beliefs of the speaker	I think . . . believe . . . imagine . . . assume . . . wonder . . . that it is going to rain
Directive	Gets the listener to perform an action	Can you . . . would you . . . (it's so warm) open the window
Commissive	Speaker makes a commitment to the listener	I will . . . promise . . . guarantee . . . warranty
Expressive	Expresses the psychological state of the speaker	I hope . . . welcome . . . congratulations . . . excellent
Declarative	A statement that brings about the state of affairs that it describes	I quit . . . hereby sentence you . . . now pronounce you

already knows that the listener has indeed finished with the salt. So why did the speaker ask the question? How should the listener respond? The listener is helped in answering these questions by knowing intuitively that messages generally fall into a small number of categories. The listener must simply decide which category has just been used.

The first decision the listener must make concerns the intent of the speaker: Is he or she asking a question, conveying a belief, or expressing a feeling? These categories are called **speech acts** because they are the actions intended by the speaker and are performed not by physical actions, but by the use of language (Austin, 1962; Searle, 1969). The ability to identify speech acts is critical for deciding what the speaker wants the listener to do. Although speech acts are universal and appear across cultures, there are cultural and gender differences in how the acts are performed (Lakoff, 1975). Five of the broadest categories of speech acts are summarized in **TABLE 10.3**.

Pragmatic Conventions

Sometimes people have difficulty grasping what a speaker has asked of them because the pragmatic conventions that we follow can be "violated" in subtle ways and thereby mislead us. These pragmatic conventions are called the reality and the cooperative principles.

The Reality Principle Unless your suspicion is aroused, you tend to believe the speaker is referring to a situation or set of ideas that are real or possible, or at least make sense. This is the **reality principle**. The speaker is supposed to construct utterances that can be understood—keeping in mind that the listener interprets the message in terms of his or her personal knowledge of the world and creates or re-creates a mental image of what is being said. If the listener can't construct a reality from the utterance, then it will not be understood.

On the other hand, we as listeners use the reality principle to fill in missing information and are able to work around the possibility that the speaker misspoke. For example, suppose an emotional parent wants to describe a narrow escape of his surfing son (*Daniel maneuvered his board toward shore and outdistanced the chasing shark*), but the parent is only able to gasp out: "Dan steered . . . shore . . . shark . . . safe." With these few elements, you, as the listener, can reconstruct a possible story. You assume that the parent was adhering to the reality principle and trying to make sense. Therefore, you would create a mental image that fit with the reality of people trying to avoid sharks. (You would not assemble odd interpretations such as *Dan steered his surfboard toward a shark swimming along the shoreline, but thankfully the shark was safe from him!*) This shows that the listener does not have to attend to every word in order to get the meaning of the sentence.

Individuals with aphasia often use key words to understand sentences because they know the speaker is trying to make sense; therefore, they do not need to consider every possible interpretation. All they need to do is apply their knowledge of the world to assemble a possible sentence from the fragments that they identify, much as you might be guided in assembling a jigsaw puzzle from your knowledge of what the picture is supposed to be (Bever, 1970; Clark & Clark, 1977). To gain a sense of this, do the activity in Demonstration 10.2.

■■■**DEMONSTRATION 10.2**

The Reality Principle

The reality principle allows us to ignore some of the words that are uttered. Try reading and answering the questions below as quickly as you can.

How many bowls of porridge did Goldilocks taste?

How many animals of each kind did Moses take on the ark?

By having an apple fall on his head, what did Galileo discover?

What kind of tree did Lincoln chop down?

Now look back at the questions. Did you answer any of them incorrectly? The first question is intended to make you think that we are obeying the reality principle, but notice the remaining three questions; they ask a question based on false information. Erikson and Mattson (1981) found that the most frequent response to "How many animals of each kind did Moses take on the ark?" is two, in spite of the fact the participants knew very well that in the Bible story, it was Noah, not Moses who took animals on the ark. This is an example of how we rely on our broad knowledge of topics to superficially understand sentences. It's as if our comprehension reflects only a partial match between what we hear and what we know (Reder & Cleeremans, 1990).

The superficial processing in Demonstration 10.2 often doesn't hurt us because the speaker adheres to the reality principle. It may be the case that even your instructors, as they are grading your essays, are not attending to the sentence structure as much as to the collection of key words that together evoke semantic ideas that match their own reality. The theory of how this is done will be discussed when we talk about reading comprehension.

TABLE **10.4**	
Cooperative Principle: Four Maxims	
Principle	**Description**
Quantity	Make your contribution as informative as required, but not more informative than is necessary.
Quality	Try to make your contribution one that is true. Do not say anything you believe to be false or for which you lack adequate evidence.
Relation	Make your contribution relevant to the aims of the ongoing conversation.
Manner	Be clear. Try to avoid obscurity, ambiguity, wordiness, and confusion.

Note: Based on Grice, 1975

The Cooperative Principle The second major pragmatic principle is the **cooperative principle**. It supposes that speaker and listener are trying to "cooperate" in the communication process. The listener assumes that the speaker is: (a) telling the listener all that he or she needs to know and no more, (b) trying to tell the truth, (c) saying things that are relevant, and (d) using sentences clearly and unambiguously. In observing the cooperative principle, speakers normally try to satisfy four requirements called **maxims** that were described by Grice (1975), a philosopher of language, and are summarized in **TABLE 10.4**. The four maxims are quantity, quality, relation, and manner. Briefly, the *principle of quantity* requires that the speaker play Goldilocks and give neither too little nor too much information. The *principle of quality* implores the speaker to be sincere and tell the truth. The *principle of relation* guarantees that the sentences are related to the ongoing conversation. Finally, the *principle of manner* asks the speaker to present the message clearly and to avoid ambiguity.

Because the listener assumes that the speaker is obeying the four maxims, the speaker doesn't have to be too precise: The listener will draw a correct inference on fragmentary information. Take the sentence about a baseball event: *Ryan Joseph Braun took a swing at the pitch*. On the face of it, this is a statement of fact. Notice, however, that the speaker has not told us whether the baseball player hit the ball or not. The listener is able to reason that Braun must have missed the ball. Why? Because the maxim of quantity says the speaker should give sufficient information to understand the event. If Braun had hit the ball, the speaker would have said so. Perhaps a critical element in the cooperative principle is respect for the intelligence of the listener, who is presumed to be capable of drawing the correct inference by relying on the speaker's adherence to the cooperative principle (Spivey, Tyler, Eberhard, & Tanenhaus, 2001).

The Given–New Contract

Once the listener has identified the general category of message being uttered, it is time to calculate the actual content of the message. It is one thing for the listener to understand that the speaker is uttering a directive (see Table 10.3); it's another thing to figure out what the listener is being asked to do. To accomplish this, the listener follows a strategy that allows him or her to isolate the actual message from background information. The strategy is based on a pragmatic convention that appears to be universally followed (Clark & Haviland, 1977):

> The speaker agrees that every message will have two components. The first is information that the <u>listener already knows</u> and can identify, called the *given* and the second part is information that the speaker believes is true, but is <u>not already known</u> to the listener; this is the *new* information.
>
> *(Clark & Clark, 1977, p. 92)*

In general, listener and speaker agree that in all sentences, one part of the sentence links to the listener's memory and another part presents the message (which presumably is not already known to the listener; if it were known, there would be no reason for the speaker to utter the sentence unless there were another agenda in the speaker's mind). This is called the **given–new contract**. The information that is in the listener's mind or generally shared by speaker and listener is called the *given* information in the sentence. The information that is supposed to be a message to the listener is called the *new* information. These are illustrated in **TABLE 10.5**. Sentences that violate the given–new contract are difficult to understand. For example, suppose your friend says, "Mary had a great time at the party." You don't remember hearing about a party and don't have any friends named Mary, so you spend quite a bit of time searching your memory for answers to the questions, who's Mary? what party?

It is easier to discuss how the listener uses the contract to understand messages by offering a few more details about the meaning of the terms *given* and *new*. Suppose you heard someone say, "Paul climbed the boulder." If the speaker is adhering to the given–new contract, then:

Given: There is someone named Paul (presumably, you know this person).

New: What this person did was climb a boulder.

TABLE **10.5**			
Examples of Given and New			
Sentence	**Given**	**New**	**Action**
Paul climbed the boulder.	Paul	Climbed the boulder	Update knowledge of Paul
Do they grow coffee in Brazil?	Brazil	Is coffee grown there?	Yes or no
Who invented the snowboard?	Someone invented the snowboard	What is the name?	Retrieve from memory ("Burton")
You got a haircut.	You	Cut your hair	Update knowledge of yourself
You got a haircut?	I	Am surprised	Update your knowledge of the speaker

It is the boy who is riding the horse.

FIGURE 10.5 The Given–New Contract Students were asked to choose the picture that matched the sentence they saw. The results suggest that people identify the given as the topic of the sentence.

Images provided courtesy of Peter A. Hornby, Department of Psychology, SUNY, Plattsburgh.

The given is often considered the topic of the sentence—what the sentence is about. In the sentence "Paul climbed the boulder," the true topic of the sentence is that Paul did something.

To demonstrate that the given is the topic of the sentence—what it is about—students listened to a sentence that was followed immediately by two pictures flashed on a screen at the same time (see **FIGURE 10.5**). The students' task was to decide which picture the *sentence* was *about*.

One picture showed a boy riding a bike, the other showed a girl riding a horse (Hornby, 1972, 1974). Notice that the sentence did not perfectly match either picture. When the students saw the sentence, "It is the boy who is riding the horse" (given = someone is riding a horse), they chose the picture of a girl riding a horse 70% of the time, which corresponds to the given of the sentence. This suggests that people identify the given as what a sentence is about.

In contrast, the new part of the sentence is the *commentary* on the topic of the sentence. When listeners decide whether a sentence is true or false, it is the new information that they are evaluating. In the sentence "It is the boy who is riding the horse," the new information is that the boy is doing something. To show this, Hornby (1974) presented the sentence aloud ("It is the boy who is riding the horse"), but this time, Hornby showed a single picture for about 50 msec. The picture might be of a girl riding a horse or of a boy riding a bike. The students' job was to say whether the picture is true or false in terms of the sentence. Listeners identified the picture of the boy riding the bike as true 75% of the time. This and other experiments suggest two principles:

PRINCIPLE 1: *When deciding what a sentence is about, people focus on the given.*

PRINCIPLE 2: *When deciding whether a sentence is true, people focus on the new.*

Creating Bridges

Suppose you return home and upon seeing you, a friend or family member asks, "How'd it go?" In this sentence, *it* is the given, but it is so abstract that you have to search your memory to figure out what *it* the speaker is asking about. The speaker has a particular event in mind and assumed it was so obvious you wouldn't have to be reminded. Your job in this situation is to try to determine how to connect the *it* to what you know. This process is called **bridging** (Haviland & Clark, 1974).

The listener can only truly understand the given when he or she creates a link between what was actually said and what it refers to. Here are some sentences that are like those in Haviland and Clark (1974) that illustrate bridging. Each pair consists of a context sentence followed by a target sentence. Students pressed a button when they finished reading each sentence. Of critical concern was how much time they required to read the target sentence of each pair (*The soda was warm*). Which pair do you find easier to understand?

1. Jack got some soda out of the car. The soda was warm.

2. Jack checked the picnic supplies. The soda was warm.

Did you find that Set 1 was easier to understand? This is because *soda* in the target sentence is an identical match with *soda* in the context sentence. In contrast, the target sentence in Set 2 will require more time to understand because *soda* must be connected to *supplies* in the context sentence: The bridge needs to be constructed between *soda* and *supplies*, which requires time. Haviland and Clark (1974) observed that the target sentence like the one in Set 2 required 181 msec longer to understand than the identical sentence in Set 1. In sum, when you unpack a sentence into given and new, you must know the given part of the sentence. If the connection isn't obvious, the listener must create a bridge between the given and what the listener already knows (Revlin & Hegarty, 1999).

Responding to the Message

Identifying the new is absolutely critical to communication because once the listener has identified the speech act, the new tells the listener what the speaker wants to convey. It might be useful now to review the basic speech acts listed in Table 10.3. Responding to these speech acts is another example of social exchange (Baumeister & Leary, 1995; Collins & Miller, 1994). There are basically five categories of actions the listener is supposed to carry out in response to the message (Clark & Clark, 1977, p. 90); these are illustrated in **TABLE 10.6**. For example, if the utterance is a representative, a commissive, or an expressive, listeners should add the new information to memory and respond in the way their culture prescribes. When people share their feelings with you, your culture might obligate you to be silent and shake your head, or reciprocate with an expressive of your own, or perhaps commiserate. In the North American culture, men tend to respond differently from women in such situations (Tannen, 1994a, 2001).

TABLE **10.6**	
Responses to Speech Acts	
Speech acts	**Responses**
Representatives (assertions)	Listen; agree/disagree; ask for justification; retrieve previous examples, etc.
Directives	Perform requested action; deny need for action; agree with the need, etc.
Commissives	Reciprocate with action that completes the social exchange.
Expressives	Smile; "thank you"; utter a reciprocating expressive of your own.
Declarative	Follow the rules for the situation.

Sometimes the utterance will be a question to which you can respond yes or no. If the utterance is a yes/no question, this obligates you to compare the new information with knowledge you possess in your memory and decide what to answer. If the utterance is a *wh* (*who*, *what*, *where*, or *when*) question, then the speaker wants you to retrieve the new information and compose an answer. The speaker does not expect a yes response to a *wh* question such as, who went to the game last night?

SECTION SUMMARY

Sentence Comprehension: The Utilization Process

Language is a communicative system that creates an exchange between speaker and listener. The speaker tries to get the listener to do something, and the listener is trying to figure out what that is. The process proceeds through three broad stages: identifying the speech act of the utterance, applying the given–new contract, and finally responding to the utterance. Speech acts are basic types of communications in which the speaker is trying to convey his or her beliefs, feelings, and intentions. In interpreting these, the listener assumes the speaker is adhering to two broad principles: the reality and cooperative principles. The given–new contract specifies that each utterance should have two identifiable parts: first, the portion that connects with what the listener already knows; and second, the message or the new piece of information. Sometimes the given information is not readily available to the listener. As a result, the listener will have to create a bridge between what should have been given and what is in the listener's long-term memory. Once this is accomplished, the listener knows how to respond.

Connected Discourse: Understanding Many Sentences

The utilization process allows us to understand single sentences in isolation, but the usual situation for language occurs when a series of sentences is strung together. This is called **connected discourse**. The strategy of identifying given and new elements from sentences can also be applied to understanding multiple sentences that are part of a connected discourse.

The Importance of Knowledge for Understanding

Knowledge is more than the definitions of words in sentences. It includes the *context* for the remarks and the *implications* of the ideas that are expressed. Let's take an example of the effect of context on understanding text. Read the following passage from a study by Bransford and Johnson (1972) and rate its ease of reading on a scale from 1 (*very difficult to comprehend*) to 3.5 (*moderately difficult to comprehend*) to 7 (*easy to comprehend*).

> The procedure is actually quite simple. First you arrange things into different groups depending on their makeup. Of course, one pile may be sufficient depending on how much there is to do. If you have to go somewhere due to lack of facilities that is the next step, otherwise you are pretty well set. It is important not to overdo any particular endeavor. That is, it is better to do too few things at once than too many. In the short run this may not seem important, but complications from doing too many can easily arise. A mistake can be expensive as well. The manipulation of the appropriate mechanisms should be self-explanatory, and we need not dwell on it here. At first the whole procedure will seem complicated. Soon, however, it will become just another facet of life. It is difficult to foresee any end to the necessity for this task in the immediate future, but then one never can tell. (p. 722)

In the original study, two groups of students heard the passage, and 2 minutes later they rated how easy it was to understand and wrote down as much as they could recall. If you are like those students, you rated this passage quite low. One group had been told that the passage was about laundry (yes, it's about washing clothes; you might want to reread it with that interpretation), but the other group was not given any advance information. The first group rated the passage twice as easy to understand, and they remembered more than twice as many ideas as the second group. One factor that contributed to this result was that students in the first group had a context for interpreting and encoding the ambiguous terms. Take the second sentence in the passage, for example. Terms such as *things* or *makeup* are so general that the normal reader is unable to understand what they refer to. Having knowledge to create the bridges is critical to understanding. Now, look at the sentence from the point of view of participants in Group 1: "First you arrange things (*clothes*) into different groups depending on their makeup (*colors or types of fabrics*)." Activating relevant knowledge makes it easier to comprehend a passage in a way that is more than just knowing the individual meaning of words (Mikulecky & Jeffries, 2007).

The Importance of Knowledge for Retrieval

When the reader or listener has an idea of the topic (e.g., washing clothes) in working memory, he or she is able to integrate the sentences into the stored "structure" or procedure for washing clothes that not only includes what was said in the discourse, but what was activated in the listener's mind from knowledge in long-term memory. Later on, this integrated knowledge and the stored facts from the discourse can act as retrieval cues when the reader tries to recall what was read or heard.

Remembering the Gist The knowledge you possess gives you more than just a clue about how to understand words or sentences; it can provide a perspective on the entire discourse and both aid in comprehension and provide a "plan" for retrieval of the conversation or story. This is because memory for discourse is primarily semantic and not verbatim. When hearing sentences for their meaning as communication, the listener constructs a kind of model of the content, a mental representation of the **gist** of the message. These mental constructions may contain more information than is literally—word for word—presented in the sentences themselves. Because of this, we sometimes forget the literal sentences in favor of an impression of what was said. An example of this can be seen in a study where students heard sentences like the following (Bransford, Barclay, & Franks, 1972, p. 201):

> There is a tree with a box beside it, and a chair is on top of the box. The box is to the right of the tree. The tree is green and extremely tall.

A few minutes later, they were asked to decide which target sentences they had heard in Group A or Group B.

Group A	**Group B**
1. The box is to the right of the tree.	5. The tree is to the left of the box.
2. The chair is to the right of the tree.	6. The tree is to the left of the chair.
3. The box is to the left of the tree.	7. The tree is to the right of the box.
4. The chair is to the left of the tree.	8. The tree is to the right of the chair.

Notice that Sentence 1 was originally presented to the students, whereas Sentences 2, 5, and 6 were not, but they are consistent with the gist and mental model of the relationships in the brief passage. The students had difficulty deciding which of these sentences they had actually seen, and "recognized" them as consistent with what they heard 70% of the time. In contrast, Sentences 3, 4, 7, and 8 were never heard and were inconsistent with the mental model. Students rejected these sentences 71% of the time (Bransford et al., 1972).

Gist and Reconstruction It should come as no surprise, then, that when we retrieve information from a passage, we use the gist memory of it to reconstruct the rest of what we heard or saw. This was shown in a clever study by Pichert and Anderson (1977; Anderson & Pichert, 1978), who had students read a story about two boys who played hooky from school and visited the home of one of the boys.

One group of readers thought they were reading a story from the perspective of a burglar and another group read it from the perspective of a potential home buyer. Twelve minutes later, both groups of students were asked to recall as much of the passage as they could. What they recalled was related to the perspective that they took in reading the passage: Nearly 65% of the idea units relevant to the perspective were recalled, whereas only 50% of the idea units not relevant were recalled.

The Importance of Knowledge for Reasoning About Sentences

The previous sections show that when we hear or read connected discourse, we activate relevant information in long-term memory to create coherence across the ideas and sentences. For example, in one study (Singer, Halldorson, Lear, & Andrusiak, 1992, p. 508) students were asked to read sentences that described a causal sequence (extinguishing a camp fire) or a temporal sequence (a series of events). The students were timed as they read the passages and answered questions.

Causal: Dorothy poured the bucket of water on the fire.

The fire went out.

Temporal: Dorothy placed the bucket of water by the fire.

The fire went out.

Students required 15% more time to read the temporal sequence than the causal one. The causal sequence is one the students would expect merely by activating their knowledge that *water extinguishes fire*. To test whether students were really activating this knowledge, they were asked for a yes/no judgment on the question, does water extinguish fire? right after they read the sentence. Students who read the causal sequence were faster at answering the question than those who read the temporal sequence. Both groups possessed the knowledge, but only the causal group had activated that knowledge while they were reading, which made them faster at answering the question (Singer et al., 1992).

SECTION SUMMARY ■

Connected Discourse: Understanding Many Sentences

In both reading and in speech, an utterance contains a series of sentences connected by a theme. The ability of the listener or reader to identify the theme, make the bridge to memory, and draw the appropriate inferences is dependent on making use of long-term knowledge. This ability helps to understand the theme of the utterance as well as the individual words. When we store the content of the message in our memories, the basic coding is in terms of the general theme—the gist of the discourse. It is the gist that we use to reconstruct the discourse later on. Knowledge is also critical to understanding the causal relationships in a discourse.

■ ■

Reading: Process, Instruction, and Individual Differences

Reading is an unnatural act. It is not a biologically based universal, the way basic spoken or gestural language is. While understanding language only requires that a child interact with a linguistic environment, reading requires deliberate instruction in interpreting written characters as representing a sound or an idea. According to the U.S. Department of Education (National Center for Education Statistics, 1992), 40% of adults in North America have difficulty reading simple labels on packages or combining ideas expressed as text. Although reading is not universal, cognitive psychology has sought to understand this highly valued skill and why it is so unevenly distributed in the population.

Kindergarteners Learn to Read Using a Phonics System Like all of us, these children were not born with the same innate ability to read that they have to speak a language; reading is a skill that must be taught.

Myrleen Pearson/Alamy

A model of the reading process is shown in **FIGURE 10.6**. The diagram portrays the reading process as including the decoding of visual characters (called *graphemic* encoding) and the translation of the visual characters into a kind of subvocal speech via a process called **speech recoding**. This involves individual speech sounds that, like standard speech, activate word and contextual knowledge in semantic memory. This in turn allows people to understand writing and speech.

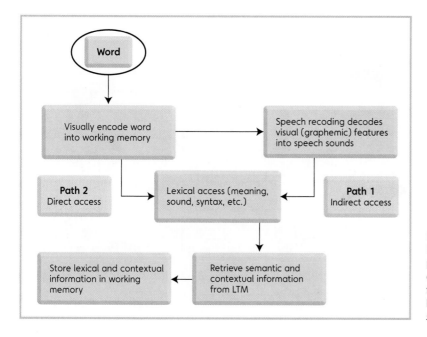

FIGURE 10.6 Model of the Reading Process The diagram portrays the reading process as including the decoding of visual characters (called *graphemic encoding*) and the translation of the visual characters into a kind of subvocal speech via a process called *speech recoding*.

Speech Recoding

The very nature of an alphabetic writing system (based on a written embodiment of speech sounds) would suggest that people read by looking at the visually presented word and translating the visual stimulus into a phonological code, which they look up in their mental lexicon. After all, that's what the whole enterprise is supposed to be, and that is certainly how it is typically taught. This is called indirect access to the lexicon because sound-based features mediate between the visual characteristics of the word and its meaning. This view of reading is embodied in Path 1 in Figure 10.6. The sounds of words are critical to early reading. Children who are best at identifying word sounds also have the highest reading scores (Wagner & Stanovich, 1996). One way of examining children's sensitivity to the sounds of words is the Auditory Analysis Test (Rosner & Simon, 1971). Children are asked to listen to a word and then delete specific sounds from the words. For example, the child hears *block* and must say the word without the /b/ sound (i.e., *lock*) or say *sour* without the /s/ (i.e., *our*). Shaywitz (1996) reported that even among 15-year-olds, who by this age are skilled readers, the ability to perform on this task was positively related to reading ability.

Men and women differ in their language processing during reading. This was discovered in an fMRI analysis of students' brains while they were listening to pairs of words (Baxter et al., 2003). The results are shown in **FIGURE 10.7**. Men tend to do more semantic processing using the left prefrontal cortex (Broca's area), whereas women tend to use both left and right prefrontal cortex (Baxter et al., 2003; Shaywitz, 1996). The fact that women's brains tend to have bilateral representation for language processing explains why, after a stroke involving the left side of the brain, women are less likely than men to have significant,

FIGURE 10.7 Language Differences in the Brain Between Men and Women In this study, men and women were tested on whether pairs of terms were semantically related (e.g., beverage–milk) or not (vehicle–carrot). The fMRI results: Men show activation primarily in the left hemisphere, whereas women show both right- and left-hemisphere activation.

Reprinted from *Brain & Language, 84,* Baxter, L. C., Saykin, A. J., Flashman, L. A., Johnson, S. C., Guerin, S. J., Babcock, D. R. & Wishart, H. A., Sex differences in semantic language processing: A functional MRI study, 272–274, Copyright 2003, with permission from Elsevier.

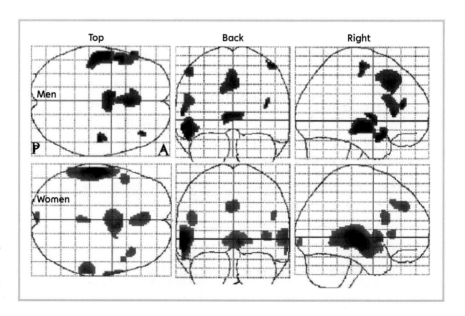

long-lasting impairments in their language skills. It also explains why women are more able than men to compensate for dyslexia.

We know that even skilled readers use the sounds of words as aids in reading. For example, McGuigan and Winstead (1974) placed recording electrodes on the lips, tongue, and throat of readers ages 11–20, who were asked to perform a silent reading task. They found that as people are reading silently, there is heightened electrical activity in the muscles associated with speaking the words they are reading, even though they are not actually speaking. Mentally processing the sounds of words also contributes to errors made during proofreading. Proofreaders are more likely to detect errors that are phonetically incompatible with the correct word (e.g., the word *burst* misspelled as *borst*) than they are to detect phonetically compatible misspellings (e.g., the word *heard* misspelled as *hurd*). Finally, you have no doubt noticed that misspellings that occur because silent letters are missing (e.g., the last *e* in *the*) are more difficult to identify than those due to missing, pronounced letters (e.g., the *t* in *bat*; Corcoran, Dorfman, & Weening, 1968).

Speech recoding seems like a sensible explanation for how all of us learned to read and how we still perform this task as adults. That does not mean we don't sometimes bypass speech recoding and go directly from the visually presented word to its meaning in long-term memory.

Visual Recoding

An alternative view to the speech recoding hypothesis is that the reader maps from the perception of the entire written word to the mental lexicon (Smith, 1983). This is Path 2 in Figure 10.6.

Reading Without Hearing The first evidence for the possibility of reading based on direct visual access is that deaf people can learn to read. Although they may not score as high as their hearing peers on the Reading Comprehension subtest of the Stanford Achievement Test (Holt, Traxler, & Thomas, 1997), deaf college students are undeniably reading and they do so without speech recoding. In one study, 11- to 16-year-old deaf and hearing children were asked to read silently a printed passage while crossing out all detected examples of a certain target letter. For example, they might be asked to cross out *e*'s; some were voiced, as in *eat*, and some were silent as in *the*. Hearing children were sensitive to the voicing of the letters and made errors by missing silent letters. Deaf children, on the other hand, made an equal number of errors in both categories of letters (Locke, 1978). Clearly, deaf children were not sensitive to the sounds of the letters, yet they were able to understand the passages they were reading. This result demonstrates that it is possible to read without speech recoding (Izzo, 2002).

Acquired Dyslexia There is a clinical condition called **acquired dyslexia** in which individuals have difficulty reading words that they already know and cannot read words they have not seen before. Such individuals usually have neurological damage in Broca's area (see Figure 9.4). When they try to read a

TABLE **10.7**		
Characteristics of Acquired Dyslexia		
Type of error	**Definition**	**Example**
Semantic	Responds with a word semantically similar to the one presented	Sees *arm* and says "finger"
Visual	Responds with a word that shares many letters	Sees *frost* and says "forest"
Syntactic	Responds with a word that is altered in syntax	Sees *duck* and says "ducks" Skips function word—sees *the* and does not pronounce it
Phonetic	Skips pronounceable nonwords	Sees *brane*—doesn't pronounce it

Note: From Patterson, Vargha-Khadem, & Polkey, 1987

word they learned prior to the neurological damage, they are unable to read it aloud and utter a word that is semantically related. For example, an individual might be presented with the word *dream* and read it aloud as *sleep* (Coltheart, 1987). If people with this condition are shown a nonword such as *widge*, they cannot read it aloud because they cannot derive the sound of new words. However, their speech perception is perfectly fine, because if they hear the sound *widge*, they can repeat it correctly. A typical cluster of symptoms for individuals with acquired dyslexia generally falls into the four categories summarized in **TABLE 10.7** (Patterson, Vargha-Khadem, & Polkey, 1987).

Notice that when a person with acquired dyslexia sees the word *arm* and says "finger," it demonstrates that the letters of the word *arm* activated some of the semantic reading that is part of the lexical entry for the word *arm*. How else could the reader respond with a word so semantically close? Therefore, it is possible to activate part of the mental lexicon without speech recoding. This is especially the case when people with acquired dyslexia read silently to themselves (Morton & Patterson, 1987).

Speech Recoding Without Reading It is possible to be able to identify the sounds of the letters of the word (called **phonemic awareness**) and still not be able to read the word. This is seen in people who have **word blindness**, also called **pure alexia** (Montant & Behrmann, 2000). People with pure alexia are able to write and spell; they are able to recognize words spelled aloud to them. Many therefore adopt the strategy of reading words letter by letter in an effort to recognize the word from the sound of the letters. As a consequence, the longer the word, the longer it takes the person to say the word aloud. Every letter takes about 3 sec to process, compared with about 9 msec for a typical reader of the same age (Behrmann & Shallice, 1995). This separation between phonemic awareness and word recognition suggests that they are neurologically separable and that phonemic awareness is not enough to produce word recognition.

The Dual Route Hypothesis

A third approach to the lexical access question for reading is the **dual route hypothesis** (both paths in Figure 10.6). It claims that the reader has the potential of using both routes to reading comprehension and actually does so under specifiable circumstances. This model is more flexible than the other explanations of reading because it can account for the fact that early readers tend to use phonological codes; skilled readers tend to do direct visual coding; and everyone slows down when they encounter new or difficult-to-pronounce words (e.g., Coltheart, Rastle, Perry, Langdon, & Ziegler, 2001; Rayner, Pollatsek, & Binder, 1998).

The dual route hypothesis views reading as if it were a horse race: Speech and visual access go on simultaneously, and whichever process is faster will finish first (Coltheart, 1978). If children are beginning reading, visual access may be slower than speech recoding, especially since teachers emphasize the letter–sound correspondences. As reading skills improve, the influence of speech recoding decreases, and direct visual access "wins" more often. Speech recoding wins when reading new words or complex sentences. We see evidence for this in cases where children are forced to suppress lip movements during silent reading, which interferes with speech recoding. This causes them to have difficulty comprehending new material, but does not impair their ability to understand easy material (Hardyck & Petrinovitch, 1970).

Instruction in Reading

The theory of reading in Figure 10.6 is not only descriptive of the cognitive processes associated with reading competency, but it can also be used to guide instruction for effective reading. The model suggests three approaches to reading instruction. The first is based on the indirect access route, the second is based on the direct access route, and the third depends upon a combination of the first two, the dual path route.

The Indirect Access Hypothesis The **indirect access hypothesis** emphasizes the basic sensory process (referred to as *bottom-up processing* in earlier chapters). A working model of reading development consistent with this hypothesis has been proposed by Chall (1983) and her skills-based approach to instruction (described in **TABLE 10.8**). This hypothesis emphasizes the phonological component in word identification. Teaching is based on rigidly sequenced phonics instruction in which children learn letter–sound correspondences by sounding out words. They then learn consonant blends, and long and short vowels. This system has children read stories using controlled vocabulary with the same letter–sound relationships and words they have just mastered. After children have learned the letter–sound correspondences, they are supposed to be prepared to read.

Evidence in support of this approach comes from a positive correlation between reading ability and phonemic awareness: the reader's ability to analyze spoken words into phonemes (e.g., Adams, 1990; Lyon, 1997; Stanovich, 1986).

TABLE **10.8**				
Six-Stage Model of Reading Development				
Stage	Age	Label	Characteristics	**Method of acquisition**
0	0.5–5	Prereading	"pretend" reading, recognizes signs, prints special names, aware of rhymes, most direction is "whole word" (top-down)	mere exposure, imitation, some direction
1	5–7	Initial reading and decoding	learns grapheme–phoneme rules, best at single-syllable words, oral reading, reading vocabulary = 600 words (bottom-up)	direct instruction on phonemic rules
2	7–8	Confirmation, fluency, and "ungluing from the print"[a]	reads simple stories, basic decoding skills, sight vocabulary = 3,000 words	direct instruction on phonemic rules
3	9–14	Reading for the new	reads to learn, growth of silent reading	reading and studying, demands for recall of reading
4	14–17	Multiple viewpoints	wide range in reading (different genres) interests, awareness of story structures and textbook structure	reading and studying, reading for different purposes
5	18	Construction and reconstruction	reading to evaluate and to integrate knowledge	reading and writing

Note: From Chall, 1983

[a]Making reading guesses based on content.

This method is evaluated by comparing children trained in phonemic awareness with those trained in other methods. The children are assessed in reading, spelling, and comprehension (e.g., Pressley, 1994; Pressley, Wharton-McDonald, Hampson, & Echevarria, 1998). Findings support initial benefits to early instruction in phonemic awareness (Adams, 1990; Chall, 1983; Stahl & Miller, 1989). However, no such benefits are shown when older students, who were given phonics-based instruction in kindergarten, are tested on reading comprehension (Bus & van Ijzendoorn, 1999). In this case, the benefits are no greater than other methods in the long run.

The Direct Access Hypothesis The **direct access hypothesis** claims that new readers are capable of going from the visual arrangement of the letters directly to the lexicon and that an appreciation for phonemic structure will be gained from experience in pronouncing recognized words. That is, phonemic awareness may result from reading rather than the other way around. This hypothesis advocates that teachers stress recognition of entire words and largely ignore the pronunciation of letter patterns in words. This is especially the case with reading in English, which has a notoriously poor correspondence between letter sounds and word sounds. For example, the *gh* in *fight* is silent, the *gh* in *tough* is pronounced /f/, and the *gh* in *ghost* is pronounced /g/. The implication is that teachers should emphasize the association between whole-word identification and word meaning (e.g., Crowder & Wagner, 1992).

The whole-word approach (e.g., Raines & Canady, 1990) assumes that children will be using top-down processing. They will identify whole words rather than decoding elements of the word. When words are difficult to map into the lexicon, the reader will use context to identify them, as well as intuitions about pronunciation gained from experience with reading a variety of words (e.g., Scholes, 1998). Because this method advocates drawing upon the child's knowledge of context and similar situations, it's often called the *whole-language approach* to reading (Smith, 1983).

Research on phonemic awareness and whole-word approaches has been compared with evidence tending to favor the whole-word approach (Krashen, 1999; Troia, 1999). There is little evidence to support the value of direct instruction on phonemic awareness as the sole form of instruction.

Many Paths to Reading It can be instructive to take another look at Chall's (1983, 1991) system because it advocates that reading instruction should be tailored to the reading level of the child. That is, which method is effective will depend upon where the child is in the reading stages. In Stage 0, any instruction should probably be at the whole-word (top-down) level as the child acquires an interest in reading and a sense that there is a phonological–meaning correspondence. In Stage 1 the child begins to acquire the graphemic–phonemic correspondences in the process of looking at the text while stories are being read to him or her. The medium of instruction in Stage 1 and the beginning of Stage 2 should be phonics based.

By Stage 2, Chall's (1983, 1991) model looks for the child to be developing a substantial sight vocabulary. The child should be reducing reliance on phonemic rules. Here the child is reading for meaning, and the mode of instruction should begin to emphasize whole-word sight-reading and using context (top-down processing) to identify words and their meanings. After a year or so of phonics instruction, some children will have substantially mastered the decoding process and will be moving through the stages and back to whole word. For them, reliance on instruction in phonemic decoding may interfere with the rapid development of reading skills.

This approach acknowledges the role of both top-down and bottom-up processing in reading. It also says that there are multiple paths to the lexicon and reading the correct word (e.g., Coltheart et al., 2001). A curriculum based on dual routes may begin with phonemic rules in the early stages but, at the same time, will enhance the child's familiarity with frequently used words in order to develop a sight vocabulary. This method also encourages the child to rely on topic knowledge to help access appropriate meanings of the individual words as part of the context of reading. Topic knowledge and contextual information facilitate comprehension in poor readers (Yekovich, Walker, Ogle, & Thompson, 1990).

A whole-language curriculum that embodies these general ideas (e.g., Samuels & Kamil, 1984) focuses on children's individual reading strategies and emphasizes comprehension of the meaning of the individual words by attending to the context provided by the sentences, paragraphs, and entire text. This approach is

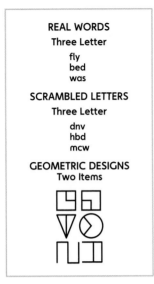

FIGURE 10.8 Reading Skill and Working Memory A sample of verbal and nonverbal experimental stimuli used to test normal and dyslexic readers: real words, nonwords, and geometric shapes.

Sample stimuli from the study: Reading Disability: Age Differences and the Perceptual-Deficit Hypothesis Frank R. Vellutino, Harry Smith, Joseph A. Steger and Mitchell Kaman, *Child Development* Vol. 46, No. 2 (Jun., 1975), pp. 487–493. Courtesy Frank R. Vellutino.

consistent with the dual route hypothesis if the curriculum offers systematic instruction in phonemic awareness and whole-word recognition concurrently with being read to and reading interesting stories and writing.

Individual Differences in Reading

Reading is a cognitive skill that is distributed unevenly across the population. Overall, it seems to be unrelated to general intelligence. Snowling (1980) compared 36 dyslexic children with 18 normal readers. They had similar IQs, although the normal readers were younger (6-11 years old) than the dyslexic readers (9-15 years old). So what is the source of the difference? One possibility is that reading skill may be related to working memory resources. We know that adolescents who are considered to be dyslexic have smaller memory for words they have just read in a text (Goldman, Hogaboam, Bell, & Perfetti, 1980) and for words they have just heard (Perfetti & Goldman, 1976).

Are these memory effects a general characteristic that distinguishes good from dyslexic readers, or are they just specific to language? To address this question, children between the ages of 8 and 15 were asked to copy a sequence of geometric shapes (Vellutino, Steger, & Kandel, 1972), real words, or nonwords (**FIGURE 10.8**). There was no difference in accuracy between children characterized as poor readers (including those with dyslexia) and normal readers when they were copying the geometric shapes or the nonwords. However, the poor readers did not do as well in copying the real words. In addition, the poor readers had more difficulty in pronouncing the real words (the poor readers were more accurate in copying the words than in pronouncing them). These data show that children are not poor or dyslexic readers because of overall perceptual problems, but rather they have word-specific difficulties in making use of their working memory resources. We assess this cognitive limitation by using a reading span measure.

Reading Span A major contribution to understanding individual differences in reading skill was the measure of reading span developed by Daneman and Carpenter (1980). They asked college students to read a series of sentences aloud. After the series, the students attempted to recall the final word of each of the sentences they had just read. **Reading span** was defined as the number of final words the students were able to recall. Reading comprehension was assessed by having the students read the passages silently and then answer questions about specific facts in the sentences. The typical college student's span is between two and seven sentences. Reading span was predictive of reading comprehension. In contrast, ordinary measures of working memory capacity (like the digit-span tests described in Chapter 5) did not predict comprehension performance as well as reading span did.

Daneman and Carpenter (1980) demonstrated that readers differ in their reading memory span. People with larger spans have greater resources available when reading. They can retain contextual elements that help them guess the meaning of unusual words (Daneman & Green, 1986). People with low reading spans tend to interpret an ambiguous word early in the reading process, whereas people with high reading spans generally keep their interpretations open until more information is available (Whitney, Ritchie, & Clark, 1991). People with high reading spans are better able to understand complex sentences and do it faster than people with low reading spans. Because measures of pure working memory capacity by themselves are inadequate to predict reading comprehension scores, the concept of reading span when combined with working memory capacity gives a better indication of a person's overall processing resources (Daneman & Merikle, 1996).

Neurological Processing Research on how the brain processes written language helps us understand why some people have difficulty reading. One of these groups is composed of people labeled as *dyslexic*. (This term was mentioned previously in this chapter without a proper definition.) **Dyslexia** literally means "faulty reading": reading that is markedly below what is expected, based on a person's intelligence. This discrepancy between reading performance and IQ distinguishes dyslexia from just poor reading, in which a person's poor reading performance is consistent with other measures of general intellectual ability.

Dyslexia is defined in the *Diagnostic and Statistical Manual of Mental Disorders* (American Psychiatric Association, 2000) as "reading difficulties that could not be the result of other cognitive problems" (p. 53). Typically this is a child who is 2 or more years behind in reading achievement, but not in school performance. This ignores the possibility that children have other problems that may be related to reading. The definition has a larger impact in lower grades, where 2 years represents a larger percentage of progress in school. Eighty-five percent of people with dyslexia have a specific deficit in assigning appropriate sounds to specific letters. The remaining percentage of people with dyslexia have difficulty identifying the letters or words themselves (Boder, 1973; Morais, Luytens, & Alegria, 1984; Shankweiler et al., 1995).

There is some evidence that the brains of males diagnosed as dyslexic have anomalies not present in the brains of typical readers. These differences are seen as regions in which migrating cells (called *ectopia*) are randomly aligned, and they suggest difficulties in early brain development (Bigler, 1992; Pennington, 1995). The locations of these misplaced cells are shown in **FIGURE 10.9**. You'll notice that they tend to cluster in language-related centers of the brain.

Are the brains of people with dyslexia operating differently when they try to read a word? Recent findings with fMRI show that neurological areas are activated a different proportion of time when dyslexic students are reading than when generally unskilled or skilled readers are reading (Pugh et al., 1996). Unskilled readers show lower levels of activity in the visual cortex (where letter patterns are sensed), Wernicke's area (where contextual meaning is sensed and processed), and the angular gyrus (where specific lexical processing occurs) than do skilled readers. In contrast, dyslexic students show significantly greater processing in Broca's area (associated with syntactic and speech-related perceptual processing; Shaywitz, 1996; Shaywitz et al., 2000). These findings support the theory that dyslexic readers are not the same as unskilled readers.

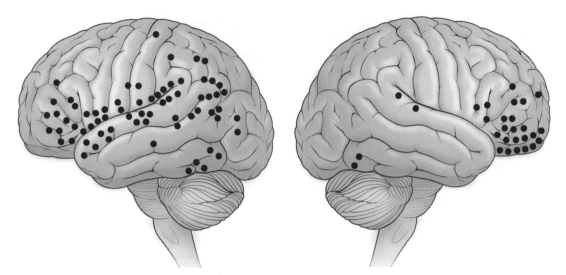

FIGURE 10.9 *Ectopia* in the Brains of Dyslexic People Typical ectopia in the left and right sides of brains of people with dyslexia. The left hemisphere is the dominant one for reading.

Source: From Ramus, 2004

They also show that dyslexic readers have phonemic coding difficulties. If this proves to be correct, then the curriculum remedies for these students are clearly in line with the indirect path hypothesis.

The Eye of the Reader The mechanics of reading seem to be the same for everyone, but skill in reading varies greatly. The mechanics are simple. When you read this sentence, your eye must focus on at least some of the words and record an image on the fovea of your eye. The *fovea* is the central part of the back of the eye called the *retina*. It is the area of the eye that is necessary for sharp, precise visual detail needed for driving or reading. The fovea is wide enough to capture about eight letters of ordinary text. As your eye moves along, it brings selected images to the fovea. These eye movements are called *saccades*. In Chapter 2 you learned the surprising fact that your brain does not process the signal from your eyes as your eyes move, but only when they stop. That is why, when you read this page, it isn't a blur.

The eyes move quickly from one spot to the next, fixate for a moment, and then make another saccadic movement. The fixation of your eyes on the text lasts only about 200–250 msec (Rayner, 1998; Starr & Rayner, 2001). The eyes gaze at a word for as long as the brain is processing the word. In a sense, the gazes reveal that the mind is at work (Just & Carpenter, 1980, 1987). The typical saccade is dictated by what is next in the display. While reading, the eyes tend to skip over short words (function words like *the*) and focus or gaze on longer words. Roughly 80% of all content words are fixated, but only about 35% of function words are fixated (Just & Carpenter, 1980; Rayner & Duffy, 1988; Rayner & Well, 1996).

People differ greatly on their pattern of eye movements when they read. Skilled readers make larger saccades, skipping over short, less meaningful words, compared with less skilled readers. When skilled readers gaze at a word, their fixations on it are shorter (200 msec) than those of less skilled readers (500 msec). All readers occasionally need to regress back to a previous word because they didn't quite get the meaning of the clause they are reading or because they want to understand what the referent for a pronoun (*he, her, them*, etc.) might be.

Skilled readers make fewer regressions to previous words than unskilled readers (Carpenter & Daneman, 1981; Just & Carpenter, 1980).

Just and Carpenter (1980) had college students read a text aloud and recorded their eye fixations as they read. The participants were primarily science and engineering students with at least a B average, yet some would be clearly described as poor readers. As expected, the poor readers tended to make more pronunciation errors than the skilled readers, but when they were correct in their pronunciation, poor readers took as much time to fixate the difficult words as the skilled readers took to read the entire sentence, about 2.5 sec (see also MacKeben et al., 2004). These poor readers typically pronounced the first syllable in a word correctly, but their accuracy declined after that on words they found difficult (often proper names, e.g., Napoleon). Although typical university readers never gave up trying to pronounce a word, students with dyslexia sometimes did. One reason that poor readers took so much time to process the text was because they had difficulty recognizing individual words and, as a result, they required longer fixations and more frequent regressions than skilled readers.

People with dyslexia spend disproportionately less time reading the ends of sentences compared with skilled readers. That is, skilled readers seem to delay final interpretation of the sentence elements until all of the information is available. At this time (at the end of the sentence) they combine the information into a coherent interpretation. In contrast, dyslexic readers make a commitment to the interpretation much earlier. This may be due to memory demands that are reflected in their lower reading span scores.

The findings from these reading, spelling, and eye fixation tasks lend clear support to the indirect access hypothesis and to previous research, which shows that people with dyslexia have problems with tasks that require knowledge of symbol–sound relations. These may be associated with their lower reading spans. They are particularly slow in retrieving such information and make significantly more errors than normal readers in encoding words and in spelling (Just & Carpenter, 1980).

Knowledge Trumps Reading Skill

It should be clear that personal knowledge comes into play when people hear or read connected discourse. You may be surprised to learn that knowledge can also improve comprehension in people who are poor readers. Two experiments by Yekovich et al. (1990) looked at the comprehension skills of high school students who were either high or low performers on the verbal portion of the Scholastic Aptitude Test (SAT). In the first experiment, the students had low verbal SAT scores (10th percentile). They read 12 passages: half from the SAT and half about football. There were two groups of these low-scoring students: One group knew a great deal about football (high knowledge) and the second group knew very little about football (low knowledge). The results are presented in **FIGURE 10.10**,

FIGURE 10.10 Comprehension of Passages Results of a study on the link between knowledge and reading comprehension skills of high school students.

Source: From Yekovich et al., 1990

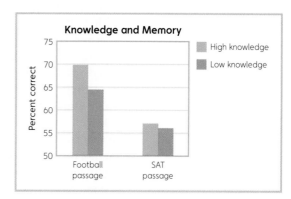

which shows that the high-knowledge students (who are poor readers) did well in understanding passages about football, but did poorly on questions derived from the actual SAT (e.g., a passage on biology). In contrast, the low-knowledge students scored poorly in understanding both types of materials.

In a second task, Yekovich et al. (1990) looked at the spoken performance of high and low verbal aptitude students who all had a high degree of knowledge about football. Although you might expect the high verbal students to perform better than the low verbal students, there was no reliable difference between these two groups when they discussed a football game they had just watched. These results tell us that comprehension of connected discourse (whether presented in a spoken or written format) depends greatly on the reader or listener's background knowledge of the topic (see also Spilich, Vesonder, Chesi, & Voss, 1979).

A paradox is at work here: It seems as if you have to know what is being said in order to understand what is being said. In other words, the more you know in general about the topic of conversation, the easier it will be for you to understand what is being said. These findings have implications for improving the reading performance of poor readers. Basically, students could compensate for lower reading abilities by using or increasing their overall knowledge of what is being read. Take a situation where a child does not understand simple narrative books. To compensate, someone could read the story to the child so that he or she would be able to identify the names, places, and causal sequences in the text. This should lead to improved reading performance later on.

SECTION SUMMARY ■

Reading: Process, Instruction, and Individual Differences

Reading is neither universal nor biologically based; it must be taught. Two main processes allow the reader to take visual or gestural elements and understand the individual words. The first is called speech recoding; the second is visual recoding. In speech recoding the reader identifies the individual letters of a word, accesses the sounds of those letters, and creates a sound pattern for the entire word. This is transformed by the reader as if he or she were hearing and understanding the spoken word. In visual recoding, the reader recognizes the entire word and directly accesses this word in his or her lexicon to understand it. Neuropsychological case histories show that it is possible to understand words without being able to pronounce them, and pronouncing the individual letters does not guarantee that the person will be able to read. Both speech recoding and visual recoding probably go on at the same time, although at different speeds. Depending on the conditions, the one that finishes first is on the route to reading. Children most likely begin with speech recoding and then move to direct visual access. We all rely on speech recoding when we encounter a new or complex word. Many of the individual differences in reading skills are related to two factors: performing the sound–letter correspondences and the working memory span. Most people diagnosed with dyslexia have difficulty in decoding the written words into sound elements. They do not suffer from memory, vision, or hearing difficulties. In general, non-dyslexic people differ in their reading ability (including comprehension) because of limitations in their working memory capacity: The greater the working memory capacity (as measured by reading span tests) the greater the reading speed and comprehension. People who are considered poor readers (not dyslexic) can compensate for lower working memory capacity by using their long-term knowledge, which will ease the memory burden in reading comprehension.

CHAPTER SUMMARY

The seeds of adult language are planted in childhood. Children's acquisition of language follows an orderly sequence toward adult language. In every aspect of language function, all the components (semantics, syntax, medium, and pragmatics) come into play and influence the other components. Three theories jointly account for human speech perception: the motor theory, the interaction models, and the fuzzy logic model. Each is able to account for some of the findings of reading research and is consistent with neurological evidence.

Many words have multiple meanings, called ambiguity. The reader or listener's ability to understand the intended meaning of ambiguous words creates a demand on working memory because all meanings of a word are carried in memory until the clause boundary, when the reader makes a commitment to the dominant meaning. A psychologically relevant account of how we interpret sentences is described by case grammar. By using it, the listener is able to identify the thematically relevant components and store them in memory.

In natural language-based communication, both speaker and listener follow the utilization process: The listener seeks to identify which speech act the speaker is using. Then the listener tries to identify the given (known information) and the new information in the utterance so that he or she will know how to respond. The speaker tries to obey the given–new contract to ease the burden on the listener. When the consequence of the interaction is stored in memory, the primary coding is meaning or gist.

It is necessary to instruct people in reading because reading is not a biologically natural act. Two approaches to the teaching of reading skill are often used: direct access, which emphasizes visually identifying the whole-word, and indirect access, which emphasizes phonemic awareness. Modern cognitive research, using brain imaging and eye fixation methodologies, has assessed the theories of reading and made recommendations about curriculum.

KEY TERMS

QUESTIONS FOR REVIEW

Check Your Knowledge

1. What are the interaction models of language processing?

2. At what age does a child start to acquire his or her mother's language?

3. What is wrong with the idea that humans hear words because they are surrounded by silence in natural speech?

4. Do people make errors in segmenting (identifying) words? Why?

5. What is meant by "we hear what we expect to hear"?

6. What is word deafness? What does it tell us about hearing linguistic and nonlingustic sounds?

7. Do hearing people read lips? Why?

8. What is the McGurk effect?

9. What happens if a noise obscures a word when we are listening to someone speak? What type of theory accounts for this?

10. What is the cohort theory? Why is it called *cohort*?

11. How is the fuzzy logic theory similar to standard theories of perception?

12. The development of which form of aphasia is the reverse pattern of how speech and language develop?

13. What does conduction aphasia tell us about brain mechanisms or speech recognition and speech production?

14. Our mental lexicon contains what sorts of facts about words in addition to meaning?

15. When you hear an ambiguous word, does it slow down your comprehension of the utterance?

16. When do readers or listeners make a commitment to a single meaning of an ambiguous word?

17. Can you name three of the major cases in case grammar?

18. What missing case is created in the mind of the reader when processing the sentence, *Anna hit the nail into the board*?

19. If you ask your dinner companion, "can you pass the salt?" do you expect her to say, "yes, I've been working out"? Why not?

20. Suppose you ask your friend, "how was your date last night?" What maxim would the following answer violate, "he had nice shoelaces"?

21. In the sentence *Kevin saw the movie*, what is the *given* and what is the *new*?

22. Suppose in the last question you don't know anyone named Kevin. What do you need to do according to the utilization theory?

23. When we remember connected discourse, what is the central coding?

24. How does knowing the topic beforehand help you understand text?

25. What are the two primary processes in reading?

26. Which instructional techniques correspond to each process in the previous question?

27. What is the primary factor in dyslexia?

28. What happens when you try to teach phonics to people who are already readers?

29. What is the dual route hypothesis? How does it affect reading familiar and unfamiliar words?

30. Which test of memory span predicts skill in reading?

31. How long do we fixate on a word while reading it?

32. Who fixates on a word longer, skilled or unskilled readers?

33. If you are a poorly skilled reader, what's one thing you can do to increase your comprehension of a passage?

Apply Your Knowledge

1. Pragmatics is a universal component of natural human languages, but can we still communicate without it? What would our language be like if there were no cooperative and reality principles?

2. We try to be unambiguous when we communicate. However, can you attribute some value

to words having multiple meanings? Does ambiguity allow us to express shades of meaning? Can poetry exist without ambiguity in language?

3. According to the utilization process, *given* refers to what you already know, and *new* refers to the message. Can you design a communication system where there is only *new*? Where there is only *given*? How useful would these systems be in communicating with others?

4. A controversy currently rages in the United States about the best way to teach reading. Now that you are armed with the theories and research, select an article on the Internet and reply to it with the facts at your disposal from this chapter. Alternatively, imagine you are creating your own blog. Write an essay describing the best reading method for instructing a typical second grader and the best method for instructing a second grader considered to be dyslexic.

"It's not that I'm so smart; it's just that
I stay with problems longer.**"**

—Albert Einstein

When people imagine what cognitive psychology is about, they usually think of problem solving, reasoning, and decision making. It is traditional for cognitive psychology books to include a unit on these critical topics, which should be familiar by now because they have been included in the previous units. Memory includes problem solving because people typically have to construct answers to questions as if they were solving a problem; memory also involves making decisions about what you know. Language involves reasoning so that you can understand people's intentions from their words. This section adds something special, however, by examing in depth the central topics of problem solving, reasoning, and decision making because these cognitive abilities have rules and properties of their own that are important to an understanding of human cognition. These topics are at the core of the thinking processes that distinguish humans as sentient beings—thinking creatures. We plan, we decide, we create, and we calculate.

We are lifelong problem solvers. In childhood we put together jigsaw puzzles; as adults, we figure out how to move a wide table through a narrow doorway or arrange a weekly schedule to handle conflicting demands. Problem solving seems to be a part of everything we do every day. So how can we distinguish problem solving from all our other activities? A useful place to start is to define what a problem is. Imagine that there are two states of affairs: a *goal state* (a desired condition to be achieved) and a second condition, the *current state*, which is the situation you are in at the present time. A **problem** exists when the goal state and the current state are different. **Problem solving** occurs when the current state is transformed into the goal state—you have achieved your goal.

To see how this works, suppose you are to meet someone in the park and you are currently at home. This problem can be easily solved: All you have to do is transform the current state of affairs (*home*) into the goal state (*park*) by taking a route from home to the park and arriving there at the specified time. Alternatively, you could ask the person to meet you at home or transform the problem further by changing the time for the meeting. We solve problems like this one every day. One reason these types of problems are easy for us to solve is that we create and store in our memories a mental library of procedures for handling them. In Chapter 6 we showed that some of these solution methods seem to be stored in procedural memory and applied automatically. Other strategies are more deliberately and consciously applied and are part of the broader, declarative semantic memory described in Chapters 6 and 7.

This chapter describes what it takes for ordinary people to solve a problem. It focuses first on the most critical aspect of problem solving: how people represent the problem to be solved. This is critical because the effectiveness of the clever procedures that we have learned over a lifetime depend greatly on what we think the problem is.

Representing a Problem

Your search of prior solutions will be effective if your understanding of the problem in front of you activates the right solution stored in long-term memory. Your understanding of a problem including what facts it specifies, what it asks of you, and the methods you can use to solve it are collectively called your **representation** of the problem. Try Silveira's (1971) problem in Demonstration 11.1 before reading on.

■■■**DEMONSTRATION 11.1**

Solving a Problem by Changing the Representation

A woman was given four gold chains for her birthday. Each chain was three links long. She wanted to join the four chains into a single closed chain to make a necklace. However, having a link opened would cost $2 and having a link closed would cost $3. The woman had her chains joined into a closed necklace for $15. How did she do this?

Did you start by trying to open the end of each chain and then closing the link on the next chain? That would cost $20. People do this because they represent the problem in terms of a necklace four chains long. The breakthrough comes when you change how you represent the problem and think in terms of opening and closing links and trying to figure out how many links you would have to open and close. *Hint*: For every link you open ($2), you must close one ($3). To sum to $15, three links would have to be opened and then closed. Now, how can that be done (solution on p. 394)?

This challenge demonstrates that representation of a problem is the key to its solution. Sometimes the correct representation does not come right away. One study compared problem solvers who were given short or long breaks (up to 4 hours). Taking a long break is called *incubation* and it increased solution rates by nearly 50%, but only for the students who had worked on the problem for many hours before they took a break (Silveira, 1971). Incubation can be an effective strategy to solve a problem but only if you do the basic work beforehand.

How you imagine the problem in Demonstration 11.1 is critical to the solution you derive. Unfortunately, in this problem, you don't have any prior experience with the situation to know how to tackle it. When we apply learned knowledge or techniques to solve a problem, it's called **routine problem solving**. This term highlights the fact that we are applying previously successful procedures from memory. Solving routine problems tends to go smoothly and quickly. In contrast, **nonroutine problem solving** stresses the use of procedures or strategies that do not guarantee a solution to a problem but offer the possibility of success. Of course, what is a routine problem for an adult could be a nonroutine problem for a child. It all depends on what the solver knows (Schoenfeld, 1992).

Cognitive psychology investigates how people represent the problems they are asked to solve. In fact, a central idea in cognitive psychology is that representation is the key to understanding cognition. Consider the following problem, a version of one first presented by Duncker (1945) long ago:

> One morning, shortly after first light, a monk leaves his home at the bottom of a mountain and takes a path to the top as part of his weekly devotional. He climbs to the top of the mountain via its one and only path. He arrives at his destination, weary from his journey, just as the sun is about to set, and begins to meditate. Though he was sleepless all that night, he is invigorated by his meditation, and the next morning he sets off eagerly down the path—the one and only path—and reaches his home at the bottom of the mountain that evening. Just as he settles in for a well-deserved rest, his mind wanders to whether every event is unique and whether, for example, there was a place on the path that he passed at the same time on both days. With this he fell asleep.
>
> *(Koestler, 1964, p. 183)*

Is there a place on the path where the monk was at the same time on both days? What do you think: yes? no? can't tell? This problem is a wonderful example of the impact that representation has on the solution. When they first encounter the problem, students quickly sort themselves into the three response options. Those who respond no think there is definitely no place that the monk passes at the same time on both days; they give as their justification that (a) there are too many facets to the path and too many seconds in the day to have the same combination on both days, or (b) the path itself is not the same on both days. This is similar to the comment attributed to Heraclitus (540–480 BCE) nearly three millennia ago: "You can't put your foot into the same river twice" (cited in Plato, 360 BCE/2008). In the first instance, the student has represented the problem as one in which the outcome is implausible. In the second option, the philosophically oriented student denies the basic presupposition of the problem—that the monk, the path, space, and time are constant entities. This latter approach is an example of a problem-solving strategy in which you first decide whether a problem really exists.

Most students choose the can't tell option and argue that they cannot calculate an answer because they have too little information. They would like to know the monk's walking rate on both days, whether there are discontinuities in his travel (did he take a break and stop walking or ever leave the path?). They want to know the precise time that he left on each day, and so forth. They represent the situation as a rate-of-travel problem, and want to calculate the relationship between time and place. Many students begin with the assumption that the "spot," if it exists, would be halfway up the trail and want to confirm this assumption or modify it with rate-of-travel data.

FIGURE 11.1 Graphical Solution to the Monk Problem This shows the path that the monk took on both days. Notice that the paths intersect. This is the same place and time where the monk is on both days.

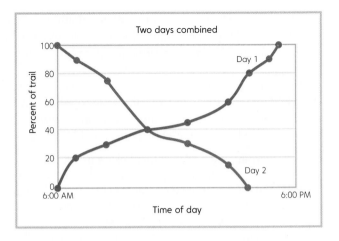

FIGURE 11.2 The Two-Monk Solution These graphs show the paths of the two monks: (A) one is going up the hill, and (B) one is going down the hill. They will meet on the path in a certain place and time.

Less than 10% of students are certain that there is a spot on the path. They generally arrive at this conclusion by imagining the problem as the intersection of two monks (one traveling up the path and one traveling down the path on the same day); they meet at some point (and time). On some occasions, students represent the problem as two graphs that describe the trajectories of the monk on 2 days. The trajectories are superimposed to make a single image that collapses the monk's 2-day activities into a single "day." The only obstacle to using this representation is seeing that the 2 days can be combined into a single graph. **FIGURES 11.1** and **11.2** graph the monk problem and show possible solutions when the solver says yes.

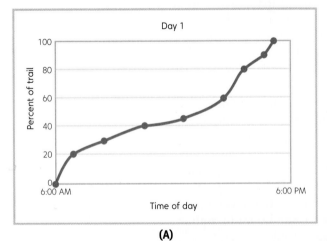

(A)

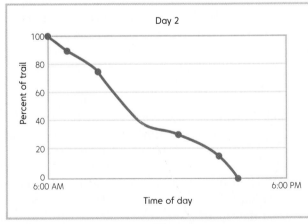

(B)

If you do not see the value of these two ways of representing the problem, fear not: One person's representation is not easily relinquished in favor of another's. Inability to solve a problem is not necessarily the result of failure to possess clever strategies, but of not creating the correct representation, which then allows you to apply a successful solution procedure. This is why the Einstein quotation that begins this chapter is so important: Einstein kept working on problems until he had the correct representation. Sometimes these came from unexpected places. After spending years working on a theory of quantum energy, Einstein was still unable to determine how atoms would behave in a gas under different temperatures. Then a former student, S. N. Bose, asked Einstein to look over his equations for a completely different problem—counting quanta of energy. These equations changed Einstein's view of the problem: Einstein then predicted that when atoms in a gas are close to absolute zero temperature, they would behave as one atom, like a wave—a fact that has now been tested and verified (e.g., Levy, Lahoud, Shomroni, & Steinhauer, 2007).

Albert Einstein in the Classroom One of the great minds of the last century solved critical problems in physics by relying on his mental imagery.

Keystone Pictures USA/Alamy

SECTION SUMMARY ▪

Representing a Problem

Problem solving is finding a way to reach a goal. The key to understanding human problem solving is how we represent the problem. This is illustrated with the gold chain and monk problems. Our understanding of the situation allows us to make use of personal knowledge or invent novel solution methods. However, as in the case of the gold chain, when we misinterpret the conditions, we may fail to appreciate the simple elements of the problem and not retrieve a successful solution method.

Types of Problems

Some problems, as we all know, are more difficult to solve than others. Some problems are so well specified that we can easily tell how to represent them, and we can then go to long-term memory to find the right solution method. Other problems seem to be wide open, with barely a hint of how to represent them. These two broad categories are called *well-defined* and *ill-defined problems* (e.g., Hayes, 1978; Newell & Simon, 1972; Reitman, 1964; Schraw, Dunkle, & Bendixen, 1995). They have special characteristics that influence the ease with which we can solve them.

Well-Defined Problems

The gold chain problem discussed before is quite simple. You need to determine the minimum number of openings and closings to connect the links. Once you see that there is basically only one option, the solution is clear. This is typical of **well-defined problems**, which possess distinctive properties: They have clearly described goals, they specify all relevant information, and a clear ending is obvious (you know when you have the solution). Well-defined problems are the kind you encounter in finding your way through a new city, planning your day, or choosing the best buy at a market. They can be difficult because you must decide how you will approach the problem, what methods you will use to solve it, and the best way to reach your goal.

Clearly Specified Goals It is characteristic of this type of problem to have unambiguous goals: how many pieces? what path is the shortest? who committed the crime? A good example is the *cryptarithmetic* problem (Newell & Simon, 1972; Schoenfeld, 1992): A student writes to his parents asking for money to complete the school term. Rather than simply stating the amount needed, he disguises it within a code, hoping his parents will be so impressed by his mathematical ability that they will be more likely to send the amount required. So the student's request is an arithmetic problem, except that the numbers are disguised as letters. There is a unique assignment of numbers (0–9) to letters (*D, E, M, O, N, R, S, Y*). Can you determine the amount the student is requesting?

$$\begin{array}{r} \text{SEND} \\ + \underline{\text{MORE}} \\ \text{MONEY} \end{array}$$

How might you tackle this problem? The first thing you need to do is to understand that the goal is to assign letters to numbers. The second step is to understand the constraints of the problem: The first constraint is that the number assignment is one-to-one, so that each letter has only one number assigned to it and each number has only one corresponding letter (*Hint*: $E = 5$). The second constraint is that the solution must conform to the rules of arithmetic, so you must process the columns of letters as you would numbers. For example, look at the *M* in MONEY. It is in the left-most column. Rules of arithmetic dictate that it must be 1 because the largest numbers that *S* and *M* can be are 8 and 9 and, even with a carry of 1, they cannot sum to more than 19. Hence the *M* in the last column can only be 1. What have you done here? You have established some arithmetic constraints and processed the column to fit with this constraint (solution on p. 394).

It is rare that you will find a real-world example of a cryptarithmetic problem like the one above (Dudeney, 1924). However, because people typically approach it in a limited number of ways, it has endured as a standard by which to judge the effectiveness of theories of problem solving for their ability to match the kinds of solutions that people produce (e.g., Ishaque et al., 2004; Newell & Simon, 1972).

All Relevant Information Another characteristic of well-defined problems is that the information necessary for a solution is given in the problem statement. This can be illustrated with a typical truth-teller/liar problem.

A crime has been committed and the police narrow the possible criminals down to four people, who each give a statement. The police deduce that one and only one statement is true, and the rest are false. Here are the statements. Who is the criminal?

Tom: Ann lied when she said I did it.

Bill: Ann did it.

Joe: I didn't do it.

Ann: Tom did it.

There are at least three ways to tackle this problem; each makes use of a little logic and the information given in the statements. Since there is only one true statement, the first way to approach the problem is to randomly (but systematically) assign *true* to one statement and *false* to the remaining ones and see whether the statements are consistent and whether they reveal the criminal. If not, you can apply this method over and over until a solution emerges. This could take a considerable period of time.

In a second approach, you could start with a hypothesis that a specific speaker is the criminal and use that information to decide which statements must be true and which must be false. You would keep doing this for each of the suspects until you arrived at a solution consistent with the problem constraints (one true statement). A third approach would be to search for any semantic inconsistencies between statements (e.g., Tom's and Ann's statements contradict each other). In such a case, you would know that one of the two statements must be true and one must be false. The rest of the statements in the problem have to be false (because the one true statement has just been used). Perhaps there are other ways to tackle the problem. The point to be made here is that any of these strategies uses only the information given in the problem (see the solution in **TABLE 11.1**).

To be effective, the methods used to solve the problems need to be sensitive to our memory limitations. At times it is difficult to solve well-defined problems because there are so many options to consider and it is difficult to keep track of the paths through the problem that have already been traversed (Hayes, 1989). One method that helps reduce the memory load in such problems and in everyday tasks is the use of a table to keep track of the facts. Table 11.1 tracks the truth-teller/liar problem. It consists of a list of speakers and whether or not they are hypothesized to be the criminal. This data structure allows you to keep track of your hypotheses and the truth-value assignments and permits you to keep applying the task constraints to tell you when you are done (when only one statement is true and the rest are false). This

TABLE 11.1

Truth-Teller/Liar Problem

Statement provider	Hypothesized criminals			
	Tom	Bill	Joe	Ann
Tom	F	T	T	T
Bill	F	F	F	T
Joe	T	T	F	T
Ann	T	F	F	F

Solution: Joe is the criminal.

example of a truth-teller/liar problem is more than a game for amusement; it reflects the kind of decisions police interrogators must make when they are trying to differentiate between pairs of truth-tellers and pairs of liars (e.g., Granhag, Stromwall, & Jonsson, 2003; Vrij et al., 2009).

A Clear Ending   The final characteristic of well-defined problems is that there is a stop rule. You are done when you have computed how many chain links have to be opened and closed, or the cryptarithmetic code has been broken and the money requested is understood, or the criminal is identified. The examples of well-defined problems that we have considered here have unique solutions: Only one solution can be derived with total certainty.

We solve well-defined problems throughout our everyday lives, from simple arithmetic to calculating the product with the best price in a supermarket; from planning the shortest route on a road trip to the most comfortable shoes to wear; and from how to bake a cake to which approach to a snowboard jump will give the longest air time. These and so many more tasks are examples of problems that have clearly specified goals, include all relevant knowledge, and have a clear ending or goal point. They are all well-defined problems.

Ill-Defined Problems

Ill-defined problems are often more challenging and more interesting than well-defined problems. With an **ill-defined problem**, it is not always clear what the question really is, or how to arrive at a solution, or what a solution would look like (VanLehn, 1989). You may have experienced these types of problems in open-ended questions where there is no fixed answer. They are **open domain** topics because you are free to consider any kind of information you want. Some examples of ill-defined problems include:

What career should I pursue?

How can I be happy?

Is this person the love of my life?

Is honesty the right action if it hurts someone's feelings?

You will notice that although there is no logically necessary solution to these four problems, some solutions will seem clearly better than others (e.g., Goel, 1992; Rittel & Webber, 1973).

Ill-defined problems can be physical as well as abstract. Demonstration 11.2 includes a well-researched ill-defined problem, the nine-dot problem, which has some well-defined components (Maier, 1930). Like other ill-defined problems, all the constraints in the nine-dot problem are not fully specified, and certainly the methods to be used are unclear. In fact, some of the constraints are actually invented by the problem solvers themselves (Kershaw & Ohlsson, 2004). It is only when the problem solver is able to relax these self-imposed constraints that a solution appears (Knoblich, Ohlsson, Haider, & Rhenius, 1999). To experience this directly, try the problem.

▪▪▪DEMONSTRATION 11.2

The Nine-Dot Problem

Your task is to draw a line through each of the dots by drawing no more than four straight lines without retracing a line or lifting the pencil from the paper. You might wish to make many copies of these dots on a separate piece of paper because the correct solution often requires a good bit of trial and error (Maier, 1930). (*Hint*: It is ok for the lines to extend outside the 3 × 3 array; solution on p. 394.)

The Neuropsychology of Moral Reasoning The nine-dot problem illustrates a major difficulty in addressing ill-defined problems: You never know what constitutes a full set of constraints or assumptions, and you can never be sure that you have constructed the "right" answer. This is even more strikingly the case in the following version of the trolley dilemma (Foot, 1978, p. 23):

> A trolley is running out of control down a track. In its path are five people who have been tied to the track by a mad philosopher. You can flip a switch, which will lead the trolley down a different track and avoid the five people. Unfortunately, there is a single person tied to that track. If you flip the switch, that person will be killed. Should you flip the switch?

What would you do? When university students are asked to make such a decision, 90–95% decide to flip the switch and sacrifice the one person for the many (e.g., J. D. Greene & Haidt, 2002; J. D. Greene, Sommerville, Nystrom, Darley, & Cohen, 2001; Valdesolo & DeSteno, 2006). In contrast, a superficially similar dilemma (Thomson, 1976, pp. 207–208) yields a different response:

> Suppose that in the trolley dilemma, you are sitting on a footbridge over the trolley tracks and a large stranger is sitting nearby. If you were to push him onto the tracks, his body would stop the trolley and save the five people. Would you push him onto the tracks?

Less than 10% of university students would sacrifice the one man to save the five people. The footbridge version of the problem produces more negative emotion in the problem solvers than does the first problem (J. D. Greene, Nystrom, Engell, Darley, & Cohen, 2004). As we noted in Chapter 5, negative emotion tends to interrupt basic cognitive processes (Klein & Boals, 2001b; Simon, 1967). To explore this consequence, students were placed in a happy mood by watching comedy clips from a TV show. Afterward, 25% chose to sacrifice the man on the footbridge to save the five people (Valdesolo & DeSteno, 2006). Positive emotions allowed them sufficient working memory to make the calculation of the greatest good for the greatest number.

The first moral problem is called **impersonal reasoning** because it relies on a calculation that can be applied to any topic and doesn't involve the reasoner (J. D. Green et al., 2001). It is so basic that even a chimpanzee can appreciate it; perhaps we actually inherited our sensitivity to this kind of reasoning from our

FIGURE 11.3 Brain Areas Activated by Personal and Impersonal Reasoning The two types of moral reasoning, personal and impersonal, are associated with the activation of different areas of the brain. When we engage in personal reasoning, there is increased activation in the medial frontal gyrus and the posterior cingulate gyrus. When we reason about impersonal dilemmas, there is increased activity in the areas associated with working memory that are required to make calculations: the dorsolateral prefrontal cortex and parietal areas.

Reprinted from *Trends in Cognitive Sciences*, 6, Greene, J.D. and Haidt, J. Moral Reasoning. How (and where) does moral judgment work? 517–523, 2002 with permission from Elsevier.

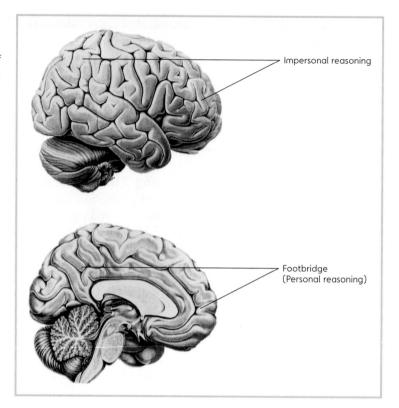

Impersonal reasoning

Footbridge
(Personal reasoning)

prehuman ancestors (J. D. Greene & Haidt, 2002). The second problem is called **personal reasoning** because it involves the deliberate inflicting of serious harm on a person by direct action ("I hurt you" or "you hurt me").

The distinctions between these two types of moral reasoning are not just based on a philosophical analysis; they are also associated with the activation of different areas of the brain (see **FIGURE 11.3**). Greene et al. (2001) asked volunteers to respond to these two types of dilemmas while their brains were being scanned and found that when they were engaged in personal reasoning (footbridge-type problems), there was increased activation in the medial frontal gyrus and the posterior cingulate gyrus. In contrast, when they were reasoning about impersonal dilemmas, such as throwing a switch, the researchers documented increased activity in the areas associated with working memory that are required to make calculations: the dorsolateral prefrontal cortex and parietal areas.

The Influence of Culture Solutions to these ill-defined dilemmas require judgments that combine moral, emotional, and cultural components. You need only have watched the TV show *24* to witness how people with different backgrounds respond to moral issues (e.g., when the lead character Jack Bauer tortures someone). To experience this interplay of moral and cultural factors further, try the activity in Demonstration 11.3.

■■■DEMONSTRATION 11.3

The Effect of Culture on Problem Solving

Your ship has sunk at sea. You are in the ocean with your mother, your spouse, and your child. Because of your poor swimming ability and the absence of any flotation device, you can only save one other person from drowning. Whom would you save, and why?

This problem has been presented to cognitive psychology classes for years. The typical solution varies with culture: The dominant response among young American university students is to save the spouse (50%), then to save the child (45%), and last, to save the mother (5%). The typical argument for saving the spouse is that

(a) you made a commitment to this person;

(b) with the spouse you can always have another child;

(c) the mother is old and would not expect to be saved.

A strikingly different solution profile occurs among Middle-Eastern cultures. There, the dominant solution is to save the mother (85%), then the child (8%), then the spouse (7%), with the last two about equally selected. The reasons given are:

(a) you only have one mother;

(b) you can always have another spouse;

(c) you can always have another child.

Cognitive Skills in Well-Defined and Ill-Defined Problem Solving

Well-defined and ill-defined problems require different types of cognitive skills. People who are skilled at well-defined problems are not necessarily successful with ill-defined problems, and vice versa (e.g., Schraw et al., 1995). Both types of problems require two of the same skills: (a) an ability to reason and draw inferences, and (b) an ability to monitor whether the reasoning is progressing correctly. This type of self-monitoring is called **metacognition**. It is a critical aspect of all reasoning and problem solving described in the chapters in this unit. In addition to these two skills, ill-defined problems also require a third skill, **epistemic monitoring** (Greeno, 1989; Kitchener, 1983). This skill reflects the problem solvers' ability to tell whether they are creating a legitimate representation and whether they are using the correct understanding and appropriate methods to solve the problem.

You can see the difference between metacognition and epistemic monitoring in the rescue at sea problem. Metacognition informs you whether you have rescued the correct number of people and whether you understand the problem correctly. Epistemic monitoring tells you whether the solution is satisfying and corresponds to your stored values. Ill-defined problems require all three skills, whereas well-defined problems typically require only the first two. Differences among people in solving ill-defined problems often reflect differences in beliefs and values (e.g., Kardash & Scholes, 1996).

Framing a Problem: The Role of Values

A special characteristic of both well-defined and ill-defined problems is that the solver's approach to the problem is influenced by how the problem is contextualized or framed. You can see this in a simple evaluation situation. If you were asked to rate a meat product, which of the following descriptions seem better?

(a) The meat is 75% lean.

(b) The meat is 25% fat.

In one study, college students rated meat as better tasting when it was labeled (a) rather than (b), even though there was no difference between the two servings (Levin & Gaeth, 1988). In another study, when condoms were said to be 95% effective in preventing the spread of HIV, college students said that they were more likely to use them than when they were described as having a 5% failure rate (Linville, Fischer, & Fischhoff, 1993). **Framing** reflects how a situation's description influences the kind of representation the solver establishes, which in turn can affect the methods used to solve the problem.

The influence of framing is especially strong in ill-defined problems. The two scenarios presented in Demonstration 11.4 were given to different groups of students to solve (Tversky & Kahneman, 1981). When you solve Problem B, pretend that you have not already solved Problem A. For an explanation of the solutions, return to the text.

■■■DEMONSTRATION 11.4

Framing in Problem Solving

Problem A

Imagine that you have decided to see a play where admission is $10 for a ticket. As you approach the ticket booth you discover that you have lost a $10 bill sometime during the day. Would you still pay $10 for a ticket to the play if you had at least $10 remaining in your wallet? (*yes* or *no*)

Problem B

Imagine that you have decided to see a play and paid the admission price of $10 for a ticket. As you enter the theater, you discover that you have lost the ticket sometime during the day. The seat was not marked and the ticket cannot be recovered. Would you pay $10 for another ticket? (*yes* or *no*)

Tversky and Kahneman (1981) reported that 88% of their university students said yes in Problem A (they would spend $10 for a ticket). In contrast, only 46% said yes in Problem B. Notice that the two problems are logically equivalent: loss of a $10 ticket or loss of a $10 bill. Yet, the judgments are different. In answer to Problem A, the students reportedly said that in life you occasionally lose money and, if you have more money, then it's acceptable to use what you have remaining to buy something. In contrast, in Problem B, the majority of the students said that because you lost the ticket, you should pay the penalty and not buy another ticket: You lost your ticket and your right to go to the show. Although the monetary value of the loss is the same in both problems, people behave differently depending on how the loss is framed. In Problem A the loss is $10 from a pool of money, but in Problem B, the loss is permission to see the show. The $10 is only part of the meaning of the loss.

In an ill-defined problem, calculation may be tempered by meaning. One characteristic of framing is that the quantities in ill-defined problems have values other than their pure numerical amounts. In the ticket problem, the value or meaning of the $10 is different in the two situations. The representation in the two situations is quite different. In the case of gains and losses, numbers are often not amounts: They are *values* whose worth is framed by the context.

SECTION SUMMARY

Types of Problems

Two broad categories of problems are related to the methods people use to solve them: well-defined and ill-defined. Well-defined problems have clearly specified goals; all of the necessary information is given in the statement of the problem. The end condition is clear: You know when you have achieved the goal, or not. In contrast, ill-defined problems have vaguely specified goals, incomplete statements of the necessary means to achieve the goal, and often it is not clear when to stop. Ill-defined problems are sensitive to the values of the reasoner. They show the influence of culture on reasoning and how important the framing of the problem is to the representation of the situation. One type of ill-defined problem is a moral dilemma. When confronting personal dilemmas, solvers show activity in their medial frontal gyrus and the posterior cingulate gyrus in addition to the areas of the frontal lobes that are found in solving impersonal dilemmas. Two cognitive skills are important to both well-defined and ill-defined problems: (a) ability to reason, and (b) metacognition (the ability to monitor whether the steps of the problem solution are proceeding correctly). An additional skill is especially necessary for ill-defined problems: epistemic monitoring (evaluating whether the solution and its components are satisfying).

Problem Solving by Analogical Reasoning

Often we encounter problems that are similar to ones we have solved before. There is a special kind of problem solving in which people compare the current problem to similar ones they have encountered in the past: **Analogical reasoning** is based on noticing similarities between current and prior problems. This way of solving problems, by analogy to what you already know, is typical of people answering common, everyday questions (Blanchette & Dunbar, 2002; Hofstadter, 2007; Pinker, 2007). When you look ahead on a road and see that the other drivers are driving into a traffic jam, you might say to yourself, "The drivers are like a herd of sheep driving into a traffic jam and creating a bigger one; I'll think for myself and take a detour." Or perhaps,

Analogies in Everyday Life
People driving into traffic like a herd of sheep.

Stephen Johnson/Getty Images

faced with a sloppy roommate, you might think, "The laundry on the floor is like a trail of cookie crumbs leading to the culprit." In wondering whether you should speak up and ask for a pay raise, you might say, "The squeaky wheel gets the grease."

We use our basic knowledge to fill in the gaps in our knowledge in order to solve everyday problems (Collins, 1978), or even technical problems about how machinery or the human body work (Console & Torasso, 1990). In fact, we do this most of the time when answering questions.

Analogical reasoning is a common means of understanding new findings in scientific domains (e.g., Dreistadt, 1968; Dunbar, 1997; Dunbar & Blanchette, 2001) and can be an enormous aid to effective problem solving (Duncker, 1945; Polya, 1957). Nearly all milk is purified for us to drink by a method called *pasteurization*. Louis Pasteur created his germ theory of disease by reasoning that germs cause fermentation in grapes, and since human diseases are like fermentation, they must be caused by germs. Unfortunately, if laboratory studies are any guide, most people are dismal failures at creating analogies on their own without special help. Even in science, analogies can often be incorrect and throw research off the track. For example, physicist Niels Bohr had the idea that the atom had a similar structure to the solar system, with the nucleus in the middle and electrons running around like planets. In fact, the structure of the atom is more like a cloud of energy around a central core, acting like a wave.

In a systematic series of studies of analogical reasoning, Duncker (1945) presented students with a challenging problem and discovered that people do poorly on analogical reasoning. Here is a version of the original problem:

Suppose you are a doctor faced with a patient who had a malignant tumor in his stomach. It is impossible to operate on the patient, but unless the tumor is destroyed, the patient will die. There is a kind of ray that may be used to destroy the tumor. If the rays reach the tumor all at once and with sufficiently high intensity, the tumor will be destroyed, but surrounding tissue may be damaged as well. At lower intensities the rays are harmless to healthy tissue, but they will not affect the tumor either. What type of procedure might be used to destroy the tumor with the rays, and at the same time avoid destroying the healthy tissue?

(Gick & Holyoak, 1980, pp. 307–308)

Student responses ranged from general solutions, such as *avoid contact with healthy tissue* or *lower intensity of rays as they're passing through tissue*, to very specific solutions: *insert a tube* or *use a lens*. Modern medical solutions to this very real problem are similar to the *use a lens* response. Physicians bombard the tumor with low-level radiation from many different angles, but all focused on the tumor. This is a difficult problem to solve; across a large number of studies, the solution rate is typically less than 10% (Mayer, 1992).

You may think that if students were given a simpler version of the problem to solve, they would reason by analogy and be able to solve the more complex tumor problem. This is just what Gick and Holyoak (1980) did. They first gave students a military problem similar to the following:

> A dictator ruled a country from a strong fortress. Many roads radiated out-ward from the fortress like spokes on a wheel. A general who vowed to capture the fortress and free the country knew that if his entire army could attack the fortress at once, it could be captured. However, the dictator had planted mines on each of the roads. The mines were set so that small bodies of men could pass over them safely, but any large force would detonate the mines. A full-scale direct attack on the fortress appeared impossible.
>
> The general was undaunted. He divided his army into small groups and dispatched each to the head of a different road. When all was ready, each group charged down a different road. All of the small groups passed safely over the mines, and the army then attacked the fortress in full strength. In this way, the general was able to capture the fortress and overthrow the dictator.
>
> *(Gick & Holyoak, 1983, p. 3)*

Do you see the parallel between the fortress and the tumor stories: *a central core to be challenged by means of dispersion of an external force*? The students seemed to understand the military story and its solution, yet only 20% used the dispersion solution for the tumor problem. Most students saw no relation between the two stories. In case the students didn't appreciate the principle involved in the fortress story, Gick and Holyoak (1983) summarized it for some of the students:

> If you need a large force to accomplish some purpose, but are prevented from applying such a force directly, many smaller forces applied from different directions may work just as well. (p. 16)

Summarizing the principle—convergence of forces—did not help students draw an analogy from the fortress to the tumor problems. Nor did drawing a picture for them. However, when some students were given direct instructions to use the solution of the fortress problem in order to solve the tumor problem, 92% solved the problem with the dispersion method (Gick & Holyoak, 1980). When diagrams are coupled with hints, the diagram can also be effective (Pedone, Hummel, & Holyoak, 2001). Based on these findings, the critical factor in solving problems by analogy is being instructed to do so; people don't do it spontaneously. This has important implications for instructing children in school (VanLehn,

1996). Teachers should not assume that showing a method of solving one problem will cause students to generalize the method to solving any other problem.

One way to help students do analogical reasoning other than directly telling them to do it is to give them many examples of the desired type of solution. In one study, students read two stories about converging forces before trying to solve the tumor problem. For some students, both stories had the same military theme. Other students read two stories with different topics: one was about the fortress and one was about firefighting. The group that read two seemingly different stories produced the best results (Gick & Holyoak, 1983). Problem solvers seem better able to identify critical elements for a solution when they solve the same kind of problem but in a different context (Holyoak & Koh, 1987).

Analogical reasoning occurs frequently when we are asked to solve problems in a **closed domain**, which is one where all the information may be learned and all questions about the contents of the domain are definitely answerable, just as in well-defined problems. If someone were to ask whether Sao Paulo is the capital of Uruguay, you could answer, "no, it is a city in Brazil," or "no, the capital of Uruguay is Montevideo." Or, you could just respond, "don't know, it's not in my database." The important thing about closed domains is how people respond to questions about them. Often when people have only fragmentary knowledge in a closed domain, they will answer about their incomplete knowledge by drawing an inference from what they know and reason by analogy (Collins & Michalski, 1989; Collins, Warnock, Aiello, & Miller, 1975). For example, if you were to ask a student how many piano tuners there are in New York City, the student might reason:

> Well, here in New Haven there are 3 or 4 in a city that has about 300,000 people. That's about 1 per 100,000. New York has about 7 million people, so that would make 70. I'll say 50 or 60.
>
> *(Collins et al., 1975, p. 405)*

This student is reasoning by analogy from facts known about New Haven and assumes that the number of piano tuners increases linearly with the population. After this, analogical reasoning is performed and the student makes a correction as if there were some upper limit to the number of piano tuners (instead of saying 70, he says 50 or 60).

SECTION SUMMARY ■

Problem Solving by Analogical Reasoning

Sometimes a solution to one problem can be used to solve a different problem. This is called analogical reasoning, and it requires that the problem solver notice a correspondence between the two problems. As important as this form of problem solving is in dealing with everyday as well as scientific problems, college students have not shown that they can readily bridge the gap between a new problem and a structurally similar one they have experienced before. They are helped, however, by being given hints on the mapping between the problems or at least being told that there is one. Problem solvers are also helped by solving the same kind of problem in different contexts (Holyoak & Koh, 1987). In classroom settings we often use analogical reasoning by using one set of facts to answer questions about another set of facts about which we only have partial information. This is a type of analogical reasoning called reasoning from incomplete knowledge and is most often used when people reason about information in closed domains, where all of the information may be learned (as occurs in well-defined problems), as opposed to open domains where the "facts" depend on your point of view (as occurs in ill-defined problems).

Problem Solving Through Insight and Creativity

People are able to solve some problems by methodically working on them, one step at a time. They know they are moving in the right direction. However, on other problems they seem to be heading for failure but then suddenly perceive the solution to the problem, a kind of *aha!* experience that we call **insight**. On occasion, solutions seem to be both useful and unusual, in which case we say that they show **creativity**.

Insight

To see the difference between problems that require insight and those that do not, try the two problems (from Restle & Davis, as cited in Metcalfe & Wiebe, 1987, p. 244) in Demonstration 11.5.

▪▪▪DEMONSTRATION 11.5

Puzzles

Problem 1

If the puzzle you solved before you solved this one was harder than the puzzle you solved after you solved the puzzle you solved before you solved this one, was the puzzle you solved before you solved this one harder than this one?

Problem 2

Without lifting your pencil from the paper, show how you could join all four dots with two straight lines.

(Solutions are shown on p. 394.)

People typically experience Problem 1 as difficult, but they can see that their procedure is leading to a solution. Problem 2, similar to the nine-dot problem presented in Demonstration 11.2, is often frustrating. In a study of problem solving with these types of problems, students were asked to indicate every 15 seconds whether they were getting closer ("warmer") to a solution or further away ("colder"; Metcalfe & Wiebe, 1987). For the noninsight problems such as Problem 1, students felt progressively warmer as they worked the problem. On an insight problem such as Problem 2, students only started feeling warmer just before they solved the problem. It is as if in order to solve the insight problem, they had to change their mental representation of it (Anderson & Lebiere, 1998; Davidson, 1995; Duncker, 1945; Knoblich, Ohlsson, & Raney, 2001). When they did that, they were able to solve the problem.

To achieve insight means to overcome an impasse and to understand the basic structure of a problem. In a sense, all problem solving is insight except for problems to which we automatically respond correctly (such as avoiding a car while we are crossing a street). To see that problems can vary in the degree to which they involve insight, try the problems (Knoblich et al., 2001) in Demonstration 11.6.

■■■DEMONSTRATION 11.6

Matchstick Problems

Here are three problems, labeled A, B, and C. In each problem you are faced with an incorrect arithmetic statement that is expressed in Roman numerals (constructed from matchsticks). Your task is to correct the arithmetic statements by moving only one matchstick in each equation (Knoblich et al., 2001, pp. 1001–1002).

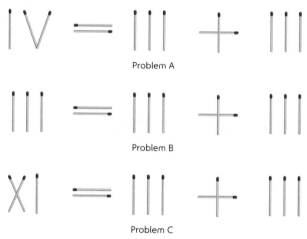

Problem A

Problem B

Problem C

In solving matchstick problems, people focus first on the quantities as the relevant object to manipulate; they do not think of the arithmetic operators (e.g., the equal or plus signs) as something that can change. Because of this, people tend to experience Problem A as the easiest, and 90% of students solve it. It simply requires moving the vertical stick on the left (that makes IV) to the right side of the V, thereby making a Roman numeral 6 (VI). Problem B is more difficult for two reasons. First, it requires changing the plus sign into another equal sign. This violates what people think can change in an equation. Second, it requires rethinking what an equation can look like: III = III = III. The solution rate for this problem is about 35%. Problem B definitely requires a change in under-standing the nature of an arithmetic equation. Problem C requires substantial insight because the problem solver needs to focus on the way the number is constructed and must slide the left-slanted stick that is part of X to the left to create a V, which results in the equation VI = III + III. Seventy-five percent of students are able to solve it.

Solving Problems B and C involves more insight than does Problem A. To show this, researchers recorded the eye movements of participants while they solved the problems, which revealed that in the first few minutes of trying and failing to solve the problems, there was no difference in where the students looked. However, in the last minute, those who ultimately solved the problem radically shifted their gazes away from the elements that are obstacles to a solution and to the area necessary to solve the problem. This new focus of attention corresponds to the *aha!* experience in which the students changed their understanding of the nature of the problem (Knoblich et al., 2001).

This research tells us that not only is the experience of insight related to a change in the mental representation of a problem, but it is also a matter of degree. All problem solving requires some amount of insight, which is occasionally experienced as a distinct change from the representation used initially. This is what gives us a sense of *aha!*

Creativity

Some solutions to ill-defined problems seem amazingly novel, somewhat unconventional, and useful: When we have all of these together, we say the solution is *creative* (Mumford & Gustafson, 1988; Newell, Shaw, & Simon, 1962; Tardif & Sternberg, 1988). To gain a sense of creative solutions, look at the examples in Demonstration 11.7.

▪▪▪DEMONSTRATION 11.7

Creative Solutions

1. What do you think the drawing in (A) (which was used on a Frank Zappa album cover) is about? (See answers to these questions on p. 394.)

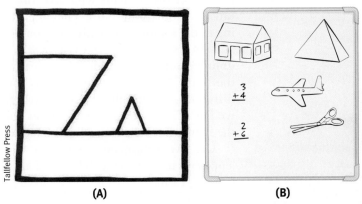

Tallfellow Press

(A) (B)

2. Circle 5 things that are alike in the picture in (B).

3. Why did the elephant stand on the marshmallow?

These simple examples capture one aspect of creative problem solving: They reflect the solver's willingness to discard preconceived assumptions and produce new ideas or actions.

One of the earliest studies of creative problem solving is now called the *two-string problem* (Maier, 1931). In that study, the participant entered a large room that contained many objects: poles, clamps, pliers, extension cords, tables, and chairs. Most important, there were two strings hanging from the ceiling to the floor. One was hung near a wall, the other in the center of the room. The situation is illustrated in **FIGURE 11.4**. The participant's task was to tie the ends of the two strings together. Alas, if the participant held either cord in one hand, he or she could not reach the other. However, the participant was allowed to use anything in the room that he or she wished. There were four basic solutions:

1. One cord was tied to a chair and placed part way between the cords and then the other cord was brought over to it.

2. One of the cords was lengthened with an extension cord and the other cord could be reached with a hand.

3. While holding one cord, the other was pulled with a pole.

4. Pliers were tied to the cord hanging from the center of the room and then put in motion, making it a pendulum; the other cord was brought near the center and the swinging cord was caught as it approached.

FIGURE 11.4 The Two String Problem The participant's task is to tie the two strings hanging from the ceiling together. This can be done if one of the strings is held and the other is swung. In the most creative solution, the participant ties one of the objects on the floor to the string so it can swing far enough to be reached (Maier, 1931).

Bianca Moscatelli/Worth Publishers

Only 39% of the participants were able to solve the problem without being given hints. The author of the study considered the fourth solution the most creative because it clearly had not been seen in other situations before. Eighty percent of the students who used this solution did so within 10 minutes. They reported coming to the solution suddenly, as a complete idea, and not incrementally. One reason why the pendulum solution is considered so creative is that the string had to be thought of as something different—a pendulum—not a string. When we fail to see a new function for an object like the string, it is called **functional fixedness**.

Creative performance on the two-string problem seems to contain the following four elements (Wallas, 1926).

1. *Preparation:* The solver thinks about what the problem requires and keeps it in memory.

2. *Incubation:* The solver's mind engages in unconscious activation of critical elements and past solutions, although they may not be available to conscious thought.

3. *Illumination/insight:* The unconscious processing bursts into conscious awareness.

4. *Verification:* The new awareness is applied to the problem.

These four characteristics of the creative process do not sound extraordinary. Indeed, a major analysis of creativity shows that it is produced by processes that everyone at one time or another experiences (Weisberg, 1993). What is critical is that the elements are assembled at a particular moment. Cognitive psychologists have studied the factors that contribute to the ability of people to activate these essential elements of creative problem solving. One of the reliable findings is somewhat surprising: Emotion promotes creativity in problem solving (Isen, Daubman, & Nowicki, 1987).

The Role of Emotion

A positive mood can influence a person's ability to solve problems. This was illustrated by the performance of university students in a problem-solving task (Isen et al., 1987). Two groups of university students were shown either a 5-minute film of comedy bloopers from TV shows (the positive mood condition) or a 5-minute film taken from a math lesson (the neutral mood condition). They were then given a problem-solving task. It consisted of looking at a table that contained a book of matches, a box of tacks, and a candle. Above the table was a corkboard. Students were told that their task was to affix the candle to the corkboard so that the candle would burn without dripping wax on the table or floor. This task has long been used to assess creative problem solving and functional fixedness (Duncker, 1945). The solution is to use the tacks to affix the box to the board, then put the candle on top of the box and light it with a match.

This is a difficult task, because the students need to see the items in an untypical way: the box as a platform, the tacks (inside the box) as tools to affix the box, and so on. In fact, only 20% of the neutral group was able to solve the problem in 10 minutes. However, 75% of the positive mood group was able to solve the problem. These effects are not limited to watching a funny movie. A person's mood can be elevated by sniffing a pleasant fragrance (R. A. Baron & Thomley, 1994) or even being given a bag of candy before a task (but not eating the candy while doing the task; Erez & Isen, 2002).

One conclusion from this and many other studies is that positive mood increases the number and range of cognitive elements available to the solver to bring together: This is the incubation process described before. Positive mood also increases flexibility, so that more diverse elements become associated: This is the insight component.

The Neuroscience of Creativity

In reading about creativity, you may have wondered how mood can affect it. What is the connection between emotion and problem solving? The simple answer is that a person's mood can affect the production of the neurotransmitter dopamine, which in turn influences the activity of parts of the brain that contribute to problem solving and to creativity (Dreisbach & Goschke, 2004; T. R. Greene & Noice, 1988). The theory that accounts for this is called the **dopaminergic theory of positive affect (DTPA)** and was developed by Ashby, Isen, and Turken (1999). It has three central elements. First, the neurotransmitter dopamine and the circuits in the brain that use it are especially active when people experience positive mood. You may already know that drugs that cause an increase in the presence of dopamine, such as morphine, cocaine, and amphetamine, elevate positive mood (e.g., Beatty, 1995). Second, the dopamine circuit is critical to activity in the prefrontal cortex, which plays a central role in human working memory (Goldman-Rakic, 1995) and problem solving. People who suffer from Parkinson's disease, for example, have reduced dopamine levels in their prefrontal cortex and as a result show losses in their working memory functioning (Williams & Goldman-Rakic, 1995). This loss is reversed when they are given medications such as L-dopa, which increase brain dopamine levels (Lange et al., 1992).

The third element of the DTPA concerns the relationship between dopamine, the prefrontal cortex, and an area of the brain called the *anterior cingulate cortex.* This connection is responsible for cognitive flexibility: the ability to switch from one way of looking at a situation to another (e.g., Moore & Oaksford, 2002; Posner & Peterson, 1990). This ability relies on both working memory and the ability to switch attention to something different. This, of course, is a characteristic of creative problem solving. With these three elements, DTPA is able to show how a person's emotional state can affect the brain, with critical results for creativity.

SECTION SUMMARY ■

Problem Solving Through Insight and Creativity

People may have difficulty solving a problem because their initial representation of it creates a kind of obstacle, causing them to focus on irrelevant elements. The solution can come relatively quickly when the solver establishes a new representation of the problem and focuses on relevant elements. In such cases, people are said to have insight into the problem. All problems require some degree of insight; some lead to a rapid solution and cause people to exclaim *aha!*

An especially valued and rare aspect of problem solving occurs when the solution is seen as creative. In such cases, solutions have four characteristics: preparation, incubation, illumination/insight, and verification. Positive mood seems to promote these kinds of solutions by means of a dopamine circuit in the brain explained by the dopaminergic theory of positive affect.

Problem Solving Through Rule Discovery

The process of making discoveries and communicating about them has characterized modern human history since the days of our ancestral hunter-gatherers, who occupied themselves trying to figure out how to catch food for their extended families (e.g., Premack & Premack, 2003). Discovering rules that help us understand nature has been true for modern humans, especially scientists. Much of psychological research on how people discover rules and test hypotheses shows that most people, even scientists, make errors in scientific reasoning (e.g., Tweney & Yachanin, 1985). How is this possible?

Disconfirmation and Confirmation Biases

To understand this finding, we first have to examine the discovery process and how it has been studied. We begin with the traditional view of scientific reasoning: Someone makes an observation, generates a hypothesis, and then tries to test the hypothesis with new observations. Philosophers of science have established rules for how hypothesis testing should be done. They tell us that anyone trying to test a hypothesis—including scientists—should follow a process called **disconfirmation** (e.g., Platt, 1964; Popper, 1972). This means that testing your hypothesis requires you to try to falsify it—to try to find a way that it might not be true.

Falsifying your hypothesis is important because, although you can always find some support for a hypothesis, support doesn't make it true. For example, suppose you have the hypothesis that *all swans are white.* It does you no good to keep looking at hundreds of white birds to see if they are swans—some of the white birds may be swans and some may not. The critical test is to look at black birds (or another color) and see if any of them are swans. If you find any (as there are in Australia), then you know your hypothesis is false. Performing disconfirming experiments does not mean that scientists want or even expect that their own hypothesis will be false; what they may want to see is that a competing hypothesis is falsified (Popper, 1972).

We use disconfirmation occasionally in our everyday lives. When we want to challenge someone's assertion, we offer a counterexample. If someone were to say, "every bird flies south for the winter," all we need to answer is, "chickens don't fly south and chickens are birds." If someone were to make a claim that some stereotype about another person or group is true, a counterexample disconfirms the assertion (Wyer, 2004).

In order to measure disconfirmation in the laboratory, researchers have used a procedure called the *2–4–6 task* (Wason, 1960, 1968). Students are asked to discover an arithmetic rule concerning triples of numbers that the experimenter has in mind. Focus on Methods invites you to try the task yourself and learn about research that investigates how we test our hypotheses.

For many people the disconfirmation sequence is counterintuitive: It asks them to formulate a rule and then come up with a triple of numbers that would violate that rule in the hopes of receiving a negative response from the experimenter.

FOCUS ON METHODS ■■■■■■■■■■■■■■■■■■■■■■■■■■■■

The 2–4–6 Task

Mother Nature is thinking of a rule that governs triples of numbers (three numbers in a group). She gives you an example of a triple that conforms to her rule. Your job is to discover her rule. You do this by formulating a hypothesis and testing it by creating a triple of numbers that tests your hypothesis. Mother Nature tells you whether the triple conforms to her rule. You in turn use this information to decide whether your hypothesis is correct or not. The example triple that Mother Nature gives you is 2–4–6.

What hypothesis would you formulate? Most people immediately imagine that the rule is either (a) even numbers, (b) numbers increasing by 2, or (c) the second number is 2 times the first and the third number is 3 times the first (Farris & Revlin, 1989b). At this point in the task you must test your hypothesis. How will you select a triple to do that? This is not an easy decision. Typical experiments offered by students are: 4–8–12; then 10–100–1,000 and 6–8–12; and sometimes 1–2–3. Did you think of any of these? Over many studies of this sort of reasoning, the success rate of university students rarely exceeds 35% (e.g., Farris & Revlin, 1989a, 1989b; Wason, 1968).

This task is equivalent to scientific investigations: Mother Nature gives us events to explain and scientists try to generate and test hypotheses about the event. If scientists follow the principles based on the philosophy of science, the procedure they would follow would be something like the following, using the 2–4–6 task as an example.

Disconfirmation Procedure

Step 1: Assume that your hypothesis (H_1) is correct

Step 2: Generate a triple that is inconsistent with H_1.

Step 3: Evaluate feedback about whether your triple fits the rule.

    a. If feedback is no, then H_1 may be correct.

    b. If feedback is yes, then H_1 cannot be correct.

Step 4: Formulate a new rule, another experiment, or stop.

The actual rule in the 2–4–6 task is numbers increasing in size. This rule is often considered disappointingly simple by many participants (Mahoney & DeMonbreun, 1977), but it forces them to perform many tests before they come upon the actual rule.

In our everyday lives, we generally produce "experiments" consistent with our hypotheses and invariably hope for a yes (J. Baron, 1985; Farris & Revlin, 1989a; Klayman & Ha, 1987). It is no wonder, then, that the pattern of "tests" by students on this task rarely shows evidence for disconfirmation. Peter Wason (1960), who invented the task, believed that people don't know how to test their hypotheses, they only know how to confirm them. That is, people gather evidence in favor of what they believe and trust in the amount of the supporting data to "prove" them right. He called this the **confirmation bias**. The evidence for this bias is that people who believe that the rule is even numbers only generate even numbers.

Counterfactual Strategy

Scientists appear to be no better than university students at this task: In one study, psychologists and physical scientists tried the task and were as poor as university students at discovering the rule (Mahoney & DeMonbreun, 1977). Scientists also do not follow the disconfirmation rule in their own research. This is because when scientists evaluate hypotheses in their own research, they follow a two-pronged attack: They look for evidence to confirm that they are on the right track in discovering a rule (like generating even numbers in the 2–4–6 task) and they also try to test competing hypotheses (Platt, 1964; Wharton, Cheng, & Wickens, 1993). In fact, many students follow this same strategy.

In the 2–4–6 task, when students announce they are sure that they have discovered the rule, the task is over even if they are wrong. If reasoners are allowed to continue their discovery efforts after announcing an incorrect rule, most of them (75%) will eventually discover the rule, but they don't use the disconfirmation procedure (Farris & Revlin, 1989a). What are the solvers doing differently the second time? The answer is that reasoners follow a procedure called the **counterfactual strategy** (Farris & Revlin, 1989a, 1989b). The strategy has four steps that are similar to the disconfirmation strategy, but it begins with a different kind of assumption. Here the reasoners assume that their favored hypothesis is incorrect by following the four steps in the counterfactual procedure:

Step 1: Assume that your hypothesis (H_1) is incorrect, even though you don't really believe that it is.

Step 2: Select another hypothesis (H_2) that is incompatible with H_1.

Step 3: Generate a triple consistent with H_2.

Step 4: Evaluate feedback.

    a. If yes, then H_1 is incorrect.

    b. If yes, then H_2 is plausible.

    c. If no, then H_2 is incorrect and H_1 is plausible.

TABLE 11.2 shows a trace of a student following a typical rule discovery sequence (Farris & Revlin, 1989b). The student is instructed to specify his or her hypothesis in one column, the test triple in another column, and finally the feedback from the experimenter is placed in the last column. Notice that in none of the rows (tests) did the reasoner generate a triple of numbers that was inconsistent with the hypothesis written in that row. Technically, there was no disconfirmation. But the hypotheses kept changing, especially on the fourth trial.

TABLE **11.2**		
Trace of a Reasoning Sequence in the 2–4–6 Task		
Hypothesis	**Test**	**Feedback**
1. *Even numbers*	4–8–12	Yes
2. *Second number 2 times first number and third number 3 times first number*	20–40–60	Yes
3. *Same with big numbers*	2,000–4,000–6,000	Yes
4. *Odd numbers*	1–3–5	Yes
5. *Any numbers*	2–3–4	Yes
6. *Any order*	4–3–2	No (Disconfirmation)
7. *Numbers getting bigger*	8–1,000–1,000,001	Yes

TABLE **11.3**		
Strategies Followed by Solvers and Nonsolvers		
Rule announcement	**Disconfirmation strategy (% of tests)**	**Counterfactual strategy (% of tests)**
First rule		
Correct	6.8	37.9
Incorrect	2.3	18.7
Second Rule		
Correct	0.0	47.4
Incorrect	11.4	13.7

Note: From Farris & Revlin, 1989a, 1989b

TABLE 11.3 shows that solvers who correctly discover the rule on the first run through tend to follow this counterfactual strategy. In fact, the average solver generates his or her first counterfactual hypothesis after 4.3 trials. The students who announce an incorrect rule, but go on to discover the correct rule, are those who begin to use the counterfactual strategy.

Can we generalize from laboratory experiments like the 2–4–6 task to situations in which people normally reason? In order to examine problem solving in more realistic situations, university students were asked to discover a mechanism by which genes control the activity of other genes (Dunbar, 1993). This was an effort to simulate the Nobel prize–winning discoveries about *E. coli* bacteria. In spite of the difficulty of this task, 70% of the students were able to solve this problem—a task that took 20 years of research by Jacob and Monod (1961)—in less than 1 hour.

The rule discovery patterns shown by these university students are similar to what was found in the more abstract 2–4–6 task. There were solvers and nonsolvers. The nonsolvers assumed that the current hypothesis was correct and attempted to generate data consistent with it. These students noted inconsistencies with their hypothesis but ignored them and continued to search for some consistent data. The solvers were students who noted the inconsistent data and understood that it disconfirmed the current hypothesis. Solvers attempted to generate new hypotheses consistent with the range of the data: They tended to switch between generating new hypotheses and searching for new data. The solvers seemed to have two goals (generating hypotheses and generating tests) in contrast with the nonsolvers' single goal (generating tests).

SECTION SUMMARY ■

Problem Solving Through Rule Discovery

In trying to discover rules, people consistently depart from the standard methods advocated by philosophers of science. Rather than using the disconfirmation process, they actually use a counterfactual strategy where they repeatedly change their hypotheses, but always generate tests that are consistent with the new hypothesis and inconsistent with the prior one. They appear to be using a defective test procedure called confirmation bias, but are in fact using the rational decision rule followed by scientists in real laboratory situations. Problem solvers behave as if they are searching through two spaces: one that contains a range of hypotheses and another that contains tests of those hypotheses. Successful solvers coordinate the two spaces; unsuccessful ones do not.

Computers and Computer Simulation of Problem Solving

We have just seen how important your representation of a problem is for a creative solution of it. Modern theories of problem solving emphasize how people mentally represent the problems that confront them and the methods they use to transform that representation to achieve their goal. Important ideas about how problem solvers do this were proposed in the 20th century by Gestalt psychologists. They were interested in how problem solvers would suddenly reimagine a problem, change their representation of it, and produce an interesting solution. Most of this work consisted of cataloging people's clever solutions. In the last half of the 20th century, however, advances in cognitive psychology allowed scientists to specify the mental operations that could account for how people actually transform their representations of problems. This deeper understanding of human problem solving was made possible by the computer models developed by Allen Newell and Herbert Simon (Newell & Simon, 1972), which could simulate human thinking, that is, computers could make the same decisions and for the same reasons that humans do.

Kasparov Versus Deep Blue On February 13, 1996, chess master Gary Kasparov played IBM's Deep Blue computer in Philadelphia as part of a six-game match. Kasparov is at left; at right is Feng-Hsiung Hsu, Deep Blue's architect and principal designer. This game ended in a draw.

AP/Wide World Photos

Simulating Human Thought

The early computers were typically used as giant calculators (McCorduck, 2004). However, by the second half of the 20th century they began to be used to manipulate symbols, solve logic problems, and store data. They quickly became a metaphor for human cognition. Terms such as *storage*, *retrieval*, *processing*, *decoding*, and *encoding* are as basic to cognitive psychology today as they are to computer science. The bridge between the two fields began with efforts by Newell, Shaw, and Simon (1958) to use the computer to solve problems that humans might confront, and also by Miller, Galanter, and Pribram (1960), who wrote a simple book showing how the computer metaphors could be applied to understand a broad array of human behavior. A half century after these initial efforts, computer programs are able to solve problems and also simulate human problem-solving strategies in the process. **Computer simulations** are programs that mimic human behavior. If they are successful, the programs can be viewed as the embodiment of theories of cognitive processing (Cummins & Cummins, 2000; Posner, 1993).

Computer simulations show steps that correspond to how people actually solve problems—or do not solve them—as the case may be. Simulating non-solutions allows us to learn about cognitive limitations to successful problem solving and to account for individual differences in problem-solving skills. The first computer program that had an impact on cognitive psychology was the Logic Theorists (Newell, Shaw, & Simon, 1963). It simulated how an educated person attempted to prove 38 of the 52 theorems of Russell and Whitehead's *Principia Mathematica*, a landmark text in the history of mathematics and logic. As part of this enterprise, Newell et al. created a broad theory of problem solving called the *general problem solver* (e.g., Newell & Simon, 1972), which we discuss later.

Problem Solving by Searching a Problem Space

In order to understand problem solving broadly, it helps to imagine that the solver is negotiating a path through a space of possibility: from the initial state to the final, or goal, state (Klahr & Dunbar, 1988). The path the problem solver takes is through this space of possibilities called a **problem space**, which is defined as the set of all relevant things that the problem solver can do (called *operations*) and all of the possible understandings that the problem solver can imagine. The difference among problem solvers, then, can be attributed to the fact that some people may be working with a more complete problem space than others (Ernst & Newell, 1969; Newell & Simon, 1972; Simon, 1978). One illustration of this is the Tower of Hanoi puzzle, which has been used extensively in cognitive research. It is described in Demonstration 11.8. Try it before you continue with the chapter.

■■■DEMONSTRATION 11.8

The Tower of Hanoi

This ancient puzzle probably originated in Benares, India, and was introduced into Europe by the French mathematician Edouard Lucas in 1883. It consists of three pegs, one of which has seven disks of decreasing size on it. The other two pegs are initially empty. The problem solver's task is to move the disks one at a time so that they are all arranged in the same order on one of the other pegs. However, a disk may not be placed on top of one that is smaller than it is. Using a piece of paper, map out how you would solve the puzzle with just the three disks illustrated on the next page.

If you are very efficient, you will be able to move the three disks in seven steps. A typical experiment presents the solver with seven disks rather than just three. Since the number of moves $= 2^n - 1$ steps (where n is the number of disks), the solution requires 127 moves. A puzzle requiring this many moves challenges the solver's working memory in order to keep track of the plan of action. It is staggering to imagine what people would do with a larger number of disks. In fact, the legend associated with the puzzle is that Brahmin monks in a tower in Benares are working on a puzzle with 64 disks. When they finish, the world will come to an end. Note that if it takes 1 second each time a disk is moved, a 64-disk puzzle will require 585 billion years to complete, so we have little to fear. **FIGURE 11.5** shows the problem space for this puzzle: all the possible

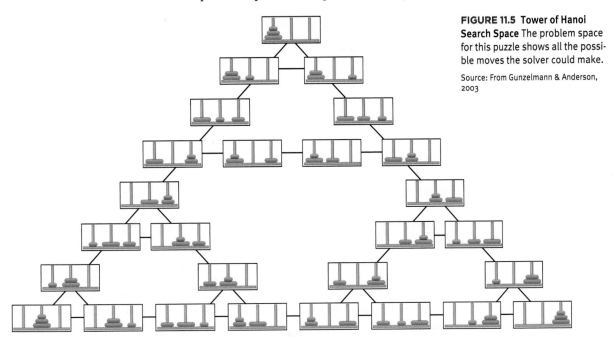

FIGURE 11.5 Tower of Hanoi Search Space The problem space for this puzzle shows all the possible moves the solver could make.

Source: From Gunzelmann & Anderson, 2003

moves the solver could make. Some are dead ends; if any of these paths are taken, the solver must backtrack to another path (Gunzelmann & Anderson, 2003).

The set of possibilities that is available to the solver at any point in solving the problem is called the *current state*. The person's task is to march through the problem space by selecting simple techniques, called **operators**, which allow you to move from one state of affairs to another (such as moving a disk to a peg). Searching through a problem space describes the problem-solving process for all types of problems. Demonstration 11.9 shows an unusual problem developed by Hayes (1989). Try to solve it yourself.

■■■DEMONSTRATION 11.9

The Fortune-Teller's Spell

A man once offended a fortune-teller by laughing at her predictions and saying that fortune-telling was all nonsense. So she cast a spell on him that turned him into both a compulsive gambler and a consistent loser. Yet instead of winding up impoverished and depressed, he soon married a wealthy woman who took him to the casino every day, gave him money, and smiled as he lost it at the roulette table. They lived happily ever after (Robertson, 2001, p. 7).

Try to think of three reasons why the man's wife was so happy to see him lose.

This problem exemplifies the use of search because the solver must examine a set of possibilities to find one or more states that could produce the desired goal of explaining the behavior. Were you able to come up with a satisfactory account? Many solutions could produce the goal state, some more satisfying than others. Here are some that students have suggested:

1. The woman is the daughter of the fortune-teller and is happy making sure her mother's curse comes true.

2. The woman owns the casino.

3. The woman knows her husband is going to lose so she makes the opposite bet and wagers twice as much as he does and wins.

Search Strategies

Successful solvers seem to use two basic strategies called breadth-first and depth-first (Newell & Simon, 1972); both are illustrated in **FIGURE 11.6**. The **breadth-first strategy** occurs when the problem solver tries all of the main possible options to see if they immediately lead to success. If they do not, the solver deepens the search and tries the next level of options. Here is an example. Suppose you are playing checkers and you have to decide on your next move. You scan the board, notice that you have three options (call them A, B, and C), and consider what would happen if you took each one. If any one clearly allows you to win directly (your ultimate goal), that's the one you would take. If none of your options achieve an immediate win, you would descend a level and search all states and moves at that level (A_1, B_1, or C_1) and keep descending until the goal is achieved

A Schooling	B Religion	C Political Organization	D Medical Beliefs	E Community
1. Importance of education	1. Believes in deities	1. Hierarchy	1. Source of illness	1. Family structure
2. Home instruction	2. Attendance at church	2. Power within hierarchy	2. Beliefs about diseases	2. Cooperation within family
3. "School" instruction	3. Disease and religion	3. Social position within hierarchy	3. Nature of cures	3. Groups of families
4. Skills acquired	4. Church hierarchy	4. Acquisition of position	4. Treatment hierarchy (shaman, doctor, etc.)	4. How they spend their day

FIGURE 11.6 Depth- and Breadth-First Diagrams In the breadth-first strategy, problem solvers try all of the main possible options to see if they immediately lead to success. They go from column A to B to C and so on, starting at the first level and going down the rows (1, 2, 3, etc.). Participants who use the depth-first strategy examine all the information in a single category (e.g., A_1, A_2, A_3, etc.) to see if it leads to a solution; if it doesn't, they search the next category. The result is a laborious process in which participants search many irrelevant categories. Participants who use the breadth-first strategy are more successful solvers.

(A_n, B_n, and C_n). In this case you would consider how your opponent would respond to each possible move and then how you would respond to the situation that results from that move. You keep doing this until your goal is achieved or your working memory is exhausted.

An alternative is called **depth-first strategy**. Continuing with the checkers example, you would select one move (e.g., A); if you win, then you would stop. If not, you would consider the move after that one (A_1) and so on (e.g., $A_2 \ldots A_n$) until you either win or end the sequence. After that you would try the second option (B) and progress downward, and continue until you've exhausted the possibilities.

These strategies have practical applications. For example, an early test of American Peace Corps applicants gave them the problem of getting a hypothetical community to build a school. The participants were given more than a dozen categories of facts about the community to select among. The solvers who were most efficient and creative were those who used the breadth-first strategy and sampled from each category (to find out what kinds of facts they truly contained) and then progressively searched deeper within the few categories that seemed most fruitful (Schroder, Driver, & Streufert, 1967; Suedfeld & Streufert, 1966; Suedfeld & Tetlock, 2001).

Participants who used the depth-first strategy were less successful. They examined all of the information in a single category to see if it would lead to a solution; if it didn't, they would search the next category. The result was a laborious process in which participants searched many irrelevant categories.

The Next Move

An ever-present question in solving a problem is what do I do next? A number of methods can guide your choice for the next move through the problem space. The first of these is called hill climbing; the second is called means–ends analysis.

Hill Climbing Imagine your job is to find the highest peak in the area so that you can see the terrain and find your way home. But, it's foggy and you can't tell where the highest peak is. In this case, you use your feet to sense your location. If you are already at the peak then your goal has been achieved: A step in any direction will lead you down. If you take a step and you go up, then you were not at the peak and you should keep going. Of course, you could go downwards and not be at the highest peek, just a lower one. **Hill climbing** is a metaphor for a technique that says each move that you take in solving a problem should at least appear to be in the direction of the goal. Do not retrace your steps or go down a different path. Most important of all, do not go in a direction that appears to move away from the goal. If you have gone as far as you can in the direction of the goal, then you have done the best that you could, given what you know. Of course, you may miss the top, but you will have made some progress.

Not all problems can be solved by using the hill-climbing method. This can be seen when people are confronted with a type called the *river-crossing problem* (Greeno, 1974; Thomas, 1974). These problems have appeared in many forms since they were introduced a thousand years ago. One version (after Thomas, 1974) is called Hobbits and Orcs, and is shown in Demonstration 11.10. Try the problem and see why it is difficult.

■■■DEMONSTRATION 11.10

Hobbits and Orcs
There are three Hobbits and three Orcs together on the left side of a river. Their goal is to use the one and only canoe to cross the river to the right side. The problem is that, at most, only three creatures can fit in the boat at any one time, and since the Orcs are nasty beasts, they should never outnumber the Hobbits (in the boat or on either shore) or they'll be very rude to them, which will demoralize the Hobbits.

Try this problem and make note of where you had difficulties. Once you have the general idea about how to transport Hobbits and Orcs to one side and have someone bring back the boat, you're off and running on the solution.

Thomas (1974) studied how students solve this problem. He created an ideal problem behavior graph to show the steps in the solution, shown in **FIGURE 11.7**. Students seem to move smoothly to a solution by employing the hill-climbing strategy: always moving in the forward direction through the problem space. They have difficulty, however, when they must reverse direction when a majority of the Hobbits and Orcs are on the right side of the river. At this point in the problem, you have to undo what was accomplished and move both a Hobbit and an Orc back to the left side of the river. Here is a case of hill climbing where the problem solvers are stumped because they must go "down hill." In fact, a third of the solvers move back to a previously successful state just to avoid the one that requires them simply to reverse direction (Jeffries, Polson, Razran, & Atwood, 1977).

Reversing direction is a common difficulty people have in everyday problem solving. When we encounter detours on the highway, the most difficult route for people to choose is the one that has them reverse direction. Taking two steps forward and then one step back may lead you to your goal, but it is exceedingly

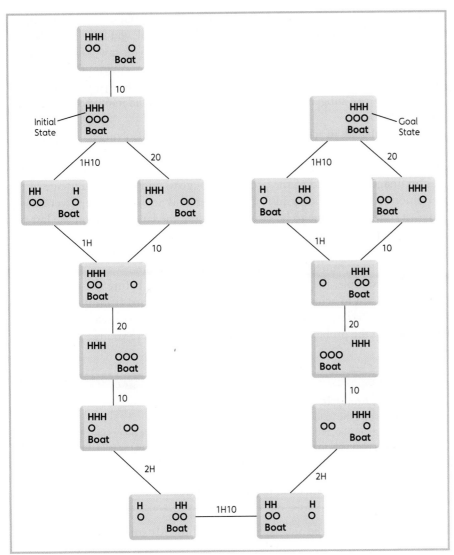

FIGURE 11.7 Hobbits and Orcs Solution This is a chart (called a *problem behavior graph*) of the choices and decisions the problem solver must make in the Hobbits and Orcs problem. With it, researchers can trace what decisions the solver has made. Problem solvers encounter difficulty at the bottom-most choice points, as predicted by hill climbing.

Source: From Thomas, 1974

difficult for people to do. We seem to follow a hill-climbing process automatically (Sperber & Wilson, 1996).

Means–Ends Analysis

Another commonly used method is **means–ends analysis**; it involves minimizing the distance between the current and goal states. To do this, the problem solver applies operators from the problem space that will transform the problem into one that is more readily solved. This intermediate state is called a **subgoal**. It is a situation that gets you to your ultimate goal. Suppose your goal is to get a box from the top shelf of a cabinet that is beyond your reach. One way to achieve your goal is to set an intermediate goal of standing on a chair or ladder to get closer to the box. To do this, you must establish another subgoal of finding a ladder to stand on. To achieve this subgoal, you have to establish a subgoal of remembering the location of the last place you saw a ladder, and so forth. Creating subgoals can lead to successful problem solving. People do this normally: In fact, the overall time a person needs to solve a problem is related to the number of subgoals he or she needs to create (Anderson, Kushmerick, & Lebiere, 1993).

To see subgoals in action, as well as another problem-solving technique called *working backward*, let's return to the Tower of Hanoi puzzle. In Figure 11.5 you may have noticed that there are subgoals for the successful solver. The solver has an image of the end of the problem (the goal) and creates an image of the condition that should occur just before the goal is achieved. The solver sets up this last condition as one to be satisfied: putting the largest disk on the last peg at the bottom. Given this situation, it is simple to arrange the smaller disks (one on either of the remaining pegs) to achieve the subgoal (Hayes, 1989). Satisfying the subgoal leads immediately to the problem solution.

In this example, the solver imagined the last step before the problem was solved and tried to achieve this goal. Working backward from the goal can be enormously effective in providing direction to the problem search. To see this firsthand, try the problem in Demonstration 11.11 before you read on.

■■■**DEMONSTRATION 11.11**

Means–Ends Analysis
See if you can solve the following problem.

An ailing frog can hop, but not swim. In order for him to get to the other side of a large lake, he has to hop from water lily to water lily. Sadly there is only one lily on the lake. However, the frog knows water lilies grow so rapidly that the amount of water surface covered by the lilies doubles every 24 hours. He calculates that in 30 days the entire surface of the lake will be covered with water lilies. On what day will the lake be half covered? (You can return to the text for a hint.)

If you haven't derived an answer, here is a hint: My students say that they are more likely to work backward when the last statement is, "Why will he celebrate on the day the lake is half covered?" This statement gets solvers to focus on what will happen the day after it is half full rather than focusing on how to calculate the day it will be half full; this shows the value of working backward.

There are three steps in the use of means–ends analysis: First, you must be aware of a difference between the current state and the goal state. If there is none, you have solved the problem or don't understand the current situation. The second step is to find an operator to reduce the difference, perhaps creating a subgoal. Finally, make sure you can apply the operator. If there is an impediment to applying the necessary operator, set the elimination of that barrier as a subgoal and try to solve that subgoal. Means–end analysis may seem obvious as a component of problem solving because it is manifested in virtually every complex task, from cooking dinner to writing an essay, and is an effective method for solving problems.

Satisficing

It is tempting to assume that a good problem solver will somehow make the optimal decisions and find the correct path or paths to the goal. In fact, even the best solvers tend not to make optimal decisions because not all of the information is known or because there is so much information that it taxes their working memory. Good solvers tend to make satisfactory decisions that are sufficient for their purposes, as with hill climbing. If you combine the words *satisfactory* and *sufficient*, you have the word **satisfice** (Goodrich, Stirling, & Boer, 2000; Simon, 1956, 1997). A person who satisfices is one who chooses a path or goal that is good enough, rather than searching endlessly for the one that is the best or optimal. In chess, for example, the total number of positions has been calculated to be approximately 10^{120}. To consider every possible consequence of a single move, at one move per second, would require 11 years, and that's just for one move!

Satisficing characterizes human decision making not only within problem-solving contexts, but also in most complex decisions because we simply do not have enough time or capacity to consider all options. It allows us to avoid being stymied by indecision (Simon, 1969). People do not always satisfice, however. When you go shopping for pants and find a pair that fits and looks attractive, do you put it aside and continue searching in the hope of finding an even better pair? If so, you are an *optimizer*, looking for the best pants no matter how long it takes. If you stop and simply purchase the first pair of pants that looks good and meets your criteria, you are a *satisficer*. In our everyday lives, it seems that some people are optimizers and others are satisficers (Bruine de Bruin, Parker, & Fischhoff, 2007). People who are identified as optimizers (e.g., when watching TV they report channel surfing even though they are already watching a show) tend to have worse decision outcomes (locked themselves out of their house, lost car keys, got divorced, etc.) than people who are identified as satisficers (Parker, Bruine de Bruin, & Fischhoff, 2007). Most of us, however, do a mixture of both optimizing and satisficing: We look for the best choice within a reasonable time and price.

The Effect of Neurological Impairments

Means–ends analysis illustrates that successful problem solving often requires an understanding of what the final state ought to look like, that is, an image of the goal. This is especially important in ill-defined problems (where the final state is not defined), but it is also critical for solving well-defined problems. When you have a sense of where you are going (the goal) and the process for achieving it (the path), you have the rudiments of a plan. Planning is crucial to reliable problem solving. In fact, it may be the case that planning in our everyday lives is simply a form of problem solving: figuring out how to get from here to there.

Some people are unable to plan because of neurological impairments. One of the earliest documented cases of the neurology of planning failure was that

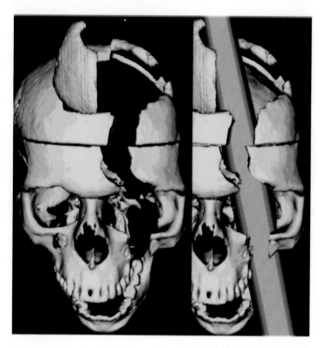

FIGURE 11.8 Phineas Gage's Injuries This is a 3-D computer reconstruction of the injury based on an image of the skull and the tamping iron. The right panel shows the reconstruction of the injury with the tamping iron in place.

From Ratiu, P., Talos, I. F., Haker, S., Lieberman, S., Everett, P. 2004. The tale of Phineas Gage, digitally remastered. *Journal of Neurotrauma, 21*, 637–643. The publisher for this copyrighted material is Mary Ann Liebert, Inc. publishers.

of Phineas Gage, a railroad foreman in Vermont, who in September 1848 experienced damage to a portion of his frontal lobe. An explosion forced a tamping iron into his cheek and out through the top of his skull, damaging the frontal cortex and severing a portion of it from the thalamus. In his post-accident life he was unable to form and maintain coherent plans: "devising many plans of future operation, which are no sooner arranged than they are abandoned in turn for others" (Harlow, 1868, pp. 339–340). When he recovered, Gage worked at odd jobs and then toiled for 7 years as a coach driver in Chile. Eventually he moved to San Francisco, became a farm worker, and lived with his mother until his death in 1861. The location of his brain injury has been estimated in various ways (e.g., Damasio, Grabowski, Frank, Galaburda, & Damasio, 1994). A recent analysis (Ratiu, Talos, Haker, Lieberman, & Everett, 2004) has generated the picture shown in **FIGURE 11.8**.

There is now evidence that Gage's inability to plan is the hallmark of frontal lobe damage and is seen in the problem-solving skills of others with similar neurological disorders. For example, individuals with lesions to the prefrontal cortex have difficulty completing the Tower of Hanoi puzzle (Goel & Grafman, 1995; Morris, Miotto, Feigenbaum, Bullock, & Polkey, 1997). Recall that one of the difficulties with the Hobbits and Orcs and Tower of Hanoi problems is that they involve a critical violation of hill climbing because the solver must undo what has already been accomplished. Goel and Grafman (1995) had people with left frontal lobe damage try to solve the Tower of Hanoi problem. They showed worse performance than people without such injuries, especially on those moves that are in conflict with hill climbing (such as taking off a disk that is already placed).

The influence of the frontal lobes in planning and problem solving is not limited to well-defined problems like the Tower of Hanoi. Goel and Grafman (2000) asked a skilled architect to design an office space that would accommodate desks, chairs, and so on. This is an ill-defined task because the architect was constrained only by the size of the space and its contents and was free to craft any solution he wished. The architect had damage to the right top prefrontal cortex (called *dorsolateral prefrontal cortex*). In spite of years of experience with such tasks, he could not go much beyond a listing of the dimensions of the furniture and the space—cursory, preliminary planning. A generalization from this and related research is that left prefrontal cortex damage seems to be implicated in difficulties with solving well-defined problems, whereas damage to the right prefrontal cortex is associated with difficulties in solving ill-defined problems.

Computers and Computer Simulation of Problem Solving

The development of computers has influenced both problem-solving research as well as the language that we use to describe human thought processes. Computer models of problem solving try to simulate the decision process used by people—both their successes and their failures. A dominant metaphor in computer simulations is the idea that solvers are searching through a problem space to create a path from the initial to the goal state. Differences among people in their ability to solve problems are related to how complete their problem space is and their search strategy: breadth-first or depth-first. Even the best problem solvers do not make optimal decisions and frequently satisfice, selecting decision paths that are good enough rather than the best.

In this context two major methods are commonly followed: hill climbing (moving in the direction of the goal) and means–ends analysis (minimizing the distance between the current and goal states). These methods involve the solver having an image of the goal in mind. Means–ends analysis illustrates that successful problem solving often requires an understanding of what the final state ought to look like, that is, an image of the goal. The frontal lobes of the brain play an important role in creating solution plans that require access to this image of the goal.

■ ■

The General Problem Solver (GPS)

Cognitive psychology contributes to the understanding of human behavior by specifying the underlying mental processes that produce the behavior. Nearly a century of research has seen the development of many successful theories of human cognition that are broad in scope, yet specific enough to help us appreciate the mental activities that explain human behavior. The basic theory presented here, the general problem solver, has been selected from an incredibly rich array of theories because it has the most successful track record over the decades for explaining human problem solving.

The cognitive analysis of successful problem solving is part of a theory called the **general problem solver (GPS)** (Newell et al., 1958). The theory is embodied as a running computer program. GPS contains four major components that humans generally possess: (a) a limited-capacity working memory with rapid storage and retrieval; (b) a large-capacity long-term memory with relatively slow storage and retrieval; (c) a serial processor that performs a single operation at a time; and (d) a library of shortcut methods (called *heuristics*) that will be described in Chapter 13. The major elements of the theory were discovered by using a technique of obtaining verbal reports (called *protocols*) from volunteers as they were solving problems (Ericsson & Simon, 1993). These participant contributions guided the development of GPS and formed the early data to be simulated with the computer model. GPS is both a theory of problem solving as well as a computer simulation that solves well-defined problems the way people do (Atwood & Polson, 1976; Newell & Simon, 1972). As a theory of human problem solving, it specifies mechanisms and processes that are broadly sufficient to fit the human data. GPS showed that human problem solving could be successfully understood through the creation of computer programs.

The lessons learned from GPS helped to form the basis of general theories of cognition that go beyond problem solving. Many theories that have been inspired by the broad visionary work of Allen Newell and GPS contain a collection of primitive problem-solving elements called **production systems**. These are libraries of condition–action pairs that are part of the solver's long-term knowledge. Each pair is called a *production* (e.g., Anderson, 1983; Brown & Van Lehn, 1980; Card, Moran, & Newell, 1983). To illustrate the simplest production, consider the reflexes a 1-day-old infant possesses:

Orienting reflex: If cheek is touched—turn face in direction of touch.

Sucking reflex: If lip is touched—close lip, suck.

These productions are automatically activated in response to environmental events. Suppose a typical infant has both reflexes: If their cheek is touched by a nipple, infants will turn in the direction of the nipple and suck.

A slightly more complex production (P) that has been learned would be hammering a nail:

P1: If head of nail is upright and nail is flush with surface—stop.

P2: If head of nail is upright and is not flush with surface—hammer.

P2a: If hammer—strike nail.

P2b: If strike nail—lift hammer up then down.

Note that P1 is both a statement of the goal as well as a production; the P2's are the actions to be taken to achieve the goal. They are part of the repertoire and can be activated in any order. Try these productions yourself, starting with either one and imagine that the nail is not initially flush with the surface.

An ambitious theory of cognition is **ACT-R (adaptive control of thought with a rational analysis)**, which employs productions (Anderson & Lebiere, 1998). It contains descriptions of multiple memory systems and buffers that are under the general "control" of productions. A selected production can cause changes in the current goal, make a retrieval request of declarative memory, shift attention, or call for new motor actions. ACT-R is extraordinary in its ability to capture the general properties of human cognition from basic perceptual processes to high-level cognitive functioning.

ACT-R is sensitive to differences among people in the way they approach and solve problems (e.g., Schunn, Lovett, & Reder, 2001). The repertoire of actions each person brings to a task can be specified in terms of the contents of each person's library of productions. For example, you can characterize the behavior of nonsolvers by the fact that they do not possess some necessary production, or they fail to apply ones that they do possess. Suppose a first grader's goal is to add

5 + 6, but she only possesses productions to add 1 or 2 to every number up to 10. The typical first grader will have difficulty with this because she does not possess the necessary math facts. In contrast, the same problem will be of minimal difficulty to a typical second grader, because the math fact is already memorized as part of her set of arithmetic productions. ACT-R and the production system approach to problem solving can be both an explanation for problem-solving behavior and a guide to instructional design to help people become better problem solvers.

SECTION SUMMARY ▪

The General Problem Solver (GPS)

Modern theories of problem solving owe their inspiration and critical ideas to the innovative work of Newell et al. (1958) in the creation of the general problem solver (GPS). GPS embodies the concepts of problem solving occurring in a problem space, which is searched by the solver using an array of search strategies and general methods. Theories that followed in the tradition of GPS such as ACT-R have advanced the concept of production systems that express the knowledge people assemble to solve problems.

CHAPTER SUMMARY

A problem exists when the current state of affairs is not our desired, or goal state. Problem solving consists of transforming the current state into the goal state by acceptable methods. Our ability to solve a problem is affected by our representation of it. Sometimes we are at an impasse because the way we represent a problem disguises it so we don't realize that the new problem is just like an old one we've already solved. The key to successful problem solving is the proper representation of the problem.

There are two broad classes of problems: well-defined and ill-defined ones. The former are usually well structured with clear goals and constraints and a defined set of operators that can be used to transform the problem into one that is solved. In contrast, ill-defined problems are not well structured. The constraints are typically unspecified, and it isn't always clear what the goal state is. These are the interesting problems that we often encounter and that occupy a lifetime such as, how can I be happy? For ill-defined problems, representation is greatly affected by the framing of the problem.

In our everyday lives we often draw parallels between a current difficulty and similar ones we have en-

countered in the past. We use past successes to help us solve current problems; this is called reasoning by analogy. People can be successful in such reasoning when they are encouraged to find analogues for current problems and are given hints about the similarities between the old and new problems.

Our representation of a problem can help us solve it or create an impediment to solution. In the latter case, we must create a different mental representation of the problem. When we are successful in doing this, we are said to have insight into the problem, which allows us to focus on the important elements leading to a rapid solution. Creative solutions are often enhanced by activity in the dopamine circuit in the brain, which can promote a positive mood.

Human problem solving has been simulated using computer programs, which reveal that much of our problem solving is like searching through a space of hypotheses and a space of tests of those hypotheses. Creative problem solving often involves a blending of input spaces to create a new representation of the problem. Two prominent types of searches are hill climbing and means–ends analysis. Because of hill climbing, one source of difficulty in problem solving is to go in the opposite direction from the goal. Means–ends analysis involves creating subgoals that mitigate the distance between the current state and the goal state. The human ability to create subgoals and search past methods of problem solving can be represented as a system of productions that are automatically applied depending on the person's representation of the problem.

When scientists and nonscientists alike seek to discover a rule, they appear to depart from the prescribed disconfirmation strategy and show a confirmation bias. Successful problem solvers follow a counterfactual reasoning strategy where they treat hypotheses as if they were correct even though they do not believe in those hypotheses. If the data support those hypotheses, then the scientists know that the original one was incorrect and has been disconfirmed.

There are many theories of human problem solving, but the general problem solver was the foundational one that provided the first successful computer simulation. Its key elements have been embodied in ACT-R theory, which provides not only a basic account of human problem solving, but also a guide for how to instruct people to be better solvers.

KEY TERMS

problem, p. 353

problem solving, p. 353

representation, p. 354

routine problem solving, p. 354

nonroutine problem solving, p. 354

well-defined problem, p. 358

ill-defined problem, p. 360

open domain, p. 360

impersonal reasoning, p. 361

personal reasoning, p. 362

metacognition, p. 363

epistemic monitoring, p. 363

framing, p. 364

analogical reasoning, p. 365

closed domain, p. 368

insight, p. 369

creativity, p. 369

functional fixedness, p. 372

dopaminergic theory of positive affect (DTPA), p. 374

disconfirmation, p. 375

confirmation bias, p. 376

counterfactual strategy, p. 377

computer simulations, p. 380

problem space, p. 380

operators, p. 382

breadth-first strategy, p. 382

depth-first strategy, p. 383

hill climbing, p. 384

means–ends analysis, p. 385

subgoal, p. 385

satisfice, p. 387

general problem solver (GPS), p. 389

production systems, p. 390

ACT-R (adaptive control of thought with a rational analysis), p. 390

QUESTIONS FOR REVIEW

Check Your Knowledge

1. What is the definition of *problem solving*?

2. If you are trying to get from your house to the library, what is the current state of affairs and what is the goal state?

3. What is the key to all problem solving that allows you to apply a successful solution procedure?

4. What are the two broad categories of problems?

5. What are the three characteristics of well-defined problems?

6. What are the three characteristics of ill-defined problems?

7. You wonder, what is the best occupation for me? What type of problem is this?

8. What part of the brain participates in resolving moral dilemmas?

9. What type of problems are moral dilemmas?

10. What are the two skills that characterize both well-defined and ill-defined problems?

11. What skill is unique to ill-defined problems?

12. How a situation is worded influences the solver's kind of representation. What is this called?

13. Under which scenario is a student most likely to buy a $10 ticket to a show: if he lost the first ticket he bought or if he lost $10 that day?

14. To promote reasoning by analogy, you give students a simple version of a problem to solve and then test to see if they can solve the more complex version. Are they successful?

15. In trying to get students to reason by analogy, which of the following is most successful: (a) summarize the basic principle; (b) draw a picture with the solution elements in it; or (c) give the students different problems to solve but with the same underlying principle?

16. Someone is asked, "do they grow coffee in Paraguay?" and the person answers, "they grow coffee in Brazil and it's near Paraguay." What kind of reasoning is this?

17. In the previous question, is this reasoning about a closed or open domain?

18. If you watch a funny movie for a few minutes, what effect might this have on your creative problem solving?

19. Why does a person's mood affect the solution to problems?

20. If someone's hypothesis is that all swans are white and never black, should that person look for white birds to see if they are swans or look for black birds to see if they are swans?

21. What is the reasoning process if that person looks only at white birds?

22. What is the reasoning process if that person looks only at black birds?

23. What is the counterfactual strategy?

24. What strategy is typically used by scientists?

25. What is a computer simulation?

26. What is the problem space for the Tower of Hanoi puzzle?

27. Describe breadth-first search.

28. Describe depth-first search.

29. What is *satisficing*? What would be an example?

30. You decide to write an essay; the first thing you do is decide to get paper and pen. Is this an example of hill climbing or means–ends analysis?

31. What is the intermediate step of getting the paper and pen called?

32. Which area of the brain is involved in planning on ill-defined problems?

33. Which area of the brain is involved in planning on well-defined problems?

34. What is the general problem solver?

35. What is a production system? List the productions for hammering a nail.

Apply Your Knowledge

1. Consider the two moral dilemma problems in the trolley story discussed in this chapter, which typically reveal values you might not have been aware that you possess. In the first scenario, would you flip the switch? In the second scenario, would you push the man onto the tracks? In both instances your choice is between killing one person or five persons. Yet, people typically treat the two situations differently. Where do you stand on this? Do you think they are different? If so, what aspects of the problems make them seem different?

2. Reconsider the rescue at sea dilemma in Demonstration 11.3. Whom would you save? Why? Under what circumstances, if any, would your answer be different?

3. Consider the importance of problem representation in the following scenario: *Two men were working on a chimney. Both fall down it, but only one gets his face dirty. There are no mirrors; which man washes his face?* (One answer: The man whose face is clean; he sees the man whose face is dirty and thinks his own face is dirty. The man whose face is dirty sees the man whose face is clean and thinks his own face is clean.) How many other outcomes and explanations can you think of?

4. Create a complete production system for tying a bow in your shoelaces. Find a child who can't tie his shoe and see if the production system you wrote could be used for instructing the child to tie his shoes. This is the basis for many instructional computer programs developed by Anderson (1983) and his associates.

SOLUTIONS

Demonstration 11.1: Solution to Gold Chain Problem

Open the three links in one of the chains (cost = $6) and attach each one to hold together the end links to the other chains (cost = $9). Total cost = $15.

Cryptarithmetic Solution

SEND
+MORE
MONEY

$M = 1, O = 0, R = 8, E = 5, S = 9, N = 6, D = 7, Y = 2$

Demonstration 11.2: Solution to Nine-Dot Problem

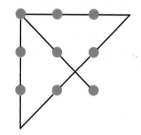

Demonstration 11.5: Solution to Problem 1

Yes. There are only two puzzles being spoken of: this one and the one before this one. The entire question could be rephrased like this:

> If the puzzle you solved before this one was harder than this one, was the puzzle you solved before this one harder than this one?

Obviously, the answer to the question is simply yes.

Demonstration 11.5: Solution to Problem 2

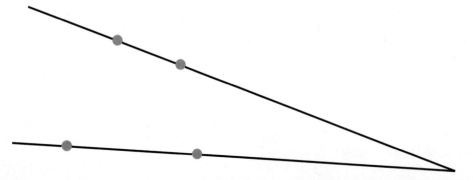

Demonstration 11.7: Solutions to Questions

1. Ship arriving too late to save a drowning witch.
2. Circle the 3 and the 2.
3. So he wouldn't fall into the hot chocolate.

Demonstration 11.11: Solution to Means–Ends Analysis Problem

The lake is half covered on the 29th day.

12

Reasoning

> **"**I know what you're thinking about," said Tweedledum; "but it isn't so, nohow." "Contrariwise," continued Tweedledee, "if it was so, it might be; and if it were so, it would be; but as it isn't, it ain't. That's logic.**"**
> —Lewis Carroll

nimals in the wild can be clever, they can learn to avoid predators, select nonpoisonous food, and respond to different cries and displays by other creatures. But because they are adapted to narrow environmental niches, a significant change in a niche threatens their survival. In contrast, humans can transcend restricted habitats, develop plans, and adapt strategies to changes in time and place. Humans' greatest adaptation is not our speed (the cheetah is faster), nor is it our strength (consider the elephant or the whale). It is not even our unique ability to make tools: Sea otters find rocks to crack open abalone shells; chimpanzees use stalks to troll for termites and carry clubs to crack open nuts at the tops of trees (Calvin, 1983; Goodall, 1971); and New Caledonian crows can make hooks to snag food (Weir, Chappell, & Kacelnik, 2002). Humanity's crucial skill is the ability to reason. **Reasoning** is the process by which we draw conclusions from given information called *premises*. It has been said that reasoning is the central intellectual activity of humanity (Rips, 1986). It organizes language, culture, and memory. Reasoning allows us to take events, assertions, suppositions, and beliefs as input and draw conclusions and create new information.

Reasoning also allows us to go beyond the given in a situation: to see the overall pattern, to find the theme, to see the plan or to create one, and to test our hypotheses to ensure that we've drawn the correct conclusion. Not even our closest primate relatives can perform all of these feats. Nor can they imagine a situation that has never occurred before (Hockett, 1966). Reasoning is even central to how people perceive the world (Helmholtz, 1910/1925; Spelke, 1990) because our minds put together fragmentary sensations of light, lines, and movement and create perceptions of people, objects, and intentions. We draw conclusions by going beyond the basic information and making sense of our experience of the world.

Reasoning and Logic

When people reason and draw sensible conclusions, we say they are rational. Do humans act irrationally? The answer is yes, especially in cases of severe time pressure or great emotion, when emotions interrupt the general flow of cognition (Evans, 2003; Simon, 1967). However, on most occasions human reasoning appears to be *sensible*. That is, we appear to follow sensible decision-making procedures without direct instructions (Farris & Revlin, 1989b). We understand cause and effect; we generally understand a well-reasoned argument when we hear one (Sperber & Wilson, 1995); and we are able to function in everyday life. In spite of our frequent complaints that other people are irrational, our everyday interactions are based on the assumption that other people will be rational. For example, if we really believed that the other drivers on the road were irrational, we would be unlikely to risk driving to work or school on a regular basis. Without rationality, human life would be difficult and social life would be impossible, because we could never count on anyone else to act in a socially acceptable way (e.g., Cheng & Holyoak, 1989; Cosmides & Tooby, 1997; Gigerenzer & Hug, 1992; Stanovich, 1999).

Is being rational the same as following the rules of logic? If you know that, under normal conditions, if it rains the crops will grow and you also know that it is raining, logic tells you to conclude that the crops will grow. However, to be rational is to be consistent and sensible. Rational thinking uses many of the same principles of standard logic, but need not because it can also include personal values and goals. Although rational thought and logic overlap, under normal conditions, people do not need to know the rules of logic in order to reason. For example, take this old chestnut, which is based on Hobbes' *Government & Society* (1651/1983):

> All men are living creatures.
>
> Socrates is a man.

Question: Can you conclude that Socrates is a living creature?

When college undergraduates are asked to consider this problem, they are capable of drawing the correct inference without ever having had any instruction on how to do it and without any special graphical aids (Calvillo, DeLeeuw, & Revlin, 2006). In fact, in cases when students understand the meaning of the first two sentences about men, living creatures, and Socrates, they are 95% accurate in drawing correct conclusions (Braine, Reiser, & Rumain, 1984). We don't need to be taught logic in order to be rational.

You may wonder why humans are endowed with the gift of reason. One answer is that reasoning ability allows us to draw conclusions from information coming from different sources and different periods of time (Braine & O'Brien, 1998). Reasoning allowed our human ancestors to notice the causal relation between water resources and crop growth. They could identify the presence of predators from the direction and size of footprints. They could communicate their findings and guesses to others (Mercier & Sperber, 2009). Their reasoning ability aided their survival and reproduction, as it does for us today.

SECTION SUMMARY ■
Reasoning and Logic

One of the great adaptations across the eons of human development is the ability to reason. It comes early in the development of the individual and underlies our ability to comprehend language, to reconstruct memories, and to understand the world around us. It is our central intellectual activity. Our conclusions are not arbitrary: We are rational beings, and in our interactions with other people, we basically assume that they are, too.

The Development of Reasoning

In many religious traditions, the rituals that connect a child voluntarily to his or her place of worship are administered when the child has reached the "age of reason." The age of reason dates back to the Middle Ages when the medieval catechism tested children's understanding of the implication of abstract concepts such as the meaning of *faith* (the Apostles' Creed), *hope* (the Lord's Prayer), and *charity* (the Ten Commandments).

In some Christian denominations, 7 years old is the critical age, but we know that children are capable of reasoning at significantly earlier ages. The development of rationality is a puzzle. Somehow we go from "the infant mewling and puking in the nurse's arms" (Shakespeare, *As You Like It*, act 22, scene 7) to the logical computer that is an adult reasoner. How does this happen? Some psychologists argue it is such a complex undertaking that logical reasoning could not possibly develop; it has to be an innate capacity in the mind, like a specialized module (Fodor, 1983). Other psychologists propose that rationality results from an ability to represent sentences by constructing models in our minds of what is said, and everything follows from the representation (e.g., Johnson-Laird & Byrne, 1991). Although we cannot resolve the basis for the ability to reason, we do know that children appear to progress through three stages before they reason at the adult level without being explicitly taught how to reason (Moshman, 1990).

Stage 1 Reasoning

One of the earliest examples of children's reasoning occurs when they hear a conditional relationship; by age 4 a child may have heard the choice:

Eat your vegetables or you will have no dessert.

The important aspect of this message is the *or* relationship. The child's ability to draw inferences from this connective characterizes the beginning of the first stage of reasoning (Moshman, 1990; Moshman & Franks, 1986). Now consider this example:

The ice cream is either chocolate or vanilla.

The ice cream is not chocolate.

Therefore, the ice cream is vanilla.

By age 5 or 6, the typical child is capable of solving such a problem as accurately as an adult. It is as if the child possesses a library of logical procedures that are automatically applied. At this stage, the child is aware of the content of the problem (e.g., ice cream), but not of the logical rules that allow him or her to actually carry out the reasoning.

Stage 2 Reasoning

In the second stage of reasoning, roughly between the ages of 6 and 10, the child shows skill at realizing that a single conclusion may not be the only possibility. Take, for example, what happens when you play 20 questions with someone at Stage 2:

What I'm thinking of is either animal, vegetable, or mineral.

It is not animal.

Therefore, is it vegetable?

A Stage 2 child will either exhibit confusion at the conclusion or say that you cannot tell if it is correct. The child seems to understand that conclusions must follow from premises and seems to appreciate that there are many possible conclusions. This is the beginning of personal awareness of their own thought processes, *metacognition* (described in Chapter 11). They seem to be aware that they are reasoning and what this implies. As a result they can detect whether a conclusion is reasonable, or plausible, or likely (Moshman & Timmons, 1982; Somerville, Hadkinson, & Greenberg, 1979).

Stage 3 Reasoning

Children in this stage are able to reason about statements that they know are false. This is not so in earlier stages. In spite of children's ability to pretend and imagine situations that are clearly false in the real world, Stage 1 children are not able to place themselves in hypothetical situations and imagine the consequences. As an example, the Russian psychologist Vygotsky (1962, p. 222) asked a 4-year-old child to look at a statue of a cow and imagine this state of affairs:

Let's pretend that this statue [of a cow] is a dog.

What sound does it make?   *Woof!*

Does it have horns?   *Yes . . . but they're very small.*

This task calls for **counterfactual reasoning**, reasoning from assertions that you disbelieve, and is key to hypothesis testing (described in Chapter 11). Children in Stages 1 and 2 find it difficult to reason counterfactually because it violates what they know of the content. It is only when children are able to function at Stage 3 (approximately 11 years old) that they would have no difficulty with Vygotsky's problem or the following:

Elephants are either animals or plants.

Elephants are not animals.

Therefore, elephants are plants.

In this argument, the child clearly knows that the premise (*elephants are not animals*) and the conclusion (*elephants are plants*) are clearly false. Yet Stage 3 children can readily evaluate whether the conclusion must definitely follow, called **validity**, even though it is not true. Stage 3 children can reason in a way that is independent of content. Try the task that has been given to children of this age in Demonstration 12.1.

■■■DEMONSTRATION 12.1

Stage 3 Reasoning

Here are three arguments; two are similar. Which two would you group together?

A	B	C
If elephants are bigger than dogs,	If adults are older than babies,	If mice are bigger than dogs,
And dogs are bigger than mice,	And children are older than babies,	And mice are bigger than elephants,
Then elephants are bigger than mice.	Then adults are older than children.	Then dogs are bigger than elephants.
Argument = Valid,	Argument = Invalid,	Argument = Invalid,
Topic = Elephant–Dogs	Topic = Adults–Babies–Children	Topic = Mice–Dogs–Elephants
Statements = True	Statements = True	Statements = False

Note: Based on Moshman & Franks, 1986 (p. 155)

The task in Demonstration 12.1 asks you to group reasoning problems on the basis of content, truthfulness of the conclusion, or validity of the logical argument. If you grouped A and B, then your judgment would be based on the truth of the propositions (the similarity between the two). If you grouped A and C, it would be based on their common theme of elephants. If you grouped B and C, it would be based on common logical property of **invalidity**: conclusions that do not definitely follow.

When children sort a stack of cards with these types of descriptions, they combine A and B or A and C, but few combine B and C before they are 11 years old unless they are given special instructions. For example, 9- and 10-year-olds sort arguments on the basis of empirical truth and appear to ignore validity even after 40 trials with feedback. Forty-five percent of 12- and 13-year-olds distinguished arguments on the basis of validity. Nearly 85% of university students combine problems based exclusively on validity (Moshman & Franks, 1986).

SECTION SUMMARY ■

The Development of Reasoning

The development of reasoning is similar to the development of language: We are born with the capacity to reason, but it takes interaction with the world to accomplish this feat. The ability to reason develops in stages. In Stage 1 reasoning, the child grasps the concept of *or* and is sensitive to the basic content of messages. By the end of this stage, children can comprehend different logical forms. In Stage 2 reasoning, children between the ages of 6 and 10 develop metacognition (awareness of their own cognitive processes) and seem to appreciate that conclusions must follow from the premises, but they are not fully sensitive to the validity of an argument. By Stage 3, 12- and 13-year-olds are able to reason on the basis of validity.

▪ ▪

Linear Reasoning

People regularly compare themselves to other people in terms of height, appearance, wealth, intelligence, or athleticism. These comparisons are based on linear relationships, in which the dimensions for comparison (e.g., height, weight, speed) can be represented as positions on a line. When people draw a conclusion that goes beyond the given "facts," we say they are reasoning. For example, if someone knows that Barbara is taller than Jessie (Fact 1) and Jessie is taller than Pam (Fact 2), then he or she can conclude that Barbara is taller than Pam. This ability to draw a conclusion from pairs of relationships on some dimension (such as height) is called **linear reasoning**.

One way to perform this kind of reasoning is to represent the quantities as points on a line or some kind of continuous scale and then mentally inspect the line for the relevant information (e.g., *who is biggest/smallest?*). Of course, it is possible to draw conclusions without imagining or mentally drawing points on a line. In fact, sometimes it is impossible to create a line even though the sentences of a problem seem to tell you that a line would be effective. To see this, try the activities in Demonstration 12.2.

▪▪▪DEMONSTRATION 12.2

Nonlinear Problems

One of the earliest studies of reasoning without images was performed by the German psychologist Buhler (1909, cited in Knauff, 2006, p. 129), who developed the following problem. Try to answer the question as quickly as possible:

Does a man have the right to marry the sister of his widow?

Try this second question:

How many birthdays does the average woman have?

It is possible to answer these questions by drawing lines or making charts. The correct solution, however, relies on understanding the definition of terms, not any linear relationship. In the first problem, if you are like typical undergraduates, you may have immediately thought, "yes, it's legal to marry a widow." However, with some reflection you should have realized that the clause, *his widow*, means that the female person in question is dead. In the second question, the definition of *birthdays* doesn't require counting, only the knowledge that every woman has a single birthday that she celebrates on the same day each year.

Because you were under time pressure in attempting the questions in Demonstration 12.2, you may have used a set of simple reasoning procedures, called

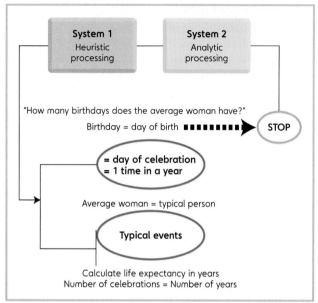

FIGURE 12.1 Reasoning Procedures: The Dual System The dual system hypothesis views human reasoning as occurring in the interplay of two systems: one reflects intuitive (heuristic) processing and the other reflects logical (analytic) processing.

Child putting rings of different sizes on a tower.

Jim Craigmyle/Getty Images

System 1 (e.g., Evans, 2003; Stanovich & West, 2000), that are often associated with intuitive ("gut level") responses. System 1 often leads to an incomplete understanding of a situation and unreflective decisions. We discuss System 1 later in the chapter, but it is illustrated in **FIGURE 12.1**.

Seriation and Transitivity

The basis of linear reasoning is the ability to (a) compare two physically present objects along a single dimension (e.g., size or weight); and (b) order those physically present items along that dimension. This is called **seriation**, the ability to place objects in a series or order. Two-year-old children show this ability when they put rings of different sizes on a tower or organize their blocks in order of size (Piaget, 1928/1966).

A child's ability to seriate has been used for nearly a century as an indicator of intelligence. A simple seriation task is included in the Binet–Simon (1916) test of intelligence (Item 22). The child is presented with five boxes that look alike but contain different weights (3, 6, 9, 12, and 15 grams). The child is asked to arrange them from heaviest to lightest, starting with the heaviest on the left. The child's arrangement is compared with the correct one, and the child receives a score based on the number of moves that are required to rearrange the child's sequence into the correct one. This score is compared with those obtained for children of different chronological ages. The child's *mental age* is equivalent to the chronological age of children who obtain the same score. The typical child is able to seriate the boxes perfectly by around the age of 7.

The simplest form of seriation occurs when the child compares every box with every other box and decides which is the heavier in each pair of boxes. For example, a 4-year-old presented with boxes A, B, and C would compare A and B and choose the heavier of the two; then compare A and C and identify the heavier; but also compare B and C. This would require a total of three comparisons. But suppose the child had the concept that, if A were heavier than B, and B were heavier than C, then A would be heavier than C. In this case, the child would have to make only two comparisons in order to place the three objects. The concept that underlies this is called **transitivity**: Given three items, if a relation (e.g., heavier) holds between the first two items and also between the second and the third items, it must hold between the first and third items. The concept of transitivity is acquired as people age (Breslow, 1981) as long as their memory is good (Trabasso, 1977).

For adults, seriation is performed effortlessly because we have achieved the concept of transitivity, but that does not mean we are flawless in our linear reasoning. We can easily be misled into thinking that some relationship terms, such as *loves* or *sees*, can be seriated. To see this, compare your reasoning process in statement (a) with that in statements (b) and (c).

(a) John is taller than Bill and Bill is taller than Charles. Who is tallest?

(b) John can see Bill and Bill can see Charles, but John can't see Charles. Why?

(c) John loves Mary and Mary loves Bill. Does John love Bill?

Notice that in (a) there is only one definite answer, whereas in (b) there are many possible solutions—everything is up for grabs. Bill might be standing at the corner of a building on a street; down one street is John and down another is Charles, neither of whom can see each other. All these questions can be seen as linear reasoning problems, yet drawing a line does not always produce a unique solution. These occasional difficulties or errors with linear relations have been noted for millennia and have prompted teachers to try to instruct their students on how to avoid reasoning errors. Aristotle's (384–322 BCE) *Organon* was written 2,500 years ago, for example (Aristotle, 1938).

Linear Syllogisms

To evaluate people's ability to reason about linear relations, cognitive psychologists use a linear syllogism task. A **syllogism** is an argument in which the conclusion follows from the premises. A typical one looks like the following:

Scott is taller than Paul.

Paul is taller than Nancy.

Who's tallest? Who's shortest?

A syllogism contains two explicit relations and asks the reasoner for a conclusion. Reasoners' decisions reflect their expectation that the information will be presented in a linear order: either left-to-right or top-down (e.g., DeSoto, London, & Handel, 1965; Handel, DeSoto, & London, 1968; Hunter, 1957). This is called an *idealized* or *canonical* form. When the information flow fits this form, reasoning is fast and accurate as in example (a) below. When it does not fit the canonical order, as in example (b), reasoning can be labored and error prone (Clark, 1969; Hunter, 1957; Huttenlocher, 1968).

(a) A is better than B; B is better than C. Who's best?

(b) B is better than C; B is worse than A. Who's best?

University students make twice as many errors answering (b) as they do when answering (a), and when students solve the problems correctly, they require more time to solve (b) than (a) (Clark, 1969). Problems like this have found their way into tests of intelligence (e.g., Burt, 1919; Sternberg, 1980) because reasoning skill with abstract problems increases with chronological age (e.g., Hunter, 1957; Sternberg, 1980, 1982). Interestingly, the linear syllogisms that are difficult for children are also relatively difficult for adults (Clark, 1969; Huttenlocher, 1968).

Language and Linear Reasoning

Because linear syllogisms are expressed in language, it is natural to suppose that human language processing plays a role in reasoning. Two basic principles of language processing explain how people solve linear syllogisms: the principle of lexical marking and the principle of congruity (Clark, 1969).

Principle of Lexical Marking When a reasoning task is presented to us using the medium of words, we may be unaware of the importance of the meaning of those words for our ability to reason. Some words are semantically more difficult to understand than others, even though we have already stored their meaning. Take the word *lion*, for example. It covers both male and female lions. However, *lioness* refers only to female lions. When we hear *lion* it is easier to understand than is *lioness* because *lion* doesn't require us to think of the gender of the animal or other details. Words like *lioness* are more complicated and are called **marked terms** (think of making a mark noting that they are more difficult). Words liked *lion* are simpler and less detailed and are called **unmarked terms** (Bierwisch, 1967). The **principle of lexical marking** says that marked terms are more difficult to reason with and to store in memory (e.g., Chase & Clark, 1971; Clark, 1969; Clark & Card, 1969).

This is also true for descriptive terms like the following pairs:

good–bad

long–short

wide–narrow

deep–shallow

intelligent–dumb

In each pair, the terms on the left are unmarked compared with the ones on the right. There are two criteria for determining which one of a pair is unmarked. First, the unmarked term names a dimension or scale like goodness, length, width, depth, or intelligence. You might ask, "how long is that board?" but you would rarely ask, "how short is that board?" You might say, "that board is three feet wide," but probably not "that board is three feet narrow" (just like the *lion–lioness* example).

The second criterion is that marked terms ask us to make a commitment to a particular point on a dimension. If you were told that the pond is shallower than the pool, you might think they are both shallow. But if you were told that the pool is deeper than the pond, you would have no expectations about their basic depth. Using the marked terms causes the listener to think of one end of the dimension.

To test the principle of lexical marking (that marked terms are more difficult to reason with than unmarked terms), Clark (1969) asked university students to solve problems like these, either asking who's best or who's worst. Problem A uses unmarked terms and problem B uses marked terms.

Problem A

    Adam is better than Bill.

    Bill is better than Chuck.

    Who's best? Who's worst?

Ans: Adam is best; Chuck is worst.

Problem B

    Chuck is worse than Bill.

    Bill is worse than Adam.

    Who's best? Who's worst?

Ans: Adam is best; Chuck is worst.

On average, university students made twice as many errors on B than they did on A and took 10% longer to solve B correctly.

Principle of Congruity As you can see from the syllogisms above, linear reasoning problems ask the solver a question. The second principle of language processing, called *congruity*, addresses how people answer questions. This process is similar to encoding specificity described in Chapter 6. The mental steps that someone may go through in order to answer a question are summarized in **FIGURE 12.2**. It shows that to answer any question, you must do three things: (a) encode the question, (b) compare your encoding of the question with your encoding of facts you have already stored, and (c) if your encoding of the question and the facts match, answer the question. If they don't, you re-encode the question to match what you do know or you re-encode your facts in an attempt to fit the question.

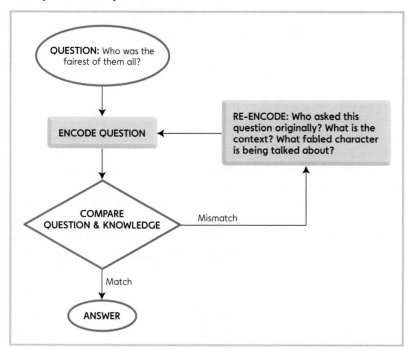

FIGURE 12.2 Question-Answering Process: Principle of Congruity When you are asked a question about information you may possess in LTM, you encode the question and compare it to your relevant knowledge. If there is a match, you answer the question; if there is no match, you try to re-encode the question to gain a different understanding of what is being asked. If there is still no match, you give up.

FIGURE 12.3 Picture Encoding (A) *High+*
and *high* (B) *Low+* and *low*.

Source: After Banks, Clark, & Lucy, 1975

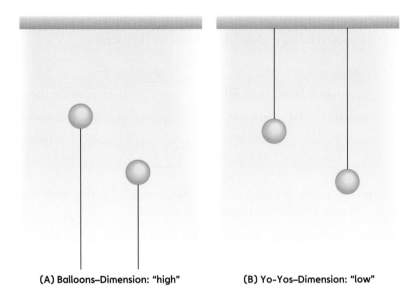

(A) Balloons–Dimension: "high"   (B) Yo-Yos–Dimension: "low"

The **principle of congruity** refers to the matching component: When the codes of the question and the codes of what is stored match, answers are fast and accurate. When they do not match, more time is consumed and the responder is likely to make an error. This was tested in a precise but lighthearted way by Banks, Clark, and Lucy (1975). They showed students drawings of pairs of balloons (**FIGURE 12.3A**) and asked them to press a button indicating which balloon was higher or which balloon was lower. When people look at balloons, they naturally think of them in terms of how high they might float. That is, the relevant dimension is height. Your encoding of the balloons diagram would have the balloons encoded, from left to right, as *high+* and *high*. That is, both balloons are encoded in terms of *high*, but the one on the left is higher so it's encoded as *high+*. If you are asked which balloon is higher, the question is encoded as *high+*: You simply compare the question with the picture encodings and select the one that matches. However, if you are asked which is lower (encoded as *low+*), the question will not match any facts, and you have to convert the question to be *high*. For the balloons pictured, higher questions should be easier to deal with than lower questions. In fact, Banks et al. found that students were quicker at answering which is higher than which is lower.

To see whether this effect of congruity would work using different drawings, half the time when the students were asked which is higher and which is lower, they saw the balloons pictured upside down so that they looked like yo-yos (a yo-yo is a toy invented in the Philippines, illustrated in **FIGURE 12.3B**). Since playing with a yo-yo requires it to descend to the end of its string, the relevant dimension for coding pictures of yo-yos is *low*. Consequently, the question, which yo-yo is lower? ought to be more congruent with the way the pictures are coded than the question, which yo-yo is higher? Banks et al. (1975) found this to be the case: For the yo-yo condition students were faster at responding to which is lower than to which is higher—exactly the opposite pattern than with the balloons.

Now if we apply the principle of congruity to linear reasoning problems like who's best and who's worst in problem A (see p. 405), who's best should be more rapidly answered than who's worst because *best* matches *better than*. In contrast, congruity also predicts that in problems like B, who's worst should be answered more quickly because *worst* matches *worse than*. The results are shown in **TABLE 12.1**, which supports the predictions of the congruity principle. Notice that problems with the marked terms (e.g., *worse*) require more time to answer than those with unmarked terms no matter what the question (Carpenter & Just, 1975; Clark & Chase, 1972).

TABLE **12.1**		
Time Required to Answer Questions		
Premises	**Who's best? (in seconds)**	**Who's worst? (in seconds)**
A is better than B; B is better than C.	5.20	5.81
A is worse than B; B is worse than C.	6.10	5.78

Note: Based on Clark, 1969

As we learned in Chapters 9 and 10, difficulties with processing language are related to the limitations in working memory capacity. In fact, working memory components described in Chapter 5, such as the visuospatial sketchpad and the phonological loop, should lead you to anticipate that different parts of working memory are active when people try to solve linear syllogisms. This is in fact what research has shown. For example, students were asked to solve a spatial four-term problem (Vandierendonck & De Vooght, 1997, p. 809): They were to read the statements (a) to (c) and answer the question (d).

(a) The guitar is to the right of the violin.

(b) The guitar is to the left of the drum kit.

(c) The drum kit is to the left of the piano.

(d) Is the violin to the right of the drum kit?

Because these are spatial relations, we should expect that the visuospatial sketchpad would be critical to a person's ability to solve this problem. This was shown to be the case: In a situation where there was a concurrent task that interfered with the visuospatial sketchpad, it interfered with the person's ability to answer the question correctly and also increased the time to make a decision (Vandierendonck & De Vooght, 1997). This shows that working memory plays a distinct role in solving linear reasoning problems.

Reasoning About Narratives

Linear reasoning has been studied in situations far more natural than syllogisms. In one series of studies (Daneman & Hannon, 2007; Potts, 1972, 1978; Potts & Peterson, 1985), students read a passage as illustrated in Demonstration 12.3, and then answered questions about it. You can see from the passage that the sentences expressed linear relations among at least four categories (e.g., *deer*, *bear*, *wolf*, and *hawk*). Some of the questions that students answered were verbatim matches with information given in the passage (e.g., the equivalent of A is greater than B: *The deer is smarter than the bear*). Other questions required an inference from the information from the paragraph (e.g., the equivalent of A is greater than D: *The deer is smarter than the hawk*).

The study was designed to determine the relationship between the number of reasoning steps needed to answer the question and the accuracy of the responses given. Common sense would tell us that the more reasoning steps, the more difficult the judgment, and therefore the greater the error rate. But science often requires some uncommon sense! The figure in the demonstration shows that terms that are farther apart on the linear scale are easier for students to evaluate. So, for example, is A greater than D? was answered more rapidly and more accurately than, is A greater than B? (Potts, 1978; Woocher, Glass, & Holyoak, 1978). This was especially surprising because the statement "A > B" was actually presented in the paragraph, while the statement "A > D" was not (Potts, 1976). Because of the way people represent linear relations, they can evaluate inferences more accurately and faster than they can with the actual information presented.

■■■DEMONSTRATION 12.3

Linear Reasoning Within a Paragraph

Read this linear ordering passage (Potts, 1972, p. 730) and see how the relations among the deer, wolf, bear, and hawk are represented symbolically (in letters).

In a small forest just south of nowhere, a deer, a bear, a wolf, and a hawk were battling for dominion over the land. It boiled down to a battle of wits, so intelligence was the crucial factor. The bear was smarter than the hawk, the hawk was smarter than the wolf, and the wolf was smarter than the deer. These relations are symbolically represented as:

1. A > B [A is greater than B]
2. B > C
3. C > D

The questions can be represented as follows:

One-step inference: A > B or B > C (these are verbatim with the story)
Two-step inference: A > C or B > D, etc.
Three-step inference: A > D

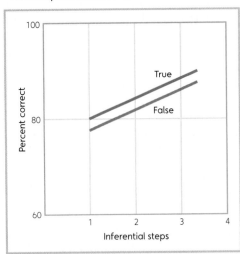

Memory for Linear Relationships
People remember the theme of what they read rather than the set of facts. In Potts (1972) students memorized a paragraph that described linear relationships. When asked to recognize both true and false relationships later on, they were more accurate at recognizing the "distant" relationships that were inferences from what they read than the "close" ones that they had actually read.

Source: After Potts, 1972

Linear Discriminability Student responses in Demonstration 12.3 illustrate that the farther apart terms are placed on a mental line, the more easily their relationship can be "seen," and therefore the more accurately people can make a judgment about which is greater or smaller. This is like the symbolic distance effect described in Chapters 1 and 8, where observers are faster at judging which object is largest or smallest when the objects are easier to discriminate. In the symbolic distance effect, it doesn't matter whether you are looking at a picture of the objects or just imagining them.

Category Discriminability These findings also generalize to other forms of inference, such as **set-inclusion relations**. Set inclusion describes the relationship among categories of objects. For example, since we know that *all lions are mammals* and that *all mammals are living things*, it allows us to draw the conclusion that *all lions are living things.* To discover whether students reason the same way with set inclusions as they do with linear relations, Nguyen and Revlin (1993) asked university students to read a passage about a mythical society and then answer questions about it (Frase, 1970; Griggs, 1976). In one passage, all of the categories were political parties (such as tribes, unions, coalitions, etc.) and so were easily related on a common dimension of political parties. These are called *convergent relations* because they all relate to the same basic concept. In another passage, the categories did not fit on a common dimension (outcasts, hill people, peace lovers). These are called *divergent relations*. The passage and questions are illustrated in Demonstration 12.4.

▪▪▪DEMONSTRATION 12.4

Category Discriminability

Convergent Narrative

All members of the Fundala tribe are members of the Outcast Union. All members of the Outcast Union are members of the Hill People Coalition. All members of the Hill People Coalition are members of the Farmers Cooperative. All members of the Farmers Cooperative are members of the Peace Party.

(Nguyen & Revlin, 1993, p. 1209)

Divergent Narrative

All Fundalas are outcasts from Central Ugalla. All Outcasts are hill people. All Hill People are Farmers. All Farmers are peace loving, as revealed in their artwork.

(Nguyen & Revlin, 1993, p. 1209)

Verbatim (True)	Verbatim (False)	Inferential (True)	Inferential (False)
All A are B	All B are A	All A are C	All C are A
All B are C	All C are B	All A are D	All D are A
All C are D	All D are C	All A are E	All E are A
All D are E	All E are D	All B are D	All D are B
		All B are E	All E are B
		All C are E	All E are C

When students answered questions about the convergent relations, the pattern of reasoning was similar to linear relations: Students were more accurate on distant relationships than more immediate ones. In contrast, with divergent relations, where categories could not be put on a common dimension, the pattern of reasoning was substantially different: Students were less accurate with regard to distant relations than they were with more immediate ones (e.g., Frase, 1970; Griggs, 1976; Potts, 1976). This shows that the pattern of linear reasoning is the same for all kinds of relationships as long as the items reasoned about can be expressed as positions on a line.

The Neuropsychology of Linear Reasoning

A key element in linear reasoning is a person's ability to lay out the terms spatially. This suggests that the brain areas related to spatial processing ought to be involved in solving linear syllogisms. To identify the critical areas for linear reasoning, Goel and Dolan (2001) asked a group of 16 men and women to solve 60 meaningful and 60 abstract linear syllogisms (examples illustrated in **TABLE 12.2**). While the participants were solving the problems, the researchers performed an fMRI analysis of the brain areas most active during the reasoning process.

They found two patterns illustrated in **FIGURE 12.4**. When students solved linear syllogisms that contained concrete or familiar words, the left hemisphere of the brain involving spatial and language processing was highly active, just as the discussion of the two language principles would suggest. However, when students solved abstract, unfamiliar problems with minimal words, the students' parietal lobes and occipital lobes were highly active. These are areas associated with spatial processing. With concrete materials, the left hemisphere spatial processing is involved. With abstract materials, the right hemisphere spatial processing is critical. This tells us that there are two neurological systems for dealing with linear syllogisms (Knauff, Mulack, Kassubek, Salih, & Greenlee, 2002).

TABLE **12.2**		
Materials Used in Goel and Dolan (2001, p. 903)		
	Concrete sentences	**Abstract sentences**
Relational arguments	Karen is in front of Larry. Larry is in front of Jane. Karen is in front of Jane.	K is in front of L. L is in front of J. K is in front of J.
	Nancy is younger than Karen. Karen is younger than Jake. Nancy is younger than Jake.	N is younger than K. K is younger than J. N is younger than J.
Baseline	Karen is in front of Larry. Larry is in front of Jane. George is above Mary.	K is in front of L. L is in front of J. K is above J.
	Nancy is younger than Karen. Karen is younger than Jake. Mary is richer than Jane.	N is younger than K. K is younger than J. K is richer than J.

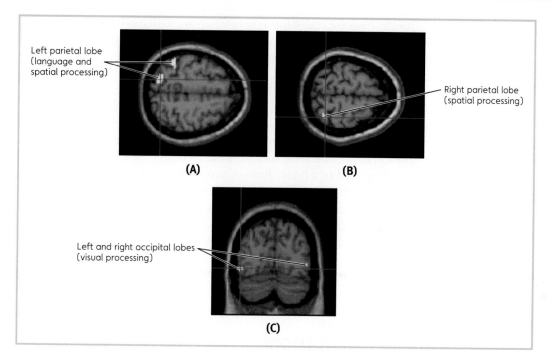

Left parietal lobe
(language and
spatial processing)

Right parietal lobe
(spatial processing)

(A)   **(B)**

Left and right occipital lobes
(visual processing)

(C)

We must be cautious, however, in assuming that one hemisphere of the brain is responsible for one kind of processing and the other hemisphere is responsible for something different. We can see this in linear reasoning studies. When people reason about simple concrete syllogisms like those on p. 410, left-hemisphere processing dominates. However, when the syllogisms are difficult for people, the brain recruits processing from other areas of the brain to help them out (Caramazza, Gordon, Zurif, & DeLuca, 1976; Hier & Kaplan, 1980; Knauff, Strube, Jola, Rauh, & Schlieder, 2004; Read, 1981). Research on the neurophysiology of linear reasoning tells us that working memory processing contributes to linear reasoning and that the type of representation of the linear relations is also critical to correct reasoning.

FIGURE 12.4 Reasoning with Different Content When solving linear syllogisms, there are two separate systems involved: left hemisphere-based spatial processing for concrete materials and right hemisphere-based spatial processing for abstract materials.

Reprinted from *Neuropsychologia, 39,* Vinod Goel, Raymond J. Dolan, Functional neuroanatomy of three-term relational reasoning, 908, 2001, with permission from Elsevier.

SECTION SUMMARY ▪

Linear Reasoning

Linear reasoning is among the earliest forms of complex reasoning to appear in human development. It is called linear reasoning because it can be performed by mentally placing objects on a line so that the distance between the objects reflects their relationship to one another. The process by which this is accomplished is called seriation. We are able to draw conclusions from our seriations because we have the concept of transitivity, which allows a conclusion to be drawn from this arrangement: If A has a relationship to B and B has the same relationship to C, then A has that relationship to C. This ability to seriate is evident in childhood and forms the basis for reasoning as measured on intelligence tests. Linear relations in the form of a series of statements are called linear syllogisms. Our ability to solve such syllogisms is influenced by the linguistic forms the syllogism takes. Language processes can account for people's decisions in cases where the reasoner is practiced at doing the task and the sentences are meaningful. When the relationships are clearly spatial or abstract, the spatial components of working memory play a distinct role in linear reasoning.

When people draw conclusions about relations expressed in a narrative form, their representation of the sentences is critical. When the relationship among the objects can be placed in a linear format, people are quite rational. The greater the distance between two objects, the more discriminable they are and the more accurate people's judgments are. People reason similarly when asked about set-inclusion problems. The critical factor is whether reasoners are able to place the information on a common dimension. If they cannot, as in the case of divergent relations, then the more inferential steps they must make to solve the problem, the less likely they are to reach the correct conclusion.

Categorical Reasoning

For more than 20 centuries university students, scientists, and people who argue before judges have been careful to use the syllogism as their guide for communication, as described by Judge Aldisert (1989, p. 3):

> Among the obvious benefits to be derived from a careful study of logic is a facility in studying law, in detecting error in the reasoning process, in learning how to avoid errors, and in thinking about difficult matters with clearness and consistency.

This is because, by adhering to the structure imposed by the syllogism, the speaker can create valid arguments with a conclusion you may or may not accept as correct or true, but with a logical basis that cannot be disputed. Cognitive research has investigated how people are able to perform this kind of reasoning and seemingly understand such logical arguments without much effort.

Categorical Reasoning Is Universal

Go back to the beginning of the chapter to the syllogism that begins, "All men are living creatures." It relates the categories *living creatures*, *men*, and *Socrates* (*all men are living creatures; Socrates is a man;* therefore, *Socrates is a living creature*). The ability to draw the appropriate inference in this syllogism is nearly universal; it does not require knowledge of logical forms (Morgan & Morton, 1944), nor does it require you to know the meaning of the category terms. Even children are capable of drawing the appropriate conclusion (Taplin, Staudenmayer, & Taddonio, 1974).

The ability to determine the logical outcome of this type of syllogism supports the idea that human beings are basically rational. In fact, drawing the correct conclusion requires only a willingness to cooperate with the task. This is illustrated in a study by Cole and Scribner (1974). They showed syllogisms similar to the following one to unschooled adults in Liberia (Kpelle rice farmers) and found that although the farmers declined to draw an inference, their explanations reveal an elegant logic. Here is a syllogism like the ones the Kpelle farmers were asked to solve (Scribner, as cited in Scribner & Tobach, 1975/1997, pp. 107–108):

> All men in Kpelle Town are farmers.
> Joe is a man in Kpelle Town.
> Is Joe a farmer?
>
> *Kpelle*: I cannot answer the question, because I only speak about people that I know and I don't know this Joe.

In the canonical form of a categorical syllogism, the man's explanation looks as follows:

I can only speak of people I know.

I don't know Joe.

Therefore, I cannot speak of Joe.

Notice that the man's refusal to solve the syllogism takes the form of a perfectly phrased logical argument. Cole and Scribner (1974) found that the critical factor in the willingness to cooperate with the task and to solve syllogisms seems to be whether a person has had more than 2 years of basic schooling, which presumably gives permission to "play" with these kinds of problems even though they violate Kpelle social norms. This pattern is not restricted to the people of West Africa. A similar pattern of reasoning has also been found among people in the Yucatan (Scribner, 1977) as well as among the nomadic people of Uzbekistan (Luria, 1976).

Three Types of Reasoning

Categorical reasoning is an example of **deduction**, which occurs when we reason from generalities to specifics. For example, if you wanted to know whether Shamu, a female whale, nurses her young, you might recall the generality, *all female mammals nurse their young* (one of the defining features of the category), and another generality, *all female whales are mammals;* therefore, *Shamu nurses her young*. People are incredibly good at drawing conclusions deductively (Calvillo & Revlin, 2005), although they often have to be reminded of the relevant facts (Sloman, 1998).

Deduction is contrasted with a type of reasoning called **induction**, in which the reasoner tries to generalize from specific facts: *Shamu nurses her young*; therefore, *all female whales nurse their young*. Inductive reasoning occurs when you go from some examples to a general rule that you think will explain all the examples.

Sherlock Holmes, with his pipe and deerstalker hat, and Dr. Watson, in a magazine illustration of the 1890s.

Stapleton Collection/Heritage/The Image Works

Although deductions from true statements result in true conclusions, inductions from true statements do not necessarily result in true generalities. For example, the fact that well-known singers Whitney Houston, Jon Bon Jovi, Queen Latifah, Bette Midler, Tracy Morrow, Ricky Nelson, Paul Simon, Frank Sinatra, Bruce Springsteen, and Dionne Warwick were born in New Jersey might lead to these false generalizations: *All well-known singers are born in New Jersey*, or *If you are born in New Jersey, you will be a well-known singer*. Even though conclusions derived from inductive reasoning are not necessarily true, that fact does not seem to stop us from jumping to conclusions based on such inferences—from belief in the Bermuda Triangle to astrology. Induction seems to come naturally.

A form of induction called **abduction** is often used by physicians, scientists, and famous detectives, like Sherlock Holmes. Abduction is a form of induction in which you draw the conclusion that offers the best explanation for the facts at hand (Dieussaert, Schaeken, Schroyens, & d'Ydewalle, 1999), but not necessarily the correct one. Take the example from Sherlock Holmes, who spoke to a terrified woman in *The Adventure of the Speckled Band*.

"You have come in by train this morning, I see."
"You know me, then?"

"No, but I observe the second half of a return ticket in the palm of your left glove. You must have started early, and yet you had a good drive in a dog-cart, along heavy roads, before you reached the station."

The lady gave a violent start and stared in bewilderment at my companion.

"There is no mystery, my dear madam," said he, smiling. "The left arm of your jacket is spattered with mud in no less than seven places. The marks are perfectly fresh. There is no vehicle save a dog-cart which throws up mud in that way, and then only when you sit on the left-hand side of the driver."

"Whatever your reasons may be, you are perfectly correct," she said.

(Doyle, 1892/2007, p. 160)

You probably are aware that alternative (and more correct) conclusions could have been drawn. This is often seen in the TV program *House*, whose two main characters (House and Wilson) are modeled after Holmes and his companion Watson. They often draw the wrong abductions throughout the story, until the final scenes.

The Importance of Representation

Cognitive research on reasoning tends to focus on two broad elements: (a) how people interpret and represent the sentences of the problem, and (b) the procedures that people use to go from the facts at hand to deriving a conclusion. In the syllogism about Socrates, whatever difficulty people have in drawing a conclusion is because of the effort to interpret the quantified sentence, *all men are living creatures*. Quantifiers are terms like *all, some*, and *few*. Reasoners have long been known to have difficulty understanding sentences with quantifiers, such as *all A are B* (e.g., Bucci, 1978; Chapman & Chapman, 1959; Revlin & Leirer, 1980; Wilkins, 1928). Many of the modern methods devised to help students reason are based on techniques developed centuries ago. For example, Euler (1775), the great 18th-century Swiss mathematician, provided instruction to the niece of Frederick the Great. To help her understand the relationship among sets and the interpretation of quantifiers, he drew circle diagrams that now bear his name, Euler circles, shown in **FIGURE 12.5**. The reasoner is supposed to understand the sentence by selecting the corresponding Euler diagram.

You can see from Figure 12.5 that most of the sentences have more than one diagram associated with them. This makes it difficult to select just the right diagram to use in reasoning (Erickson, 1978; Johnson-Laird & Steedman, 1978). Even when students are instructed on the use of Euler diagrams, they still make errors (Calvillo et al., 2006) and fail to draw the correct conclusions (Calvillo et al., 2006; Revlin & Leirer, 1980).

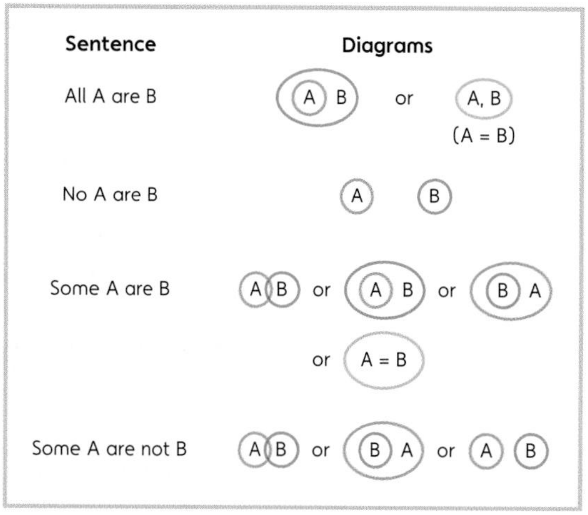

FIGURE 12.5 Euler Diagrams
Euler, the great 18th-century Swiss mathematician, drew circle diagrams, which now bear his name, to his student to explain the relationship among sets and the interpretation of quantifiers. Here the reasoner is supposed to understand the sentence by selecting the corresponding Euler diagram.

Sentence	Diagrams
All A are B	(A B) or (A, B) (A = B)
No A are B	(A) (B)
Some A are B	(A B) or (A B) or (B A) or (A = B)
Some A are not B	(A B) or (B A) or (A) (B)

For example, take two sentences with quantifiers such as *all A are B* and *some C are A*. How many different combinations of diagrams would you need before you have a complete understanding of the pair of sentences? The answer is 8. Other diagram systems such as the one developed by John Venn (1880), which you may have studied in high school, have similar limitations.

Conversion Representation

One reason people have difficulty with diagram representations is that their understanding of sentences may not correspond to the correct interpretation of the pictures. One source of difficulty in understanding sentences is that people use an interpretation procedure called **conversion**, in which they treat sentences as reversible. For example, since they know that *all A are B*, they assume that the reverse, *all B are A*, is also true (Cohen & Nagel, 1934; Revlin & Leirer, 1980). This is equivalent to concluding that A = B. To see that conversion could be incorrect, take the sentence, *all men are mortal*. The reverse, *all mortals are men*, is not true because women are also mortal. Many reasoning errors can be explained by noticing that reasoners may have converted one or more of the premises of the syllogism (e.g., Chapman & Chapman, 1959; Wilkins, 1928). Take the true statement that "most people with severe lung cancer have been heavy smokers of cigarettes" (about 90%; Peto, Lopez, Boreham, Thun, & Heath, 1994). This leads to the common—though incorrect—interpretation that most cigarette smokers will get lung cancer.

Conversion is so natural that it is not easy to train students to avoid it. In one study (Revlin, Ammerman, Petersen, & Leirer, 1978), two groups of students were given 16 reasoning problems to solve. One group solved symbolic problems (e.g., *all A are B; some B are C*), and students tended to use a converted interpretation (e.g., A = B). A second group solved problems in which the natural semantics would prevent a converted interpretation (e.g., *all birds are animals* would not be interpreted to mean *all animals are birds*). On the 17th problem, both groups of students were shown a symbolic problem with As, Bs, and Cs. The first group continued to use the interpretation it had used on the previous 16 problems. The second group switched its interpretation on the 17th problem and, just like the first group, used a converted interpretation. Conversion is a habit that is difficult to break.

Why would the converted interpretation of the symbolic problem be so readily available? To gain a sense of this, try the activity in Demonstration 12.5 and then continue reading.

■■■**DEMONSTRATION 12.5**

Implied Transitivity

Read the following set of facts and then answer the questions as rapidly as you can at the end. You'll notice that a relationship marked by a long dash (—) is undefined in the task and relies on you to provide an interpretation.

There are four people: Bob, Lou, Pat, and Fred
Either Pat (—) Bob, or Pat (—) Fred.
Either Lou (—) Fred, or Bob (—) Lou.
Pat (—) Bob.
Either Fred (—) Bob, or Pat (—) Fred.
Either Lou (—) Fred, or Fred (—) Bob.

Which of the following statements are true and which are false?

Lou (—) Fred.
Pat (—) Lou.
Bob (—) Lou.

(Tsal, 1977, p. 679)

In the original task (Tsal, 1977), university students were shown the set of facts, in which the relationship marked by (—) was undefined. However, most students chose to interpret (—) as symmetrical or transitive. In this case the question, Pat (—) Lou is true, Lou (—) Fred is false, and Bob (—) Lou is true.

The demonstration shows that there is a tendency to interpret relations in the simplest way. Using the converted interpretation treats the *A are B* relationship as symmetrical, A = B (Tsal, 1977) and thereby reduces the need to keep track of exceptions (Dawes, 1964).

People are not doomed to convert sentences. Their representation depends on the semantics of the sentence. Consider problem A on the next page. Students report that their mental image of the situation (see **FIGURE 12.6**) has Bill's books on a shelf crowded with books that are difficult to differentiate. They use a symmetrical interpretation and incorrectly conclude (70% of the time) that at least some of the psychology books are Bill's (some think that all of the psychology books are Bill's). In contrast, their reported image of the situation in problem B is that Bill's books are among a substantial number of volumes in a library, and therefore they rarely conclude (35% of the time) that some of the psychology books are Bill's, and never conclude that all of the psychology books are Bill's (Revlis, 1975a, p. 123).

FIGURE 12.6 Mental Representation and Reasoning (A) Students report that their mental image of the situation in this problem has Bill's books on a shelf crowded with books that are difficult to differentiate. (B) In contrast, their reported image of the situation in this problem is that Bill's books are among a substantial number of volumes in a library.

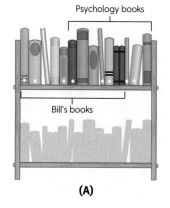

Psychology books

Bill's books

(A)

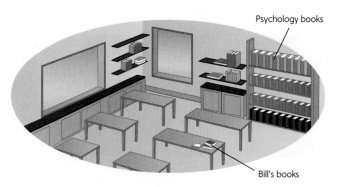

Psychology books

Bill's books

(B)

Problem A

All of Bill's books are on the top shelf.

All of the psych books are on the top shelf.

Some of the psych books are Bill's.

Problem B

All of Bill's books are on the 4th floor.

All of the psych books are on the 4th floor.

Some of the psych books are Bill's.

Therefore a person's semantic analysis and representation of the statements play a key role in how that reasoner draws conclusions with categorical relations (Johnson-Laird, 1983; Johnson-Laird & Steedman, 1978).

FIGURE 12.7 Reasoning and the Brain A broad circuitry in the human brain participates in deductive reasoning.

Reprinted from *Trends in Cognitive Science, 11,* Vinod Goel, Anatomy of deductive reasoning, 438, Copyright 2007, with permission from Elsevier.

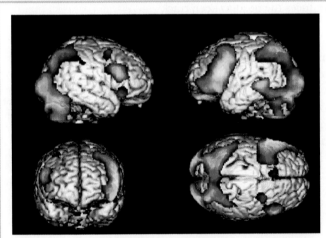

(A) Main Effect of Reasoning

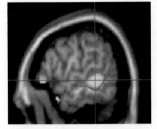

(B) Reasoning with Familiar Material

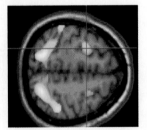

(C) Reasoning with Unfamiliar Material

The Neuropsychology of Categorical Reasoning

Earlier in the chapter we learned that linear reasoning relies on the right parietal lobe as well as the left temporal lobe when people read meaningful text. What areas of the brain are important for categorical reasoning? To identify the general brain areas involved in this form of deduction, Goel, Buchel, Frith, and Dolan (2000) presented categorical syllogisms to volunteers and performed an fMRI analysis while they were reasoning. Participants were asked to solve two sorts of deduction problems. One set of problems contained concrete syllogisms such as *all dogs are pets; all poodles are dogs;* therefore, *all poodles are pets.* Solving these problems was associated with language-related, left-hemisphere processing. The second set of problems contained syllogisms with abstract material, such as *all P are B; all C are P;* therefore, *all C are B.* Solving these abstract syllogisms was associated with right-hemisphere spatial processing. These findings are similar to what was observed when solving linear reasoning problems (Osherson et al., 1998).

The studies suggest that what appear to be different kinds of reasoning—linear and categorical—are treated similarly in the human brain. In fact, we can conclude that a broad circuitry in the human brain participates in deductive reasoning. This circuitry is illustrated in **FIGURE 12.7** (Goel, 2007). It shows that the main differences in brain processing of deduction occur when dealing with familiar versus unfamiliar materials. It is quite possible that for familiar material, people have stored away special procedures for dealing with it in the left hemisphere. But with unfamiliar material, right-hemisphere processing has to be added. Inspection of Figure 12.7, however, also reveals that there is no special reasoning center of the brain—no one system deals with all reasoning. A considerable portion of our brains is recruited all of the time to perform even the most basic deduction.

SECTION SUMMARY ▪

Categorical Reasoning

When we reason from categorical information, we can deduce conclusions or induce them. Deduction requires drawing conclusions from general rules to specific facts. Induction occurs when we draw a general rule based on specific facts. When these rules are believed to be the best at explaining the facts, the reasoning process is called abduction. Categorical reasoning is a form of deduction that occurs when we reason from generalities to specifics. It is a universal skill as widely distributed as language. The ability of untrained people to reason correctly on this type of syllogism supports the argument that people are rational beings.

When reasoners draw an invalid conclusion or fail to draw a valid one, it is primarily because of the way they have interpreted the categorical relationship. An important source of reasoners' difficulties in interpreting sentences is the natural human tendency to simplify the sentences and to use an interpretation procedure called *conversion*, where reasoners interpret *all A are B* to mean that *A are B* and *B are A*. When there is only a single possible interpretation, students rarely make errors in reasoning. Studies of brain functioning during reasoning show that two major centers of the cortex are critical to reasoning: the left-hemisphere language centers and the right-hemisphere pattern recognition centers. These findings provide cognitive neuropsychological support for the similarity between linear and categorical reasoning.

▪ ▪

Belief Bias in Reasoning

> The barber of Seville shaves all those men and only those men of Seville who do not shave themselves. If the barber is also a resident of Seville, who shaves the barber?
>
> *(Russell, as cited in Slateer, 1986, p. 228)*

This puzzle is a **paradox** (a self-contradictory statement): The barber has to shave himself, but if he does shave himself, then he can't! Paradoxes are useful because they focus our attention on how we implicitly define terms and situations. In this case, the present paradox rests on our assumption that the barber is a man. It is not a puzzle at all if the barber is a woman. Our beliefs and biases enter into our interpretations not only as part of understanding puzzles, but also when understanding sentences and engaging in many forms of reasoning. This is especially powerful in a phenomenon called the **belief-bias effect**, where people are said to allow their personal knowledge and beliefs to affect their decision as to whether or not a conclusion is logically valid.

Bias Effect

In the case of the syllogism, people's knowledge often plays a role in evaluating the logical validity of a conclusion: If you believe a conclusion is true, then you're more likely to think it is a correct conclusion, the result of a logically valid process. On the other hand, if you disbelieve a conclusion, you're more likely to think it is not valid. Put simply, your decision is influenced by your beliefs and biases. These beliefs not only come into play when you are drawing or evaluating a conclusion, they also come along for the ride when you begin interpreting the sentences of a logical argument (Revlin & Leirer, 1978; Wilkins, 1928). What makes the paradox so difficult for people to deal with is that they often don't see how their personal beliefs and assumptions interact with their reasoning.

Our belief in conclusions affects our willingness to test them (e.g., Klauer, Musch, & Naumer, 2000). The classic study of this phenomenon was performed during World War II (Morgan & Morton, 1944). College students had to solve two types of syllogisms. One type was abstract, with category labels, X, Y, and Z. The other type had a potentially personal content for the reasoner and ranged from everyday problems (*all troubles are unpleasant*; *some insults are troubles*; therefore, *some insults are unpleasant*) to dealing with personal convictions, like this one related to a Nazi called Heydrich, who was, for a time, in charge of the Gestapo and responsible for overseeing the deaths of millions of people:

Some ruthless men deserve a violent death

One of the most ruthless men was Heydrich, the Nazi hangman.

1. Heydrich, the Nazi hangman, deserved a violent death.
2. Heydrich, the Nazi hangman, may have deserved a violent death.
3. Heydrich, the Nazi hangman, did not deserve a violent death.
4. Heydrich, the Nazi hangman, may not have deserved a violent death.
5. None of the given conclusions seem to follow logically.

(Morgan & Morton, 1944, p. 39)

This syllogism does not have a valid conclusion. Using only the relationships expressed in the premises, none of the conclusions unambiguously follow, even though a reasoner might agree with the appropriateness or believability of one or more of them. The correct answer would be Option 5. In the original study, only 1 student chose this correct option and 37 chose Option 1. In contrast, when the identical problem with X, Y, and Z was solved, 16 students chose Option 5 and only 1 student chose Option 1. Morgan and Morton (1944) found that the distortions in reasoning become more marked when the terms in the syllogism are related to the personal convictions of the reasoner: "The only circumstances under which we can be relatively sure that the inferences of a person will be logical is when they lead to a conclusion which he has already accepted" (p. 39).

Although there is ample proof that our attitudes and beliefs affect our evaluation of the validity of an argument, as in this one (e.g., Evans, 1989; Feather, 1965; Gordon, 1953; Janis & Frick, 1943; Kaufman & Goldstein, 1967; Lefford, 1946; Markovits & Nantel, 1989; Thistlethwaite, 1950), this does not necessarily mean that humans are irrational creatures swayed by their emotions. If that were the case, then studies of reasoning would uncover massive errors in evaluating conclusions. That doesn't happen, either in the laboratory or in real life (Gigerenzer, 1996a; Henle, 1962).

Reasoners are basically trying to accomplish two things. First, they are trying to formulate a coherent interpretation of the premises that are presented to them. This is difficult to do in cases where people don't believe the premises because they don't make much sense when they are not believable (Cherubini, Garnham, Oakhill, & Morley, 1998). Second, reasoners are trying to *combine* the premises with the conclusion. When the conclusion is believable, the reasoner is biased toward finding a way to integrate it. When the conclusion is disbelieved, the reasoner is biased toward rejecting it and so tries to find a way for the premises and the conclusion to be separate. This is the same sort of thing we do when we are trying to comprehend sentences: We try to establish a "model" of what is being said and integrate it with what has come earlier in the conversation (Henle, 1971). Suppose someone says "hey, that bread was good." By itself, you can understand the basic sentence, but until you know that the previous sentence was "I've checked the use-by date on the package," you don't really know its true meaning. Integration is the essence of comprehension. It appears, then, that biases are part and parcel of rational processes.

Another way to look at this phenomenon is to think of human reasoning as resulting from the operation of two cognitive systems. System 1 is a basic-level processing, which is at the mercy of conflicts between logic and belief, and often responds at an emotional, heuristic level. System 2 is responsible for more deliberate, rational processing (Evans, 2003, 2008; Stanovich & West, 2000). These two systems are often in conflict, resulting in the belief-bias effect (Evans, Handley, & Harper, 2001). They are often referred to as dual processing (e.g., Wason & Evans, 1975) and are described in the next section.

Dual Processing

The idea that high-level cognition reflects the operation of two basic systems is called **dual processing** (e.g., Evans, 2008; Kahneman & Frederick, 2002; Stanovich, 1999). System 1 is generally conceived as a set of unconscious processes that are automatic, rapid, and able to accommodate many activities at once. System 2 contains processes that are more deliberate, conscious, and slow, and relies heavily on working memory. This is similar to the features of attentional processing described in Chapter 3. Other names for these two systems are *heuristic* and *analytic* (e.g., Evans, 2003, 2008). These two systems do not stand alone; they interact with each other. On some occasions, there is a conflict between automatic, shoot-from-the hip, kind of processing and analytic thinking. For example, when a conclusion is generated that is consistent with our beliefs, but not our sense of logic, the conflict is detected and System 2 may be called upon to resolve it (Evans, 2003, 2008; Goel & Dolan, 2003). To appreciate how these systems work to explain the belief-bias effect in reasoning, read the Focus on Methods.

FOCUS ON METHODS ■■■■ ■ ■■■■ ■

Dual Task Methodology

Our belief in the truth or falsity of a statement will affect whether we see it as a logically correct conclusion. This has an effect on our reasoning accuracy. For reasoning problems with valid conclusions, any disbelief in the conclusion might cause us to reject it and make an error. For an invalid conclusion (which we should logically reject) any belief in the truth of the conclusion could lead us to accept it and make an error. The belief bias reflects the influence of System 1. However, if System 2 enters into the reasoning process, we would be less likely to make an error. Put another way, if System 2 is interfered with by a secondary task that uses up the cognitive resources of System 2, it will not function efficiently, and we will have to make more efforts than if System 2 were free to normally function. The dual task methodology selectively affects the functioning of System 2. Researchers add a task that affects one system and should leave the other one less affected. If the predictions are correct, it demonstrates that two separate systems influence the performance of the task.

In one study (De Neys, 2006), students performed two tasks: a reasoning task where belief should cause errors, and a second task that uses up spatial working memory. The reasoning problems were like the following:

Major premise: All fruits can be eaten;

Minor premise: Bananas can be eaten;

Conclusion: Bananas are fruit.

1. The conclusion follows logically from the premises.
2. The conclusion does not follow logically from the premises.

Notice that while the conclusion is true, it does not follow from the premises. The second (memory load) task required the participants to look at a matrix with three or four dots before doing the reasoning task and then to reproduce the matrix after doing the reasoning task (see above right). One third of the students had to memorize a low-load, three-dot pattern; one third of the students had to memorize a more complex high-load, four-dot pattern; and one third of the students had no memory load task.

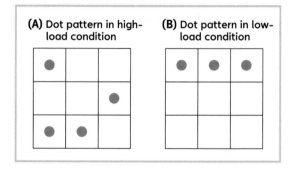

The results of the study are presented in the graph below, which shows that the students' accuracy in reasoning decreased as the memory load increased.

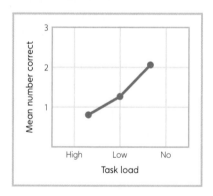

These findings illustrate that the cognitive load introduced by the dot matrix task affected reasoning performance on tasks where System 2 should help the reasoner make a rational judgment. When the task doesn't provide a load (the no load) condition, performance is better than when there is a low or high load: The greater the load, the poorer the reasoning accuracy. These findings provide just one example of the dual task methodology and its effectiveness in testing theories of reasoning.

SECTION SUMMARY

Belief Bias in Reasoning

It is natural for people to let their personal knowledge and beliefs affect their decisions. This happens because we cannot stop ourselves from using all the knowledge at our disposal to understand the sentences of an argument. However, at times this leads people to draw incorrect conclusions. This is called the belief-bias effect. It does not necessarily mean that human beings are always swayed by their emotions. However, strong beliefs in the validity of conclusions may pose difficulties for people in formulating a coherent interpretation of the premises and conclusions and can make them less motivated to verify the conclusions. Many of the cognitive processes that lead to belief bias in reasoning are the same rational processes that work in our favor in everyday life. They seem to reflect two overlapping systems, one more rational than the other, often referred to as System 1 and System 2.

Reasoning Schemas

We have learned that people are capable of rational thinking both in solving reasoning problems and in their everyday lives. One way they do this is to employ strategies called **reasoning schemas**, a set of rules and procedures that the reasoner automatically follows to draw or evaluate conclusions. The basic idea of schemas in memory processes was first described in Chapter 7. This section describes reasoning schemas and how they help people make decisions in many situations. To do this, we must first consider a standard task that has been used to reveal the presence of reasoning schemas, the selection task.

The Wason Selection Task

Peter Wason, a truly imaginative cognitive psychologist, developed a situation called the **selection task** (Wason, 1966), which offers an excellent opportunity to see reasoning in action (Newstead & Evans, 1995). In the task, reasoners were asked to listen to a rule that described an arbitrary relationship among numbers and letters and then were asked to see if the rule was true or false. To experience this task first hand, try the activity in Demonstration 12.6, based on Wason (1966) and Griggs and Cox (1982).

■■■DEMONSTRATION 12.6

Selection Task

You will see four squares; imagine these are cards with a front and a back. On each of these cards facing you is either a letter or a number. Your job is to read the rule and decide which card or cards you'd like to flip over to see what is written on the other side in order to test the rule.

Rule 1. *If there is a vowel on one side of the card, there is an even number on the other side.*

Which card or cards would you like to turn over to see if this rule is true?

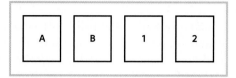

After you make your decision for Rule 1, try the situation for Rule 2.

Rule 2. *If you are drinking alcohol, you must be at least 21 years old.*

Which card or cards would you like to turn over to see if this rule is true?

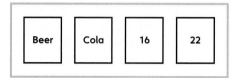

These are logically identical rules, yet people tend to turn over the first and fourth cards for Rule 1 and the first and third cards for Rule 2 (Griggs & Cox, 1982; Wason, 1966).

When presented with the first rule in Demonstration 12.6, 45% of the participants want to turn over the A and the 2 card (Wason & Johnson-Laird, 1972) and 33% want to turn over just the A card. Notice that these are just the instances of the categories mentioned in the rule (vowels and even numbers). Are these the ones you selected? How did you do with Rule 2? Accuracy on this problem, turning over the first and third cards, is nearly universal among college students. Why is Rule 1 so difficult? Let's review the options.

What are the consequences of different decisions? If you were to turn over the A card and there was an odd number written on the other side, it would falsify the rule (you would have a vowel on one side and an odd number on the other). So it is correct to turn over the A card because it would truly test the rule. What about the 2 card? The rule said that if there is a vowel there will be an even number, but it did not say that if there were an even number there would be a vowel. If you thought that the rule implied this, then you would be using a conversion interpretation of the rule (vowel = even number). Perhaps there is an even number on the other side of every card that is facing you. The rule would be correct, but a little uninformative (Sperber & Wilson, 1995). A comedian popular in the 1950s and 1960s, Oscar Levant, used to bid his audience good-bye by saying, "May your house be free from tigers." When asked about this farewell in New York, where wandering tigers are rarely (if ever) a problem, he cleverly responded that ever since he used this greeting, a tiger had not eaten a single one of his friends and he was afraid to stop. Similarly, if the 2 card is turned over, nothing on the other side could falsify the rule.

What about the B card? The rule speaks of vowels and even numbers, but it says nothing about consonants. So this card is irrelevant. Finally, we come to the 1 card, which shows an odd number. If you turn it over and there is a vowel, then you have the case where there is a vowel on one side and an odd number on the other. This would falsify the rule. In sum, the cards that would truly test the rule because they could falsify it are the A and the 1 cards. It is noteworthy that from 67% to 94% of college students fail to make the correct deduction and appropriately test the rule (see review by Evans, 1980). This is surprising because developmental psychologists (e.g., Beth & Piaget, 1966; Moshman, & Timmons, 1982) claim that children who reach 12 years of age are capable of the kind of falsification required in the selection task. Surely, college students should be successful at testing the rule. Why aren't they?

Schemas for Everyday Life

You might suppose from these findings that humans have limited reasoning ability and are not rational. But there is surprising data to come: When the rules are "realistic," such as Rule 2, people can be highly skilled in making the correct deductions. Why is this the case? Before launching into an explanation, let me briefly describe what happens with realistic information. Wason and Shapiro (1971, p. 68) gave participants the rule: *"Every time I go to Manchester, I go by train."* The cards showing were two cities in England (Manchester and Leeds) and two modes of transportation (car and train). Like the other selection tasks, the participants' task was to determine and test to see if the rule was true. The logical approach is to turn over the Manchester and car cards (like the A and 1 cards). This realistic situation improved performance over the basic vowel–even number rule, though not every time (see Manktelow & Evans, 1979).

Another realistic situation, and one that produces reliable decisions, occurs when students are presented with a drinking age rule logically similar to Rule 2 in Demonstration 12.6. Griggs and Cox (1982, p. 415) asked students to decide whether a permission rule was true: *"If a person is drinking beer, then that person must be over 18 years of age."* The following conditions were presented: person drinking beer, person drinking cola, person 16 years old, and person 22 years old. Notice that these correspond logically to the abstract situations described in the vowel–even number problem (A, B, 3, 2, respectively). Seventy-five percent of university students made the correct choices and selected the card with person drinking beer and the card that shows the person's age as 16 years old (i.e., not over 18).

At first the accuracy for these problems seems easy to explain. Participants may just recall specific examples from their memory of similar cases and reason by analogy (Griggs, 1983; Klaczynski, Gelfand, & Reese, 1989; Manktelow & Evans, 1979; Pollard, 1990; Riesbeck & Schank, 1989). However, the rules that result in accurate performance are examples of a broader range of rules to which reasoners are sensitive.

The drinking problem is an example of a **deontic rule**: a rule that involves permission and obligation. Such rules are common in everyday life and are learned because they are integral to how people in society get along (e.g., Cheng & Holyoak, 1985; Cheng, Holyoak, Nisbett, & Oliver, 1986). We use deontic rules to negotiate with people: *If you do X, you may have Y* (Cummins, 1996). They are also important in self-protection against law violators (e.g., Cosmides, 1989). One reason students may be successful at solving the drinking problem is that they have vast experience with testing deontic rules.

Another reason we are so successful at this sort of everyday reasoning is that we constantly use inference rules defined in terms of goals and actions to be taken. These are reasoning schemas. A small set of these that applies to the deontic situations is called **pragmatic reasoning schemas**, and their general format has the following four features (Cheng & Holyoak, 1985, p. 397):

(a) If the action is to be taken, then the precondition must be satisfied.

(b) If the action is not to be taken, then the precondition need not be satisfied.

(c) If the precondition is satisfied, then the action may be taken.

(d) If the precondition is not satisfied, then the action must not be taken.

Although these sound abstract, when you flesh them out, they allow a broad range of inferences. If a reasoner employed this four-part schema on the selection task, then component (a) leads the reasoner to test the connection between *is drinking* and *is over 21* by turning over the *is drinking beer* card. The schema, via part (d), leads the reasoner to examine the *under 21* and *drinking* connection by turning over the 16 (*under 21 card*). These are the responses reasoners actually make on this selection task. But if we all possess these schemas, why don't people use them in the vowels–even numbers problem? The answer is simple: Arbitrary rules don't evoke any pragmatic reasoning schema. For example, in one selection task, students were given the rule, *"If I eat haddock, then I drink gin."* Since there was no obvious realistic condition that this rule addressed, performance was as poor as in the vowel–even number condition (Manktelow & Evans, 1979). Applying conditional reasoning depends on whether the context evokes the reasoning schema.

The power of the pragmatic schemas is shown even when the reasoner is given an arbitrary rule to evaluate, but it is presented in a way that suggests the four-part schema is relevant. When this happens, reasoning is improved. Take the case presented by Jackson and Griggs (1990). They asked students to decide whether or not this regulation was being followed: *"If one is to take action A, one must first satisfy precondition P"* (p. 358). Although it sounds like the reasoning schema, performance was not much better than on other arbitrary problems. However, when reasoners were given the same rule and their motivation was "You are an authority checking whether or not people are obeying certain regulations" (p. 358), accuracy tripled, from 19% to 61% (Cheng & Holyoak, 1985; Cheng et al., 1986; Jackson & Griggs, 1990). This rule is no less abstract than vowels and numbers, but it evokes the schema framework.

Where Reasoning Schemas Come From

Cognitive psychologists want to know how we happen to learn rules for obligations and permissions. Do we learn them in the same way that we learn other schemas (described in Chapter 7), or are we somehow genetically endowed with this knowledge? One answer is that the permissions and obligations rules are really instances of **social exchange rules**. In its simplest expression, social exchange takes the form of "I'll scratch your back if you scratch mine." Cosmides (1989) asserted that humans are inherently social animals and come evolutionarily equipped to engage in social contracts. It is as if we all possess a biologically based reasoning module in our brains that is attuned to critical aspects of social exchanges. These exchanges may be just the sort of situations that are described by the pragmatic reasoning schemas. Broadly speaking, the social exchange rules are of the form: *If you take the benefit, then you pay the cost.*

Such rules have specialized procedures for dealing with social exchanges, especially for detecting cheating (Fiddick, Cosmides, & Tooby, 2000). Fiddick et al. argued that the enhanced performance on the selection task with permission rules is really just the result of activating the cheater detector rule. To see how this would work, let's suppose that the reasoner, confronted with the drinking rule, is looking for people who are cheating: people who are getting the *benefit* of drinking, without paying the *cost* of being 21. When you look for cheaters in this context, you'd want to know if a drinker has paid the cost and whether someone who has not paid the cost (e.g., age 16) is drinking. Together, these two elements predict correct selections in the task.

To show that the critical element in good performance on the selection task is activation of the social contract and not merely because the scenario was a permission, Cosmides, Barrett, and Tooby (2010, p. 9012) had participants read stories that involved permissions, but were either contracts or noncontracts. Before performing the selection task, two groups of participants were exposed to either of two scenarios. Both groups were told that in order to attend a school outside their district (Grover City), they needed permission. In one scenario, they needed permission because the school was supported by taxpayers ("Grover City residents pay higher taxes to have a good school"), hence there is a *cost* for attending. In the second scenario, there was no *cost* for attending ("You need permission because all the schools should have the right number of teachers"). Participants who experienced the social contract version of the story (the first scenario) were 75% correct in their selections, but students who experienced the nonsocial contract version (the second scenario) were only 30% correct in their selections.

Reasoning in applied contexts like the selection task involves two major processing stages: (a) interpretation of the rule, and (b) deliberative reasoning, where the person tries to apply rational procedures to evaluate the situation given the interpretation. Reasoning performance appears to be closely related to how people interpret the scenario that contains the rule they are to evaluate. Typically, the reader supplies relevant knowledge to make sense of the situation, and it is this knowledge that is being used to decide which rule to apply. So the critical factor is rule interpretation. Sometimes we make reasoning errors because we not only fail to interpret the rule correctly, we also fail to remember our own interpretations. To show this, Almor and Sloman (2000) assessed people's memory for the information in the scenarios compared with the selections they actually made in the task. They found that the memory for the rule wasn't always accurate and that the participants were more likely to choose the cards consistent with the rule that they recalled, rather than with the rule as it was actually stated in the problem (Almor & Sloman, 1996; Evans, Newstead, & Byrne, 1993; Liberman & Klar, 1996; Sperber & Wilson, 1995). Once again, memory is basic to problem solving and reasoning.

Understanding the Reasoning Task Itself

As we have just seen, interpreting the rules that we are asked to test is critical for applying the appropriate reasoning schema. However, it is also important to understand what the task itself is asking the reasoner to do: Is the reasoner supposed to determine if the rule is false (as in the vowel–number rule) or if the rule is violated (as in the drinking rule)? To see this, college students in New York and Brazil were given the following situations (S1 and S2; O'Brien, Dias, Roazzi, & Cantor, 1998, p. 451):

> S1: Tourists renting an automobile are told by the car rental agent that if someone drives on the expressway, they must stay below 100 km per hour. Later, the tourists notice <u>some drivers are traveling at a higher speed.</u>

Then the students were asked whether the underlined phrase "violated" the driving rule or "falsified" the rule. Ninety percent of the students said that it violated the rule. O'Brien et al. (1998) also gave students the following situation:

> S2: The tourist tells his wife that if someone drives in this country, he or she must stay on the left side of the road. Later, the tourist notices that <u>some drivers stay on the right side.</u>

Students view this instance as falsifying the rule. These two scenarios tell us that depending on the wording of the overall situation, the critical statement will be interpreted in different ways. If reasoners see S1 as a selection task and are asked to look for *violators*—as is done in selection tasks with pragmatic rules—they will select the underlined statement as critical and be scored as reasoning consistent with a pragmatic rule. However, if the reasoners are asked to select information to determine if the rule in S1 is *falsified* (i.e., true or false), the underlined statement will not be selected because it is not relevant to falsification: It is only relevant to violation (Noveck & O'Brien, 1996). The opposite applies to solving S2. These outcomes are summarized in **TABLE 12.3**. As a result, the same

TABLE **12.3**	
Falsification and Violation of Rules	
True rule that was violated	**False rule**
S1: If someone drives on the expressway, they must stay below 100 km per hour.	S2: If someone drives in this country, he or she must stay on the left side of the road.
<u>Some drivers are traveling at a higher speed.</u>	<u>Some drivers stay on the right side.</u>
Speed rules are often violated. Violations do not falsify a rule.	Side-of-road driving rules are rarely violated. Since there are clear violations in this case, the rule must not be a true one.
"Look for violators" will select critical sentence and be scored as correct.	"Look for violators" will not select critical sentence and be scored as wrong.
"Is the rule false?" will miss critical sentence and be scored as wrong.	"Is rule false?" will select critical sentence and be scored as correct.

reasoners who were correct in searching for violations will be scored as having made an error in searching for falsification. Obviously, it is not the reasoner's rationality that is at issue, it is how the reasoner has framed the situation and what the situation calls upon the reasoner to do.

SECTION SUMMARY ▪

Reasoning Schemas

The selection task offers an opportunity to see reasoning in action. People seem to experience difficulty in critically testing arbitrary rules; they have difficulty applying reasoning schemas. However, they perform quite well when they test deontic rules—rules that involve permission and obligation. Consistent with research on problem solving, reasoning performance depends greatly upon people's interpretation of the rules they are testing and what "testing" means to them. People perform best when they are able to use their understanding of social exchange rules that are a universal part of normal human interaction, such as *if you take the benefit, then you must pay the cost*. The understanding of these higher-order rules of social interaction is part of cognitive processes that are present even in early childhood. When even arbitrary situations are framed as social exchanges, people are good reasoners. Critical to correct reasoning, however, is how the reasoner interprets the situation and, of course, how the reasoner interprets the goals of the task.

▪ ▪

Clinical Aspects of Categorical Reasoning

As we have seen, the ability to reason develops with age and that there is a biological contribution to reasoning just as there is with language. Recent research into the brain mechanisms related to reasoning has helped us to understand both the importance of age and how neurological functioning affects the way people interact with the world. This includes reasoning by typical members of society as well as people suffering from psychiatric difficulties.

Age and Reasoning

It is part of Western folklore that reasoning ability declines with age (e.g., Craik & Salthouse, 1992; Levy, 1994; Paykel et al., 1994). Evidence for such a decline comes primarily from cross-sectional studies where younger and older people are tested on reasoning and memory ability. However, when researchers do longitudinal studies (i.e., monitor the same people across years of their lives), the data do not support the stereotype of a decline with age (Bolla, Lindgren, Bonaccorsy, & Bleecker, 1991; Schaie & Willis, 1999; but see Cullum et al., 2000). In general, when decline in reasoning is related to the increasing age of a person,

An older adult performs demanding work.

JGI/Getty Images

the effects of age are primarily a result of diseases, neurological deficits (brain damage, reduced production of dopamine, overactive serotonin uptake, etc.), or depression (e.g., Girling et al., 1995).

Teaching appropriate reasoning strategies can successfully mitigate some of the difficulties that do occur in older adults as a result of neurological deficits (e.g., Baltes, Kliegal, & Dittmann-Kohli, 1988; Schaie & Willis, 1986). In one such study, people 73 years of age and older were trained on a reasoning task and a spatial ability task. Although performance on both tasks tends to decline with age (Barash, 1994; Kirasic, 2000; Salthouse, 1992), 7 years after training (when the participants averaged 80 years of age), their spatial ability skills had declined, but no decline in reasoning ability was observed (Saczynski, Willis, & Schaie, 2002).

Schizophrenic Reasoning

Teachers throughout the ages have used the categorical syllogism as an instructional tool to help their students understand "right reasoning" (Hobbes, 1651/1983). In modern times, syllogisms have found their way onto tests of intelligence (Guilford, 1959; Thurstone, 1938), as well as tests that diagnose and distinguish among clinical groups and reveal different aspects of personality (French, Ekstrom, & Price, 1963; Kupermintz, 2002). Syllogisms have even been used as a diagnostic tool to identify people with schizophrenia and to characterize their thought disorders (see Kasanin, 1954).

The statements of individuals with schizophrenia reveal the presence of logical conversion (described previously), which helps them draw syllogistic-like conclusions. In one well-known case study, a person with schizophrenia claimed that Jesus, cigar boxes, and sex were identical. He justified his belief by saying, "The head of Jesus is encircled by a halo; the package of cigars is encircled by the tax band; and the woman is encircled by the sex glance of a man" (Von Domarus, 1954, pp. 108–109). This kind of thinking is called **paralogical thinking** because it follows the format of normal logic except that the speaker sees two things as identical based on similarity between them. If you reasoned this way, the following syllogism would make sense to you:

Gazelles can jump while running.

LeBron James can jump while running.

Therefore, LeBron James is a gazelle.

The paralogical utterances of some people with schizophrenia appear nonsensical because we would not draw the same conclusions, but surprisingly, we can often understand the reasoning because it resembles normal reasoning. In fact, the kinds of conclusions drawn by people with schizophrenia are not qualitatively different from some of the conclusions drawn by typical people. This was shown in a study by Gottesman and Chapman (1960, p. 251), who compared 30 people with schizophrenia with 30 people without schizophrenia on their ability to solve categorical syllogisms, such as this:

All of Tom's ties are red.

Some of the things Ada is holding are red.

Therefore,

1. at least some of the things Ada is holding are Tom's ties.

2. at least some of the things Ada is holding are not Tom's ties.

3. none of these conclusions are proved.

4. none of the things Ada is holding are Tom's ties.

5. all of the things Ada is holding are Tom's ties.

You won't be surprised that the participants with schizophrenia were less successful than the other participants in solving the problems: Participants with schizophrenia made about 20% more errors overall than the other participants. However, on problems where both groups made an error, they tended to make the same error (see also Watson & Wold, 1981; Williams, 1964). This is not the result of some special problem that all the participants had with the content. The pattern appeared even with a symbolic version of the problems, such as

All A are B.

Some C are B.

The invalid conclusion, *some C are A*, is drawn by about 75% of college students (Revlis, 1975b) as well as by people with schizophrenia. This challenges the notion that such errors in reasoning are distinctly pathological (unless you think that university students are pathological). The pattern of reasoning shown by people with schizophrenia is merely an extreme form of normal response tendencies (Arieti, 1948, 1955; Black & Overton, 1990).

But why would this be the case? People with schizophrenia tend to relate categories according to superficial features rather than deeper semantic relationships. In part, this may be due to a greater emphasis on System 1 so that System 2 is not called upon to evaluate the conclusions they draw. This leads them to give unusual or low probability interpretations to events (Broen & Storms, 1966). The finding is consistent with a view of schizophrenia as resulting in some part from dysfunction in the prefrontal cortex (Meyer-Lindenberg et al., 2002), especially that portion of the prefrontal cortex associated with dopamine circuits (Seeman & Kapur, 2000).

This result also manifests itself in tasks other than categorical syllogisms. Consider the Wisconsin Card Sorting Test (Berg, 1948). The individual with schizophrenia is shown cards or blocks with designs of different shapes and colors and has to group the objects given only feedback from the tester. This task requires

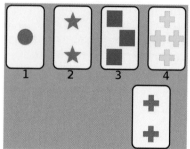

Wisconsin Card Sorting Test
People are asked decide how cards should be sorted. Some patients have difficulty creating a hypothesis; others have difficulty changing their hypothesis.

Reproduced by special permission of the Publisher, Psychological Assessment Resources, Inc., 16204 North Florida Avenue, Lutz, Florida 33549, from the Wisconsin Card Sorting Test by David A. Grant., PhD and Esta A. Berg, PhD, Copyright 1981, 1993 by Psychological Assessment Resources, Inc. (PAR). Further reproduction is prohibited without permission of PAR.

the person to formulate and test hypotheses. Persons with schizophrenia tend to vacillate among competing hypotheses—not only before they make a selection, but afterward as well—because they tend to see endless possibilities and cannot discard the illogical ones. They try to find a way to accept all options. Kasanin (1954, p. 54) described one such individual: "When he starts to sort the blocks according to color, he becomes attracted by the shape and then does not know which way to turn or how to classify the blocks."

This is one reason why responses by people with schizophrenia tend to be of low probability: Everything is equally possible (Storms & Broen, 1972). This leads to systematic errors in reasoning (called *thought disorder*) and in language production (*neologisms* and *word salad*), and it explains why people with schizophrenia tend to solve categorical syllogisms by principles of association rather than the logic of set inclusion.

SECTION SUMMARY ■

Clinical Aspects of Categorical Reasoning

Longitudinal studies that monitor people across the life span show that reasoning ability does not necessarily decline with age. Age has an effect on reasoning because the longer people live, the more likely they are to show the cumulative effects of neurological damage. Age by itself has no effect.

Categorical syllogisms have been used to examine the thought processes of schizophrenia, an illness that shows a tendency to reason based on similarity of categories instead of inclusion within categories. People with schizophrenia tend to make the same reasoning errors as people without schizophrenia, except that they make them to a greater degree.

■ ■

CHAPTER SUMMARY

Humans are rational creatures who follow a set of rational rules to guide their reasoning. These rules are not the ones of standard logic. Human reasoning allows us to think beyond our narrow experiences, formulate plans beyond our environment, and communicate with one another.

Reasoning develops in childhood through three broad stages. In Stage 1, children understand the basic concept of sentences, and some logical relations. In Stage 2, children are aware of their own cognitive processes (metacognition) and sense that conclusions must follow from given information. In Stage 3, children and adolescents are able to assess whether an argument is valid.

One of the forms of reasoning that comes earliest in our lives is transitive inference, which allows us to seriate objects (to put them in order). It shows itself in all forms of comparison and is embodied in linear syllogisms. The cognitive models of this kind of reasoning incorporate rules of language understanding as well as representation of information. As in all forms of reasoning, how sentences are represented affects the decisions that are made. The brain responds differently depending on the different content that we are asked to reason about: abstract or concrete relationships.

Reasoning can be divided into two broad categories: deductive and inductive. Reasoning with categories or with conditional statements are forms of deduction that are manifested in a vast array of human behavior—from language comprehension to legal decision making. The human ability to reason comes early in our lives and may not only reflect our earliest experiences, but may also result from innate mechanisms similar to those associated with language.

Categorical deduction is a common form of reasoning that does not require special instructions; people around the world do it naturally. What distinguishes one group of people from another on categorical reasoning is their willingness to participate in the task. Even when they refuse to draw a conclusion, their justification is invariably in the form of a deductive argument. Categorical reasoning is universal and basic.

Humans are not infallible reasoners. Our beliefs in the conclusions to logical arguments affect our willingness to evaluate them critically. This is not an isolated aspect of human behavior, but reflects the rational processes that also come into play when we are interpreting language and social situations. Our beliefs about the world can also

help us reason. In everyday situations, when the reasoner understands the situation as related to permissions and obligations, correct reasoning flows from that understanding. Some reasoning schemas appear to be universal, such as permissions and cheater detection.

Reasoning ability seems to be tied to human biology. It not only comes early in life, it persists throughout a person's life span. People who find certain forms of reasoning to be difficult can be trained, and their new ability endures longer than other trained skills. Because of neurological conditions, the reasoning skills of some people can become distorted. People with schizophrenia, for example, show paralogical reasoning. They make inferences about categories based on how similar the categories appear rather than their logical relations. This is such a distinctive pattern that their mode of reasoning can be used to diagnose their neurological condition. Laboratory studies of human reasoning may someday lead to a better understanding of why this very human skill can become distorted.

KEY TERMS

reasoning, p. 396

counterfactual reasoning, p. 399

validity, p. 400

invalidity, p. 400

linear reasoning, p. 401

seriation, p. 402

transitivity, p. 402

syllogism, p. 403

marked terms, p. 404

unmarked terms, p. 404

principle of lexical marking, p. 404

principle of congruity, p. 406

set-inclusion relation, p. 409

deduction, p. 413

induction, p. 413

abduction, p. 414

conversion, p. 416

paradox, p. 419

belief-bias effect, p. 420

dual processing, p. 421

reasoning schemas, p. 423

selection task, p. 423

deontic rule, p. 425

pragmatic reasoning schemas, p. 426

social exchange rules, p. 426

paralogical thinking, p. 430

QUESTIONS FOR REVIEW

Check Your Knowledge

1. What is a definition for *reasoning*?

2. What properties does reasoning have that makes it central to human cognition?

3. People often think that other people are irrational. Why would this be wrong?

4. Is being rational the same as being logical?

5. What is Stage 1 reasoning, and when does it normally occur?

6. What are Stage 2 and Stage 3 reasoning, and when do they normally occur?

7. What is linear reasoning?

8. What are the two primary components to linear reasoning?

9. Define *transitivity*. Give an example of a relationship that is transitive and one that is not.

10. What are the principles of lexical marking and congruity? Give an example of both.

11. How do the two principles of lexical marking and congruity account for the pattern of human linear reasoning?

12. What major principle accounts for the pattern of linear reasoning or set inclusion from information in a narrative?

13. What areas of the brain are involved in linear reasoning?

14. Why doesn't categorical reasoning appear to be universal? What explains this?

15. Define *deduction*, *induction*, and *abduction*. Give an example of each from everyday life.

16. Are diagrams always helpful in categorical reasoning? Why or why not?

17. What are conversion and symmetry representations?

18. What are the key brain areas involved in categorical reasoning?

19. Define the *belief-bias effect*. Does it mean that people are primarily irrational?

20. What is a reasoning schema? Name and illustrate at least two of these.

21. Can correct reasoning be trained?

22. What is paralogical thinking? Illustrate it.

23. What types of people typically use paralogical thinking?

Apply Your Knowledge

1. Use your knowledge of conditional reasoning to solve the following problem:

    You are visiting a strange island where there are two kinds of villagers: some who always tell the truth and some who always lie. It is impossible to tell them apart. As luck would have it, your pet frog has been captured by evil men who want to eat it. They have taken it to their cave. You chase after them but come to a fork in the road where a villager stands. You want to know which direction the cave is, but can't tell whether the villager is a truth-teller or liar.

    Write down a series of questions that you could ask this person to determine if he was a truth-teller or a liar. Then see if you can reduce this set of questions to a single question that would both allow you to get directions to the cave and know that the directions are correct.

2. The chapter emphasizes that normally functioning humans are capable of reasoning correctly. Based on what you've read, what is the major source of reasoning errors? If you were designing a curriculum that would teach the kind of reasoning illustrated here, what critical elements would you want to include?

3. If reasoning ability comes early in life, is it wired in? If so, why does it still develop through three stages? Draw on what you've also learned about the development of language when you answer this question.

4. If people are generally rational reasoners, how is it possible for us to have different political and moral beliefs?

5. Teaching people how to use Euler and Venn diagrams does not seem to help them and demands resources of working memory. Why do you think people still teach the use of these diagrams? Might there be a value in using them?

6. A dominant reasoning process of persons with schizophrenia is to make judgments based on the similarity of objects and categories. Can you think of any cases where nonschizophrenic politicians employ the same reasoning process?

7. If you and another person draw a different conclusion about an issue and you assume that you both are rational, where should you look for the source of the difference?

13

Decision Making

> **"**The great decisions of human life have as a rule far more to do with the instincts and other mysterious unconscious factors than with conscious will and well-meaning reasonableness.**"**
>
> —Carl Jung

People solve problems and reason every day. Chapters 11 and 12 described some of the cognitive processes involved in these activities—some that lead to failure, others that lead to success. The missing piece to the cognitive puzzle of human behavior is described in this chapter: how people go from the process of finding a solution to making choices or taking action. In Ecclesiastes (a chapter of the Hebrew Bible written more than 20 centuries ago) it was noted that the only certainty in life was that there are precious few events we can absolutely count on. It was also noted that some events are more likely to happen than others, and we should use this fact in making predictions. In short, a rational person takes into account the likelihood of events before making a decision. But do we? The quotation that begins this chapter, written by Swiss psychologist Carl Jung, is based on years of clinical observations and concludes that, more often than not, people base their judgments on intuitions and what they wish were true and not what is true. Our motives and emotions are part of the decision-making process.

Let's start with a commonplace example. Suppose you are thirsty and hungry and have only $1. A vending machine nearby has a drink for $1 and a bag of cookies for $1. You could put your money in the machine and get either the drink or the cookies. Both would be equally likely to come out of the machine after you put your dollar into it. How do you decide which item to choose? We select among possible courses of action like this every day: we decide on travel routes and times; we choose among items to purchase or shows to watch on TV; we make moral and ethical decisions about how to behave. With all the experience that people have making decisions, you would think we would be flawless in our choices. Not so: We are all prone to error. Let's see how we make mistakes and how we prevent those mistakes from happening by examining research findings on human decision making.

Weighing Options

Benjamin Franklin, writer, diplomat, and inventor, who proved that lightning is electricity, offered one of the earliest descriptions of a method for making decisions. He said that he made decisions by listing the "pros" and "cons" of each choice and then weighed the options:

> My way is to divide half a sheet of paper by a line into two columns; writing over the one Pro, and over the other Con. Then, during three or four days' consideration, I put down under the different heads short hints of the different motives, that at different times occur to me, for or against the measure. When I have thus got them all together in one view, I endeavor to estimate their respective weights; and where I find two, one on each side, that seem equal, I strike them both out . . . and thus proceeding I find at length where the balance lies; and . . . come to a determination accordingly. . . . I have found great advantage from this kind of equation, and what might be called moral or prudential algebra.
>
> *(Franklin, 1772; reprinted in Smyth, 1906)*

Corbis Flirt/Alamy

Franklin's system works well in situations where the decision maker is able to imagine all the positive and negative consequences of a course of action. It certainly could be applied effectively in the vending machine problem, in which the machine works well and contains food and drink items that would satisfy both your hunger and your thirst.

Unequal Likelihoods

Franklin's list of pros and cons has a built-in expectation that the choices are equally likely to occur. That is, if you are choosing between eating a chocolate cake or a banana for dessert, or deciding which of two TV shows to watch at 8 p.m., you will have equal access to the choices. Unfortunately, the likelihood of events isn't always equal. Sometimes we put money in a vending machine and it works perfectly; at other times, nothing comes out, emotions flare, and perhaps we pound the machine or swear instinctively, as Carl Jung (1933) would predict. If we are going to make good decisions, the procedures we follow need to take into consideration the likelihood that the events will occur. For example, the first time a drink does not come out of the machine, what do people do? Typically, they put another dollar in the machine because they think the problem will not repeat; in fact, many people hypothesize that the first dollar is stuck so that putting in a second one will release two drinks.

Researchers who investigate the effect of reinforcements on human and animal behavior notice that because people typically get what they want 100% of the time from machines, when one fails, 25% of people will put in more money. Many people will also press the buttons with more force and pound on the machine. This behavior is called an *extinction burst* (e.g., Cooper, Heron, & Howard, 1987; Lerman & Iwata, 1995). In the economics of decision making, putting money in the machine because you have already invested some money (and lost) comes under the general heading of sunk costs and the sunk cost fallacy, topics we cover later in the chapter. What is important to keep in mind, however, is that the likelihood of events (the probability that an event will occur) varies, and our behavior varies with it.

Suppose someone tells you that the drink machine doesn't always work properly and that about 10% of the time the drink cans are not dispensed. No such difficulties have been encountered for the cookie dispenser. In this case, the likelihood of getting a cookie remains close to 1.00 (100%); the likelihood that a drink will be dispensed is about .90 (90%). Following Franklin's method, the cons for the drink would have to include the chance that your money will be lost. Which choice should you make if you are equally hungry and thirsty? If you were judging solely based on the likely outcome of inserting your money in the vending machine, you would select the cookies. However, if you want one option more than another, a different decision process is called for. In it, you take into consideration your values.

Unequal Values

If you are much more thirsty than you are hungry and would value a drink much more than a cookie, you must decide not only the likelihood of each option, but also the value of each one to you. Your personal evaluation of an outcome is called its **subjective utility**, a term associated with a method a bit more complicated than Ben Franklin's. For example, on a scale of 1 to 5 (where 5 is the highest value), rate how much you would value the cookies and how much you would value the drink. Let's suppose you valued the cookies at 2 and the drink at 4. A careful decision maker will select the course of action with the highest subjective utility: the action leading to the outcome most valued by him or her.

This approach can be derived mathematically using a method developed by economists called *subjective expected utility* (Keynes, 1937; von Neumann & Morgenstern, 1947). All you do is multiply the likelihood of an event by its subjective utility (its value to you):

subjective utility$_{cookie}$ = 2 × 1.00 = 2.00
subjective utility$_{drink}$ = 4 × .90 = 3.60,

where

2 and 4 = values of the cookie and the drink, respectively.
1.00 and .90 = probabilities that the item will be correctly dispensed.

In this case, a careful decision maker would take a chance on purchasing the drink because it has the highest subjective utility even though it is slightly less likely to be dispensed by the machine.

In this kind of simple situation, it is easy for a decision maker to use subjective utility to help make the choice. If at all possible, it is a good method to follow. Unfortunately, in everyday life, we rarely know the probabilities of events. There is no sign on a vending machine telling us the probability of it working at any moment, and our evaluation of the outcomes (the "subjective" part) may vary from moment to moment depending on how hungry or thirsty we are, or even how much we expect to enjoy the outcome (Shafir & LeBoeuf, 2002). The example has the decision maker compare two possible gains (positive outcomes). We will see later that subjective expected utility doesn't work well at all when the choice includes a loss.

Unconsciously Weighing Options

For the types of choices Benjamin Franklin was talking about, it seems sensible that a deliberate, conscious approach is the rational route to take. But then why do people suggest that for complicated choices, they should not make an immediate decision but wait to have more time to think about it, "to sleep on it"? Recent research in decision making suggests that this bit of folk wisdom has a psychological reality. Humans may actually make better decisions in certain kinds of situations when they don't consciously think about it too much. Suppose you are trying to decide which of four apartments to rent. Should you try to list the pros and cons of each one and calculate the maximum value as Franklin suggested, or should you rely on less conscious processes that produce an impression, a gut reaction?

Research by the Dutch psychologist Dijksterhuis and his colleagues suggests that relying on impressions often produces better judgments than more conscious reactions (e.g., Dijksterhuis, 2004; Dijksterhuis & Nordgren, 2006; Dijksterhuis & van Olden, 2006). In the situation of choosing an apartment, students were given dozens of pieces of information about possible apartments. Afterward, one group had to make a decision immediately, a second group could think about it for a few minutes, and a third group (the unconscious group) had to delay making a decision. The unconscious group was prevented from consciously thinking about the apartment information because it had to perform an interfering task. Of the three groups, the unconscious group made the best apartment selections (Dijksterhuis, 2004). A more detailed description of the basic methodology is given in the Focus on Methods box.

The findings described previously and those in the Focus on Methods box led researchers to develop the **unconscious thought theory (UTT**; Dijksterhuis & Nordgren, 2006). It has many principles, but here are three key ones:

Capacity. *Unconscious thought is like automatic attentional processing and requires little cognitive capacity. Conscious thought consumes high cognitive capacity.*

FOCUS ON METHODS ■

Unconscious Thinking

The method used to investigate the merits of sleeping on it—of putting the problem out of your mind for a few minutes—follows commonsense thinking on incubation in problem solving or decision making. First, you give people a set of facts to assimilate and to consider. Then, you have them think about something else for a few minutes. Finally, you ask for their judgment about the problem at hand. To see the effect, you compare their decisions with those of people who, for the same period of time, were to consider the set of facts intently. This is just what has been done in innumerable studies of unconscious thinking (e.g., Dijksterhuis & Nordgren, 2006; Dijksterhuis & Van Olden, 2006; Wilson & Schooler, 1991). The prototypical study was conducted by the psychologists Bos, Dijksterhuis, and van Baaren (2011).

Participants were told they would be presented with 12 pieces of information about four cars (48 facts in all). The attributes of the cars were presented one at a time on a computer screen for 4 seconds each. Unknown to the participants, two of the cars are designated "quality cars" because they have 4 important positive attributes and 8 unimportant negative ones. Two cars are called "frequency cars" because they have 8 unimportant positive attributes and 4 important negative ones. Here is a sample list of attributes for one of the quality cars and one of the frequency cars (Dijksterhuis, Bos, Nordgren, & van Baaren, 2006) (These attributes were rated *important* or *unimportant* by students in a previous study.):

Quality Car Features	Frequency Car Features
No cup holders	Cup holders
No sliding roof	Sliding roof
Comes in few colors	Comes in many colors
No light metal rims	Light metal rims
No spare tire	Spare tire
One exhaust pipe	Two exhaust pipes
No tinted windows	Tinted windows
No spoiler	Spoiler
Good roadholding	No good roadholding
Easy transmission	Difficult transmission
Environmentally friendly	Not environmentally friendly
Good mileage	Bad mileage

Two groups of students were randomly assigned to the immediate decision and the unconscious thought conditions. As you would suspect, in the immediate decision group, students were asked to express their attitude toward each of the four cars on a 20-point rating scale from 1 (*extremely negative*) to 20 (*extremely positive*). The unconscious thought group performed the same task, but not right away. They were delayed for 5 minutes performing a demanding task that made it difficult for them to consciously consider the cars.

The results are easy to calculate. If the students were making the most judicious judgments, they should rate the quality cars higher than the frequency cars. To see if this is true for the two groups, each person's score for the frequency cars was subtracted from their score for the quality cars to determine if they gave the quality cars a higher rating. The data are graphed in the figure, which shows that the unconscious thought group gave the quality cars a consistently higher rating than did the immediate group. This suggests that unconscious thought allows decision makers to weigh the evidence and make the best choice, even though they are not consciously aware of doing it.

Research using similar methods has shown that unconscious thinking allows people to make better choices in selecting an apartment (Nordgren, Bos, & Dijksterhuis, 2011), a roommate (Dijksterhuis, 2004), and even art posters (Wilson, Lisle, Schooler, Hodges, Klaaren, & LaFleur, 1993).

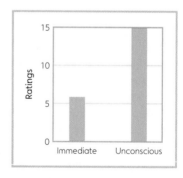

The greater ratings given to the quality cars by the conscious (immediate) and unconscious (delayed) decision groups.

Bottom-up versus top-down. *Unconscious thought slowly integrates informa-tion to form an objective summary judgment. Conscious thought tends to be guided by expectations and schemas.*

Weighing of evidence. *Unconscious thought naturally weighs the relative importance of various attributes. Conscious thought leads to biased weighing.*

These principles say that because conscious thought requires a lot of cogni-tive capacity to function well, it may have to forgo high-quality decision choices. Unconscious thought, in contrast, is relatively automatic and is sparing of re-sources. This allows it to process more information than conscious thinking (see Chapter 3 for a discussion of automatic and controlled processing). Conscious thought occasionally allows people to jump to conclusions, whereas the quality of unconscious thought improves with time. Decisions often require weighing the importance of elements, and the longer a person spends unconsciously process-ing the various pros and cons, the more consistent the judgment. The quick gut reactions of conscious processing tend to be less reliable and less accurate than long unconscious processing.

SECTION SUMMARY

Weighing Options

In a simple world of choosing between two roughly equal courses of action, the decision maker can easily make a list enumerating the pros and cons associated with each choice. However, if one option is more likely than another and if some of the benefits (or costs) are more important than others, then merely listing and weighing the benefits is not enough. In such cases, the careful decision maker must take these additional factors into consideration. One method for doing so, called subjective utility, allows the decider to compare various opportunities in terms of their likelihood and value for the decider. Subjective utility is a basic element in conscious decision making. However, under certain circumstances, unconscious decision making is more reliable and produces a higher quality of decisions. This is described by the UTT, the unconscious thought theory.

Heuristics

In everyday life, people are often quite good at determining the likelihood of outcomes they frequently encounter. These shortcuts, or rules of thumb, are called **heuristics**; they often lead to a correct solution, but they occasionally fail. Other sources of errors occur because people make the wrong assumption about the relationships among events. Assumptions are based on certain reasoning fallacies (Gilovich, Griffin, & Kahneman, 2002; Kahneman, Slovic, & Tversky, 1982); a few are described in the next section.

Heuristics Versus Algorithms

People invariably look for ways to make judgments more quickly or to reduce the load on their working memory. But heuristics, although useful, do not guarantee a correct solution. A procedure that does guarantee a solution is called an **algorithm**, which consists of a clearly defined set of rules or procedures that, if given enough time, will always solve a problem.

The difference between heuristics and algorithms can be seen in strategies for running through a typical maze to find your way out through an exit in the wall. A heuristic would be to create a mental list of turns as you proceed through the maze. If there are fewer than nine turns, you should be able to keep track of your path (see working memory capacity in Chapter 5). With a complex maze of many turns, this may not work. An algorithm to follow would be to keep your right hand on the wall as you enter and never put it down until you have reached the goal. You may go down a large number of blind alleys, but a solution—in the fullness of time—is guaranteed.

Many heuristics that people employ in their everyday lives are effective: the more expensive product tends to be the best; a well-dressed person at an interview will make the best employee; the shortest line at the market moves the fastest. Although they are not true algorithms, heuristics are often correct enough to be valuable to their users. Three such heuristics are widely, although not always correctly, used: representativeness, availability, and anchoring and adjustment.

Representativeness On occasion, problem solvers will judge the likelihood of an event—not by the standard methods for calculating probabilities—but rather by how similar that event is to another event of known probability. This is called **representativeness**. Suppose you meet someone wearing work clothes covered with grease and oil stains and holding a wrench. Which is more likely, that the person is a neurosurgeon or a mechanic? Of course, your judgment could be wrong, but the tendency is to use the similarity to some other situation to judge the present one (Kahneman & Tversky, 1973). Representativeness is especially useful in cases where medical practitioners have to deal with complex situations (e.g., Cioffi & Markham, 1997). If a physician is trying to determine whether a patient with chest pain has coronary artery disease, the patient's symptoms are compared to the stereotype of someone with that disease. The degree of match tells the physician what tests to perform (Sox, Blatt, Higgins, & Marton, 2006).

An experiment conducted by Kahneman and Tversky (1973) illustrates this. There were two groups of participants. One group of participants (engineer–high group) was told there was a study in which 100 people were interviewed and it was found that 70 of the interviewees were engineers and 30 were lawyers. A second group (engineer–low group) was told the same story with the percentages reversed. The two groups were asked to read descriptions of some of the interviewees and judge how likely they were to have been written about someone who is an engineer. Here's one that is consistent with the stereotype of an engineer (Kahneman & Tversky, 1973, p. 241):

> Jack is a 45-year-old man. He is married and has four children. He is generally conservative, careful and ambitious. He shows no interest in political and social issues and spends most of his free time on his many hobbies, which include home carpentry, sailing, and mathematical puzzles.
>
> How likely is it that Jack is an engineer in the interview sample?

Participants in both groups rated the likelihood that Jack is an engineer to be greater than 90%. They appear to have based their judgments solely on how representative the profile was of an engineer, rather than taking into consideration the proportion of engineers in the sample. This proportion is called the **base rate** and should have influenced their judgments. For example, if there were no engineers in the sample, no matter how well the description portrayed an engineer, the probability that it referred to an interviewee in this sample is zero. Or if there were no lawyers in our sample, no matter how poor the description was of an engineer, Jack had to be one. So, how likely is it that Jack is an engineer? The mathematics is a bit complicated and is described in Demonstration 13.1.

▪▪▪DEMONSTRATION 13.1

Calculation of Conditional Probability

To do the calculation, you need to know four things: (a) how likely it is that a randomly selected person would be an engineer (base rate); (b) the likelihood that an engineer would show this profile; (c) the likelihood that a lawyer would be selected (base rate); and (d) the likelihood that a lawyer would show this profile. The formula is shown next in words.

The probability that Jack is an engineer given the profile equals: (1) the probability that an *engineer* selected from the sample will show the profile, divided by (2) the probability that *anyone* selected from the sample will show the profile.

(1) is calculated as $a \times b$.

(2) is calculated as $(a \times b) + (c \times d)$.

To make this concrete, let's suppose that in the engineer-high group with 70% engineers the profile is 80% descriptive of an engineer (b) and only 40% descriptive of a lawyer (d). The equation would look as follows if you were in the engineer–high group (probablilty of engineer given the profile):

$$(.70 \times .80) / [(.70 \times .80) + (.30 \times .40)] = .82$$

If you were in the engineer–low group, the probability that someone with the description was an engineer would be .49 (where $a = .30$ and $c = .70$). Obviously, participants in the two groups did not use the base rates or they would have generated a different probability that the interviewee was an engineer. They appear to be overwhelmed by how well the profile fits their stereotype, that is, how representative the description is of an engineer.

Using probabilities in this problem can be daunting. It is difficult for the solver to get a sense of the base rates and make the necessary calculations. However, this largely reflects how the problems are presented and not a lack of competence. When conditions such as in the engineer–lawyer problem are presented in percentages instead of probabilities, people are significantly better at computing the rational choice (Cosmides & Tooby, 1996; Gigerenzer, 1991, 1996a; but see also Kahneman & Tversky, 1996).

Availability Let's suppose you are asked which of two situations is more likely: Are there more words in English that begin with the letter *K*, or are there more words that have *K* as their third letter? Since you don't have absolute direct knowledge of this information, it's useful to try to imagine words that either begin with *K* or have *K* as the third letter. For example, you might have thought of *key, know, king, kite*. Alternately, you might think of words that have *K* as the third letter. If you did this and based your answer on the ease with which you could retrieve instances, you are using the availability heuristic.

Availability is the use of ease of retrieval as the basis for judging frequency. It is much easier to think of words that begin with a given letter, say *k*, than words that have a given letter in another position. This gives you the false impression that there are many more words with *k* as the first letter, when in fact there are more words with *k* as the third letter. About 70% of students asked this question in the original study by Tversky and Kahneman (1973) estimated there were more words that begin with *k*.

Events that occur often in our lives are easier to recall and reconstruct than those that are rare. As a result, availability can be an effective basis for judging frequency and can protect us against dangerous situations such as automobile accidents, cigarette smoke, or snakes on a trail. But availability is a fickle master because it can be influenced by the odd spectacular event or news report or movie that causes rare events to come to mind (e.g., Steinbrugge, McClure, & Snow, as cited in Lichtenstein, Slovic, Fischoff, Layman, & Combs, 1978). Perhaps more insidious than the spectacular but unusual event is how the availability of events is affected by their treatment in newspapers and other news media. Combs and Slovic (1979) looked at the relationship among three factors: frequency of reported deaths in newspapers, ordinary people's estimates of the frequency of those deaths, and actual mortality rates. Some of their findings are presented in **TABLE 13.1**.

The table shows that newspapers underreport frequently occurring causes of death such as diabetes, emphysema, and cancer. In contrast, they heavily report violent and catastrophic events such as tornadoes, fires, drownings, homicides, and accidents. If you add up the mortality rates for diseases and for accidents in the table, you will notice that diseases take about 16 times as many lives as accidents, but there were more than 3 times more articles about accidents than disease. In fact, people's ratings of the frequency of the events correspond more closely to how often the newspapers report the events than their true frequency (Slovic, 1987; Slovic, Fischhoff, & Lichtenstein, 1976). Look, for example, at tornadoes and homicides versus breast cancer and diabetes.

The availability heuristic can be a harmful force in our lives. It makes us fear events that are rare (plane crashes) and fail to anticipate and thereby prevent more frequent dangers like the development of alcohol poisoning. The availability heuristic also contributes to superstitious beliefs such as "whenever I forget to carry an umbrella, it rains." Of course, there is no relationship between failing to carry an umbrella and rain. When we do carry an umbrella and it rains, we just don't notice a relationship because we are dry. When we get wet (because we don't have an umbrella), it reminds us of other times the same thing has happened, not of all the times that we didn't carry an umbrella and the sun shined.

TABLE **13.1**			
Mortality Estimates			
Causes of death	Actual rates (per 205 million)	Ordinary people's estimates	Newspaper reports (averaged)
Botulism	2	102	0
Measles	5	168	0
Polio	17	97	0
Tornado	90	564	30
Flood	205	736	7
Pregnancy & abortion	451	1,344	0
Appendicitis	902	605	0
Train collision	1,517	689	1
Asthma	1,886	506	1
Firearm accident	2,255	1,345	5
Fire	7,380	3,336	70
Drowning	7,380	1,684	54
Leukemia	14,555	2,496	1
Homicide	18,860	5,582	243
Emphysema	21,730	2,848	1
Breast cancer	31,160	2,964	0
Diabetes	38,950	1,476	0
Motor accidents	55,350	41,161	298
Lung cancer	75,850	9,764	3
All cancers	328,000	45,609	19
All accidents	112,750	88,876	656

Note: From Lichtenstein, Slovic, Fischhoff, Layman, and Combs, 1978 (pp. 551–578)

Anchoring and Adjustment Before you read this section, try the activity in Demonstration 13.2. Tversky and Kahneman's (1974) study, which is related to the demonstration, featured two groups of participants: one group was asked to judge whether the Mississippi River is longer or shorter than 500 miles. Another group was asked whether it is longer or shorter than 5,000 miles. After giving their responses, the participants were also asked to guess the actual length of the river. The Mississippi starts as a trickle from Lake Itasca in Minnesota (where you can actually stand in the stream where it begins) and travels to the Gulf of Mexico. It is 2,348 miles long. The 500-mile group estimated that the river is approximately 1,000 miles long, but the 5,000-mile group estimated that it is 2,000 miles long. The phenomenon is called **anchoring and adjustment** (Tversky & Kahneman, 1974) because the people in the study used the initial number as a starting point and then made adjustments from it. Just as an anchor weighs down a boat, the anchoring heuristic prevents the problem solver from deviating from the initial information, even in the face of contradictory information.

■■■DEMONSTRATION 13.2

Anchoring Effects

This demonstration requires two people: one to answer Question 1 in Set A and Set B and the other to answer Question 2 in each set. The two respondents should *not* see one another's questions before answering their own question. If a second person is unavailable, try Set B a few minutes after trying Set A.

Set A

1. Is the percentage of African countries in the UN greater than 10%? Guess the percentage.

2. Is the percentage of African countries in the UN greater than 65%? Guess the percentage.

Set B

1. Look at the following series, and taking no more than 5 seconds, estimate the final product.

   $1 \times 2 \times 3 \times 4 \times 5 \times 6 \times 7 \times 8 =$

2. Look at the following series, and taking no more than 5 seconds, estimate the final product.

   $8 \times 7 \times 6 \times 5 \times 4 \times 3 \times 2 \times 1 =$

Answers: 28% of UN member states are from Africa; product = 40,320

Photo of merchandise showing normal and sale prices. (This photo happens to be of clothing in Belgium, so the amounts are in euros.)

age fotostock/SuperStock

How did the answers of each respondent vary? Typically, people with the second set of numbers give higher estimates of African states and the product of the numbers. What might explain the differences in the answers? The starting point (initial percentages, initial number in the series) anchors our judgment; everything is a stretch from there. In everyday life, the anchoring bias is occasionally used in marketing in order to give people a sense of a good deal or "fair" price. You may have seen a listing that shows a "normal" price and then a "sale" price. The normal price anchors your estimate of the amount from which you compute the value of the sale. This anchoring effect occurs even when the participant knows that the starting number is false or believes that the starting number is randomly selected. People may adjust their decisions after consideration, but it is rarely enough to overcome the anchoring effect (Cervone & Palmer, 1990; Kahneman et al., 1982).

Even experts are subject to this heuristic. In one study, real estate agents were asked to estimate the value of a house; they were given 10 pages of information about the house that varied only by the listing price. The agents who saw the high listing price gave higher estimates of the value of the house than the agents who saw the low listing price. In general, the agents said that they disregarded the listing price in their judgments. The same pattern of anchoring was shown with a group of business students who had no real estate experience (Northcraft & Neale, 1987). Anchoring can have a powerful, unconscious influence on our judgments (Kristensen & Garling, 2000).

Anchoring and adjustment is also found in clinical situations. For example, the intake interview, which in many hospital settings precedes treatment, can establish an anchoring point for the clinician. The intake interview is a means by which the clinician develops an initial impression of the patient and makes a preliminary diagnosis. Later, the clinician may make only slight adjustments to this diagnosis based on the results of laboratory tests, prior conditions, and so on. The concept of anchoring and adjustment should be a warning that clinicians may place too much emphasis on early information and fail to adjust their initial impressions and diagnosis even when additional, more extensive and reliable information is available (Alegriak et al., 2008; Gigerenzer, Todd, & ABC Research Group, 1999). Anchoring and adjustment may also lead to a kind of conservatism (Phillips & Edwards, 1966) in which clinicians make only small adjustments in the face of other evidence because their decisions are anchored by the initial impression (e.g., Plous, 1993).

The Value of Heuristics

Since our use of heuristics can mislead us, you may well wonder why people would so often rely on them. There are two basic reasons. First, they are often found to be adaptive and lead to a correct judgment (Hutchinson & Gigerenzer, 2005). Second, and perhaps more important to cognitive psychologists, is that they reflect low-level processing—methods we use when we are not being completely rational. They reflect the kind of thinking that characterizes System 1 processing described in Chapter 12. They are fast and require little working memory capacity (Evans, 2008). In contrast, rational inferences that are the result of using System 2 are not automatic and require effort (De Neys & Schaeken, 2007; Sperber & Wilson, 1995).

One way to look at the range of human reasoning, both when we are accurate and when we are in error, is to think of human reasoning and problem solving as a dual process system where two systems are in conflict. When the more reflective processing of System 2 holds sway, it is because it is able to inhibit the basic heuristic, System 1 operation. This dual process explanation is called *default-interventionist processing* (Evans, 2008) because System 2 competes with and can override System 1. People vary in their ability to accomplish this and therefore in their reasoning accuracy (Stanovich, 1999). These two systems are based in two basic systems of neurological processing.

The Neuropsychology of Heuristic Processing

System 1 and System 2 The dual process explanation of heuristic processing says that there are two systems functioning when people are confronted with problems in which the heuristic decisions are in conflict with rational ones. In these kinds

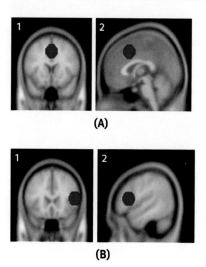

(A)

(B)

FIGURE 13.1 Heuristic and Control Areas of the Frontal Lobes These are brain scans of reasoners confronted with problems where heuristic and logical processing conflict (System 1 vs. System 2). (A) The two images show the brain activity when the reasoner automatically detects a conflict between System 1 and System 2. (B) Images of brain activity when System 2 dominates.

De Neys, Vartanian, O., & Goel, V. *Psychological Science, 19*, 483–489 © 2008. Reprinted by Permission of SAGE Publications.

of problems, System 1 is heuristic processing and is fast and automatic. System 2 processing is analytic and controlled (see analysis by Franssens & De Neys, 2009). The two systems have separate brain circuits.

This theoretical account is clearly supported in a recent study (De Neys, Vartanian, & Goel, 2008). In it, 27-year-old volunteers solved problems like the engineer problem, which illustrates the representativeness heuristic. Only 45% of these college graduates were able to overcome the tendency to reason using the heuristic. While they were making the decisions, their brains were scanned using the fMRI methodology. The results are shown in **FIGURE 13.1**. In Figure 13.1A you see the brain activity when there is a conflict between the heuristic and rational responses; the anterior cingulate cortex is highly active when the reasoner's brain detects a conflict between System 1 and System 2, shown in photo 1. When a heuristic decision is made, activity in the left hemisphere is shown in photo 2. Figure 13.1B shows that when the reasoner is able to suppress the heuristic and make a rational judgment, the right prefrontal cortex is highly active.

Why don't people always reach a correct decision? To do this, they must engage System 2 and their right prefrontal cortex must inhibit activation of System 1 (left temporal lobe). People invariably detect the conflict in decisions between the heuristic and the rational processes, but only those who can activate System 2 will consistently solve the problem.

Emotion and the Somatic Marker Hypothesis An important aspect of System 1 and heuristic decision making is its broad connection to the human emotional system. You may recall that Chapter 11 mentioned how researchers have found that positive emotions can improve speed of problem solving (Isen, Daubman, & Nowicki, 1987). This is also true of decision making. The reason is that the emotion circuit in the human brain participates in the decision-making process (e.g., Bechara, 2004). The general theory of how this happens is called the **somatic marker hypothesis** (Bechara, Damasio, & Damasio, 2000). It states that the entire body's emotion-related circuitry (hence the term *somatic*) is the basic system in which decision making occurs. This is manifested in the ventromedial prefrontal cortex (VM), shown in **FIGURE 13.2**. A person with damage to this area of the brain has difficulty making decisions. Individuals with right-side lesions of the VM cortex show severe difficulties making personal and social decisions. After the

FIGURE 13.2 The Somatic Marker Hypothesis The somatic marker hypothesis correctly predicts that damage to the ventromedial prefrontal cortex disrupts social behavior and the ability to make rational choices. When someone with an undamaged brain makes an optimum decision, the heightened brain activity is shown in red.

Bechara, Damasio, and Damasio, Emotion, Decision Making and the Orbitofrontal Cortex, *Cerebral Cortex*, 2000, 10, 3, 295–307, by permission of Oxford University Press.

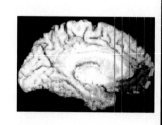
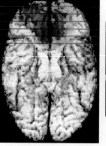
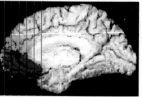

damage, they develop difficulties in planning their workday and their future and have difficulties in choosing friends, partners, and activities (Bechara, Damasio, & Damasio, 2000; Bechara, Tranel, & Damasio, 2002). Yet, their normal intellectual functions are still preserved.

In laboratory studies (Bechara, Tranel, & Damasio, 2002), participants with and without injury to the VM area were asked to perform a gambling task and were forced to decide between options that led to modest gains now but future losses, or small losses now but high future gains. The optimal decision is to choose future gains, but participants with VM damage do not, either in the laboratory task or in their daily lives. In contrast, people without damage to the VM make the optimal judgment (the long-term large gain) in the laboratory task and in their daily lives. This effect on decision making is also seen in children. Adolescents who have had damage to their VM prefrontal cortex in early childhood also show an inability to make appropriate decisions throughout their lives, just as adults who have suffered such damage late in life do (Anderson, Bechara, Damasio, Tranel, & Damasio, 1999). These data support the somatic marker hypothesis and give researchers selected brain areas to examine for their importance to decision making and emotion.

SECTION SUMMARY ▪

Heuristics

Heuristics are procedures that often lead to a correct solution, but there is no guarantee that they will be successful. In contrast, algorithms are procedures that will inevitably lead to a solution if there is one. Using heuristics is a rational process, because they typically are successful in everyday life and they are often faster to apply than are algorithms. Three heuristics are often successful but can also lead us astray: representativeness, availability, and anchoring and adjustment.

When we judge the likelihood of an event by how similar it is to another event whose likelihood we know, we are applying the representativeness heuristic. This is often the case when a physician, for example, performs a diagnosis of a complex situation based on "what it looks like." When we judge our certainty of something happening based on how readily it comes to mind, we are using the availability heuristic. When our treatment of another person is based on first impressions, or when the negotiated sale price of an object is influenced by the starting amount, we are using the anchoring and adjustment heuristic.

Heuristic methods reflect the operation of low-level processing, called System 1. This is associated with activation in the left temporal lobe. It can be interfered with in the service of more rational decision making by the activity of System 2, associated with the right prefrontal cortex. Jointly, these reflect dual reasoning processes. System 1 processing and its use of heuristics are related more broadly to the human emotional system. As described in the somatic marker hypothesis, people with damage to the VM area, which controls the emotional system, also show difficulties making rational choices. Emotion and decision making are connected.

Decision Fallacies

A broad type of decision error is called a **decision fallacy**. A major example of such fallacies occurs when people falsely believe that two events, which are independent of each other, are actually dependent. The two main examples of such fallacies are called sunk costs and gambler's fallacy.

Sunk Costs

Let's suppose you decide to follow a recipe to make a special meal. After spending time and money to prepare the dish, you discover halfway along that you added the wrong ingredients and you don't know how it will turn out. Since you can't get your time and money back, the cost of the preparation is a **sunk cost**: money or resources already invested that cannot be recovered. You now have options: You can continue cooking and risk having an unpleasant dish, or you can start over, cook something different, or go out for a meal.

If you take the first option, you have committed more of your resources (e.g., time and ingredients) in an unprofitable activity only because you have already invested time and money in it. When people do this, they are said to have fallen victim to the **sunk cost fallacy**. It's a fallacy because additional resources put into an initial, failing investment may simply increase the cost of the investment and not increase the likelihood of a positive outcome. In the failing vending machine example that began this chapter, the first dollar inserted into the machine is independent of the second dollar. Putting additional money into the machine simply doubles the cost of the drink (if ultimately successful) and doesn't change the likelihood of success. It is the equivalent of "throwing good money after bad."

One explanation for the sunk cost effect is that people believe their desired goal is more likely to be achieved if they add to the investment, even though the first investment has failed to produce a result. It is as if the first investment and the second are connected, when in fact, from the point of view of decision making, these are independent events: a failed activity and then a decision to re-create or regenerate the failed activity. It is difficult for people not to make this type of error because once having made an investment, their belief in its value increases beyond its objective value. This was shown in a test of people who were betting on horse races. Half of them had just placed a $2 bet and half of them were about to place a bet. Both groups were asked to estimate the likelihood that their choice would win. Those who made a bet 30 seconds before the question were more confident that their horse would win than were those who were about to make a bet but had not yet done so (Knox & Inkster, 1968). A prior commitment increases confidence in a win (Arkes & Hutzel, 2000). There is a second type of sunk cost effect. To experience this, see how you would fare in a typical scenario shown in Demonstration 13.3.

▪▪▪DEMONSTRATION 13.3

Sunk Cost Effect

Assume that you have spent $100 on a ticket for a weekend ski trip to Nebraska. Several weeks later you buy a $50 ticket for a weekend ski trip to Vermont. You think you will enjoy the Vermont ski trip more than the Nebraska ski trip. As you are putting the Vermont mountain trip ticket in your wallet, you notice that the Nebraska and the Vermont trips are for the same weekend. It's too late to sell either ticket, and you cannot return either one. You must use one ticket and not the other. Which trip will you go on? Why?

(Arkes & Blumer, 1985, p. 126)

In the original study described in Demonstration 13.3, more than half of the participants chose to go on the least desirable trip rather than "wasting" their money. Since the story character has equal access to both events, the subjective utility equation (see Demonstration 13.1) points the person to choose the option that has the highest value for him or her. Yet the typical participant does not. He or she chooses the option he or she had paid most for, not the one that is most desirable: the bigger the sunk cost, the bigger the commitment to a failed gamble. This is the quintessential sunk cost effect. The sunk cost effect has real implications for real-world decision making. In fact, it is sometimes referred to as the *Concorde fallacy* (Weatherhead, 1979) because the British and French governments spent hundreds of millions of dollars to fund the building of the Concorde aircraft long after it was obvious that it was not needed, because they had already invested vast sums of money.

The sunk cost fallacy shows that people have a tendency to see independent events as connected. In this case, they sense that the occurrence of one event is dependent on a prior event. This notion of "dependence" promotes the sunk cost effect as well as an equally irrational one, the gambler's fallacy.

Gambler's Fallacy

Humans cannot escape seeing events as causally related and dependent on each other. Children as young as 6 months of age, shown geometric shapes moving on a screen, readily perceive one shape as causing the other one to move (e.g., Leslie & Keeble, 1987; Michotte, 1963). It should not be surprising, then, that adults perceive completely independent events as causally connected. This is easily shown in the **gambler's fallacy**, where the behavior of some gamblers suggests that they mistakenly believe past events will affect future events. For example, many gamblers believe that a random event like throwing an 8 on a pair of dice is more likely to occur because it has not happened for a period of time; it's as if the gambler assumes that the dice have a memory. To experience the power of the gambler's fallacy, try the activity in Demonstration 13.4.

■■■DEMONSTRATION 13.4

Gambler's Fallacy

1. If you flip a coin 1 time, what will be the likelihood of getting a head?

   (a) 1/2   (b) 1/4   (c) 1/8   (d) 1/32

2. Now suppose you flip a coin 5 times in a row and it comes up heads each time and someone asks you to flip the coin 1 more time. What is the likelihood that the 6th flip will produce a head?

   (a) 1/2   (b) 1/4   (c) 1/8   (d) 1/32

Did you think that a head was less likely following a run of 5 heads as in Question 2? People are often surprised when a run of outcomes deviates from randomness. They expect a kind of correction to the deviation; they feel as if they are "due" for a correction. This is the gambler's fallacy. People are so overwhelmed by the sequence they forget that the chance of a head is 1/2, no matter how many have already occurred, because each coin flip is independent of the last. It is true that the likelihood of a run of 5 heads is 1/32 before the first coin is flipped, but because each flip is independent of the previous one, the likelihood of a head (or a tail for that matter) is 1/2 for each flip. In answer to both questions, the actual likelihood of a head is 1/2, assuming it is a fair coin; yet, a person suffering from the gambler's fallacy will think that the probability of a head on the second question is more like 1/32 than 1/2.

Sometimes gamblers believe that in the long run (after they start to lose) everything will even out, as in the following discussion:

Paul: Let's start shopping for a sailboat.

Kelly: Did you get a raise?

Paul: No, but I just bought a lottery ticket.

Kelly: You've been buying tickets for years and haven't won.

Paul: I know, but I'm due for a big win.

People who operate according to the gambler's fallacy occasionally pursue a doubling strategy called the *Martingale system*. When gambling at casinos, they start with a $4 bet. If they lose, they bet $8 on the next gamble, then $16 on the next, and so forth until they win. This method assumes that the gamblers have an infinite amount of money at their disposal and can place an unlimited number of bets. Because of such strategies, most casinos limit the size of the wager. To see the ultimate fallacy in the Martingale system, read Demonstration 13.5. You can see that the gambler's fallacy is similar to the sunk cost effect: Both assume that independent events are really connected, and the participants in both instances are overly optimistic about the probability of a return on their investment (Weinstein, 1980).

■■■DEMONSTRATION 13.5

Doubling Strategy

The Martingale system refers to a set of betting strategies employed during the 18th century in France. It is a doubling strategy: If you lose on a bet, you keep making subsequent bets of double the previous amount until you ultimately win. Underlying this is the gambler's fallacy that within a short period of time you're due for a win.

With unlimited money at your disposal, it is effective. However, three practical flaws undermine this system. First, even though it is true that in the long run you win, the time could exceed any practical limits. Second, the casinos often set betting limits at a table, so you may reach the betting limit before you are able to win. Third, considering the amount you are risking, the amount you win may not be much. For example, suppose you are playing roulette, in which there are an equal number of red and black numbers (in most cases there is a third option, but we will not deal with that). Say you choose black at $4 and lose. Following the Martindale system, you keep doubling the next 6 times until maybe you win. You have gambled a total of $508 ($4 + $8 + $16 + $32 + $64 + $128 + $256 = $508). Suppose you won on the last bet of $256 and received $512. Your total investment was $508, so in reality your net win was $4, a return of 0.8%: definitely not a good investment.

fStop/Alamy

The Monty Hall Dilemma

When people are caught in the grip of sunk costs or the gambler's fallacy, they fail to appreciate the independence of events and treat them as somehow connected. Occasionally people do the opposite: They treat events as independent, even though they should be treated as dependent. Nowhere is this better shown than in the classic case of the **Monty Hall dilemma**.

In the 1970's version of the TV show *Let's Make a Deal,* the host, Monty Hall, would show a contestant three curtains: behind one would be a desirable prize like a new automobile; behind another would be an undesirable prize like a goat; behind a third would be something equally strange or useless. If the contestant chose the curtain concealing the automobile, he or she would get to keep it.

The contestant would select one of the three curtains. However, before it was opened, Monty (who knew which curtain held the big prize), would open one of the other curtains and show an undesirable prize like a goat. What should the contestant now do? Stay with the curtain originally selected, or switch to the other closed curtain? What would you do? The correct answer may surprise you. The person should switch curtains! Most people, including

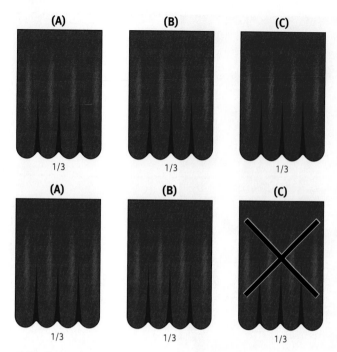

FIGURE 13.3 Monty Hall Dilemma: Version 1 The typical way people represent the choices in the Monty Hall Dilemma before and after one of the options has been eliminated—as independent events.

many mathematicians, are astonished by this solution (vos Savant, 1990).

The key factor in understanding the problem is that the events are not independent, as most people imagine. In the explanation that follows, keep in mind that like the monk problem in Chapter 11, seeing the solution depends on how you represent the problem. Even though people have been taught the correct answer, they do not always accept the new representation (Franco-Watkins, Derks, & Dougherty, 2003). Let's start with **FIGURE 13.3**, which illustrates a common way of representing this problem. Inspect the figure to see if it corresponds to your representation. Most people interpret the chances of finding the automobile behind each curtain as 1/3 (three curtains, one is correct). When the goat is revealed, one of the options has been eliminated. This leaves two curtains, one of which holds the prize.

People now perceive the choices as if they are between two independent events, each with a 50% chance of being correct. Therefore, they believe there is nothing to be gained by switching curtains; each is equally likely to conceal the prize. An alternative representation is shown in **FIGURE 13.4**. Notice that the initial choice has a 1/3 chance of being correct and the remaining curtains collectively have a 2/3 chance of being correct, as indicated by a line drawn around them. This 2/3 likelihood of being correct is not altered by Monty Hall showing that one of the curtains hides a goat. Monty Hall knew which curtain held the goat; he was not selecting randomly from the three options. Since one of the curtains is now eliminated from the set, the entire burden of the 2/3 likelihood is carried by the remaining, unassigned curtain. It alone has a 2/3 chance of revealing the automobile. Therefore, the contestant's best bet is to shift to this curtain.

This is a deceptively difficult dilemma: Less than 20% of psychology students are usually able to solve it correctly (e.g., De Neys & Vershueren, 2006; Krauss & Wang, 2003). The typical decision maker adopts a plausible heuristic, called the *number of cases heuristic* (Shimojo & Ichikawa, 1989), in which each option (curtain) has an equal chance of being the correct one. Therefore, each choice will be correct $1/n$ where n is the number of options. Cognitive resources such as working memory are necessary to overcome the use of this heuristic. For example, university students asked to solve the dilemma had to decide whether to switch, stick with their original pick, or decide that their chances were equal. All participants were also given a test of the working memory capacity of their central executive (for a reminder of this, see Chapter 5). Students who successfully solved the problem and decided to switch (5.2% of 239 students) were those with the highest working memory capacity (De Neys & Vershueren, 2006).

De Neys and Vershueren (2006) reasoned that if working memory capacity was important to solve the Monty Hall problem, then reducing memory capacity should hurt performance. To test this, in another experiment half of the students were given a second task while solving the problem in order to tax their memory resources. The remaining half of the participants, the control group, was not given an extra memory load. The memory load group was less successful than the control group in solving the problem (7.8% and 21.6%, respectively). Memory load and, indirectly, memory capacity affects the ability to solve this dilemma. One reason is that people have to have the memory resources to overcome the tendency to see the events as independent and create a new mental representation of the problem that allows them to see the dependent relationship among the options (Burns & Wieth, 2004).

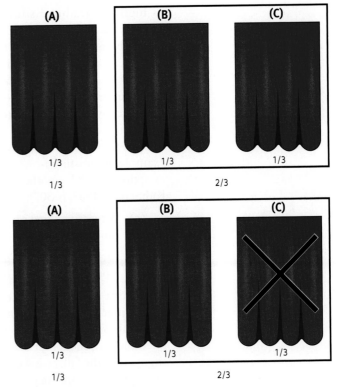

FIGURE 13.4 **Monty Hall Dilemma: Version 2** The way correct solvers represent the Monty Hall Dilemma—as dependent events.

The Conjunction Fallacy

Often people correctly see events as independent, but believe the likelihood of the two independent events *together* is greater than the likelihood of any one of them *alone*. This violates the basic idea of independence and is called the **conjunction fallacy**, which is illustrated in the following situation. Read the description and then answer the question that follows it (Tversky & Kahneman, 1983, p. 297):

> Linda is 31 years old, single, outspoken, and very bright. She majored in philosophy. As a student, she was deeply concerned with issues of discrimination and social justice, and also participated in anti-nuclear demonstrations.

Given what you have just read, decide which is more likely:

(a) Linda is a bank teller.

(b) Linda is a bank teller and is active in the feminist movement.

Which option did you select? In this simple situation, being a bank teller is the larger set of possibilities; it includes bank tellers who are active in the feminist movement as well as bank tellers who are not. As a result, being a bank teller is the most likely event (a); all of the subsets of the main category are necessarily less likely. However, when given this narrative, nearly 90% of the students selected option (b) and committed the conjunction fallacy. They argued that Linda is more likely to be a feminist bank teller than she is likely to be a bank teller, because she resembles an active feminist more than she resembles a bank teller. This tendency to commit the conjunction fallacy is as high for graduate students and professors as it is for undergraduates (Tversky & Kahneman, 1983).

People are susceptible to this fallacy because the combination of events satisfies a person's sense of what naturally goes together. That is, the conjunction of events is more representative of the situation that it describes than are the individual events alone (Tversky & Kahneman, 1983). The representativeness heuristic says that people judge the likelihood of an event by estimating how similar it is to another event whose likelihood they know.

The conjunction fallacy occurs in many areas of decision making. Take, as an example, forecasting future events. One group of students rated the likelihood of option (c) while another group rated the likelihood of option (d) (Tversky & Kahneman, 1983, p. 307):

(c) A massive flood somewhere in North America, in which more than a thousand people drown.

(d) An earthquake in California causing a flood in which more than a thousand people drown.

Notice that while option (c) contains a single event, a flood, option (d) contains the conjunction of two events: an earthquake and a flood. Therefore, objectively this conjunction is less likely than the single event (c). However, students rated the conjunction of events (d) 50% more likely than (c). The likelihood of engaging in the fallacy is somewhat greater when the events are as vivid as in the earthquake example (e.g., Nisbett & Ross, 1980). People show this pattern not only when they are estimating the likelihood of future events, but also when they are asked to wager money on various events (Sides, Osherson, Bonini, & Viale, 2002; Tentori, Bonini, & Osherson, 2004).

One view of why people commit the conjunction fallacy is that it reflects how people interpret the information (Gigerenzer, 1996a). Look back at the Linda problem. Did you interpret option (a) to mean that Linda was a bank teller *and* not a feminist? Some estimates claim that more than half of the participants in these studies use this interpretation when they make their decisions (Hertwig & Gigerenzer, 1999; Macdonald & Gilhooly, 1990). However, when these relationships are clarified and students are simply asked to estimate how many people out of 100 like Linda would be bank tellers *and* feminists, the conjunction fallacy still persists (Mellers, Hertwig, & Kahneman, 2001). Although the interpretation of the situation may affect some people, it is not the dominant explanation. So far, the most viable explanation is the representative heuristic, because, like the engineer problem described earlier, people are not using the base rates given the situation; they are not inhibiting their automatic processing (and use the right frontal lobe).

SECTION SUMMARY ■

Decision Fallacies

Sunk cost, which is the nonrefundable cost that you have already incurred in your original investment, often influences whether you should continue on a course of action even if the likelihood of success has been lowered. In fact, people often assume that success is more likely if they have made an initial investment in a project. This tendency to continue investing, even in the face of a clear loss, is called the sunk cost fallacy. It is based on an erroneous belief that an initial investment is causally related to the ultimate outcome. The sunk cost fallacy is also related to people's desire not to be "wasteful" or to "throw away" their initial investment, as when people resist selling a stock that is diminishing in value because they invested so much in the stock originally. This type of thinking guarantees that they will lose even more of their initial investment. The gambler's fallacy is a decision error where random events are assumed to be connected and dependent on one another. In contrast, the difficulty that people have with the Monty Hall dilemma is in seeing that some events are not random and are dependent on each other. Avoiding making an error in the Monty Hall dilemma requires cognitive effort and relies on available processing in working memory. The conjunction fallacy occurs when people correctly see events as independent, but they assume that two events together are more likely to occur than either of the events apart.

Base Rates and the Truth

Although most laboratory experiments that study decision making do not involve life or death decisions, we can nevertheless learn from those studies about how people interpret medical information, such as the outcomes of diagnostic tests. Suppose, for example, that you go to a physician to see if you have disease x. You are told that you do not have the disease and that the test is 90% accurate. For most people and some physicians, this means that the patient should be 90% sure that she or he doesn't have the disease. **TABLE 13.2** shows an idealized chart of what "90% accurate" means to the typical person. It shows that 90% of the people who have the disease are told that they have it and 90% of the people who do not have the disease are told that they do not have it. The medical test should only "miss" 10% of each of these two groups.

However, it is possible to define 90% accuracy as being correct on 90% of the people and not the likelihood that a specific person has the disease. This is different from the common interpretation. To see this, notice that the top of the table shows the number of people who actually have the disease—the base rate. This is important because it is the true proportion of people who have the disease. Because of the base rate—in this case 10% (100 out of 1,000 people)—it is possible for the medical test to simply indicate that none of the 1,000 people have it. In this situation, the test would be right 90% of the time. This is what is shown in **TABLE 13.3**. Unfortunately, it would miss all of those who actually have the disease. Since 90% of the patients do not have the disease, the test is still calculated to be 90% accurate (Hastie & Dawes, 2001), a distressing state of affairs.

TABLE 13.2				
Commonsense Idea of 90% Accurate				

Medical test indicates	Reality		Total no. of people (1,000)	True accuracy (%)
	No. of people who really have disease x (Base rate = 100)	No. of people who really do not have disease x (Base rate = 900)		
Have disease x	90	90	180	18
Do not have disease x	10	810	820	82
Total error	10	90	100	90

TABLE 13.3				
Medical Test Indicates that Someone Does Not Have Disease x				

Medical test indicates	Reality		Total no. of people (1,000)	True accuracy (%)
	No. of people who really have disease x (Base rate = 100)	No. of people who really do not have disease x (Base rate = 900)		
Have disease x	0	0	0	0
Do not have disease x	100	900	900	90
Total accuracy	0	900	900	90

TABLE 13.4				
Medical Test Indicates You Do Not Have Disease x 80% of the Time When You Do Not Have It and 20% of the Time When You Do Have It				

Medical test indicates	Reality		Total no. of people (1,000)	True accuracy (%)
	No. of people who really have disease x (Base rate = 100)	No. of people who really do not have disease x (Base rate = 900)		
Have disease x	20	180	200	20
Do not have disease x	80	720	800	80
Total accuracy	20	720	740	74

Using Base Rates to Find the Truth

This example shows that even when you know the accuracy of the test, you need to know the base rates in order to interpret the diagnosis. This situation is potentially serious: Dawes (1986) showed that the statistical basis for surgeries to treat a certain type of cancer (in advance of its discovery in a patient) was flawed by failing to take into account base rates. Although a test says that you have disease x, what's the probability that you really do? The data in **TABLE 13.4** show the situation when a test matches the base rate and indicates that people don't have the disease with 80% accuracy when they do not have it and 20% accuracy when they do have it. Using the data in Table 13.4, you can estimate whether a person actually has the disease.

Bayes' theorem will allow you to make the necessary calculation. The probability of having disease *x* is determined by the following equation:

$$P_{(x|d)} = (P_{(x)} \times P_{(d|x)}) / [(P_{(x)} \times P_{(d|x)}) + (P_{(not\ x)} \times P_{(d|not\ x)})],$$

where

> $P_{(x|d)}$ = probability (*p*) of having disease *x* given that the diagnosis (*d*) said you did (this answers the question);
>
> $P_{(x)}$ = base rate of the disease (the probability that you have it);
>
> $P_{(d|x)}$ = probability of being diagnosed with the disease given that you actually have it; and
>
> $(P_{(not\ x)} \times P_{(d|not\ x)})$ = probability that you don't have the disease multiplied by the probability that you are *incorrectly* diagnosed with the disease.

Let's see how this can be used to understand whether the patient has disease *x* by plugging in the appropriate values:

> $P_{(x)}$ = .10 (the base rate of the disease = .10);
>
> $P_{(d|x)}$ = .20 (probability that the text will say you have the disease when you do have it = .20);
>
> $(P_{(not\ x)} \times P_{(d|not\ x)})$ = .90 × .20 (the probability that you don't have disease *x* multiplied by the probability that you are incorrectly diagnosed = .18).

If you substitute these values into Bayes' equation, you will find the probability that the patient has been correctly diagnosed as having the disease is only 10% in spite of the fact that the test is 80% accurate. This is because the overall likelihood of the disease is quite low. In fact, sometimes in real life we are tested for diseases that are extremely rare. Assuming that a highly accurate test diagnoses us with having one of these rare diseases, should we believe it immediately without further testing? To decide this, we need to proceed cautiously and employ the base rates. We can see from the example that when base rates are low, even highly accurate tests can be wrong. This situation is covered by a rule of thumb taught to medical students, and it is paraphrased here: If you hear hoofbeats on Main Street, don't look for zebras. (The actual quotation is attributed to the lectures of Dr. T. E. Woodward of the University of Maryland, around 1950: "Don't look for zebras on Greene Street.") It's wise to look for common diseases before considering rare ones.

Base rates and the neglect of them in understanding evidence has been a factor in the interpretation of DNA evidence in the courtroom (Hastie & Dawes, 2001). Rather than describing the intricacies of DNA, the difficulties can be illustrated with a standard task for which there is research evidence. It is called the taxicab problem. It is considered the classic demonstration of the importance of base rates for decision making and also how difficult it is for people to use base rates in making decisions. To appreciate this, consider Demonstration 13.6.

■■■**DEMONSTRATION 13.6**

The Taxicab Problem

A cab was involved in a hit-and-run accident at night. Two cab companies, the Green and the Blue, operate in the city. You are given the following data: (i) 85% of the cabs in the city are Green and 15% are Blue. (ii) A witness identified the cab as a Blue cab. The court tested his ability to identify cabs under the appropriate visibility conditions. When presented with a sample of cabs (half of which were Blue and half of which were Green) the witness made correct identifications in 80% of the cases and erred in 20% of the cases.

Question: What is the probability that the cab involved in the accident was Blue rather than Green?

(Tversky & Kahneman, 1982, pp. 156–157)

In the taxicab problem, most people estimate the probability as over 50%, and some as over 80%. However, the correct answer (found through adding and multiplying the probabilities) is actually lower than these estimates.

In the taxicab problem there are four facts:

(i) A cab was involved in a hit-and-run accident:

(ii) 85% of the cabs in the city are green and 15% are blue.

(iii) A witness identified the cab as a blue cab.

(iv) The witness is 80% accurate (20% inaccurate).

What is the probability that the cab involved in the accident was blue rather than green? There are two ways to compute the true state of affairs given the base rates. One is to use the probabilities in the formula of Bayes' theorem. The other is to draw a diagram. We illustrate both methods here with the information provided in the problem.

What we really want to know in this case is the probability that the cab was really blue given that the observer said it was blue. This quantity equals the following: probability of a blue cab multiplied by probability that someone would say blue when it really was blue, divided by probability someone would say blue when it was blue plus probability someone would say blue when the cab was really green. This is expressed arithmetically as:

$$(.15 \times .80) / [(.15 \times .80) + (.85 \times .20)] = [.12 / (.12 + .17)] = .41$$

Two Ways of Representing a Decision Problem One way to derive the probabilities of various outcomes in the cab problem is to draw a diagram starting from the left side where the initial two options are easily calculated: 85% chance of a green cab and 15% of a blue cab. Then the witness is 80% accurate (or 20% inaccurate) in identification. The results require minimal calculation and only careful drawing of possibilities.

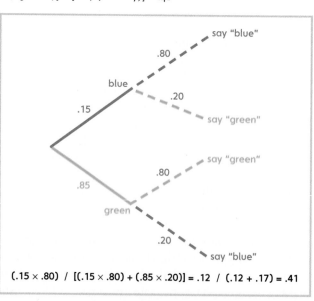

$$(.15 \times .80) / [(.15 \times .80) + (.85 \times .20)] = .12 / (.12 + .17) = .41$$

A second way to calculate the likelihood that it was truly a blue cab is to draw a diagram: After you draw the diagram, you simply calculate the probability of saying blue when the cab was really blue and divide this by all the ways that a person would say blue.

Did you find the graph method for solving the problem easier than Bayes' formula? They are logically equivalent, but the graph can be more intuitively appealing.

Representation of Base Rates

It has long been known that people of all backgrounds have difficulty in solving problems like the one in Demonstration 13.6. Indeed, even medical students have difficulty calculating the likelihood that a person has a certain disease given the diagnosis (Hastie & Dawes, 2001). We now know that the difficulty is not because the calculations are particularly difficult (though they are a bit), but because of how people represent these sorts of problems. It's possible to illustrate this by changing the way the problem is presented and therefore how people will represent it. In fact, even elementary schoolchildren can solve these problems when they are presented in a way that evokes an effective representation (Gigerenzer & Hoffrage, 1995). In one study (Zhu & Gigerenzer, 2006) the problem below was shown to 4th, 5th, and 6th graders and adults. The problem is similar to the taxicab problem, with the various outcomes specified as probabilities. Try to solve it yourself:

> Pingping goes to a small village to ask for directions. In this village, the probability that the person he meets will lie is 10%. If a person lies, the probability that he/she has a red nose is 80%. If a person doesn't lie, the probability that he/she also has a red nose is 10%. Imagine that Pingping meets someone in the village with a red nose. What is the probability that the person will lie?
>
> *(Zhu & Gigerenzer, 2006, p. 289)*

How did you do on this one? It should be as difficult as all of the other problems presented here:

$$(.10 \times .80) / [(.10 \times .80) + (.90 \times .10)] = [.08 / (.08 + .09)] = .47$$

So, it should come as no surprise that none of the children were able to solve the problem. However, another group of children and adults was given the same problem, but expressed differently using numbers that show how often something has occurred (called *frequencies*) rather than probabilities. See if this presentation is easier for you to solve:

> Pingping goes to a small village to ask for directions. In this village, 10 out of every 100 people will lie. Of the 10 people who lie, 8 have a red nose. Of the remaining 90 people who don't lie, 9 also have a red nose. Imagine that Pingping meets a group of people in the village with red noses. How many of these people will lie?
>
> *(Zhu & Gigerenzer, 2006, p. 289)*

In this presentation, you can see that 8 of the people have red noses and are liars; 9 people have red noses but are not liars. So, there are 17 red-nosed people and only 8 of them are liars: 8 out of 17 = .47, or 47%. Perhaps this problem will

FIGURE 13.5 Bayesian Reasoning with Natural Frequencies This is a diagram of the Pingping problem. Instead of presenting the options as probabilities or percentages, they are presented as frequencies: the number of people with red noses and the number with blue noses, and so on. (There are 17 people with red noses; 8 red-nosed people are liars; therefore, 8/17 = 47%.) Children's accuracy increases with age and eventually parallels that of adults.

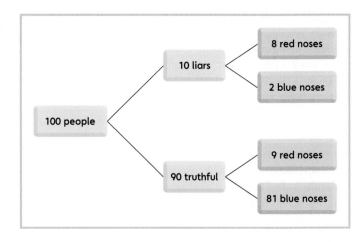

FIGURE 13.6 Two Ways of Representing the Pingping Problem Adults and children of various ages tried to solve problems like the Pingping problem presented as percentages or frequencies. In the graph, the frequency presentation shows a steady increase in accuracy with age in two studies.

Source: From Zhu, L., & Gigerenzer, G., Children Can Solve Bayesian Problems: The Role of Representation in Mental Computation. *Cognition*, 2006, 98, 287–308

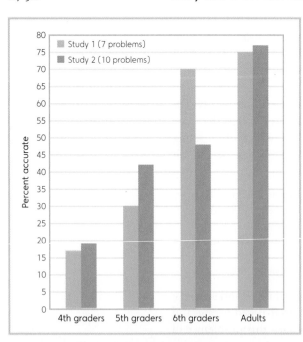

be easier to understand if you glance at **FIGURE 13.5**. When the children were given the problem in this configuration, they showed an increase in accuracy from 4th to 6th grade, reaching a maximum accuracy of 53%. Even adults show an improvement over reasoning with probabilities, as illustrated in **FIGURE 13.6**. Reasoning with frequencies is considerably easier than with probabilities (e.g., Cosmides & Tooby, 1996; Gigerenzer, 1996b).

Natural Use of Base Rates

You may have gotten the impression from these examples that people are not normally able to use base rates in calculating the likelihood of outcomes. The truth of the matter is that under normal circumstances, people are actually pretty sensitive to base rates even if they do not actually make the calculations. Take sports, for example. In baseball, there is a slight advantage for hitters batting against pitchers with opposite handedness—it increases a batter's average by .032 (Lindsey, 1959). A good baseball manager plays the percentages by having left-handed batters face right-handed pitchers and right-handed batters face left-handed pitchers, no matter what the batting average of the batter. Indeed, sometimes team managers will substitute pitchers who have the same handedness as the batter, just to force the opposing manager to change the batter (presumably for one who is not as good). In such instances, base rate probabilities are considered and are given substantial weight (Hirostu & Wright, 2005). But do the managers actually make the calculations? Probably not. However, they may make intuitive judgments as described in the unconscious thought theory discussed at the beginning of the chapter.

If people can at least occasionally appreciate base rates in the real world, why do they seem to neglect them in laboratory studies? The primary answer is that the studies present unfamiliar formats. We can see this when the information is presented in terms of frequencies (how often events occur) rather than probabilities, as in the previous study with children. The second difference between the laboratory and real-world situations is that reasoners treat the "accuracy" of diagnostic tests or the eyewitnesses to an event as of paramount importance. Take the famous taxicab problem. Reasoners are aware that there are many more green cabs than blue cabs and assume that the witness in the problem also knows this and has taken it into consideration in his report. Therefore, decision makers reason that the witness's accuracy is the only critical factor to his observation. It isn't that people necessarily ignore base rates, it's that they assume accuracy somehow includes that knowledge (Birnbaum, 1983).

SECTION SUMMARY ■
Base Rates and the Truth
Base rates are critical in order to determine the true likelihood of events, such as how likely it is that a medical diagnosis is true. People do not have difficulty appreciating base rates in their everyday lives, but they do have difficulty making the correct calculations. When the relevant information for calculating base rates is presented as natural frequencies, people (including children and physicians) are more accurate.

Seeing Patterns in Randomness

Suppose you tossed a coin 4 times and it came up heads each time. You would be surprised and might begin to wonder whether the coin was properly balanced or whether you were flipping it in a special way. This is because you know that the likelihood of a head (or tail) on any single toss is 50%. If you were to flip the coin 100 times, roughly half of the results would be heads. In fact, we generally expect to see alternations of heads and tails. When the pattern looks different, the representativeness heuristic begins to activate and tell us that there may be something wrong because some sequences seem consistent with a random coin toss and others do not.

Humans seem to have an appreciation for the ratio of possible outcomes over the long run. The 18th-century mathematician Bernoulli called this the **law of large numbers**. However, people also seem to be thrown off occasionally by small numbers: clusters of events that deviate from expectations. This is because we believe that small numbers of events should repeat the pattern that we expect from large numbers of events (Tversky & Kahneman, 1971).

Looking at small series of numbers often misleads us. Suppose someone asked you to state the first 10 prime numbers (a prime number has only two divisors, 1 and the number itself). If you quickly wrote down the odd numbers 3, 5, 7, you might draw the conclusion that all odd numbers are prime numbers; after all, the first three odd numbers are also the first three prime numbers. Of course, the fourth odd number, 9, is not a prime. This tendency to extrapolate to large sets by drawing conclusions from small samples is the **law of small numbers** (Guy, 1988) and leads to many decision-making errors.

False Clusters

It is difficult for humans to perceive events as being randomly generated. For example, six coin flips might produce the sequence: (a) H, H, H, T, T, T, or (b) H, H, T, H, T, T. Which sequence do you think is more likely to be produced at random? People are often surprised to learn that both sequences are equally likely; however, only the (b) sequence seems random to people because they expect random events to "look random" (Kahneman & Tversky, 1973). Chapter 4 described the pattern recognition processes that cause us to see shapes even in randomly configured clouds. We detect regularities when the pattern we experience (however random) fits stories or narratives in our memories (Falk & Konold, 1997; Siegrist, Cvetkovich, & Gutscher, 2001).

The **clustering illusion** is a decision-making error that stems from our perception that clusters of random events are not really random (Gilovich, 1993). For example, we often read that disease rates in certain cities are many times the normal, expected rate. Although these rates may be statistically unusual, they are not necessarily rare. Some of these disease clusters have as much to do with where we draw the boundary of a neighborhood or a city as they do with any causal element. Consider, for example, the joke about the Texas (or New York, or California) sharpshooter—a cowboy who liked to fire his shotgun at a big target and then paint a bull's-eye around the tightest cluster of holes and boast about his accurate shooting to his friends. Clearly, the significance of clusters depends on where you draw the boundaries. Disease clusters, for example, are not typically predicted, but are usually noticed after the fact (Dolk, Busby, Armstrong, & Walls, 1998).

The surgeon, Atul Gawande (1999), described the situation of McFarland, California. This farming town of 6,400 people had 11 cases of childhood cancer, a rate 4 times higher than the national average. People were understandably alarmed and began investigating groundwater and other possible sources of pollution, but none were found. In fact, the children had different forms of cancer that could not have developed in the same way from the same source (Neutra, 1990). These sorts of examples suggest that in many cases, we see patterns where none exist. Disease clusters may arise from chance variation and, like the Texas sharpshooter, we draw the bull's-eye after the fact.

This does not mean that all identifications of clusters are in error. There are some striking, but rare, cases where illness clusters have specific causes. For example, the Turkish village of Karain had a high instance of lung cancer that was traced to erionite, a mineral in the soil. Residents of the Love Canal neighborhood in Niagara Falls, New York,

Sign warns of contamination at a school in Love Canal, which was evacuated in 1978. This photo was taken around 1992.

Galen Rowell/Corbis

had high rates of cancer and birth defects, which were traced to toxic wastes buried in an adjoining area (Zavestoski, Agnello, Mignano, & Darroch, 2004). The evidence, however, shows that few identifications of disease clusters are valid.

The Hot Hand Fallacy

Most sports fans believe that players have hot and cold streaks and they want the ball to be put in the hands of their favored player. They'll call out for a quarterback to pass the ball to Terrell Owens, or they'll scream for his teammates to give the basketball to LeBron James because he's got the "hot hand." The term **hot hand** refers to the belief that players have clusters of success in which one successful play leads to another. This belief is pervasive among fans. Of 100 basketball fans surveyed, 91% thought "a player has a better chance of making a shot after having just made his last two or three shots than he does after having just missed his last two or three shots" (Gilovich, Vallone, & Tversky, 1985, p. 297). Eighty-four percent of people surveyed thought "in basketball, it's important to pass the ball to someone who has just made several shots in a row" (p. 298).

Are these perceived clusters like the examples of cluster illusions mentioned before? To answer this question, Gilovich et al. (1985) analyzed the shooting of players in more than 80 games played by the Philadelphia 76ers, the New Jersey Nets, and the New York Knicks basketball teams during the 1980–1981 season. **TABLE 13.5** shows that none of the players have more runs of hits or misses than would be expected by chance, given their basic rate of baskets. These expert players were no more likely to make a basket following three misses (*cold hand*) than they were to make a basket following three previous baskets (*hot hand*). The study

TABLE **13.5**							
Hot Hand Findings							
Player	$P(x\|ooo)$	$P(x\|oo)$	$P(x\|o)$	$P(x)$	$P(x\|x)$	$P(x\|xx)$	$P(x\|xxx)$	r
C. Richardson	.50	.47	.56	.50	.49	.50	.48	−.02
J. Erving	.52	.51	.51	.52	.53	.52	.48	.02
L. Hollins	.50	.49	.46	.46	.46	.46	.32	.00
M. Cheeks	.77	.60	.60	.56	.55	.54	.59	−.04
C. Jones	.50	.48	.47	.47	.45	.43	.27	−.02
A. Toney	.52	.53	.51	.46	.43	.40	.34	−.08
B. Jones	.61	.58	.58	.54	.53	.47	.53	−.05
S. Mix	.70	.56	.52	.52	.51	.48	.36	−.02
D. Dawkins	.88	.73	.71	.62	.57	.58	.51	−.14
Means =	.56	.53	.54	.52	.51	.50	.46	−.04

Note: *x* = a hit; *o* = a miss, *r* = the correlation between the outcomes of consecutive shots.
Source: From Gilovich, Vallone, & Tversky, 1985

also analyzed free throws by the Boston Celtics over two seasons and found that when a player made his first shot, he made the second shot 75% of the time; when he missed the first shot he made the second shot 75% of the time. Basketball players do shoot in streaks, but within the bounds of chance (see also Bar-Eli, Avugos, & Raab, 2006; Koehler & Conley, 2003; Larkey, Smith, & Kadane, 1989).

A similar pattern has been shown in investigations of the hot hand among 35 professional golfers on the 1997 PGA tour. These golfers were just as likely to score a birdie (one stroke less than the par for that hole) or better when following a hole on which they scored worse than a birdie, as they were on a hole on which they scored better than a birdie (Clark, 2005). In another study, the batting records of all major league baseball games from 1984–1987 were analyzed searching for cold and hot streaks; the results showed that batters were as likely to increase their batting averages after a hot streak as after a cold streak (Siwoff, Hirdt, & Hirdt, 1988).

Belief in the hot hand is pervasive and invades many aspects of our lives, including our personal finances. People purchase mutual funds based on past performance of fund managers (Sirri & Tufano, 1988) as if some are hot and some are cold. The gambler's fallacy notoriously guides stock investing. People will sell stocks that have appreciated and hold on to those that have lost value. They argue that if a stock has risen, it's due for a downturn, and therefore it's time to sell. If stocks have lost value, they are due to appreciate so one should hold on to them (Odean, 1998; Shefrin & Statman, 1985).

Are you convinced by these findings that there is no hot hand? Two decades have passed since the original study, which has been followed by many more, yet fans persist in their belief that successes and failures come in streaks.

The Hot Hand Versus the Gambler's Fallacy

Students often view the gambler's fallacy and the hot hand fallacy as contradicting each other. These two decision-making errors are not opposites, however. The gambler's fallacy expresses a person's belief about the outcome of a random process. The hot hand fallacy expresses a person's belief in what an individual will accomplish. In the gambler's fallacy, the coin or card or some other inanimate object "is due." The hot hand refers to a person or another animate object (Sundali, 2006) and asserts that whatever the person is doing will continue. The gambler's fallacy assumes that the pattern (not the person) will change ("I'm due").

The two fallacies focus on different aspects of the environment. It is possible for someone to believe both in the gambler's fallacy (that after three coin flips of heads, a tail is due) and the hot hand (that after three wins of a correctly guessed coin toss, they will be more likely to correctly guess the next outcome).

The gambler's fallacy however, is the opposite of a different decision-making fallacy that has a name similar to the hot hand. It is called the **hot outcome fallacy**, which is the belief that the last type of outcome will continue to occur. For example, after three red numbers appear on the spin of a roulette wheel, if you believe in the hot outcome, you will expect another red number to appear—red numbers are hot. Notice that here the *outcomes* are hot (e.g., red numbers), rather than individuals, as in the hot hand (Edwards, 1961). If you don't gamble, perhaps you had an experience in grade school where the teacher picked names out of a bag for who would be first up in baseball, or dismissed early. After 2 days in a row of being picked first (or last) you might assume that the pattern is fixed and would persist on the 3rd day as well. If you were subject to the gambler's fallacy, you would not believe in the hot outcome and would predict that something was going to change.

The hot outcome and the hot hand are different: One refers to outcomes and the other refers to people. Someone who believes in the hot outcome believes that a particular outcome is going to continue to occur. A person who believes in the hot hand believes that someone will continue to be effective (hot) or ineffective (cold) in some endeavor.

Why do people adopt these decision-making beliefs? The gambler's fallacy may be the consequence of the representativeness heuristic. People expect small sequences to look like large sequences (the law of small numbers mentioned earlier; e.g., Ayton & Fischer, 2004; Gilovich et al., 1985; Roney & Trick, 2003; Tversky & Gilovich, 1989). Because of this, people are led to reject the randomness of sequences: Even though four heads come up in a row, which is quite likely in a sequence of 20 flips, it doesn't look random. In studies where people were asked to generate strings of random numbers, they produced strings of numbers with significantly fewer runs of the same number than a truly random sequence would. People are more likely to produce 2 3 5 7 9 8 2 6 as a random sequence than 2 3 4 3 2 9 8 2 2 (e.g., Wagenaar, 1972). The first string only duplicates one of the nine numbers in the string, whereas the second string repeats two of the numbers, including one that occurs four times.

Why are people susceptible to these heuristics and fallacies? A major explanation is the illusion of control (Langer, 1975): Individuals believe they can control outcomes that are, in fact, random. This is related to the broader psychological concept called **locus of control**, which refers to an individual's perception of the main causes of events in his or her life. Put simply, do you believe that you control your destiny, or is it controlled by external forces such as fate or other people? People with an internal locus of control believe that winning is a result of skill; they reject the idea that the process producing the outcomes is random (Rotter, 1966; Weiner, 1980). Someone with an internal locus of control sees that outcomes of random events, such as gambling on a roulette wheel, are controlled by some process that can be learned or discerned by the use of skill. When the internal locus of control person wins, it is confirmation that he or she has ascertained the pattern. This confidence leads the person to bet more on the next spin of the wheel (hot hand, hot outcome). This would be the case even when you're just observing other people's performance.

People with external locus of control believe that their behavior is guided by fate or luck. These people explain the hot hand in gambling behavior (not skilled performance as in sports) in terms of people possessing a "stock of luck." We are each endowed with a package of luck, either positive (hot) or negative (cold), and things will stay the same no matter what options we select until the stock of luck runs out. In general, a person with an internal locus of control will view the hot hand as skill, and someone with an external locus of control will view the hot hand as a result of luck coming his or her way.

SECTION SUMMARY ■

Seeing Patterns in Randomness

Humans often perceive a relationship among events that is quite different from reality. One specific difficulty people have is noticing when a sequence of events is actually random. We are susceptible to the clustering illusion and tend to see events as being grouped together and causally related. Although people have a good appreciation for the law of large numbers and correctly identify the pattern in many recurring events, we are often incorrect in judging the pattern in small numbers of events.

One source of decision errors is called the hot hand fallacy. This is the belief that skilled performers, such as athletes or decision makers, have clusters of success in which one successful play leads to another or one unsuccessful play will lead to more errors. We are susceptible to this illusion because we believe that a player's success is the result of inherent competence. Once the player masters the correct performance, he or she will continue to do so throughout the event.

■ ■

Gains and Losses: Prospect Theory

In Chapter 11, we learned about the effect of framing for problem solving and how it can influence the interpretation of numerical values. Framing can also affect how those values are used in making decisions and solving problems. The theory that explains the relationship between framing and the choices we make is called **prospect theory** (Kahneman & Tversky, 1979; recently modified as **cumulative prospect theory,** Tversky & Kahneman, 1992). It is graphically presented in **FIGURE 13.7** as an S-shaped function that predicts framing effects. Before discussing the graph, let's look at some situations that have been used to test prospect theory.

> Imagine that the United States is preparing for the outbreak of an unusual disease, which is expected to kill 600 people. Two alternative programs to combat the disease have been proposed. Assume that the exact scientific estimate of the consequences of the program is as follows:
>
> If Program A is adopted, 200 people will be saved.
>
> If Program B is adopted, there is a 1/3 probability that 600 people will be saved and a 2/3 probability that no people will be saved.
>
> *(Tversky & Kahneman, 1981, p. 453)*

Which of the two programs would you favor? Tversky and Kahneman (1981) found that 72% of students choose Program A. Since the expected number of people is the same for A and B (1/3 probability of 600 people = 200 people) the students must be basing their choice on the framing of the problem. The participants seem to go with the option that is phrased in terms of a guaranteed gain rather than a risky gain (Program B).

Another group of students was given a mathematically equivalent choice, but phrased in terms of losses, that is, in terms of people dying.

If Program C is adopted, 400 people will die.

If Program D is adopted, there is a 1/3 probability that nobody will die, and a 2/3 probability that 600 people will die.

(Tversky & Kahneman, 1981, p. 453)

When presented with these choices, 78% of university students selected Program D. When the problem is framed in terms of losses, people appear willing to take a risk to avoid the loss. It's as if the certain death of 400 people is less acceptable than the 2/3 chance that 600 people will die. These examples show that framing is important for decision making. The specifics of how framing affects people's behavior are detailed in prospect theory. The theory states that people are *risk averse* when gains are involved, but *risk seeking* when there are potential losses. We are presumably not willing to take risks when gains are involved, such as saving lives or winning a gamble. Small risks in such cases don't get us very much, and people prefer a "sure thing." In contrast, people are willing to take risks when losses are involved (deaths or money), because if the outcome is positive, a tremendous increase in value will result.

Prospect theory, as graphed in Figure 13.7, matches the outcomes here. There are two principles to note. First, when there is a possible gain (lives saved) to the right of A, people tend to prefer a sure thing rather than just a possible outcome. Second, when there is a possible loss (deaths) to the left of A, people tend to prefer a choice that reduces the loss even if they have to take a risk. If you compare the bottom left quadrant (losses) with the upper right quadrant (gains), you will see that the line for losses is steeper than that for gains. This is because losses loom larger than gains. A gamble in which you would lose $100 is felt more than a gain of $100.

How does prospect theory affect our everyday lives? In some stores retailers charge slightly more if you use a credit card than if you pay in cash. There are two ways they could present this to their customers: (a) as a *surcharge* for using the card (think of this as a loss); or (b) as a *discount* for using cash (consider this a gain). Prospect theory predicts that a customer is less likely to use a credit card if the charge is considered a loss. If a merchant doesn't want people to use the credit card, presenting its use as a loss will be more effective than saying there is

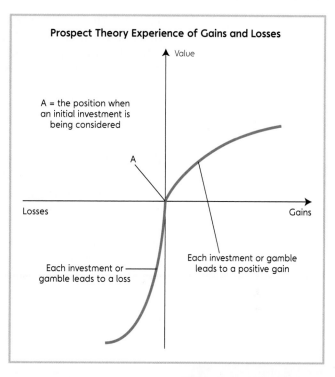

FIGURE 13.7 Prospect Theory of Gains and Losses If a gamble leads to a loss, it weighs more heavily on us than if it leads to an equal gain. We are willing to take risks to avoid more losses and want to avoid risks to keep a gain.

Source: From Kahneman & Tversky (1979, p. 279)

a benefit to using cash. Prospect theory can also be seen in the world of investing. Investors often show a notorious reluctance to sell stocks that have already lost value; they are willing to hold on to them and take a risk in the hope of reducing their future loss (Odean, 1988). In contrast, many investors will sell too soon if their stock has shown a gain because they are risk averse (Shleifer, 2000).

SECTION SUMMARY ■

Gains and Losses: Prospect Theory

Prospect theory (cumulative prospect theory) expresses how the choices we make are influenced by whether the choices are framed in terms of gains or losses. When an outcome is framed in terms of a gain, people are risk averse and want a sure thing. When the outcome is framed in terms of a loss, people are risk seeking to avoid the loss. Gains and losses don't have the same value to people: losses loom larger than gains. A gamble in which you would lose $100 is felt more than a gain of $100. Prospect theory not only predicts people's behavior in simple gambles, it is informative in explaining people's investment behavior in the stock market.

CHAPTER SUMMARY

People use many different ways to make a decision and choose among options. They sometimes make lists of pros and cons; or compare options in terms of their likelihood and overall value; or select options based on their confidence that they will lead to positive results. On occasion, each of these methods can lead to a successful outcome, even in cases where conscious thought plays only a minimal role. Each one of these decision methods can also lead to failure because people are susceptible to reasoning fallacies.

We often employ rules of thumb called heuristics to solve well-defined problems. Three major heuristics that influence our behavior are: representativeness, availability, and anchoring and adjusting.

A major source of decision errors is related to our perception of the connection between events. When we falsely believe that events are causally connected, we might commit the gambler's fallacy and believe that a series of losses means we are due for a success. Or we might view random events as having a common cause. In addition, we might commit the sunk cost fallacy and "throw good money after bad" because we believe that since we have invested in one option, we should continue to do so even though it has not been successful.

People are also susceptible to the clustering illusion: They tend to see events as being grouped together and causally related.

Having a clear understanding of the independence or dependence of events can be helpful, but it is no guarantee of correct decision making. People are still susceptible to the conjunction fallacy when they assume that two independent events are more likely to occur than either event apart. People also have difficulty using the base rates of events (such as diseases) in making decisions when the base rates are presented as probabilities. People are far better at using base rates when they are expressed as frequencies (how often something has occurred). Under such conditions, even children can make good decisions.

We may also have to guess the future behavior of other people. In the hot hand fallacy, we sometimes believe that skilled people will be either hot or cold in their behavior and have runs of highly successful or highly unsuccessful behavior because of some inherent skill. In fact, the runs are deceptive: People's behavior tends toward their long-term average.

Prospect theory explains how our choices are influenced by whether they are framed in terms of gains or losses. The theory is expressed as a graph that shows that losses weigh more heavily on our choices than do gains. When an outcome is framed in terms of a gain, people are risk averse, but when they are expressed in terms of a loss, people are risk seeking.

Even though we can list many types of decision-making errors, the truth is that under ordinary circumstances people are good decision makers. Unfortunately, they extend their normally successful strategies and understandings into domains where they should be more cautious.

KEY TERMS

subjective utility, p. 438

unconscious thought theory (UTT), p. 439

heuristics, p. 441

algorithm, p. 442

representativeness, p. 442

base rate, p. 443

availability, p. 444

anchoring and adjustment, p. 445

somatic marker hypothesis, p. 448

decision fallacy, p. 450

sunk cost, p. 450

sunk cost fallacy, p. 450

gambler's fallacy, p. 451

Monty Hall dilemma, p. 453

conjunction fallacy, p. 455

Bayes' theorem, p. 459

law of large numbers, p. 463

law of small numbers, p. 464

clustering illusion, p. 464

hot hand, p. 465

hot outcome fallacy, p. 466

locus of control, p. 467

prospect theory, p. 468

cumulative prospect theory, p. 468

QUESTIONS FOR REVIEW

Check Your Knowledge

1. What is Benjamin Franklin's decision-making technique?

2. What is a major limitation of Franklin's system?

3. What is an extinction burst, and how does it show up in our decision making?

4. Are peoples' decisions value free? How do you know?

5. What is subjective utility?

6. How does subjective utility influence a rational decision?

7. Contrast heuristics and algorithms.

8. Define *representativeness*, *availability*, and *anchoring and adjustment* heuristics.

9. Which heuristic relies most on retrieving facts from memory?

10. What are System 1 and System 2, and how do they relate to heuristic processing?

11. What would be an example of the sunk cost effect?

12. How is the expression "throwing good money after bad" related to the sunk cost effect?

13. What is the gambler's fallacy, and what is its underlying basis?

14. Is the Martingale (doubling) strategy in gambling effective? Why not?

15. What is the Monty Hall dilemma?

16. What is the underlying cause for the fallacy exemplified by the Monty Hall dilemma?

17. Give an example of the conjunction fallacy. Why is it a fallacy?

18. Define *base rate*.

19. What is the basic purpose of Bayes' theorem?

20. How does the frequency approach accomplish the same thing as Bayes' theorem?

21. Which is easier for people to use to make decisions: Bayes' theorem or frequency?

22. Cite an example where people use base rates correctly.

23. What is the Texas sharpshooter fallacy? How is it related to other cluster illusions?

24. What is the hot hand fallacy?

25. How are the hot hand and gambler's fallacies related?

26. How does the locus of control concept relate to people's judgments about the hot hand?

27. In what situations are we most likely to take a risk: when a gain is involved or when a loss is involved?

28. What is the name of the theory that helps you to answer the preceding question?

Apply Your Knowledge

1. Given what you have learned about decision making in this and previous chapters, write a letter to Benjamin Franklin commenting on his pros and cons method.

2. If humans constantly fall into the kinds of fallacies enumerated in this chapter, how is it that we are able to make decisions at all? Is there any benefit to people derived from the tendency to succumb to fallacies?

3. The hot hand has been assessed by examining the successes or failures of athletes. The research concludes that there is no true hot hand. Can you think how the phenomenon would apply to other areas of expertise, such as investors, authors, or farmers? How would you go about testing whether the hot hand applies to these domains?

4. Using base rates can help determine the validity of a diagnosis. Recently, DNA evidence has been used to convict people accused of a crime. Apply the concept of base rates to determine the likelihood that person x committed crime y given a DNA match between x and a DNA sample left at the crime scene. Note that there are roughly 6.5 billion people in the world. The chance that someone other than the suspect left the DNA sample is 1 in 7,000. Would you convict or exonerate someone based on a DNA sample?

Glossary

A

abduction A form of induction in which a conclusion is made that offers the best explanation for the available facts, although it is not necessarily a correct conclusion.

accounts A type of narrative schema initiated by the speaker (not in response to a question).

ACT-R (adaptive control of thought with rational analysis) An ambitious theory of cognition that has the ability to capture general properties of human cognition, from basic perceptual processes to high-level cognitive functioning; its production systems reflect the knowledge people assemble to solve problems.

acquired dyslexia Difficulty reading words already known and inability to read words not seen before.

advance organizers Preview materials that help people learn new information based on the ordering of the material before they are asked to learn specific details.

algorithm A clearly defined set of procedures that, if given enough time, will always solve a problem.

amnesia Inability to store and retrieve information; loss of memory.

analog code A way to describe a mental image that preserves the relationship among elements of the image as if they were being experienced (e.g., a map).

analogical reasoning Problem solving based on noticing similarities between a current problem and one that was encountered in the past.

anchoring and adjustment Using initial information as a starting point and then adapting from it to make judgments about other measurements; this prevents the problem solver from deviating from the initial information, even in the face of contradictory information.

angular gyrus An area of the brain located next to the auditory cortex in the parietal lobes that provides an understanding of categories of words.

anomia Avoidance or inability to recall the names of objects in categories; individuals with anomia often sound inarticulate although their intellectual abilities are unaffected.

aphasias Any of the numerous impairments that cause an inability to understand language or express oneself through language; most aphasias are the result of head injuries, strokes, or tumors.

articulatory control process A component of the phonological loop that automatically refreshes and maintains the elements in the phonological store as if they were being rehearsed through a subvocal process (no sound is actually made).

attention Cognitive processes that allow us to concentrate on one set of events in our environment while ignoring other events; it controls our mental environment by choosing the events that enter our consciousness.

attentional blink The moment when a person is shifting focus and is unable to attend fully to a new target event.

attentional processing Processing an event within the first second after it is captured by sensory storage.

attentional spotlight The cognitive ability to focus or sharpen attention on a previously peripheral stimulus.

attention-deficit/hyperactivity disorder (ADHD) A neurobehavioral disorder that manifests itself in symptoms such as restlessness, distractibility, inattention, and difficulty in self-control. People with ADHD focus on too many stimuli and have difficulty filtering out unnecessary information in their environment, and are therefore easily distracted.

autism spectrum disorder A congenital disorder involving deficits in social and communication skills that covers a wide range and intensity of symptoms. Children with this disorder do not appear to attend to faces in early childhood as much as children typically do.

autobiographical memory Memory for personal past experiences; retrospective memory of events in your life.

automatic processing Processing that leads to decisions that are not consciously controlled and which requires minimal attentional resources.

availability A heuristic that uses the ease by which facts are retrieved as an indicator of how important they are or how frequently they occur.

B

base rate A known proportion of a sample or population.

Bayes' theorem A formula that relates two conditional probabilities: The probability of event x if event y has occurred, and the probability of event y if event x has occurred.

behaviorist A scientist who looks exclusively at observable actions (what can be seen), rather than hypothesizing about mental processes (what cannot be seen).

belief-bias effect Allowing personal knowledge and convictions to affect one's decision as to whether or not a conclusion is logically valid.

bilingualism The ability to speak two or more languages fluently.

bottom-up processing (bottom-up analysis) Extracting primitive or basic elements from a stimulus and creating a higher-level understanding of it.

bridging A process in which the listener creates a link between what was actually said by the speaker and the unmentioned object, event, or idea the speaker was referring to; if the listener is unable to create a link, then he or she will be unable to understand what the speaker was referring to.

breadth-first strategy A process in which the problem solver tries all the main possible options to see if any lead to immediate success; if not, the problem solver proceeds to the next level of options.

Broca's aphasia Difficulty in speaking and writing. Expressions tend to be short and ungrammatical with some difficulty in comprehending complex sentences (also called *nonfluent aphasia*).

Broca's area An area of the brain typically located in the left prefrontal cortex that has two primary functions: activating a program for speech production in the motor area of the cortex involved in speech, and communicating a syntactic analysis of an incoming stream of words to Wernicke's area.

C

capacity The amount of information a memory system can hold.

capacity theory of attention The idea that attention is a resource distributed among tasks and that the ability to focus attention varies with the number and complexity of tasks.

case grammar A universal set of concepts that is expressed in the sentences of all languages and used to compute the meaning of utterances. Case grammar is divided into five syntactic–semantic elements (*cases*): agent, instrument, patient, object, and locative.

central executive A component of working memory that coordinates the activities of the visuospatial sketchpad, phonological loop, and episodic buffer; it also communicates with long-term memory via the episodic buffer. It is not a memory store, but rather a control system that guides attention and allocates resources to maximize performance.

change blindness The inability to notice changes between similar scenes or pictures unless they are compared side by side (cf. attentional blink).

characterizing features In the feature comparison model theory, aspects that describe commonly occurring characteristics of many (though not necessarily all) members of a category.

chunking Relating items to what you already know increases the capacity of short-term memory by storing items in groups; the average adult can hold 5–9 items (or chunks) in short-term memory.

chunks Single units of information.

closed domain An area or topic that contains all the information needed to find a clear solution to a problem, such as in a well-defined problem.

closed skill A task that can be reliably accomplished under a variety of predictable circumstances (e.g., typing).

clustering illusion A decision-making error that stems from the perception that groups of random events are not really random.

cocktail-party phenomenon The ability to shift attention immediately when a word or voice from a peripheral stream of speech "grabs" your attention (e.g., someone in a noisy room says your name).

coding How information is retained in a memory system.

cognition Those processes by which the sensory input is transformed, reduced, elaborated, stored, recovered, and used.

cognitive interview A method used to enhance recall of an observed or experienced event.

cognitive neuroscience The scientific study of the relationship between brain structures, neurological activity, and cognitive function.

cognitive psychology The branch of psychology that identifies our mental processes and how they affect our ability to interact with the world around us.

cognitive science An interdisciplinary field that embraces research and theory from many areas of specialization (e.g., anthropology, artificial intelligence, linguistics, philosophy, as well as cognitive psychology and cognitive neuroscience) and is devoted to studying mental activity and intelligent behavior.

cohort model A theory that divides speech recognition into two stages at the word level. The first stage detects the beginning sounds of the word, which activates all possible words in long-term memory with a similar set of sounds. The second stage processes information to eliminate words that are not the target word, including the broad context of the word and acoustic information coming from other parts of the sound stream that make up the word.

computer simulation Programs that mimic human behavior; if successful, they can be viewed as the embodiment of theories of cognitive processing.

conduction aphasia A rare form of language difficulty in which a person can understand what is being said but cannot repeat it correctly, although spontaneous speech is largely unimpaired.

confirmation bias Attempting to prove that a hypothesis is correct by gathering only information in support of it.

congenital blindness A condition afflicting individuals who are blind since birth.

conjunction fallacy The belief that the likelihood of two independent events occurring together is greater than the likelihood of either one occurring alone.

connected discourse A series of sentences strung together.

connectionist model A broad model of knowledge that incorporates the best aspects of network theories, the feature comparison model, and the perceptual symbol system model. This model asserts that the ability to answer questions depends on the entire pattern of connections in the brain (often referred to as *neural networks*). It posits that every node of knowledge is connected to every other node and that perceptual experiences are a key component of the network.

controlled processing Processing that requires conscious, attentional resources, in contrast with automatic processing.

conversion An interpretation procedure people use that (erroneously) treats sentences as reversible.

cooperative principle A pragmatic principle: The speaker and listener are assisting each other in the communication process. The listener supposes that the speaker is telling enough information and no more, trying to tell the truth, saying things that are relevant, and using sentences clearly and unambiguously.

corpus callosum The largest of a collection of fibers (*commissures*) that connects the right and left hemispheres of the brain.

cortex The outer surface of the brain, composed of cell bodies and their axons.

counterfactual reasoning Reasoning from assumptions or hypotheses that the reasoner believes to be false (e.g., "If I had studied for the test, I would have gotten a good grade.").

counterfactual strategy A process in which reasoners assume that their favored hypothesis is incorrect (cf. disconfirmation).

creativity Problem solutions that are both novel and useful.

Creole A pidgin that becomes a native language and takes on the characteristics of the grammar of the dominant group.

cross-race effect Difficulty recognizing faces of people from a different race.

cumulative prospect theory A modified version of prospect theory that predicts framing effects.

D

decision fallacy The false belief that two events, which are independent of each other, are causally related.

declarative memory Memory that can be described to others if you are asked to recall it. (*See* **explicit memory**.)

deduction Reasoning that proceeds from generalities to specifics.

defining features In the feature comparison model theory, aspects that are necessary and sufficient to specify the requirements of a category.

deontic rule Common rules in everyday life that consist of permissions and obligations, and are often used in negotiations.

depth-first strategy A process in which the problem solver selects one option, and if successful, stops; if unsuccessful, the problem solver tests the next option and continues until the goal is achieved or all options have been exhausted.

direct access hypothesis The theory that new readers are able to go from the visual arrangement of the letters of words directly to the lexicon, and that an appreciation for phonemic structure is gained from pronouncing recognized words.

disconfirmation Attempting to falsify a hypothesis in order to find a way to show that it might not be true.

distinctive features theory This theory assumes that all complex perceptual stimuli are composed of distinctive and separable attributes that allow observers to distinguish one object from another. It focuses on how humans and other animals recognize patterns by attending to low-level features of objects such as lines, angles, and dots.

dopaminergic theory of positive affect (DTPA) The theory that mood affects the production of the neurotransmitter dopamine, which in turn activates parts of the brain that contribute to problem solving and creativity.

Down syndrome A mild to severe developmental delay caused by the presence of three (rather than two) copies of the 21st chromosome in each cell of the body. Children with this syndrome have slow linguistic development, but usually acquire a basic working vocabulary and are able to articulate simple sentences by puberty.

dual code hypothesis (or **dual coding theory**) Some words, especially abstract ones, are primarily represented verbally, while other words, especially concrete ones, can be represented both by imaginal or verbal codes. The coding of words and concepts affects the ease of memory retrieval.

dual processing The idea that high-level cognition reflects two basic systems: unconscious processes that are automatic, rapid, and able to accommodate many activities at once; and processes that are more deliberate, conscious, slow, and rely heavily on working memory.

dual route hypothesis A flexible model of reading that accounts for the fact that early readers tend to use phonological codes, skilled readers tend to do direct visual coding, and all readers slow down when encountering new or difficult-to-pronounce words.

duration The length of time information is held in a memory system.

dyslexia Reading ability that is markedly below what would be expected based on a person's IQ.

E

early-selection filter Active when attention is captured by the physical properties of the stimulus (e.g., someone coughing during a lecture).

ecological validity The degree to which experiments are based on how people operate in the real world, and are more realistic.

eidetic imagery Exceptional (and rare) imagery ability that allows a person to maintain a mental image that has the quality of reviving an earlier perceptual event with great clarity.

elaborative rehearsal Thinking about meaningful relationships among items to be learned and focusing on how they connect to other things you know. This type of strategy often results in long-term recall and recognition of the items learned.

electroencephalography (EEG) The oldest neuroimaging technique in which a cap containing electrodes is placed on a person's head; the electrodes reflect the total electrical output of neurons near them, which varies according to the person's state of arousal. This activity is shown as waves that vary in height (*amplitude*) and how rapidly they repeat (*frequency*). EEG identifies broad areas of the brain involved in specific cognitive events.

encoding specificity The way in which information stored in memory will be recalled better (or worse) depending on the retrieval cue used to elicit the stored information.

environmental spatial ability The ability to navigate in new places successfully, including the ability to form accurate mental representations of large-scale environments such as buildings, campuses, or cities.

episodic buffer A component of working memory that acts as an integrative system that places events occurring in the visuospatial sketchpad and the phonological loop into a coherent sequence, along with the memory of the goals that initiated those events.

episodic memory The portion of long-term memory that stores and connects specific times, places, and events in a person's life, and is therefore autobiographical in nature.

epistemic monitoring In an ill-defined problem, the ability to determine if a legitimate representation of the problem is being made, along with the correct understanding and appropriate methods needed to reach a solution.

eventcasts A type of narrative schema that consists of a running commentary of present or future events.

event-related potential (ERP) Momentary changes in the EEG signal that occur as an immediate response to something the participant has observed or thought about.

explicit memory All information that we consciously seek to store and retrieve, such as personal history and general knowledge. (*See* **declarative memory**.)

F

feature comparison model A theory that portrays human knowledge as a vast semantic space with clusters of knowledge that represent categories and form consistent patterns.

feeling of knowing The inability to recall something that you believe is stored somewhere in your memory.

fictionalized stories An imaginative tale about a make-believe character or event that can be told in any schema structure style (recount, eventcast, or account).

flashbulb memories Memories of distinctive, surprising, or significant events that seem to be stored in memory with photograph-like details; research has shown that such memories are not always completely accurate.

focal colors Eight colors (red, yellow, green, blue, brown, pink, orange, and purple) that are universally recognized even among people whose languages do not have words for all or some of these colors.

focused attentional processing Those processes by which the attentional system deeply processes stimuli in the environment.

forebrain The outer portion of the brain that surrounds the midbrain and is composed of the cortex; the forebrain regulates higher mental processes, such as complex learning, memory, thought, and language.

forgetting The inability to recall information in a memory system.

framing A description of a situation that influences the kind of representation and methods a person uses to solve a problem.

frontal lobe Lobe of the brain that performs many functions, especially those related to memory, problem solving, and communication.

functional fixedness Failure to see a different use for an object; inability to change the organization of a problem.

functional magnetic resonance imaging (fMRI) A neuroimaging technique that locates areas of cognitive activity by measuring blood changes, called the BOLD (blood oxygen level dependent) response. This electromagnetic system creates an image of the electrical activity by indirectly measuring the amount of blood flow and, therefore, the amount of brain activity.

fuzzy logic model A theory of speech perception composed of three stages (evaluation, integration, and assessment and decision), which assumes the listener matches the incoming stream of sounds against speech prototypes stored in memory and makes a decision based on all possible factors.

G

gambler's fallacy The mistaken belief that independent past events will affect future events.

general problem solver (GPS) The cognitive analysis of human problem solving embodied as a running computer program. GPS contains four major components that humans possess: (a) a limited-capacity working memory with rapid storage and retrieval; (b) a large-capacity LTM with relatively slow storage and retrieval; (c) a serial processor that performs a single operation at a time; and (d) a library of shortcut methods (heuristics).

geons Any of 36 primitive shapes (geometric ions) that are the building blocks for identifying 3-D objects. Such shapes are critical to pattern recognition because objects can be rotated in three dimensions and create an unlimited number of impressions on the retina.

gestalt The idea that we perceive the form or configuration of things before we understand their parts. (*Gestalt* is a German word that roughly translates as "whole" or "configuration.")

Gestalt psychology The study of principles that determine how people's perception of the whole is derived from their perception of individual parts.

gist A mental model a listener constructs that contains a semantic—rather than verbatim—representation of a communication; the model may contain more information than was given and/or be an impression of what was said.

given–new contract An agreement consisting of two components between a speaker and listener: information already known and identified by the listener (*given*), and information conveyed by the speaker that is unknown to the speaker (*new*).

H

habituation Situation in which we do not orient toward a stimulus because it is no longer novel and does not capture our attention.

haptic Used to describe imagery that involves touch (e.g., imagining the feeling of sandpaper in your hands or how it feels to wear shoes that pinch your toes).

hemisphere Split down the middle, from front to back, the brain contains two hemispheres, each serving different cognitive functions.

hemispherectomy Surgical removal of one of the cerebral hemispheres of the brain.

hemispheric neglect (hemineglect) An attentional (not visual) disease in which individuals are only able to see half of what they should be able to see (i.e., the right visual field only). Hemineglect is a symptom of a broader neurological difficulty (parietal lobe syndrome).

heuristic A shortcut or rule of thumb that often, but not always, helps to solve a problem.

hill climbing A metaphor for a problem-solving technique: Each step in the process should at least be in the direction of the goal.

hindbrain The bottom (or ventral) portion of the brain, which controls automatic processes that regulate life-support functions, such as breathing, heart rate, swallowing, and sleep cycles.

holophrastic speech A tendency to find meaning beyond what is superficially expressed in speech utterances; this process begins in young childhood and continues through adulthood.

hot hand The belief that a person has clusters of success in which one successful play leads to another (refers to people).

hot outcome fallacy The belief that the last type of outcome will continue to occur (refers to outcomes).

human factors Research that focuses on our mental capacities and how they constrain our actions, which helps us to perform tasks more efficiently and safely.

I

ill-defined problem A problem that does not contain a clearly specified goal, information, or solution.

imagery value A component of the dual code hypothesis: The greater the vividness of a mental representation, the easier it will be to remember a word.

images Perceptual experiences that occur without the presence of an external source (e.g., imagining or picturing something).

impersonal reasoning A calculation that can be applied to any topic and doesn't involve the reasoner.

implicit memory A semiautonomous memory system that frees up cognitive resources so that you can concentrate on more demanding tasks; it allows you to put important mental functions that can be performed automatically in the background.

inattentional blindness Failure to notice stimuli when the focus of attention is elsewhere (e.g., performing two attention-demanding tasks simultaneously, such as driving and talking on a cell phone).

indirect access hypothesis A theory that emphasizes basic sensory processes and the phonological components of word identification in reading.

induction Reasoning that proceeds from specifics to generalities.

infantile (or childhood) amnesia Difficulty in retrieving autobiographical information of early childhood.

information processing A way of thinking about human behavior: analyzing the flow of events, in both our external and internal environments, shows how past knowledge helps us understand present events.

inner scribe A component of the visuospatial sketchpad that performs at least two functions. First, it refreshes all the information in the visuospatial sketchpad; and second, it briefly stores spatial relationships associated with bodily movements.

insight Perceiving the solution to a problem at an unexpected time or in an unanticipated way (e.g., the *aha!* experience).

interaction models Theories of speech perception that evaluate the entire context of the interaction among linguistic and social elements (e.g., the semantics of words, the syntax of the utterance, and theme of the social exchange).

invalidity A property of conclusions that do not logically follow a premise.

irrelevant speech effect The ability of inconsequential background speech to interfere with silent verbal rehearsal.

isomorphic In mental rotation, the ability to rotate objects in a 2-D or 3-D manner in the same way objects are physically rotated in a 2-D or 3-D way.

K

key-word method A memory technique that forms a bridge between a foreign word, for example, and one in your own language.

Korsakoff's syndrome Amnesia that usually results from malnutrition due to excessive alcohol consumption; it is associated with damage to the mamillothalamic tract of the temporal lobes.

L

language A system of communication that presumes there is a speaker and a listener (interpreter): The speaker must figure out the best way to communicate the message, and the listener must figure out the meaning of the message.

late-selection filter The unconscious retention of stimuli not necessarily related to current mental processes, but always relevant or pertinent (e.g., the sound of your name, the odor of gas, someone yelling "Fire!").

late-selection theory This theory presumes that even supposedly unattended stimuli enter the sensory storage system and are only filtered out late in the process if not relevant.

law of closure The experience of seeing a figure as a closed unit, even when the observer knows that there are open spaces.

law of common fate If two or more objects are moving in the same direction at the same speed, they will tend to be perceived as a group and share the same destiny.

law of good continuation The tendency to connect elements in a way that makes the elements seem continuous or flowing in a particular direction; this can exert a powerful affect on what is perceived.

law of large numbers An appreciation for the ratio of possible outcomes over the long run (i.e., repetition of the pattern expected from large numbers of events).

law of proximity Elements that are close together will be perceived as a coherent group and be differentiated from items that are far from them.

law of similarity Elements that look similar will be perceived as part of the same form or group; similarity can be based on size, brightness, color, shape, or even orientation.

law of small numbers Drawing conclusions from small sets of events and extrapolating those conclusions to large sets of events, which leads to many decision-making errors.

law of symmetry First, images that are perceived as symmetrical are experienced as belonging together; second, people tend to find symmetry in a figure even if it is otherwise disorganized.

learning The permanent change in behavior that results from experience.

lesions Damage or destruction to the structure of any major organ that causes a disruption in normal functioning; lesions can result from many causes (stroke, injury, tumors, surgery, etc.).

lexicon A mental dictionary that matches words to specific meanings.

linear reasoning The ability to draw a conclusion from pairs of relationships on some dimension (e.g., height).

linguistic relativity In its strongest version, the idea that a person's language determines their perception of the world (i.e., language controls cognition).

localization of function A hypothesis that different functions of thought are performed in different areas in the brain.

locus of control Individuals' perception of the main causes of events in their lives: whether they control their own destiny, or their destiny is controlled by external forces (fate or other people).

logographic systems Systems of writing that use a symbol to convey an entire spoken word (e.g., modern Chinese).

long-term memory (LTM) The aspect of memory that consists of all the knowledge and experience acquired throughout life.

M

maintenance rehearsal Saying something repeatedly to keep it in mind. This sort of rote learning keeps items in short-term memory, but does not guarantee permanent ability to recall them.

marked terms A word that is noted or "marked" because it is difficult to understand as a result of its specificity or complexity (e.g., lioness is more complicated than lion because it specifies a subset of a larger group).

masking When events occur simultaneously, or less than 80 msec apart, the second event can interfere with the first event and displace it from sensory storage: One event hides the other from conscious awareness.

maxims Four requirements of the cooperative principle: quantity, quality, relation, and manner.

McGurk effect The inability to hear sounds correctly when a speaker's utterances and lip movements do not match; the listener hears something that is neither in the mouth movements of the speaker nor in the auditory signal.

means–ends analysis A problem-solving technique that minimizes the distance between the current state and the goal state.

memory The mental operations that store information as well as recover and retrieve it at appropriate times.

memory chunks Perceptual units of knowledge, acquired through years of practice, that allow experts to encode new information in their area of expertise and perceive configurations of events that are invisible to others.

metacognition The ability to reason and draw inferences coupled with the ability to determine if the reasoning process is progressing correctly.

metamemory The awareness of your memory system and what resides there. Metamemory is helpful in deciding whether a fact that isn't immediately recalled is worth retrieving or not.

method of loci and imagines A memory technique for associating information (in the form of images) with locations.

midbrain The middle portion of the brain, which serves as a relay center for sensory information entering the brain, such as hearing and vision; a bundle of fibers associated with voluntary movement also passes through the midbrain.

mindlessness Failing to evaluate what you are doing; performing activities by rote (not paying attention).

modality effect The different recall pattern of list items when they are visually or auditorily presented.

Monty Hall dilemma A decision situation where people believe events are independent of each other when they actually are dependent. Named after a popular TV show where people were confronted with such situations.

motoric *See* **motoric imagery**.

motoric imagery Describes imagery that contains movement (e.g., imagining a dance routine or athletic play).

motor theory The idea that people try to unconsciously simulate a sound they hear, and if the sound they hear matches the sound the brain has registered, they will be able to identify it.

N

narrative (or story) schema A basic story structure that develops over the life span from two-word stories of 2-year-olds to complex, detailed stories of adults that usually contain a starting event with possible responses to it and a conclusion.

native language A person's first language.

natural language A communication system that contains four basic components: a message, rules or physical constraints, a medium of communication, and social constraints.

negative recency A tendency to recall items from the beginning of list (because they have been rehearsed) better than items from the end of a list.

neurogenesis A process in which brain cells grow new connections, which occurs before birth and throughout life.

neuroimaging Methods that reveal the structure and functioning of the brain and show the relationship between neurological activity and cognitive processes.

neurons Specialized cells in the brain composed of three parts: (a) a cell body that processes and transmits information; (b) fibers, called dendrites, that conduct input to the cell body; and (c) an axon that conducts electrical activity from the cell body to a junction with other cells, called a synapse.

neurotransmitters Packets of chemicals that fill the gaps (synapses) between neurons when an electrical signal is transmitted via the axon.

node–link system Network theories, words, images, and facts are represented as nodes that are connected to each other via links, which express a semantic relationship.

nonredundancy of words principle When children learn their native language, they act as if there is only one name for an object and every name has only one single referent; if children hear an unfamiliar word, they try to connect it to something that they do not know the name of in their field of vision.

nonroutine problem solving The use of strategies or procedures that do not guarantee a solution, but offer the possibility of success.

O

occipital lobe The area of the cortex that does the complex job of processing signals from the eyes.

open domain An area or topic without restrictions; any information can be considered.

open skill A task that requires conscious attention to perform in unpredictable circumstances (e.g., swimming in a backyard pool vs. swimming in the ocean).

operators Techniques that allow problem solvers to move from one state to another in a problem space.

orienting reflex The basic biological reaction to turn our attention to any change in the environment;

a universal component of the human cognitive architecture.

P

paradox A self-contradictory statement.

paralogical thinking Thinking that follows the format of normal logic, except that the speaker sees two things as identical based on the similarities between them.

parietal lobe Each hemisphere contains one (located above the occipital lobe) that registers sensory experiences such as touch, taste, and sight.

Parkinson's disease (Parkinson's dementia) An irreversible, neurodegenerative disease caused by the death of dopamine-producing neurons in the substantia nigra of the brain; a classic symptom is muscle tremors. Advanced stages of the disease are accompanied by attentional deficits, such as difficulty engaging in an activity that is not well learned or formulating a hypothesis, suppressing a habitual response or resisting temptation, or staying focused on a task.

partial report procedure A method in which a person is asked to recall particular items in a briefly presented array of multiple items.

pattern recognition The use of fragmentary pieces of sensory information to create a higher-level identification of what has been experienced. Although it often seems instantaneous, it can take years of experience to develop the ability to recognize patterns effortlessly (e.g., reading).

peg-word method A mnemonic technique that involves visual imagery and a fixed ordering of information to be remembered.

perception Becoming aware of something through the senses.

perceptual memory Awareness of physically based patterns that are difficult to describe, but are effortlessly recalled (e.g., the scent of roses, the taste of licorice, or the sights and sounds of your childhood neighborhood).

perceptual symbol system A theory that seemingly abstract knowledge is based on the perceptual mode (visual, auditory, etc.) in which we experience them.

permastore The phenomenon that once facts are stored in long-term memory they endure for nearly a lifetime.

person schema A universally used framework that connects common personality traits (e.g., outgoing) with the behavior such traits usually produce (e.g., makes friends easily).

personal reasoning A form of inference (i.e., some aspects of moral reasoning of which values and beliefs dominate).

phonemes The individual sounds that make up words.

phonemic awareness The ability to analyze spoken words into their basic sound units.

phonological confusion Memory that is worse for words or sentences that sound alike than for those that sound different; it can occur when words or sentences are presented visually or auditorily.

phonological loop A subsystem in working memory dedicated to the temporary storage of sound-based information and representations.

phonological store A component of the phonological loop that acts as a reservoir to store acoustic representations of a stimulus.

phonological (or alphabetic) system A system of writing in which a letter or group of letters corresponds to the sounds of the spoken language (e.g., English).

picture superiority effect A component of the dual coding hypothesis: Pictures are better remembered than words because they are represented as images (in analog code) and verbally (in propositional code).

pidgins Blended fragments of two (or more) languages with simple rules and vocabulary, often created to achieve trade or marriage between groups speaking different languages.

plasticity The brain's ability to make new connections and preserve its functions.

Pollyanna principle A tendency for people to recall more pleasant than unpleasant life experiences.

positron emission tomography (PET) A neuroimaging technique in which a radioactive dose of glucose is injected into the bloodstream that emits particles (called *positrons*) as it is processed by neurons. Blood flow to specific areas of the brain can then be indirectly measured when the brain is scanned to detect energy released when the positrons interact with the electrons of the brain cells. This technique is helpful in determining the specific parts of the brain that are involved during a cognitive event.

pragmatic reasoning schemas A small set of reasoning precondition action pairs that specify four social rules that will specify when an action can or cannot be taken.

pragmatics A system of rules for social cooperation in language that limits what can be spoken about, how to speak, and the listener's expectations about how information will be presented. Pragmatics also describes nonspeech elements that are used to coordinate with the spoken sentence to convey the message.

preattentive processing (preattentive analysis) The ability to focus on a relevant event to the exclusion of all else, which can happen so quickly that the perceiver is unaware of all the stimuli that have been excluded.

precategorical storage Sensory information that has been stored before it can be categorized.

prevaricating The tendency of people with Korsakoff's syndrome to make up answers to questions rather than indicate that they do not remember; their feeling of knowing is usually incorrect.

primacy effect Better recall of the first items of a list.

primary progressive aphasia A steady deterioration in the ability to understand language; individuals gradually lose the ability to speak, understand other people's speech, and comprehend written words, and eventually become mute.

principle of congruity The mental steps that must be used to answer a question: encoding the question, comparing the encoded question with encoded facts stored in memory, and if the encoding of the question and facts match, answer the question.

principle of lexical marking A semantically complicated term that is difficult to reason with and to store in memory.

principle of Prägnanz The perception of a stimulus is organized into as cohesive a figure as possible (symmetrical, simple, closed, and regular), called a "good" figure by Gestalt psychologists. (The German word *Prägnanz* means "terseness.")

proactive interference Interference that occurs when previously learned information inhibits the ability to remember new information.

problem A situation that occurs when the goal state and the current state are different.

problem solving Transforming the current state into the goal state.

problem space The mental path a problem solver negotiates through a space of possibilities from the initial state to the goal state.

procedural memory Stored knowledge that allows the skillful performance of tasks even though individual parts of the task cannot be recalled or explained to others (e.g., typing or tying your shoelaces).

production system Primitive problem-solving elements (condition–action pairs) that are part of the solver's long-term memory.

propositional code A way to describe a mental image that is similar to a series of words or a sentence, although more abstract (e.g., a list of directions).

prosody The rhythm, stress, and intonation pattern (singsong quality) of the voice.

prosopagnosia A condition usually caused by brain disease or injury in which people are unable to recognize familiar faces; it is not the result of visual, intellectual, or memory deficits.

prospective memory An aspect of episodic memory that allows a person to travel forward mentally in time (e.g., remembering to keep a dental appointment next week).

prospect theory A theory that explains the relationship between framing effects (presented as gains or losses) and the choices people make. Generally, people are more affected by the fear of loss than the prospect of equivalent gain.

prototype An average, or typical instance, of many different views of an object.

prototype theory The idea that pattern recognition occurs when the features of the object to be recognized overlap in some way with the features of the prototype.

pure alexia (or **word blindness**) A condition in which individuals face extreme difficulty reading, even though they are able to identify sounds and letters; such individuals often read words letter by letter in an effort to recognize words from the sounds of the letters.

pure word deafness Individuals with this condition can hear sounds, read, write, and speak, but are unable to understand spoken language.

Q

question interface A component of the teachable language comprehender that serves as a sensibility test to determine whether or not to pursue answering a question. The question interface prevents taxing the memory to search for information that clearly would not be found.

R

reading span A metric for assessing a person's memory capacity that affects their reading ability. It is measured by the number of final words in each of a series of sentences that a person can recall.

reality monitoring The ability to discriminate between genuine memories acquired from real-world experiences and memories generated by the imagination.

reality principle A pragmatic principle: In order to be understood, a speaker must construct utterances that can be interpreted by a listener according to the listener's personal knowledge of the world and the mental image being created in the listener's mind.

reasoning The process by which conclusions are drawn from information (*premises*); a crucial skill that sets humanity apart from all other animals.

reasoning schemas A set of rules and procedures used to draw or evaluate conclusions.

recency effect Better recall of the last items of a list.

recognition by components theory (RBC theory) The pattern recognition process that identifies features of 3-D objects.

recounts A type of narrative schema that involves the speaker's personal experiences; typically the first type of story children tell, usually in response to a question.

reference principle When learning their native language, children interpret utterances to be about whole objects and not the feelings of the speaker.

reflexes An innate fixed response triggered by certain environmental stimuli; such unconscious responses are often quicker than responses that require conscious thought, and can be thought of as a kind of schema.

regularization A downward language-learning trajectory that occurs in children around the age of 4 and lasts about a year in which children apply standard grammatical or syntactic rules incorrectly (e.g., saying *mouses* instead of *mice*; *goed* instead of *went*).

rehearsal Paying attention to items in short-term memory.

reminiscence bump Heightened retrospective recall for autobiographical events that occurred between the ages of 10 and 25.

repeated path hypothesis The idea that it takes less time to answer a question that travels the same routes as those used by a previous question; this is a consequence of spreading activation.

repetition blindness A decrease in the ability to perceive repeated stimuli during a rapid serial presentation of events.

repetitive transcranial magnetic stimulation (rTMS) A neuroimaging technique that influences an area of the brain by creating a weak electrical current using magnets over a person's head. Repetitive magnetic pulses can increase or decrease a specific brain area's activity, which helps identify that area's function.

representation The understanding of a problem: what facts it specifies, what action is required, and what possible methods can be used to solve it.

representativeness The likelihood of an event, judging by how similar it is to another event of known probability.

response latency (response time; reaction time) The amount of time it takes for participants to make a response; usually considered the time between the moment a stimulus is presented and the moment a participant makes a response.

retroactive interference Hindrance that occurs when new information makes it difficult to remember previously learned information.

retrospective memory An aspect of episodic memory that allows a person to travel back mentally in time to retrieve a fact, or to relive an experience (e.g., remembering the first time you drove a car, or what you wore to the senior prom).

routine problem solving The application of learned knowledge or techniques to find a solution.

S

saccade Ballistic movements of the eyes that permit rapid visual fixation from one point to another, at which time most information is gathered.

Sapir–Whorf hypothesis The theory that the language you speak unconsciously shapes your thinking about the world.

satisficing Choosing a path or goal in problem solving that is good enough, rather than searching endlessly for the most optimal one.

schema A piece of knowledge that can apply to many situations for many purposes; schemas may be thought of as correct in overall form but containing wrong or missing details (e.g., a sketch, not a detailed drawing).

schizophrenia A disorder in which people suffer difficulties with abnormal perceptions, moods, actions, and the ability to express themselves in a logical manner. An additional symptom of this disorder is difficulty recognizing faces.

script A type of schema that indicates what type of behavior is required in certain kinds of situations.

selection restrictions The conditions under which the definitions of words in the mental lexicon apply, as well as how the words should be treated in sentences.

selection task A research procedure in which reasoners decide how to test a rule to see if it is true or false, or being followed or violated.

semantic distance effect In spreading activation, the farther apart two nodes are in the network, the longer it takes to discover how they are related.

semantic features Word meanings stored as collections of meaning elements (e.g., the mental representation of *woman* is composed of human, female, and adult).

semantic memory The aspect of long-term memory that retains conceptual knowledge stored as an independent knowledge base containing discrete facts (e.g., dogs bark and birds lay eggs).

semantic relatedness effect In semantic networks, the existence of inequalities across categories such that related items are verified faster than unrelated items that are closer together in a network.

semantics Words or gestures that convey packets of meaning to a listener; all systems of communication, no matter how primitive, have a semantic component.

sensory information storage (SIS) *See* **sensory storage**.

sensory memory *See* **sensory storage**.

sensory storage A buffer memory system that hosts an incoming stream of information long enough for us to pay attention to it and separates incoming information from everything else occurring in our cognitive system. We are rarely conscious of its actions in everyday life. Sometimes referred to as **sensory information storage (SIS)**.

serial exhaustive search Examining every item in short-term memory in its entirety and continuing to search even after the item has been found.

serial position effect The probability of recalling items at the beginning and end of a list is higher than the probability of recalling items in the middle of a list.

seriation The basis of linear reasoning: the ability to place objects in order along a dimension (e.g., from shortest to tallest).

set-inclusion relations The inferred relationship among categories of objects.

short-term memory (STM) Memory that contains our moment-to-moment conscious thoughts and perceptions; its contents endure only as long as we are paying attention to them.

simultanagnosia A neuropsychological condition, sometimes caused by stroke, in which the individual is unable to recognize two or more objects at the same time (also referred to as Bálint's syndrome).

skilled memory theory This theory is composed of the meaningful encoding principle, the retrieval structure principle, and the speed-up principle; It explains how people with normal memory ability are able to amass staggering amounts of information in a specific domain.

social exchange rules The idea that rules containing obligations and permissions are not learned like other rules but are the result of the inherently human tendency to be social animals who come evolutionarily equipped to engage in social contacts.

somatic marker hypothesis The theory that the entire body's emotion-related circuitry is the basic system in which decision making occurs.

source monitoring Identifying where knowledge comes from; the ability to distinguish between new information about an event that was actually observed or experienced and information that was heard about the event. Inaccuracy of source monitoring can lead to false recollections.

span of apprehension What we can attend to at one time without an incredible effort of attention.

spatial imagery Mental representation of spatial relationships between parts of an object or its location in space.

specific language impairment (SLI) A condition with no clear genetic basis in which individuals possess more or less normal intelligence and understand normal speech, but their own speech tends to violate grammatical rules.

speech acts Universal categories of speech (e.g., asking a question, conveying a belief, expressing a feeling) that convey actions intended by the speaker through language. The listener must decide what is intended by the speaker in order to respond.

speech recoding The translation of visual characters into a kind of subvocal speech; individual speech sounds activate word and contextual knowledge in memory, which allows people to understand writing and speech.

spina bifida A congenital defect in which the vertebrae of the spinal cord are exposed, sometimes causing excessive cerebrospinal fluid that requires a shunt for drainage. The placement of the shunt can cause developmental delays, but language ability is typically preserved.

split brain (divided brain) A condition that results when one hemisphere of the brain has little knowledge of the signals of the other hemisphere; this occurs when the corpus callosum is not fully developed or has been surgically severed.

spreading activation In the teachable language comprehender, when a question is asked, a search is performed to see if there is a network connection; energy spreads from the nodes activated by the question in all directions, one node at a time, which also activates many unnecessary nodes. The greater the distance between the subject and predicate in the question, the longer it takes to find the answer.

state-dependent learning The ability to recall information is superior when a person is in the same physical state as when he or she learned the information (e.g., sober or intoxicated).

stereotype A person schema applied to an entire group; an oversimplified understanding of supposed positive or negative qualities of groups of people, nearly always inaccurate (e.g., all college professors are absentminded).

strokes Loss of blood to any area of the brain caused by a blockage or a blood vessel bursting, resulting in damage to brain tissue through oxygen deprivation.

Stroop effect It takes longer to name the color of ink a word is printed in when the name of the color and the color of the ink do not match (e.g., the word *green* printed in brown ink).

subgoal An intermediate state in means–ends analysis: The problem solver transforms the problem into a more readily solvable one through the use of operators in the problem space.

subitizing The ability to determine small numbers of items presented simultaneously; four or fewer items can be estimated automatically, but more than four items have to be counted.

subjective organization A unique way of encoding events specific to each person.

subjective utility The personal evaluation of a decision outcome.

sunk cost Invested money or resources that cannot be recovered.

sunk cost fallacy Committing additional money or resources into an unprofitable activity because one has already invested in it; additional resources increase the cost of the investment but not the likelihood of a positive outcome.

syllabary system A system of writing in which a letter or symbol corresponds to a syllable of a spoken word (e.g., hiragana and katakana in modern Japanese).

syllogism An argument in which the conclusion follows from the premises.

symbolic distance effect The more discriminable two objects are (larger or smaller), the faster the judgment of which is larger or smaller.

synapse A junction that allows neurons to communicate.

syntax Rules for how sentences should be put together; syntax permits distinctions to be made for tense, mood, and aspect.

T

teachable language comprehender (TLC) A network theory that has two main components: the node–link system and a question interface.

template-matching theory This theory assumes that we have stored away an unlimited number of patterns, literal copies corresponding to every object that we have experienced. These patterns are labeled with the name of the object and can be instantly matched to a new instance of the object.

temporal lobe Each hemisphere contains one that processes sound, language, and long-term memory; damage to one does not necessarily produce complete loss of cognitive functioning.

tip-of-the-tongue (TOT) phenomenon Temporary inaccessibility of word or fact in memory.

top-down processing (top-down analysis) After a preliminary guess is made about a stimulus (by using bottom-up processing), the pattern recognition process reduces the set of possibilities by selecting only low-level features that merit further analysis in order to complete the identification.

TRACE model A theory related to the cohort model that assumes listeners use all the information at their disposal simultaneously (in parallel) to identify what is being said.

transfer of training (transfer of learning) A technique researchers use to determine whether one method of presenting information contributes to better understanding than another method, often determined by whether the participant can use the information in different circumstances.

transitivity Given three items, if a relation holds between the first two items and also between the second and third items, then it must hold between the first and third items.

trepanning (trephining) A surgical process practiced since ancient times in which a hole is made in the skull.

turnabout A universal form of interaction between infants and caregivers that is used to get the infant to engage in "conversation" and serves to model communicative behavior to the infant.

Turner's syndrome For females, the absence or damage of one of the X chromosomes that results in a number of overt physical, cardiac, and hormonal difficulties. Such girls show difficulty in social relations and nonverbal problem-solving tasks, but their spoken language skills are within the normal range.

typicality effect In network theory, the difference in time it takes to answer questions about ordinary instances of a category versus unusual instances of a category.

U

unconscious thought theory (UTT) Described in 3 principles: Unconscious thought requires little cognitive capacity; it tends to be guided by expectations and schemas; and it weighs the relative importance of various attributes in an unbiased way.

unmarked terms A semantically simple word to understand.

utilization process The idea that language is a communication system intended to facilitate an exchange between a speaker and a listener; the listener is supposed to use the speaker's message in some way, even if it is only remembering what the speaker has said.

utterances Linguistic expressions that may be either speech sounds or gestures.

V

validity Conclusions that logically follow a premise.

visual cache A component of the visuospatial sketchpad that temporarily stores visual information from perceptual experience and contains color, form, and some spatial information of what is perceived.

visual imagery The appearance of an object (e.g., its color, shape, size, brightness, etc.).

visualizer–verbalizer The cognitive style that expresses the degree to which people use visuospatial representations (images or diagrams) or words while solving problems.

visuospatial sketchpad A component of working memory responsible for storing visually presented information, such as drawings, or remembering kinesthetic (motor) movements, such as dance steps.

W

way finding (or **route learning**) Cognitive processes used to navigate in a spatial environment in order to arrive at a goal.

well-defined problem Problems that have definite goals, specify all relevant information, and for which a clear answer is obvious.

Wernicke's aphasia Loss of the ability to understand sounds or speech and writing. Individuals with this condition produce effortless speech, sometimes with ill-chosen words or phrases, but do not realize that they are not making sense.

Wernicke's area An area of the brain located in the auditory cortex and parietal lobe that computes the overall message of sounds and language.

where/what circuit Two brain circuits process information about the spatial location of objects and allow us to name them. The where circuit runs from the visual cortex to the parietal lobe for visual stimuli and from the auditory cortex to the parietal lobe for sound stimuli. The what circuit runs from the visual or auditory cortex to the temporal lobe, which allows memories to be activated in order to recognize the object.

whole-object principle When learning their native language, children show a preference for identifying words with whole objects rather than part of an object.

Williams syndrome A mild to moderate developmental delay associated with a defective gene on chromosome 7, resulting in failure to thrive and in elfin facial characteristics. Children with this condition are often sociable and exceptional conversationalists with a sophisticated vocabulary.

word deafness The ability to hear sounds but not be able to identify them.

word-length effect Short-term memory span decreases when the length of words to be memorized increases.

word-superiority effect The ability to recognize letters embedded in words more easily than when they are in random strings of letters or when they appear alone.

working memory The set of mechanisms that underlies short-term memory and communicates with long-term memory; a semipermanent memory store that endures for a lifetime and aids in learning new information.

References

Abramson, L. Y., Metalsky, G. I., & Alloy, L. B. (1989). Hopelessness depression: A theory based subtype. *Psychological Review, 96,* 358–372.

Adams, B., Breazeal, C., Brooks, R., & Scassellati, B. (2009). Humanoid robots: A new kind of tool. *IEEE Intelligent Systems, 15,* 94.

Adams, M. J. (1990). *Beginning to read: Thinking and learning about print.* Cambridge, MA: MIT Press.

Aggleton, J. P., & Brown, M. W. (1999). Episodic memory, amnesia, and the hippocampal–anterior thalamic axis. *Behavioral and Brain Sciences, 22,* 425–444.

Akshoomoff, N. A., & Courchesne, E. (1992). A new role for the cerebellum in cognitive operations. *Behavioral Neuroscience, 106,* 731–738.

Aldisert, R. J. (1997). *Logic for lawyers.* South Bend, IN: National Institute for Trial Advocacy.

Alegriak, M. K., Nakash, O., Lapatin, S., Oddo, V., Gao, S., Lin, J., & Normand, S.-L. (2008). How missing information in diagnosis can lead to disparities in the clinical encounter. *Journal of Public Health Management and Practice, 14,* 826–835.

Allard, F., & Starkes, J. L. (1991). Motor-skill experts in sports, dance, and other domains. In K. A. Ericsson & J. Smith (Eds.), *Toward a general theory of expertise* (pp. 129–152). Cambridge: Cambridge University Press.

Allen, C. N., Goldstein, G., Heyman, R. A., & Rondinelli, T. (1998). Teaching memory strategies to persons with multiple sclerosis. *Journal of Rehabilitation Research and Development, 35,* 405–410.

Allopenna, P. D., Magnuson, J. S., & Tanenhaus, M. K. (1998). Tracking the time course of spoken word recognition using eye movements: Evidence for continuous mapping models. *Journal of Memory and Language, 38,* 419–439.

Allport, G. W. (1924). Eidetic imagery. *British Journal of Psychology, 15,* 99–120.

Allport, G. W. (1935). Attitudes. In C. Murchison (Ed.), *A handbook of social psychology* (pp. 798–844). Worcester, MA: Clark University Press.

Alm, H., & Nilsson, L. (1995). The effects of a mobile telephone task on driver behaviour in a car following situation. *Accident Analysis & Prevention, 27*(5), 707–715.

Almor, A., & Sloman, S. A. (1996). Is deontic reasoning special? *Psychological Review, 103,* 374–380.

Almor, A., & Sloman, S. A. (2000). Reasoning versus text processing in the Wason selection task: A non-deontic perspective on perspective effects. *Memory & Cognition, 28,* 1060–1070.

Altmann, S. A. (1967). The structure of primate social communication. In S. A. Altmann (Ed.), *Social communication among primates* (pp. 352–362). Chicago: University of Chicago Press.

American Psychiatric Association. (1994). *Diagnostic and statistical manual of mental disorders* (4th ed.). Washington, DC: Author.

American Psychiatric Association. (2000). *Diagnostic and statistical manual of mental disorders* (4th ed., text rev.). Washington, DC: Author.

Ambrose, S. (1998). Late Pleistocene human population bottlenecks, volcanic winter, and differentiation of modern humans. *Journal of Human Evolution, 35,* 115–118.

Ames, L. (1966). Children's stories. *Genetic Psychological Monographs, 73,* 307–311.

Anderson, J. A. (1973). A theory for the recognition of items from short memorized lists. *Psychological Review, 80,* 417–438.

Anderson, J. R. (1974). Retrieval of propositional information from long-term memory. *Cognitive Psychology, 6,* 451–474.

Anderson, J. R. (1983). *The architecture of cognition.* Cambridge, MA: Harvard University Press.

Anderson, J. R. (2005a). *Cognitive psychology and its implications.* New York: Worth Publishers.

Anderson, J. R. (2005b). Human symbol manipulation within an integrated cognitive architecture. *Cognitive Science, 29,* 313–341.

Anderson, J. R., Bothell, D., Lebiere, C., & Matessa, M. (1998). An integrated theory of list memory. *Journal of Memory and Language, 38,* 341–380.

Anderson, J. R., & Bower, G. H. (1972). Recognition and retrieval processes in free recall. *Psychological Review, 79,* 97–123.

Anderson, J. R., Kushmerick, N., & Lebiere, C. (1993). Navigation and conflict resolution. In J. R. Anderson (Ed.), *Rules of the mind* (pp. 93–120). Hillsdale, NJ: Erlbaum.

Anderson, J. R., & Lebiere, C. (1998). *The atomic components of thought.* Hillsdale, NJ: Erlbaum.

Anderson, J. R., & Reder, L. M. (1999). The fan effect: New results and new theories. *Journal of Experimental Psychology: General, 128,* 186–197.

Anderson, R. C., & Pichert, J. W. (1978). Recall of previously unrecallable information following a shift in perspective. *Journal of Verbal Learning and Verbal Behavior, 17,* 1–12.

Anderson, R. C., Spiro, R. J., & Anderson, M. C. (1978). Schemata as scaffolding for the representation of information in connected discourse. *American Educational Research Journal, 15,* 433–440.

Anderson, R. E. (1984). Did I do it or did I only imagine doing it? *Journal of Experimental Psychology: General, 113,* 594–613.

Anderson, S. W., Bechara, A., Damasio, H., Tranel, D., & Damasio, A. R. (1999). Impairment of social and moral behavior related to early damage in the human prefrontal cortex. *Nature Neuroscience, 2,* 1032–1037.

Angelone, B., Levin, D. T., & Simons, D. J. (2003). The relationship between change detection and recognition of centrally attended objects in motion pictures. *Perception, 32,* 947–962.

Anschutz, L., Camp, C. J., Markley, R. P., & Kramer, J. J. (1985). Maintenance and generalization of mnemonics for grocery shopping by older adults. *Experimental Aging Research, 11,* 157–160.

Archibald, C. J., & Fisk, J. D. (2000). Information-processing efficiency in MS. *Journal of Clinical and Experimental Neuropsychology, 22,* 686–701.

Arieti, S. (1948). Special logic of schizophrenic and other types of autistic thought. *Psychiatry, 11,* 325–338.

Arieti, S. (1955). *Interpretation of schizophrenia.* New York: Brunner.

Aristotle. (1938). *The organon* (H. Tredennick, Trans.). Cambridge, MA: Harvard University Press.

Arkes, H. R., & Blumer, C. (1985). The psychology of sunk cost. *Organizational Behavior and Human Decision Processes, 35,* 124–140.

Arkes, H. R., & Hutzel, L. (2000). The role of probability of success estimates in the sunk cost effect. *Journal of Behavioral Decision Making, 13,* 295–306.

Arnett, P. A., Higginson, C. I., Voss, W. D., Wright, B., Bender, W. I., Wurst, J. M., & Tippin, J. M. (1999). The relationship between coping, cognitive dysfunction, and depression in multiple sclerosis. *Neuropsychology, 13,* 434–446.

Arthur, P., & Passini, R. (1992). *Wayfinding: People, signs, and architecture.* New York: McGraw-Hill.

Ashby, F. G., Isen, A. M., & Turken, U. (1999). A neuropsychological theory of positive affect and its influence on cognition. *Psychological Review, 106,* 529–550.

Ashcraft, M. H. (1982). The development of mental arithmetic: A chronometric approach. *Developmental Review, 2,* 213–236.

Ashcraft, M. H. (1995). Cognitive psychology and simple arithmetic: A review and summary of new directions. *Mathematical Cognition, 1,* 3–34.

Ashcraft, M. H., & Stazyk, E. H. (1981). Mental addition: A test of three verification models. *Memory & Cognition, 9,* 185–196.

Atkinson, R. C. (1975). Mnemotechnics in second-language learning. *American Psychologist, 30,* 821–828.

Atkinson, R. C., & Raugh, M. R. (1975). An application of the mnemonic keyword method to the acquisition of Russian vocabulary. *Journal of Experimental Psychology: Human Learning and Memory, 104,* 126–133.

Atkinson, R. C., & Shriffin, R. M. (1969). Storage and retrieval processes in long-term memory. *Psychological Review, 76,* 179–193.

Atwood, M. E., & Polson, P. G. (1976). A process model for water jug problems. *Cognitive Psychology, 8,* 191–216.

Au, T. K.-F. (1983). Chinese and English counterfactuals: The Sapir–Whorf hypothesis revisited. *Cognition, 15,* 155–187.

Au, T. K.-F. (1984). Counterfactuals: In reply to Alfred Bloom. *Cognition, 17,* 289–302.

Austin, J. L. (1962). *How to do things with language.* Oxford, England: Oxford University Press.

Ausubel, D. P. (1960). The use of advance organizers in the learning and retention of meaningful verbal material. *Journal of Educational Psychology, 51,* 267–272.

Ausubel, D. P. (1963). *The psychology of meaningful verbal learning.* New York: Grune & Stratton.

Ausubel, D. P. (1968). *Educational psychology: A cognitive view.* New York: Holt, Rinehart and Winston.

Averbach, E., & Coriell, A. S. (1961). Short-term memory in vision. *Bell System Technical Journal, 40,* 309–328.

Avons, S. E., Wright, K. L., & Pammer, K. (1994). The word-length effect in probed and serial recall. *Quarterly Journal of Experimental Psychology: Human Experimental Psychology, 47,* 207–231.

Awh, E., Jonides, J., Smith, E. E., Schumacher, E. H., Koeppe, R. A., & Katz, S. (1996). Dissociation of storage and rehearsal in verbal working memory: Evidence from positron emission tomography. *Psychological Science, 7,* 25–31.

Aylward, E. H., Reiss, A. L., Reader, M. J., Singer, H. S., Brown, J. E., & Denckla, M. B. (1996). Basal ganglia volumes in children with attention-deficit/hyperactivity disorder. *Journal of Child Neurology, 11,* 112–115.

Ayton, P., & Fischer, I. (2004). The hot hand fallacy and the gambler's fallacy: Two faces of subjective randomness. *Memory & Cognition, 32,* 1369–1378.

Baddeley, A. D. (1976). *The psychology of memory.* New York: Basic Books.

Baddeley, A. D. (1986). *Working memory.* New York: Oxford University Press.

Baddeley, A. D. (1998). The central executive: A concept and some misconceptions. *Journal of the International Neuropsychological Society, 4,* 523–526.

Baddeley, A. D. (2000). The episodic buffer: A new component of working memory? *Trends in Cognitive Sciences, 4,* 417–423.

Baddeley, A. D. (2002). Is working memory still working? *European Psychologist, 7,* 85–97.

Baddeley, A. D., & Hitch, G. J. (1974). Working memory. In G. A. Bower (Ed.), *Recent advances in learning and motivation* (Vol. 8, pp. 47–89). New York: Academic Press.

Baddeley, A. D., & Hitch, G. J. (1976). Verbal reasoning and working memory. *Quarterly Journal of Experimental Psychology, 28,* 603–621.

Baddeley, A. D., & Hitch, G. J. (1977). Recency re-examined. In S. Dornic (Ed.), *Attention and performance* (Vol. 6, pp. 647–667). Hillsdale, NJ: Erlbaum.

Baddeley, A. D., & Logie, R. H. (1999). Working memory: The multiple component model. In A. Miyake & P. Shah (Eds.), *Models of working memory* (pp. 28–61). New York: Cambridge University Press.

Baddeley, A. D., Thomson, N., & Buchanan, M. (1975). Word length and the structure of short-term memory. *Journal of Verbal Learning and Verbal Behavior, 14,* 575–589.

Baddeley, A. D., Vallar, G., & Wilson, B. B. (1987). Sentence comprehension and phonological memory: Some neuropsychological evidence. In M. Coltheart (Ed.), *Attention and performance* (Vol. 12, pp. 509–529). Hillsdale, NJ: Erlbaum.

Baddeley, A. D., & Wilson, B. A. (2002). Prose recall and amnesia: Implications for the structure of working memory. *Neuropsychologia, 40,* 1737–1743.

Bahrick, H. P. (1984). Semantic memory content in permastore: 50 years of memory for Spanish learned in school. *Journal of Experimental Psychology: General, 113,* 1–31.

Bahrick, H. P., Bahrick, L. E., Bahrick, A. S., & Bahrick, P. E. (1993). Maintenance of foreign language vocabulary and the spacing effect. *Psychological Science, 4,* 316–321.

Bahrick, H. P., & Phelps, E. (1987). Retention of Spanish vocabulary over eight years. *Journal of Experimental Psychology: Leaning, Memory, and Cognition, 13,* 344–349.

Balakrishnan, J. D., & Ashby, F. G. (1991). Is subitizing a unique numerical ability? *Perception & Psychophysics, 50,* 555–564.

Balakrishnan, J. D., & Ashby, F. G. (1992). Subitizing: Magical numbers or mere superstition? *Psychological Review, 54,* 80–90.

Balota, D. A., & Black, S. (1997). Semantic satiation in healthy young and older adults. *Memory & Cognition, 25,* 190–202.

Balota, D. A., Dolan, P. O., & Duchek, J. M. (2000). Memory changes in healthy older adults. In

E. Tulving & F. I. M. Craik (Eds.), *The Oxford handbook of memory* (pp. 395–405). Oxford, England: Oxford University Press.

Baltes, P. B., & Kliegl, R. (1992). Further testing of limits of cognitive plasticity: Negative age differences in a mnemonic skill are robust. *Development Psychology, 28,* 121–125.

Baltes, P. B., Kliegl, R., & Dittmann-Kohli, F. (1988). On the locus of training gains in research on the plasticity of fluid intelligence in old age. *Journal of Educational Psychology, 80*(3), 392–400.

Banks, W. P. (1977). Encoding and processing of symbolic information in comparative judgments. In G. H. Bower (Ed.), *The psychology of learning and motivation* (Vol. 11, pp. 101–159). New York: Academic Press.

Banks, W. P., Clark, H. H., & Lucy, P. (1975). The locus of the semantic congruity effect in comparative judgments. *Journal of Experimental Psychology: Human Perception and Performance, 1,* 35–47.

Banks, W. P., Fujii, M., & Kayra-Stuart, F. (1976). Semantic congruity effects in comparative judgments of magnitude of digits. *Journal of Experimental Psychology: Human Perception and Performance, 2,* 435–447.

Banse, R., & Scherer, K. R. (1996). Acoustic profiles in vocal emotion expression. *Journal of Personality and Social Psychology, 70,* 614–636.

Baradell, J. G., & Klein, K. (1993). The relationship of life stress and body consciousness to hypervigilant decision making. *Journal of Personality and Social Psychology, 64,* 267–273.

Barash, J. (1994). Age-related decline in route learning ability. *Developmental Neuropsychology, 10,* 189–201.

Barbizet, J. (1970). *Human memory and its pathology* (D. K. Jardine, Trans.). San Francisco: W. H. Freeman and Company.

Barclay, J. R., Bransford, J. D., Franks, J. J., McCarrel, N. S., & Nitsch, K. (1974). Comprehension and semantic flexibility. *Journal of Verbal Learning and Verbal Behavior, 13,* 471–481.

Bar-Eli, M., Avugos, S., & Raab, M. (2006). Twenty years of "hot hand" research: Review and critique. *Psychology of Sport and Exercise, 7,* 535–553.

Bar-Haim, Y., Ziv, T., Lamy, D., & Hodes, R. M. (2006). Nature and nurture in own-race face processing. *Psychological Science, 17,* 159–163.

Barkley, R. A. (1990). *Attention-deficit/hyperacitivty disorder: A handbook for diagnosis and treatment.* New York: Guilford Press.

Barkley, R. A. (1995). *Taking charge of ADHD: The complete, authoritative guide for parents.* New York: Guilford Press.

Baron, J. (1985). *Rationality and intelligence.* Cambridge, England: Cambridge University Press.

Baron, R. A., & Thomley, J. (1994). A whiff of reality: Positive affect as a potential mediator of the effects of pleasant fragrance on task performance and helping. *Environment and Behavior, 26,* 766–784.

Barrett, M. (1982). The holophrastic hypothesis: Conceptual and empirical issues. *Cognition, 11,* 47–76.

Barsalou, L. W. (1999). Perceptual symbol systems. *Behavioral and Brain Science, 22,* 577–660.

Barsalou, L. W., Simmons, W., Barbey, A. K., & Wilson, C. D. (2003). Grounding conceptual knowledge in modality-specific systems. *Trends in Cognitive Sciences, 7,* 84–91.

Bartlett, F. C. (1932). *Remembering: A study in experimental and social psychology.* Cambridge, England: Cambridge University Press.

Bartlett, J. C., & Santrock, J. W. (1979). Affect-dependent episodic memory in young children. *Child Development, 50,* 513–518.

Bates, E. (1976). *Language and context: The acquisition of pragmatics.* New York: Academic Press.

Bates, E., & Goodman, J. C. (2001). On the inseparability of grammar and the lexicon: Evidence from acquisition. In M. Tomasello & E. Bates (Eds.), *Language development: The essential readings* (pp. 134–162). Malden, MA: Blackwell.

Bates, E., Marchman, V., Thal, D., Fenson, L., Dale, P. S., Reznick, J. S., . . . Hartung, J. (1994). Developmental and stylistic variation in the composition of early vocabulary. *Journal of Child Language, 21,* 85–123.

Bates, E., Reilly, J., Wulfec, B., Dronkers, N., Opie, M., Fenson, J., . . . Herbst, K. (2001). Differential effects of unilateral lesions on language production in children and adults. *Brain and Language, 79,* 223–265.

Battista, M. T. (1990). Spatial visualization and gender differences in high school geometry. *Journal of Research in Mathematics Education, 21,* 47–60.

Baumeister, R. F., & Leary, M. R. (1995). The need to belong: Desire for interpersonal attachment as a fundamental human motivation. *Psychological Bulletin, 117,* 497–529.

Baxter, L. C., Saykin, A. J., Flashman, L. A., Johnson, S. C., Guerin, S. J., Babcock, D. R., & Wishart, H. A. (2003). Sex differences in semantic language processing: A functional MRI study. *Brain and Language, 84,* 272–274.

Beaman, C. P., & Morton, J. (2000). The separate but related origins of the recency effect and the modality effect in free recall. *Cognition, 77,* 59–65.

Beatty, J. (1995). *Principles of behavioral neuroscience.* Dubuque, IA: Brown & Benchmark.

Bechara, A. (2004). The role of emotion in decision making: Evidence from neurological patients with orbitofrontal damage. *Brain and Cognition, 55,* 30–40.

Bechara, A., Damasio, H., & Damasio, A. R. (2000). Emotion, decision making, and the orbitofrontal cortex. *Cerebral Cortex, 10,* 295–307.

Bechara, A., Tranel, D., & Damasio, A. R. (2002). The somatic marker hypothesis and decision making. In F. Boller & J. Grafman (Eds.), *Handbook of neuropsychology: Vol. 7. The frontal lobes* (2nd ed., pp. 117–143). Amsterdam: Elsevier.

Beck, A. T. (1976). *Cognitive therapy and emotional disorders.* New York: International Universities Press.

Beck, I. L., & McKeown, M. G. (1991). Conditions of vocabulary acquisition. In R. Barr, M. Kamil, P. Mosenthal, & P. D. Pearson (Eds.), *Handbook of reading research* (Vol. 2, pp. 789–814). White Plains, NY: Longman.

Bediou, R., Krolak-Salmon, P., Saoud, M., Henaff, M.-A., Burt, M., Dalery, J., & D'Amato, T. (2005).

Facial expression and sex recognition in schizophrenia and depression. *Canadian Journal of Psychiatry, 50,* 525–533.

Behrmann, M., Moscovitch, M., & Winocur, G. (1994). Intact visual imagery and impaired visual perception in a patient with visual agnosia. *Journal of Experimental Psychology: Human Perception and Performance, 30,* 1068–1087.

Behrman, M., & Shallice, T. (1995). Pure alexia: A nonspatial visual disorder affecting letter activation. *Cognitive Neuropsychology, 12,* 409–454.

Belin, P., Van Eeckhout, P., Zilbovicius, M., Remy, P., François, C., Guillaume, S., . . . Samson, Y. (1996). Recovery from nonfluent aphasia after melodic intonation therapy: A PET study. *Neurology, 47,* 1504–1511.

Bellugi, U., Korenberg, J. R., & Klima, E. S. (2001). Williams syndrome: An exploration of neurocognitive and genetic features. *Journal of Clinical Neuroscience Research, 1,* 217–229.

Ben-Chaim, D., Lappan, G., & Houang, R. T. (1986). Development and analysis of a spatial visualization test for middle school boys and girls. *Perceptual and Motor Skills, 63,* 659–669.

Benjamin, A. S., & Bjork, R. A. (2000). On the relationship between recognition speed and accuracy for words rehearsed via rote versus elaborative rehearsal. *Journal of Experimental Psychology: Learning, Memory, and Cognition, 26,* 638–648.

Berg, E. A. (1948). A simple objective treatment for measuring flexibility in thinking. *Journal of General Psychology, 39,* 15–22.

Berk, L. S., Tan, S. A., Fry, W. F., Napier, B. J., Lee, J. W., Hubbard, R. W., . . . Eby, W. C. (1989). Neuroendocrine and stress hormone changes during mirthful laughter. *American Journal of the Medical Sciences, 298,* 390–396.

Berlin, B., & Kay, P. (1969). *Basic color terms.* Berkeley: University of California Press.

Best, C. T., McRoberts, G. W., & Sithole, N. T. (1988). Examination of perceptual reorganization for non-native speech contrasts: Zulu click discrimination by English-speaking adults and infants. *Journal*

of Experimental Psychology: Human Perception and Performance, 14, 345–360.

Beth, E. W., & Piaget, J. (1966). *Mathematical epistemology and psychology.* New York: Reidel.

Bever, T. (1970). The cognitive basis for linguistic structures. In J. R. M. Hayes (Ed.), *Cognition and the development of language* (pp. 279–352). New York: Wiley.

Bever, T., Garrett, M. F., & Hurtig, R. (1973). The interaction of perceptual processes and ambiguous sentences. *Memory & Cognition, 1,* 277–286.

Bhatnagar, S. C., & Andy, O. J. (1995). *Neuroscience for the study of communicative disorders.* Baltimore: Williams & Wilkins.

Biederman, I. (1985). Human image understanding: Recent research and a theory. *Computer Vision Graphics Image Processing, 32,* 29–73.

Biederman, I. (1987). Recognition-by-components: A theory of human image understanding. *Psychological Review, 94,* 115–147.

Biederman, I. (1995). Visual object recognition. In S. M. Kosslyn & D. N. Osherson (Eds.), *An invitation to cognitive science* (2nd ed., Vol. 2, pp. 121–165). Cambridge, MA: MIT Press.

Biederman, I., Cooper, E. E., Fox, P. W., & Mahadevan, R. S. (1992). Unexceptional spatial memory in an exceptional memorist. *Journal of Experimental Psychology: Learning, Memory, and Cognition, 18,* 654–657.

Bierwisch, M. (1967). Some semantic universals of German adjectivals. *Foundations of Language, 3,* 1–36.

Bigler, E. D. (1992). The neurobiology and neuropsychology of adult learning disorders. *Journal of Learning Disabilities, 25,* 488–506.

Binet, A., & Simon, T. (1916). *The development of intelligence in children: The Binet–Simon Scale.* (Publication of the Training School at Vineland, NJ, Department of Research Rep. No. 11; E. S. Kite, Trans.). Baltimore: Williams & Wilkins.

Birnbaum, M. H. (1983). Base rates in Bayesian inference: Signal detection analysis of the cab problem. *American Journal of Psychology, 96,* 85–93.

Bisiach, E., & Luzzatti, C. (1978). Unilateral neglect of representational space. *Cortex, 14,* 129–133.

Bisiach, E., Luzzatti, C., & Perani, D. (1979). Unilateral neglect, representational schema, and consciousness. *Brain, 102,* 609–618.

Bjork, R. A., & Whitten, W. B. (1974). Recency-sensitive retrieval processes in long-term free recall. *Cognitive Psychology, 6,* 173–189.

Bjorklund, D. F. (1987). How age changes in knowledge base contribute to the development of children's memory: An interpretive review. *Developmental Review, 7,* 93–130.

Black, J. S., & Overton, W. F. (1990). Reasoning, logic, and thought disorder: Deductive reasoning and developmental psychopathology. In W. F. Overton (Ed.), *Reasoning, necessity, and logic: Developmental perspectives* (pp. 255–297). Hillsdale, NJ: Erlbaum.

Blanchette, I., & Dunbar, K. (2002). Representational change and analogy: How analogical inferences alter target representations. *Journal of Experimental Psychology: Learning, Memory, and Cognition, 28,* 672–685.

Bloom, A. (1981). *The linguistic shaping of thought: A study of the impact of language on thinking in China and the West.* Hillsdale, NJ: Erlbaum.

Bloom, A. (1984). Caution—The words you use may affect what you say: A response to Terry Kit-Fong Au's "Chinese and English counterfactuals: The Sapir–Whorf hypothesis revisited." *Cognition, 17,* 275–287.

Bloom, F. E., & Lazerson, A. (1988). *Brain, mind, and behavior* (2nd ed.). New York: W. H. Freeman and Company.

Bloom, F. E., & Lazerson, A. (2001). Hemineglect figure. In B. Kolb & I. Q. Whishaw, *Fundamentals of human neuropsychology* (6th ed., p. 390). New York: Worth Publishing. (Reprinted from *Brain, mind, and behavior*, 2nd ed., p. 300, by F. E. Bloom & A. Lazerson, 1988, New York: W. H. Freeman and Company.)

Boder, E. (1973). Developmental dyslexia: A diagnostic approach based on three atypical reading–spelling patterns. *Developmental Medicine and Child Neurology, 15,* 663–687.

Boll, T. (1981). The Halstead–Reitan Neuropsychology Battery. In S. B. Filskov & T. J. Boll (Eds.), *Handbook of clinical neuropsychology* (pp. 577–607). New York: Wiley-Interscience.

Bolla, K. I., Lindgren, K. N., Bonaccorsy, C., & Bleecker, M. L. (1991). Memory complaints in older adults: Fact of fiction? *Archives of Neurology, 48,* 61–64.

Bonvillian, J., Garber, A. M., & Dell, S. B. (1997). Language origin accounts: Was the gesture in the beginning? *First Language, 17,* 219–239.

Bonvillian, J., Orlansky, M., & Novack, L. (1983). Developmental milestones: Sign language acquisition and motor development. *Child Development, 54,* 1435–1445.

Bookheimer, S. Y., Zeffiro, T. A., Blaxton, T., Gaillard, W., & Theodore, W. (1995). Regional cerebral blood flow during object naming and word reading. *Human Brain Mapping, 3,* 93–106.

Boon, J. C., & Davies, G. M. (1987). Rumours greatly exaggerated: Allport and Postman's apocryphal study. *Canadian Journal of Behavioural Science, 19,* 430–440.

Bornstein, M. H., Ferdinandsen, K., & Gross, C. G. (1981). Perception of symmetry in infancy. *Developmental Psychology, 17,* 82–86.

Bornstein, M. H., & Krinsky, S. (1985). Perception of symmetry in infancy: The salience of vertical symmetry and the perception of pattern wholes. *Journal of Experimental Child Psychology, 39,* 1–19.

Borovsky, A. A., & Abrams, L. (2001, June). *The interactions of syntax, lag, and age in influencing repetition blindness.* Poster presented at the 13th annual meeting of the American Psychological Society, Toronto, Canada.

Bos, M. W., Dijksterhuis, A., & Van Baaren, R. B. (2011). The benefits of "sleeping on things": Unconscious thought leads to automatic weighting. *Journal of Consumer Psychology, 21,* 4–8.

Boucher, J., & Lewis, V. (1992). Unfamiliar face recognition in relatively able autistic children. *Journal of Child Psychology and Psychiatry, 33,* 843–859.

Bousfield, W. A. (1953). The occurrence of clustering in recall of randomly arranged associates. *Journal of General Psychology, 30,* 149–165.

Bower, G. H. (1970). Analysis of a mnemonic device. *American Scientist, 58,* 496–510.

Bower, G. H. (1981). Mood and memory. *American Psychologist, 36,* 129–148.

Bower, G. H., Black, J. B., & Turner, T. J. (1979). Scripts in memory for text. *Cognitive Psychology, 11,* 177–220.

Bower, G. H., & Clark, M. C. (1969). Narrative stories as mediators for serial learning. *Psychonomic Science, 14,* 181–182.

Bower, G. H., Clark, M. C., Lesgold, A. M., & Winzenz, D. (1969). Hierarchical retrieval schemes in recall of categorical word lists. *Journal of Verbal Learning and Verbal Behavior, 8,* 323–343.

Bower, G. H., & Forgas, J. R. (2000). Affect, memory, and social cognition. In J. Forgas, K. Eich, G. H. Bower, & P. M. Niedenthal (Eds.), *Cognition and emotion* (pp. 87–168). Oxford, England: Oxford University Press.

Bower, G. H., Karlin, M. B., & Dueck, A. (1975). Comprehension and memory for pictures. *Memory & Cognition, 3,* 216–220.

Boyer, P. (2008). Evolutionary economics of mental time travel? *Trends in Cognitive Sciences, 12,* 219–224.

Braddock, B. A., Farmer, J. E., Deidrick, K. W., Iverson, J. M., & Maria, B. L. (2006). Oromotor and communication findings in Joubert syndrome: Further evidence of multisystem apraxia. *Journal of Child Neurology, 21,* 160–163.

Bradshaw, J. L., & Nettleton, N. C. (1981). The nature of hemispheric specialization in man. *Behavioral and Brain Sciences, 4,* 51–91.

Braine, M. D. S., & O'Brien, D. P. (Eds.). (1998). How to investigate mental logic and the syntax of thought. In M. D. S. Braine & D. P. O'Brien (Eds.), *Mental logic* (pp. 45–61). Mahwah, NJ: Erlbaum.

Braine, M. D. S., Reiser, B. J., & Rumain, B. (1984). Some empirical justifications for a theory of natural propositional logic. In G. Bower (Ed.), *The psychology of learning and motivation* (pp. 313–371). New York: Academic Press.

Bransford, J. D., Barclay, J. R., & Franks, J. J. (1972). Sentence memory: A constructive versus interpretative approach. *Cognitive Psychology, 3,* 193–209.

Bransford, J. D., & Johnson, M. K. (1972). Contextual prerequisites for understanding: Some investigations of comprehension and recall. *Journal of Verbal Learning and Verbal Behavior, 11,* 717–726.

Breitmeyer, B., & Ganz, L. (1976). Implications of sustained and transient channels for theories of visual pattern masking, saccadic suppression, and information processing. *Psychological Review, 83,* 1–36.

Breitmeyer, B., & Ogmen, H. (2000). Recent models and findings in visual backward masking: A comparison, review, and update. *Perception & Psychophysics, 62,* 1572–1595.

Breslow, L. (1981). Reevaluation of the literature on the development of transitive inferences. *Psychological Bulletin, 90,* 325–351.

Brewer, M. B. (1999). The psychology of prejudice: Ingroup love or outgroup hate? *Journal of Social Issues, 55,* 429–444.

Brewer, W. F. (1996). Good and bad story endings and story completeness. In R. J. Kreuz & M. S. MacNealy (Eds.), *Empirical approaches to literature and aesthetics*. Norwood, NJ: Ablex.

Brewer, W. F., & Treyens, J. C. (1981). Role of schemata in memory for places. *Cognitive Psychology, 13,* 207–230.

Briem, V., & Hedman, L. R. (1995). Behavioural effects of mobile telephone use during simulated driving. *Ergonomics, 38,* 2536–2562.

Briggs, R., & Hocevar, D. J. (1975). A new distinctive feature theory for uppercase letters. *Journal of General Psychology, 93,* 87–93.

Broadbent, D. E. (1956). Growing points in multi-channel communication. *Journal of the Acoustical Society of America, 28,* 533–535.

Broadbent, D. E. (1958). *Perception and communication*. London: Pergamon Press.

Broadbent, D. E. (1982). Task combination and selective intake of information. *Acta Psychologica, 50,* 253–290.

Broca, P. P. (1861). Perte de la parole, ramollissement chronique et destruction partielle du lobe antérieur gauche du cerveau [Loss of speech, chronic softening and parietal destruction of the anterior left lobe of the brain]. *Bulletin de la Société Anthropologique, 2,* 235–238.

Broen, W. E., & Storms, L. H. (1966). Lawful disorganization: The process underlying a schizophrenic syndrome. *Psychological Review, 73,* 265–279.

Bronnick, K., Emre, M., Lane, R., Tekin, S., & Aarsland, D. (2007). Profile of cognitive impairment in dementia associated with Parkinson's disease compared with Alzheimer's disease. *Journal of Neurology, Neurosurgery, and Psychiatry, 78,* 1064–1068.

Brookhuis, K. A., De Vries, G., & De Waard, D. (1991). The effects of mobile telephoning on driving performance. *Accident Analysis & Prevention, 23,* 309–316.

Brooks, L. R. (1968). Spatial and verbal components of the act of recall. *Canadian Journal of Psychology, 22,* 349–368.

Brookshire, R. H. (1997). *An introduction to neurogenic communication disorders* (5th ed.). St Louis, MO: Mosby.

Brown, A. S. (1991). The tip of the tongue experience: A review and evaluation. *Psychological Bulletin, 10,* 204–223.

Brown, I. D., Tickner, A. H., & Simmonds, D. C. (1969). Interfering between concurrent tasks of driving and telephoning. *Journal of Applied Psychology, 53,* 419–424.

Brown, J. A. (1958). Some tests of the decay theory of immediate memory. *Quarterly Journal of Experimental Psychology, 10,* 12–21.

Brown, J. S., & VanLehn, K. (1980). Repair theory: A generative theory of bugs in procedural skills. *Cognitive Science, 4,* 379–426.

Brown, R. (1973). *A first language: The early stage.* Cambridge, MA: Harvard University Press.

Brown, R., & Kulik, J. (1977). Flashbulb memories. *Cognition, 5,* 73–99.

Brown, R., & McNeill, D. (1966). The "tip of the tongue" phenomenon. *Journal of Verbal Learning and Verbal Behavior, 5,* 325–337.

Brown, R., & Marsden, C. D. (1988). Internal vs. external cues and the control of attention in Parkinson's disease. *Brain, 111,* 323–345.

Brown, R., & Marsden, C. D. (1990). Cognitive function in Parkinson's disease: From description to theory. *Trends in Neurosciences, 13,* 21–29.

Brown, T. L., Joneleit, K., Robinson, C. S., & Brown, C. R. (2002). Automaticity in reading and the Stroop task: Testing the limits of involuntary word processing. *American Journal of Psychology, 115,* 515–543.

Bruce, V., & Young, A. (1986). Understanding facial recognition. *British Journal of Psychology, 77,* 305–327.

Bruce, V., & Young, A. (1998). *In the eye of the beholder: The science of face perception.* Oxford, England: Oxford University Press.

Bruck, M., Ceci, S. J., & Hembrooke, H. (1998). Reliability and creditability of young children's reports: From research to policy and practice. *American Psychologist, 53,* 136–151.

Bruine de Bruin, W., Parker, A. M., & Fischhoff, B. (2007). Individual differences in adult decision-making competence. *Journal of Personality and Social Psychology, 92,* 938–956.

Bruyer, R., & Scailquin, J.-C. (1998). The visuo-spatial sketchpad for mental images: Testing the multicomponent model of working memory. *Acta Psychologica, 1,* 17–36.

Bucci, W. (1978). The interpretation of universal affirmative propositions: A developmental study. *Cognition, 6,* 55–77.

Bucher, J., & Osgood, C. (1969). The Pollyanna hypothesis. *Journal of Verbal Learning and Verbal Behavior, 8,* 1–8.

Buchsbaum, B. R., & D'Esposito, M. (2008). The search for the phonological store: From loop to convolution. *Journal of Cognitive Neuroscience, 5,* 762–778.

Buckner, R. L., & Logan, J. M. (2001). Functional neuroimaging methods: PET and fMRI. In R. Cabeza & A. Kingstone (Eds.), *Handbook of functional neuroimaging of cognition* (pp. 27–48). Cambridge, MA: MIT Press.

Budney, A. J., Moore, B. A., Rocha, H. L., & Higgins, S. T. (2006). Clinical trial of abstinence-based vouchers and cognitive behavior therapy for cannabis dependence. *Journal of Consulting and Clinical Psychology, 74,* 307–316.

Buffart, H., Leeuwenberg, E., & Restle, F. (1983). Analysis of ambiguity in visual pattern completion. *Journal of Experimental Psychology: Human Perception and Performance, 9,* 980–1000.

Bühler, K. (1909). Zur Kritik der Denkexperimente [For a critique of the thought experiment]. *Zeitschrift für Psychologie, 51,* 108–118.

Bulgren, J. A., Schumaker, J. B., & Deshler, D. D. (1994). The effects of a recall enhancement routine on the test performance of secondary students with and without learning disabilities. *Learning Disabilities Research and Practice, 9,* 2–11.

Bunting, M., Cowan, N., & Saults, J. S. (2006). How does running memory span work? *Quarterly Journal of Experimental Psychology, 59,* 1691–1700.

Bunuel, L. (1983). *My lost sigh* (A. Israel, Trans.). New York: Knopf.

Burke, D., MacKay, D. G., Worthley, J., & Wade, E. (1991). On the tip of the tongue: What causes word finding failures in young and older adults? *Journal of Memory and Language, 30,* 542–579.

Burns, B., & Wieth, M. (2004). The collider principle in causal reasoning: Why the Monty Hall dilemma is so hard. *Journal of Experimental Psychology: General, 133,* 434–446.

Burr, D. C., Morgan, M. J., & Morrone, M. C. (1999). Saccadic suppression precedes visual motion analysis. *Currrent Biology, 9,* 1207–1209.

Burt, C. (1919). The development of reasoning in school children. *Journal of Experimental Pedagogy, 5,* 68–77, 121–127.

Bus, A. G., & Van Ijzendoorn, M. H. (1999). Phonological awareness and early reading: A meta-analysis of experimental training studies. *Journal of Educational Psychology, 91,* 403–414.

Bush, G., Luu, P., & Posner, M. I. (2000). Cognitive and emotional influences in anterior cingulate cortex. *Trends in Cognitive Sciences, 4,* 215–222.

Bushnell, I. W. R. (2001). Mother's face recognition in newborn infants: Learning and memory. *Infant and Child Development, 10,* 67–74.

Bushnell, I. W. R., Sai, F., & Mullin, J. T. (1989). Neonatal recognition of mother's face. *British Journal of Developmental Psychology, 7,* 3–15.

Bybee, J. L., & Slobin, D. I. (1982). Rules and schemas in the development and use of the English past tense. *Language, 58,* 265–289.

Calvillo, D. P., DeLeeuw, K., & Revlin, R. (2006). Deduction with Euler circles: Diagrams that hurt. In D. Barker-Plummer, R. Cox, & N. Swoboda (Eds.), *Proceedings of the 4th conference on Theory and Application of Diagrams (Diagrams 2006*; pp. 199–203). Berlin/Heidelberg, Germany: Springer.

Calvillo, D. P., & Revlin, R. (2005). The role of similarity in deductive categorical inference. *Psychonomic Bulletin & Review, 12,* 938–944.

Calvin, W. H. (1983). *The throwing Madonna: Essays on the brain.* New York: McGraw-Hill.

Campbell, J. (2008). *The hero with a thousand faces* (3rd ed.). Novato, CA: New World Library.

Campbell, R., Zihl, J., Massaro, D., Munhall, K., & Cohen, M. (1997). Speechreading in the akinetopsic patient, L.M. *Brain, 120,* 1793–1803.

Campbell, W. W., DeJong, R. N., & Haerer, A. F. (2005). *DeJong's neurological exam* (6th ed.). Philadelphia: Lippincott, Williams, & Wilkins.

Canellopoulou, M., & Richardson, J. T. E. (1998). The role of executive function in imagery mnemonics: Evidence from multiple sclerosis. *Neuropsychologia, 36,* 1181–1188.

Caramazza, A., Gordon, J., Zurif, E. G., & DeLuca, D. (1976). Right hemispheric damage and verbal problem solving behavior. *Brain and Language, 3,* 41–46.

Caramazza, A., & Zurif, E. G. (1976). Dissociation of algorithmic and heuristic processes in language comprehension: Evidence from aphasia. *Brain and Language, 3,* 572–582.

Card, S., Moran, T., & Newell, A. (1983). *The psychology of human–computer interaction.* Hillsdale, NJ: Erlbaum.

Carey, S. (1978). The child as word learner. In M. Halle, J. Bresner, & G. A. Miller (Eds.), *Linguistic theory and psychological reality* (pp. 264–293). Cambridge, MA: MIT Press.

Carey, S., & Diamond, R. (1977). From piecemeal to configurational representation of faces. *Science, 195,* 312–314.

Carlesimo, G., Perri, R., Turriziani, P., Tomaiuolo, F., & Caltagirone, C. (2001). Remembering what but not where: Independence of spatial and visual working memory in the human brain. *Cortex, 36,* 519–534.

Carney, R. N., & Levin, J. R. (2000). Mnemonic instruction, with a focus on transfer. *Journal of Educational Psychology, 92,* 783–790.

Carpenter, P. A., & Daneman, M. (1981). Lexical retrieval and error recovery in reading: A model based on eye fixations. *Journal of Verbal Learning and Verbal Behavior, 20,* 137–160.

Carpenter, P. A., & Eisenberg, P. (1978). Mental rotation and the frame of reference in blind and sighted individuals. *Perception & Psychophysics, 23,* 117–124.

Carpenter, P. A., & Just, M. A. (1975). Sentence comprehension: A psycholinguistic processing model of verification. *Psychological Review, 82,* 45–73.

Carrasco, M., Ling, S., & Read, S. (2004). Attention alters appearance. *Nature Neuroscience, 7,* 308–313.

Carroll, L. (1871). *Through the looking glass and what Alice found there.* London: Macmillan.

Casey, P. J. (1993). "That man's father is my father's son": The roles of structure, strategy, and working memory in solving convoluted verbal problems. *Memory & Cognition, 21,* 506–518.

Castiello, U., & Umiltà, C. (1990). Size of the attentional focus and efficiency of processing. *Acta Psychologica, 73,* 195–209.

Cave, K. R., & Bichot, N. P. (1999). Visuospatial attention: Beyond a spotlight model. *Psychonomic Bulletin & Review, 6,* 204–223.

Cervone, D., & Palmer, B. W. (1990). Anchoring biases and the perseverance of self-efficacy beliefs. *Cognitive Therapy and Research, 14,* 401–416.

Chafe, W. (1970). *Meaning and the structure of language.* Chicago: University of Chicago Press.

Chaffin, R., & Imreh, G. (2002). Practicing perfection: Piano performance as expert memory. *Psychological Science, 13,* 342–349.

Chall, J. S. (1983). *Stages of reading development.* New York: McGraw-Hill.

Chambers, D., & Reisberg, D. (1985). Can mental images be ambiguous? *Journal of Experimental Psychology: Human Perception and Performance, 11,* 317–328.

Chambers, D., & Reisberg, D. (1991). Neither pictures nor propositions: What can we learn from a mental image? *Canadian Journal of Psychology, 45,* 336–352.

Chambers, D., & Reisberg, D. (1992). What an image depicts depends on what an image means. *Cognitive Psychology, 24,* 145–174.

Chance, J., Goldstein, A. G., & McBride, L. (1975). Differential experience and recognition memory for faces. *Journal of Social Psychology, 97,* 243–253.

Chance, J., Turner, A. L., & Goldstein, A. G. (1982). Development of differential recognition for own- and other-race faces. *Journal of Psychology: Interdisciplinary and Applied, 112,* 29–37.

Chandrasekaran, B., Smith, J. W., & Sticklen, J. (1989). Deep models and their relation to diagnosis. *Artificial Intelligence in Medicine, 1,* 29–40.

Chapman, L. J., & Chapman, J. P. (1959). Atmosphere effects re-examined. *Journal of Experimental Psychology, 58,* 220–226.

Charness, N. (1979). Components of skill in bridge. *Canadian Journal of Psychology, 33,* 1–16.

Charness, N. (1989). Expertise in chess and bridge. In D. Klahr & K. Kotovsky (Eds.), *Complex information processing: The impact of Herbert A. Simon* (pp. 183–208). Hillsdale, NJ: Erlbaum.

Chase, W. G., & Clark, H. H. (1971). Semantics in the perception of verticality. *British Journal of Psychology, 62,* 311–326.

Chase, W. G., & Ericsson, K. A. (1981). Skilled memory. In J. R. Anderson (Ed.), *Cognitive skills and their development* (pp. 141–189). Hillsdale, NJ: Erlbaum.

Chase, W. G., & Simon, H. A. (1973a). The mind's eye in chess. In W. G. Chase (Ed.), *Visual information processing* (pp. 215–281). New York: Academic Press.

Chase, W. G., & Simon, H. A. (1973b). Perception in chess. *Cognitive Psychology, 4,* 55–81.

Chatwin, B. (1987). *The songlines.* New York: Penguin Books.

Chen, C.-C., & Tyler, C. W. (2010). Symmetry: Modeling the effects of masking noise, axial cueing, and salience. *PLoS ONE.* doi:10.1371/journal.pone.009840

Cheng, P. W., & Holyoak, K. J. (1985). Pragmatic reasoning schemas. *Cognitive Psychology, 17,* 391–416.

Cheng, P. W., & Holyoak, K. J. (1989). On the natural selection of reasoning theories. *Cognition, 33,* 285–313.

Cheng, P. W., Holyoak, K. J., Nisbett, R. E., & Oliver, L. M. (1986). Pragmatic versus syntactic approaches to training deductive reasoning. *Cognitive Psychology, 18,* 293–328.

Cherry, E. C. (1953). Some experiments on the recognition of speech, with one and two ears. *Journal of the Acoustical Society of America, 25,* 975–979.

Cherry, R. S., & Kruger, B. (1983). Selective auditory attention abilities of learning disabled and normal achieving children. *Journal of Learning Disabilities, 16,* 202–205.

Cherubini, P., Garnham, A., Oakhill, J. V., & Morley, E. (1998). Can an ostrich fly? New data on belief bias in syllogistic reasoning. *Cognition, 69,* 179–218.

Chi, M. T. H. (1978). Knowledge structure and memory development. In R. Siegler (Ed.), *Children's thinking: What develops* (pp. 73–96). Hillsdale, NJ: Erlbaum.

Chi, M. T. H., Feltovich, P. J., & Glaser, R. (1981). Categorization and representation of physics problems by experts and novices. *Cognitive Science, 5,* 121–152.

Chi, M. T. H., Glaser, R., & Farr, M. J. (Eds.). (1988). *The nature of expertise.* Hillsdale, NJ: Erlbaum.

Chiesi, H. L., Spilich, G. J., & Voss, J. F. (1979). Acquisition of domain-related information in relation to high and low domain knowledge. *Journal of Verbal Learning and Verbal Behavior, 18,* 257–273.

Chomsky, N. (1959). Review of verbal behavior. *Language, 35,* 26–58.

Chomsky, N. (1980). *Rules and representation.* Oxford, England: Blackwell.

Chow, S. L. (1986). Iconic memory, location information, and partial report. *Journal of Experimental Psychology: Human Perception and Performance, 12,* 455–465.

Chow, S. L. (1991). Partial report: Iconic store or two buffers? *Journal of General Psychology, 118,* 147–169.

Chui, H. C., & Damasio, A. R. (1980). Human cerebral asymmetries evaluated by computed tomography. *Journal of Neurology, Neurosurgery, and Psychiatry, 43,* 873–878.

Cioffi, J., & Markham, R. (1997). Clinical decision making by midwives: Managing case complexity. *Journal of Advanced Nursing, 25,* 265–272.

Clahsen, H., Aveledo, F., & Roca, I. (2002). The development of regular and irregular verb inflection in Spanish child language. *Journal of Child Language, 29,* 591–622.

Clark, E. V. (1970). How children describe events in time. In G. B. Flores d'Arcais & W. J. M. Levelt (Eds.),

Advances in psycholinguistics (pp. 275–284). Amsterdam: North-Holland.

Clark, E. V. (1971). On the acquisition of the meaning of *before* and *after*. *Journal of Verbal Learning and Verbal Behavior, 10,* 266–275.

Clark, E. V. (1987). The principle of contrast: A constraint on language acquisition. In B. MacWhinney (Ed.), *Mechanisms of language acquisition* (pp. 1–33). Hillsdale, NJ: Erlbaum.

Clark, H. H. (1969). Linguistic processes in deductive reasoning. *Psychological Review, 76,* 387–404.

Clark, H. H., & Card, S. K. (1969). Role of semantics in remembering comparative sentences. *Journal of Experimental Psychology, 82,* 545–553.

Clark, H. H., & Chase, W. G. (1972). On the process of comparing sentences against pictures. *Cognitive Psychology, 3,* 472–517.

Clark, H. H., & Clark, E. V. (1977). *Psychology and language.* New York: Harcourt.

Clark, H. H., & Haviland, S. E. (1977). Comprehension and the given–new contract. In R. O. Freedle (Ed.), *Discourse production and comprehension* (pp. 1–40). Norwood, NJ: Ablex.

Clark, R. D. (2005). An examination of the "hot hand" in professional golfers. *Perceptual and Motor Skills, 101,* 935–942.

Clifton, C., Staub, A., & Rayner, K. (2007). Eye movements in reading words and sentences. In R. P. Van Gompel, M. Fischer, W. S. Murray, & R. L. Hill (Eds.), *Eye movements: A window on mind and brain* (pp. 341–371). Amsterdam: Elsevier.

Cocchini, G., Logie, R. H., Della Sala, S., MacPherson, S. E., & Baddeley, A. D. (2002). Concurrent performance of two memory tasks: Evidence for domain-specific working memory systems. *Memory & Cognition, 30,* 1086–1095.

Code, C. (1987). *Language, aphasia, and the right hemisphere.* New York: Wiley.

Cohen, A., & Shoup, R. (1997). Perceptual dimensional constraints on response selection processes. *Cognitive Psychology, 32,* 128–181.

Cohen, J. D., Dunbar, K., & McClelland, J. L. (1990). Automaticity, attention, and the strength of processing: A parallel distributed processing account of the Stroop effect. *Psychological Review, 97,* 332–361.

Cohen, M. R., & Nagel, E. (1934). *An introduction to logic and scientific method.* New York: Harcourt, Brace.

Cole, M., & Scribner, S. (1974). *Culture and thought: A psychological introduction.* New York: Wiley.

Colle, H. A., & Welsh, A. (1976). Acoustic masking in primary memory. *Journal of Verbal Learning and Verbal Behavior, 15,* 17–32.

Collins, A. M. (1978). Fragments of a theory of human plausible reasoning. In D. Waltz (Ed.), *Proceedings of the Conference on Theoretical Issues in Natural Language Processing, 2,* 194–201.

Collins, A. M., & Loftus, E. F. (1975). A spreading-activation theory of semantic processing. *Psychological Review, 82,* 407–428.

Collins, A. M., & Michalski, R. (1989). The logic of plausible reasoning: A core theory. *Cognitive Science, 13,* 1–49.

Collins, A. M., & Quillian, M. R. (1969). Retrieval time from semantic memory. *Journal of Verbal Learning and Verbal Behavior, 8,* 240–247.

Collins, A. M., & Quillian, M. R. (1970). Facilitating retrieval from semantic memory: The effect of repeating part of an inference. *Acta Psychologica, 33,* 304–314.

Collins, A. M., & Quillian, M. R. (1972). Experiments on semantic memory and language comprehension. In L. W. Gregg (Ed.), *Cognition in learning and memory* (pp. 240–247). New York: Wiley.

Collins, A. M., Warnock, E. H., Aiello, N., & Miller, M. L. (1975). Reasoning from incomplete knowledge. In D. G. Bobrow & A. M. Collins (Eds.), *Representation and understanding: Studies in cognitive science* (pp. 383–415). New York: Academic Press.

Collins, N. L., & Miller, L. C. (1994). Self-disclosure and liking: A meta-analytic review. *Psychological Review, 116,* 457–475.

Coltheart, M. (1980). Iconic memory and visible persistence. *Perception & Psychophysics, 27,* 183–228.

Coltheart, M. (1987). *The cognitive neuropsychology of language*. London: Erlbaum.

Coltheart, M., & Glick, M. J. (1974). Visual imagery: A case study. *Quarterly Journal of Experimental Psychology, 26,* 438–453.

Coltheart, M., Rastle, K., Perry, C., Langdon, R., & Ziegler, J. (2001). DRC: A dual route cascaded model of visual word recognition and reading aloud. *Psychological Review, 108,* 204–256.

Combs, B., & Slovic, P. (1979). Causes of death: Biased newspaper coverage and biased judgments. *Journalism Quarterly, 56,* 837–843, 849.

Conrad, R., & Hull, A. J. (1964). Information, acoustic confusion, and memory span. *British Journal of Psychology, 55,* 429–432.

Console, L., & Torasso, P. (1990). Hypothetical reasoning in causal models. *International Journal of Intelligent Systems, 5,* 83–124.

Conway, A. R., Kane, M. J., & Engle, R. W. (2003). Working memory capacity and its relation to general intelligence. *Trends in Cognitive Sciences, 7,* 547–552.

Conway, M. A., Wang, Q., Hanyu, K., & Hague, S. (2005). A cross-cultural investigation of autobiographical memory: On the universality and cultural variation of the reminiscence bump. *Journal of Cross-Cultural Research, 36,* 739–749.

Cooke, N. J., Atlas, R. S., Lane, D. M., & Berger, R. C. (1993). Role of high-level knowledge in memory for chess positions. *American Journal of Psychology, 106,* 321–351.

Cooper, J. O., Heron, T. E., & Howard, W. L. (1987). *Applied behavior analysis*. Columbus, OH: Merrill.

Cooper, L. A. (1995). Varieties of visual representation: How are we to analyze the concept of mental image? *Neuropsychologia, 33,* 1575–1582.

Cooper, L. A., & Shepard, R. N. (1973). Chronometric studies of the rotation of mental images. In W. G. Chase (Ed.), *Visual information processing* (pp. 75–176). Oxford, England: Academic Press.

Cooper, R. P., & Aslin, R. N. (1990). Preference for infant-directed speech in the first month after birth. *Child Development, 61,* 1584–1595.

Corballis, M. C. (2002). *From hand to mouth: The origins of language*. Princeton, NJ: Princeton University Press.

Corballis, M. C., & Sergent, J. (1988). Imagery in a commissurotomized patient. *Neuropsychologia, 26,* 13–26.

Corballis, M. C., & Sergent, J. (1989). Hemispheric specialization for mental rotation. *Cortex, 25,* 15–25.

Corballis, M. C., & Sergent, J. (1992). Judgments about numerosity by a commissurotomized subject. *Neuropsychologia, 30,* 865–876.

Corcoran, D. W., Dorfman, D. D., & Weening, D. L. (1968). Perceptual independence in the perception of speech. *Quarterly Journal of Experimental Psychology, 20,* 336–350.

Corkin, S., Amaral, D. G., Gonzalez, R. G., Johnson, K. A., & Hyman, B. T. (1997). HM's medial temporal lobe lesion: Findings from magnetic resonance imaging. *The Journal of Neuroscience, 17,* 3964–3979.

Cornoldi, C., & De Beni, R. (1991). Memory for discourse: Loci mnemonics and the oral presentation effect. *Applied Cognitive Psychology, 5,* 511–518.

Corteen, R. S., & Wood, B. (1972). Autonomic responses to shock-associated words in an unattended channel. *Journal of Experimental Psychology, 94,* 308–313.

Cosmides, L. (1989). The logic of social exchange: Has natural selection shaped how humans reason? Studies with the Wason selection task. *Cognition, 31,* 187–276.

Cosmides, L., Barrett, H. C., & Tooby, J. (2010). Adaptive specializations, social exchange, and the evolution of human intelligence. *Proceedings of the National Academy of Sciences, 107,* 9007–9014.

Cosmides, L., & Tooby, J. (1996). Are humans good intuitive statisticians after all? Rethinking some conclusions from the literature on judgment under uncertainty. *Cognition, 58,* 1–73.

Cosmides, L., & Tooby, J. (1997). Dissecting the computational architecture of social inference mechanisms. In G. Bock & G. Cardew (Eds.), *Characterizing human psychological adaptations*

(Ciba Foundation Symposium No. 208; pp. 132–161). Chichester, England: Wiley.

Courtney, S. M., Ungerleider, L. G., Keil, K., & Haxby, J. V. (1997). Object and spatial visual working memory activate separate neural systems in human cortex. *Cerebral Cortex, 6,* 39–49.

Craik, F. I. M. (1970). The fate of primary items in free recall. *Journal of Verbal Learning and Verbal Behavior, 9,* 143–148.

Craik, F. I. M. (2002). Levels of processing: Past, present . . . and future? *Memory, 10,* 305–318.

Craik, F. I. M., & Lockhart, R. (1972). Levels of processing: A framework for memory research. *Journal of Verbal Learning and Verbal Behavior, 11,* 671–684.

Craik, F. I. M., & Salthouse, T. A. (Eds.). (1992). *Handbook of aging and cognition.* Hillsdale, NJ: Erlbaum.

Cress, C. J., & King, J. M. (1999). AAC strategies for people with primary progressive aphasia without dementia: Two case studies. *AAC: Augmentative & Alternative Communication, 15,* 248–259.

Cromer, R. (1994). A case study of dissociations between language and cognition. In H. Tager-Flusberg (Ed.), *Constraints on language acquisition: Studies of atypical children* (pp. 141–153). Hillsdale, NJ: Erlbaum.

Croson, R., & Sundali, J. (2005). The gambler's fallacy and the hot hand: Empirical data from casinos. *Journal of Risk and Uncertainty, 30,* 195–209.

Cross, I. (2009). Communicative development: Neonate crying reflects patterns of native language speech. *Current Biology, 19,* R1078–R1079.

Crovitz, H. F. (1971). The capacity of memory loci in artificial memory. *Psychonomic Science, 24,* 187–188.

Crovitz, H. F., & Daniel, W. F. (1984). Measurements of everyday memory: Toward the prevention of forgetting. *Bulletin of the Psychonomic Society, 22,* 413–414.

Crovitz, H. F., & Shiffman, H. (1974). Frequency of episodic memories as a function of their age. *Bulletin of the Psychonomic Society, 4,* 517–518.

Crowder, R. G. (1989). Imagery for musical timbre. *Journal of Experimental Psychology: Human Perception and Performance, 15,* 472–478.

Crowder, R. G. (1992). Eidetic imagery. In L. R. Squire (Ed.), *Encyclopedia of learning and memory* (pp. 154–157). New York: Macmillan.

Crowder, R. G., & Morton, J. (1969). Precategorical acoustic storage (PAS). *Perception & Psychophysics, 5,* 365–373.

Crowder, R. G., & Wagner, R. K. (1992). *The psychology of reading: An introduction* (2nd ed.). Oxford, England: Oxford University Press.

Cullum, S., Huppert, F., McGee, M., Dening, T., Ahmed, A., Paykel, E. S., & Brayne, C. (2000). Decline across different domains of cognitive function in normal ageing: Results of a longitudinal population-based study using CAMCOG. *International Journal of Geriatric Psychiatry, 15,* 853–862.

Cummins, D. D. (1996). Evidence of deontic reasoning in 3- and 4-year-old children. *Memory & Cognition, 24,* 823–829.

Cummins, R., & Cummins, D. D. (Eds.). (2000). *Minds, brains, and computers.* Malden, MA: Blackwell.

Curtis, H. S. (1899/1900). Automatic movements of the larynx. *American Journal of Psychology, 11,* 237–239.

Curtiss, S. (1977). *Genie: A psycholinguistic study of a modern-day "wild child."* New York: Academic Press.

Damasio, A. R. (1985a). Disorders of complex visual processing: Agnosia, achromatopsia, Bálint's syndrome, and related difficulties of orientation and construction. In M. M. Mesulam (Ed.), *Principles of behavioral neurology* (pp. 259–288). Philadelphia: Davis.

Damasio, A. R. (1985b). Prosopagnosia. *Trends in Neurosciences, 8,* 132–135.

Damasio, A. R. (1989). The brain binds entities and events by multiregional activation from convergence zones. *Neural Computation, 1,* 123–132.

Damasio, H., & Damasio, A. R. (1980). The anatomical basis of conduction aphasia. *Brain, 103,* 337–350.

Damasio, H., Grabowski, T., Frank, R., Galaburda, A. M., & Damasio, A. R. (1994). The return of Phineas Gage: Clues about the brain from the skull of a famous patient. *Science, 264,* 1102–1105.

Daneman, M., & Carpenter, P. A. (1980). Individual differences in working memory and reading. *Journal of Verbal Learning and Verbal Behavior, 19,* 450–466.

Daneman, M., & Carpenter, P. A. (1983). Individual differences in integrating information between and within sentences. *Journal of Experimental Psychology: Learning, Memory, and Cognition, 9,* 561–584.

Daneman, M., & Green, I. (1986). Individual differences in comprehending and producing words in context. *Journal of Memory and Language, 25,* 1–18.

Daneman, M., & Hannon, B. (2007). What do working memory span tasks like reading span really measure? In N. Osaka, R. H. Logie, & M. D'Esposito (Eds.), *The cognitive neuroscience of working memory* (pp. 21–42). Oxford, England: Oxford University Press.

Daneman, M., & Merikle, P. M. (1996). Working memory and language comprehension: A meta-analysis. *Psychonomic Bulletin & Review, 3,* 422–433.

Das, J. P., & Mishra, R. K. (1991). Relation between memory span, naming time, speech rate, and reading competence. *Journal of Experimental Education, 59,* 129–139.

Davidson, D. (1996). The role of schemata in children's memory. In H. W. Reese (Ed.), *Advances in child development and behavior* (Vol. 26, pp. 35–58). San Diego, CA: Academic Press.

Davidson, J. E. (1995). The suddenness of insight. In R. J. Sternberg & J. E. Davidson (Eds.), *The nature of insight* (pp. 125–155). Cambridge, MA: MIT Press.

Davis, Z. T. (1994). Effects of prereading story mapping on elementary readers' comprehension. *Journal of Educational Research, 87,* 353–360.

Dawes, R. M. (1964). Cognitive distortion. *Psychological Reports, 14,* 443–459.

Dawes, R. M. (1986). Representative thinking in clinical judgment. *Clinical Psychology Review, 6,* 425–441.

De Beni, R., & Cornoldi, C. (1985). Effects of the mnemotechnique of loci in the memorization of concrete words. *Acta Psychologica, 60,* 11–24.

De Beni, R., & Cornoldi, C. (1997). Learning from texts or lectures: Loci mnemonics can interfere with reading but not with listening. *European Journal of Cognitive Psychology, 9,* 401–415.

DeCasper, A. J., & Fifer, W. P. (1980). Of human bonding: Newborns prefer their mothers' voices. *Science, 208,* 1174–1176.

DeCasper, A. J., & Spence, M. J. (1986). Prenatal maternal speech influences newborns' perception of speech sounds. *Infant Behavior & Development, 9,* 133–150.

Deese, J. (1959). On the prediction of occurrence of particular verbal intrusions in immediate recall. *Journal of Experimental Psychology, 58,* 17–22.

de Gelder, B., Bachoud-Levi, A. C., & Degos, J. D. (1998). Inversion superiority in visual agnosia may be common to a variety of orientation polarized objects besides faces. *Vision Research, 38,* 2855–2861.

Demb, J. B., Boynton, G. M., & Heeger, D. J. (1997). Brain activity in visual cortex predicts individual differences in reading performance. *Science, 94,* 13363–13366.

Dempster, F. N. (1981). Memory span: Sources of individual and developmental differences. *Psychological Bulletin, 89,* 63–100.

De Neys, W. (2006). Dual processing in reasoning: Two systems but one reasoner. *Psychological Science, 17,* 428–433.

De Neys, W., & Schaeken, W. (2007). When people are more logical under cognitive load. *Experimental Psychology, 54,* 128–133.

De Neys, W., Vartanian, O., & Goel, V. (2008). Smarter than we think: When our brains detect that we are biased. *Psychological Science, 19,* 483–489.

De Neys, W., & Vershueren, N. (2006). Working memory capacity and a notorious brain teaser: The case of the Monty Hall dilemma. *Experimental Psychology, 53,* 123–131.

Denis, M., & Whitaker, H. (1976). Language acquisition following hemidecortication: Linguistic superiority of the left over the right hemisphere. *Brain and Language, 3,* 404–433.

De Renzi, E. (2000). Prosopagnosia. In M. J. Farah & T. E. Feinberg (Eds.), *Patient-based approaches to cognitive neuroscience: Issues in clinical and cognitive neuropsychology* (pp. 85–96). Cambridge, MA: MIT Press.

De Renzi, E., & Vignolo, L. (1962). The Token Test: A sensitive test to detect disturbances in aphasics. *Brain, 85,* 655–678.

Descartes, R. (1989). *The passions of the soul* (S. Voss, Trans.). Indianapolis, IN: Hackett Publishing. (Original work published 1649)

DeSoto, C. G., London, M., & Handel, S. (1965). Social reasoning and spatial paralogic. *Journal of Personality and Social Psychology, 2,* 513–521.

D'Esposito, M., Detre, J. A., Alsop, D. C., & Shin, R. K. (1995). The neural basis of the central executive system of working memory. *Nature, 378,* 279–281.

D'Esposito, M., Onishi, K., Thompson, H., Robinson, K., Armstrong, C., & Grossman, M. (1996). Working memory impairments in multiple sclerosis: Evidence from a dual-task paradigm. *Neuropsychology, 10,* 51–56.

Dethier, V. G. (1987). Sniff, flick, and pulse: An appreciation of interruption. *Proceedings of the American Philosophical Society, 131,* 159–176.

Deutsch, J. A., & Deutsch, D. (1963). Attention: Some theoretical considerations. *Psychological Review, 70,* 80–90.

de Villiers, P. A., & de Villiers, J. G. (1972). Early judgments of semantic and syntactic acceptability by children. *Journal of Psycholinguistic Research, 1,* 299–310.

Dewhurst, S. A., & Robinson, C. A. (2004). False memories in children: Evidence for a shift from phonological to semantic associations. *Psychological Science, 15,* 782–786.

Diamond, R., & Carey, S. (1986). Why faces are not special: An effect of expertise. *Journal of Experimental Psychology, 114,* 107–117.

Dieussaert, K., Schaecken, W., Schroyens, W., & d'Ydewalle, G. (1999). Strategies for dealing with complex deductive problems: Combining and dividing. *Psychologica Belgica, 34,* 215–234.

Dijksterhuis, A. (2004). Think different: The merits of unconscious thought in preference development and decision making. *Journal of Personality and Social Psychology, 87,* 586–598.

Dijksterhuis, A., Bos, M. W., Nordgren, L. F., & van Baaren, R. B. (2006). On making the right choice: The deliberation-without-attention effect. *Science, 311,* 1005–1007.

Dijksterhuis, A., & Nordgren, L. F. (2006). A theory of unconscious thought. *Perspectives on Psychological Science, 1, 95–109.*

Dijksterhuis, A., & van Olden, Z. (2006). On the benefits of thinking unconsciously: Unconscious thought can increase post-choice satisfaction. *Journal of Experimental Social Psychology, 42,* 627–631.

DiPietro, J. A., Hodgson, D. M., Costigan, K. A., Hilton, S. C., & Johnson, T. R. B. (1996). Fetal neurobehavioral development. *Child Development, 67,* 2553–2567.

Dolk, H., Busby, A., Armstrong, B. G., & Walls, P. H. (1998). Geographical variation in anopthalmia and microphthalmia in English, 1988–1994. *British Medical Journal, 317,* 905–910.

Donaldson, M., & Balfour, G. (1968). Less is more: A study of language comprehension in children. *British Journal of Psychology, 59,* 461–472.

Donders, F. C. (1969). On the speed of mental processes (W. G. Koster, Trans.). *Acta Psychologica, 30,* 412–431. (Original work published 1868)

Dooling, D. J., & Christiaansen, R. E. (1977). Levels of encoding and retention of prose. In G. H. Bower (Ed.), *The psychology of learning and motivation* (Vol. 11, pp. 1–39). New York: Academic Press.

Down, J. L. H. (1886). Observations on an ethnic classification of idiots. *London Hospital Reports, 3,* 259–262.

Doyle, A. C. (2007). *The treasury of Sherlock Holmes: 7 in 1 omnibus edition*. Radford, VA: Wilder. (Original work published 1892)

Dreisbach, G., & Goschke, T. (2004). How positive affect modulates cognitive control: Reduced perseveration at the cost of increased distractibility. *Journal of Experimental Psychology: Learning, Memory, and Cognition, 30*, 243–253.

Dreistadt, R. (1968). An analysis of the use of analogies and metaphors in science. *Journal of Psychology, 68*, 97–116.

Dretzke, B. J. (1993). Effects of pictorial mnemonic strategy usage on prose recall of young, middle-aged, and older adults. *Educational Gerontology, 19*, 489–502.

Drevenstedt, J., & Bellezza, F. S. (1993). Memory for self-generated narration in the elderly. *Psychology and Aging, 8*, 187–196.

Driskell, J. E., Copper, C., & Moran, A. (1994). Does mental practice enhance performance? *Journal of Applied Psychology, 79*, 481–492.

Driver, J., & Mattingley, J. B. (1998). Parietal neglect and visual awareness. *Nature Neuroscience, 1*, 17–22.

Dronkers, N. F., Plaisant, O., Iba-Zizen, M. T., & Cabanis, E. A. (2007). Paul Broca's historic cases: High resolution MRI imaging of the brains of Leborgne and Lelong. *Brain, 130*, 1432–1441.

Dubois, B., Defontaines, B., Deweer, B., Malapani, C., & Pillon, B. (1995). Cognitive and behavioral changes in patients with focal lesions of the basal ganglia: Behavioral neurology of movement disorders. In W. J. William & A. D. Lang (Eds.), *Advances in neurology* (Vol. 65, pp. 29–41). New York: Raven Press.

Duchaine, B., & Nakayama, K. (2005). Dissociations of face and object recognition in developmental prosopagnosia. *Journal of Cognitive Neuroscience, 17*, 249–261.

Dudeney, H. E. (1924, July). Puzzles. *Strand Magazine, 68*, 97, 124.

Duffy, J. R., & Petersen, R. C. (1992). Primary progressive aphasia. *Aphasiology, 6*, 1–16.

Dunbar, K. (1997). How scientists think: On-line creativity and conceptual change in science. In T. B. Ward, S. M. Smith, & J. Vaid (Eds.), *Conceptual structures and processes: Emergence, discovery, and change* (pp. 461–493). Washington, DC: American Psychological Association.

Dunbar, K. & Blanchette, I. (2001). The invivo/invitro approach to cognition: The case of analogy. *Trends in Cognitive Sciences, 5*, 334–339.

Dunbar, K., & MacLeod, C. M. (1984). A horse race of a different color: Stroop interference patterns with transformed words. *Journal of Experimental Psychology: Human Perception and Performance, 10*, 622–639.

Duncker, K. (1945). On problem solving. *Psychological Monographs, 58*(5, Whole No. 270).

Ebbinghaus, H. (1913). *Memory* (H. A. Ruger & C. E. Busenius, Trans.). New York: Teachers College Press. (Original work published 1885)

Edmondson, A. C. (2003). Speaking up in the operating room: How team leaders promote learning in interdisciplinary action teams. *Journal of Management Studies, 40*, 1419–1452.

Edwards, W. (1954). The theory of decision making. *Psychological Bulletin, 51*, 380–417.

Edwards, W. (1961). Probability learning in 1,000 trials. *Journal of Experimental Psychology, 62*, 385–394.

Egan, D. E., & Schwartz, B. J. (1979). Chunking in the recall of symbolic drawings. *Memory & Cognition, 7*, 149–158.

Egan, P., Carterette, E. C., & Thwing, E. J. (1954). Some factors affecting multichannel listening. *Journal of the Acoustic Society of America, 26*, 774–782.

Eichenbaum, H., Otto, T., & Cohen, N. J. (1994). Two functional components of the hippocampal memory system. *Behavioral and Brain Sciences, 17*, 449–517.

Einstein, G. O., & McDaniel, M. A. (1990). Normal aging and prospective memory. *Journal of Experimental Psychology: Learning, Memory, and Cognition, 16*, 717–726.

Einstein, G. O., McDaniel, M. A., Richardson, S. L., Guynn, M. J., & Cunfer, A. R. (1995). Aging and prospective memory: Examining the influence of self-initiated retrieval processes. *Journal of Experimental Psychology: Learning, Memory, and Cognition, 21,* 996–1007.

Eisenstadt, M., & Kareev, Y. (1975). Aspects of human problem solving: The use of internal representation. In D. A. Norman & D. E. Rumelhart (Eds.), *Explorations in cognition* (pp. 551–564). San Francisco: W. H. Freeman and Company.

Ellis, A. W., & Young, A. W. (1989). Face processing in A. W. Ellis & A. W. Young (Eds.), *Human cognitive neuropsychology: A textbook with readings* (pp. 87–111). London: Psychology Press.

Ellis, H. D. (1975). Recognizing faces. *British Journal of Psychology, 66,* 409–426.

Ellis, N. C., & Hennelly, R. A. (1980). A bilingual word-length effect: Implications for intelligence testing and the relative ease of mental calculations in Welsh and English. *British Journal of Psychology, 7,* 43–51.

Emerson, R. W. (1876). *Letters and social aims*. Boston: James R. Osgood & Co.

Emmorey, K. (1999). Do signers gesture? In L. Messing & R. Campbell (Eds.), *Gesture, speech, and sign* (pp. 133–159). New York: Oxford University Press.

Emmorey, K., Klima, E., & Hickok, G. (1998). Mental rotation within linguistic and nonlinguistic domains in users of American Sign Language. *Cognition, 68,* 221–246.

Enns, J. T., & Di Lollo, V. (2000). What's new in visual masking? *Trends in Cognitive Sciences, 4,* 345–352.

Erez, A., & Isen, A. M. (2002). The influence of positive affect on the components of expectancy motivation. *Journal of Applied Psychology, 87,* 1055–1067.

Erickson, J. R. (1978). Research on syllogistic reasoning. In R. Revlin & R. Mayer (Eds.), *Human reasoning* (pp. 39–50). Washington, DC: Winston.

Erickson, J. R., & Allred, S. (2001). A model of repetition priming for lexical decisions. In D. S. Gorfein

(Ed.), *On the consequences of meaning selection: Perspectives on resolving lexical ambiguity. Decade of behavior* (pp. 191–214). Washington, DC: American Psychological Association.

Ericsson, K. A. (1988). Analysis of memory performance in terms of memory skill. In R. S. Sternberg (Ed.), *Advances in the psychology of human intelligence* (Vol. 4, pp. 137–179). Hillsdale, NJ: Erlbaum.

Ericsson, K. A., & Kintsch, W. (1995). Long-term working memory. *Psychological Review, 102,* 211–245.

Ericsson, K. A., & Polson, P. G. (1988). An experimental analysis of the mechanisms of a memory skill. *Journal of Experimental Psychology: Learning, Memory, and Cognition, 14,* 305–316.

Ericsson, K. A., & Simon, H. A. (1993). *Protocol analysis: Verbal reports as data* (2nd ed.) Cambridge, MA: MIT Press.

Eriksen, B. A., & Eriksen, C. W. (1974). Effects of noise letters upon the identification of a target letter in a nonsearch task. *Perception & Psychophysics, 16,* 143–149.

Eriksen, C. W., & Yeh, Y. (1985). Allocation of attention in the visual field. *Journal of Experimental Psychology: Human Perception and Performance, 11,* 583–597.

Erikson, T. A., & Mattson, M. E. (1981). From words to meaning: A semantic illusion. *Journal of Verbal Learning and Verbal Behavior, 20,* 540–552.

Erlanger, E. M., Kutner, K. C., Barth, J. T., & Barnes, R. (1999). Neuropsychology of sports-related head injury: Dementia pugilistica to post-concussion syndrome. *The Clinical Neuropsychologist, 13,* 193–209.

Ernst, G., & Newell, A. (1969). *GPS: A case study in generality and problem solving*. New York: Academic Press.

Ervin-Tripp, S., Guo, J., & Lambert, M. (1990). Politeness and persuasion in children's control acts. *Journal of Pragmatics, 14,* 307–331.

Euler, L. (1775). *Lettres à une princesse d'Allemagne sur divers sujets de physique et de philosophie [Letters to a German princess on various subjects of physics and philosophy]*. Berne, Switzerland: Société Typographique.

Evans, J. St. B. (1980). Current issues in the psychology of reasoning. *British Journal of Psychology, 71,* 227–239.

Evans, J. St. B. (1989). *Bias in human reasoning: Causes and consequences*. Hillsdale, NJ: Erlbaum.

Evans, J. St. B. (2003). In two minds: Dual-process accounts of reasoning. *Trends in Cognitive Sciences, 7,* 454–458.

Evans, J. St. B. (2008). Dual-processing accounts of reasoning, judgment, and social cognition. *Annual Review of Psychology, 59,* 255–278.

Evans, J. St. B., Handley, S. J., & Harper, C. N. J. (2001). Necessity, possibility, and belief: A study of syllogistic reasoning. *Quarterly Journal of Experimental Psychology: Human Experimental Psychology, 54A,* 935–958.

Evans, J. St. B., Newstead, S. E., & Byrne, R. M. J. (1993). *Human reasoning: The psychology of deduction*. Hove, England: Erlbaum.

Everhart, D. E., Shucard, J. L., Quatrin, T., & Shucard, D. W. (2001). Sex-related differences in event-related potentials, face recognition, and facial affect processing in prepubertal children. *Neuropsychology, 15,* 329–341.

Faglioni, P., Saetti, M. C., & Botti, C. (2000). Verbal learning strategies in Parkinson's disease. *Neuropsychology, 14,* 456–470.

Falk, R., & Konold, C. (1997). Making sense of randomness: Implicit encoding as a basis for judgment. *Psychological Review, 104,* 301–318.

Fantz, R. L. (1963). Pattern vision in newborn infants. *Science, 140,* 296–297.

Farah, M. J. (1988). Is visual imagery really visual? Overlooked evidence from neuropsychology. *Psychological Review, 85,* 307–317.

Farah, M. J. (1990). *Visual agnosia: Disorders of object recognition and what they tell us about normal vision*. Cambridge, MA: MIT Press.

Farah, M. J., Hammond, K. M., Levine, D. N., & Calvanio, R. (1988). Visual and spatial mental imagery: Dissociable systems of representation. *Cognitive Psychology, 20,* 439–462.

Farah, M. J., Levine, D. N., & Calvanio, R. (1988). A case study of mental imagery deficit. *Brain and Cognition, 8,* 147–164.

Farah, M. J., Wilson, K. D., Drain, H. M., & Tanaka, J. R. (1998). What is "special" about face perception? *Psychological Review, 105,* 482–498.

Farris, H. H., & Revlin, R. (1989a). The discovery process: A counterfactual strategy. *Social Studies of Science, 19,* 497–513.

Farris, H. H., & Revlin, R. (1989b). Sensible reasoning in two tasks: Rule discovery and hypothesis evaluation. *Memory & Cognition, 17,* 221–232.

Faust, M., Dimitrovsky, L., & Davidi, S. (1997). Naming difficulties in language-disabled children: Preliminary findings with the application of the tip-of-the-tongue paradigm. *Journal of Speech, Language, and Hearing Research, 40,* 1037–1047.

Feather, N. (1965). Acceptance and rejection of arguments in relation to attitude strength, critical ability, and intolerance of inconsistency. *Journal of Abnormal and Social Psychology, 69,* 127–136.

Feltz, D. L., & Landers, D. M. (1983). The effects of mental practice on motor skill learning and performance: A meta-analysis. *Journal of Sport Psychology, 5,* 25–57.

Ferber, S., & Karnath, H.-O. (2001). Size perception in hemianopia and neglect. *Brain, 124,* 527–536.

Fernald, A. (1989). Intonation and communicative intent in mother's speech to infants: Is melody the message? *Child Development, 60,* 1497–1510.

Fernald, A., Taeschner, T., Dunn, J., Pepousek, M., Boysson-Bardies, B., & Fukui, I. (1989). A cross-language study of prosodic modifications in mothers' and fathers' speech to preverbal infants. *Journal of Child Language, 1,* 477–501.

Fernandez-Duque, D., & Johnson, M. L. (1999). Attention metaphors: How metaphors guide the cognitive psychology of attention. *Cognitive Science, 23,* 83–116.

Ferraro, F. R., & Balota, D. A. (1999). Memory scanning performance in healthy young adults, healthy older adults, and individuals with dementia of the Alzheimer type. *Aging, Neuropsychology, and Cognition, 6,* 260–272.

Ferreira, F., Christianson, K., & Hollingworth, A. (2001). Misinterpretations of garden-path sentences: Implications for models of sentence processing and reanalysis. *Journal of Psychliinguistic Research, 30,* 3–20.

Fiddick, L., Cosmides, L., & Tooby, J. (2000). No interpretation without representation: The role of domain-specific representations in the Wason selection task. *Cognition, 77,* 1–79.

Fillenbaum, S. (1966). Memory for gist: Some relevant variables. *Language and Speech, 9,* 217–227.

Fillenbaum, S. (1974). Information amplified: Memory for counterfactual conditionals. *Journal of Experimental Psychology, 102,* 44–49.

Fillmore, C. (1968). The case for case. In E. Bach & R. Harms (Eds.), *Universals in linguistic theory* (pp. 1–87). New York: Holt, Rinehart and Winston.

Finger, S., & Clower, T. W. (2003). On the birth of trepanation: The thoughts of Paul Broca and Victor Horsley. In R. Arnott, S. Finger, & C. Smith (Eds.), *Trepanation: History, discovery, theory* (pp. 19–42). Lisse, the Netherlands: Swets & Zeitlinger.

Finke, R. A., & Pinker, S. (1982). Spontaneous imagery scanning in mental extrapolation. *Journal of Experimental Psychology: Learning, Memory, and Cognition, 8,* 142–147.

Fisher, R. P., & Geiselman, R. E. (1992). *Memory enhancing techniques for investigative interviewing: The cognitive interview*. Springfield, IL: Charles C Thomas.

Fisher, R. P., Geiselman, R. E., & Amador, M. (1989). Field test of the cognitive interview: Enhancing the recollection of actual victims and witnesses of crime. *Journal of Applied Psychology, 74,* 722–727.

Fiske, S. T., & Linville, P. W. (1980). What does the schema concept buy us? *Personality and Social Psychology Bulletin, 6,* 543–557.

Fitts, P. M. (1947). *Psychological research on equipment design* (Research Report No. 19). Washington, DC: U.S. Army Air Forces Aviation Psychology Program.

Fitzgerald, J. M. (1988). Vivid memories and the reminiscence phenomenon: The role of the self-narrative. *Human Development, 31,* 260–270.

Fitzgerald, J. M. (1996). The distribution of self-narrative memories in younger and older adults: Elaborating the self-narrative hypothesis. *Aging, Neuropsychology, and Cognition, 3,* 229–236.

Fleet, W. S., Valenstein, E., Watson, R. T., & Heilman, K. M. (1987). Dopamine agonist therapy for neglect in humans. *Neurology, 37,* 1765–1770.

Fleming, P., Ball, L. J., Collins, A. F., & Ormerod, T. C. (2004). Spatial representation and processing in the congenitally blind. In S. Ballesteros & M. A. Heller (Eds.), *Touch, blindness, and neuroscience*. Madrid: UNED Press.

Fodor, J. A. (1983). *Modularity of mind: An essay on faculty psychology*. Cambridge, MA: MIT Press.

Foldi, N. S., Cicone, M., & Gardner, H. (1983). Pragmatic aspects of communication in brain damaged patients. In S. J. Segalowitz (Ed.), *Language functions and brain organization* (pp. 51–86). New York: Academic Press.

Foot, P. (1978). The problem of abortion and the doctrine of the double effect. In P. Foot (Ed.), *Virtues and vices* (pp. 19–32). Oxford, England: Blackwell.

Fox, M. D., Snyder, A. Z., Vincent, J. L., Corbetta, M., Van Essen, D. C., & Raichle, M. E. (2005). The human brain is intrinsically organized into dynamic, anticorrelated functional networks. *Proceedings of the National Academy of Sciences, USA, 102,* 9673–9678.

Franco-Watkins, A. M., Derks, P. L., & Dougherty, M. R. (2003). Reasoning in the Monty Hall problem: Examining choice behaviour and probability judgements. *Thinking & Reasoning, 9,* 67–90.

Frank, M. J. (2005). Dynamic dopamine modulation in the basal ganglia: A neurocomputational account of cognitive deficits in medicated and nonmedicated

Parkinsonism. *Journal of Cognitive Neuroscience, 17,* 51–73.

Franklin, M. S., Moore, K. S., Yip, D.-Y., Jonides, J., Rattray, K., & Moher, J. (2008). The effects of musical training on verbal memory. *Psychology of Music, 36,* 353–365.

Franssens, S., & De Neys, W. (2009). The effortless nature of conflict detection during thinking. *Thinking & Reasoning, 15,* 105–128.

Frase, L. T. (1970). Influence of sentence order and amount of higher level text processing upon reproductive memory. *American Educational Research Journal, 7,* 307–319.

Frazier, L., & Rayner, K. (1982). Making and correcting errors during sentence comprehension: Eye movements in the analysis of structurally ambiguous sentences. *Cognitive Psychology, 14,* 178–210.

French, J. W., Ekstrom, R. B., & Prince, L. A. (1963). *Kit of reference tests for cognitive factors.* Princeton, NJ: Educational Testing Service.

Freud, S. (1974). The psychopathology of everyday life. In J. Strachey (Ed. & Trans.), *The standard edition of the complete psychological works of Sigmund Freud* (Vol. 6, pp. 1–291). London: Hogarth Press. (Original work published 1901)

Fu, W.-T., Bothell, D., Douglass, S., Haimson, C., Sohn, M.-H., & Anderson, J. A. (2006). Toward a real-time model-based training system. *Interacting with Computers, 18,* 1216–1230.

Gabrieli, J. D., Cohen, N. J., & Corkin, S. (1988). The impaired learning of semantic knowledge following bilateral medial temporal lobe resection. *Brain and Cognition, 7,* 157–177.

Gaddes, W. H., & Edgell, D. (1994). *Learning disabilities and brain functions* (3rd ed.). Berlin: Springer-Verlag.

Galaburda, A. M., LeMay, M., Kemper, T. L., & Geschwind, N. (1978). Right–left asymmetries in the brain: Structural differences between the hemispheres may underlie cerebral dominance. *Science, 199,* 852–856.

Gall, F. J. (1835). *On the functions of the brain and of each of its parts: The influence of the brain on the form of the head: The difficulties and means of determining the fundamental qualities and faculties, and of discovering the seat of their organs* (W. Lewis, Trans.). Boston: Marsh, Capen & Lyon.

Gallistel, C. R., & Gelman, R. (1992). Preverbal and verbal counting and computation. *Cognition, 44,* 43–74.

Galton, F. (1883). *Inquiries into human faculty and its development.* London: Macmillan.

Galton, F. (1907). *Statistics of mental imagery* (2nd ed.). New York: Everyman's Library. (Original work published 1880)

Gardner, H. (1975). *The shattered mind: The person after brain damage.* New York: Knopf.

Gardner, R. A., & Gardner, B. T. (1969). Teaching sign language to a chimpanzee. *Science, 165,* 664–672.

Gawande, A. (1999, February 8). The cancer-cluster myth. *The New Yorker,* pp. 34–37.

Gazzaniga, M. S. (1989). Organization of the brain. *Science, 245,* 947–952.

Gazzaniga, M. S. (2005). Forty-five years of split brain research and still going strong. *Nature Reviews Neuroscience, 6,* 653–659.

Gegenfurtner, K. R., & Sperling, G. (1993). Information transfer in iconic memory experiments. *Journal of Experimental Psychology: Human Perception and Performance, 19,* 845–866.

Geisel, S. (1957). *The cat in the hat.* New York: Random House.

Geiselman, R. E., & Callot, R. (1990). Reverse versus forward order recall of script-based texts. *Applied Cognitive Psychology, 4,* 141–144.

Geiselman, R. E., & Fisher, R. P. (1997). Ten years of cognitive interviewing. In D. Payne & F. Conrad (Eds.), *Intersections in basic and applied memory research* (pp. 291–310). Mahwah, NJ: Erlbaum.

Gentner, D. (1982). Why nouns are learned before verbs: Linguistic relativity versus natural partitioning. In S. A. Kuczaj (Ed.), *Language development.*

Vol. 2: Language, thought, and culture (pp. 301–334). Hillsdale, NJ: Erlbaum.

George, A. R. (2003). *The Babylonian Gilgamesh epic.* Oxford, England: Oxford University Press.

George, M. S., Lisanby, S. H., & Sackheim, H. A. (1999). Transcranial magnetic stimulation: Applications in neuropsychiatry. *Archives of General Psychiatry, 56,* 300–311.

Geschwind, N., & Levitsky, W. (1968). Human brain: Left–right asymmetries in temporal speech region. *Science, 161,* 186–187.

Gibbs, K. W. (1989). Individual differences in cognitive skills related to reading ability in the deaf. *American Annals of the Deaf, 134,* 214–218.

Gibson, E. J. (1969). *Principles of perceptual learning and development.* New York: Appleton-Century-Crofts.

Gick, M. L., & Holyoak, K. J. (1980). Analogical problem solving. *Cognitive Psychology, 12,* 306–355.

Gick, M. L., & Holyoak, K. J. (1983). Schema induction and analogical transfer. *Cognitive Psychology, 15,* 1–38.

Gigerenzer, G. (1991). How to make cognitive illusions disappear: Beyond "heuristics and biases." *European Review of Social Psychology, 2,* 83–115.

Gigerenzer, G. (1996a). On narrow norms and vague heuristics: A reply to Kahneman and Tversky. *Psychological Review, 103,* 592–596.

Gigerenzer, G. (1996b). Why do frequency formats improve Bayesian reasoning? Cognitive algorithms work on information, which needs representation. *Behavioral and Brain Sciences, 19,* 23–24.

Gigerenzer, G., & Hoffrage, U. (1995). How to improve Bayesian reasoning without instruction: Frequency formats. *Psychological Review, 102,* 684–704.

Gigerenzer, G., & Hug, K. (1992). Domain-specific reasoning: Social contracts, cheating, and perspective change. *Cognition, 43,* 127–171.

Gigerenzer, G., Todd, P., & ABC Research Group. (1999). *Simple heuristics that make us smart.* New York: Oxford University Press.

Gill, N. F., & Dallenbach, K. M. (1926). A preliminary study of the range of attention. *American Journal of Psychology, 37,* 247–256.

Gilligan, S. G., & Bower, G. H. (1983). Reminding and mood-congruent memory. *Bulletin of the Psychonomic Society, 21,* 431–434.

Gilligan, S. G., & Bower, G. H. (1984). Cognitive consequences of emotional arousal. In C. Izard, J. Kagan, & R. Zajonc (Eds.), *Emotions, cognitions, and behavior* (pp. 547–588). New York: Cambridge University Press.

Gilovich, T. (1993). *How we know what isn't so: The fallibility of human reason in everyday life.* New York: Free Press.

Gilovich, T., Griffin, D., & Kahneman, D. (Eds.). (2002). *Heuristics and biases: The psychology of intuitive judgment.* New York: Cambridge University Press.

Gilovich, T., Vallone, R., & Tversky, A. (1985). The hot hand in basketball: On the misperception of random sequences. *Cognitive Psychology, 17,* 295–314.

Girling, D. M., Huppert, F. A., Brayne, C., Paykel, E. S., Gill, C., & Mathewson, D. (1995). Depressive symptoms in the very elderly—Their prevalence and significance. *International Journal of Geriatric Psychiatry, 10,* 497–504.

Glanzer, M., & Adams, J. K. (1990). The mirror effect in recognition memory: Data and theory. *Journal of Experimental Psychology: Learning, Memory, and Cognition, 16,* 5–16.

Glanzer, N., & Clark, W. H. (1964). The verbal loop hypothesis: Conventional figures. *American Journal of Psychology, 77,* 621–626.

Glenberg, A. M. (1997). What memory is for. *Behavioral and Brain Sciences, 10,* 1–55.

Glenberg, A. M., Smith, S. M., & Green, C. (1977). Type I rehearsal: Maintenance and more. *Journal of Verbal Learning and Verbal Behavior, 16,* 339–352.

Glucksberg, S., & McCloskey, M. (1981). Decisions about ignorance: Knowing that you don't know. *Journal of Experimental Psychology: Human Learning and Memory, 7,* 311–325.

Gobert, J. D. (1999). Expertise in the comprehension of architectural plans (knowledge acquisition and inference making). In J. S. Gero & B. Tversky (Eds.), *Visual and spatial reasoning in design* (pp. 184–205). Cambridge, MA: MIT Press.

Gobet, F. (2000). Some shortcomings of long-term working memory. *British Journal of Psychology, 91,* 551–570.

Gobet, F., Lane, P. C. R., Croker, S., Cheng, P. C. H., Jones, G., Oliver, I., & Pine, J. M. (2001). Chunking mechanisms in human learning. *Trends in Cognitive Sciences, 5,* 236–243.

Godden, D. R., & Baddeley, A. D. (1975). Context-dependent memory in two natural environments: On land and underwater. *British Journal of Psychology, 66,* 325–331.

Goel, V. (1992). A comparison of well-structured and ill-structured task environments and problem spaces. *Proceedings of the Fourth Annual Conference of the Cognitive Science Society* (pp. 130–135). Hillsdale, NJ: Erlbaum.

Goel, V. (2007). Anatomy of deductive reasoning. *Trends in Cognitive Sciences, 11,* 435–441.

Goel, V., Buchel, C., Frith, C., & Dolan, R. J. (2000). Dissociation of mechanisms underlying syllogistic reasoning. *NeuroImage, 12,* 504–514.

Goel, V., & Dolan, R. J. (2001). Functional neuroanatomy of three-term relational reasoning. *Neuropsychologia, 39,* 901–909.

Goel, V., & Dolan, R. J. (2003). Explaining modulation of reasoning by belief. *Cognition, 87,* B11–B22.

Goel, V., & Grafman, J. (1995). Are the frontal lobes implicated in "planning" functions? Interpreting data from the Tower of Hanoi. *Neuropsychologia, 33,* 623–642.

Goel, V., & Grafman, J. (2000). The role of the right prefrontal cortex in ill-structured problem solving. *Cognitive Neuropsychology, 17,* 415–436.

Goffman, E. (1959). *The presentation of self in everyday life.* London: Penguin.

Goffman, E. (1967). *Interaction ritual.* New York: Pantheon.

Goldenberg, G. (1998). Is there a common substrate for visual recognition and visual imagery? *Neurocase, 4,* 141–147.

Goldman, S. R., Hogaboam, I. W., Bell, L. C., & Perfetti, C. A. (1980). Short-term retention of discourse during reading. *Journal of Educational Psychology, 72,* 547–655.

Goldman-Rakic, P. S. (1995). Cellular basis of working memory. *Neuron, 14,* 477–485.

Goldstein, A. G., & Chance, J. E. (1971). Visual recognition memory for complex configurations. *Perception & Psychophysics, 9,* 237–241.

Goldstein, G., McCue, M., Turner, S. M., Spanier, C., Malec, E. A., & Shelly, C. (1988). An efficacy study of memory training for patients with closed-head injury. *Clinical Neuropsychology, 2,* 251–259.

Golinkoff, R., Mervis, C., & Hirsh-Pasek, K. (1994). Early object labels: The case for a developmental lexical principles framework. *Journal of Child Language, 21,* 125–155.

Gollin, E. S. (1960). Developmental studies of visual recognition of incomplete objects. *Perceptual and Motor Skills, 11,* 289–298.

Gonsalves, B., Reber, P. J., Gitelman, D. R., Parrish, T. B., Mesulam, M. M., & Paller, K. A. (2004). Neural evidence that vivid imaging can lead to false remembering. *Psychological Science, 13,* 655–660.

Goodall, J. (1971). *In the shadow of man.* Boston: Houghton Mifflin.

Goodglass, H., & Kaplan, E. (1983). *Boston Diagnostic Aphasia Examination (BDAE).* Philadelphia: Lea & Febiger.

Goodglass, H., & Kaplan, E. (1983). *The assessment of aphasia and related disorders* (2nd ed.). Philadelphia: Lea & Febiger.

Goodrich, M. A., Stirling, W. C., & Boer, E. R. (2000). Satisficing revisited. *Minds and Machines, 10,* 79–109.

Goodwin, D. W., Powell, B., Bremer, D., Hoine, H., & Stern, J. (1969). Alcohol and recall: State-dependent effects in man. *Science, 163,* 1358–1360.

Gopnik, A., Meltzoff, A. N., & Kuhl, P. K. (1999). *The scientist in the crib: Minds, brains, and how children learn.* New York: William Morrow.

Gordon, C. J., & Braun, C. (1983). Using story schema as an aid to reading and writing. *Reading Teacher, 37,* 116–121.

Gordon, R. (1953). Attitudes toward Russia on logical reasoning. *Journal of Social Psychology, 37,* 103–112.

Gottesman, L., & Chapman, L. J. (1960). Syllogistic reasoning errors in schizophrenia. *Journal of Consulting Psychology, 24,* 250–255.

Gould, D., Hodge, K., Peterson, K., & Giannini, J. (1989). An exploratory examination of strategies used by elite coaches to enhance self-efficacy in athletes. *Journal of Sport & Exercise Psychology, 11,* 128–140.

Graesser, A. C., Gordon, S. E., & Sawyer, J. D. (1979). Recognition memory for typical and atypical actions in scripted activities: Tests of a script pointer plus tag hypothesis. *Journal of Verbal Learning and Verbal Behavior, 18,* 319–322.

Graesser, A. C., Kassler, M. A., Kreuz, R. J., & McLain-Allen, B. (1998). Verification of statements about story worlds that deviate from normal conceptions of time: What is true about *Einstein's Dreams? Cognitive Psychology, 35,* 256–301.

Graesser, A. C., Singer, M., & Trabasso, T. (1994). Constructing inferences during narrative text comprehension. *Psychological Review, 101,* 371–395.

Graf, P., & Schacter, D. L. (1985). Implicit and explicit memory for new associations in normal and amnesic subjects. *Journal of Experimental Psychology: Learning, Memory, and Cognition, 11,* 501–518.

Grammer, K., & Oberzaucher, E. (2008). Face to face: The perception of automotive designs. *Human Nature, 19,* 3310–3346.

Granhag, P. A., Stromwall, L. A., & Jonsson, A. C. (2003). Partners in crime: How liars in collusion betray themselves. *Journal of Applied Social Psychology, 33,* 848–868.

Green, R. L. (1987). Effects of maintenance rehearsal on human memory. *Psychological Bulletin, 102,* 404–413.

Greenbaum, J., & Revlin, R. (1989). PSN: A Prolog declarative model of conceptual knowledge. *Behavior Research Methods, Instruments & Computers, 21,* 15–23.

Greenberg, J. H. (1966). *Language universals.* The Hague: Mouton.

Greene, G. (1999). Mnemonic multiplication fact instruction for students with learning disabilities. *Learning Disabilities Research and Practice, 14,* 141–148.

Greene, J. D., & Haidt, J. (2002). Moral reasoning: How (and where) does moral judgment work? *Trends in Cognitive Sciences, 6,* 517–523.

Greene, J. D., Nystrom, L. E., Engell, A. D., Darley, J. M., & Cohen, J. D. (2004). The neural bases of cognitive conflict and control in moral judgment. *Neuron, 44,* 389–400.

Greene, J. D., Sommerville, R. B., Nystrom, L. E., Darley, J. M., & Cohen, J. D. (2001). An fMRI investigation of emotional engagement in moral judgment. *Science, 293,* 2105–2108.

Greene, T. R., & Noice, H. (1988). Influence of positive affect upon creative thinking and problem solving in children. *Psychological Reports, 63,* 895–898.

Greeno, J. G. (1974). Hobbits and Orcs: Acquisition of a sequential concept. *Cognitive Psychology, 6,* 270–292.

Greeno, J. G. (1989). A perspective on thinking. *American Psychologist, 44,* 134–141.

Gregory, R. L. (1970). *The intelligent eye.* Englewood Cliffs, NJ: McGraw-Hill.

Grice, H. P. (1975). Logic and conversation. In P. Cole & J. L. Morgan (Eds.), *Syntax and semantics. Vol. 3: Speech acts* (pp. 41–58). New York: Seminar Press.

Griggs, R. A. (1983). Memory cueing and instructional effects on Wason's selection task. *Current Psychological Research & Reviews, 3,* 3–10.

Griggs, R. A., & Cox, J. R. (1982). The elusive thematic materials effect in Wason's selection task. *British Journal of Psychology, 73,* 407–420.

Grimes, B. F., & Grimes, J. E. (Eds.). (2000). *Ethnologue. Vol. 1: Languages of the world; Vol. 2: Maps and indexes* (14th ed.). Dallas: SIL International.

Grimes, J. (1996). On the failure to detect changes in scenes across saccades. In K. Akins (Ed.), *Vancouver studies in cognitive science. Vol. 2: Perception* (pp. 89–110). New York: Oxford University Press.

Grodzinsky, Y. (2004). Variations in Broca's region: Preliminary cross-methodological comparisons. In L. Jenkins (Ed.), *Variations and universals in biolinguistics* (pp. 171–193). Amsterdam: Elsevier/North-Holland.

Grodzinsky, Y., Pinango, M. M., Zurif, E., & Drai, D. (1999). The critical role of group studies in neuropsychology: Comprehension regularities in Broca's aphasia. *Brain and Language, 67,* 134–147.

Groen, G. J., & Parkman, J. M. (1972). A chronometric analysis of simple arithmetic. *Psychological Review, 79,* 329–343.

Gronwall, D. (1977). Paced auditory serial addition task: A measure of recovery from concussion. *Perceptual and Motor Skills, 44,* 367–373.

Gronwall, D., & Sampson, H. (1974). *The psychological effects of concussion.* Oxford, England: Auckland University Press.

Gross, C. G. (1999). A hole in the head. *The Neuroscientist, 5,* 263–269.

Guajardo, N. R., & Best, D. L. (2000). Do preschoolers remember what to do? Incentive and external cues in prospective memory. *Cognitive Development, 15,* 75–97.

Guilford, J. P. (1959). Three faces of intellect. *American Psychologist, 14,* 469–479.

Gunzelmann, G., & Anderson, J. R. (2003). Problem solving: Increased planning with practice. *Cognitive Systems Research, 4,* 57–76.

Guthrie, E. R. (1935). *The psychology of learning.* Oxford: Harper.

Guy, R. K. (1988). The strong law of small numbers. *American Mathematics Monthly, 95,* 697–712.

Haber, R. N. (1979). Twenty years of haunting eidetic imagery: Where's the ghost? *Behavioral and Brain Sciences, 2,* 583–629.

Haber, R. N., & Haber, R. B. (1964). Eidetic imagery: I. Frequency. *Perceptual and Motor Skills, 19,* 131–138.

Habib, R., Nyberg, L., & Tulving, E. (2003). Hemispheric asymmetries of memory: The HERA model revisited. *Trends in Cognitive Sciences, 7,* 241–245.

Hadamard, J. (1945). *The psychology of invention in the mathematical field.* Princeton, NJ: Princeton University Press.

Hall, C., Mack, D., Paivio, A., & Hausenblas, H. (1998). Imagery use by athletes: Development of the sport imagery questionnaire. *International Journal of Sport Psychology, 29,* 73–89.

Hall, J. W., Wilson, K. P., & Patterson, R. J. (1981). Mnemotechnics: Some limitations of the mnemonic keyword method for the study of foreign language vocabulary. *Journal of Educational Psychology, 73,* 345–357.

Hall, L. L. (2005). Turner syndrome. In *Encyclopedia of life sciences* (pp. 1–2). New York: Wiley.

Halpern, A. R., & Zatorre, R. J. (1999). When that tune runs through your head: A PET investigation of auditory imagery for familiar melodies. *Cerebral Cortex, 9,* 697–704.

Hamilton, W. (1859). *Lectures in metaphysics and logic* (Vol. 1). Edinburgh, Scotland: Blackwood.

Handel, S., De Soto, C. B., & London, M. (1968). Reasoning and spatial representation. *Journal of Verbal Learning and Verbal Behavior, 7,* 351–357.

Hardyck, C. D., & Petrinovitch, L. R. (1970). Subvocal speech and comprehension level as a function of the difficulty level of reading material. *Journal of Verbal Learning and Verbal Behavior, 9,* 647–652.

Harlow, J. M. (1868). Recovery from the passage of an iron bar through the head. *Publication of the Massachusetts Medical Society, 2,* 327–347.

Harris, J. C. (2004). The cure of folly. *Archives of General Psychiatry, 61,* 1187.

Harris, J. E. (1984). Remember to do things: A forgotten topic. In J. E. Harris & P. E. Morris (Eds.), *Everyday memory, actions, and absent-mindedness* (pp. 71–92). New York: Academic Press.

Harris, J. E., & Wilkins, A. J. (1982). Remembering to do things: A theoretical framework and illustrative experiment. *Human Learning, 1,* 1–14.

Harris, N., Bellugi, U., Bates, E., Jones, W., & Rossen, M. (1997). Contrasting profiles of language development in children with Williams and Down syndromes. *Developmental Neuropsychology, 13,* 345–370.

Harris, R. J., Schoen, L. M., Lawrence, M., & Hensley, D. L. (1992). A cross-cultural study of story memory. *Journal of Cross-Cultural Psychology, 23,* 133–147.

Hart, J. T. (1965). Memory and the feeling-of-knowing experience. *Journal of Educational Psychology, 56,* 208–216.

Hastie, R., & Dawes, R. M. (2001). *Rational choice in an uncertain world: The psychology of judgment and decision making.* Thousand Oaks, CA: Sage.

Hauck, M., Fein, D., Maltby, N., Waterhouse, L., & Feinstein, C. (1998). Memory for faces in children with autism. *Child Neuropsychology, 4,* 187–198.

Haviland, S. E., & Clark, H. H. (1974). What's new? Acquiring new information as a process in comprehension. *Journal of Verbal Learning and Verbal Behavior, 13,* 512–521.

Hawkins, H. L., & Shigley, R. H. (1970). Short-term retention and similarity of word length. *Psychonomic Science, 20,* 111–112.

Hayes, J. R. (1973). On the function of visual imagery in elementary mathematics. In J. R. Hayes & W. G. Chase (Eds.), *Visual information processing* (pp. 177–214). San Diego, CA: Academic Press.

Hayes, J. R. (1978). *Cognitive psychology: Thinking and creating.* Homewood, IL: Dorsey Press.

Hayes, J. R. (1989). *The complete problem solver.* Hillsdale, NJ: Erlbaum.

Head, H. (1926). *Aphasia and kindred disorders of speech.* New York: Macmillan.

Head, H., & Holmes, G. (1911). Sensory disturbances from cerebral lesions. *Brain, 34,* 102.

Heeger, D. J., Huk, A. C., Geisler, W. S., & Albrecht, D. G. (2000). Spikes versus BOLD: What does neuroimaging tell us about neuronal activity? *Nature Neuroscience, 3,* 631–633.

Hegarty, M. (1992). Mental animation: Inferring motion from static displays of mechanical systems. *Journal of Experimental Psychology: Learning, Memory, and Cognition, 18,* 1084–1102.

Hegarty, M. (2004). Mechanical reasoning as mental simulation. *Trends in Cognitive Sciences, 8,* 280–285.

Hegarty, M., & Just, M. A. (1989). Understanding machine from text and diagrams. In H. Mandl & J. R. Levin (Eds.), *Knowledge acquisition from text and pictures* (pp. 171–194). New York: North-Holland.

Hegarty, M., & Kozhevnikov, M. (1999). Spatial abilities, working memory and mechanical reasoning. In J. Gero & B. Tversky (Eds.), *Visual and spatial reasoning in design* (pp. 684–689). Sydney, Australia: Key Centre of Design and Cognition.

Hegarty, M., & Sims, V. K. (1994). Individual differences in mental animation during mechanical reasoning. *Memory & Cognition, 22,* 411–430.

Hegarty, M., & Steinhoff, K. (1997). Individual differences in use of diagrams as external memory in mechanical reasoning. *Learning and Individual Differences, 9,* 19–42.

Hegarty, M., & Waller, D. (2006). Individual differences in spatial abilities. In P. Shah & A. Miyake (Eds.), *Handbook of visuospatial thinking* (pp. 121–169). Cambridge, England: Cambridge University Press.

Helmholtz, H. (1925). *Physiological optics: Vol. 3. The perception of vision* (J. P. Southall, Trans.). Rochester, NY: Optical Society of America (Original work published 1910)

Henkel, L. A., & Franklin, N. (1998). Reality monitoring of physically similar and conceptually related objects. *Memory & Cognition, 26,* 659–673.

Henle, M. (1962). On the relation between logic and thinking. *Psychological Review, 69,* 366–378.

Henle, M. (1971). Of the scholler of nature. *Social Research, 38,* 93–107.

Henry, L. A. (1994). The relationship between speech rate and memory span in children. *International Journal of Behavioral Development, 17,* 37–56.

Hepper, P. G. (1996). Fetal memory: Does it exist? What does it do? *Acta Paediatrica, 416,* 16–20.

Hepper, P. G., Dornan, J. C., & Little, J. F. (2005). Maternal alcohol consumption during pregnancy may delay the development of spontaneous fetal startle behavior. *Physiology & Behavior, 83,* 711–714.

Hernandez, A., Martinez, A., & Kohnert, K. (2000). In search of the language switch: An fMRI study of picture naming in Spanish–English bilinguals. *Brain and Language, 73,* 421–431.

Hertwig, R., & Gigerenzer, G. (1999). The "conjunction fallacy revisited": How intelligent inferences look like reasoning errors. *Journal of Behavioral Decision Making, 12,* 275–305.

Hess, T. M. (1985). Aging and context influences on recognition memory for typical and atypical script actions. *Developmental Psychology, 21,* 1139–1151.

Hetts, S., Werne, A., & Hieshima, G. B. (1995). " . . . and do no harm." *American Journal of Neuroradiology, 16,* 1–5.

Hickok, G., Klima, E. S., & Bellugi, U. (1996). The neurobiology of signed language and its implications for the neural basis of language. *Nature, 381,* 699–702.

Hickok, G., Wilson, M., Clark, K., Klima, E., Kritchevsky, M., & Bellugi, U. (1999). Discourse deficits following right-hemisphere damage in deaf signers. *Brain and Language, 66,* 233–248.

Hier, D., & Kaplan, J. (1980). Verbal comprehension deficits after right hemispheric damage. *Applied Psycholinguistics, 1,* 279–294.

Hill, R. D., Allen, C., & McWhorter, P. (1991). Stories as a mnemonic aid for older learners. *Psychology and Aging, 6,* 484–486.

Hirotsu, N., & Wright, M. (2005). Modeling a baseball game to optimize pitcher substitution strategies incorporating handedness of players. *IMA Journal of Management Mathematics, 15,* 179–194.

Hobbes, T. (1983). *Philosophical rudiments concerning government and society* (H. Warrender, Ed.). Oxford, England: Oxford University Press. (Original work published 1651)

Hockett, C. F. (1966). The problem of universals in language. In J. H. Greenberg (Ed.), *Universals of language* (2nd ed., pp. 1–29). Cambridge, MA: MIT Press.

Hodges, J. R., Graham, N., & Patterson, K. (1995). Charting the progression in semantic dementia: Implications for the organization of semantic memory. *Memory, 3,* 463–495.

Hofstadter, D. (2007). *I am a strange loop.* New York: Basic Books.

Holding, D. H. (1975). Sensory storage reconsidered. *Memory & Cognition, 3,* 31–41.

Holmes, A., Vuilleumier, P., & Eimer, M. (2003). The processing of emotional facial expression is gated by spatial attention: Evidence from event-related brain potentials. *Cognitive Brain Research, 16,* 174–184.

Holt, J. A., Traxler, C. B., & Thomas, A. (1997). *Interpreting the scores: A user's guide to the 9th edition Stanford Achievement Test for educators of deaf and hard-of-hearing students* (Gallaudet Research Institute Tech. Rep. No. 97-1). Washington, DC: Gallaudet University.

Holyoak, K. J., & Koh, K. (1987). Surface and structural similarity in analogical transfer. *Memory & Cognition, 15,* 332–340.

Hoosain, R., & Salili, F. (2005). Dimensions of language in multicultural education. In R. Hoosain & F. Salili (Eds.), *Language in multicultural education* (pp. 3–9). Greenwich, CT: Information Age Publishing.

Horgan, D. D., & Morgan, D. (1990). Chess expertise in children. *Applied Cognitive Psychology, 4,* 109–128.

Hornby, P. A. (1972). The psychological subject and predicate. *Cognitive Psychology, 2,* 632–642.

Hornby, P. A. (1974). Surface structure and presupposition. *Journal of Verbal Learning and Verbal Behavior, 13,* 530–538.

Horowitz, M. J. (1991). Person schemas. In M. J. Horowitz (Ed.), *Person schemas and maladaptive interpersonal behavior patterns* (pp. 13–31). Chicago: University of Chicago Press.

Howe, M., & Courage, M. (1993). On resolving the enigma of infantile amnesia. *Psychological Bulletin, 113,* 305–326.

Hubel, D. H. (1989). *Eye, brain, and vision.* New York: W. H. Freeman and Company.

Hubel, D. H., & Wiesel, T. N. (1962). Receptive fields, binocular interaction and functional architecture in the cat's visual cortex. *Journal of Physiology, 160,* 106–154.

Hubel, D. H., & Wiesel, T. N. (1968). Receptive fields and functional architecture of monkey striate cortex. *Journal of Physiology, 195,* 215–243.

Huber, M., Siol, T., Herholz, K., Lenz, O., Kohle, K., & Heiss, W. D. (2001). Activation of thalamo-cortical systems in posttraumatic flashbacks: A positron emission tomography study. *Traumatology, 7,* 131–141.

Hudson, J., & Nelson, K. (1983). Effects of script structure on children's story recall. *Developmental Psychology, 19,* 625–635.

Hulme, C., Thomson, N., Muir, C., & Lawrence, A. (1984). Speech rate and the development of short-term memory span. *Journal of Experimental Child Psychology, 38,* 241–253.

Hunt, E. B. (1978). Mechanics of verbal ability. *Psychological Review, 85,* 109–130.

Hunt, E. B., & Love, T. (1972). How good can memory be? In A. W. Melton & E. Martin (Eds.), *Coding processes in human memory* (pp. 237–260). New York: Holt.

Hunt, G. M., & Holmes, A. E. (1975). Some factors relating to intelligence in treated children with *spina bifida cyystica. Developmental Medicine & Child Neurology, 17,* 65–70.

Hunter, I. M. L. (1957). The solving of three-term series problems. *British Journal of Psychology, 48,* 286–298.

Hurford, P., Stringer, A. Y., & Jann, B. (1998). Neuorpharmacologic treatment of hemineglect: A case report comparing bromocriptine and methylphenidate. *Archives of Physical Medicine and Rehabilitation, 79,* 346–349.

Hutchins, E. (1996). *Cognition in the wild.* Cambridge, MA: MIT Press.

Hutchinson, J. M., & Gigerenzer, G. (2005). Simple heuristics and rules of thumb: Where psychologists and behavioural biologists might meet. *Behavioural Processes, 69,* 97–124.

Huttenlocher, J. (1968). Constructing spatial images: A strategy in reasoning. *Psychological Review, 75,* 550–560.

Huttenlocher, J., & Burke, D. (1976). Why does memory span increase with age? *Cognitive Psychology, 8,* 1–31.

Hyland, D. T., & Ackerman, A. M. (1988). Reminiscence and autobiographical memory in the study of the personal past. *Journal of Gerontology: Psychological Sciences, 43,* 35–39.

Hyman, I. E., & Billings, F. J. (1998). Individual differences and the creation of false childhood memories. *Memory, 6,* 1–20.

Hyman, I. E., Husband, T. H., & Billings, F. J. (1995). False memories of childhood experiences. *Applied Cognitive Psychology, 9,* 181–197.

Ingvar, D. H., & Philipon, L. (1977). Distribution of cerebral blood flow in the dominant hemisphere during motor ideation and motor performance. *Annals of Neurology, 2,* 230–237.

Intons-Peterson, M. J., & Roskos-Ewoldsen, B. B. (1989). Sensory perceptual qualities of images. *Journal of Experimental Psychology: Learning, Memory, and Cognition, 15,* 188–199.

Intraub, H., & Hoffman, J. E. (1992). Reading and visual memory: Remembering scenes that were never seen. *American Journal of Psychology, 105,* 101–114.

Intriligator, J., & Cavanaugh, J. (2001). The spatial resolution of visual attention. *Cognitive Psychology, 43,* 171–216.

Isen, A. M., Daubman, K. A., & Nowicki, G. P. (1987). Positive affect facilitates creative problem solving. *Journal of Personality and Social Psychology, 52,* 1122–1131.

Ishaque, A. S., Haider, M. B., Wasid, M., Alaul, S. M., Hassan, M. K., Ahsan, T., & Alam, M. S. (2004). An evolutionary algorithm to solve cryptarithmetic problems. *Transactions on Engineering, Computing, and Technology, 6,* 494–496.

Itard, J. M. G. (1962). *The wild boy of Aveyron* (G. Humphrey & M. Humphrey, Trans.). New York: Appleton-Century-Crofts. (Original work published 1801 and 1806)

Iverson, J., Reed, H., & Revlin, R. (1989). The effect of music on the personal relevance of lyrics. *Psychology, 26,* 15–22.

Ivry, R. B., & Robertson, L. C. (1998). *The two sides of perception.* Cambridge, MA: MIT Press.

Ivry, R. B., Spencer, R. M., Zelanik, H. N., & Diedrichsen, J. (2006). The cerebellum and event timing. *Annals of the New York Academy of Sciences, 978,* 302–317.

Izzo, A. (2002). Phonemic awareness and reading ability: An investigation with young readers who are deaf. *American Annals of the Deaf, 147,* 18–28.

Jackson, S. L., & Griggs, R. A. (1990). The elusive pragmatic reasoning schemas effect. *Quarterly Journal of Experimental Psychology: Human Experimental Psychology, 42A,* 353–373.

Jacob, F., & Monod, J. (1961). Genetic regulatory mechanisms in the synthesis of proteins. *Journal of Molecular Biology, 3,* 318–356.

Jacoby, L. L. (1991). A process-dissociation framework: Separating automatic from intentional uses of memory. *Journal of Memory and Language, 30,* 513–541.

James, L. E., & Burke, D. M. (2000). Phonological priming effects on word retrieval and tip-of-the-tongue experiences in young and older adults. *Journal of Experimental Psychology: Learning, Memory, and Cognition, 26,* 1378–1391.

James, W. (1890). *The principles of psychology.* New York: Dover.

Jang, Y. G., Hoi, H. I., & Hong, K. S. (2010). Visual contents adaptation for color vision deficiency using customized ICC profiles. *Disability and Rehabilitation: Assistive Technology, 5,* 258–265.

Janis, I., & Frick, P. (1943). The relationship between attitude toward conclusions and errors in judging logical validity of syllogisms. *Journal of Experimental Psychology, 33,* 73–77.

Jansari, A., & Parkin, A. J. (1996). Things that go bump in your life: Explaining the reminiscence bump in autobiographical memory. *Psychology and Aging, 11,* 85–91.

Janssen, S. M. J., Chessa, A. G., & Murre, J. M. J. (2005). The reminiscence bump in autobiographical memory: Effects of age, gender, culture, and education. *Memory, 13,* 658–668.

Janssen, S. M. J., & Murre, J. M. J. (2008). Reminiscence bump in autobiographical memory: Unexplained by novelty, emotionality, valence, or importance of personal events. *Quarterly Journal of Experimental Psychology, 61,* 1847–1860.

Jeannerod, M. (1994). The representing brain: Neural correlates of motor intention and imagery. *Behavioral and Brain Sciences, 17,* 187–243.

Jeffries, R., Polson, P. G., Razran, L., & Atwood, M. E. (1977). A process model for missionaries–cannibals and other river-crossing problems. *Cognitive Psychology, 9,* 412–440.

Johnson, D. M. (1939). Confidence and speed in the two-category judgment. *Archives of Psychology, 241,* 1–52.

Johnson, M. H. (2001). The development and neural basis of face recognition: Comment and speculation. *Infant and Child Development, 10,* 31–33.

Johnson, M. K., Bransford, J. D., & Solomon, S. K. (1973). Memory for tacit implications of sentences. *Journal of Experimental Psychology, 98,* 203–205.

Johnson, M. K., Foley, M. A., & Leach, K. (1988). The consequences for memory of imagining in another person's voice. *Memory & Cognition, 16,* 337–342.

Johnson, M. K., Foley, M. A., Suengas, A. G., & Raye, C. L. (1988). Phenomenal characteristics of memories for perceived and imagined autobiographical events. *Journal of Experimental Psychology: General, 117,* 371–376.

Johnson, M. K., Hashtroudi, S., & Lindsay, D. S. (1993). Source monitoring. *Psychological Bulletin, 114,* 3–28.

Johnson, M. K., & Raye, C. L. (1981). Reality monitoring. *Psychological Review, 88,* 67–85.

Johnson, M. K., Raye, C. L., Wang, A. Y., & Taylor, T. H. (1979). Fact and fantasy: The roles of accuracy and variability in confusing imaginations with perceptual experiences. *Journal of Experimental Psychology: Human Learning and Memory, 5,* 229–240.

Johnson, S. (1963). Memory rarely deficient. In W. J. Bate, J. M. Bullitt, & L. F. Powell (Eds.), *The works of Samuel Johnson, L.L.D.* (Vol. 2). Oxford: Clarendon Press. (Reprinted from The Idler #74, *Universal Chronicle,* September 15, 1759, London: Talboys & Wheeler)

Johnson-Laird, P. N. (1983). *Mental models.* Cambridge, MA: Harvard University Press.

Johnson-Laird, P. N., & Byrne, R. M. J. (1991). *Deduction.* Hillsdale, NJ: Erlbaum.

Johnson-Laird, P. N., & Steedman, M. (1978). The psychology of syllogisms. *Cognitive Psychology, 10,* 64–99.

Jolicoeur, P. (1999). Concurrent response-selection demands modulate the attentional blink. *Journal of Experimental Psychology: Human Perception and Performance, 25,* 1097–1113.

Jolicoeur, P., & Kosslyn, S. M. (1985). Is time to scan visual images due to demand characteristics? *Memory & Cognition, 13,* 320–332.

Jones, W., Bellugi, U., Lai, Z., Chiles, M., Reilly, J., Lincoln, A., & Adolphs, R. (2001). Hypersociability: The social and affective phenotype of Williams syndrome. In U. Bellugi & M. St. George (Eds.), *Journey from cognition to brain to gene: Perspectives from Williams syndrome* (pp. 43–72). Cambridge, MA: MIT Press.

Jonides, J. (1983). Further toward a model of the mind's eye's movement. *Bulletin of the Psychonomic Society, 21,* 247–250.

Joseph, R. (2003). Emotional trauma and childhood amnesia. *Journal of Consciousness and Emotion, 4,* 151–178.

Joseph, R. M., & Tager-Flusberg, H. (1997). An investigation of attention and affect in children with autism and Down syndrome. *Journal of Autism and Developmental Disorders, 4,* 385–396.

Joseph, R. M., & Tanaka, J. (2003). Holistic and part-based face recognition in children with autism. *Journal of Child Psychology and Psychiatry, 43,* 1–14.

Jowdy, D. P., & Harris, D. V. (1990). Muscular responses during mental imagery as a function of motor skill level. *Journal of Sport & Exercise Psychology, 12,* 191–201.

Joyner, C. (2009). *Down by the riverside.* Chicago: University of Chicago Press.

Jung, C. G. (1933). *Modern man in search of a soul* (W. S. Dell & C. F. Baynes, Trans.). London: Routledge & Kegan Paul.

Jusczyk, P. W. (1997). *The discovery of spoken language.* Cambridge, MA: MIT Press.

Just, M. A., & Carpenter, P. A. (1980). A theory of reading: From eye fixations to comprehension. *Psychological Review, 87,* 329–354.

Just, M. A., & Carpenter, P. A. (1987). *The psychology of reading and language comprehension.* Needham Heights, MA: Allyn & Bacon.

Kahneman, D. (1973). *Attention and effort.* Englewood Cliffs, NJ: Prentice Hall.

Kahneman, D., & Frederick, S. (2002). Representativeness revisited: Attribute substitution in intuitive judgment. In T. Gilovich, D. Griffin, & D. Kahneman (Eds.), *Heuristics and biases: The psychology of intuitive judgment* (pp. 49–81). New York: Cambridge University Press.

Kahneman, D., Slovic, P., & Tversky, A. (Eds.). (1982). *Judgment under uncertainty: Heuristics and biases.* New York: Cambridge University Press.

Kahneman, D., & Treisman, A. (1984). Changing views of attention and automaticity. In R. Parasuraman,

D. R. Davies, & J. Beatty (Eds.), *Variants of attention* (pp. 29–61). New York: Academic Press.

Kahneman, D., & Tversky, A. (1973). On the psychology of prediction. *Psychological Review, 80,* 237–251.

Kahneman, D., & Tversky, A. (1979). Prospect theory: An analysis of decision under risk. *Econometrica, 47,* 263–291.

Kahneman, D., & Tversky, A. (1996). On the reality of cognitive illusions: A reply to Gigerenzer's critique. *Psychological Review, 103,* 582–591.

Kail, R., & Salthouse, T. A. (1994). Processing speed as a mental capacity. *Acta Psychologica, 86,* 199–225.

Kajikawa, S., Amano, S., & Kondo, T. (2004). Speech overlap in Japanese mother–child conversations. *Journal of Child Language, 3,* 215–230.

Kandel, E. R. (2007). *In search of memory—The emergence of a new science of mind.* New York: W. W. Norton.

Kanizsa, G. (1976). Subjective contours. *Scientific American, 234,* 48–52.

Kantowitz, B. H., & Sorkin, R. D. (1983). *Human factors: Understanding people–system relationships.* New York: Wiley.

Kanwisher, N. (1987). Repetition blindness: Type recognition without token individuation. *Cognition, 27,* 117–143.

Kanwisher, N., McDermott, J., & Chun, M. M. (1997). The fusiform face area: A module in human extrastriate cortex specialized for face perception. *The Journal of Neuroscience, 17,* 4302–4311.

Kanwisher, N., & Potter, M. C. (1990). Repetition blindness: Levels of processing. *Journal of Experimental Psychology: Human Perception and Performance, 16,* 30–47.

Kaplan, E., Goodglass, H., & Weintraub, S. (1983). *The Boston Naming Test* (2nd ed.). Philadelphia: Lea & Febiger.

Kara, S., & Güven, A. (2007). Neural network-based diagnosing for optic nerve disease from visual-evoked potential. *Journal of Medical Systems, 31,* 391–396.

Kardash, C., & Scholes, R. J. (1996). Effects of preexisting beliefs, epistemological beliefs, and need for cognition on interpretation of controversial issues. *Journal of Education Psychology, 88,* 260–271.

Karwowski, P. (Ed.). (2006). *International encyclopedia of ergonomics and human factors* (2nd ed.). Boca Raton, FL: CRC Press.

Kasanin, J. S. (1954). The disturbance of conceptual thinking in schizophrenia. In J. S. Kasanin (Ed.), *Language and thought in schizophrenia* (pp. 41–49). Berkeley: University of California Press.

Kasper, L. F. (1993). The keyword method and foreign language learning: A rationale for its use. *Foreign Language Annals, 26,* 244–251.

Kassin, S. M., Ellsworth, P., & Smith, V. L. (1989). The "general acceptance" of psychological research on eyewitness testimony. *American Psychologist, 44,* 1089–1098.

Kaufman, E. L., Lord, M. W., Reese, T. W., & Volkmann, J. (1949). The discrimination of visual number. *American Journal of Psychology, 62,* 498–525.

Kaufman, H., & Goldstein, S. (1967). The effects of emotional value of conclusions upon distortions in syllogistic reasoning. *Psychonomic Science, 7,* 367–368.

Kaye, K., & Charney, R. (1980). How mothers maintain "dialogue" with two-year-olds. In D. R. Olson (Ed.), *The social foundations of language and thought* (pp. 211–230). New York: W. W. Norton.

Keele, S. W., & Mayr, U. (2005). A tribute to Michael I. Posner. In U. Mayr, E. Awh, & S. W. Keele (Eds.), *Developing individuality in the human brain: A tribute to Michael I. Posner* (pp. 3–16). Washington, DC: American Psychological Association.

Keeler, M. L., & Swanson, H. L. (2001). Does strategy knowledge influence working memory in children with mathematical disabilities? *Journal of Learning Disabilities, 34,* 418–434.

Kelley, W. M., Miezin, F. M., McDermott, K. B., Buckner, R. L., Raichle, M. E., Cohen, N. J., . . . Peterson, S. E. (1998). Hemispheric specialization in human dorsal frontal cortex and medial temporal lobe for verbal and nonverbal memory encoding. *Neuron, 20,* 927–936.

Kemper, S., & Edwards, L. (1986). Children's expression of causality and their construction of narratives. *Topics in Language Disorders, 7,* 11–20.

Kendall, P. C., & Hammen, C. (1995). *Abnormal psychology.* Boston: Houghton-Mifflin.

Kennedy, Q., Mather, M., & Carstensen, L. L. (2004). The role of motivation in the age-related positivity effect in autobiographical memory. *Psychological Science, 15,* 208–214.

Keppel, G., & Underwood, B. J. (1962). Proactive inhibition in short-term retention of single items. *Journal of Verbal Learning and Verbal Behavior, 1,* 153–161.

Kerns, K. A. (2000). An investigation of development of prospective memory in children. *Journal of the International Neuropsychological Society, 6,* 62–70.

Kerr, N. H. (1983). The role of vision in "visual imagery" experiments: Evidence from the congenitally blind. *Journal of Experimental Psychology: General, 112,* 265–277.

Kershaw, T. C., & Ohlsson, S. (2004). Multiple causes of difficulty in insight: The case of the nine-dot problem. *Journal of Experimental Psychology: Learning, Memory, and Cognition, 30,* 3–13.

Keynes, J. M. (1937). General theory of employment. *Quarterly Journal of Economics, 51,* 209–223.

Kihlstrom, J. F., Beer, J. S., & Klein, S. B. (2003). Self and identity as memory, In M. R. Leary & J. P. Tangney (Eds.), *Handbook of self and identity* (pp. 47–67). New York: Guilford Press.

Kihlstrom, J. F., Eich, E., Sandbrand, D., & Tobias, B. A. (2000). Emotion and memory: Implications for self-report. In A. Stone, J. Turkan, J. Jobe, H. Kutzman, & V. Cain (Eds.), *The science of self-report: Implications for research and practice* (pp. 81–99). Mahwah, NJ: Erlbaum.

Kihlstrom, J. F., & Harackiewicz, J. M. (1982). The earliest recollection: A new survey. *Journal of Personality, 50,* 134–149.

Kimura, D. (1993). Sex differences in the brain. In *Mind and brain: Readings from Scientific American magazine* (pp. 79–89). New York: W. H. Freeman and Company.

King-Sears, M. E., Mercer, C. D., & Sindelar, P. T. (1992). Toward independence with keyword mnemonics: A strategy for science vocabulary instruction. *Remedial and Special Education, 13,* 22–33.

Kinjo, H., & Snodgrass, J. G. (2000). Is there a picture superiority effect in perceptual implicit tasks? *European Journal of Cognitive Psychology, 12,* 145–164.

Kintsch, W. (1968). Recognition and free recall of organized lists. *Journal of Experimental Psychology, 78,* 481–487.

Kintsch, W., & Keenan, J. (1973). Reading rate and retention as a function of the number of propositions in the base structure of sentences. *Cognitive Psychology, 5,* 257–274.

Kintsch, W., Patel, V. L., & Ericsson, K. A. (1999). The role of long-term working memory in text comprehension. *Psychologia, 42,* 186–198.

Kirasic, K. C. (2000). Age differences in adults' spatial abilities, learning environmental layout, and wayfinding behavior. *Spatial Cognition and Computation, 2,* 117–134.

Kitchener, E. G., Hodges, J. R., & McCarthy, R. (1998). Acquisition of postmorbid vocabulary and semantic facts in the absence of episodic memory. *Brain, 121,* 1313–1327.

Kitchener, K. S. (1983). Cognition, metacognition, and epistemic cognition. *Human Development, 26,* 222–232.

Klaczynski, P. A., Gelfand, H., & Reese, H. W. (1989). Transfer of conditional reasoning: Effects of explanations and initial problem types. *Memory & Cognition, 17,* 208–220.

Klahr, D., & Dunbar, K. (1988). Dual space search during scientific reasoning. *Cognitive Science, 12,* 1–48.

Klatzky, R. L., & Rafnel, K. J. (1976). Labeling effects on memory for nonsense pictures. *Memory & Cognition, 41,* 717–720.

Klauer, K. C., Musch, J., & Naumer, B. (2000). On belief bias in syllogistic reasoning. *Psychological Review, 107,* 852–884.

Klayman, J., & Ha, Y. (1987). Confirmation, disconfirmation, and information in hypothesis testing. *Psychological Review, 94,* 211–228.

Klein, K. (2011). Writing can improve working memory. *LitSite Alaska: Narrative and healing.* Retrieved from http://www.litsite.org

Klein, K., & Boals, A. (2001a). Expressive writing can increase working memory capacity. *Journal of Experimental Psychology: General, 130,* 520–533.

Klein, K., & Boals, A. (2001b). The relationship of life event stress and working memory capacity. *Applied Cognitive Psychology, 15,* 565–579.

Klein, S. B., German, T. P., Cosmides, L., & Rami, G. (2004). A theory of autobiographical memory: Necessary components and disorders resulting from their loss. *Social Cognition, 22,* 460–490.

Klein, S. B., Loftus, J., & Kihlstrom, J. F. (1996). Self-knowledge of an amnesic patient: Toward a neuropsychology of personality and social psychology. *Journal of Experimental Psychology: General, 125,* 250–260.

Klein, S. B., Loftus, J., & Kihlstrom, J. F. (2002). Memory and temporal experience: The effects of episodic memory loss on an amnesic patient's ability to remember the past and imagine the future. *Social Cognition, 25,* 353–379.

Kleinecke, D. (1959). An etymology of "Pidgin." *International Journal of American Linguistics, 25,* 271–272.

Kleinfeld, J. (1971). Visual memory in village Eskimo and urban Caucasian children. *Arctic, 24,* 132–138.

Knauff, M. (2006). A neurocognitive theory of relational reasoning with mental models and visual images. In C. Held, M. Knauff, & G. Vosgerau (Eds.), *Mental models of the mind* (pp. 127–154). Amsterdam: Elsevier.

Knauff, M., Mulack, T., Kassubek, J., Salih, H. R., & Greenlee, M. W. (2002). Spatial imagery in deductive reasoning: A functional MRI study. *Cognitive Brain Research, 13,* 203–212.

Knauff, M., Strube, G., Jola, C., Rauh, R., & Schlieder, C. (2004). The psychological validity of qualitative spatial reasoning in one dimension. *Spatial Cognition and Computation, 4,* 167–188.

Knoblich, G., Ohlsson, S., Haider, H., & Rhenius, D. (1999). Constraint relaxation and chunk decomposition in insight problem solving. *Journal of Experimental Psychology: Learning, Memory, and Cognition, 25,* 1534–1555.

Knoblich, G., Ohlsson, S., & Raney, G. (2001). An eye movement study of insight problem solving. *Memory & Cognition, 29,* 1000–1009.

Knox, R. E., & Inkster, J. A. (1968). Postdecision dissonance at post time. *Journal of Personality and Social Psychology, 8,* 319–323.

Kobayashi, S. (1986). Theoretical issues concerning superiority of pictures over words and sentences in memory. *Perceptual and Motor Skills, 63,* 783–792.

Koehler, J. J., & Conley, C. A. (2003). The "hot hand" myth in professional basketball. *Journal of Sport & Exercise Psychology, 25,* 253–259.

Koestler, A. (1964). *The act of creation.* London: Hutchinson.

Koffka, K. (1922). Perception: An introduction to the gestalt theory. *Psychological Bulletin, 19,* 531–585.

Koffka, K. (1935). *Principles of Gestalt psychology.* London: Lund Humphries.

Kohnken, G., Milne, R., Memon, A., & Bull, R. (1999). The cognitive interview: A meta-analysis. *Psychology, Crime, & Law, 5,* 3–27.

Kolb, B. (1995). *Brain plasticity and behavior.* Mahwah, NJ: Erlbaum.

Kolb, B., & Whishaw, I. Q. (2001). *An introduction to brain and behavior.* New York: Worth Publishers.

Kolb, B., & Whishaw, I. Q. (2009). *Fundamentals of human neuropsychology* (6th ed.). New York: Worth Publishers.

Kolb, B., & Whishaw, I. Q. (2011). *An introduction to brain and behavior* (3rd ed.). New York: Worth Publishers.

Kolers, P. A., & Palef, S. R. (1976). Knowing not. *Memory & Cognition, 4,* 553–558.

Kopelman, M. D., Wilson, B. A., & Baddeley, A. D. (1989). The autobiographical memory interview: A new assessment of autobiographical and personal semantic memory in amnesic patients. *Journal of Clinical Experimental Neuropsychology, 11,* 723–744.

Koriat, A. (2000). The feeling of knowing: Some metatheoretical implications for consciousness and control. *Consciousness and Cognition, 9,* 149–171.

Koriat, A., & Goldsmith, M. (1996). Memory metaphors and the real-life/laboratory controversy: Correespondence versus storehouse conceptions of memory. *Behavioral and Brain Sciences, 19,* 167–228.

Korkman, M., Kirk, U., & Kemp, S. (1998). *NEPSY: A developmental neuropsychological assessment.* San Antonio, TX: The Psychological Corporation.

Korsakoff, S. S. (1955). Psychic disorder in conjunction with peripheral neuritis (M. Victor & P. E. Yakovlev, Trans.). *Neurology, 5,* 394–406. (Original work published 1889)

Kosslyn, S. M. (1975). Information representation in visual images. *Cognitive Psychology, 7,* 341–370.

Kosslyn, S. M. (1980). *Image and mind.* Cambridge, MA: Harvard University Press.

Kosslyn, S. M. (1983). *Ghosts in the mind's machine.* New York: W. W. Norton.

Kosslyn, S. M., Alpert, N., Thompson, W., Maljkovic, V., Weise, S., Chabris, C., . . . Buonanno, F. (1993). Visual mental imagery activates topographically organized visual cortex: PET investigations. *Journal of Cognitive Neuroscience, 5,* 263–287.

Kosslyn, S. M., Ball, T. M., & Reiser, B. J. (1978). Visual images preserve metric spatial information: Evidence from studies of image scanning. *Journal of Experimental Psychology: Human Perception and Performance, 4,* 47–60.

Kosslyn, S. M., Ganis, G., & Thompson, W. L. (2001). Neural foundations of imagery. *Nature Reviews Neuroscience, 2,* 635–642.

Kosslyn, S. M., Koenig, O., Barrett, A., & Cave, C. B. (1989). Evidence for two types of spatial representations: Hemispheric specialization for categorical and coordinate relations. *Journal of Experimental*

Psychology: Human Perception and Performance, 15, 723–735.

Kosslyn, S. M., Pascual-Leone, A., Felician, O., Camposano, S., Keenan, J. P., Thompson, W. L., . . . Alpert, N. M. (1999). The role of area 17 in visual imagery: Convergent evidence from PET and rTMS. *Science, 284,* 167–170.

Kosslyn, S. M., & Thompson, W. L. (2003). When is early visual cortex activated during visual mental imagery? *Psychological Bulletin, 129,* 723–746.

Kotchoubey, B., Lang, S., Winter, S., & Bierbaumer, N. (2003). Cognitive processing in completlely paralyzed patients with amyotrophic lateral sclerosis. *European Journal of Neurology, 10,* 551–558.

Kovner, R., Mattis, S., & Goldmeier, E. (1983). A technique for promoting robust free recall in chronic organic amnesia. *Journal of Clinical Neuroscience, 5,* 65–71.

Kozhevnikov, M., Hegarty, M., & Mayer, R. E. (2002). Revising the visualizer–verbalizer dimension: Evidence for two types of visualizers. *Cognition and Instruction, 20,* 47–78.

Krashen, S. (1999). What the research really says about structured English immersion: A response to Keith Baker. *Phi Delta Kappan, 80,* 705–706.

Krauss, S., & Wang, X. T. (2003). The psychology of the Monty Hall problem: Discovering psychological mechanisms for solving a tenacious brain teaser. *Journal of Experimental Psychology: General, 132,* 3–22.

Kristensen, H., & Garling, T. (2000). Anchoring induced biases in consumer price negotiations. *Journal of Consumer Policy, 23,* 445–460.

Kristjansson, A., & Nakayama, K. (2002). The attentional blink in space and time. *Vision Research, 42,* 2039–2050.

Kroger, J. K., Sabb, F. W., Fales, C. L., Bookheimer, S. Y., Cohen, M. S., & Holyoak, K. J. (2002). Recruitment of anterior dorsolateral prefrontal cortex in human reasoning: A parametric study of relational complexity. *Cerebral Cortex, 12,* 477–485.

Kroll, N. E., & Tu, S.-F. (1988). The bizarre mnemonic. *Psychological Research, 50,* 28–37.

Krutetskii, V. A. (1976). *The psychology of mathematical abilities in school children.* Chicago: University of Chicago Press.

Kuhl, P. K., Williams, K. A., Lacerda, F., Stevens, K. N., & Lindblom, B. (1992). Linguistic experience alters phonetic perception in infants by 6 months of age. *Science, 255,* 606–608.

Kunst-Wilson, W. R., & Zajonc, R. B. (1980). Affective discrimination of stimuli that cannot be recognized. *Science, 207,* 557–558.

Kupermintz, H. (2002). Affective and conative factors as aptitude resources in high school science achievement. *Educational Assessment, 8,* 123–137.

Kutas, M., & Van Petten, C. K. (1994). Psycholinguistics electrified: Event-related brain potential investigations. In M. A. Gernsbacher (Ed.), *Handbook of psycholinguistics* (pp. 83–143). San Diego, CA: Academic Press.

Kvavilashvili, L. (1987). Remembering intention as a distinct form of memory. *British Journal of Psychology, 79,* 507–518.

Kwong, K. K., Belliveau, J. W., Chesler, D. A., Goldberg, I. E., Weisskoff, R. M., Poncelet, B. P., . . . Turner, R. (1992). Dynamic magnetic resonance imaging of human brain activity during primary sensory stimulation. *Proceedings of the National Academy of Sciences, USA, 89,* 5675–5679.

Kyllonen, P. C., & Christal, R. E. (1990). Reasoning ability is (little more than) working memory capacity?! *Intelligence, 14,* 389–433.

LaBerge, D. (1983). Spatial extent of attention to letters and words. *Journal of Experimental Psychology: Human Perception and Performance, 9,* 371–379.

Lahar, C. J., Isaak, M. I., & McArthur, A. D. (2001). Age differences in the magnitude of the attentional blink. *Aging, Neuropsychology, and Cognition, 8,* 149–159.

Lakoff, R. (1975). *Language and a woman's place.* New York: Harper & Row.

Lampinen, J. M., Arnal, J., & Hicks, J. L. (2009). The effectiveness of supermarket posters in helping to find missing children. *Journal of Interpersonal Violence, 24,* 406–423.

Lampinen, J. M., Copeland, S. M., & Neuschatz, J. S. (2001). Recollections of things schematic: Room schemas revisited. *Journal of Experimental Psychology: Learning, Memory, and Cognition, 27,* 1211–1222.

Langdell, T. (1978). Recognition of faces: An approach to the study of autism. *Journal of Child Psychology and Psychiatry, 19,* 255–268.

Lange, K. W., Robbins, T. W., Marsden, C. D., James, M., Owen, A. M., & Paul, G. M. (1992). L-dopa withdrawal in Parkinson's disease selectively impairs cognitive performance. *Psychopharmacology, 107,* 394–404.

Langer, E. J. (1975). The illusion of control. *Journal of Personality and Social Psychology, 32,* 311–328.

Langer, E. J., & Moldoveanu, M. (2000). The construct of mindfulness. *Journal of Social Issues, 56,* 1–9.

Larkey, P., Smith, R., & Kadane, J. B. (1989). It's okay to believe in the hot hand. *Chance, 2,* 22–30.

La Rochefoucauld, F. de (1871). *Reflections, or sentences and moral maxims* (J. W. Bund & J. H. Friswell, Trans.). London: Simpson Low, Son, & Marston. (Original work published 1678)

Larsen, J. D., Baddeley, A. D., & Andrade, J. (2000). Phonological similarity and the irrelevant speech effect: Implications for models of short-term memory. *Memory, 8,* 145–157.

Latora, V., & Marchiori, M. (2004). How the science of complex networks can help developing strategies against terrorisms. *Chaos, Solutions, and Fractals, 20,* 69–75.

Lawton, C. A., & Kallai, J. (2002). Gender differences in wayfinding strategies and anxiety about wayfinding: A cross-cultural comparison. *Sex Roles, 47,* 389–401.

Lea, G. (1975). Chronometric analysis of the method of loci. *Journal of Experimental Psychology: Human Perception and Performance, 1,* 95–104.

Lean, G., & Clements, M. A. (1981). Spatial ability, visual imagery, and mathematical performance. *Educational Studies in Mathematics, 12,* 267–299.

Lecanuet, J., Granier-Deferre, C., & Jacquet, A. (1992). Decelerative cardiac responsiveness to acoustic stimulation in the near-term fetus. *Quarterly Journal of Experimental Psychology, 44,* 279–303.

LeDoux, J. E. (1994). In search of an emotional system in the brain: Leaping from fear to emotion and consciousness. In M. S. Gazzaniga (Ed.), *The cognitive neurosciences* (pp. 356–368). Cambridge, MA: MIT Press.

LeDoux, J. E., Wilson, D. H., & Gazzaniga, M. S. (1977). Manipulo-spatial aspects of cerebral lateralization: Cues to the origin of lateralization. *Neuropsychologia, 15,* 743–750.

Lee, A. Y. (2002). Effects of implicit memory on memory-based versus stimulus-based brand choice. *Journal of Marketing Research, 39,* 440–454.

LeFevre, J. A., Sadesky, G. S., & Bisanz, J. (1996). Selection of procedures in mental addition: Reassessing the problem size effect in adults. *Journal of Experimental Psychology: Learning, Memory, and Cognition, 22,* 216–230.

Lefford, A. (1946). The influence of emotional subject matter on logical reasoning. *Journal of General Psychology, 34,* 127–151.

Lengenfelder, J., Chiaravalloti, N. D., Ricker, J. H., & DeLuca, J. (2003). Deciphering components of impaired working memory in multiple sclerosis. *Cognitive and Behavioral Neurology, 16,* 28–39.

Lenneberg, E. H. (1967). *Biological foundations of language.* New York: Wiley.

Lenton, A. P., Blair, I. V., & Hastie, R. (2001). Illusions of gender: Stereotypes evoke false memories. *Journal of Experimental Social Psychology, 37,* 3–14.

Lerman, D. C., & Iwata, B. A. (1995). Prevalence of the extinction burst and its attenuation during treatment. *Journal of Applied Behavior Analysis, 28,* 93–94.

Lesgold, A., Rubinson, H., Feltovich, P., Glaser, R., Klopfer, D., & Wang, Y. (1988). Expertise in a complex skill: Diagnosing x-ray pictures. In M. T. H. Chi, R. Glaser, & M. J. Farr (Eds.), *The nature of expertise* (pp. 311–341). Hillsdale, NJ: Erlbaum.

Leslie, A. M., & Keeble, S. (1987). Do six-month-old infants perceive causality? *Cognition, 25,* 265–288.

Levelt, W. J. M. (1989). *Speaking: From intention to articulation.* Cambridge, MA: MIT Press.

Levin, I. P., & Gaeth, G. J. (1988). How consumers are affected by the framing of attribute information before and after consuming the product. *Journal of Consumer Research, 15,* 374–378.

Levin, J. R. (1981). The mnemonic '80s: Keywords in the classroom. *Educational Psychologist, 16,* 65–82.

Levin, J. R. (1993). Mnemonic strategies and classroom learning: A twenty-year report card. *Elementary School Journal, 94,* 235–244.

Levin, J. R., Shriberg, L. K., & Berry, J. K. (1983). A concrete strategy for remembering abstract prose. *American Education Research Journal, 20,* 277–290.

Levin, J. R., Shriberg, L. K., Miller, G. E., McCormick, C. B., & Levin, B. B. (1980). The keyword method in the classroom: How to remember the states and their capitals. *Elementary School Journal, 80,* 185–191.

Levy, R. (1994). Aging-associated cognitive decline (Report of the working party of the International Psychogeriatric Association in collaboration with the World Health Organization). *International Psychogeriatric Association, 6,* 63–68.

Levy, R., & Goldman-Rakic, P. S. (2000). Segregation of working memory functions within the dorsolateral prefrontal cortex. *Experimental Brain Research, 133,* 23–32.

Levy, S., Lahoud, E., Shomroni, I., & Steinhauer, J. (2007). The a.c. and d.c. Josephson effects in a Bose–Einstein condensate. *Nature, 449,* 579–583.

Lewinsohn, P. M., Danaher, B. G., & Kikel, S. (1977). Visual imagery as a mnemonic aid for brain-injured persons. *Journal of Consulting and Clinical Psychology, 45,* 717–723.

Lewis, M., & Freedle, R. (1973). Mother–infant dyad: The cradle of meaning. In P. Pliner, L. Kramer, &

T. Alloway (Eds.), *Communication and affect* (pp. 127–155). New York: Academic Press.

Lewis, M. B. (2003). Thatcher's children: Development and the Thatcher illusion. *Perception, 32,* 1415–1421.

Lewkowicz, D. J. (2002). Heterogeneity and heterochrony in the development of intersensory perception. *Cognitive Brain Research, 14,* 41–63.

Liberman, A. M. (1982). On finding that speech is special. *American Psychologist, 37,* 148–167.

Liberman, A. M., & Mattingly, I. G. (1985). The motor theory of speech perception revised. *Cognition, 21,* 1–36.

Liberman, A. M., & Mattingly, I. G. (1989). A specialization for speech perception. *Science, 243,* 489–494.

Liberman, N., & Klar, Y. (1996). Hypothesis testing in Wason's selection task: Social exchange, cheating detection, or task understanding. *Cognition, 58,* 127–156.

Lichtenstein, S., Slovic, P., Fischhoff, B., Layman, M., & Combs, B. (1978). Judged frequency of lethal events. *Journal of Experimental Psychology: Human Learning and Memory, 4,* 551–578.

Liddell, S. K., & Metzger, M. (1998). Gesture in sign language discourse. *Journal of Pragmatics, 30,* 657–697.

Lieberman, P. (1970). Towards a unified phonetic theory. *Linguistic Inquiry, 1,* 307–322.

Lieberman, P. (1984). *The biology and the evolution of language.* Cambridge, MA: Harvard University Press.

Light, L. L., & Carter-Sobell, L. (1970). Effects of changed semantic context on recognition memory. *Journal of Verbal Learning and Verbal Behavior, 9,* 1–11.

Light, L. L., & Anderson, P. A. (1983). Memory for scripts in young and older adults. *Memory & Cognition, 11,* 435–444.

Likert, R., & Quasha, W. H. (1970). *Revised Minnesota Paper Form Board Test.* San Antonio, TX: The Psychological Corporation.

Lindenberger, U., Kliegl, R., & Baltes, P. B. (1992). Professional expertise does not eliminate age differences in imagery-based memory performance during adulthood. *Psychology and Aging, 7,* 585–593.

Lindsay, D. S., & Johnson, M. K. (2000). False memories and the source-monitoring framework: Reply to Reyna and Lloyd (1997). *Learning and Individual Differences, 12,* 145–161.

Lindsey, G. R. (1959). Statistical data useful for the operation of a baseball team. *Operations Research, 7,* 197–207.

Linton, M. (1979). Real-world memory after six years: An in-vivo study of very long-term memory. In M. M. Gruneberg, P. E. Morris, & R. N. Sykes (Eds.), *Practical aspects of memory: Current research and issues: Vol. 1. Memory in everyday life* (pp. 69–76). New York: Academic Press.

Linville, P. W., Fischer, G. W., & Fischhoff, B. (1993). AIDS risk perceptions and decision biases. In J. B. Pryor & G. D. Reeder (Eds.), *The social psychology of HIV infection* (pp. 35–38). Hillsdale, NJ: Erlbaum.

Liotti, M., Mayberg, H. S., McGinnis, S., Brannan, S. L., & Jerabek, P. (2002). Unmasking disease-specific cerebral blood flow abnormalities: Mood challenge in patients with remitted unipolar depression. *American Journal of Psychiatry, 159,* 1830–1840.

Lippmann, W. (1922). *Public opinion.* Oxford, England: Harcourt, Brace.

Locke, J. L. (1978). Phonemic effects in the silent reading of hearing and deaf children. *Cognition, 6,* 175–187.

Loess, H., & Waugh, N. C. (1967). Short-term memory and inter-trial interval. *Journal of Verbal Learning and Verbal Behavior, 5,* 455–460.

Loftus, E. F. (1975). Leading questions and the eyewitness report. *Cognitive Psychology, 7,* 560–572.

Loftus, E. F. (1980). *Memory.* Reading, MA: Addison-Wesley.

Loftus, E. F. (1997). Memory for a past that never was. *Current Directions in Psychological Science, 6,* 60–65.

Loftus, E. F. (2003). Make-believe memories. *American Psychologist, 58,* 867–873.

Loftus, E. F., & Burns, T. W. (1982). Mental shock can produce retrograde amnesia. *Memory & Cognition, 10,* 318–323.

Loftus, E. F., Miller, D. G., & Burns, H. J. (1978). Semantic integration of verbal information into a visual memory. *Journal of Experimental Psychology: Human Learning and Memory, 4,* 19–31.

Loftus, E. F., & Palmer, J. C. (1974). Reconstruction of automobile destruction: An example of the interaction between language and memory. *Journal of Verbal Learning and Verbal Behavior, 13,* 585–589.

Loftus, E. F., & Zanni, G. (1975). Eyewitness testimony: The influence of the wording of a question. *Bulletin of the Psychonomic Society, 5,* 86–88.

Loftus, G. R. (1983). The continuing persistence of the icon. *Behavioral and Brain Sciences, 6,* 28.

Loftus, G. R., & Bell, S. M. (1975). Two types of information in picture memory. *Journal of Experimental Psychology: Human Learning and Memory, 1,* 103–113.

Loftus, G. R., & Kallman, H. J . (1979). Encoding and use of detail information. *Journal of Experimental Psychology: Human Learning and Memory, 1,* 197–211.

Loftus, G. R., & Mackworth, N. H. (1978). Cognitive determinants of fixation location during picture viewing. *Journal of Experimental Psychology: Human Perception and Performance, 4,* 565–572.

Logan, G. D. (2002). Parallel and serial processing. In H. Pashler & J. Wixted (Eds.), *Stevens' handbook of experimental psychology* (3rd ed., Vol. 4, pp. 271–300). Hoboken, NJ: Wiley.

Logie, R. H. (1995). *Visuo-spatial working memory.* Hove, England: Erlbaum.

Logie, R. H. (2003). Spatial and visual working memory: A mental workspace. In D. Irwin & B. Ross (Eds.), *Cognitive vision: The psychology of learning and motivation* (Vol. 42, pp. 37–78). San Diego, CA: Academic Press.

Lorch, E. P., Diener, M. B., van den Broek, P., Sanchez, R. P., Milich, R., & Welsh, R. (1999). The effects of story structure on the recall of stories in children with attention deficit/hyperactivity disorder. *Journal of Educational Psychology, 91,* 273–283.

Losh, M., Bellugi, U., Reilly, J., & Anderson, D. (2000). Narrative as a social engagement tool: The excessive use of evaluation in narratives from children with Williams syndrome. *Narrative Inquiry, 10,* 265–290.

Lovaas, O. I., Cross, S., & Revlin, S. (2006). Autistic disorder. In J. E. Fisher & W. O'Donohue (Eds.), *Practioner's guide to evidence-based psychotherapy* (pp. 101–114). New York: Springer.

Lucariello, J. M., & Mindolovich, C. (2002). The best laid plans . . . : Beyond scripts are counterscripts. *Journal of Cognition and Development, 3,* 91–115.

Lucy, J. A. (1992). *Language diversity and thought: A reformulation of the linguistic relativity hypothesis.* Cambridge, England: Cambridge University Press.

Luria, A. R. (1968). *The mind of a mnemonist: A little book about a vast memory* (L. Solotaroff, Trans.). New York: Basic Books.

Luria, A. R. (1976). *Cognitive development: Its cultural and social foundations* (M. Lopez-Morillas & L. Solotaroff, Trans.). Cambridge, MA: Harvard University Press.

Lynch, K. (1960). *The image of the city.* Cambridge, MA: MIT Press.

Lyon, G. R. (1997). *Report on learning disabilities research.* Washington, DC: U.S. House of Representatives, Committee on Education and the Workforce.

Macdonald, R., & Gilhooly, K. (1990). More about Linda, *or* conjunctions in context. *European Journal of Cognitive Psychology, 2,* 57–70.

Mack, A., & Rock, I. (1998). *Inattentional blindness.* Cambridge, MA: MIT Press.

MacKay, D. G. (1966). To end ambiguous sentences. *Perception & Psychophysics, 1,* 426–436.

MacKay, D. G. (1973). Aspects of the theory of comprehension, memory and attention. *Quarterly Journal of Experimental Psychology, 25,* 22–40.

MacKay, D. G., & Miller, M. D. (1994). Semantic blindness: Repeated concepts are difficult to encode and recall under time pressure. *Psychological Science, 5,* 52–55.

MacKay, D. G., Miller, M. D., & Schuster, S. P. (1994). Repetition blindness and aging: Evidence for a binding deficit involving a single, theoretically specified connection. *Psychology and Aging, 5,* 52–65.

MacKay, D. G., Shafto, M., & Taylor, J. K. (2004). Relations between emotion, memory, and attention: Evidence from taboo Stroop, lexical decision and immediate memory tasks. *Memory & Cognition, 32,* 474–488.

MacKay, D. G., Wulf, G., Yin, C., & Abrams, L. (1993). Relations between word perception and production: New theory and data on the verbal transformation effect. *Journal of Memory and Language, 32,* 624–646.

MacKeben, M., Trauzettel-Klosinski, S., Reinhard, J., Durrwachter, U., Adler, M., & Klosinski, G. (2004). Eye movement control during single-word reading in dyslexics. *Journal of Vision, 4,* 388–402.

Mackworth, N. H. (1948). The breakdown of vigilance during prolonged visual search. *Quarterly Journal of Experimental Psychology, 1,* 6–21.

Mackworth, N. H. (1950). *Researches on the measurement of human performance* (Medical Research Council Special Report No. 268). London: HMSO.

MacLin, O. H., & Malpass, R. S. (2001). Racial categorization of faces: The ambiguous race face effect. *Psychology, Public Policy, and Law, 7,* 98–118.

MacLin, O. H., & Malpass, R. S. (2003). The ambiguous race face illusion. *Perception, 32,* 249–252.

Macnamara, J. (1982). *Names for things: A study of human learning.* Cambridge, MA: MIT Press.

MacWhinney, B. (1998). Models of the emergence of language. *Annual Review of Psychology, 49,* 199–227.

Mahoney, M. J., & DeMonbreun, B. G. (1977). Psychology of the scientist: An analysis of problem-solving bias. *Cognitive Therapy and Research, 1,* 229–238.

Maier, N. R. F. (1930). Reasoning in humans: I. On direction. *Journal of Comparative Psychology, 10,* 115–143.

Maier, N. R. F. (1931). Reasoning in humans: II. The solution of a problem and its appearance in consciousness. *Journal of Comparative Psychology, 12,* 181–194.

Maki, W. S., & Padmanabhan, G. (1994). Transient suppression of processing during rapid serial visual presentation: Acquired distinctiveness of probes modulates the attentional blink. *Psychonomic Bulletin & Review, 1,* 499–504.

Malpass, R. S., & Kravitz, J. (1969). Recognition for faces of own and other race. *Journal of Personality and Social Psychology, 13,* 330–334.

Mampe, B., Friederici, A. D., Christophe, A., & Wermke, K. (2009). Newborns' cry melody is shaped by their native language. *Current Biology, 19,* 1994–1997.

Mandler, G. (1980). Recognizing: The judgment of previous occurrence. *Psychological Review, 87,* 252–271.

Mandler, G., & Shebo, B. J. (1982). Subitizing: An analysis of its component processes. *Journal of Experimental Psychology: General, 11,* 1–22.

Mandler, J. M., & Johnson, N. S. (1977). Remembrance of things parsed: Story structure and recall. *Cognitive Psychology, 9,* 111–151.

Manktelow, K. I., & Evans, J. St. B. (1979). Facilitation of reasoning by realism: Effect or non-effect. *Journal of Psychology, 70,* 477–488.

Manning, S. K. (1980). Tactual and visual alphanumeric suffix effects. *Quarterly Journal of Experimental Psychology, 32,* 257–267.

Marchman, V. A., & Bates, E. (1994). Continuity in lexical and morphological development: A test of the critical mass hypothesis. *Journal of Child Language, 21,* 339–366.

Marcus, G. F. (1996). Why do children say "breaked"? *Current Directions in Psychological Science, 5,* 81–85.

Markman, E. M., & Wachtel, G. F. (1988). Children's use of mutual exclusivity to constrain the meaning of words. *Cognitive Psychology, 20,* 121–157.

Markovits, H., & Nantel, G. (1989). The belief-bias effect in the production and evaluation of logical conclusions. *Memory & Cognition, 17,* 11–17.

Marmor, G. S., & Zaback, L. A. (1976). Mental rotation by the blind: Does mental rotation depend on visual imagery? *Journal of Experimental Psychology: Human Perception and Performance, 2,* 515–521.

Marsh, R. L., & Hicks, J. L. (1998). Event-based prospective memory and executive control of working memory. *Journal of Experimental Psychology: Learning, Memory, and Cognition, 24,* 336–349.

Marshall, J. C., & Halligan, P. W. (1994). The yin and the yang of visuo-spatial neglect: A case study. *Neuropsychologia, 32,* 1037–1057.

Marshall, J. C., & Halligan, P. W. (1995). Seeing the forest but only half the trees? *Nature, 373,* 521–523.

Marslen-Wilson, W. D. (1987). Functional parallelism in spoken word recognition. *Cognition, 25,* 71–102.

Martin, G. (2003). Why trepan? Contributions from medical history and the South Pacific. In R. Arnott, S. Finger, & C. Smith (Eds.), *Trepanation: History, discovery, theory* (pp. 323–345). Lisse, the Netherlands: Swets & Zeitlinger.

Martin, K. A., & Hall, C. R. (1995). Using mental imagery to enhance intrinsic motivation. *Journal of Sport & Exercise Psychology, 17,* 54–69.

Martin, K. A., Moritz, S., & Hall, C. R. (1999). Imagery use in sport: A literature review and applied model. *Sport Psychologist, 13,* 245–268.

Martin, L. (1986). "Eskimo words for snow": A case study in the genesis and decay of an anthropological example. *American Anthropologist, 88,* 418–423.

Martin, R. C., & Freedman, M. L. (2001). Relations between language and memory deficits. In R. S. Berndt (Ed.), *Handbook of neuropsychology: Vol. 3. Language and aphasia* (2nd ed., pp. 239–256). Amsterdam: Elsevier.

Massaro, D. M. (1987). *Speech perception by ear and eye: A paradigm for psychological inquiry.* Hillsdale, NJ: Erlbaum.

Massaro, D. M. (1998). *Perceiving talking faces: From speech perception to a behavioral principle.* Cambridge, MA: MIT Press.

Mastropieri, M. A. (1988). Using the keyword method. *Teaching Exceptional Children, 20,* 4–8.

Mastropieri, M. A., Scruggs, T. E., & Fulk, B. J. M. (1990). Teaching abstract vocabulary with the keyword method: Effects on recall and comprehension. *Journal of Learning Disabilities, 23,* 92–96, 107.

Mastropieri, M. A., Scruggs, T. E., & Levin, J. R. (1985). Maximizing what exceptional children can learn: A review of research on the keyword method and related mnemonic techniques. *Remedial and Special Education, 6,* 39–45.

Mather, M., & Carstensen, L. L. (2005). Aging and motivated cognition: The positivity effect in attention and memory. *Trends in Cognitive Sciences, 9,* 496–502.

Matlin, M. W., & Stang, D. J. (1978). *The Pollyanna principle: Selectivity in language, memory, and thought.* Cambridge, MA: Schenkman.

Matthews, G., Davies, D., Westerman, S., & Stammers, R. (2000). *Human performance, cognition, stress and individual differences.* Philadelphia: Taylor & Francis.

Maugham, W. S. (1963). *Ten novels and their authors.* London: Mercury Books.

Maujean, A., Sum, S., & McQueen, R. (2003). Effect of cognitive demand on prospective memory in individuals with traumatic brain injury. *Brain Impairment, 4,* 135–145.

Maunsell, J. H. R., & Newsome, W. T. (1987). Visual processing in monkey extrastriate cortex. *Annual Review of Neuroscience, 10,* 365–367.

Mayer, R. E. (1979). Twenty years of research on advance organizers: Assimilation theory is still the best predictor of results. *Instructional Science, 8,* 133–167.

Mayer, R. E. (1992). *Thinking, problem solving, cognition*. New York: W. H. Freeman and Company.

Mayer, R. E. (2003). *Learning and instruction*. Upper Saddle River, NJ: Pearson.

Mayer, R. E., & Anderson, R. B. (1991). Animations need narrations: An experimental test of a dual-coding hypothesis. *Journal of Educational Psychology, 82,* 484–490.

Mayer, R. E., & Gallini, J. K. (1990). When is an illustration worth ten thousand words? *Journal of Educational Psychology, 82,* 715–725.

Mayer, R. E., Heiser, H., & Lonn, S. (2001). Cognitive constraints on multimedia learning: When presenting more material results in less understanding. *Journal of Educational Psychology, 93,* 187–198.

Mayes, A. R. (1992). What are the functional deficits that underlie amnesia? In L. R. Squire & N. Butters (Eds.), *Neuropsychology of memory* (2nd ed., pp. 23–35). New York: Guilford Press.

McClelland, J. L., & Elman, J. L. (1986). The TRACE model of speech perception. *Cognitive Psychology, 18,* 1–86.

McClelland, J. L., & Rogers, T. T. (2003). The parallel distributed processing approach to semantic cognition. *Nature Reviews Neuroscience, 4,* 310–322.

McClelland, J. L., & Rumelhart, D. E. (1981). An interactive activation model of context effects in letter perception: Part I. An account of basic findings. *Psychological Review, 88,* 375–407.

McCorduck, P. (2004). *Machines who think* (2nd ed.). Natick, MA: A. K. Peters.

McDaniel, M. A., & Einstein, G. O. (1993). The importance of cue familiarity and cue distinctiveness in prospective memory. *Memory, 1,* 23–41.

McDaniel, M. A., Glisky, E. L., Rubin, S. R., Guynn, M. J., & Routhieaux, B. C. (1999). Prospective memory: A neuropsychological study. *Neuropsychology, 13,* 103–110.

McDaniel, M. A., & Pressley, M. (1984). Putting the keyword method in context. *Journal of Educational Psychology, 76,* 598–609.

McDermott, K. B. (1996). The persistence of false memories in list recall. *Journal of Memory and Language, 35,* 212–230.

McDonald, J. J., Teder-Sälejärvi, W. A., Di Russo, F., & Hillyard, S. A. (2003). Neural substrates of perceptual enhancement by cross-modal spatial attention. *Journal of Cognitive Neuroscience, 15,* 10–19.

McEachin, J. J., Smith, T., & Lovaas, O. I. (1993). Long-term outcome for children with autism who received early intensive behavioral treatment. *American Journal on Mental Retardation, 97,* 359–372.

McGee, M. G. (1979). Human spatial abilities: Psychometric studies and environmental, genetic, hormonal, and neurological influences. *Psychological Bulletin, 86,* 889–918.

McGuigan, F. L., & Winstead, C. L. (1974). Discriminative relationship between covert oral behavior and the phonemic system in internal information processing. *Journal of Experimental Psychology, 103,* 885–890.

McGurk, H., & MacDonald, J. (1976). Hearing lips and seeing voices. *Nature, 264,* 746–748.

McKnight, A. J., & McKnight, A. S. (1993). The effect of cellular phone use upon driver attention. *Accident Analysis & Prevention, 25,* 259–265.

McKone, E., Martini, P., & Nakayama, K. (2001). Categorical perception of face identity in noise isolates configural processing. *Journal of Experimental Psychology: Human Percpetion and Performance, 3,* 573–599.

McLean, R. S., & Gregg, L. W. (1967). Effects of induced chunking on temporal aspects of serial recitation. *Journal of Experimental Psychology, 74,* 455–459.

McNeill, D. (1970). *The acquisition of language: The study of developmental psycholinguistics*. New York: Harper & Row.

Meacham, J. A. (1982). A note on remembering to execute planned actions. *Journal of Applied Developmental Psychology, 3,* 121–133.

Meacham, J. A., & Singer, J. (1977). Incentive effects in prospective remembering. *Journal of Psychology, 97,* 191–197.

Mehler, J., Jusczyk, P., Dehaene-Lambertz, G., Halsted, N., Bertoncini, J., & Amiel-Tison, C. (1988). A precursor of language acquisition in young infants. *Cognition, 29,* 143–178.

Meissner, C. A., & Brigham, J. C. (2001). Thirty years of investigating the own-race bias in memory for faces: A meta-analytic review. *Psychology, Public Policy, and Law, 7,* 3–35.

Melara, R. D., & Mounts, J. R. W. (1993). Selective attention to Stroop dimensions: Effects of baseline discriminability, response mode, and practice. *Memory & Cognition, 21,* 627–645.

Mellers, B., Hertwig, R., & Kahneman, D. (2001). Do frequency representations eliminate conjunction effects? An exercise in adversarial collaboration. *Psychological Science, 12,* 269–275.

Meltzoff, A. N., & Brooks, R. (2001). "Like me" as a building block for understanding other minds: Bodily acts, attention, and intention. In B. F. Malle, L. J. Moses, & D. A. Baldwin (Eds.), *Intentions and intentionality: Foundations of social cognition* (pp. 171–191). Cambridge, MA: MIT Press.

Meltzoff, A. N., & Moore, M. K. (1977). Imitation of facial and manual gestures by human neonates. *Science, 198,* 74–78.

Meltzoff, A. N., & Moore, M. K. (1997). Explaining facial imitation: A theoretical model. *Early Development and Parenting, 6,* 179–192.

Meltzoff, A. N., & Prinz, W. (2002). *The imitative mind: Development, evolution, and brain bases.* New York: Cambridge University Press.

Memon, A., & Higham, P. A. (1999). A review of the cognitive interview. *Psychology, Crime, & Law, 5,* 177–196.

Merabet, L. B., Maguire, D., Warde, A., Alterescu, K., Stickgold, R., & Pascual-Leone, A. (2004). Visual hallucinations during proonged blindfolding in sighted subjects. *Journal of Neuro-Opthalmology, 24,* 109–113.

Mercier, H., & Sperber, D. (2009). Intuitive and reflective inferences. In J. St. B. Evans & K. Frankish (Eds.), *In two minds* (pp. 149–170). New York: Oxford University Press.

Merikle, P. M. (1980). Selection from visual persistence by perceptual groups and category membership. *Journal of Experimental Psychology: General, 109,* 279–295.

Merritt, L. (2003). Recognition of the clinical signs and symptoms of Joubert syndrome. *Advances in Neonatal Care, 3,* 178–188.

Mervis, C., Catlin, J., & Rosch, E. (1975). Development of the structure of color categories. *Developmental Psychology, 11,* 54–60.

Merzenich, M., Jenkins, W., Johnston, P., Schreiner, C., Miller, S., & Tallal, P. (1996). Temporal processing deficits of language-learning impaired children ameliorated by training. *Science, 271,* 81–84.

Mesulam, M. M. (1998). From sensation to cognition. *Brain, 125,* 1013–1052.

Mesulam, M. M. (2001). Primary progressive aphasia. *Annals of Neurology, 49,* 425–432.

Metcalfe, J., & Wiebe, D. (1987). Intuition in insight and noninsight problem solving. *Memory & Cognition, 15,* 236–246.

Meudell, P. R., Mayes, A. R., Ostergaad, A., & Pickering, A. (1985). Recency and frequency judgments in alcoholic amnesics and normal people with poor memory. *Cortex, 21,* 487–511.

Mewhort, D. J. K., & Butler, B. E. (1983). On the nature of brief visual storage: There never was an icon. *Behavioral and Brain Sciences, 6,* 31–33.

Meyer-Lindenberg, A., Miletich, R. S., Kohn, P. D., Esposito, G., Carson, R. E., Quarantelli, M., . . . Berman, K. F. (2002). Reduced prefrontal activity predicts dopaminergic function in schizophrenia. *Nature Neuroscience, 5,* 267–271.

Michael, E. B., Keller, T. A., Carpenter, P. A., & Just, M. A. (2001). fMRI investigation of sentence comprehension by eye and by ear: Modality fingerprints on cognitive processes. *Human Brain Mapping, 13,* 239–252.

Michel, F., & Henaff, M.-A. (2004). Seeing without the occipitoparietal cortex. Simultanagnosia as a shrinkage of the attentional visual field. *Behavioural Neurology, 15,* 3–13.

Michotte, A. (1963). *The perception of causality.* Andover, MA: Methuen.

Mikels, J. A., Reuter-Lorenz, P. A., Beyer, A., & Frederiskson, B. L. (2008). Emotion and working memory: Evidence for domain-specific processes for affective maintenance. *Emotion, 8,* 256–266.

Mikulecky, B. S., & Jeffries, L. (2007). *Advanced reading power: Extensive reading, vocabulary building, comprehension skills, reading faster.* Tokyo: Pearson.

Miller, G. A. (1956). The magical number seven plus or minus two: Some limits on our capacity for processing information. *Psychological Review, 63,* 81–97.

Miller, G. A. (1991). *The science of words.* New York: Scientific American.

Miller, G. A. (2003). The cognitive revolution: A historical perspective. *Trends in Cognitive Sciences, 3,* 141–144.

Miller, G. A., Galanter, E. H., & Pribram, K. H. (1960). *Plans and structure of behavior.* New York: Holt.

Miller, G. A., & Isard, S. (1963). Some perceptual consequences of linguistic rules. *Journal of Verbal Learning and Verbal Behavior, 2,* 217–228.

Miller, K. F., Smith, C. M., Zhu, J., & Zhang, H. (1995). Preschool origins of cross-national differences in mathematical competence: The role of number-naming systems. *Psychological Science, 6,* 65–60.

Miller, M. D., & MacKay, D. G. (1994). Repetition deafness: Repeated words in computer-compressed speech are difficult to encode and recall. *Psychological Science, 5*(5), 47–51.

Milner, B. (1962). Les troubles de la mémoire accompagnant des lésions hippocampiques bilatérales [Memory problems accompanying bilateral hippocampal lesions]. In *Physiologie de l'hippocampe* (pp. 257–272). Paris: Centre de la Recherche Scientifique.

Milner, B. (1965). Visually guided maze learning in man: Effects of bilateral hippocampal, bilateral frontal, and unilateral cerebral lesions. *Neuropsychologia, 3,* 317–338.

Milner, B. (1970). Memory and the temporal regions of the brain. In K. H. Pribram & D. E. Broadbent (Eds.), *Biology of memory* (pp. 29–50). New York: Academic Press.

Milner, B., Corkin, S., & Teuber, H.-L. (1968). Further analysis of the hippocampal amnesic syndrome. *Neuropsychologia, 6,* 215–234.

Milner, B., Squire, L. R., & Kandel, E. R. (1998). Cognitive neuroscience and the study of memory. *Neuron, 20,* 445–468.

Mintzer, M. Z., & Snodgrass, J. G. (1999). The picture superiority effect: Support for the distinctiveness model. *American Journal of Psychology, 112,* 113–146.

Mishkin, M., Ungerleider, L. G., & Macko, K. A. (1983). Object vision and spatial vision: Two cortical pathways. *Trends in Neurosciences, 6,* 414–417.

Mitchell, A. A. (1986). The effect of verbal and visual components of advertisements on brand attitudes and attitude toward the advertisement. *Journal of Consumer Research, 13,* 12–24.

Miura, I. T. (1987). Mathematics achievement as a function of language. *Journal of Educational Psychology, 79,* 79–82.

Mofidi, R., Duff, M., Madhavan, K., Garden, O., & Parks, R. (2006). Identification of severe acute pancreatitis using an artificial neural network. *Surgery, 14*(1), 59–66.

Mondor, T. A. (1998). A transient processing deficit following selection of an auditory target. *Psychonomic Bulletin & Review, 5,* 305–311.

Montant, M., & Behrmann, M. (2000). Pure alexia: A case review. *Neurocase, 6,* 265–294.

Moore, S. C., & Oaksford, M. (2002). An information value for mood: Negative mood biases attention to global information in a probabilistic classification task. In S. Moore & M. Oaksford (Eds.), *Emotional cognition* (pp. 221–243). Amsterdam: John Benjamins.

Morais, J., Luytens, M., & Alegria, J. (1984). Segmentation abilities of dyslexics and normal readers. *Perceptual and Motor Skills, 58,* 221–222.

Moray, N. (1959). Attention in dichotic listening: Affective cues and the influence of instruction. *Quarterly Journal of Experimental Psychology, 11,* 56–60.

Morcom, A. M., Good, C. D., Frackowiak, R. S. J., & Rugg, M. D. (2003). Age effects on the neural correlates of successful memory encoding. *Brain, 126,* 213–229.

Moreno, R., & Mayer, R. E. (1999). Cognitive principles of multimedia learning: The role of modality and contiguity. *Journal of Educational Psychology, 91,* 358–368.

Morgan, J., & Morton, J. (1944). The distortion of syllogistic reasoning produced by personal conviction. *Journal of Social Psychology, 20,* 39–59.

Moritz, S. E., Hall, C. R., Vadocz, E., & Martin, K. A. (1996). What are confident athletes imagining? An examination of image content. *Sport Psychologist, 10,* 171–179.

Morris, A. L., & Harris, C. L. (1999). A sublexical focus of repetition blindness: Evidence from illusory words. *Journal of Experimental Psychology: Human Perception and Performance, 25,* 1060–1075.

Morris, A. L., Still, M. L., & Caldwell-Harris, C. L. (2009). Repetition blindness: An emergent property of interitem competition. *Cognitive Psychology, 58,* 338–375.

Morris, R. G., Miotto, E. C., Feigenbaum, J. D., Bullock, P., & Polkey, C. E. (1997). The effect of goal–subgoal conflict on planning ability after frontal- and temporal-lobe lesions in humans. *Neuropsychologia, 35,* 1147–1157.

Morrongiello, B. A., & Clifton, R. K. (1984). Effects of sound frequency on behavioral and cardiac orienting in newborn and five-month-old infants. *Journal of Experimental Child Psychology, 38,* 429–446.

Morton, J., & Patterson, K. (1987). A new attempt at an interpretation, or, and attempt at a new interpretation. In M. Coltheart, K. E. Patterson, & J. C. Marshall (Eds.), *Deep dyslexia* (pp. 286–306). London: Routledge.

Moshman, D. (1990). The development of metalogical understanding. In W. Overton (Ed.), *Reasoning, necessity, and logic: Developmental perspectives* (pp. 205–225). Hillsdale, NJ: Erlbaum.

Moshman, D., & Franks, B. A. (1986). Development of the concept of inferential validity. *Child Development, 57,* 153–165.

Moshman, D., & Timmons, M. (1982). The construction of logical necessity. *Human Development, 25,* 309–323.

Most, S. B., Simons, D. J., Scholl, B. J., Jimenez, R., Clifford, E., & Chabris, C. F. (2001). How not to be seen: The contribution of similarity and selective ignoring to sustained inattentional blindness. *Psychological Science, 12,* 9–17.

Mottaghy, F. M., Gangitano, M., Sparing, R., Krause, B. J., & Pascual-Leone, A. (2002). Segregation of areas related to visual working memory in the prefrontal cortex revealed by rTMS. *Cerebral Cortex, 12,* 369–375.

Motter, A. E., de Moura, A. P. S., Lai, Y.-C., & Dasgupta, P. (2002). Topology of the conceptual network of language. *Physical Review, E65,* 65102-1–65102-4.

Moutard, M. L., Kieffer, V., Feingold, J., Kieffer, F., Lewin, F., Adamsbaum, C., . . . Ponsot, G. (2003). Agenesis of corpus callosum: Prenatal diagnosis and prognosis. *Child's Nervous System, 19,* 471–476.

Moyer, R. S. (1973). Comparing objects in memory: Evidence suggesting an internal psychophysics. *Perception & Psychophysics, 13,* 180–184.

Moyer, R. S., & Bayer, R. H. (1976). Mental comparison and the symbolic distance effect. *Cognitive Psychology, 8,* 228–246.

Mumford, M., & Gustafson, S. (1988). Creativity syndrome: Integration, application, and innovation. *Psychological Bulletin, 103,* 27–43.

Murdock, B. B. (1961). The retention of individual items. *Journal of Experimental Psychology, 62,* 618–625.

Murdock, B. B. (1962). The serial position effect of free recall. *Journal of Experimental Psychology, 64,* 482–488.

Nadel, L., & Zola-Morgan, S. (1984). Infantile amnesia: A neurobiological perspective. In M. Moscovitch (Ed.), *Infant memory: Its relation to normal and pathological memory in humans and other animals* (Vol. 9, pp. 145–172). New York: Plenum Press.

Naito, E., Kochiyama, T., Kitada, R., Nakamura, S., Matsumura, M., Yonekura, Y., & Sadato, N. (2002). Internally simulated movement sensations during motor imagery activate cortical motor areas and the cerebellum. *The Journal of Neuroscience, 22,* 3683–3691.

Nakamura, G., Graesser, A., Zimmerman, J., & Riha, J. (1985). Script processing in a natural situation. *Memory & Cognition, 13,* 140–144.

Nakazima, S. A. (1962). A comparative study of the speech development of Japanese and American English in childhood. *Studio Phonologica, 2,* 27–46.

Narr, K. L., Bilder, R. M., Luders, E., Thompson, P. M., Woods, R. P., Robinson, D., . . . Toga, A. W. (2007). Asymmetries of cortical shape: Effects of handedness, sex and schizophrenia. *NeuroImage, 34,* 939–948.

National Center for Education Statistics. (1992). *Executive summary of adult literacy in America: A first look at the results of the National Adult Literacy Survey.* Washington, DC: U.S. Government Printing Office.

Navon, D. (1977). Forest before trees: The precedence of global features in visual perception. *Cognitive Psychology, 9,* 353–383.

Navon, D. (2003). What does a compound letter tell the psychologist's mind? *Acta Psychologica, 114,* 273–309.

Neath, I. (2000). Modeling the effects of irrelevant speech on memory. *Psychonomic Bulletin & Review, 7,* 403–423.

Neisser, U. (1964). Visual search. *Scientific American, 210,* 94–102.

Neisser, U. (1967). *Cognitive psychology.* New York: Appleton-Century-Crofts.

Neisser, U. (1976). *Cognition and reality.* San Francisco: W. H. Freeman and Company.

Neisser, U. (1979). The control of information pickup in selective looking. In A. D. Pick (Ed.), *Perception and its development: A tribute to Eleanor J. Gibson* (pp. 201–219). Hillsdale, NJ: Erlbaum.

Neisser, U. (1982). *Memory observed.* San Francisco: W. H. Freeman and Company.

Nelson, C. (1995). The ontogeny of human memory: A cognitive neuroscience perspective. *Developmental Psychology, 31,* 723–738.

Nelson, D. L., Reed, V. S., & Walling, J. R. (1976). Pictorial superiority effect. *Journal of Experimental Psychology: Human Learning and Memory, 2,* 523–528.

Nelson, T. D. (2006). *The psychology of prejudice* (2nd ed.). London: Pearson.

Nelson, T. O., Gerler, D., & Narens, L. (1984). Accuracy of feeling-of-knowing judgments for predicting perceptual identification and relearning. *Journal of Experimental Psychology: General, 113,* 282–300.

Nelson, T. O., Metzler, J., & Reed, D. A. (1974). Role of details in the long-term recognition of pictures and verbal descriptions. *Journal of Experimental Psychology, 102,* 184–186.

Nerlich, A., Peschel, O., Zink, A., & Rosing, F. W. (2003). The pathology of trepanation: Differential diagnosis, healing and dry bone appearance in modern cases. In R. Arnott, S. Finger, & C. Smith (Eds.), *Trepanation: History, discovery, theory* (pp. 43–51). Lisse, the Netherlands: Swets & Zeitlinger.

Neutra, R. R. (1990). Counterpoint from a cluster buster. *American Journal of Epidemiology, 132,* 1–8.

Neville, H. J., Snyder, E. D., Woods, D., & Galambos, R. (1982). Recognition and surprise alter the human visual evoked response. *Proceedings of the National Academy of Sciences, USA, 79,* 2121–2123.

New, J., Cosmides, L., & Tooby, J. (2007). Category-specific attention for animals reflects ancestral priorities, not expertise. *Proceedings of the National Academy of Sciences, USA, 104,* 16598–16603.

Newell, A., & Simon, H. A. (1956). The logic theory machine: A complex information processing system. *IEE Transactions on Information Theory, 2,* 61–79.

Newell, A., & Simon, H. A. (1972). *Human problem solving.* Englewood Cliffs, NJ: Prentice Hall.

Newell, A., Shaw, J. C., & Simon, H. A. (1958). Elements of a theory of human problem solving. *Psychological Review, 65,* 151–166.

Newell, A., Shaw, J. C., & Simon, H. A. (1962). The processes of creative thinking. In H. E. Gruber, G. Terrell, & M. Wertheimer (Eds.), *Contemporary approaches to creative thinking* (pp. 63–119). New York: Atherton Press.

Newell, A., Shaw, J. C., & Simon, H. A. (1963). The logic theory machine. In E. A. Feigenbaum & J. Feldman (Eds.), *Computers and thought* (pp. 109–133). New York: McGraw-Hill.

Newstead, S. E., & Evans, J. St. B. (Eds.). (1995). *Perspectives on thinking and reasoning: Essays in honour of Peter Wason.* Hillsdale, NJ: Erlbaum.

Ng, W.-J., & Lindsay, R. C. L. (1994). Cross-race facial recognition: Failure of the contact hypothesis. *Journal of Cross-Cultural Psychology, 25,* 217–232.

Nguyen, D. B., & Revlin, R. (1993). Transitive inferences from narrative relations. *Journal of Experimental Psychology: Learning, Memory, and Cognition, 19,* 1197–1210.

Nicholas, L. E., & Brookshire, R. H. (1993). A system for quantifying the informativeness and efficiency of the connected speech of adults with aphasia. *Journal of Speech and Hearing Research, 36,* 338–350.

Nickerson, R. S. (1968). A note on long-term recognition memory for pictorial material. *Psychonomic Science, 11,* 58.

Nickerson, R. S., & Adams, M. J. (1979). Long-term memory for a common object. *Cognitive Psychology, 11,* 287–307.

Nielsen, L. I., & Sarason, I. G. (1981). Emotion, personality and selective attention. *Journal of Personality and Social Psychology, 41,* 945–960.

Nieoullon, A. (2002). Dopamine and the regulation of cognition and attention. *Progress in Neurobiology, 57,* 53–83.

Nisbett, R., & Ross, L. (1980). *Human inference: Strategies and shortcomings of social judgment.* Englewood Cliffs, NJ:. Prentice Hall

Noordzij, M. L., Zuidhoek, S., & Postma, A. (2007). The influence of visual experience on visual and spatial imagery. *Perception, 36,* 101–112.

Nordgren, L. F., Bos, M. W., & Dijksterhuis, A. (2011). The best of both worlds: Integrating conscious and unconscious thought best solves complex decisions. *Journal of Experimental Social Psychology, 47,* 509–511.

Norman, D. A. (1968). Toward a theory of memory and attention. *Psychological Review, 75,* 522–536.

Norman, D. A. (1976). *Memory and attention: An introduction to human information processing* (2nd ed.). Oxford, England: Wiley.

Norman, D. A., & Shallice, T. (2000). Attention to action: Willed and automatic control of behavior. In M. S. Gazzaniga (Ed.), *Cognitive neuroscience: A reader* (pp. 376–390). Malden, MA: Blackwell.

Northcraft, G. B., & Neale, M. A. (1987). Experts, amateurs, and real estate: An anchoring-and-adjustment perspective on property pricing decisions. *Organizational Behavior and Human Decision Processes, 39,* 84–97.

Novak, J., & Gowin, G. J. (1984). *Learning how to learn.* New York: Cambridge University Press.

Noveck, I. A., & O'Brien, D. P. (1996). To what extent do pragmatic reasoning schemas affect performance on Wason's selection task. *Quarterly Journal of Experimental Psychology, 49A,* 463–489.

Nyberg, L., & Cabeza, R. (2000). Brain imaging of memory. In E. Tulving & F. I. M. Craik (Eds.), *The Oxford handbook of memory* (pp. 501–519). New York: Oxford University Press.

Oaksford, M., Morris, F., Grainger, B., & Williams, J. M. G. (1996). Mood, reasoning, and central executive processes. *Journal of Experimental Psychology: Learning, Memory, and Cognition, 22,* 476–492.

O'Brien, D., Dias, M. G., Roazzi, A., & Cantor, J. B. (1998). Pinocchio's nose knows: Preschool children recognize that a pragmatic rule can be violated, an indicative conditional can be falsified, and that a broken promise is a false promise. In M. D. S. Braine & D. P. O'Brien (Eds.), *Mental logic* (pp. 447–458). Mahwah, NJ: Erlbaum.

Odean, T. (1988). Are investors reluctant to realize their losses? *Journal of Finance, 53,* 1775–1798.

Ofan, R. H., & Zohary, E. (2007). Visual cortex activation in blilingual blind individuals during use of native and second language. *Cerebral Cortex, 17,* 1249–1259.

Ogawa, S., Tank, D. W., Menon, R., Ellermann, J., Kim, S.-G., Merkle, H., & Ugurbil, K. (1992). Intrinsic signal changes accompanying sensory stimulation: Functional brain mapping with magnetic resonance imaging. *Proceedings of the National Academy of Sciences, USA, 89,* 5951–5955.

Oller, D. K. (1980). The emergence of the sounds of speech in infancy. In G. Yeni-Komshian, J. Kavanagh, & C. Ferguson (Eds.), *Child phonology: Perception and production* (pp. 93–112). New York: Academic Press.

Oller, D. K., & Eilers, R. E. (1988). The role of audition in infant babbling. *Child Development, 59,* 441–449.

Olson, J. N., & MacKay, D. G. (1974). Completion and verification of ambiguous sentences. *Journal of Verbal Learning and Verbal Behavior, 13,* 457–470.

Onitsuka, T., Shenton, M. E., Kasai, K., Nestor, P. G., Toner, S. K., Kikinis, R., . . . McCarley, R. W. (2003). Fusiform gyrus volume reduction and facial recognition in chronic schizophrenia. *Archives of General Psychiatry, 60,* 349–355.

Orliaguet, J. P., & Coello, Y. (1998). Differences between actual and imagined putting movements in golf: A chronometric analysis. *International Journal of Sport Psychology, 29,* 157–169.

Osgood, C. E. (1971). Where do sentences come from? In D. A. Steinberg & L. A. Jakobovits (Eds.), *Semantics: An interdisciplinary reader in philosophy, linguistics, and psychology* (pp. 497–529). Cambridge, England: Cambridge University Press.

Osherson, D., Perani, D. A., Cappa, S., Schnir, T., Grassi, F., & Fazio, F. (1998). Distinct brain loci in deductive versus probabilistic reasoning. *Neuropsychologia, 36,* 369–376.

Osterling, J. A., Dawson, G., & Munson, J. A. (2002). Early recognition of 1-year-old infants with autism spectrum disorder versus mental retardation. *Development and Psychopathology, 14,* 239–251.

O'Toole, A. J., Deffenbacher, K. A., Valentin, D., & Abdi, H. (1994). Structural aspects of face recognition and the other-race effect. *Memory & Cognition, 22,* 208–224.

Owen, A. M., Evans, A. C., & Petrides, M. (1996). Evidence for a two-stage model of spatial working memory processing within the lateral frontal cortex: A positron emission tomography study. *Cerebral Cortex, 6,* 31–38.

Paivio, A. (1969). Mental imagery in associative learning and memory. *Psychological Review, 76,* 241–263.

Paivio, A. (1971). *Imagery and verbal processes.* New York: Holt, Rinehart and Winston.

Paivio, A. (1985). Cognitive and motivational functions of imagery in human performance. *Canadian Journal of Applied Sport Sciences, 10,* 22S–28S.

Paivio, A., & Csapo, K. (1973). Picture superiority in free recall: Imagery or dual encoding? *Cognitive Psychology, 5,* 176–206.

Paivio, A., & Desrochers, A. (1981). Mnemonic techniques in second language learning. *Journal of Educational Psychology, 73,* 780–795.

Paivio, A., Rogers, T. B., & Smythe, P. C. (1968). Why are pictures easier to recall than words? *Psychonomic Science, 11,* 137–138.

Paivio, A., Yuille, J. C., & Madigan, S. A. (1968). Concreteness, imagery, and meaningfulness values for 925 nouns. *Journal of Experimental Psychology, 76,* 1–25.

Pallrand, G. J., & Seeber, F. (1984). Spatial ability and achievement in introductory physics. *Journal of Research in Science Teaching, 21,* 507–516.

Paris, S. G., & Lindauer, B. K. (1976). The role of inference in children's comprehension and memory for sentences. *Cognitive Psychology, 8,* 217–227.

Parker, A. M., Bruine de Bruin, W., & Fischhoff, B. (2007). Maximizers versus satisficers: Decision-making styles, competence, and outcomes. *Judgment and Decision Making, 2,* 342–350.

Parkinson, J. (2002). An essay on the shaking palsy. *Journal of Neuropsychiatry & Clinical Neurosciences, 14,* 223–236. (Original work published 1817)

Parkman, J. M. (1971). Temporal aspects of digit and letter inequality judgments. *Journal of Experimental Psychology, 91,* 191–205.

Parkman, J. M., & Groen, G. J. (1971). Temporal aspects of simple addition and comparison. *Journal of Experimental Psychology, 89,* 333–342.

Pascalis, O., de Haan, M., & Nelson, C. A. (2002). Is face processing species-specific during the first year of life? *Science, 296,* 1321–1323.

Pascalis, O., de Schonen, S., Morton, J., Deruelle, C., & Fabre-Grenet, M. (1995). Mother's face recognition by neonates: A replication and an extension. *Infant Behavior and Development, 18,* 79–85.

Pascual-Leone, A., Walsh, V., & Rothwell, J. (2000). Transcranial magnetic stimulation in cognitive neuroscience—Virtual lesion, chronometry, and functional connectivity. *Opinion in Neurobiology, 10,* 232–237.

Patel, V. L., Arocha, J. F., & Zhang, J. (2005). Thinking and reasoning in medicine. In K. J. Holyoak & R. G. Morrison (Eds.), *The Cambridge handbook of thinking and reasoning* (pp. 727–750). New York: Cambridge University Press.

Patterson, K., Vargha-Khadem, F., & Polkey, C. (1987). Reading with one hemisphere. *Brain, 112,* 39–63.

Paulescu, E., Frith, C. D., & Frackowiak, R. S. J. (1993). The neural correlates of the verbal component of working memory. *Nature, 362,* 342–345.

Pavani, F., Ladavas, E., & Driver, J. (2002). Selective deficit of auditory localization in patients with visuospatial neglect. *Neuropsychologia, 40,* 291–301.

Paykel, E. S., Brayne, C., Huppert, F. A., Gill, C., Barkley, C., Gehlhaar, E., . . . O'Connor, D. (1994). Incidence of dementia in a population older than 75 years in the United Kingdom. *Archives of General Psychiatry, 51,* 325–332.

Payne, B. R. (1993). Evidence for visual cortical area homologs in cat and macaque monkey. *Cerebral Cortex, 3,* 1–25.

Payne, B. R., & Rushmore, R. J. (2003). Animal models of cerebral neglect and its cancellation. *The Neuroscientist, 9,* 445–454.

Pearson, D. G. (2001). Imagery and the visuo-spatial sketchpad. In J. Andrade (Ed.), *Working memory in perspective* (pp. 33–59). London: Psychology Press.

Pedone, R., Hummel, J. E., & Holyoak, K. J. (2001). The use of diagrams in analogical problem solving. *Memory & Cognition, 29,* 214–221.

Penfield, W., & Perot, P. (1963). The brain's record of auditory and visual experience: A final summary and conclusions. *Brain, 86,* 568–693.

Penn Center, Inc. (2011). *Penn Center: Preserving the past, enriching the future* [Brochure]. St. Helena's Island, SC: Author. (Available from www.penncenter.com)

Pennington, B. F. (1995). Genetics of learning disabilities. *Journal of Child Neurology, 10,* 69–77.

Perfetti, C. A., & Goldman, S. R. (1976). Discourse memory and reading comprehension skill. *Journal of Verbal Learning and Verbal Behavior, 15,* 33–42.

Perky, C. W. (1910). An experimental study of imagination. *American Journal of Psychology, 21,* 422–452.

Perrotin, A., Isingrini, M., Souchay, C., Clarys, D., & Taconnat, L. (2006). Episodic feeling-of-knowing accuracy and cued recall in the elderly: Evidence for double dissociation involving executive functioning and processing speed. *Acta Psychologica, 122,* 58–73.

Péruch, P., Chabanne, V., Nesa, M.-P., Thinus-Blanc, C., & Denis, M. (2006). Comparing distances in mental images constructed from visual experience or verbal descriptions: The impact of survey versus route perspective. *Quarterly Journal of Experimental Psychology, 59,* 1950–1967.

Peters, A., & Jones, E. G. (1984). Classification of cortical neurons. In A. Peters & E. G. Jones (Eds.), *Cerebral cortex* (Vol. 1, pp. 107–121). New York: Plenum Press.

Peters, M. J. V., Jelicic, M., Verbeek, H., & Merckelbach, H. (2007). Poor working memory predicts false memories. *European Journal of Cognitive Psychology, 19,* 213–232.

Peters, R., & McGee, R. (1982). Cigarette smoking and state-dependent memory. *Psychopharmacology, 76,* 232–235.

Peterson, L. R., & Peterson, M. J. (1959). Short-term retention of individual verbal items. *Journal of Experimental Psychology, 58,* 193–198.

Petitto, L. A. (1987). On the autonomy of language and gesture: Evidence from the acquisition of personal pronouns in American Sign Language. *Cognition, 27,* 1–52.

Petitto, L. A., & Marentette, P. F. (1991). Babbling in the manual model: Evidence for the ontogeny of language. *Science, 251,* 1493–1495.

Peto, R., Lopez, A. D., Boreham, J., Thun, M., & Heath, C. Jr. (1994). *Mortality from smoking in developed countries 1950–2000.* Oxford, England: Oxford University Press.

Pezdek, K. (2003). Event memory and autobiographical memory for the events of September 11, 2001. *Applied Cognitive Psychology, 17,* 1033–1045.

Pezdek, K., Maki, R., Valencia-Laver, D., Whetstone, T., Stoeckert, J., & Dougherty, T. (1988). Picture memory: Recognizing added and deleted details. *Journal of Experimental Psychology: Learning, Memory, and Cognition, 14,* 468–476.

Pham, M., Hinterberger, R., Neumann, N., Kübler, A., Hofmayer, N., Grethere, A., . . . Birbaumer, N. (2005). An auditory brain–computer interface based on the self-regulation of slow cortical potentials. *Neurorehabilitation & Neural Repair, 19,* 206–218.

Phillips, L. D., & Edwards, W. (1966). Conservatism in a simple probability inference task. *Journal of Experimental Psychology, 72,* 346–354.

Phillips, W. A., & Christie, D. F. M. (1977). Components of visual memory. *Quarterly Journal of Experimental Psychology, 29,* 117–133.

Piaget, J. (1966). *Judgment and reasoning in the child* (M. Warden, Trans.). Totowa, NJ: Littlefield, Adams & Co. (Original work published 1928)

Piazza, M., Mechelli, A., Butterworth, B., & Price, C. J. (2002). Are subitizing and counting implemented as separate or functionally overlapping processes? *NeuroImage, 15,* 435–446.

Pichert, J. W., & Anderson, R. C. (1977). Taking different perspectives on a story. *Journal of Educational Psychology, 69,* 309–315.

Pierce, K., Muller, R.-A., Ambrose, J., Allen, G., & Courchesne, E. (2001). Face processing occurs outside the fusiform "face area" in autism: Evidence from functional MRI. *Brain, 124,* 2059–2073.

Pillemer, D. B., & White, S. H. (1989). Childhood events recalled by children and adults. *Advances in Child Development and Behavior, 21,* 297–340.

Pinek, B., & Brouchon, M. (1992). Head turning versus manual pointing to auditory targets in normal subjects and in subjects with right parietal damage. *Brain and Cognition, 18,* 1–11.

Pinker, S. (1994). *The language instinct: How the mind creates language.* New York: HarperCollins.

Pinker, S. (2007). *The stuff of thought.* New York: Penguin.

Plato. (2008). *Cratylus* (B. Jowett, Trans.). Available at ForgottenBooks.org (Original work 360 BCE)

Platt, J. R. (1964). Strong inference. *Science, 146,* 347–353.

Plous, S. (1993). *The psychology of judgment and decision making.* New York: McGraw-Hill.

Podgorny, P., & Shepard, R. N. (1983). Distribution of visual attention over space. *Journal of Experimental Psychology: Human Perception and Performance, 9,* 380–393.

Poeppel, D. (2001). Pure word deafness and the bilateral processing of the speech code. *Cognitive Science: A Multidisciplinary Journal, 25,* 679–693.

Poizner, H., Klima, E., & Bellugi, U. (1987). *What the hands reveal about the brain.* Cambridge, MA: MIT Press.

Poldrack, R. A., & Gabrieli, J. D. (1998). Memory and the brain: What's right and what's left? *Cell, 93,* 1091–1093.

Polk, T. A., Simen, P. O., Lewis, R. L., & Freedman, E. (2002). A computational approach to control in complex cognition. *Cognitive Brain Research, 1,* 71–83.

Pollack, I., Johnson, I., & Knaff, P. R. (1959). Running memory span. *Journal of Experimental Psychology, 57,* 137–146.

Pollard, P. (1990). Natural selection for the selection task: Limits to social exchange theory. *Cognition, 36,* 195–204.

Pollitzer, W. S. (1999). *The Gullah people and their African heritage.* Athens: University of Georgia Press.

Polya, G. (1957). *How to solve it* (2nd ed.). Princeton, NJ: Princeton University Press.

Pompi, K. F., & Lachman, K. R. (1967). Surrogate processes in the short-term retention of connected discourse. *Journal of Experimental Psychology, 75,* 143–150.

Popper, K. R. (1972). *Objective knowledge.* Oxford, England: Oxford University Press.

Posner, M. I. (1975). Psychobiology of attention. In M. S. Gazzaniga & C. Blakemore (Eds.), *Handbook of psychobiology* (pp. 441–480). New York: Academic Press.

Posner, M. I. (1980). Orienting of attention. *Quarterly Journal of Experimental Psychology, 32,* 3–25.

Posner, M. I. (1993). *Foundations of cognitive science.* Cambridge, MA: MIT Press.

Posner, M. I., Goldsmith, R., & Welton, K. E., Jr. (1967). Perceived distance of distorted patterns. *Journal of Experimental Psychology, 73,* 28–38.

Posner, M. I., & Keele, S. W. (1968). On the genesis of abstract ideas. *Journal of Experimental Psychology, 77,* 353–363.

Posner, M. I., & Petersen, S. E. (1990). The attention system of the human brain. *Annual Review of Neuroscience, 13,* 25–42.

Posner, M. I., & Raichle, M. E. (1997). *Images of the mind.* New York: Scientific American Library.

Posner, M. I., & Snyder, C. R. (1975). Attention and cognitive control. In R. I. Solso (Ed.), *Information processing and cognition* (pp. 55–85). Hillsdale, NJ: Erlbaum.

Posner, M. I., Snyder, C. R., & Davidson, B. J. (1980). Attention and the detection of signals. *Journal of Experimental Psychology: General, 109,* 160–174.

Potts, G. R. (1972). Information processing strategies used in the encoding of linear orderings. *Journal of Verbal Learning and Verbal Behavior, 11,* 727–740.

Potts, G. R. (1976). Artificial logical relations and their relevance to semantic memory. *Journal of Experimental Psychology: Human Learning and Memory, 2,* 746–758.

Potts, G. R. (1978). The role of inference in memory for real and artificial information. In R. Revlin & R. Mayer (Eds.), *Human reasoning* (pp. 139–161). Washington, DC: Winston.

Potts, G. R., & Peterson, S. B. (1985). Incorporation versus compartmentalization in memory for discourse. *Journal of Memory and Language, 24,* 107–118.

Premack, D. (1985). "Gavagai!" or the future history of the animal language controversy. *Cognition, 19,* 207–296.

Premack, D., & Premack, A. J. (2003). *Original intelligence: Unlocking the mystery of who we are*. New York: McGraw-Hill.

Presidential votes disqualified in Florida. (2000, November 15). Retrieved from *Sun-Sentinel* website: http//www.sun-sentinel.com

Presmeg, N. (1992). Prototypes, metaphors, metonymies, and imaginative rationality in high school mathematics. *Educational Studies in Mathematics, 23,* 595–610.

Pressley, M. (1994). Commentary on the ERIC whole language debate. In C. B. Smith (Moderator), *Whole language: The debate* (pp. 155–178). Bloomington, IN: ERIC/REC.

Pressley, M., Levin, F. R., & Miller, G. E. (1981). The keyword method and children's learning of foreign vocabulary with abstract meanings. *Canadian Journal of Psychology, 34,* 283–287.

Pressley, M., Wharton-McDonald, R., Hampson, J. M., & Echevarria, M. (1998). The nature of literacy instruction in ten grade-4/5 classrooms in upstate New York. *Scientific Studies of Reading, 2,* 159–191.

Pribyl, J. R., & Bodner, G. M. (1987). Spatial ability and its role in organic chemistry: A study of four organic courses. *Journal of Research in Science Teaching, 24,* 229–240.

Price, R. (1953). *Droodles*. New York: Simon & Schuster.

Prinzmetal, W., Presti, D. E., & Posner, M. I. (1986). Does attention affect visual feature integration? *Journal of Experimental Psychology: Human Perception and Performance, 12,* 361–369.

Ptito, M., Moesgaard, S. M., Gjedde, A., & Kupers, R. (2005). Cross-modal plasticity revealed by electro-tactile stimulation of the tongue in the congenitally blind. *Brain, 128,* 606–614.

Puce, A., Allison, T., Gore, J. C., & McCarthy, G. (1995). Face-sensitive regions in human extrastriate cortex studied by functional MRI. *Journal of Neurophysiology, 74,* 1192–1199.

Pugh, K., Shaywitz, B., Constable, T., Shaywitz, S., Skudlarski, P., Fulbright, R., . . . Gore, J. (1996).

Cerebral organization of component processes in reading. *Brain, 119,* 1221–1238.

Quilici, J. L., & Mayer, R. E. (1996). Role of examples in how students learn to categorize statistics word problems. *Journal of Educational Psychology, 88*(1), 144–161.

Quillian, M. R. (1968). Semantic memory. In M. Minsky (Ed.), *Semantic information processing* (pp. 216–260). Cambridge, MA: MIT Press.

Quinn, P. C., Eimas, P. D., & Tarr, M. J. (2001). Perceptual categorization of cat and dog silhouettes by 3- to 4-month-old infants. *Journal of Experimental Child Psychology, 79,* 78–94.

Quinn, P. C., Kelly, D. J., Lee, K., Pascalis, O., & Slater, A. (2008). Preference for attractive faces in human infants extends beyond conspecifics. *Developmental Science, 11,* 76–83.

Quinn, P. C., Yahr, J., Kuhn, A., Slater, A. M., & Olivier, P. (2002). Representation of the gender of human faces by infants: A preference for female. *Perception, 31,* 1109–1121.

Rafnel, K. J., & Klatzky, R. L. (1978). Meaningful-interpretation effects on codes of nonsense pictures. *Journal of Experimental Psychology: Human Learning and Memory, 4,* 631–646.

Raines, S., & Canady, R. J. (1990). *The whole language kindergarten*. New York: Teachers College Press.

Rajaram, S. (1993). Remembering and knowing: Two means of access to the personal past. *Memory & Cognition, 21,* 89–102.

Rakic, P. (2002). Neurogenesis in adult primate neocortex: An evaluation of the evidence. *Nature Reviews Neuroscience, 3,* 65–71.

Ramachandran, V. S., & Blakeslee, S. (1988). *Phantoms in the brain: Probing the mysteries of the human mind*. New York: William Morrow.

Ramsey, W., & Stich, S. (1991). *Philosophy and connectionist theory*. Hillsdale, NJ: Erlbaum.

Ramus, F. (2004). Neurobiology of dyslexia: A reinterpretation of the data. *Trends in Neurosciences, 27,* 720–726.

Ramus, F., Hauser, M. D., Miller, C. T., Morris, D., & Mehler, J. (2000). Language discrimination by human newborns and cotton-top tamarin monkeys. *Science, 288,* 349–351.

Rasmussen, T., & Milner, B. (1977). The role of early left-brain injury in determining lateralization of cerebral speech functions. *Annals of the New York Academy of Sciences, 299,* 355–375.

Ratcliff, R., Hockley, W., & McKoon, G. (1985). Components of activation: Repetition and priming effects in lexical decision and recognition. *Journal of Experimental Psychology: General, 114,* 435–450.

Ratiu, P., Talos, I. F., Haker, S., Lieberman, S., & Everett, P. (2004). The tale of Phineas Gage, digitally remastered. *Journal of Neurotrauma, 21,* 637–643.

Raugh, M. R., & Atkinson, R. C. (1975). A mnemonic method for learning a second language vocabulary. *Journal of Educational Psychology, 67,* 1–16.

Rauscheker, J. P. (2011). An expanded role for the dorsal auditory pathway in sensorimotor control and integration. *Hearing Research, 271,* 16–25.

Rawlinson, G. E. (1976). *The significance of letter position in word recognition.* Unpublished doctoral dissertation, University of Nottingham, Nottingham, England.

Raymond, J. E., Shapiro, K. L., & Arnell, K. M. (1992). Temporary suppression of visual processing in an RSVP task: An attentional blink? *Journal of Experimental Psychology: Human Perception and Performance, 18,* 849–860.

Rayner, K. (1998). Eye movements in reading and information processing: 20 years of research. *Psychological Bulletin, 124,* 372–422.

Rayner, K., & Duffy, S. A. (1988). On-line comprehension processes and eye movements in reading. In M. Daneman, G. E. MacKinnon, & T. G. Waller (Eds.), *Reading research: Advances in theory and practice* (Vol. 6, pp. 13–66). New York: Academic Press.

Rayner, K., Pollatsek, A., & Binder, K. S. (1998). Phonological codes and eye movements in reading. *Journal of Experimental Psychology: Learning, Memory, and Cognition, 24,* 476–497.

Rayner, K., & Well, A. D. (1996). Effects of contextual constraint on eye movements in reading: A further examination. *Psychonomic Bulletin & Review, 3,* 504–509.

Raz, N. (2000). Aging of the brain and its impact on cognitive performance: Integration of structural and functional findings. In F. I. M. Craik & T. A. Salthouse (Eds.), *Handbook of aging and cognition* (2nd ed., pp. 1–90). Mahwah, NJ: Erlbaum.

Read, D. B. (1981). Solving deductive reasoning problems after unilateral temporal lobectomy. *Brain and Language, 12,* 116–127.

Reason, J. (1990). *Human error.* New York: Cambridge University Press.

Reder, L. M., & Cleeremans, A. (1990). The role of partial matches in incomprehension: The Moses illusion revisited. In A. C. Graesser & G. H. Bower (Eds.), *Inferences and text comprehension* (pp. 233–258). San Diego, CA: Academic Press.

Reed, S. K., & Johnsen, J. A. (1975). Detection of parts in patterns and images. *Memory & Cognition, 3,* 569–575.

Rees, G. (2008). Vision: The evolution of change detection. *Current Biology, 18,* r40–r42.

Reicher, G. M. (1969). Perceptual recognition as a function of meaningfulness of stimulus material. *Journal of Experimental Psychology, 81,* 275–280.

Reilly, J. S., Bates, E. A., & Marchman, V. A. (1998). Narrative discourse in children with early focal brain injury. *Brain and Language, 61,* 335–375.

Reitman, W. R. (1964). *Heuristic decision procedures open constraints and the structure of ill-defined problems.* New York: Wiley.

Rensink, R. A., O'Regan, J. K., & Clark, J. J. (1997). To see or not to see: The need for attention to perceive changes in scenes. *Psychological Science, 8,* 368–373.

Reutzel, D. R. (1985). Story maps improve comprehension. *Reading Teacher, 38,* 400–404.

Reutzel, D. R. (1986). Investigating a synthesized comprehension instructional strategy: The Cloze story map. *Journal of Educational Research, 79,* 343–349.

Revlin, R., Ammerman, K., Petersen, K., & Leirer, V. O. (1978). Category relations and syllogistic reasoning. *Journal of Educational Psychology, 70,* 613–625.

Revlin, R., & Hegarty, M. (1999). Resolving signals to cohesion: Two models of bridging inferences. *Discourse Processes, 27,* 77–102.

Revlin, R., & Leirer, V. (1978). Effects of personal biases on syllogistic reasoning: Rational decisions from personalized representations. In R. Revlin & R. Mayer (Eds.), *Human reasoning* (pp. 51–81). Washington, DC: Winston.

Revlin, R., & Leirer, V. O. (1980). Understanding quantified categorical expressions. *Memory & Cognition, 8,* 447–458.

Revlis, R. (1975a). Syllogistic reasoning: Logical decisions from a complex data base. In R. J. Falmagne (Ed.), *Reasoning: Representation and process in children and adults* (pp. 93–132). New York: Halsted Press.

Revlis, R. (1975b). Two models of syllogistic reasoning: Feature selection and conversion. *Journal of Verbal Learning and Verbal Behavior, 14,* 180–195.

Reyna, V. F., & Titcomb, A. L. (1997). Constraints on the suggestibility of eyewitness testimony: A fuzzy-trace theory analysis. In D. G. Payne & F. G. Conrad (Eds.), *A synthesis of basic and applied approaches to human memory* (pp. 157–174). Hillsdale, NJ: Erlbaum.

Rhoades, H. M. (1981). Training and spatial ability. In E. Klinger (Ed.), *Imagery, concepts, results, and applications* (Vol. 2, pp. 247–256). New York: Plenum Press.

Richardson, A. (1969). *Mental imagery.* Oxford, England: Springer.

Richardson, J. T. E. (1992). Imagery mnemonics and memory remediation. *Neurology, 42,* 283–286.

Riddoch, M. J. (1990). Loss of visual imagery: A generation deficit. *Cognitive Neuropsychology, 7,* 249–273.

Riddoch, M. J., Humphreys, G. W., Gannon, T., Blott, W., & Jones, V. (1999). Memories are made of this: The effects of time on stored visual knowledge in a case of visual agnosia. *Brain, 122,* 537–559.

Riesbeck, C. K., & Schank, R. C. (1989). *Inside case-based reasoning.* Hillsdale, NJ: Erlbaum.

Rips, L. J. (1986). Mental muddles. In M. Brand & R. M. Harnish (Eds.), *Problems in the representation of knowledge and belief* (pp. 258–286). Tucson: University of Arizona Press.

Rips, L. J. (1989). Similarity, typicality, and categorization. In S. Vosniadou & A. Ortony (Eds.), *Similarity and analogical reasoning* (pp. 21–59). New York: Cambridge University Press.

Rips, L. J., Shoben, E. J., & Smith, E. E. (1973). Semantic distance and the verification of semantic relations. *Journal of Verbal Learning and Verbal Behavior, 12,* 1–20.

Rittel, H. W., & Webber, M. M. (1973). Dilemmas in a general theory of planning. *Policy Sciences, 4,* 155–159.

Rivera, S. M., Reiss, A. L., Eckert, M. A., & Menon, V. (2005). Developmental changes in mental arithmetic: Evidence for increased functional specialization in the left inferior parietal cortex. *Cerebral Cortex, 15,* 1779–1790.

Rizzo, M. (1993). Bálint's syndrome and associated visuospatial disorders. *Clinical Neurology, 2,* 415–437.

Rizzo, M., & Vecera, S. P. (2002). Psychoanatomical substrates of Bálint's syndrome. *Journal of Neurology, Neurosurgery, and Psychiatry, 72,* 162–178.

Robert, P., Migneco, V., Marmod, D., Chaix, I., Thauby, S., Benoit, M., . . . Darcourt, G. (1997). Verbal fluency in schizophrenia: The role of semantic clustering in category instance generation. *European Journal of Psychiatry, 12,* 124–129.

Roberts, S., & Sternberg, S. (1993). The meaning of additive reaction-time effects: Tests of three alternatives. In D. E. Meyer & S. Kornblum (Eds.), *Attention and performance* (Vol. 14, pp. 611–653). Cambridge, MA: MIT Press.

Robertson, S. I. (2001). *Problem solving*. Phildadelphia: Taylor & Francis.

Robey, R. R. (1994). The efficacy of treatment for aphasic persons: A meta-analysis. *Brain and Language, 47,* 582–608.

Röder, R., Demuth, L., Steb, J., & Rösler, F. (2003). Semantic and morpho-syntactic priming in auditory word recognition in congenitally blind adults. *Language and Cognitive Processes, 18,* 1–20.

Roediger, H. L., III. (2003, August). *Aging and false memory: Exploring Mark Twain's conjecture*. Paper presented at the annual meeting of the American Psychological Association, Toronto, Canada.

Roediger, H. L., III, & McDermott, K. B. (1995). Creating false memories: Remembering words not presented in lists. *Journal of Experimental Psychology: Learning, Memory, and Cognition, 21,* 803–814.

Roland, P. E., & Friberg, L. (1985). Localization of cortical areas activated by thinking. *Journal of Neurophysiology, 53,* 1219–1243.

Roman, K. (2009). *The King of Madison Avenue*. New York: Palgrave Macmillan.

Romans, S. M., Stefanatos, G., Roeltgen, D. P., Kushner, H., & Ross, J. L. (1998). Transition to young adulthood in Ullrich–Turner syndrome: Neurodevelopmental changes. *American Journal of Medical Genetics, 79,* 140–147.

Roney, C. J., & Trick, L. M. (2003). Grouping and gambling: A gestalt approach to understanding the gambler's fallacy. *Canadian Journal of Experimental Psychology, 57,* 69–75.

Rosch, E. (1973a). Natural categories. *Cognitive Psychology, 4,* 328–350.

Rosch, E. (1973b). On the internal structure of perceptual and semantic categories. In T. Moore (Ed.), *Cognitive development and the acquisition of language* (pp. 111–144). New York: Academic Press.

Rosch, E., & Mervis, C. B. (1975). Family resemblances in the internal structure of categories. *Cognitive Psychology, 7,* 573–605.

Rosch Heider, E. (1972). Universals in color naming and memory. *Journal of Experimental Psychology, 93,* 10–20.

Rosenbaum, R. S., Kohler, S., Schacter, D. L., Moscovitch, M., Westmacott, R., Black, S. E., . . . Tulving, E. (2005). The case of KC: Contributions of a memory-impaired person to memory theory. *Neuropsychologia, 43,* 989–1021.

Roser, M., & Gazzaniga, M. S. (2004). Automatic brains—Interpretive minds. *Current Directions in Psychological Science, 13,* 56–59.

Rosner, J., & Simon, D. P. (1971). The auditory analysis test: An initial report. *Journal of Learning Disabilities, 4,* 384–392.

Ross, L., & Nisbett, R. E. (1991). *The person and the situation: Perspectives of social psychology*. New York: McGraw-Hill.

Rotter, J. B. (1966). Generalized expectancies for internal versus external control of reinforcement. *Psychological Monographs, 80* (Whole No. 609).

Roure, R., Collet, C., Deschaumes-Molinaro, C., Delhomme, G., Dittmar, A., & Vernet-Maury, E. (1999). Imagery quality estimated by autonomic response is correlated to sporting performance enhancement. *Physiology & Behavior, 66,* 63–72.

Rovee, C. K., & Rovee, D. T. (1969). Conjugate reinforcement of infant exploratory behavior. *Journal of Experimental Child Psychology, 8,* 33–39.

Rovee-Collier, C. (1999). The development of infant memory. *Current Directions in Psychological Science, 8,* 80–85.

Rovee-Collier, C., & Giles, A. (2010). Why a neuro-maturational model of memory fails: Exuberant learning in early infancy. *Behavioural Processes, 83,* 197–206.

Rowland-Bryant, E., Skinner, C. H., Skinner, A., Saudargas, R., Robinson, D., & Kirk, E. (2009). Investigating the interaction of studies in the internal structure of graphic organizers and seductive details: Can a graphic organizer imitate the seductive details effect? *Research in the Schools, 16,* 29–40.

Rubin, D. C., Rahhal, T. A., & Poon, L. W. (1998). Things remembered in early life are remembered best. *Memory & Cognition, 26,* 3–19.

Rubin, D. C., & Schulkind, M. D. (1997a). Distribution of autobiographical memories across the life span. *Memory & Cognition, 25,* 859–866.

Rubin, D. C., & Schulkind, M. D. (1997b). Distribution of important and word-cued autobiographical memories in 20-, 35-, and 70-year-old adults. *Psychology and Aging, 12,* 524–535.

Rubin, D. C., Wetzler, S. E., & Nebes, R. D. (1986). Autobiographical memory across the adult life span. In D. C. Rubin (Ed.), *Autobiographical memory* (pp. 202–221). Cambridge, England: Cambridge University Press.

Rumelhart, D. E. (1975). Notes on a schema for stories. In D. G. Bobrow & A. Collins (Eds.), *Representation and understanding: Studies in cognitive science* (pp. 185–210). New York: Academic Press.

Rumelhart, D. E. (1980). Schemata: The building blocks of cognition. In R. J. Spiro, B. C. Bruce, & W. F. Brewer (Eds.), *Theoretical issues in reading comprehension* (pp. 38–58). Hillsdale, NJ: Erlbaum.

Rumelhart, D. E., & Norman, D. A. (1981). Analogical processes in learning. In J. R. Anderson (Ed.), *Cognitive skills and their acquisition* (pp. 335–361). Hillsdale, NJ: Erlbaum.

Rumelhart, D. E., & Ortony, A. (1977). The representation of knowledge in memory. In R. C. Atkinson, R. J. Herrnstein, G. Lindzey, & R. D. Luce (Eds.), *Steven's handbook of experimental psychology: Learning and cognition* (pp. 99–135). Hillsdale, NJ: Erlbaum.

Rumelhart, D. E., Smolensky, P., McClelland, J. L., & Hinton, G. E. (1986). Schemata and sequential thought processes in PDP models. In D. E. Rumelhart & J. L. McClelland (Eds.), *Parallel distributed processing: Explorations in the microstructure of cognition* (Vol. 2, pp. 7–57). Cambridge, MA: MIT Press.

Ryan, J. (1969). Temporal grouping, rehearsal and short-term memory. *Quarterly Journal of Experimental Psychology, 21,* 148–155.

Rybash, J., Monaghan, M., & Brynn, E. (1999). Episodic and semantic contributions to older adults' autobiographical recall. *Journal of General Psychology, 126,* 85–86.

Rymer, R. (1992a, April 13). A silent childhood (I). *The New Yorker,* pp. 41–81.

Rymer, R. (1992b, April 20). A silent childhood (II). *The New Yorker,* pp. 43–77.

Sabatino, M., Gravante, G., Ferraro, G., Savatteri, V., & La Grutta, V. (1988). Inhibitory control by substantia nigra of generalized epilepsy in the cat. *Epilepsy Research, 2,* 380–386.

Sachs, J. (1967). Recognition memory for syntactic and semantic aspects of connected discourse. *Perception and Psychophysics, 2,* 437–442.

Sacks, O. (1985). *The man who mistook his wife for a hat.* New York: Summit Books.

Sacks, O. (1995). *An anthropologist on Mars.* New York: Knopf.

Saczynski, J. S., Willis, S. L., & Schaie, K. W. (2002). Strategy use in reasoning training with older adults. *Aging, Neurology, and Cognition, 9,* 48–60.

Sadato, N., Pascual-Leone, A., Grafman, J., Deiber, M. P., Ibanez, V., & Hallett, M. (1998). Neural networks for Braille reading by the blind. *Brain, 121,* 1213–1229.

Saffran, E. M., Marin, O. S., & Yeni-Komshian, G. H. (1976). An analysis of speech perception in word deafness. *Brain and Language, 3,* 209–228.

Sala, J. B., Rama, P., & Courtney, S. M. (2003). Functional topography of a distributed neural system for spatial and nonspatial information maintenance in working memory. *Neuropsychologia, 41,* 341–356.

Salame, P., & Baddeley, A. (1989). Effects of background music on phonological short-term memory. *Quarterly Journal of Experimental Psychology, 41,* 107–122.

Salthouse, T. A. (1992). Reasoning and spatial abilities. In F. I. M. Craik & T. A. Salthouse (Eds.), *The handbook of aging and cognition* (pp. 167–211). Hillsdale, NJ: Erlbaum.

Salthouse, T. (1996). The processing-speed theory of adult age differences in cognition. *Psychological Review, 103,* 403–428.

Samuels, S. J., & Kamil, M. L. (1984). Models of the reading process. In P. D. Pearson, P. Mosenthal, M. L. Kamil, & R. Barr (Eds.), *Handbook of reading research* (Vol. 1, pp. 185–224). New York: Longman.

Sangrigoli, S., & de Schonen, S. (2004). Recognition of own-race and other-race faces by three-month-old infants. *Journal of Child Psychology and Psychiatry, 45,* 1219–1227.

Santos, F. H., & Bueno, O. F. A. (2003). Validation of the Brazilian children's test of pseudoword repetition in Portuguese speakers aged 4 to 10 years. *Brazilian Journal of Medical and Biological Research, 36,* 1533–1547.

Sarason, I. G., Johnson, J. H., & Siegel, J. M. (1979). Assessing the impact of life changes: Development of the life experiences survey. *Journal of Consulting and Clinical Psychology, 46,* 932–946.

Savage-Rumbaugh, E., McDonald, K., Sevcik, R., Hopkins, W., & Rubert, E. (1986). Spontaneous symbol acquisition and communicative use by pygmy chimpanzees (*Pan paniscus*). *Journal of Experimental Psychology: General, 115,* 211–235.

Schab, F. R. (1990). Odors and the remembrance of things past. *Journal of Experimental Psychology: Learning, Memory, and Cognition, 16,* 648–655.

Schacter, D. L. (1996). *Searching for memory: The brain, the mind, and the past.* New York: Basic Books.

Schacter, D. L. (2001). *The seven sins of memory: How the mind forgets and remembers.* Boston: Houghton Mifflin.

Schacter, D. L., Chiu, C. Y. P., & Ochsner, K. M. (1993). Implicit memory: A selective review. *Annual Review of Neuroscience, 16,* 159–182.

Schacter, D. L., & Tulving, E. (1994). What are the memory systems of 1994? In D. L. Schacter & E. Tulving (Eds.), *Memory systems 1994* (pp. 39–63). Cambridge, MA: MIT Press.

Schacter, D. L., Wagner, A. D., & Buckner, R. L. (2000). Memory systems of 1999. In E. Tulving & F. I. M. Craik (Eds.), *The Oxford handbook of memory* (pp. 627–643). New York: Oxford University Press.

Schaie, K. W., & Willis, S. L. (1986). Can decline in intellectual functioning be reversed? *Developmental Psychology, 22,* 223–232.

Schaie, K. W., & Willis, S. L. (1999). Theories of everyday competence and aging. In V. L. Bengtson & K. W. Schaie (Eds.), *Handbook of theories of aging* (pp. 174–195). New York: Springer.

Schank, R. C., & Abelson, R. (1977). *Scripts, plans, goals, and understanding.* Hillsdale, NJ: Erlbaum.

Scherer, K. R. (1986). Vocal affect expression: A review and a model for future research. *Psychological Bulletin, 99,* 143–165.

Schmidt, H. G., Boshuizen, H. P., & van Breukelen, G. J. (2002). Long-term retention of a theatrical script by repertory actors: The role of context. *Memory, 10,* 21–28.

Schmidt, H. G., Peeck, V. H., Paas, F., & Van Bruekelen, G. J. (2000). Remembering the street names of one's childhood neighborhood: A study of very long-term retention. *Memory, 8,* 37–49.

Schneider, W., & Shiffrin, R. M. (1977). Controlled and automatic human information processing: I. Detection, search, and attention. *Psychological Review, 84,* 1–66.

Schnorr, J. A., & Atkinson, R. C. (1969). Repetition versus imagery instructions in the short- and long-term retention of paired associates. *Psychonomic Science, 15,* 183–184.

Schnorr, J. A., & Atkinson, R. C. (1970). Study position and item differences in the short- and long-term retention of paired associates learned by imagery. *Journal of Verbal Learning and Verbal Behavior, 9,* 614–622.

Schoenfeld, A. H. (1992). On paradigms and methods: What do you do when the ones you know don't do what you want them to? *Journal of the Learning Sciences, 2,* 179–214.

Scholes, R. J. (1998). The case against phonemic awareness. *Journal of Research in Reading, 21,* 177–189.

Schraw, G. (1995). Measures of feeling-of-knowing accuracy: A new look at an old problem. *Applied Cognitive Psychology, 9,* 321–332.

Schraw, G., Dunkle, M. E., & Bendixen, L. D. (1995). Cognitive processes in well-defined and ill-defined problem solving. *Applied Cognitive Psychology, 9,* 523–538.

Schroder, H. M., Driver, M. J., & Steufert, S. (1967). *Human information processing.* New York: Holt, Rinehart and Winston.

Schultz, R. T., Gauthier, L., Klin, A., Fulbright, R. K., Anderson, A. W., Volkmar, F., . . . Gore, J. C. (2000). Abnormal ventral temporal cortical activity during face discrimination among individuals with autism and Asperger syndrome. *Archives of General Psychiatry, 57,* 331–340.

Schultz, W., Romo, R., Ljungberg, T., Mirenowicz, J., Hollerman, J., & Dickinson, A. (1995). Reward-related signals carried by dopamine neurons. In J. Houk, J. Davis, & D. G. Beiser (Eds.), *Models of information processing in the basal ganglia* (pp. 233–248). Cambridge, MA: MIT Press.

Schunn, C. D., Lovett, M. C., & Reder, L. M. (2001). Awareness and working memory in strategy adaptivity. *Memory & Cognition, 29,* 254–266.

Schwartz, B. L. (1999). Sparkling at the end of the tongue: The etiology of tip-of-the-tongue phenomenology. *Psychonomic Bulletin & Review, 6,* 379–393.

Schweikert, R., & Boruff, B. (1986). Short-term memory capacity: Magic number or magic spell? *Journal of Experimental Psychology: Learning, Memory, and Cognition, 12,* 419–425.

Scribner, S. (1977). Modes of thinking and ways of speaking: Culture and logic reconsidered. In P. N. Johnson-Laird & P. C. Wason (Eds.), *Thinking and reasoning in cognitive science* (pp. 481–500). Cambridge, England: Cambridge University Press.

Scribner, S., & Tobach, E. (1997). Recall of classical syllogisms: A cross-cultural investigation of error on logical problems. In E. Tobach, R. J. Falmagne, M. B. Parlee, L. M. W. Martin, & A. S. Kapelman (Eds.), *Mind and social practice: Selected writings of Sylvia Scribner* (pp. 106–124). Cambridge, England: Press Syndicate of the University of Cambridge.

Scruggs, T. E., & Mastropieri, M. A. (2000). The effectiveness of mnemonic instruction for students with learning and behavior problems: An update and research synthesis. *Journal of Behavioral Education, 10,* 163–173.

Searle, J. R. (1969). *Speech acts.* Cambridge, England: Cambridge University Press.

Seeman, P., & Kapur, S. (2000). Schizophrenia: More dopamine, more D2 receptors. *Proceedings of the National Academy of Sciences, USA, 97,* 7673–7675.

Segal, S. J. (1971). Processing of the stimulus in imagery and perception. In S. J. Segal (Ed.), *Imagery: Current cognitive approaches* (pp. 73–100). New York: Academic Press.

Segal, S. J., & Fusella, V. (1971). Effects of images in six sense modalities on detection of visual signal from noise. *Psychonomic Science, 24,* 55–56.

Segalowitz, N. (1997). Individual differences in second language acquisition. In A. de Groot & J. Kroll (Eds.), *Tutorials in bilingualism* (pp. 85–112). Hillsdale, NJ: Erlbaum.

Segalowitz, N. (2000). Automaticity and attentional skill in fluent performance. In H. Riggenbach (Ed.), *Perspectives on fluency* (pp. 200–219). Ann Arbor: University of Michigan Press.

Seidenberg, M. (1997). Language acquisition and use: Learning and applying probabilistic constraints. *Science, 275,* 1599–1603.

Sergent, J., Signoret, J.–L., Bruce, V., & Rolls, E. T. (1992). Functional and anatomical decomposition of face processing: Evidence from prosopagnosia and PET study of normal subjects. *Philosophical Transactions of the Royal Society, 335,* 55–62.

Seyfarth, R. M., & Cheney, D. L. (2003). Meaning and emotion in animal vocalizations. *Annals of the New York Academy of Sciences, 1000,* 32–55.

Shafir, E., & LeBoeuf, R. A. (2002). Rationality. *Annual Review of Psychology, 53,* 491–517.

Shafto, M. (1973). The space for case. *Journal of Verbal Learning and Verbal Behavior, 12,* 551–562.

Shallice, T., & Vallar, G. (1990). The impairment of auditory–verbal short-term storage. In G. Vallar & T. Shallice (Eds.), *Neuropsychological impairments of short-term memory* (pp. 11–53). New York: Cambridge University Press.

Shankweiler, D., Crain, S., Katz, L., Fowler, A. E., Liberman, A. M., Brady, S. A., . . . Shaywitz, B. A. (1995). Cognitive profiles in reading disabled children: Comparison of language skills in phonology, morphology, and syntax. *Psychological Science, 6,* 149–156.

Shapiro, K. L., Arnell, K. M., & Raymond, J. E. (1997). The attentional blink. *Trends in Cognitive Sciences, 1,* 291–296.

Shapiro, K. L., Caldwell, J. I., & Sorensen, R. E. (1997). Personal names and the attentional blink: The cocktail party revisited. *Journal of Experimental Psychology: Human Perception and Performance, 23,* 504–514.

Shapiro, K. L., Raymond, J. E., & Arnell, K. M. (1994). Attention to visual pattern information produces the attentional blink in rapid serial visual presentation. *Journal of Experimental Psychology: Human Perception and Performance, 20,* 357–371.

Shaywitz, S. E. (1996). Dyslexia. *Scientific American, 275,* 98–104.

Shaywitz, S. E., Morris, R., & Shaywitz, B. A. (2008). The education of dyslexic children from childhood to young adulthood. *Annual Review of Psychology, 59,* 451–475.

Shaywitz, S. E., Pugh, K. R., Jenner, A. R., Fulbright, R. K., Fletcher, J. M., Gore, J. C., & Shaywitz, B. A. (2000). The neurobiology of reading and reading disability (dyslexia). In M. L. Kamil, P. B. Mosenthal, P. D. Pearson, & R. Barr (Eds.), *Handbook of reading research* (Vol. 3, pp. 229–249). Mahwah, NJ: Erlbaum.

Shefrin, H., & Statman, M. (1985). The disposition to sell winners too early and ride losers too long: Theory and evidence. *Journal of Finance, 40,* 777–790.

Shelly, R. K. (1996). "Feminine speech" in homogeneous gender groups. *Current Research in Social Psychology, 1,* 50–59.

Shepard, R. N. (1967). Recognition memory for words, sentences, and pictures. *Journal of Verbal Learning and Verbal Behavior, 6,* 156–163.

Shepard, R. N., & Metzler, J. (1971). Mental rotation of three-dimensional objects. *Science, 171,* 701–703.

Shepherd, G. M., & Koch, C. (1998). Introduction to synaptic circuits. In G. M. Shepherd (Ed.), *The synaptic organization of the brain* (pp. 1–36). New York: Oxford University Press.

Sherman, J. (1979). Predicting mathematics performance in high school girls and boys. *Journal of Educational Psychology, 71,* 242–249.

Shields, J. (1991). Semantic–pragmatic disorder: A right-hemisphere syndrome? *British Journal of Disorders of Communication, 26,* 383–392.

Shiffrin, R. M., & Schneider, W. (1977). Controlled and automatic human information processing: II. Perceptual learning, automatic attending, and a general theory. *Psychological Review, 84,* 127–190.

Shimamura, A. P., Landwehr, R. E., & Nelson, T. O. (1981). FACTRETRIEVAL: A program for assessing someone's recall of general information facts, feeling of knowing judgments for nonrecalled facts, and recognition of nonrecalled facts. *Behavior Research Methods & Instrumentation, 13,* 691–692.

Shimamura, A. P., & Squire, L. R. (1986). Memory and metamemory: A study of the feeling-of-knowing phenomenon in amnesic patients. *Journal of Experimental Psychology: Learning, Memory, and Cognition, 112,* 452–460.

Shimamura, A. P., & Squire, L. R. (1987). Neuropsychological study of fact memory and source amnesia. *Journal of Experimental Psychology: Learning, Memory, and Cognition, 13,* 464–473.

Shimojo, S., & Ichikawa, S. (1989). Intuitive reasoning about probability: Theoretical and experimental analyses of the "problem of three prisoners." *Cognition, 32,* 1–24.

Shing, Y. S., & Heyworth, R. M. (1992). Teaching English vocabulary to Cantonese-speaking students with the keyword method. *Education Journal, 20,* 113–129.

Shleifer, A. (2000). *Inefficient markets: An introduction to behavioral finance.* Oxford, England: Oxford University Press.

Shriberg, L. D., Paul, R., McSweeny, J. L., Klin, A., Cohen, D. J., & Volkmar, F. R. (2001). Speech and prosody characteristics of adolescents and adults with high-functioning autism and Asperger syndrome. *Journal of Speech, Language, and Hearing Research, 44,* 1097–1115.

Siakaluk, P., Buchanan, L., & Westbury, C. (2003). The effect of semantic distance in yes/no and go/no-go semantic categorization. *Memory & Cognition, 3,* 100–113.

Sides, A., Osherson, D., Bonini, N., & Viale, R. (2002). On the reality of the conjunction fallacy. *Memory & Cognition, 30,* 191–198.

Siegler, R. S. (1992). The other Alfred Binet. *Developmental Psychology, 28,* 179–190.

Siegrist, M., Cvetkovich, G. T., & Gutscher, H. (2001). Shared values, social trust, and the perception of geographic cancer clusters. *Risk Analysis, 21,* 1047–1053.

Siekmeier, P. J., Hasselmo, M. E., Howard, M. W., & Coyle, J. (2007). Modeling of context-dependent retrieval in hippocampal region CA1: Implications for cognitive function in schizophrenia. *Schizophrenia Research, 89,* 177–190.

Silveira, J. (1971). *Incubation: The effect of interruption timing and length on problem solution and quality of problem processing.* Unpublished doctoral dissertation, University of Oregon, Eugene.

Simion, F., Cassia, V. M., Turati, C., & Valenza, E. (2001). The origins of face perception: Specific versus nonspecific mechanisms. *Infant and Child Development, 10,* 59–65.

Simon, H. A. (1956). Rational choice and the structure of the environment. *Psychological Review, 63,* 129–138.

Simon, H. A. (1967). Motivational and emotional controls of cognition. *Psychological Review, 74,* 29–39.

Simon, H. A. (1969). *The sciences of the artificial.* Cambridge, MA: MIT Press.

Simon, H. A. (1978). Induction and representation of sequential patterns. In E. L. J. Leeuwenberg & H. F. J. M. Buffart (Eds.), *Formal theories of visual perception* (pp. 315–331). New York: Wiley.

Simon, H. A. (1996). *The sciences of the artificial* (3rd ed.). Cambridge, MA: MIT Press.

Simon, H. A. (1997). Satisficing. In H. A. Simon (Ed.), *Models of bounded rationality: Vol. 3. Empirically grounded economic reason* (pp. 295–298). Cambridge, MA: MIT Press.

Simon, H. A., & Gilmartin, K. (1973). A simulation of memory for chess positions. *Cognitive Psychology, 5,* 29–46.

Simons, D. J. (2000). Current approaches to change blindness. *Visual Cognition, 7,* 1–15.

Simons, D. J., & Chabris, C. F. (1999). Gorillas in our midst: Sustained inattentional blindness for dynamic events. *Perception, 28,* 1059–1074.

Simons, D. J., & Levin, D. T. (1997). Change blindness. *Trends in Cognitive Sciences, 1*(7), 261–267.

Simons, D. J., & Levin, D. T. (1998). Failure to detect changes to people in a real-world interaction. *Psychonomic Bulletin & Review, 5*(4), 644–649.

Simpson, G., & Burgess, C. (1985). Activation and selection processes in the recognition of ambiguous words. *Journal of Experimental Psychology: Human Perception and Performance, 11,* 28–39.

Sinclair-de Zwart, H. (1967). *Acquisition du langage et développement de la pensée* [Acquisition of language and development of thought]. Paris: Dunod.

Singer, M. (1979). Temporal locus of inference in the comprehension of brief passages: Recognizing and verifying implications about instruments. *Perceptual and Motor Skills, 49,* 539–550.

Singer, M., Halldorson, M., Lear, J., & Andrusiak, P. (1992). Validation of causal bridging inferences in discourse understanding. *Journal of Memory and Language, 31,* 507–524.

Siqueland, E. R., & DeLucia, C. A. (1969). Visual reinforcement of nonnutritive sucking in human infants. *Science, 165,* 1144–1146.

Siraisi, N. G. (2001). *Medicine and the Italian universities, 1250–1600.* Boston: Brill.

Sirri, E., & Tufano, P. (1988). Costly search and mutual fund flows. *Journal of Finance, 53,* 1589–1622.

Siwoff, S., Hirdt, S., & Hirdt, P. (1988). *The 1988 Elias baseball analyst.* New York: Collier.

Skarakis-Doyle, E. (2002). Young children's detection of violations in familiar stories and emerging comprehension monitoring. *Discourse Processes, 33,* 175–197.

Sklar, M. (1983). Relation of psychological and language test scores and autopsy findings in aphasia. *Journal of Speech and Hearing Research, 6,* 84–90.

Slater, A., Bremner, G., Johnson, S. P., Sherwood, P., Hayes, R., & Brown, E. (2000). Newborn infants' preference for attractive faces: The role of internal and external facial features. *Infancy, 1,* 265–274.

Slater, A., & Quinn, P. C. (2001). Face recognition in the newborn infant. *Infant and Child Development, 10,* 21–24.

Slater, A., Quinn, P. C., Hayes, R., & Brown, E. (2000). The role of facial orientation in newborn infants' preference for attractive faces. *Developmental Science, 3,* 181–185.

Slateer, J. G. (Ed.). (1986). *The collected papers of Bertrand Russell, 1914–19* (Vol. 8). London: Taylor & Francis.

Sleeman, D., & Brown, J. S. (Eds.). (1982). *Intelligent tutoring systems.* New York: Academic Press.

Slezak, P. (1991, August). *Can images be rotated and inspected?* Paper presented at the 13th annual meeting of the Cognitive Science Society, Chicago.

Slobin, D. (1970). Universals of grammatical development in children. In G. B. Flores d'Arcais & W. J. M. Levelt (Eds.), *Advances in psycholinguistics* (pp. 174–186). Amsterdam: North-Holland.

Slobin, D. (1973). Cognitive prerequisites for the development of grammar. In C. A. Ferguson & D. I. Slobin (Eds.), *Studies of child language development* (pp. 175–208). New York: Holt, Rinehart and Winston.

Sloman, S. A. (1998). Categorical inference is not a tree: The myth of inheritance hierarchies. *Cognitive Psychology, 35,* 1–33.

Slovic, P. (1987). Perception of risk. *Science, 236,* 280–285.

Slovic, P., Fischhoff, B., & Lichtenstein, S. (1976). Cognitive processes and societal risk taking. In J. S. Carroll & J. W. Payne (Eds.), *Cognition and social behavior* (pp. 165–184). Hillsdale, NJ: Erlbaum.

Smith, A. T., & Over, R. (1976). Color-selective tilt aftereffects with subjective contours. *Attention, Perception, & Psychophysics, 20,* 305–308.

Smith, E. E., & Jonides, J. (1999). Storage and executive processes in the frontal lobes. *Science, 283,* 1657–1661.

Smith, E. E., Jonides, J., Koeppe, R. A., Awh, E., Schumacher, E. H., & Minoshima, S. (1995). Spatial versus object working memory: PET investigations. *Journal of Cognitive Neuroscience, 7,* 337–356.

Smith, E. E., & Larson, D. E. (1970). The verbal loop hypothesis and the effects of similarity on recognition and communication in adults and children. *Journal of Verbal Learning and Verbal Behavior, 9,* 237–242.

Smith, E. E., Shoben, E. J., & Rips, L. J. (1974). Structure and process in semantic memory: A featural model for semantic decisions. *Psychological Review, 81,* 214–241.

Smith, F. (1983). *Essays into literacy.* Portsmouth, NH: Heinemann.

Smith, I. M. (1964). *Spatial ability.* San Diego, CA: Knapp.

Smith, L. C., & Klein, R. (1990). Evidence for semantic satiation: Repeating a category slows subsequent semantic processing. *Journal of Experimental Psychology: Learning, Memory, and Cognition, 16,* 852–861.

Smith, M. C., & Phillips, M. R. (2001). Age differences in memory for radio advertisements: The role of mnemonics. *Journal of Business Research, 53,* 103–109.

Smith, S. J. (2005). EEG in the diagnosis, classification, and management of patients with epilepsy. *Journal of Neurology, Neurosurgery, and Psychiatry, 76,* 2–7.

Smith, S. M. (1979). Remembering in and out of context. *Journal of Experimental Psychology: Human Learning and Memory, 5,* 460–471.

Smith, S. M. (1994). Frustrated feelings of imminent recall: On the tip-of-the-tongue. In J. Metcalfe & A. P. Shimamura (Eds.), *Metacognition: Knowing about knowing* (pp. 27–46). Cambridge, MA: MIT Press.

Smyth, A. H. (Ed.). (1906). *The writings of Benjamin Franklin* (Vol. 5). New York: Macmillan.

Smyth, M., & Pendleton, L. R. (1989). Working memory for movements. *Quarterly Journal of Experimental Psychology: Human Experimental Psychology, 42,* 235–250.

Snowden, J. S., Goulding, P. J., & Neary, D. (1989). Semantic dementia and form of circumscribed cerebral atrophy. *Behavioral Neurology, 2,* 167–182.

Snowling, M. J. (1980). The development of grapheme–phoneme correspondences in normal and dyslexic readers. *Journal of Experimental Child Psychology, 29,* 294–305.

Sohlberg, M. M., & Mateer, C. A. (1989). *Introduction to neuropsychological rehabilitation.* New York: Guilford Press.

Solet, D., Norvell, J., Rutan, G., & Frankel, R. (2005). Lost in translation: Challenges and opportunities in physician-to-physician communication during patient handoff. *Academic Medicine, 80,* 1094–1099.

Solomon, K. O., & Barsalou, L. W. (2001). Representing properties locally. *Cognitive Psychology, 43,* 129–169.

Solso, R. L., & McCarthy, J. E. (1981). Prototype formation of faces: A case study of pseudo-memory. *British Journal of Psychology, 72,* 499–503.

Somerville, S. C., Hadkinson, B. A., & Greenberg, C. (1979). Two levels of inferential behavior in young children. *Child Development, 50,* 119–131.

Souchay, C., Isingrini, M., & Espagnet, L. (2000). Aging, episodic memory feeling of knowing, and frontal functioning. *Neuropsychology, 14,* 299–309.

Sox, H. C., Blatt, M. A., Higgins, M. C., & Marton, K. I. (2006). *Medical decision making.* Philadelphia: ACP Press.

Spelke, E. S. (1990). Principles of object segregation. *Cognitive Science, 14,* 29–56.

Spelt, D. K. (1948). The conditioning of the foetus *in utero. Journal of Experimental Psychology, 38,* 338–346.

Sperber, D., & Wilson, D. (1995). *Relevance: Communication and cognition* (2nd ed.). Oxford, England: Blackwell.

Sperber, D., & Wilson, D. (1996). Fodor's frame problem and relevance theory (reply to Chiappe & Kukla). *Behavioral and Brain Sciences, 19,* 530–532.

Sperling, G. (1960). The information available in brief visual presentations. *Psychological Monographs, 74* (Whole No. 48).

Sperry, R. W. (1964). The great cerebral commissure. *Scientific American, 210,* 42–52.

Spezio, M. L., Adolphs, R. S., Hurley, R., & Piven, J. (2007). Abnormal use of facial information in high-functioning autism. *Journal of Autism and Developmental Disorders, 5,* 929–939.

Spilich, G. J., Vesonder, G. T., Chiesi, H. L., & Voss, J. F. (1979). Text processing of domain-related information for individuals with high and low domain knowledge. *Journal of Verbal Learning and Verbal Behavior, 18,* 275–290.

Spiro, R. J. (1977). Remembering information from text: The "state of schema" approach. In R. C. Anderson, R. J. Spiro, & W. E. Montague (Eds.), *Schooling and the acquisition of knowledge* (pp. 137–177). Hillsdale, NJ: Erlbaum.

Spivey, M., Tyler, M., Eberhard, K., & Tanenhaus, M. (2001). Linguistically mediated visual search. *Psychological Science, 12,* 282–286.

Spreen, O., & Strauss, E. (1991). *A compendium of neuropsychological tests.* New York: Oxford University Press.

Spurzheim, J. G. (1815). *The physiognomical system of Drs. Gall and Spurzheim: Founded on an anatomical and physiological examination of the nervous system in general, and of the brain in particular; and indicating the dispositions and manifestations of the mind. Being at the same time a book of reference for Dr. Spurzheim's demonstrative lectures.* London: Baldwin, Cradock, and Joy.

Squire, L. R. (1992). Memory and the hippocampus: A synthesis from findings with rats, monkeys, and humans. *Psychological Review, 99,* 195–231.

Stahl, S. A., & Miller, P. D. (1989). Whole language and language experience approaches for beginning reading: A quantitative research synthesis. *Review of Educational Research, 59,* 87–116.

Stanovich, K. E. (1986). Matthew effects in reading: Some consequences of individual differences in the acquisition of literacy. *Reading Research Quarterly, 21,* 360–407.

Stanovich, K. E. (1999). *Who is rational? Studies of individual differences in reasoning.* Mahwah, NJ: Erlbaum.

Stanovich, K. E., & West, R. F. (2000). Individual differences in reasoning: Implications for the rationality debate? *Behavioral and Brain Sciences, 23,* 645–726.

Starr, M. S., & Rayner, K. (2001). Eye movements during reading: Some current controversies. *Trends in Cognitive Sciences, 5,* 156–163.

Stein, N. L. (2002). Memories for emotional, stressful, and traumatic events. In N. L. Stein, P. J. Bauer, & M. Rabinowitz (Eds.), *Representation, memory, and development: Essays in honor of Jean Mandler* (pp. 247–265). Mahwah, NJ: Erlbaum.

Stein, N. L., & Glenn, C. G. (1979). An analysis of story comprehension in elementary children. In R. Freedle (Ed.), *New directions in discourse processing* (pp. 53–120). Norwood, NJ: Ablex.

Stenbert, G., Radeborg, K., & Hedman, L. R. (1982). The picture superiority effect in a cross-modality recognition task. *Journal of Experimental Psychology: Learning, Memory, and Cognition, 8,* 584–598.

Sternberg, R. J. (1980). Sketch of a componential sub-theory of human intelligence. *Behavioral and Brain Sciences, 3,* 573–584.

Sternberg, R. J. (Ed.). (1982). *Handbook of human intelligence.* New York: Cambridge University Press.

Sternberg, S. (1966). High-speed scanning in human memory. *Science, 153,* 652–654.

Sternberg, S. (2004). *Memory-scanning: Mental processes revealed by reaction-time experiments.* New York: Psychology Press.

Stevens, A., & Coupe, P. (1978). Distortions in judged spatial relations. *Cognitive Psychology, 10,* 422–437.

Stevens, K. N. & Halle, M. (1967). Remarks on analysis by synthesis and distinctive features. In W. Wathen-Dunn (Ed.), *Models for the perception of speech and visual form* (pp. 88–102). Cambridge, MA: MIT Press.

Stevenson, H. W., Lee, S.-Y., Stigler, J. W., Hsu, C.-C., Kitamura, S., & Hatano, G. (1990). Context of achievement: A study of American, Chinese, and Japanese children. *Monographs of the Society for Research in Child Development, 55*(1–2), 1–123.

St. George, M., Kutas, M., Martinez, A., & Sereno, M. I. (1999). Semantic integration in reading: Engagement of the right hemisphere during discourse processing. *Brain, 122,* 1317–1325.

Stone, J. L., & Urcid, J. (2002). Pre-Columbian skull trepanation in North America. In R. Arnott, S. Finger, & C. Smith (Eds.), *Trepanation: History, discovery, theory* (pp. 237–249). Lisse, the Netherlands: Swets & Zeitlinger.

Storms, L. H., & Broen, W. E. (1972). Intrusion of schizophrenics' idiosyncratic associations into their conceptual performance. *Journal of Abnormal Psychology, 79,* 280–284.

Strange, P. G. (2001). Antipsychotic drugs: Importance of dopamine receptors of mechanisms of therapeutic actions and side effects. *Pharmacological Review, 53,* 119–134.

Strayer, D. L., & Drews, F. A. (2006). Profiles in driver distraction: Effects of cell phone conversations on younger and older drivers. *Human Factors, 46,* 640–649.

Strayer, D. L., & Drews, F. A. (2007). Cell phone induced driver distraction. *Current Directions in Psychological Science, 16,* 128–131.

Strayer, D. L., Drews, F. A., & Johnston, W. A. (2003). Cell phone induced failures of visual attention during simulated driving. *Journal of Experimental Psychology: Applied, 9,* 23–32.

Strayer, D. L., & Johnston, W. A. (2001). Driven to distraction: Dual-task studies of simulated driving and conversing on a cellular telephone. *Psychological Science, 12,* 462–466.

Strohmeyer, C. F., & Psotka, J. (1970). The detailed texture of eidetic images. *Nature, 224,* 346–349.

Stroop, J. R. (1935). Studies of interference in serial verbal reactions. *Journal of Experimental Psychology, 18,* 643–662.

Suedfeld, P., & Streufert, S. (1966). Information search as a function of conceptual and environmental complexity. *Psychonomic Science, 4,* 351–352.

Suedfeld, P., & Tetlock, P. E. (2001). Individual differences in information processing. In A. Tesser & N. Schwartz (Eds.), *The Blackwell handbook of social psychology. Vol. 1: Intraindividual processes* (pp. 284–304). London: Blackwell.

Sulin, R. A., & Dooling, D. J. (1974). Intrusion of a thematic idea in retention of prose. *Journal of Experimental Psychology, 103,* 255–262.

Sullivan, E. V., Deshmukh, A., Desmond, J. E., Lim, K. O., & Pfefferbaum, A. (2000). Cerebellar volume decline in normal aging, alcoholism, and Korsakoff's syndrome: Relation to ataxia. *Neuropsychology, 14,* 341–352.

Sundali, J. (2006). Biases in casino betting: The hot hand and the gambler's fallacy. *Judgment and Decision Making, 1,* 1–12.

Sutton-Smith, B. (1986). The development of fictional narrative performances. *Topics in Language Disorders, 7,* 1–10.

Suzuki, K., & Takahashi, R. (1997). Effectiveness of color in picture recognition memory. *Japanese Psychological Research, 39,* 25–32.

Swanson, H. L. (1999). Instructional components that predict treatment outcomes for students with learning disabilities: Support for a combined strategy and direct instruction model. *Learning Disabilities Research and Practice, 14,* 129–140.

Swanson, H. L., & Jerman, O. (2007). The influence of working memory on reading growth in subgroups of children with reading disabilities. *Journal of Experimental Child Psychology, 96,* 249–283.

Szpir, M. (1992). Accustomed to your face. *American Scientist, 80,* 537–539.

Talarico, J. M., & Rubin, D. C. (2003). Confidence not consistency characterizes flashbulb memories. *Psychological Science, 14,* 455–461.

Talarico, J. M., & Rubin, D. C. (2009). Flashbulb memories result from ordinary memory processes and extraordinary event characteristics. In O. Luminet & A. Curci (Eds.), *Flashbulb memories:*

New issues and new perspectives (pp. 79–97). New York: Psychology Press.

Talgar, C., Pelli, D. G., & Carrasco, M. (2004). Covert attention enhances letter identification without affecting channel tuning. *Journal of Vision, 41,* 23–32.

Tan, L., & Ward, G. (2000). A recency-based account of the primacy effect in free recall. *Journal of Experimental Psychology: Learning, Memory, and Cognition, 26,* 1589–1625.

Tanaka, J. W., & Farah, M. J. (1993). Parts and wholes in face recognition. *Quarterly Journal of Experimental Psychology, 46,* 225–245.

Tannen, D. (1994a). *Gender and discourse.* New York: Oxford University Press.

Tannen, D. (1994b). *Talking 9 to 5.* New York: William Morrow.

Tannen, D. (2001). *You just don't understand: Women and men in conversation.* New York: HarperCollins.

Taplin, J. E., Staudenmayer, H., & Taddonio, J. L. (1974). Developmental changes in conditional reasoning: Linguistic or logical? *Journal of Experimental Child Psychology, 17,* 360–373.

Tardif, T. Z., & Sternberg, R. J. (1988). What do we know about creativity? In R. J. Sternberg (Ed.), *The nature of creativity: Contemporary psychological perspectives* (pp. 429–440). Cambridge, England: Cambridge University Press.

Taylor, A. E., & Saint-Cyr, J. A. (1995). The neuropsychology of Parkinson's disease. *Brain and Cognition, 28,* 281–296.

Taylor, J. G., & Fragopanagos, N. F. (2005). The interaction of attention and emotion. *Neural Networks, 18,* 353–369.

Taylor, L. K., Alber, S. R., & Walker, D. W. (2002). The comparative effects of a modified self-questioning strategy and story mapping on the reading comprehension of elementary students with learning disabilities. *Journal of Behavioral Education, 11,* 69–87.

Tehan, G., & Lalor, D. M. (2000). Individual differences in memory span: The contribution of rehearsal, access to lexical memory, and output speed. *Quarterly Journal of Experimental Psychology, 53A,* 1012–1038.

Tentori, K., Bonini, N., & Osherson, D. (2004). The conjunction fallacy: A misunderstanding about conjunction? *Cognitive Science, 29,* 467–477.

Terrace, H., Petitto, L., Sanders, R., & Bever, T. (1979). Can an ape create a sentence? *Science, 26,* 891–902.

Terry, W. S. (2005). Serial position effects in recall of television commercials. *Journal of General Psychology, 13,* 151–163.

Theios, J. (1973). Reaction time measurements in the study of memory processes: Theory and data. In G. H. Bower (Ed.), *The psychology of learning and motivation* (Vol. 7, pp. 43–85). New York: Academic Press.

Theodore, W. H. (2006). Expanding the geography of epilepsy: Imaging evidence for basal ganglia involvement. *Epilepsy Currents, 6,* 40–41.

Thistlethwaite, D. (1950). Attitude and structure as factors in the distortion of reasoning. *Journal of Abnormal and Social Psychology, 45,* 422–448.

Thomas, J. C. (1974). An analysis of behavior in the Hobbits–Orcs problem. *Cognitive Psychology, 6,* 257–269.

Thompson, P. (1980). Margaret Thatcher: A new illusion. *Perception, 9,* 483–484.

Thomson, J. J. (1976). Killing, letting die, and the trolley problem. *The Monist, 59,* 204–217.

Thorndike, E. L., & Woodworth, R. S. (1901). The influence of improvement in one mental function upon the efficiency of other functions (I). *Psychological Review, 8,* 247–261.

Thorndyke, P. (1977). Cognitive structures in comprehension and memory of narrative discourse. *Cognitive Psychology, 9,* 77–110.

Thurstone, L. L. (1938). *Psychometric monograph* (No. 1). Chicago: University of Chicago Press.

Townsend, J. T. (1971). A note on the identifiability of parallel and serial processes. *Perception & Psychophysics, 10,* 161–163.

Townsend, J. T. (1990). Serial vs. parallel processing: Sometimes they look like Tweedledum and Tweedledee but they can (and should) be distinguished. *Psychological Science, 1,* 46–54.

Trabasso, T. (1977). The role of memory as a system in making transitive inferences. In R. V. Kail, J. W. Hagen, & J. M. Belmont (Eds.), *Perspectives on the development of memory and cognition* (pp. 333–366). Hillsdale, NJ: Erlbaum.

Trehub, S. (1976). The discrimination of foreign speech contrasts by infants and adults. *Child Development, 47,* 466–472.

Treisman, A. (1960). Contextual cues in selective listening. *Quarterly Journal of Experimental Psychology, 12,* 242–248.

Treisman, A. (1964). Selective attention in man. *British Medical Bulletin, 20,* 12–16.

Treisman, A., & Gelade, G. (1980). A feature integration theory of attention. *Cognitive Psychology, 12,* 97–136.

Treisman, A., & Gormican, S. (1988). Feature analysis in early vision: Evidence from search asymmetries. *Psychological Review, 95,* 15–48.

Trick, L. M., & Pylyshyn, Z. W. (1994). Why are small and large numbers enumerated differently? A limited-capacity preattentive stage in vision. *Psychological Review, 101,* 80–102.

Troia, G. A. (1999). Phonological awareness intervention research: A critical review of the experimental methodology. *Reading Research Quarterly, 34,* 28–52.

Tsal, Y. (1977). Symmetry and transitivity assumptions about a nonspecified logical relation. *Quarterly Journal of Experimental Psychology, 29,* 677–684.

Tucker, G. R. (1998). A global perspective on multilingualism and multilingual education. In J. Cenoz & F. Genesee (Eds.), *Beyond bilingualism: Multilingualism and multilingual education* (pp. 3–63). Philadelphia: Multilingualism Matters.

Tulving, E. (1962). Subject organization in free recall of "unrelated" words. *Psychological Review, 69,* 344–354.

Tulving, E. (1972). Episodic and semantic memory. In E. Tulving & W. Donaldson (Eds.), *Organization of memory* (pp. 382–402). New York: Academic Press.

Tulving, E. (1982). Synergistic ecphory in recall and recognition. *Canadian Journal of Psychology, 36,* 130–147.

Tulving, E. (1984). Precis of elements of episodic memory. *Behavioral and Brain Sciences, 7,* 223–268.

Tulving, E. (1985). How many memory systems are there? *American Psychologist, 40,* 385–398.

Tulving, E. (2002). Episodic memory: From mind to brain. *Annual Review of Psychology, 53,* 1–25.

Tulving, E., & Craik, F. I. M. (Eds.). (2000). *The Oxford handbook of memory*. Oxford, England: Oxford University Press.

Tulving, E., Kapur, S., Craik, F. I. M., Moscovitsch, M., & Houle, S. (1994). Hemispheric encoding/retrieval asymmetry in episodic memory: Positron emission tomography findings. *Proceedings of the National Academy of Sciences, USA, 91,* 2016–2020.

Tulving, E., & Osler, S. (1968). Effectiveness of retrieval cues in memory for words. *Journal of Experimental Psychology, 77,* 593–601.

Tulving, E., & Thomson, D. M. (1973). Encoding specificity and retrieval processes in episodic memory. *Psychological Review, 80,* 352–373.

Turner, H. H. (1938). A syndrome of infantilism, congenital webbed neck, and *cubitus valgus. Endocrinology, 23,* 566–574.

Turner, M. L., & Engle, R. W. (1989). Is working memory capacity task dependent? *Journal of Memory and Language, 28,* 127–154.

Tversky, A., & Gilovich, T. (1989). The cold facts about the hot hand in basketball. *Chance, 2,* 16–21.

Tversky, A., & Kahneman, D. (1971). Belief in the law of small numbers. *Psychological Bulletin, 76,* 105–110.

Tversky, A., & Kahneman, D. (1973). Availability: A heuristic for judging frequency and probability. *Cognitive Psychology, 5,* 297–232.

Tversky, A., & Kahneman, D. (1974). Judgment under uncertainty: Heuristics and biases. *Science, 185,* 1124–1131.

Tversky, A., & Kahneman, D. (1981). The framing of decisions and the psychology of choice. *Science, 211,* 453–458.

Tversky, A., & Kahneman, D. (1982). Evidential impact of base rates. In D. Kahneman, P. Slovic, & A. Tversky (Eds.), *Judgment under uncertainty: Heuristics and biases* (pp. 201–208). New York: Cambridge University Press.

Tversky, A., & Kahneman, D. (1983). Extensional vs. intuitive reasoning: The conjunctive fallacy in probability judgment. *Psychological Review, 90,* 293–315.

Tversky, A., & Kahneman, D. (1992). Advances in prospect theory: Cumulative representation of uncertainty. *Journal of Risk and Uncertainty, 5,* 297–323.

Tversky, B. (1981). Distortions in memory for maps. *Cognitive Psychology, 13,* 407–433.

Twain, M. (1924). *Mark Twain's autobiography* (Vol. 1). New York: Harper & Brothers.

Tweney, R. D., & Yachanin, S. A. (1985). Can scientists rationally assess conditional inference? *Social Studies of Science, 15,* 155–172.

Uberti, H. Z., Scruggs, T. E., & Mastropieri, M. A. (2003). Keywords make the difference! Mnemonic instruction in inclusive classrooms. *Teaching Exceptional Children, 10,* 56–61.

United Nations. (2009). *Human development report.* New York: Palgrave Macmillan.

Usher, A., & Neisser, U. (1993). Childhood amnesia and the beginnings of memory for four early life events. *Journal of Experimental Psychology: General, 122,* 155–165.

U.S. National Transportation Safety Board (2005, September 29). *Collision between the U.S. Navy submarine USS Greeneville and Japanese motor vessel Ehime Maru near Oahu, Hawaii, 9 February 2001* (Marine Accident Brief, Accident No. DCA-01-MM-022). Retrieved from http://www.ntsb.gov/doclib/reports/MABO501.pdf

Uttal, W. R. (2001). *The new phrenology: The limits of localizing cognitive processes in the brain.* Cambridge, MA: MIT Press.

Vaidya, C. J., Austin, G., Kirkorian, G., Ridlehuber, H. W., Desmond, J. E., Glover, G. H., & Gabrieli, J. D. E. (1998). Selective effects of methylphenidate in attention deficit hyperactivity disorder: A functional magnetic resonance study. *Proceedings of the National Academy of Sciences, USA, 95,* 14494–14499.

Vaidya, C. J., & Gabrieli, J. D. E. (1999). Searching for a neurobiological signature of attention deficit hyperactivity disorder. *Molecular Psychiatry, 4,* 206–208.

Valdesolo, P., & DeSteno, D. (2006). Manipulations of emotional context shape moral judgment. *Psychological Science, 17,* 476–477.

Valentine, T. (1988). Upside-down faces: A review of the effect of inversion upon face recognition. *British Journal of Psychology, 79,* 471–491.

Valentine, T., & Endo, M. (1992). Towards an exemplar model of face processing: The effects of race and distinctiveness. *Quarterly Journal of Experimental Journal, 44A,* 671–703.

Valentine, T., Harris, N., Piera, A. C., & Darling, S. (2003). Are police video identifications fair to African-Caribbean suspects? *Applied Cognitive Psychology, 17,* 459–476.

Valenza, E., Simion, F., Macchi Cassia, V., & Umiltà, C. (1996). Face preference at birth. *Journal of Experimental Psychology: Human Perception and Performance, 22,* 892–903.

Van den Dikkenberg-Pot, I., & Van der Stelt, J. M. (2001). Mother–child interaction in two-year-old deaf and hearing children. *Proceedings of the Institute of Phonetic Sciences, Amsterdam, 23,* 1–13.

Vandierendonck, A., & De Vooght, G. (1997). Working memory constraints on linear reasoning with spatial and temporal contents. *Quarterly Journal of Experimental Psychology, 50,* 803–820.

Vanetti, E. J., & Allen, G. L. (1988). Communicating environmental knowledge: The impact of verbal and spatial abilitiles on the production and comprehension of route directions. *Environment and Behavior, 20,* 667–682.

VanLehn, K. (1989). Problem solving and cognitive skill acquisition. In M. I. Posner (Ed.), *Foundations of cognitive science* (pp. 526–579). Cambridge, MA: MIT Press.

VanLehn, K. (1996). Cognitive skill acquisition. *Annual Review of Psychology, 47,* 513–539.

Van Overschelde, J. P. (2002). The influence of word frequency on recency effects in directed free recall. *Journal of Experimental Psychology: Learning, Memory, and Cognition, 28,* 611–615.

van Rossum, I., Tenback, D., & van Os, J. (2009). Bipolar disorder and dopamine dysfunction: An indirect approach focusing on tardive movement syndromes in a naturalistic setting. *BioMedical Central Psychiatry, 9,* 1–9.

Vargha-Khadem, F., Gadian, D. G., Watkins, K. E., Connelly, A., Van Paesschen, W., & Mishkin, M. (1997). Differential effects of early hippocampal pathology on episodic and semantic memory. *Science, 277,* 376–380.

Vellutino, F. R., Smith, H., Steger, J. A., & Kaman, M. (1975). Reading disability: Age differences and the perceptual deficit hypothesis. *Child Development, 46,* 487–493.

Vellutino, F. R., Steger, J. A., & Kandel, A. (1972). Reading disability: An investigation of the perceptual deficit hypothesis. *Cortex, 8,* 106–118.

Venn, J. (1880). On the diagrammatic and mechanical representation of propositions and reasoning. *The London, Edinburgh, and Dublin Philosophical Magazine and Journal of Science, 9,* 1–18.

Vercelletto, M., Bourin, M., Lacomblez, L., Verpillat, P., & Derkinderen, P. (2005). Neurotransmitter dysfunction and neurotransmitter replacement therapy as part of frontotemporal dementia treatment. *Current Psychiatry Reviews, 1,* 345–351.

Verhaeghen, P., & Marcoen, A. (1996). On the mechanisms of plasticity in young and older adults after instruction in the method of loci: Evidence for an amplification model. *Psychology and Aging, 11,* 164–178.

Verster, J. C., van Duin, D., Volkerts, E. R., Schreuder, A., & Verbaten, M. N. (2003). Alcohol hangover effects on memory functioning and vigilance performance after an evening of binge drinking. *Neuropsychopharmacology, 28,* 740–748.

Vilberg, K. L., & Rugg, M. D. (2008). Memory retrieval and the parietal cortex: A review of evidence from a dual-process perspective. *Neuropsychologia, 46,* 1787–1799.

Vokey, J. R., & Read, J. D. (1992). Familiarity, memorability, and the effect of typicality on the recognition of faces. *Memory & Cognition, 20,* 291–302.

Volkow, N. D., Fowler, J. S., Wang, G., Ding, Y., & Gatley, S. J. (2002). Role of dopamine in the therapeutic and reinforcing effects of methylphenidate in humans: Results from imaging studies. *European Neuropsychopharmacology, 12,* 557–566.

Volle, E., Kinkingnehun, S., Pochon, J. P., Mondon, K., Thiebaut de Schotten, M., Sessau, M., . . . Levy, R. (2008). The functional architecture of the left posterior and lateral prefrontal cortex in humans. *Cerebral Cortex, 18,* 2460–2469.

Von Domarus, E. (1954). The specific laws of logic in schizophrenia. In J. S. Kasanin (Ed.), *Language and thought in schizophrenia* (pp. 104–114). Berkeley: University of California Press.

von Frisch, K. (1974). Decoding the language of the bee. *Science, 185,* 663–668.

Von Neumann, J., & Morgenstern, O. (1947). *Theory of games and economic behavior* (2nd ed.). Princeton, NJ: Princeton University Press.

Voorhees, E. M. (1999). Natural language processing and information retrieval. In M. T. Pazienza (Ed.), *Information extraction: Towards scalable, adaptable systems* (pp. 48–32). New York: Springer.

vos Savant, M. (1990, February 17). "Ask Marilyn" column. *Parade Magazine,* p. 12.

Vrij, A., Leal, S., Granhag, P. A., Mann, S., Fisher, R. P., Hillman, J., & Sperry, K. (2009). Outsmarting the liars: The benefit of asking unanticipated questions. *Law and Human Behavior, 33,* 159–166.

Vuilleumier, P., Armony, J. L., Driver, J., & Dolan, R. J. (2001). Effects of attention and emotion on face processing in the human brain: An event-related study. *Neuron, 20,* 1–20.

Vygotsky, L. S. (1962). *Thought and language.* New York: Wiley.

Wada, J. (1949). A new method for the determination of the side of cerebral speech dominance. A preliminary report of the intracarotid injection of sodium amytal in man. *Igaku to Seibutsugaki, Tokyo, 14,* 221–222.

Wagemans, J., Verhulst, F., & De Winter, J. (2003, September). *The time course of the attentional blink for objects.* Paper presented at the European Conference for Visual Perception, Paris.

Wagenaar, W. A. (1972). Generation of random sequences by human subjects: A critical survey of the literature. *Psychological Bulletin, 77,* 65–72.

Wagner, R. K., & Stanovich, K. W. (1996). Expertise in reading. In A. Ericsson (Ed.), *The road to excellence: The acquisition of expert performance in the arts and sciences, sport and games* (pp. 189–225). Mahwah, NJ: Erlbaum.

Walker, R. W., Skowronski, J. J., Gibbons, J. A., Vogl, R. J., & Thompson, C. P. (2003). On the emotions that accompany autobiographical memories: Dysphoria disrupts the fading affect bias. *Cognition & Emotion, 17,* 703–723.

Walker, R. W., Skowronski, J. J., & Thompson, C. P. (2003). Life is pleasant—and memory helps to keep it that way! *Review of General Psychology, 7,* 203–210.

Wallas, G. (1926). *The art of thought.* New York: Harcourt Brace.

Walton, G. E., Armstrong, E. S., & Bower, T. G. R. (1998). Newborns learn to identify a face in eight-tenths of a second? *Developmental Science, 1,* 79–84.

Walton, G. E., Bower, N. J., & Bower, T. G. R. (1992). Recognition of familiar faces by newborns. *Infant Behavior & Development, 15,* 265–269.

Walton, G. E., & Bower, T. G. R. (1993). Newborns form "prototypes" in less than 1 minute. *Psychological Science, 4,* 203–205.

Wang, A. Y., Thomas, M. H., & Ouellette, J. A. (1992). Keyword mnemonic and retention of second-language vocabulary words. *Journal of Educational Psychology, 84,* 520–542.

Warburton, D. M., Skinner, A., & Martin, C. D. (2001). Improved incidental memory with nicotine after semantic processing, but not after phonological processing. *Psychopharmacology, 153,* 258–263.

Warren, R. M. (1970). Perceptual restoration of missing speech sounds. *Science, 167,* 392–393.

Warren, R. M., & Sherman, G. L. (1974). Restorations based on subsequent context. *Perception & Psychophysics, 16,* 150–156.

Warren, R. M., & Warren, R. P. (1970). Auditory illusions and confusions. *Scientific American, 223,* 30–36.

Warrington, E. K. (1971). Neurological disorders of memory. *British Medical Bulletin, 27,* 243–247.

Warrington, E. K. (1975). The selective impairment of semantic memory. *Quarterly Journal of Experimental Psychology, 27,* 635–657.

Wason, P. C. (1960). On the failure to eliminate hypotheses in a conceptual task. *Quarterly Journal of Experimental Psychology, 12,* 129–140.

Wason, P. C. (1966). Reasoning. In B. M. Foss (Ed.), *New horizons in psychology* (pp. 135–151). Harmondsworth, England: Penguin Books.

Wason, P. C. (1968). On the failure to eliminate hypotheses: A second look. In P. C. Wason & P. N. Johnson-Laird (Eds.), *Thinking and reasoning* (pp. 165–174). Harmondsworth, Middlesex, England: Penguin.

Wason, P. C., & Evans, J. St. B. (1975). Dual processes in reasoning. *Cognition, 3,* 141–154.

Wason, P. C., & Johnson-Laird, P. N. (1972). *Psychology of reasoning: Structure and content.* Cambridge, MA: Harvard University Press.

Wason, P. C., & Shapiro, D. (1971). Natural and contrived experience in a reasoning problem. *Quarterly Journal of Experimental Psychology, 23,* 63–71.

Watkins, M. J., & Tulving, E. (1975). Episodic memory when recognition fails. *Journal of Experimental Psychology: General, 104,* 5–29.

Watkins, M. J., & Watkins, O. C. (1974). The tactile suffix effect. *Memory & Cognition, 2,* 176–180.

Watkins, O. C., & Watkins, M. J. (1980). The modality effect and echoic persistence. *Journal of Experimental Psychology: General, 109,* 251–278.

Watson, C. G., & Wold, J. (1981). Logical reasoning deficits in schizophrenia and brain damage. *Journal of Clinical Psychology, 37,* 466–471.

Watson, J. B. (1916). Behavior and the concept of mental disease. *Journal of Philosophy, Psychology, and Scientific Methods, 13,* 589–597.

Watson, J. B. (1925). *Behaviorism.* New York: W. W. Norton.

Watt, W. C. (1970). On two hypotheses concerning psycholinguistics. In J. R. Hayes (Ed.), *Cognition and the development of language* (pp. 130–220). New York: Wiley.

Weatherhead, P. J. (1979). Do Savannah sparrows commit the Concorde fallacy? *Behavioral Ecology and Social Biology, 5,* 373–381.

Weber, A. M. (1988). A new clinical measure of attention: The attentional capacity test. *Neuropsychology, 2,* 59–71.

Wegner, D. M., & Bargh, J. A. (1998). Control and automaticity in social life. In T. D. Gilbert, S. T. Fiske, & G. Lindzey (Eds.), *Handbook of social psychology* (4th ed., Vol. 1, pp. 446–496). New York: McGraw-Hill.

Weinberger, D. R. (1987). Implications of normal brain development for the pathogenesis of schizophrenia. *Archives of General Psychiatry, 44,* 660–669.

Weiner, B. (1980). *Human motivation.* New York: Holt, Rinehart and Winston.

Weinstein, N. D. (1980). Unrealistic optimism about future life events. *Journal of Personality and Social Psychology, 39,* 806–820.

Weintraub, S., Rubin, N., & Mesulam, M. M. (1990). Primary progressive aphasia: Longitudinal course, neurological profile, and language features. *Archives of Neurology, 47,* 1329–1335.

Weir, A. A., Chappell, J., & Kacelnik, A. (2002). Shaping of hooks in New Caledonian crows. *Science, 297,* 981.

Weisberg, R. W. (1993). *Creativity: Beyond the myth of genius.* New York: W. H. Freeman & Company.

Wellbrink, J. C. G., & Buss, A. H. (2004). Vigilance performance modeled as a complex adaptive system with listener event graph objects (LEGOS). In R. G. Ingalls, M. D. Rossetti, J. S. Smith, & B. A. Peters (Eds.), *Proceedings of the 2004 Winter Simulation conference* (pp. 755–759). San Diego, CA: Society for Computer Simulation International.

Wells, G. L. (1993). What do we know about eye-witness identification? *American Psychologist, 48,* 553–571.

Werker, J. F., Gilbert, J. H. V., Humphrey, K., & Tees, R. C. (1981). Developmental aspects of cross-language speech perception. *Child Development, 52,* 349–355.

Werker, J. F., & Tees, R. C. (1984). Cross-language speech perception: Evidence for perceptual reorganization during the first year of life. *Infant Behavior & Development, 7,* 49–63.

Wertheimer, M. (1938). Examining the teachings of Gestalt psychology. In W. Ellis (Ed.), *A source book of Gestalt psychology* (pp. 71–78). London: Routledge & Kegan Paul. (Original work published 1923)

Wharton, C. M., Cheng, P. W., & Wickens, T. D. (1993). Hypothesis-testing strategies: Why two goals are better than one. *Quarterly Journal of Experimental Psychology, 46A,* 743–758.

Wheeler, M. A., Stuss, D. T., & Tulving, E. (1995). Frontal lobe damage produces episodic memory impairment. *Journal of the International Neuropsychological Society, 1,* 524–536.

Wheeler, M. A., Stuss, D. T., & Tulving, E. (1997). Toward a theory of episodic memory: The frontal lobes and autonoetic consciousness. *Psychological Bulletin, 121,* 331–354.

Whitney, P., Ritchie, B. G., & Clark, M. B. (1991). Working memory capacity and the use of elaborative inferences in text comprehension. *Discourse Processes, 14,* 133–145.

Whittaker, J. F., Deakin, J. F. W., & Tomenson, B. (2001). Face processing in schizophrenia: Defining the deficit. *Psychological Medicine, 31,* 499–507.

Whorf, B. J. (1956). *Language, thought, and reality: The selected writings of Benjamin Lee Whorf.* Cambridge, MA: MIT Press.

Wickelgren, W. A. (1964). Size of rehearsal group and short-term memory. *Journal of Experimental Psychology, 68,* 413–419.

Wickelgren, W. A. (1979). Chunking and consolidation: A theoretical synthesis of semantic networks, configuring, in conditioning, S–R versus cognitive learning, normal forgetting, the amnesic syndrome, and the hippocampal arousal system. *Psychological Review, 86,* 44–60.

Wickens, C. (1992). *Engineering psychology and human performance.* New York: HarperCollins.

Wickens, D. D. (1970). Encoding categories of words: An empirical approach to meaning. *Psychological Review, 77,* 1–15.

Wickens, D. D., Born, D. G., & Allen, C. K. (1963). Proactive inhibition and item similarity in short-term memory. *Journal of Verbal Learning and Verbal Behavior, 2,* 440–445.

Widner, R. L., Jr., Otani, H., Adams, D., & Mueller, M. (1998, November). *Age-related differences between young and older adults in the attentional blink.* Paper presented at the meeting of the Psychonomic Society, Dallas, TX.

Wiens, A., Fuller, K. H., & Crossan, J. R. (1997). Paced Auditory Serial Addition Test: Adult norms and moderator variables. *Journal of Clinical and Experimental Neuropsychology, 19,* 473–483.

Wilde, N., & Strauss, E. (2002). Functional equivalence of WAIS-III Digit and Spatial span under forward and backward recall conditions. *The Clinical Neuropsychologist, 16,* 322–330.

Wilkens, A. J., & Baddeley, A. D. (1978). Remembering to recall in everyday life: An approach to absentmindedness. In M. M. Gruneberg, P. E. Morris, & R. N. Sykes (Eds.), *Practical aspects of memory* (pp. 27–34). New York: Academic Press.

Wilkins, M. C. (1928). The effect of changed material on ability to do formal syllogistic reasoning. *Archives of Psychology, 16,* 1–83.

Williams, E. B. (1964). Deductive reasoning in schizophrenia. *Journal of Abnormal and Social Psychology, 69,* 47–61.

Williams, G. V., & Goldman-Rakic, P. S. (1995). Modulation of memory fields by dopamine D1 receptors in prefrontal cortex. *Nature, 376,* 572–575.

Williams, J. C. P., Barratt-Boyes, B. G., & Lowe, J. B. (1961). Supravalvular aortic stenosis. *Circulation, 24,* 1311–1318.

Williams, R. W., & Herrup, K. (1988). The control of the neuron number. *Annual Review of Neuroscience, 11,* 423–453.

Wilson, B. A., & Davidoff, J. (1993). Partial recovery from visual object agnosia: A 10-year follow-up study. *Cortex, 29,* 529–542.

Wilson, D. H., Reeves, A., & Gazzaniga, M. (1982). Central commissurotomy for intractable generalized epilepsy (Series 2). *Neurology, 32,* 687–697.

Wilson, T. (2011). *The arte of rhetorique* Available in the Renascence collection at https://scholarsbank .uoregon.edu (Original work published 1553)

Wilson, T. D., Lisle, D. J., Schooler, J. W., Hodges, S. D., Klaaren, K. J., & LaFleur, S. J. (1993). Introspecting about reasons can reduce post-choice satisfaction. *Personality and Social Psychology Bulletin, 19,* 331–339.

Wilson, T. D., & Schooler, J. W. (1991). Thinking too much: Introspection can reduce the quality of preferences and decisions. *Journal of Personality and Social Psychology, 60,* 181–192.

Winner, E., & Gardner, H. (1977). The comprehension of metaphor in brain-damaged patients. *Brain, 100,* 717–729.

Winograd, E. (1988). Some observations on prospective remembering. In M. M. Gruneberg, P. E. Morris, & R. N. Sykes (Eds.), *Practical aspects of memory. Vol. 1: Memory in everyday life* (pp. 348–353). Chichester, England: Wiley.

Witelson, S. F., Kigar, D. L., & Harvey, T. (1999). The exceptional brain of Albert Einstein. *The Lancet, 353,* 2149–2153.

Woocher, F. D., Glass, A. L., & Holyoak, K. J. (1978). Positional discriminability in linear orderings. *Memory & Cognition, 6,* 165–173.

Wood, N. L., & Cowan, N. (1995). The cocktail party phenomenon revisited: Attention and memory in the classic selective listening procedure of Cherry (1953). *Journal of Experimental Psychology: General, 124,* 243–262.

Woodworth, R. S. (1938). *Experimental psychology.* Oxford, England: Holt.

Wright, D. B., & McDaid, A. T. (1996). Comparing system and estimator variables using data from real line-ups. *Applied Cognitive Psychology, 10,* 75–84.

Wright, D. B., & Stroud, J. N. (2002). Age differences in lineup identification accuracy: People are better with their own age. *Law and Human Behavior, 26,* 641–654.

Wyer, N. A. (2004). Not all stereotypic biases are created equal: Evidence for a stereotype-disconfirming bias. *Personality and Social Psychology Bulletin, 30,* 706–720.

Yamadori, A., Osumi, Y., Masuhara, S., & Okubo, M. (1977). Preservation of singing in Broca's aphasia. *Journal of Neurology, Neurosurgery, and Psychiatry, 40,* 221–224.

Yamamoto, M., & Hatta, T. (1980). Hemispheric asymmetries in a tactile thought task for normal subjects. *Perceptual and Motor Skills, 50,* 469–471.

Yantis, S. (1993). Stimulus-driven attentional capture and attentional control settings. *Journal of Experimental Psychology: Human Perception and Performance, 3,* 676–681.

Yates, F. A. (1966). *The art of memory.* Chicago: University of Chicago Press.

Yekovich, F. R., Walker, C. H., Ogle, L. T., & Thompson, M. A. (1990). The influence of domain knowledge on inferences in low-aptitude individuals. In A. Graesser & G. Bower (Eds.), *Inferences and text comprehension* (pp. 259–278). San Diego, CA: Academic Press.

Yeni-Komshian, G. H. (1998). Speech perception. In J. B. Gleason & N. B. Ratner (Eds.), *Psycholinguistics* (pp. 107–156). Fort Worth, TX: Harcourt Brace.

Yin, R. K. (1969). Looking at upside-down faces. *Journal of Experimental Psychology, 81,* 141–145.

Young, A. W., & Ellis, H. D. (1989). Childhood prosopagnosia. *Brain and Cognition, 9,* 16–47.

Young, A. W., Hay, D. C., & Ellis, A. W. (1985). The faces that launched a thousand slips: Everyday difficulties and errors in recognizing people. *British Journal of Psychology, 76,* 495–523.

Yue, G. H., Wilson, S. L., Cole, K. J., & Darling, W. G. (1996). Imagined muscle contraction training increases voluntary neural drive to muscle. *Journal of Psychophysiology, 10,* 198–208.

Zangwill, O. L. (1972). Remembering revisited. *Quarterly Journal of Experimental Psychology, 24,* 123–138.

Zaragoza, M. S., & Lane, S. M. (1994). Source misattributions and the suggestibility of eyewitness memory. *Journal of Experimental Psychology: Learning, Memory, and Cognition, 20,* 934–945.

Zaragoza, M. S., Payment, K. E., Ackil, J. K., Drivdahl, S. B., & Beck, M. (2001). Interviewing witnesses: Forced confabulation and confirmatory feedback increase false memories. *Psychological Science, 12,* 473–477.

Zatorre, R. J., Halpern, A. R., Perry, D. W., Meyer, E., & Evans, A. C. (1996). Hearing in the mind's ear: A PET investigation of musical imagery and perception. *Journal of Cognitive Neuroscience, 8,* 29–46.

Zavestoski, S., Agnello, K., Mignano, F., & Darroch, F. (2004). Issue framing and citizen apathy toward local environmental contamination. *Sociological Forum, 19,* 255–283.

Zelinski, E. M., & Miura, S. A. (1988). Effects of thematic information on script memory in young and older adults. *Psychology and Aging, 3,* 292–299.

Zhao, W., Chellappa, R., Phillips, P. J., & Rosenfeld, A. (2003). Face recognition: A literature survey. *ACM Computing Survey, 35,* 399–458.

Zhaoping, L., & Dayan, P. (2006). Preattentive visual selection. *Neural Networks, 19,* 1437–1439.

Zhu, L., & Gigerenzer, G. (2006). Children can solve Bayesian problems: The role of representation in mental computation. *Cognition, 98,* 287–308.

Zimler, J., & Keenan, J. M. (1983). Imagery in the congenitally blind: How visual are visual images? *Journal of Experimental Psychology: Learning, Memory, and Cognition, 9,* 269–282.

Zimmer, C. (2004). *The soul made flesh: The discovery of the brain—and how it changed the world.* New York: Simon & Schuster.

Name Index

Subject Index